PRACTICAL PSYCHOLOGY FOR PASTORS

SECOND EDITION

William R. Miller

Kathleen A. Jackson

The University of New Mexico

PRENTICE HALL, Englewood Cliffs, New Jersey 07632

Library of Congress Cataloging-in-Publication Data

Miller, William R.
    Practical psychology for pastors/William R. Miller, Kathleen A. Jackson.—2nd ed.
        p.   cm.
    Includes bibliographical references and index.
    ISBN 0-13-171829-0
    1. Pastoral psychology.   2. Pastoral counseling.   I. Jackson, Kathleen A.   II. Title.
BV4012.M55   1994
253.5'2—dc20   94-34115
                                                                                CIP

Editor/Production Supervision: *Betsy Winship*
Executive Editor: *Pete Janzow*
Senior Editor: *Heidi Freund*
Editorial Assistant: *Jennifer Fader*
Cover Designer: *Rosemarie Votta*
Page Layout: *Lorraine Paul*
Manufacturing Buyer: *Tricia Kenny*

©1995, 1985 by Prentice-Hall, Inc.
A Simon & Schuster Company
Englewood Cliffs, New Jersey 07632

Printed in the United States of America

10 9 8 7 6 5 4 3 2 1

ISBN   0-13-171829-0

Prentice-Hall International (UK) Limited, *London*
Prentice-Hall of Australia Fty, Limited, *Sydney*
Prentice-Hall Canada Inc., *Toronto*
Prentice-Hall Hispanoamericans, S.A., *Mexico*
Prentice-Hall of India Private Limited, *New Delhi*
Prentice-Hall of Japan, Inc., *Tokyo*
Simon & Schuster Asia Pte. Ltd., *Singapore*
Editora Prentice-Hall do Brasil, Ltda., *Rio de Janeiro*

CONTENTS

PREFACE

Besides being complicated, reality, in my experience, is usually odd. It is not neat, not obvious, not what you expect.

—C. S. Lewis, *Mere Christianity*

These words of C. S. Lewis capture an eternal truth about nature, or human nature at least. Reality is not only complicated but full of surprises. One who would discern reality by armchair intuiting or by force of logic from superficial observations may spend many years in mental gymnastics without coming much closer to its nature. Just when the answer seems simple, neat, obvious, clearcut, black and white—at that very moment one ought to become suspicious. Reality seldom comes in such tidy packages. The Creator of us all seems to have had a penchant for surprise and the unexpected, combined with no small sense of humor.

Yet here we are, seeking to translate complex reality into usable information and principles. We propose to try to make sense of some major areas of human life and problems, to provide an orderly framework for understanding them, and to describe effective ways of intervening that are accessible to the pastoral counselor. The potential for oversimplification is immense.

Still, the task is not hopeless. We write in the belief that there *is* an underlying order within complexity. In describing such order we draw not only upon our personal counseling experience, but also on a large body of psychological theory and research that sheds light on the nature of these human problems and their solutions. A pastor friend, who had been out of the country for ten years, told us after returning: "I can't believe how pastoral counseling has changed! It's not just Rogerian any more. You need skills, but there's so much you can do!" Not surprisingly, the answers emerging from this new knowledge are complex. No single approach, theory, technique, or way of perceiving reality seems to be sufficient. Different problems require different perspectives and unique interventions. Like the individuals who experience them, different types of problems have a certain amount in common with each other but also a substantial degree of uniqueness.

At the very outset we hasten to acknowledge that this is *not* a pastoral counseling textbook, at least not in the traditional sense. If it were, our chapters would be devoted to the uses and applications within a counseling setting of the pastor's special expertise and role—prayer and the sacraments, interpretation of scripture, and spiritual direction. Numerous texts are available on this subject, and they are rightly written by pastors who are well experienced in counseling within a spiritual context. Instead, we intend to offer something different—a range of new skills and knowledge helpful and directly useful to the pastor who counsels, effective methods developed within the realm of scientific and professional psychology. We hope to bridge a gap that has existed between useful psychological knowledge and the many pastors who can apply it. Over the past three decades, there has been a virtual explosion of psychological knowledge and research, and one result of this has been the discovery and refinement of specific and practical counseling methods that are effective in helping people deal with their problems in living. We have drawn on this rapidly growing body of knowledge, extracting concepts and approaches helpful to the pastor who counsels. The fact that we are privileged to be writing this second edition of our text encourages us that our somewhat different, practical approach meets a need in the field.

We have not attempted, to any considerable extent, to integrate this knowledge within a particular doctrinal system. Instead, we have focused on information and methods that are applicable and effective across a broad range of perspectives and problem areas. We have also sought, wherever possible, to offer valid alternative perspectives and counseling approaches. We leave it to your expertise to understand and manifest the material within your own faith (and that of those you counsel). Some readers may find our book "not Christian enough" or unclear in its theological basis. Again, we reply that there are already many doctrinal texts on pastoral counseling. Rather than instructing you in how to apply pastoring to psychology, we hope to explain in clear and applicable terms how you can use modern psychology in the process of pastoring.

At the same time, it would be dishonest of us to claim that there is no particular theological perspective embedded in or underlying our writing. As practicing and believing Christians, our world view and perspectives are greatly influenced and, we hope, enriched by the traditions and heritage of the Judeo-Christian faith. As elders in our own denomination, we are most familiar with its particular form of church government, liturgical style, and pastoral role. Thus, our examples, at least, will be closer to the experience of some pastors than of others. Beyond this we want to acknowledge several of our views and beliefs that underlie this book and that have some theological implications.

First, we believe that God is real and alive, and has an active purpose and will for each individual life. We understand purpose in life to be the finding and following of that will. In part the task of the pastor who counsels, then, is always spiritual direction, but another vital task, and the one to which this book is addressed, is the resolution or removal of obstacles in the path. The human problems now often treated by psychologists and other mental health professionals can also be understood as barriers to the individual's journey. We believe that it is the task of the pastoral counselor not to prescribe every step along the way but rather to help remove the obstacles and get the person back on the road of his or her own journey toward God. This is a book about helping to remove those obstacles.

Furthermore, we believe that there is enormous power to be found in faith. Every healer knows this. The will to live, the desire for health, the belief that one has a purpose or reason to continue living, the placebo effect, trust in the counselor—all of these tap more or less directly the healing resources of faith. (By *faith* we mean here not the endorsement of a particular creed, but rather a trusting relationship, be it with the counselor or with God.) We believe in the power of personal and intercessory prayer. God also has given to humankind the gift of reason and through it the marvelous healing techniques of modern medicine and psychology. We view such secular technology as a set of tools to be employed within any faith system that does not exclude it. Just as few pastors shun the ministrations of physicians in overcoming physical illness, so pastors can avail themselves of modern psychological knowledge as they counsel on problems with mood, anxiety, relationships, self-concept, and alcohol. We believe that God's will for humanity is health—physical, psychological, and spiritual health. We offer no new theological solution to the problem of suffering. Instead, we hope that what you find here will be of practical help to you in the alleviation of suffering.

Finally, we express our belief in the ability of people to choose and to change, to turn around (repent), to be new and renewed. Change is usually neither sudden nor dramatic, as we shall see, but it is almost always a real potential. We believe that within each individual there is a kind of wisdom—God within—that is a powerful ally for the counselor. We know from our own counseling that profound and lasting change can and does occur, even when things look darkest. The miracle of change may come through an experience of grace, through the giving or accepting of forgiveness, through a pastor's skillful use of such methods as are described later in this book, or through some combination of these.

A common sermon illustration comes to mind. A priest and a parishioner are golfing together, and the latter notices that every time the priest is about to putt he crosses himself. And every putt goes right in! After four holes of that, the parishioner asks, "Father, does that really work for you?" "Oh, yes indeed!" the priest replies. So on the fifth green, the parishioner crosses himself, draws back the putter, taps the ball, and misses the hole by a good foot and a half. "I thought you said it works," the frustrated golfer complains. "Ah, it does," the priest replies, "but you also have to know how to putt!"

So it is with the pastor who counsels. God works through us all, using the potential and skills we have developed. God's healing will is manifest, at least in part, through the skills of healers. We hope, through what follows, to add to your skills, your knowledge, and your confidence in the pastoral ministry of counseling.

Acknowledgments

So many people have contributed to the organized complexity of this book that we hardly know where to begin with thanks. We have, both together and individually, led counseling skills workshops for clergy, and the participants in these seminars have taught us much about the needs and concerns of the frontline pastor who counsels. We particularly want to thank pastoral colleagues who took special time to give us comments and suggestions through the writing and revisions of this text, among them the Revs. Rob Craig, Daniel Erdman, Svein-Alf Gerdt, Bob Hillman, Kay Huggins, Sherry Johnston, Dave McConaughy, Howard Paul, Bill Scholes, Ed Steinmetz, and Joyce Thompson. Our own clients and students have also provided continuous relearning by challenging us to specify and apply our knowledge.

We owe much to the countless psychologists and other researchers who have devoted their time to the tedious but rewarding process of operationalizing, testing, and communicating the results of their ideas through systematic research. The mainstreams of psychological research have provided important guidelines for us as we have attempted to organize the complicated and often surprising realities of human change.

As the manuscript took shape, other friends and colleagues made important contributions. Rev. Kenneth Eaton read early drafts of more than 700 pages and made extensive and helpful comments from the perspective of a seasoned pastor and counselor. Our faithful and patient editors at Prentice-Hall, Pete Janzow, Heidi Freund, Maureen Richardson, and Betsy Winship, coaxed, cajoled, and encouraged us through two editions. We also thank the following reviewers for their thoughtful suggestions that led to substantial improvements from earlier manuscripts: W. Eastwood Atwater, Montgomery Community College; Dennis Klass, Webster University; Nelson S. T. Thayer, Drew University; William J. Baugh, Hospital of Saint Raphael and Yale Divinity School; Joseph A. Kloba, Christian Broadcasting Network University; John M. Mackey, Pittsburgh Pastoral Institute.

But more than anything else, we wrote this book specifically for *pastors* because of those who have pastored to us along the way, helping us to blend our own professions with the sensitivities, concerns, and callings of faith. There have been many, but we particularly want to acknowledge the important influence in our lives of these pastors: Bob Butziger, Larry Collins, Rob Craig, Harold Daniels, Walter Dodds, Eduardo Guerra, Sherry Johnston, Norman Marden, Mark Miller, Wesley Nicholson, Dick Symes, Barbara Troxell, and George Wilson. Their loving concern, witness, and very personal humanity have ever called us to see our vocations within the larger context of faith and thus to the writing of this book.

William R. Miller
Kathleen A. Jackson
The University of New Mexico
Albuquerque, New Mexico

1

THE PASTOR AS COUNSELOR

It is my conviction that pastoral counseling theory and practice are at a crossroads and must turn a corner if they are to respond to the opportunity for a renewal ministry of enlarged dimensions. If the corner can be turned, a new chapter will begin in the church's ministry to the heavy-laden. This new chapter can be without equal in the history of our faith. Never before have we had such rich resources as are provided by the contemporary renaissance in pastoral care and counseling, the renewal movement in the churches, the sparkling new insights from the behavioral sciences, and the new techniques from the psychotherapeutic disciplines. As these converge in the pastoral counseling ministry, a broad stream of healing will be released through the churches.

— Howard J. Clinebell Jr., *Basic Types of Pastoral Counseling*

Among all my patients in the second half of life—that is to say, over thirty-five—there has not been one whose problem in the last resort was not that of finding a religious outlook on life. It is safe to say that every one of them fell ill because [they] had lost that which the living religions of every age have given to their followers, and none of them has been really healed who did not regain [a] religious outlook.

— Carl Gustav Jung, *Modern Man in Search of a Soul*

Members of the clergy are called upon to play many roles in modern society—to be priest and prophet, administrator and pastor. Within each of these are many specific and demanding areas of expertise. One pastoral role ever in demand is that of the counselor, the one to whom a person turns at life's moments of distress, despair, and decision.

This is not a new role for clergy. Historically, the priest and the healer have a common ancestor in the ancient *shaman*, the one to whom people came seeking wisdom and health.[1] Jesus manifested both prophetic and healing roles in his ministry. In the American Southwest, this traditional unity is reflected today in the Navajo *yataalii* (medicine men and women) and the Hispanic *curandero* and *curandera*, folk healers with ancient spiritual heritage. It is only in recent history that the two roles of priest and healer have become separated and alienated, with priestly and pastoral professions on one hand and the disciplines of psychology and medicine on the other.

Some clergy gladly accept this division of roles, feeling some measure of relief at being freed of the burdens involved in helping people deal with their personal problems. Others take on the mantle of the counselor but continue to be haunted by its ambiguities and questions: "Am I qualified? What if I do harm? Is this my true calling? Am I getting in over my head?" These are legitimate questions not only for pastors but for all counselors and therapists. Yet these concerns should not dissuade pastors from considering counseling as a vital part of their ministry. There are, in fact, several good reasons why pastors should be involved in the ministry of counseling.

WHY PEOPLE COME TO PASTORS

Contemporary society is filled with helpers of every stripe and color: psychologists, psychiatrists, social workers, counselors, consultants, marriage and family specialists, self-help organizations, psychiatric nurses, family practice physicians, group facilitators, faith healers, hypnotists, sex therapists, art therapists, dance therapists, educational and career guidance specialists, and authors of self-change books. Even in the midst of all of this, many people— in some communities most people—turn first and sometimes solely to their pastor for help, often long before they would be willing to enter into other types of professional treatment or therapy. Why?

One obvious answer is that the pastor is *accessible*. In contrast to the confusing maze of professional helpers, the pastor is a known quantity, a familiar and reassuring face in a world crowded with strangers. There is already a kind of relationship with the pastor, making it easier and safer to take the risk of asking for help. From a pragmatic standpoint, the pastor is also more financially accessible to the average person, as the fee for a fifty-minute hour approaches or exceeds $100 in the office of the typical metropolitan psychologist or psychiatrist. If current trends toward cutbacks of public funding for social services continue, the demand for pastoral counseling is likely to increase still further.

The pastoral rites of access also extend much further than do those of the average mental health professional. The pastor's prerogative of home visitation is invaluable in identifying and intervening in life problems. Because of his or her ongoing relationship with parishioners, the pastor can initiate contact when a problem seems to be emerging and can continue with follow-up care long after the average mental health clinic has lost touch with the individual. In short, the pastor is in a unique position to be able to recognize, counsel, and even prevent problems.

Beyond these advantages of two-way pastoral accessibility, however, is a more important reason why people seek the counseling of a man or woman of the cloth. They come to their pastors because they wish to be understood within a spiritual context; as whole people. They do not, in most cases, view the pastor as a psychological professional who happens to chargeless, but as a spiritual leader who will be able to help them in their journey toward wholeness. The fact that the pastor also has a priestly, spiritual dimension is not a coincidence—it is *essential* to what they are seeking. This is crucial for pastoral counselors to remember; otherwise they may be tempted to abandon the pastoral role in an attempt to be "objective" counselors, thus repeating the mistake made by society in general—the divorce of psychological from spiritual.[2] Bergin and Jensen observed that "a large number of distressed persons appear to be hungry for help that is friendly and not foreign to their way of thinking, for in their deepest moments of change many of them see, feel and act in spiritual terms."[3] Pastoral counselors have something unique and important to offer.

This is so, in part, because the spiritual dimension has been so often overlooked in the training and practice of traditional mental health professionals. Secular therapists have been found, on the whole, to profess less belief in God and religious affiliation and fewer traditional values than do the general populations they serve.[3] In professional training, religious beliefs may be either ignored as irrelevant to healing or regarded as psychologically immature, if not mildly pathological.[4] There are encouraging signs that this is changing. Since 1975, there has been an official Division of Psychologists Interested in Religious Issues within the American Psychological Association. Still, the gap between theology and therapy remains wide, and many believe it should remain that way. Consequently, individuals to whom spiritual dimensions are important find themselves turned off (in several senses) by many traditional mental health professionals. They turn instead to their pastors.

WHAT IS COUNSELING?

Counseling is a special kind of helping relationship. It follows from an agreement between two people to enter into a relationship whereby one (the counselor) applies special skills to assist the other in the resolution of a personal or interpersonal problem. If the counselor sees more than one person at a time, as in family counseling or group counseling, this special relationship exists between the counselor and each individual.

Under certain circumstances the person being counselled is not the one with whom the agreement was originally made. A parent may bring a child for counseling; a spouse may come under duress; an offender may seek treatment under pressure from the courts. In such situations it is prudent for the counselor to be aware of the question, "Who is my client?" As a general rule, the client is the person seeking a change, the one who perceives a problem and desires its resolution. This is not always the one being counseled. Throughout most of this book, however, we will be using the term *client* to refer to the individual who is *participating* in counseling.*

WHAT AM I *DOING*?

Most pastors have had, in the course of their seminary training, at least some instruction in counseling. Some have had practicum experience through a clinical pastoral education program. Yet most find their training insufficient in preparing them to deal with the rich diversity of problems that people actually bring to the pastor's office: anxieties and guilt, depressions in all shapes and sizes, sexual concerns, alcohol and other drug problems, marital and family difficulties, delusions, difficult decisions, physical abuse, chronic stress, life transitions and thoughts, threats, and acts of suicide. The pastor who communicates an openness to counseling with human problems finds all of these and more among the people who make their way to the private study or counseling room. And there come those moments, as to all others who counsel, when the pastor asks, "What am I *doing*?"

One response to this disquieting question is to default on the pastoral role of counselor. This is, of course, one possible choice. Some pastors are simply not well suited by skill or calling or temperament to the demands of counseling with their parishioners' deeply personal and disturbing problems. Some find it too difficult to integrate this role with other functions of the clergy because of either the time required or the difficulty of transitions into and back out of a counseling relationship. These are legitimate concerns and will be addressed in this and later chapters. In general, however, we urge pastors *not* to abandon counseling from some general sense of disqualification. There is nothing inherent in a Ph.D., M.D., or M.S.W. that qualifies the individual as a good therapist, nor is effective counseling limited to the practices of professionals holding such degrees.[5] There is more than ample evidence that per-

---

*There is no one term that we find wholly satisfactory to describe the individual with whom one enters into a helping relationship. *Counselee* and *helpee* sound awkward. *Patient* is a medical term and implies a very uneven and hierarchical relationship (doctor/patient). *Student* is preferred by some but it does not capture the special relationship inherent in counseling. In addition to *person* and *individual*, we have chosen to use *client* because it is a reasonably neutral term and, though it sounds a bit businesslike, it is the term most rooted in the history of counseling.

sons from a broad range of backgrounds can learn effective counseling skills and apply them to the benefit of others.[6] Therapeutic effectiveness is determined by many factors, only one of which is formal professional training.

This is not to say that there is no value in advanced training in psychology or other mental health fields. In fact, the highly trained professional in psychology, psychiatry, or another mental health discipline can provide valuable and effective consultation within his or her specialty area—knowledge not likely to be available to the average pastor. Nor do we wish to imply that all therapeutic approaches are equally effective, for nothing could be further from the truth. There *is* a large knowledge base upon which to draw when helping people change. The best approach varies with the particular person, problem, and pastor, but this does not mean that it doesn't matter what you do as long as you are genuinely concerned. Perhaps the most complex challenge facing the modern counselor is that of finding the best approach for each individual. This requires specific knowledge and skill.

Needless to say, this book cannot make you a psychologist, nor should you try to be, for you are first and foremost a *pastor*, and this is as it should be. At the same time, your pastoral counseling can and should be informed by modern psychological knowledge and discoveries. An unfortunate consequence of the historical divorce between psychology and religion has been the development of pastoral counseling in relative isolation from the mainstream of clinical psychology. Each can benefit from the perspective of the other.[7]

FIVE PRACTICAL QUESTIONS

The purpose of this book, then, is to share with you current psychological thinking and research as they bear on the practical questions that face you as a pastoral counselor. This *practical* psychology is necessarily focused; it cannot and does not pretend to cover all possibilities or angles. Rather, we intend to provide you with carefully selected information and methods most likely to be useful in dealing with the kinds of problems that are most often confronted by the pastor who counsels. More specifically, the material presented is intended to help you in addressing five questions that arise in every counseling situation.

1. *Should I intervene?* The first question is, "Should I do anything?" or "Is there a problem here?" Some of the material that we offer is designed to help you develop a way of thinking about human problems, to recognize early signs of problem development, and to decide whether to intervene.
2. *What is the problem?* Related to the first question, this second issue requires a systematic way of conceptualizing human adjustment problems that incorporates both psychological knowledge and spiritual perspectives. This is a crucial though often deemphasized stage. Until you know what the real problem is, you

cannot choose an appropriate intervention (unless you believe that there is one answer for every problem, in which case you can stop reading here). Some of the material we present is intended to give you a working knowledge of major areas of human psychopathology.

3. *When should I intervene?* Another question encountered frequently by pastors is, "Should I do something now or wait?" This is always a judgment call, but an important one. It involves understanding the process of change and recognizing where an individual is in this process, issues addressed in chapter 8.

4. *What should I do?* This is the next most difficult question after identifying the problem. Sometimes it follows directly from a diagnosis, because some problems require a specific kind of treatment. In other cases there are several approaches from which to choose, all of which have been supported as effective. In still other cases there is simply too little knowledge to guide us in making decisions. The challenge here is finding the right approach for a particular person with a certain kind of problem. For better or for worse, there is no single approach or set of approaches that can be endorsed as effective across the board. No single counseling strategy will help all of the people all of the time or even most of the people most of the time. We present a variety of counseling strategies in parts IV and V.

5. *Should I refer?* Having dealt with the other questions, this one still remains: Should *I* be the one to intervene, or should I get other professional help? Here the skill is in knowing your own gifts as well as limitations. You may wish to make a referral when help is beyond your own expertise. Referral is not a cop-out. To the contrary, it is itself a professional skill. Helping to find the *right* treatment with the *right* professional can save an individual or a family years of suffering as well as unnecessary expense. The answer to this fifth question depends upon the first four. Once you have a clear sense of the problem and what is needed, it becomes more apparent whether you have the time and skills necessary to help.

AM I THE RIGHT KIND OF PERSON?

Another question that pastors ask themselves about counseling is whether they have the right temperament, personality, or character for this kind of work. There is no simple answer here, in part because different people are well suited for different kinds of counseling.

What personal characteristics mark an effective pastoral counselor? Our pastor colleagues most often mention genuine *caring* as a fundamental prerequisite. This is communicated not only in counseling, but in virtually every aspect of the pastor's work—in meetings, sermons, casual conversations, funerals, pastoral calls, and sacraments. It is often this deeply felt sense of God-based caring that draws pastors to a counseling ministry and strengthens them in it. Carl Rogers described this as "unconditional positive regard." Paul called it *agape*.

Another often mentioned characteristic of effective pastoral counselors is *accessibility*. By this we do not mean primarily availability in terms of time and space, though that is important, too. Rather, we mean emotional accessibility—a clear and communicated sense of openness to the inner world. This is reflected in how you respond when people take risks with you, providing an opening or confiding in you. How approachable are you? How safe is it to talk to you? Will you listen or flip quickly into judgment or advice? Chapters 4 and 5 are meant to help you develop and practice this kind of accessibility.

Yet another factor, emphasized both by Rogers and by our pastoral colleagues, is *genuineness*. This has to do with being in touch with your own feelings, values, issues, limits, and strengths. It is difficult, even dangerous to help others explore their inner worlds if you are out of touch with your own (cf. Matt. 7:2–5; Luke 6:39–42). Genuineness involves sharing of yourself, being vulnerable, expressing your feelings. We acknowledge that this departs from the psychoanalytic tradition in which self-disclosure is anathema and the analyst remains a mystery, a blank screen onto which images are projected. To be sure, pastoral counselors, like all mental health professionals, must be judicious in revealing personal feelings and experiences. Not all thoughts and feelings are best shared with your clients. Some are better discussed with a supervisor or trusted colleague. Yet we believe that the sharing of self is a vital strength for the counselor. Tears are okay for the counselor as well as for the client. Genuineness means counseling as a real person, not as a distant expert who speaks in jargon and remains aloof.

If there is a single personal characteristic that seems, from the available research, to facilitate a counselor's effectiveness, it is the capacity to be *empathic*, to listen with accurate understanding. People differ in their capacity for empathy, but it is also, to a considerable extent, a learnable skill (to which we return in chapter 5). Personal situations or characteristics that interfere with this ability to listen reflectively (see our discussion of "roadblocks" in chapter 4) may impair counseling effectiveness. More directive and authoritarian counselors, for example, tend to evoke greater resistance but less change from their clients.[8]

What interferes with your ability to counsel effectively? Besides the issues already discussed, we have encountered three broad themes in our work with pastors. First, there is the issue of time consciousness. It is hard to counsel effectively when you are fatigued, overscheduled, keeping one eye on the clock and the other on your to-do list. Counseling takes quality time and so must be given priority. We will return to this issue shortly. Second, there is impatience. It's natural enough to want to help, but the sense of having to fix it *now* can really get in the way. This impatience also extends to, "Why can't he do it *my* way?" or "Why won't she just take my advice?" Counseling, like spiritual direction, involves a good bit of patient listening, following, trusting, and exploring, with a prudent nudge here and there at the right time. Third, there is the matter of an issue being too close to home. It happens to us all that material arising in counseling is all too familiar, too near to our own sensitivities, difficulties, or blind spots. For pastors, who often have multiple relationships with their clients, the needed counseling directions may be too intertwined with other roles. There are some clients and problems just too close to counsel effectively. Counseling such people can make it difficult to have enough distance and avoid overidentification. This is where good supervision, consultation, and referral can be important (see chapter 19).

Relatedly, any counselor may be better suited to deal with certain kinds of problems or clients and ill-suited for others. It is often experience that teaches this. Some find it immensely rewarding to work with alcoholics, for example, and obtain excellent results; others find they are ineffective and frustrated with such clients. Some have the energy and compassionate patience to treat depression or schizophrenia. Others work well with the victims or perpetrators of violence. Still other counselors prefer the exciting work of fostering psychological and spiritual growth among relatively well-functioning individuals or couples.

What we want to emphasize is that good counselors are not born to it. There are tangible, learnable, and vital *skills* involved in effective counseling. Don't expect it all to come naturally. Skillfulness can be increased with good training, experience, and some supervision. If you are called to a ministry of counseling as part of your pastoral role, there is much you can learn that will help you work effectively. The primary purpose of this book is to support you in that learning process.

HOW DOES COUNSELING FIT WITH MY OTHER PASTORAL ROLES?

We have met few pastors with time to spare. Some are quite gifted at conveying to most everyone they see the sense that there is plenty of time and that nothing or no one is more important right now. Yet the demands of pastoring are great. Where does counseling fit? There are at least two important questions for you to sort out here. How does counseling fit within your own philosophy of ministry? How does counseling affect your other duties or roles as a pastor?

The place of counseling within your philosophy of ministry determines its importance for you. For some, pastoral care in general and counseling in particular is quintessential ministry—caring for one person at a time, dealing with their personal struggles, hopes, fears, and choices. It is an opportunity for meaningful influence in lives, beyond preaching and teaching. Some give pastoral counseling top priority; everything else can wait. Some, in fact, make pastoral counseling the primary focus of their ministry. Others understand their gifts and calling as lying in other areas—administration, preaching, prophetic and social action, teaching, or writing—and find that counseling distracts them from the focus of their work. It is time well spent to consider where counseling fits in your own understanding of and calling for ministry.

This includes a consideration of how your counseling is integrated with spiritual direction. Experienced pastors have told us in recent years that they find their clients increasingly asking for spiritual direction as part and even as the essence of counseling. Again, we urge you not to see these as separate roles. In a telling article, Richard Rohr asked, "Why does psychology always win?" when it comes into contact with the spiritual.[9] Formal or informal, in crisis or for growth, counseling is a journey toward wholeness. "I try to remember that my objective is salvation," said one pastor, "and counseling is part of that journey." Viewed another way, pastoral counseling is the process of removing obstacles that stand in the way of a person's natural journey and growth toward God. What are your own objectives in counseling?

Whatever its place in your ministry, there is no denying that counseling takes *time*, which means that it competes with your availability for other types of ministry. Effective counseling involves not only the face-to-face time, but also preparation (study, prayer and centering, reflection, reviewing notes) and residual tasks (recording notes, following up with contacts and information, dealing with related phone calls, etc.). Counseling may increase the urgency of your availability to deal with crises, although this is a common aspect of pastoral ministry in general. The weight of dealing face to face with counseling issues can also be substantial, carried over into your personal and other pastoral hours. It is wise to have clear time priorities for counseling in relation to other roles and an understanding of these that is shared with your family and governing board.

Beyond time, how does counseling affect your other pastoral roles? Many find that it enriches their preaching, their teaching, and their understanding of interpersonal dynamics crucial to effective administration and pastoral care. It is also vital, we believe, to have clear limits and boundaries on your counseling role, so that it does not blend and interfere with other pastoral functions. "I never turn anybody away," a pastor told us, "but I counsel them in special times and places. Then when I meet them in other contexts, I am careful to pretend not to know anything of what we discussed." This is a new idea for some pastors—to set counseling apart as a special relationship. To do so offers many advantages and can prevent some of the more serious problems of role conflict inherent in pastoral counseling. We will return to this issue in chapters 2 and 3.

A PERSONAL NOTE

No book can be wholly objective, for it comes necessarily from the writers' own perceptions and beliefs about the world and human nature. You have already begun to see some of ours. In this regard we want to be explicit about five perspectives that undergird the approach we have chosen to take within this practical handbook.

First, as discussed in the preface, we acknowledge our grounding in the Judeo-Christian tradition and the fact that we are writing specifically for the *pastoral* counselor, for the professional whose primary expertise and training is in theology and ministry but whose work includes helping people to wrestle with and resolve their own personal problems.

A second perspective that we bring to this book is the kinship of spiritual and psychological processes. This *holistic* perspective chooses to see a whole person rather than an isolated psyche or problem. In this regard, religious issues (broadly defined) *can* be part of the problem as well as part of the solution. The extent to which spiritual issues are directly involved in the genesis or resolution of a problem will vary greatly. It is equally absurd to insist either that religious beliefs always cause pathological conditions or that they never do. Similarly, spiritual considerations may play a greater or lesser role in counseling. The pastor who is open to this can assess the extent to which the spiritual dimension of a problem is crucial. Unlike most psychologists, a pastor also has at his or her disposal the training, authority, ordination, and permission to integrate, as needed, the process of counseling with the sacraments, prayer, and spiritual direction.

A third perspective that permeates this book is the view that human behavior, both "normal" and "abnormal" is *complex* and influenced by a wide range of factors, any one of which may be crucial to the resolution of a problem. This perspective eschews counseling viewpoints that begin with the words "All it takes is . . ." Those who emphasize techniques ("All it takes is the right method") may miss the tremendous influence of the relationship within which such treatment procedures are practiced. Others emphasize milieu ("All it takes is the right relationship between counselor and client") and overlook the vast body of research on the effectiveness of specific treatment methods. Some attribute responsibility wholly to the client ("All it takes is motivation to change"), which again denies the complexity of the change process while freeing the counselor of any responsibility to keep up his or her skills and knowledge. Finally, there are those who adhere to one particular approach ("All it takes is prayer"), a bias that has already been mentioned as naively simplistic.

Related to this appreciation of human complexity is a kind of *eclecticism* that necessarily follows. No one theoretical framework can contain all the answers, nor can any single profession or therapeutic school of thought. The infighting among rival schools of psychology has generated more heat than light. The viewpoint that we have tried to maintain here is that the merit of an idea is to be judged by its helpfulness and effectiveness in the counseling process rather than by the theory or author from which it originated.

Finally, we have maintained a pragmatic bias that is *scientific* in the broadest sense of that word. We place credence in the evidence that emerges from properly conducted scientific research, selecting appropriate treatment methods on the basis of empirical proof of their effectiveness. To be sure, there are other avenues to truth. Our own predisposition, however, is to choose among the dizzying array of alternative treatment methods by examining the relative support that each has received from current research. It is this method of systematic and programmatic controlled research that advanced medicine from the standard practice of superstitious and harmful methods such as bloodletting to the marvelous, albeit still limited, technologies of current medical science. Similarly, through research, psychologists have identified more effective methods for treating depression, sexual problems, anxiety, alcoholism, and marital and family distress. In selecting material to be presented in this book, particularly in part V, we have intentionally focused on methods that are more strongly grounded in clinical research and can be applied by a broad range of professional counselors.

The final task and test of this material is to be found in your own counseling. A wide variety of strategies and methods will be presented along with guidelines for when and how to use them, but only you can choose from these the ones most appropriate to your work, and only you can find the means for integrating these into your general pastoral style. It is our hope that from the array of "practical psychology" presented here you will find at least a few insights and methods to assist you in the challenging and rewarding work of pastoral counseling.

ADDITIONAL READINGS

At the conclusion of each chapter we will provide more advanced or specialized readings. These include professional/technical resources, handbooks and guidelines for counselors on specific topics, and self-help resources for clients (where applicable) that we have found to be particularly useful.

We cannot, of course, endorse the entire content of every book listed in these sections. The readings provided are intended to offer you resources for extending your expertise and knowledge within given areas. Before recommending any book to a client, you should read it yourself to become familiar with its content and approach. Properly used, these readings can supplement and complement your counseling.

For many of the readings in these sections, we have added brief comments as guidelines to their content and use. Many of the books that we list are available in paperback editions.

The Integration of Psychology and Religion

ALPERT, NANCY L. *Religion and Psychology: A Medical Subject Analysis and Research Index with Bibliography*. Washington, DC: ABBE Publishers Association, 1985.

ARNOLD, WILLIAM V. *Introduction to Pastoral Care*. Philadelphia: Westminster Press, 1982. Discusses the broader concept of pastoral *care* within a biblical context. Addresses grief, illness, stress, sexuality, marital and family problems, suggesting biblical and theological resources for each.

KOTESKEY, RONALD L. *Psychology from a Christian Perspective.* Lanham, MD: University Press of America, 1991. A general introduction to psychology, written for a Christian lay audience.

PECK, M. SCOTT *The Road Less Traveled.* New York: Simon & Schuster, 1978.

PROPST, L. REBECCA *Psychotherapy in a Religious Framework: Spirituality in the Emotional Healing Process.* New York: Human Sciences Press, 1988.

SUMMERLIN, FLORENCE A., ed. *Religion and Mental Health: A Bibliography.* Rockville, MD: National Institute on Mental Health, 1980. A dated but still useful list of references with a subject index.

WEATHERHEAD, LESLIE D. *Psychology, Religion and Healing* (rev. ed.). Nashville: Abingdon, 1951.

Pastoral Counseling

The field of pastoral counseling proper focuses on the application of spiritual content and processes to the alleviation of human distress. Here the primary functions of the pastor are brought into play—spiritual direction, prayer, administration of the sacraments, pastoral guidance, and interpretation of scripture. Although this text does not concentrate on pastoral counseling in this sense, there are many books devoted to this subject.

CLINEBELL, HOWARD J. JR. *Basic Types of Pastoral Care and Counseling.* Nashville: Abingdon, 1984. This standard text reviews different styles and settings for pastoral counseling—family, group, crisis, supportive, educative, confrontational, marital, depth counseling, and so on.

COLLINS, GARY *Christian Counseling.* Waco, TX: Word, 1988. This volume contains some sound professional material and provides integrations of scriptural references and types of problems.

ESTADT, BARRY K., MELVIN BLANCHETTE, and JOHN R. COMPTON, eds. *Pastoral Counseling* (2d ed.). Englewood Cliffs, NJ: Prentice-Hall, 1990.

HULME, WILLIAM *Pastoral Care and Counseling: Using the Unique Resources of the Christian Tradition.* Minneapolis: Augsburg, 1981.

OATES, WAYNE E. *Pastoral Counseling.* Philadelphia: Westminster Press, 1982.

WISE, CARROLL *Pastoral Psychotherapy: Theory and Practice* New York: Aronson, 1983.

Special Series on Pastoral Care and Counseling

Various publishers have produced special series of books focusing on pastoral care and counseling. Within each series can be found some helpful titles. Information can be obtained directly from the publisher.

"Successful Pastoral Counseling" series, Russell Dicks, ed., Prentice-Hall
"Creative Pastoral Care and Counseling" series, Howard J. Clinebell Jr., ed., Fortress Press

"Christian Care Books" series, Wayne E. Oates, ed., Westminster John Knox Press. The small two-volume *Pastor's Handbook* gives brief discussions of the major topics covered in the Christian Care Books.

NOTES

[1]For an historical analysis see E. Mansell Pattison, "Psychiatry and Religion circa 1978: Analysis of a Decade, Part I," *Pastoral Psychology* 27 (1978): 8–25.

[2]This point is eloquently stated by Paul Pruyser in *The Minister as Diagnostician* (Philadelphia: Westminster Press, 1976). Also see note 9 below.

[3]Allen E. Bergin and Jay P. Jensen, "Religiosity of Psychotherapists: A National Survey," *Psychotherapy* 27 (1990): 3–7. Also see Allen E. Bergin, "Psychotherapy and Religious Values," *Journal of Consulting and Clinical Psychology* 48 (1980): 95–105.

[4]For a discussion see Paul W. Clement, "Getting Religion," *APA Monitor* 9, no. 6 (1978): 2. Freud stated his case against religion in two books: *The Future of an Illusion* and *Totem and Taboo* (New York: Norton, trans. 1962). Antitheistic views continue to be expressed by popular psychologists for example, Albert Ellis, "Psychotherapy and Atheistic Values: A Response to A. E. Bergin's 'Psychotherapy and Religious Values,' " *Journal of Consulting and Clinical Psychology* 48 (1980): 635–39.

[5]Andrew Christensen, William R. Miller, and Ricardo F. Muñoz, "Paraprofessionals, Partners, Peers, Paraphernalia, and Print: Expanding Mental Health Service Delivery," *Professional Psychology* 9 (1978): 249–70.

[6]For a review see J. A. Durlak, "Comparative Effectiveness of Paraprofessional and Professional Helpers," *Psychological Bulletin* 86 (1979): 80–92. See also Sam Alley, Judith Blanton, and Ronald E. Feldman, eds., *Paraprofessionals in Mental Health* (New York: Human Sciences Press, 1979), and Michael Gershon and Henry B. Biller, *The Other Helpers* (Lexington, MA: Lexington Books, 1977).

[7]William R. Miller and John E. Martin, eds., *Behavior Therapy and Religion* (Newbury Park, CA: Sage Publications, 1988).

[8]Gerald R. Patterson and Marion S. Forgatch, "Therapist Behavior as a Determinant for Client Noncompliance: A Paradox for the Behavior Modifier," *Journal of Consulting and Clinical Psychology* 53 (1985): 846–51. For a review see William R. Miller and Stephen Rollnick, *Motivational Interviewing: Preparing People to Change Addictive Behavior* (New York: Guilford Press, 1991).

[9]Richard Rohr, "Why Does Psychology Always Win? The Process of Conversion from Self-actualization to Self-transcendence," *Sojourners* (November 1991): 10–15.

2

THE FOUR PHASES OF COUNSELING

For everything there is a season, and a time for every matter.

—Ecclesiastes 3

Classical symphonies are written in four movements, each of which has its own unique form and pace. Chess players talk about opening, middle, and endgame phases of play, each of which requires specific knowledge and strategies. It is helpful to apply this same kind of developmental thinking to the process of counseling. Although content and progress of counseling will vary widely, there are four general phases or waves that characterize the flow of this process. Each represents different tasks and concerns, and each requires its own kind of skill on the part of the counselor. They are clarification, formulation, intervention, and termination.

These four phases are not discrete or mutually exclusive. They overlap like waves on the ocean. Sometimes counseling is brief and only one or two phases are encountered. Sometimes a particular phase is short; at other times it may require the work of many months. Sometimes it is necessary to backtrack to an earlier phase and start the process anew. In general, however, these four phases occur in order, and the counselor who is aware of this flow can better understand what is happening and choose his or her approach accordingly.

1. CLARIFICATION

The first phase, clarification, begins at the moment that either the pastor or the client initiates contact for the purpose of counseling. This can be as simple as the request, "Do you have a few minutes?" or "I wonder if I could talk to you sometime this week?"

When the pastor-person relationship expands to include that of counselor-client, it takes on a new dimension. For several reasons we recommend that pastors recognize that a transition is occurring here and make at least mental if not overt note of this change.

Herein lies a somewhat unique aspect of pastoral counseling. For the psychologist, initiation of therapeutic contact is a simple matter. The client calls the office and makes an appointment. Psychologists do not usually initiate therapy, and the relationship ends, in most cases, when the therapeutic process is over. For the pastor it is often quite different. The relationship with this person who becomes *client* probably existed for some time before the beginning of counseling and may continue long after the formal counseling process has ended. This poses unique problems as well as special advantages. The advantages have been discussed in chapter 1, but the problems may not be recognized until the pastor has been counseling for some time. These involve confusing and conflicting roles.

Some of this role conflict involves confidentiality. Parishioners who are or have been in counseling with the pastor may, for example, perceive that certain things said during a sermon were aimed at them or were derived from confidential sessions. The counseling pastor must continually remember who knows (and who can be told) what. These issues will be addressed further in chapter 3.

What we wish to address here is how to maintain gracefully two somewhat different relationships with people. We emphasize again that we do not want to divorce the pastoral context from the counseling relationship, for that would be a grave error. The problem is more one of placing some practical boundaries on the counseling relationship so that it does not expand to fill the whole pastoral context. When the pastor fails to do this, the client's emotional involvement in the counseling process can generalize to the entire relationship with the pastor or even with the church. The results can include the projection of counseling material into worship settings, the filling of every pastoral contact with therapeutic overtones, and sometimes a severing of the pastoral relationship itself, as when a parishioner leaves the congregation after the termination (albeit quite successful) of the counseling process.

The first task in this initial phase of counseling, then, is to clarify that you are embarking on a somewhat special process. One simple way of doing this is to make specific appointments for counseling and to avoid having the counseling relationship extend to every contact (which may be many if the person is an active member of your congregation). Another simple way to communicate uniqueness is to have counseling sessions occur in a consistent setting, usually behind closed doors in the pastor's study, although some pastors may prefer to set aside a special counseling room to separate roles further. This means not counseling in hallways, in doorways, or in the narthex just before worship begins. Of course, counseling cannot be totally contained within appointments and certain locations, but there are good reasons to take steps in this direction. One graceful way to deal with parishioners who corner you for "just a few minutes," particularly when you have somewhere else to go or something else to do, is to say something like, "I think you deserve my full attention, and I'd like to be able to give you some quality listening time. Let's find a time soon when I can give you my best. How about . . ." The message is clear: "You are too important to take just a few minutes." At the same time this helps to contain the counseling relationship within some reasonable limits. Also, at this point it may be helpful not to use words that imply formal counseling, since some people find that a bit threatening at first and may protest, "I just want to talk to you."

We do not recommend trying to make a formal counseling contract in early sessions for the same reason. During this clarification phase you must come to a common understanding of the type of counseling work that you will be doing together, but this process is best done gradually. The earliest communications are nonverbal: the special appointment, the closed door, your full attention. This is not to separate you from a pastoral context, but rather to indicate that a special aspect of your pastoral role is now beginning. This also makes it easier at the termination phase, when you must facilitate the transition back out of a counseling framework.

Beyond this initial context-setting, the major task of the clarification phase is for you to *listen*. Most pastors entering our workshops on practical counseling skills have regarded themselves to be good listeners, but we have found that only a minority listen well in practice. Good listening is a surprisingly difficult and specific skill that goes far beyond learning not to talk all the time. The particular listening method explained in part II of this book has been shown to do much more than clarify. It helps the client feel accepted and understood. It creates a safe atmosphere for exploration, growth, and change. This process of *relationship building* through listening is the hallmark of the clarification stage. It is a time of searching together for an understanding of the client's situation and of his or her unique way of perceiving the world.

Pastors sometimes misunderstand the purpose of this first phase. Following instincts drawn from common perceptions of how a counselor should behave, they attempt to rush in with advice, consolation, persuasion, exhortation, or questions. The true task in this clarification stage is at once more simple and more difficult than these. It is to come to share common ground with the client, to step as much as possible into his or her perceptual framework, to communicate acceptance and understanding, to help the client feel safe.[1] All of this is accomplished by the simple yet profoundly complicated process of listening in a therapeutic manner.

2. FORMULATION

Through the process of clarification, the counselor begins to approach the second phase, that of formulation. In this phase the style of interviewing shifts toward more directed inquiry, intermixing empathic listening with selective and purposeful questioning. Here the pastor needs a system for how to *think* clearly about people and their problems. Without such an organizing system, the pastor remains stuck at the first phase of listening or leaps prematurely to the third phase of intervention.

The task in this second phase is to arrive at an accurate understanding of the nature of the client's situation, a formulation that ultimately leads to the proper intervention. Part of the skill of formulation (*diagnosis* in the broadest sense) is knowing the right questions to ask, what to look for. Here it is very helpful to have some working knowledge of the major types of psychological problems that people encounter. If, for example, there is a high probability of a biological source of the problem (as in schizophrenia and certain types of depression), this must be recognized and appropriate treatment obtained. There are characteristic signs of biologically based depression, and recognizing these can save many useless and dangerous weeks of counseling (see chapter 12). There are, of course, many different causes of human problems. To know how to intervene most effectively, the counselor must be able to think clearly and accurately, to recognize types of problems and their probable causes. To begin an intervention phase without at least a tentative formulation might be likened to a surgeon operating blindfolded and without a diagnosis.

We hasten to distinguish the formulation process from the exercise of diagnostic labeling. The usefulness of the latter has been widely debated, and certainly there are good reasons to avoid labeling when possible.[2] We are not advocating that pastors mimic the process of psychiatric diagnosis. We *are* asserting that it is essential to have a clear process for formulation, for thinking, for making the transition from listening to intervention. Paul Pruyser proposed a fascinating provisional system for pastoral diagnosis based upon theological constructs.[3] In part III we provide some further guidelines to help you in the process of formulation, in deciding what (if any) problems or goals there are for counseling, in choosing how best to proceed, and in avoiding some major mistakes. There is, of course, a much larger body of knowledge regarding types of human problems than can be presented here. Some of the basics are included in part IV. A university course in psychopathology or "abnormal" psychology can be a worthwhile pursuit for the pastor who counsels.[4] Again, the challenge is to arrive at a holistic understanding that incorporates both the pastoral context and current knowledge regarding human problems and their proper treatment.

3. INTERVENTION

Still other skills are needed as the third phase is reached, that of active intervention. This phase overlaps with the formulation process in that the first decision to be made is how (and whether) to intervene. The choice of intervention approach or strategy should be closely tied to formulation.

Here again there is a large knowledge base upon which to draw. An approach that is very effective with one type of person or problem will be quite useless or even harmful with another. Fortunately, knowledge has grown beyond the trial-and-error stage in many areas, and since the 1970s there has been accumulating a systematic research literature to help in selecting approaches to use with different types of problems and people.[5] This is a complicated process and is an area of primary expertise for clinical psychologists. Nevertheless, there are some helpful guidelines that you can use in deciding whether, when, and how to intervene and when you should refer the individual for further consultation. Such guidelines are provided in part IV on a problem-by-problem basis.

Having decided what intervention is most appropriate, the pastor must then ask, "Should *I* undertake this process?" Because all of us have limited competencies, this a question not only for pastoral counselors, but also for all therapists. It may well be that, after a careful clarification and formulation process, you will determine that the client needs an intervention that is beyond your gifts and skills. A sound referral is then the appropriate intervention. The ability to make appropriate referrals is itself a crucial skill, one that is used often by the pastor who does much counseling. It is an invaluable service to help the client sort out and understand his or her situation, arrive at a tentative formulation, and provide referral to the right professional. Without this kind of guidance, the individual is left to wander with distressing helplessness and randomness through the yellow pages or through the confusing maze of the mental health service delivery system. Some guidelines for making good referrals are presented in part VI.

4. TERMINATION

Like the first phase of clarification, the final termination phase represents a transition, a shift in relationship. This phase is easier for the psychologist, as the client simply stops coming to the office. For the parish pastor, this transition poses unique challenges that contain both potential benefits and perils.

The purpose of this phase is to celebrate symbolically the end of the formal counseling relationship and the transition back into a "normal" pastoral relationship. This sentence implies that the pastor is not normally a counselor; the reasons for this distinction (as well as its limitations) have been discussed earlier. There are some practical and intuitive reasons for providing this transition. It facilitates for the client a comfortable settling back into a less intense pastor-person relationship in which there is not the assumption of continued sharing in such exhausting depth. It represents a kind of permission to be a parishioner again and to let go of the role of client (even though that term may never have been used during counseling).

Of course, the transition is never complete as long as the relationship continues, and that can be an advantage. The pastor remains a resource should the same or other problems emerge at a future time. The pastor can also ask discreetly how things are going, exercising a part of the continuing pastoral relationship. Very few psychologists can retain this kind of ongoing supportive relationship, and many are happy to be free of it. The continuing presence of the pastor, however, represents an invaluable and important support. The pastor also has permission by virtue of her or his role to check back either formally or informally or to initiate new contact if emerging problems are perceived.

The transition out of a counselor role need not be elaborate, and as with the initiation of counseling it may take place mostly through nonverbal symbols. One of these is the termination of formal appointments with a counseling goal. Some pastors use special chairs when counseling, different from those in which parishioners normally sit when making routine visits to the pastor's study. The transition may be marked simply by changing where the pastor sits (see chapter 3) or by meeting in a new place if the church maintains a separate counseling room or suite.

Certain verbal statements may also mark the transition. These are discussed in greater detail in chapter 19. These statements serve several purposes, including (a) summarizing the counseling process as it has unfolded, (b) providing a transition back to a normal pastor-person relationship, and (c) leaving the door open for future counseling contacts that may be needed. Dealing with the termination phase properly can mean the difference between having the person remain in the congregation and having him or her seek another fellowship because of some unfinished discomfort.

The pastor can also take steps to develop a caring and supportive community within the local congregation, so that the burden of pastoral care does not rest solely upon his or her shoulders. In chapter 20 we examine ways in which a local congregation can be encouraged and aided in the process of becoming a safer and more supportive place in which to live and grow.

SUMMARY

These, then, are the four general phases of the counseling process. Each differs from the others in its purpose and in the skills required of the pastoral counselor.

Not all phases occur in every case. For many clients the clarification process will be all that is needed. The listening process of this first phase is itself highly therapeutic, and through this process many individuals find within themselves the resources they need. For others, a clear understanding of their situation is what they are seeking, and the process of formulation is the end. With still others there will be a full and prolonged intervention process with a more gradual termination.

Keeping these phases in mind can help you to clarify what you are doing and to know the purpose or goal that you are pursuing at any point in time (Table 2-1). It goes without saying that this is not the *only* way of thinking about counseling. An existential theorist might seriously object to our description of formulation and intervention, preferring to see the entire process as one of a mutual journey in the search for meaning (perhaps closest to the clarification phase). A therapist committed totally to a "client-centered" approach would also probably eschew a differentiation between clarification and intervention. We present this four-phase process not as the one true light for pastoral counseling, but as a model that we have found very useful both in our own clinical practice and in our work with pastors who counsel. We acknowledge, however, that this way of thinking about counseling makes certain implicit assumptions that should perhaps be made more explicit, including the following:

The counseling process, while occurring clearly within a pastoral context, needs to be set off from the rest of the pastor's roles.

The process of mutual exploration and clarification, though invaluable for most and sufficient for some, is not enough in many cases. For many clients a clear

TABLE 2-1   The Four Phases of Counseling

COUNSELING PHASE	PURPOSE	SKILLS NEEDED
Clarification	Make transition into counseling Build therapeutic relationship Clarify goals	Reflective listening Acceptance and empathy
Formulation	Reach an accurate conception of the client's situation or problems	Working knowledge of psychological problems Organized system for thinking about people and their problems
Intervention	Move actively toward the counseling goals	Specific intervention skills Knowledge of how to choose appropriate interventions Referral skills
Termination	Make transition back to normal pastoral relationship	Smooth transition skills Continuing support skills Development of supportive community

formulation and active intervention are required, going well beyond the listening skills that characterize the first phase.

The pastoral counselor can develop skills appropriate to all of these phases, although at times referral will also be necessary.

Knowledge of psychology is beneficial to the pastoral counselor, who must be able to recognize major forms of psychological problems that require specific treatment.

A clear and organized system for thinking about people and their problems is necessary if pastoral counseling is to proceed. This system must incorporate the theological concepts of the pastor's own profession as well as essential elements from other disciplines. To proceed without such a system is to wander in the wilderness, a sometimes valuable but often woefully inefficient and insufficient process.

Effective intervention requires an informed matching of the individual with the approach most likely to be helpful. *Informed* here includes drawing on available research knowledge regarding the relative efficacy of alternative treatment approaches.

Clearly, not all of these assumptions are shared by all psychologists or counselors. We commend this approach to you, however, as having integrity as a general framework for counseling because it is flexible, draws on knowledge and skills from a broad range of theories and techniques, and is compatible with a wide range of individual counseling styles. The four phases are intended to be *descriptive* rather than prescriptive —to help you observe and understand what is happening in your counseling, not to require you to do things in a certain fashion or order. As with all of the material presented in this book, you will have to determine for yourself the usefulness and applicability of these guidelines within your own counseling.

The remainder of this book is organized around these four phases, providing specific skills and knowledge to be used at each step in the counseling process. Part II focuses on the skills most needed during the clarification phase: accurate, empathic listening and acceptance. Part III elaborates on the process of formulation, the second and very crucial phase of counseling in which you arrive at a conscious conceptualization of the problem. This in turn leads to intervention, the third phase of counseling discussed in part IV. Here chapters 8 through 11 discuss general intervention processes of increasing motivation, facilitating choice making, reducing confusion, and supporting change. Then chapters 12 through 18 of part V focus on specific problem areas commonly dealt with by pastors who counsel. In each of these chapters, basic diagnostic knowledge is introduced and then alternative interventions are suggested. Finally, part VI deals with the termination phase of counseling, the process of referral, and the building of a more caring and supportive community within the local congregation. Working within such a community, the pastor does not bear the total burden of pastoral care alone. There is a larger base of support into which the client makes a transition at the termination of formal counseling. The supportive congregation also provides opportunities for *preventive pastoring*, decreasing the occurrence and severity of problems among its members. Finally, in chapter 21, we address the important topic of pastoral self-care.

Before proceeding to part II and the skills of clarification, however, we turn to a consideration of some very important pragmatic issues that affect the context and integrity of a pastor's counseling.

ADDITIONAL READINGS

BRAMMER, LAWRENCE The Helping Relationship: Process and Skills (4th ed.). Englewood Cliffs, NJ: Prentice-Hall, 1988.

IVEY, ALLEN E., MARY B. IVEY, and LYNN SIMEK-DOWNING Counseling and Psychotherapy: Integrating Skills, Theory, and Practice (2d ed.). Englewood Cliffs, NJ: Prentice-Hall, 1987.

KANFER, FREDERICK H., and ARNOLD P. GOLDSTEIN Helping People Change: A Textbook of Methods (4th ed.). New York: Pergamon Press, 1991.

MOURSUND, JANET The Process of Counseling and Therapy (2d ed.). Englewood Cliffs, NJ: Prentice-Hall, 1990.

NOTES

[1]For elaboration on the process of forming a therapeutic relationship, see Susan K. Gilmore, *The Counselor-in-Training* (Englewood Cliffs, NJ: Prentice-Hall, 1973), and the additional readings at the end of this chapter.

[2]David L. Rosenhan, "On Being Sane in Insane Places," *Science* 179 (1973): 250–58; Thomas S. Szasz, *The Myth of Mental Illness* (New York: Harper, 1961).

[3]Paul W. Pruyser, *The Minister as Diagnostician: Personal Problems in Pastoral Perspective* (Philadelphia: Westminster Press, 1976).

[4]Two enduring standard references in this field are Robert C. Carson and James N. Butcher, *Abnormal Psychology and Modern Life*, 9th ed. (New York: Harper Collins, 1992), and Gerald C. Davison and John M. Neale, *Abnormal Psychology*, 5th ed. (New York: John Wiley, 1990).

[5]Arnold P. Goldstein and Norman Stein, *Prescriptive Psychotherapies* (Elmsford, NY: Pergamon Press, 1976); Arnold P. Goldstein, ed., *Prescriptions for Child Mental Health and Education* (Elmsford, NY: Pergamon Press, 1978). For examples from the alcoholism field, see William R. Miller and Reid K. Hester, "Matching Problem Drinkers with Optimal Treatments," in William R. Miller and Nick Heather, eds., *Treating Addictive Behaviors: Processes of Change* (New York: Plenum Press, 1986), 175–203.

3

BEFORE BEGINNING: PRACTICAL AND ETHICAL ISSUES

It is a high privilege to be able to share the experiences of so many different people; counselors are in an enviable role because they are able to interact with a very wide range of unique individuals at much more than a superficial, small-talk level.

—Susan K. Gilmore, *The Counselor-in-Training*

Thus far, we have considered the role of the pastor as counselor and some general phases of the counseling process. Before embarking on the exposition of specific skills and approaches, it is appropriate to consider some ethical and practical issues that affect all pastoral counseling and that are too often overlooked. These factors can powerfully influence the willingness of your parishioners to come to you for counseling and carry significant potential for harmful consequences.

CONFIDENTIALITY

Confidentiality is a fundamental and crucial issue in all types of counseling. Although it seems that this should be obvious, we have at times encountered distressing violations of professional standards of confidentiality among pastors. This occurs most often not through conscious carelessness or disregard, but rather through insufficient awareness of the nature and the potential effects of these issues. Difficulties can also arise because the pastor and client are unclear which interactions are and are not covered by the confidential mantle of *counseling*. This is one more good reason to demarcate counseling clearly from the rest of your pastoral roles, as discussed in chapter 2.

Rules of Confidentiality

The basic rule, to which some exceptions are necessary, is this: *whatever a client reveals to you within the context of counseling must be kept in total confidence*. This specifically includes not revealing such information to members of the client's family, to strangers, to other members of the congregation, to officers of the church, to your own colleagues, or to your family members. In short, don't tell *anyone*. The counselor is like a novelist in reverse. The novelist crafts one story and tells it to many people. The counselor hears many stories and tells them to no one.

This is a significant burden to carry, but it is an essential one. For the pastor, who maintains multiple relationships with a large number of people, the occasions for accidental violations are many. The simplest solution to remembering "who knows what" is to tell *no one* what occurs behind the closed doors of counseling sessions.

This raises another perhaps obvious but sometimes overlooked rule: *the doors should be closed*. Furthermore, the soundproofing of your counseling area should be very carefully secured, so that the sessions cannot be inadvertently or intentionally overheard by office staff or by visitors to the outer office. Any intercom arrangement with your secretary should include a safeguard controlled by you to guarantee that the system cannot be used to overhear counseling sessions. The potential for gossip within a congregation is substantial, and it is your responsibility to protect your clients from this possibility. Even if your secretary is of professional status and privy to confidential matters, it is inappropriate for him or her to have access to the content of pastoral counseling sessions.

A related rule is that any discussion of a client must occur behind closed doors. If the process of counseling requires you to place or receive telephone calls regarding the client, this must be done within the confidence of your office and in a manner that cannot be monitored by others who may pick up the telephone. You can modify your office equipment to assure confidentiality. If it is necessary to discuss a client with a colleague, this should *never* be done in a hallway, in an office with an open door, in a public restaurant, and so forth. A good rule is to be paranoid: pretend that there are people consciously attempting to overhear your remarks and gain information about your clients. The probability may be very low that there is anyone nearby who could know or care about the person you are discussing, but we have seen some very painful examples of unfortunate incidents and coincidences. Leaving out names and identifying details does not make it any more acceptable to discuss cases in a public place. Discussing clients publicly will, in general, discourage people from seeking counseling and will demean your own trustworthiness in the eyes of a person who happens to overhear. *Be careful*. Taking such precautions can only increase the confidence of the congregation that, should they decide to seek counseling, they will be similarly protected.

Client records must also be carefully safeguarded. Some pastors prefer not to keep any written records of counseling, but if you do any volume of counseling we strongly recommend that you keep notes. It is very difficult to retain in memory the significant content of every session with every client. Having a running record helps you to retain the whole picture with each person, and reviewing the total process can often be helpful in finding new directions. In any event, if you do keep written records of counseling these must be protected. A securely locked filing cabinet within your inner office is usually sufficient. With the possible exception of a confidential secretary who assists in typing client records or reports, absolutely no one besides you should have a key. This file should not be used for other purposes that permit others to have access to the cabinet.

Exceptions to Confidentiality

There are certain conditions under which the rule of total confidentiality may be broken. The most obvious of these is an understanding between pastor and client, preferably written, that information from counseling sessions may be shared with another individual. A sample permission form for exchange of information is shown in Figure 3-1, specifying the type of information to be exchanged, the individual(s) with whom such exchange is to occur, and the purpose and limitations of this exchange. If a client is also seeing another professional for counseling, it is wise to obtain such written permission for exchange of information. A clear verbal understanding may be sufficient if it is agreed that information can be shared with another family member, such as the client's spouse. When in doubt, however, obtain written permission before sharing any information about a client. Even the fact that you are seeing a certain person for counseling is confidential, and it is unprofessional to divulge this information without the client's consent. Suppose, for example, that you receive a telephone call from a colleague who says, "I believe that you are seeing John Warren for counseling, and I'd like to talk to you about him." Not only should you disclose nothing about your counseling without written permission, but you should protect the fact of your counseling relationship by saying something like: "Of course whatever happens in my pastoral counseling is confidential, and I can't even confirm whether I am seeing someone without their permission."

If the person being counseled is a minor, special issues arise with regard to divulging counseling information to the parents. When dealing with minors, it is wise to be clear from the outset what information can and will be shared with the parents and to make this known both to the child and to the parents. Confidentiality with minors is a delicate issue, and it is advisable to know about applicable laws in your state.

It is also possible that under certain circumstances you could be required by a court of law to release information or face legal consequences. The records

PARKWOOD COMMUNITY CHURCH

Permission for Exchange of Information

I hereby grant permission for an exchange of professional information between Rev. Pat Brown and

_____

of _____

The nature of specific information to be exchanged is:

_____ unrestricted, as deemed appropriate by those
named above

_____ limited to: _____

_____

The purpose for this exchange of information is: _____

_____

Exchange of information is to be:

_____ one time only   _____ ongoing

Expiration date for permission: _____

Signature: _____ Date _____

Witness: _____ Date _____

FIGURE 3-1   Sample Exchange of Information Form

of any mental health professional can be subpoenaed under particular conditions, and these statutes may apply to a pastoral counselor as well. Again, you should be informed about the applicable state laws.

Under certain other conditions, you may have a moral obligation to break confidentiality. Licensed health professionals are required by law, for example, to break confidentiality if a client reveals an intent to do violence to another person.[1] If a therapist fails to warn the threatened individual, the therapist may be found liable should the client carry out the threat. A still more difficult decision is whether to violate client confidentiality if you perceive the client to be in danger. For example, under what conditions might you notify family members of the suicidal thoughts of a client, divulged to you in confidence, without the client's permission? These are difficult professional judgments and are best shared with a colleague or supervisor when possible.

As a pastor who counsels, you will at times be privy to information that by law should be reported to legal, protective, or social service authorities. A case in point is the discovery of abuse of a child or an elderly person. Such abuse may be physical, sexual, or both. In many states, pastoral counselors (like many other professionals) are required to report incidents of suspected child abuse. Whether or not you are bound by law to report such incidents, you should be alert to signs that may indicate abuse: bruises, cuts, substantial mood changes, torn or dirty clothing, inability to concentrate, or fearful avoidance of physical contact with adults. Because children and frail elderly are largely unable to protect themselves and often frightened even to discuss their victimization, counselors have a special responsibility to explore and to provide protection when abuse is suspected. Usually the state's protective services personnel, who are experienced and empowered in such cases, will be best equipped to evaluate and intervene appropriately.

This raises another possible exception to confidentiality: the use of a colleague or supervisor as a sounding board in your counseling work. This is a common and valuable practice, but it should not be done without a client's knowledge. If information about the client is to be shared with another professional for purposes of consultation or supervision, the client should be informed of that relationship. Under certain conditions a written consent for release of information should be obtained.

For several reasons, it can be wise to review and sign a general agreement about confidentiality in addition to specific releases of information as discussed above. This may seem a bit formal for pastoral counseling, but it serves both to signal that this is a special relationship (see chapter 2) and to clarify the sometimes complex conditions of counseling confidentiality. You are on solid ground if you have specified in advance the conditions and limits of confidentiality and have followed these agreed-upon conditions. One sample of such an agreement is shown in Figure 3-2.

Another important confidentiality issue is what, if anything, the pastor

PARKWOOD COMMUNITY CHURCH

Confidentiality Agreement

Pastoral counseling is a special type of relationship between people and their pastor. I will keep in total confidence whatever you tell me during counseling sessions. I will not share any information that you have given me during counseling or discuss your counseling with anyone else. The only exceptions to this general condition of counseling are in the following circumstances:

1. If you give me written permission, below or by a separate Release of Information form, to share certain information with specific people

2. If I have reason to believe that my failure to disclose otherwise confidential information would clearly endanger the health and safety of yourself or someone else

3. If I need to obtain advice regarding your counseling from my professional consultant/supervisor, who is

_____ .

If you wish, you may grant me permission to share appropriate information from your conseling with specific people who are close to you. (Write "None" below if you so choose.)

- -

I understand and agree to the above conditions of counseling. I do request that my pastor share appropriate information from my counseling with only those people named here: _____

_____

Sigurature: _____ Date: _____

Pastor's Signature: _____ Date: _____

FIGURE 3-2   Sample Language for a Confidentiality Agreement

tells his or her spouse. Some find it difficult after a long day of counseling when their spouses ask, "What did you do at the office today?" to reply, "Oh, nothing!" Many parishioners also seem to assume that counselors share the content of sessions with their spouses. Sometimes clients approach the pastor's spouse and begin discussing their personal situations from therapy, only to discover that the spouse knows nothing about it, nor even that they were in counseling with the pastor. This kind of surprise, of course, is much preferred to the opposite. If you decide that you wish to share your counseling work with your spouse, then you are obliged to make this fact known to your clients. If you do generally share counseling experiences with your spouse, there will certainly be specific cases in which you must choose not to do so. In any event, the client should know, and you should have a clear agreement about who will be told what.

The general rule about exceptions is this: if there is to be *any* exception to the principle of total confidentiality, this should be negotiated with the client in advance. Only under the rarest of circumstances should information be divulged without the client's specific verbal if not written consent, and in these cases it is wise to share the decision with an informed colleague for your own protection. As a rule, then, no one is to be given confidential information obtained during counseling, and the very information that a person *is in* counseling with you is confidential. Because what a person reveals within a noncounseling context may ordinarily be shared at your discretion, it is best to have a clear understanding as to what constitutes the counseling context. When in doubt, protect your client.

The requirement of total confidentiality is the most basic of obligations for the pastoral counselor. It should be practiced so that it is absolutely routine. Personal matters of clients are simply not discussed with others. Period.

OTHER ETHICAL ISSUES

To take on a counseling relationship is to accept a serious professional responsibility. What you do as a counselor may alter the life course of your clients and those around them. Though you experience yourself as an ordinary person while you sit in the counselor's chair, it is important to remember the extent to which clients ascribe to their counselors special wisdom, knowledge, insight, and trustworthiness. If this is so for secular counselors, it is doubly true for pastors, who are also invested with spiritual leadership. It is vital to be conscious of your power in counseling and to guard carefully against situations and motivations that may lead you to misdirect or misuse your influence.

A community expectation of professional counselors is that they will operate within the general moral and ethical guidelines of the culture, including but not limited to the applicable legal codes. For a pastor, this extends to the standards of your own denomination. Violations of these community standards is particularly problematic within the unique context of a counseling relationship and can undermine your work and pastoral roles.

Relatedly, it is vital to be aware of the role of values in counseling. The notion that counseling can be objective and value-free is a dangerous misconception. Your own values color the ways in which you interact with people, conceptualize problems and solutions, set goals, give advice, and judge progress. For this reason it is important to be conscious of and open about your own values and assumptions and to be aware of how these may influence the process and effectiveness of your counseling.

The Appreciation of Differences

Values and assumptions are particularly important to consider when working with people different from yourself (which is, in one sense, all of the time). Stereotypes or lack of knowledge about a client's culture, gender, religion, age group, or social class can lead to problems in counseling. To counsel effectively, pastoral counselors benefit from knowledge of role expectations—not only their own, but also those of their clients. Further, as a pastoral counselor, your concern often extends beyond helping the client work on emotional concerns to helping clients look at how their spirituality ties into emotional struggles. To do so requires knowledge of social role expectations as they relate to spiritual health.

A landmark study in 1970 reported that mental health professionals had different standards for mental health for men, women, and adults.[2] The descriptors for mentally healthy adults and mentally healthy men were similar, but the descriptions of mentally healthy women matched those given for mentally *un*healthy adults. Two decades later, Long and Heggen conducted a parallel survey of clergy to study their perceptions of spiritual health as it pertains to the ideal for adults in general, men, and women.[3] They found that "(a) spiritual health is defined differently for adult men and women by clergy, (b) spiritual health for men is perceived to be equivalent to the ideal standards for adults, and (c) spiritual health for women is perceived by clergy to be significantly different from the ideal standard for adults." Said another way, the clergy surveyed saw spiritual health for men as almost identical to ideal spiritual health for adults in general, but they saw spiritual health for women as different from spiritual health for adults in general (e.g., men). Many of the characteristics of spiritual health for women identified by clergy in this study are opposite from those found in other research to predict psychological health. One could infer that pastors who counsel women might find it difficult to meet their expectations for spiritual health and also develop behaviors that lead to psychological health. We detail this research to illustrate how values and expectations, often below awareness, could affect counseling in important ways.

Different families and cultures can have dramatically different standards of appropriate behavior, including standards for subtle social behaviors such as eye contact, volume of speech, physical contact, and the proper distance between people when talking. Such differences can lead to misinterpretation and miscommunication between counselor and client. What seems normal to one may look pathological to the other.

Even among demographically similar people, personal styles vary in healthy, valuable ways. Behavior that is normal for an introvert may appear abnormal to (and indeed be abnormal for) an extrovert. An understanding and appreciation of normal variation in psychological types can be invaluable for the counselor[4]—a point to which we shall return when we discuss relationship counseling in chapter 18.

How does one guard against difference bias in counseling? Because all of us are somewhat unaware of the lenses through which we view the world, it is useful to have a supervisor or colleagues with whom to discuss professional issues. It is important, too, to take time to understand how your client thinks and perceives. When counseling people from a cultural background different from your own, for example, it is acceptable and wise to ask them to help you understand their culture, what it means to them, and how it affects the issues raised in counseling. Asking and listening, rather than assuming, can go a long way toward bridging diversity (see chapter 5).

Competence

Another important ethical issue for all counselors, not only for pastors, is that of professional competence. The guiding principle here is straightforward: Don't try to counsel beyond your own areas of competency and training. We do not mean here to discourage you from counseling, but only to say that all counselors encounter types of problems and clients for whom they simply do not have the knowledge and skills (and sometimes the time) needed to help. The ability to counsel effectively can also be affected by temporary or personal issues, as when a client's difficulties are too close to current problems and sore spots of your own.

There are two general possibilities when you reach the limits of your competency. One is to refer the person to a colleague who has the requisite training, skill, and time to offer what is needed. The art of selecting and making referrals will be discussed in detail in chapter 19. Sometimes, however, referral is not feasible. There may be no available or affordable referral options. The difficult issue may be just one part of a larger counseling picture, most of which you do feel able to address. The client may be unwilling to accept a referral. In this case, it may be possible for you to obtain advice and assistance from a colleague or supervisor with the needed competencies.

It is also possible, of course, to expand your own areas of professional competency. We hope that this book will serve as a practical handbook for you, offering relevant knowledge and skills in common counseling areas. If you regularly encounter among those you serve a particular counseling need for which you are not adequately prepared, continuing education resources may be available to strengthen your skills (see chapter 20). Specialized courses of counselor training are available through many universities, seminaries, and professional organizations.

Dual Relationships

Mental health professionals are traditionally prohibited from entering into a dual relationship. This occurs when, in addition to the counselor-client roles, there is another relationship that prescribes different roles that could cause conflicting interests or otherwise interfere with counseling (e.g., teacher-student, employer-employee, business or sexual partners).

Strictly applied, this rule would obviate most pastoral counseling because by definition you have two roles in relation to your clients: pastor and counselor. We have argued in chapter 1, however, that this is the unique heart and strength of pastoral counseling! The reconciliation here lies in the fact that counseling is just one of the historic and accepted roles within pastoring; that is, counseling is a *part* of the superordinate pastoral relationship.

Nevertheless, dual relationship issues pose serious risks and challenges for pastors. Many of the conflicting roles proscribed for counselors in general also apply to pastoral counselors. As discussed below, it is never acceptable to become sexually involved with a client. It is extremely unwise to enter into a counseling relationship with an employee, family member, trainee, relative of a supervisor, or current member of a congregational or denominational governing body to which you report or by which you are evaluated. The troubles that can emerge from such dual relationships can be devastating.

It is, however, almost unavoidable that some people you counsel were in the past in other relationships to you or will be in the future. A former client may wind up sitting across the table from you on the committee that determines your salary or may apply for a staff position that you supervise. A contentious former member of your governing board may turn up in the office seeking counseling. All of these are judgment calls. Just remember three principles:

1. Stringently avoid counseling people with whom you *currently* or will in the near future have power relationships.
2. Honor confidentiality absolutely when a former client enters into a new power relationship with you.
3. If you or the client feel uncomfortable with a possible or actual dual relationship, don't enter into or continue the counseling.

PASTORAL COUNSELING AND SEXUAL ETHICS

Some of the most sensitive and potentially destructive issues for pastoral counselors pertain to sexual ethics. The fact is that some pastoral counselors do succumb to accusations and temptations of sexual involvement with clients, despite their best intentions at the outset. How does this happen?

One experienced counselor of clergy observed two common patterns among those who became ensnared in sexual problems.[5] One involved clergy who had never resolved fundamental sexual issues in their own lives and who showed "a long history of poor sexual self-management." The other was a pattern of deterioration in the pastor's marital relationship, often related to poor management of time and stress and neglect of spiritual disciplines. These two patterns do not, of course, account for all pastoral violations of professional sexual ethics.

Neither are all accusations of pastoral sexual misconduct founded in fact. Some factors that can lead to false accusations and some practical self-protection measures will be discussed later in this chapter. Our concern here is with the pastoral counselor's own sexual conduct.

One prudent guideline is to set your own limits of conduct well short of any behaviors that could be construed as sexual misconduct. As C. S. Lewis observed, what may seem to be small and unimportant day-to-day decisions have a way of escalating, and in effect they constitute our ethical standards.[6] Societal problems related to sexual conduct in the workplace have led to a practical clarification and federal law regarding what constitutes sexual harassment, an issue that is both helpful and important for pastoral counselors to understand.

Sexual harrassment has been defined as "any attention—verbal, visual, or physical contact—that is unwanted by the recipient."[7] What is crucial here is that, by legal definition, it is the *recipient* of the behavior who defines its acceptability or welcomeness. It is when unacceptable sexual communication or behavior is imposed on another that harassment occurs.

> Harassment can be a matter of a risque joke or innuendo, an unacceptable glance, a personal insult, overly solicitous behavior, an unwelcome touch, hug, or kiss, attempted seduction, fondling, or intercourse. However subtle or blatant, whatever the degrees of seriousness one might attach to various words or action, what makes it sexual harassment is that it is unacceptable to the person on the receiving end.[7]

In a pastoral counseling context, the potential for sexual harassment may be heightened. Pastoral counselors work with clients who are distressed and who may be emotionally needy in ways that leave them vulnerable to sexual exploitation.

The "welcomeness" standard, however, is wholly insufficient within the context of pastoral counseling. No sexual intimacy is appropriate between counselor and client, regardless of its apparent acceptability to the client. Sexual behavior between counselor and client is always a violation of moral trust and of professional ethics. Furthermore, well short of overt intimacy, there is reason to be particularly cautious in pastoral counseling of any behaviors that could be construed as sexual. The uneven power context of counseling places the pastoral counselor de facto in a relationship where imposition and therefore harassment is easily inferred after the fact. Therefore, we advise that in your counseling you avoid any behavior that could be construed as sexual or suggestive. This means taking particular professional caution in physical contact.

Finally, it is wise to have a clear understanding of your denomination's code of ethics for clergy and to live by it. It can also be wise to have a clear agreement or policy with your church board regarding how sensitive situations are to be handled in counseling in particular and in other individual contacts in general.[8]

THE USE OF CASE MATERIAL

One practical issue related to ethical standards is the use of case material for other than counseling purposes. Often an experience from counseling provides an illuminating or inspiring example to include in sermons or homiletic presentations. For the pastor who writes, case materials are colorful and interesting illustrations. Case material may also be used in other talks, in conversations, in teaching, or even with other clients in similar circumstances. Herein, however, lie potential pitfalls.

The most basic concern is confidentiality. Whenever such material is used outside the context of counseling, every care must be taken to ensure that the individual being discussed cannot be identified. Names should be changed; the same initials should not be retained, nor should similar names be chosen. Critical identifying details such as occupation must be changed. It is a good general rule *never* to use in public a case example from the same community. There are just too many possibilities for problems.

Another less frequently considered aspect is that the use of such case material may be worrisome to current and potential clients. The individual who hears a sermon containing a case example cannot help but wonder, "Will my pastor use *me* as an example some day if I go for counseling?" For this reason it is desirable to let your congregation know that case materials are used only with two precautions: (a) that all critical details are changed to protect the individual and (b) that no one from the present community is mentioned. This saves the congregation from looking around the room and asking, "I wonder who *that* was!" It also lets people know that their own revelations are fully protected. Finally, care should be taken in presenting case material *never* to ridicule but always to hold the individual (even if fictitious) in total respect as if he or she were present. This is done to model for the congregation that their own confidences will be treated respectfully.

NOTE-TAKING

If you decide to keep written records of sessions, there are a few practical matters to consider. First, the decision must be made whether to keep notes during the session or to write them afterward. This is a matter of personal choice, but there is no reason why notes cannot be kept during sessions. If this method is chosen, here are a few guidelines.

1. Use small notepaper. A large clipboard or tablet can serve as a nonverbal barrier.
2. Keep notes brief. Extensive writing interferes with the counseling process, breaks eye contact, and makes clients uncomfortable.
3. Inform your client at the outset that you routinely take a few notes so that you can remember important points.
4. Be careful about timing. Writing down certain material immediately after it is given is a communication to the client and can influence further material that is offered. Delay note-taking for a time, and make the record at a less obvious break in the process.
5. As much as possible maintain eye contact with the client. This requires that notes be brief. Perhaps a form of shorthand can be used.

Regardless of the recording method used, it is wise to finish your case notes immediately after a session to retain freshness and accuracy.

Under certain circumstances it may be desirable to tape-record sessions. These include sessions that you wish to review yourself or with a supervisor and those where the specific content may be crucial later. In any event the client's permission should be obtained, and recordings should never be made without the client's knowledge. The uses to be made of a recording (or any notes) should be made clear to the client, and no other use should be allowed.

THE OFFICE

The setting in which you conduct counseling sessions is also an important consideration. The implications for confidentiality have already been discussed. The setting should allow no possibility of eavesdropping. If your office has external windows, you should provide a window covering or glazing that prevents outsiders from looking in. Various types of glazing, shades, and curtains are translucent, permitting light into the office and even a view from the inside out without allowing a person outside to determine whether there are people inside. Some pastors find this type of shade to be desirable as a general provision in their offices.

Minimization of interruptions is also essential. Random visitors should not be able to tap on the door or pop their heads into your office. Telephone calls should be diverted to a secretary or answering machine. Until you have been in the client's chair, it is difficult to appreciate the distress and anger that a client can experience when the counselor takes incoming calls. When you are counseling you should not be doing anything else. A pastor who sorts through the day's mail while listening to a client communicates (albeit unintentionally) a disregard that is quite annoying. Even if you really can do more than one thing at a time, *don't.*

The clients' comfort in coming and going from counseling sessions must be remembered. Your counseling sessions may be held away from your regular office, so that the client does not emerge to the usual traffic of the church office. A private entrance is desirable. Some pastors exchange offices with each other for counseling hours to increase confidentiality. On the other hand, one advantage of using your regular office is that no one can then determine whether a person is coming for counseling or for some other, more routine purpose. In any event your clients should be protected from embarrassment, no matter how irrational, about coming and going from counseling sessions.

The arrangement of furnishings is also significant. If you have a desk in your office, we strongly recommend that you get out from behind it when counseling. Some pastors find it comfortable to sit behind a desk for normal business transactions but come around in front of the desk and sit in proximal chairs for counseling sessions. The desk is a formidable obstacle to forming a relationship, and it certainly is not needed to establish pastoral authority.

Levels of seating should be considered. It is not desirable for the counselor to be seated in a chair that is lower than that of the client. Seating at about the same height is probably optimal. The pastor's chair being higher than that of the client implies an uneven relationship. Be aware of this communication, and don't underestimate its power.

The relative position of chairs of the counselor and client also is significant. A head-on, face-to-face arrangement is very uncomfortable for most clients. It requires the client to turn the head to look away, and at a nonverbal level this chair arrangement is highly confrontational. Also, in terms of practicalities, it can be uncomfortable for the male pastor and female client if the latter wears a short skirt. The exact angle and distance of chairs can vary. Somewhere between 90 and 140 degrees seems to work best, but don't get out the measuring tool. The best angle is one that allows you to look at each other easily but also allows you to look away from the other person by looking forward without turning your head. As for the distance between chairs, this will vary from one client to another according to their own personal comfort zone. If the chairs move easily, you may observe clients moving closer to or further from you according to their optimal personal space.

One option is to have several chairs available and allow the client to choose where to sit. You can then determine where you want to sit after the client has made a selection. If you know which chair you want, an easy way to announce this is to leave a book, notebook, or other material on that chair.

Finally, the set-up of your counseling office should take into account your own protection. Although your secretary should not have access to sessions, it may be advisable to have another person close at hand should assistance be desired. This is particularly advisable when seeing unfamiliar clients of the opposite sex. The proximal presence of another person can protect you both from unpredictable developments in counseling and from later accusations regarding your own conduct. The pastor should be aware of these issues because of the rich possibilities for transference in this relationship.

TRANSFERENCE

The term *transference* is derived from a psychoanalytic model of therapy, but it describes a process that is universal in counseling. Transference occurs when a client *transfers* to the therapist feelings and perceptions that pertain to other relationships, actual or imaginary. The stereotyped example is to transfer onto a therapist the parental image and to begin treating the therapist as if he or she were the parent. This occurs in all types of counseling, as well as in noncounseling relationships.

If therapists are ripe targets for transference, counseling pastors are doubly so. Not only are there all of the transference themes that adhere to the therapist role, but also the fertile ground of the pastoral role. Thus, clients may project onto the pastor (with or without awareness) the image of parent, sibling, authority, moralist, or even God. As this occurs, all of the client's feelings and inclinations toward the projected image can also transfer. For this reason pastors may suddenly find themselves the target of intense anger, enveloping dependency, or flagrant seduction.

The process of psychoanalysis itself, which works through this type of transference relationship, is very complex and is not to be embarked upon without extensive training. The phenomenon of transference is mentioned here simply to alert you to the possibility of the rapid emergence of these reactions. Several courses of action are worth considering in this regard.

One strategy is to be aware of counselor behaviors that amplify transference and to avoid these behaviors. The more distant and ambiguous the therapist, the greater the spontaneous transference. This is one reason why the classic psychoanalyst sits behind the couch, in darkness and out of the client's vision, and says very little. The pastor who is silent, distant, and mysterious *fosters* transference. The opposite of this style is what Carl Rogers called *genuineness*, a style that includes self-disclosure and the sharing of your own reactions with the client. This does not prevent transference, but it decreases the spontaneous variety.

Some of us are more prone than others to transference projections. Some pastors learn through supervision and their own clinical experience that clients very quickly project onto them their worst fears regarding rejection and disapproval unless active steps are taken to prevent this from happening. This may have something to do with the pastor's physical appearance or with his or her natural tendency to keep quiet while listening. If the pastor does not take specific steps to prevent transference, clients often begin imagining what the pastor is thinking about them. Of course that, too, can be useful in counseling, but you must be aware of the process and be prepared to use it if you foster it.

If you choose *not* to encourage transference nor to use it as a primary vehicle in counseling, you must at least be aware that these intense feelings will occur in your clients, be prepared to deal with them constructively, and even in some cases be prepared to protect yourself from them. It is likely that you will encounter some clients who will rage at you or at God in your presence. It is likely that some will try to seduce you. Others will become very dependent on you and try to ensnare you in deadly cycles of responsibility that often appeal strongly to guilt and may involve threats of suicide if you fail to comply. These are not everyday examples, but they are quite likely to be encountered more than once by the pastor who counsels.

A few specific guidelines may be helpful here.

1. Set clear limits for yourself regarding what you will and will not do within counseling relationships. These include limits for demands on your time, for physical contact, and so forth. When such issues arise in counseling, communicate these limits and stick by them.
2. Become more comfortable in counseling people who have intense feelings. Very angry people pose special challenges, but the listening skills presented in chapter 5 often prove quite effective in dealing with even high levels of anger.
3. Help your clients to separate reality from fantasy. Where a transference issue is emerging, discuss it directly to separate yourself from the projected image.
4. Have contingency plans to protect yourself against unpredictable violence or sexual behavior.
5. Maintain an ongoing relationship with a competent professional colleague to discuss more difficult issues.

COUNTERTRANSFERENCE

It is also common for therapists to develop strong and irrational feelings about certain clients, a process called *countertransference* in classic analytic thinking. In some cases feelings about a client are justified and natural reactions; in other cases they emerge from the counselor's own background and unresolved material. These reactions are particularly dangerous when they happen to fit into a pattern of transference from the client, as when a dependent client finds a therapist with rescue needs or a seductive client finds a counselor with a strong need to be admired and loved. Every counselor sets out with the thought that "It will never happen to me," but many become ensnared in these difficult situations. Where a pastoral role is involved, such relationships can further evolve into emotional or even financial blackmail and the potential loss of position and profession.

The possibilities for complementary countertransference relationships are so many that they cannot be addressed within a chapter such as this. A good general rule, however, is to monitor your own reactions to clients and to determine the reason for your reactions. Again, consultation with a supervisor or colleague can be valuable in sorting out these reactions. Another rule is to restrain yourself from acting on strong emotional reactions to clients. Under no circumstances is it justifiable or therapeutic to become sexually involved with a client during the counseling process. Therapist rage is usually best directed elsewhere than to the client, preferably within a different context where it can be dealt with in a healthy manner. Personal therapy for the pastor may be important when such reactions emerge. In cases where strong countertransference persists, referral is in order. In situations with a high potential for problems (as in a home visit, a night office call, etc.), it is wise to take someone with you. Finally, pay attention to and deal with *early* signs of such reactions to clients, rather than ignoring these as irrelevant or trivial.

SUPERVISION

For these and other reasons, it is usually wise for a pastoral counselor to have ongoing supervision or at least some backup consultation from a competent professional person working within the mental health system. This is helpful in cases where medication or institutionalization is required, where diagnosis is questionable, or where new and unfamiliar problems are encountered. Some pastors work together in groups and obtain consultation from a psychologist or psychiatrist for regular case discussions.

A mental health professional within your own congregation is an obvious choice, both because of his or her proximity and because of a higher likelihood of sensitivity to important pastoral issues. Some psychologists and psychiatrists do retain hostile or suspicious attitudes toward religion and are disinclined to enter into a truly collaborative professional relationship with a pastor.[9] It is best to work with a professional who has an understanding of the spiritual dimension of life and who is inclined to regard the pastor as a colleague.

The supervisory relationship or consultation group can also be helpful in your continued growth and learning as a counselor. It can provide valuable backup when complicated legal, psychological, or medical issues arise. In this regard, malpractice is an increasingly serious issue for pastoral counselors. You would be well advised to inquire regarding current legal standards in your area and to arrange appropriate supervisory relationships for your own legal protection. Various types of malpractice insurance are available if needed and may be purchased either by an individual or by an institution.

FEES

For the average pastor who counsels within a local parish setting, fees are not an issue because they are not charged. Counseling is seen as part of the larger pastoral role and not as a service to be exchanged for remuneration.

An increasing number of pastoral counselors, however, are setting up professional offices and operating on a fee-for-service basis. Such independent practice represents a vocational preference or an alternative to full-time ministry in a congregation. This raises the question of how to set and collect fees.

Fees are normally set according to professional standards within the community. What do comparably trained counselors charge? It is customary to charge on a per-session basis (with a normal session approximating forty-five to fifty minutes) even though individual sessions vary in length. Marital and family counseling sessions are usually billed at the same rate as individual sessions. In group counseling, on the other hand, the fee per client per session is typically reduced substantially, relative to the charge for private individual sessions. Many professionals are willing to make adjustments in fees based on a client's ability to pay, and some assess fees according to a sliding scale similar to those used by public agencies, taking into account the client's income and financial responsibilities. Many professionals regard it a part of their community service to offer counseling without fee or with very minimal fee to some clients who are unable to obtain services otherwise.

Whenever counseling fees are charged, questions of collection arise. How should the counselor deal with a client who does not pay? Whether such accounts are turned over to a collection agent is a matter of individual choice for the counselor, though some find this inconsistent with their pastoral role. Some counselors avoid such problems and the paperwork of billing by working with clients on a pay-as-you-go basis whereby fees are collected after each session.

Although most health insurers will reimburse for services of licensed psychologists or psychiatrists, pastoral counselors are often ineligible for such third-party reimbursement. In some states a legal supervision arrangement can be made between a counselor and a licensed professional, whereby reimbursement is paid to the supervisor and then passed on in full or in part to the supervisee. The legality of such arrangements must be checked in each locale. The emergence of health maintenance organizations (HMOs) and other prepaid health care systems has further restricted the ability of pastoral counselors to collect fees for service.

The vast majority of pastors who counsel, however, derive their personal income from other sources and do not charge fees. What effect does this have on counseling? Some therapists maintain that the payment of fees is an important and beneficial aspect of the therapeutic process, increasing the client's motivation, investment, or personal involvement and commitment. We disagree with this assertion and believe that fees are largely a matter of the counselor's needs and not the client's. Certainly, it is legitimate for a professional to collect fees in exchange for competent services. But there is nothing *necessary* about this, and there is no evidence that the payment of fees increases a client's benefit from counseling. Over the years we have treated and supervised the treatment of hundreds of clients who have received and responded well to services offered without fee.

Alternatives to fees can also be considered. Some professionals offer services on a barter basis, exchanging counseling time for specified goods or services. (Incidentally, it may be illegal not to report such arrangements as income for purposes of taxation.) Another option is available to pastors who counsel in regular congregational settings. In lieu of fees, a client could identify services that he or she might offer to others. An agreement could then be negotiated whereby the client offers such service to others without expectation of any return.

PRAYER AND THE PRIESTLY ROLE

Finally, some pastors wonder to what extent they can feel free to mix their roles and to include prayer, spiritual direction, or other "priestly" functions within the counseling setting. Our own perspective on this is perhaps already obvious. We believe that people come to a pastoral counselor specifically to be understood within a holistic framework that includes the spiritual dimension of humanity. If appropriate, there is no reason why prayer, confession, or other priestly functions should not be incorporated.

The pastor should not feel *obliged* to include prayer in counseling sessions, but neither should he or she feel inhibited from doing so. One approach is to ask the client whether this would be helpful. (Of course, many will find it difficult to say no to this question.) If your intuition suggests that a priestly function might support your counseling process, you can suggest this by saying, "I wonder whether it might be helpful to . . ." or "I wonder if you would like to . . ."

Another aspect of the priestly role that should not be underestimated is the power of suggestion and permission. In some cases, a person comes with the underlying, perhaps even unconscious agenda of determining whether a certain feeling or behavior is acceptable in God's eyes. Here, what you say has power by virtue of *who you are*. Other themes of unforgivable sin, grace, forgiveness, meaning, direction, absolution, confession, repentence, reconciliation, and faith frequently run parallel to the psychological issues in counseling, and the pastor should listen for (though not superimpose) these as they emerge. Paul Pruyser discussed these aspects of pastoral counseling in eloquent and helpful fashion.[10]

In this rich mixture of priestly and psychological expertise lies the uniquely challenging field of pastoral counseling. The spiritual dimensions are never to be forgotten, and their incorporation into the counseling process must rely upon your own creativity, intuition, and training. It is to the more psychological side, to practical theory and useful technique, to the deep art of listening "with the third ear," that we now turn our attention.

ADDITIONAL READINGS

BRENNER, DAVID The Effective Psychotherapist: Conclusions from Practice and Research. Elmsford, NY: Pergamon Press, 1982.

FORTUNE, MARIE M. Is Nothing Sacred? When Sex Invades the Pastoral Relationship. San Francisco: Harper, 1989.

OATES, WAYNE E. Pastoral Counseling. Philadelphia: Westminster Press, 1982. This popular text includes good discussion of the practicalities of pastoral counseling— short-term versus long-term counseling, confrontational versus nondirective stances, individual versus group approaches, how aggressive to be in intitiating pastoral care and counseling, and so on.

REDIGER, G. LLOYD Ministry and Sexuality: Cases, Counseling, and Care. Minneapolis: Augsburg Fortress, 1990. Discusses the vulnerability of pastors to sexual misconduct issues and recommends guidelines for a clergy sexual ethic and for self-protection.

ROSENBAUM, MAX, ed. Ethics and Values in Psychotherapy: A Guidebook. New York: Free Press, 1982. Contains chapters on a range of specific ethical quandries.

RUTTER, P. Sex in the Forbidden Zone: When Men in Power—Therapists, Doctors, Clergy, Teachers, and Others—Betray Women's Trust. New York: Fawcett, 1989.

SCHWITZGEBEL, ROBERT L., and R. KIRKLAND SCHWITZGEBEL Law and Psychological Practice. New York: John Wiley, 1980.

VESPER, JOYCE H., and GREGORY W. BROCK Ethics, Legalities and Professional Practice Issues in Marriage and Family Therapy. Needham Heights, MA: Allyn & Bacon, 1991.

NOTES

[1] For a thoughtful discussion of this and other health issues related to law and the criminal justice system, consult John Monahan, ed., *Who Is the Client? The Ethics of Psychological Intervention in the Criminal Justice System* (Washington, DC American Psychological Association, 1980); Robert L. Schwitzgebel and R. Kirkland Schwitzgebel, *Law and Psychological Practice* (New York: John Wiley, 1980); Thomas S. Szasz, *Psychiatric Justice* (New York: Macmillan, 1965).

[2] Inge K. Broverman, Donald M. Broverman, Frank E. Clarkson, Paul S. Rosenkrantz, and Susan R. Vogel, "Sex-Role Stereotypes and Clinical Judgments in Mental Health," *Journal of Consulting and Clinical Psychology* 34 (1970): 1–7.

[3] Vonda O. Long and Carolyn H. Heggen, "Clergy Perceptions of Spiritual Health for Adults, Men, and Women," *Counseling and Values* 32 (1988): 213–20.

[4] Isabel B. Myers and Peter B. Myers, *Gifts Differing* (Palo Alto, CA: Consulting Psychologists Press, 1980).

[5] G. Lloyd Rediger, *Ministry and Sexuality: Cases, Counseling, and Care* (Minneapolis: Fortress Press; 1990), 18–19.

[6] C. S. Lewis, *Mere Christianity* (New York: Macmillan, 1986).

[7] Rediger, *Ministry and Sexuality*, 67.

[8]For some practical guidelines for a clergy sexual ethic, see Rediger, *Ministry and Sexuality*, 110–11.

[9]Paul W. Clement, "Getting Religion," *APA Monitor* 9, no. 6 (1978): 2; Albert Ellis, "The Case against Religion," *Mensa Bulletin* 38 (September 1970): 5–6.

[10]Paul Pruyser, *The Minister as Diagnostician* (Philadelphia: Westminster Press, 1976).

Chapter 4

NOT LISTENING

Love asks no questions. Its natural state is one of extension and expansion, not comparison and measurement.

—Gerald G. Jampolsky, *Love Is Letting Go of Fear*

SELF-ASSESSMENT

Before beginning part II, take a few minutes to complete this self-assessment exercise. It is relatively simple but will provide you with important information later. It is essential that you do this *now*, because once you start reading part II your responses are likely to change, and the value of this exercise will have been lost.

The following six paragraphs are things that a person might say to you. With each paragraph, imagine that someone you know is talking to you and explaining a problem that he or she is having. You want to help by saying the right thing. Think about each paragraph. On a clean sheet of paper write, for each paragraph, the *next thing* you might say if you wanted to be helpful. Write only one or two sentences for each situation.

1. A forty-one-year-old woman says: "Last night Joe really got drunk and he came home late and we had a big fight. He yelled at me and I yelled back and then he hit me hard! He broke a window and the TV set, too! It was like he was crazy. I just don't know what to do!"

2. A thirty-six-year-old man says: "My neighbor really makes me mad. He's always over here bothering us or borrowing things that he never returns. Sometimes he calls us late at night after we've gone to bed, and I really feel like telling him to get lost."

3. A fifteen-year-old girl says: "I'm really mixed up. A lot of my friends, they stay out real late and do things their parents don't know about. They always want

me to come along and I don't want them to think I'm weird or something, but I don't know what would happen if I went along either."

4. A thirty-five-year-old parent says: "My Mary is a good girl. She's never been in trouble, but I worry about her. Lately she wants to stay out later and later and sometimes I don't know where she is. She just had her ears pierced without asking me! And some of the friends she brings home—well, I've told her again and again to stay away from that kind. They're no good for her, but she won't listen."

5. A forty-three-year-old man says: "I really feel awful. Last night I got drunk and I don't even remember what I did. This morning I found out that the screen of the television is busted and I think I probably did it, but my wife isn't even talking to me. I don't think I'm an alcoholic, you know, 'cause I can go for weeks without drinking. But this has got to change."

6. A fifty-nine-year-old unemployed teacher says: "My life just doesn't seem worth living any more. I'm a lousy father. I can't get a job. Nothing good ever happens to me. Everything I try to do turns rotten. Sometimes I wonder whether it's worth it."

At this moment someone in your congregation or very nearby is feeling the pain of depression and wondering whether it's really worth it to go on living. A problem drinker is reaching for that next drink. Someone else is feeling panic, a fear that fills the whole body, and is wondering whether he or she is going crazy. Not far away is a family torn apart by arguments and misunderstandings and, perhaps, by violence. There is a teenager who has run away from home or who is now thinking about it. There is a senior citizen who is lonely and who wonders what life means after all these years. There are some afraid of dying, some afraid of living; some who feel lost, others distressed by what they have found.

How can you reach out to them and let them know that it is safe to talk? And if they do, how can you help?

If we had to choose only one skill to teach to pastors, it would be the skill of *listening*, which is the subject of this chapter and the next. On the surface, most pastors take it for granted that listening is important, but quality listening involves much more than being quiet or waiting a longer than average time before giving advice. The kind of listening that we will describe here is a whole way of thinking, even a way of living in relation to others. It is a skill which, if you succeed in mastering it, will leave you a different person and will continue to teach you and to enrich your relationships throughout the rest of your life. It's that good.

This kind of listening is not easy to learn, nor is it easy to teach. It is especially challenging to try to capture the essence of this skill on the printed page, as opposed to teaching it in workshops where demonstration and feedback are possible.

The best way to begin is by explaining what good listening is *not*. You must first be aware of the things that are commonly confused with listening and that people often do instead of listening. Usually, these things are done with the best of intentions and sometimes even in the name of good listening.

This whole chapter is devoted to *not* listening. Read it carefully. It is a preparation for learning what listening *is*, just as one must wipe a blackboard clean before anything new can be written on it.

THE PICTURE WITHOUT THE SOUND

Imagine a person you know whom you believe to be a poor listener, one who does not pay attention to what others have to offer. Imagine that you are watching a videotape recording of this person talking to another and that the sound has been turned off. All you have is the picture. What do you see?

If this nonlistener is like most, several things can be observed. There will be relatively little eye contact. He or she looks away, stares at the floor or a wall or a watch, or perhaps looks around the room to see if there is someone more interesting available. In various ways his or her posture may betray lack of interest—perhaps turned away, closed up, leaning back from the other. The spans of time when the nonlistener is not talking are fairly short. He or she listens to the first few words of the other person and then begins an impatient nodding of the head as if the other's meaning were already understood, hoping to hurry the person along to a breath or a break where his or her own wisdom can again be inserted. There are long spans of time when the nonlistener does not stop talking—apparent monologues. Facial expression doesn't change much, at least not while the other person is talking, and what there is communicates a kind of boredom at having to endure listening to the other person talk. If there is anything else at hand to do—stir the soup, open the mail, polish fingernails, look for a lost paper, fill the salt shakers, alphabetize books on the shelf—the nonlistener is likely to be doing it. Otherwise, his or her fingers may be engaged in fiddling with something on the desk, picking at clothing, rubbing skin. If sitting, the nonlistener looks restless, moving about in the chair as if cramps were setting in.

Of course, it's a rare nonlistener who shows all of these. This is a catalog of the ways in which, intentionally or not, people communicate nonverbally to others that they are at best mildly interested in what others have to say. There are variations based on individual habit—the perpetual smile, the intent frown, the bobbing head that looks ever so much like one of those spring-necked puppy dogs in the back window of a car. Everyone has nonverbal quirks. It is usually a crushing shock to observe oneself on videotape for the first time. Many of these quirks are small and insignificant, but certain characteristic patterns communicate inattention, even if that is not the intent. This can be especially confusing if the words the person is saying express the opposite.

If you have the opportunity to observe yourself on videotape, we recommend that you take advantage of it. Many counselors discover through this process that they have been nonverbally communicating inattention through simple behaviors of which they were quite unaware. What does *your* picture look like without the sound?

ROADBLOCKS

As we turn on the sound, we encounter a different kind of information, but one that is also very subject to habit. All of us have learned through our life experiences certain "natural" or typical ways of responding to what other people say. These vary widely from one person to another, but usually they consist of responding with one's own material: one's own views, beliefs, feelings, judgments, opinions, reactions. That is not always wrong, for it is important to let other people know about you. Yet doing this, we will argue, is different from good listening.

Almost all "normal" ways of responding turn out to be roadblocks to the other person. What is a roadblock? It is an obstacle in the road which you must go around in order to keep going. That is exactly what happens in conversations. As an individual, you have some important things to say. If you begin saying them to another person—for convenience we will call him Joe—what will happen? If Joe is like most folks, he will listen for a few seconds until he thinks he knows what you mean, and then he will react with his own material—his own experience, criticism, evaluation, opinion. This will probably have an interrupting effect on you; it will move you away from your own train of thought, and now you have to react to his reaction. If you want to keep on telling Joe about you, you will have to find a way around the roadblock that he put in your way. Otherwise the conversation will soon be only about Joe. If Joe is really proficient with roadblocks, you will soon give up trying to go where you were originally headed, and you may even forget what it was you originally had wanted to say.

Roadblocks have the effect of interrupting, of stopping the other person from saying what he or she wants to say. They are communication stoppers. They stand in the way of understanding.

Usually, the person setting up the roadblock doesn't mean to be nasty or selfish. Typically, the intentions are good. Perhaps the person is trying to be helpful or even to be a good listener. Unfortunately, that's not the message that comes across. Behind a roadblock there is usually at least one of these messages.

> "I know how to solve your problems better than you do. Listen to me."
> "There's something wrong with you. I'm better than you are. Listen to me."
> "You're not important enough to listen to. Listen to me."

Again, that may not be what the person means to say, but by setting up a roadblock instead of listening, that is the message the person communicates. "Listen to me!" Everyone is hungry to be listened to. That's why it is such a great gift to listen to someone *without* using roadblocks.

A helpful description of these roadblocks comes from psychologist Thomas Gordon, a student of Carl Rogers whose "effectiveness training" books became well known in the 1970s. Perhaps more than anyone else, he succeeded in translating Roger's valuable concepts into language that people can understand. The roadblocks that follow were first described by Dr. Gordon in his excellent book, *Parent Effectiveness Training*.[1] They have been modified slightly and examples have been added, but these are the most common roadblocks that Gordon called "the typical twelve." They represent twelve ways in which people often respond or try to be helpful.

1. Ordering, directing, or commanding. Here a direction is given with the force of some authority behind it. There may be actual authority (as with a parent or employer), or the words may simply be phrased in an authoritarian way. Some examples:

> Don't say that.
> You've got to face up to reality.
> Go right back there and tell her you're sorry!

2. Warning or threatening. These messages are similar to directing, but they also carry an overt or covert threat of impending negative consequences if the advice or direction is not followed. It may be a threat that the individual will carry out or simply a prediction of a bad outcome if the other doesn't comply.

> You'd better start treating him better or you'll lose him.
> If you don't listen to me, you'll be sorry.
> You're really asking for trouble when you do that.

3. Giving advice, making suggestions, providing solutions. Here the individual draws on her or his own store of knowledge and experience to recommend a course of action. These roadblocks often begin with the words

> What I would do is . . .
> Why don't you . . .
> Have you tried . . ?

4. Persuading with logic, arguing, lecturing. The underlying assumption in these roadblocks is that the person has not adequately reasoned it through and needs help in doing so. An American archetype for this way of responding is the character Spock in the original Star Trek series. Such responses may begin

The facts are that . . .
Yes, but . . .
Let's reason this through . . .

5. Moralizing, preaching, telling them their duty.   An underlying moral code is invoked in "should" or "ought" language. The implicit
communication is instruction in proper morals. ("Preaching" here is used in
its more negative sense, of course.) Such communication might start

You should . . .
You really ought to . . .
It's your duty as a _____ to . . .

6. Judging, criticizing, disagreeing, blaming.   The common element here is an implication that there is something wrong with the person or
with what he or she has said. Note that simple disagreement is included in
this group.

It's your own fault.
You're being too selfish.
You're wrong.

7. Agreeing, approving, praising.   Some people are surprised to
find this included with the roadblocks. This kind of message gives a sanction
or approval to what has been said. This, too, stops the communication process
and may also imply an uneven relationship between speaker and listener.
True listening is different from approving and does not require approval.

I think you're absolutely right . . .
That's what I would do . . .
You're a good _____.

8. Shaming, ridiculing, name-calling.   Here the disapproval is
more overt and is directed at the individual in hopes of shaming or correcting a behavior or attitude.

That's really stupid.
You should be ashamed of yourself.
How could you do such a thing?

9. Interpreting, analyzing.   This is very common and tempting for
counselors: to seek out the hidden meaning for the person and give your own
interpretation.

You don't really mean that.

Do you know what your *real* problem is . . ?

You're just trying to make me look bad.

10. Reassuring, sympathizing, consoling.   The intent here is usually to help the person feel better. What's wrong with that? Nothing, perhaps, but it's not listening. It is a roadblock because it interferes with the spontaneous flow of communication. Examples:

There, there, it's not all that bad.

I'm sure things are going to work out all right.

Don't worry, you'll look back on this in a year and laugh.

11. Questioning, probing.   People also mistake asking questions for good listening. Here the intent is to probe further, to find out more. A hidden communication from the questioner, however, is that he or she will be able to find a solution as soon as enough questions have been asked. Questions interfere with the spontaneous flow of communication, diverting it in directions of interest to the questioner but not, perhaps, to the speaker.

What makes you feel that way?

How are you going to do that?

Why?

12. Withdrawing, distracting, humoring, changing the subject. Finally, this very obvious roadblock is an attempt to "take the person's mind off it." It directly diverts communication and indirectly implies that what the person was saying is not important or should not be pursued.

Let's talk about that some other time.

That reminds me of the time . . .

Hey, what's all the fuss about?

You think *you've* got problems, let me tell you . . .

I hear it's going to be a nice day tomorrow.

Oh, don't be so gloomy. Look on the bright side . . .

Two reactions are common after the roadblocks have been presented. One is defensive: "What's wrong with that?" At the risk of being repetitious, it must be emphasized that these responses are not *bad*. Each of them has its time and place, its appropriate use. However, none of these represents good listening. All of them have the effect of blocking and diverting the person's own exploration of meaning. To listen is to do something else.

The second reaction is, "My word, that's everything I say! What else is

The second reaction is, "My word, that's everything I say! What else is there?" We assure you that there is something more. To listen is to do something else, and that something else is the subject of chapter 5.

Self-assessment

Before proceeding, take a moment now to look back at the self-assessment you completed at the beginning of this chapter. Examine each of your responses carefully for roadblocks. As you identify them, place beside your response a number that corresponds to the roadblock numbers listed in this chapter. If, for example, you had said to the fifteen-year-old girl, "I think it's very brave of you to stand up to your friends. That's what you should do," you might score the first sentence 7 for praising and approving and the second sentence 5 for moralizing. Had you asked her a question instead, you would score it 11, unless the question was a hidden form of another roadblock like 8: "Don't you think your parents would feel terrible if you got mixed up with those kids and got in trouble?" which also has overtones of 2.

This exercise is not intended to make you feel bad or to say that you have been doing things all wrong. Rather, it is to acquaint you with the types of roadblocks that you may be most prone to use through the communication habits you have acquired over the years. These are the easy "reflex" responses that you fall back on instead of listening.

SUMMARY

A first step in learning how to be a good listener is the removal of obstacles. Various nonverbal habits can communicate disinterest or otherwise disrupt the development of a working therapeutic relationship. Likewise, the twelve "roadblocks" represent common ways of responding to people's statements. They are nonlistening responses, even though they constitute most of the repertoire of many people who regard themselves to be good listeners. There is nothing inherently wrong or inappropriate in using such responses: advising, questioning, consoling, persuading, etc. Indeed, these represent valid parts of pastoral counseling. Yet they are *not* listening, and they do disrupt the client's natural process. When listening is your goal (as in the clarification phase of counseling), it is helpful to avoid the temptation to use verbal and nonverbal roadblocks and to rely instead on the skills of reflective listening, to which we now turn our attention.

ADDITIONAL READINGS

BRAMMER, LAWRENCE *The Helping Relationship* (4th ed.). Englewood Cliffs, NJ: Prentice-Hall, 1988.

EGAN, GERARD *The Skilled Helper: A Systematic Approach to Effective Helping* (4th ed.). Monterey, CA: Brooks/Cole, 1990.

GORDON, THOMAS *Parent Effectiveness Training*. New York: Wyden, 1970.

IVEY, ALLEN. *Intentional Interviewing and Counseling: Facilitating Client Development* (2d ed.). Monterey, CA: Brooks/Cole, 1988.

IVEY, ALLEN, M. B. IVEY, and L. SIMEK-DOWNING *Counseling and Psychotherapy: Integrating Skills, Theory, and Practice* (2d ed.). Englewood Cliffs, NJ: Prentice-Hall, 1987.

NOTES

[1]Thomas Gordon, *Parent Effectiveness Training* (New York: Wyden, 1970).

5

LISTENING

It takes two to speak truth—one to speak, and another to hear.
—Henry David Thoreau, *A Week on the Concord and Merimack Rivers*

WHAT IT REALLY MEANS TO LISTEN

It is a sacrifice to listen. Listening means being willing to give up something. To know other people better, to understand their meaning and their perception of the world, you are voluntarily refraining from inserting your own material into the process. All of your attention—100 percent—is devoted to understanding what the other person is saying. Good listening means refraining from roadblocks, from putting in your own material, at least for the time being.

Anyone with a friend who is this kind of listener, who will sit with them and listen without judging, blaming, or giving advice, interpreting, approving, or disapproving—who just listens and understands—is very fortunate. The average person receives very little of this high-quality listening from other people, probably less than five or ten minutes a week. When you learn how to be a true listener and you do this for other people, you give them a rare gift. You are communicating: "You are so important to me that I want to understand exactly what you mean, and I'll keep my own material out of it for now so that it doesn't get in the way." Most people will like and respect you for caring enough to give them this gift. Good listening is caring.

It may sound like a good listener should sit in complete silence and say nothing at all. That's good sometimes, but silence alone is not enough. Many people are disturbed by a listener's silence and, as noted earlier, this can foster projection and transference. The good listener is far from passive but is engaging in a special kind of involved concentration. Thomas Gordon captured this essence in his term *active listening*.[1] The listener actively (and accurately) mirrors the client's internal processes—his or her thoughts and feelings, insights and conflicts.

A good mirror does not distort. It gives the person a true and clear picture of her or his present state. It neither flatters nor degrades, for judgment is not part of the mirroring process. Mirrors allow people to seek knowledge of themselves. They make it possible to see at least part of the image that is presented to others.

This is precisely what good listening does, and for this reason we prefer the term *reflective listening* because it reminds us of the purpose. The process of reflective listening gives back to the client (as much as possible) an undistorted and accurate image of his or her own internal process. In this way, reflective listening is deeper than the superficial imagery of a mirror. Without such mirrors—good reflective listeners—there is less opportunity for self-knowledge. A poor listener, on the other hand, is like a funhouse mirror. The reflected image bears some resemblance to the original, but the mirror adds something and the resulting picture may not be very pleasant.

Reflective listening is the same process that Carl Rogers who first described it for the psychological world, termed *accurate empathy* or *understanding*.[2] It is a universal skill for counselors, a basic process by which to deepen therapeutic relationships and facilitate change. Research has supported Rogers' original hypothesis that counselors showing high levels of this process in their work tend to be more helpful to their clients.[3] Before considering the elements of this skill, however, it is important to examine the basic attitude that underlies the reflective listening process.

THE ATTITUDE OF REFLECTIVE LISTENING

Implicit Messages

As emphasized in chapter 4, people who use roadblocks when they listen to others are communicating certain unspoken assumptions, most of which come back to the demand, "Listen to me!" In the same way there are several unspoken messages communicated when one engages in reflective listening. Although these may never be said directly, the very process of reflection communicates them to the other person. These messages include the five listed.

1. *You are important.* It is a privilege and a gift to be listened to. By taking the time to listen reflectively, the listener tells the other person that he or she matters, is important, and is cared about.

2. *I respect you.* Reflective listening also communicates personal respect for the other person. Rather than imposing his or her own material, the listener chooses to pursue and trust the individual's own process.

3. *I want to understand.* Although perhaps not truly understanding how the other person feels or thinks or perceives at the moment, the reflective listener moves

toward such understanding and at the same time communicates the desire to understand.

4. *You have within you the resources and wisdom to find your own solutions.* A reflective listening stance does not treat people as if they were sick, helpless, or dependent. Rather, it communicates an assumption that people have within themselves the wisdom and power to find good solutions and healing. To Rogers, this is a built-in natural tendency for people to grow in a positive direction if distorting obstacles are removed.[4]

   For the theologically minded, it is a very short step from this belief to the belief that God is within each of us, that each has available that still, small voice of guidance within, and that the search for God and growth in the direction of God's will are as natural as breathing. The reflective listening process not only communicates belief in that inner wisdom, but also helps the person to get in touch with it. In a real sense the person's own inner beauty and wisdom are reflected back in a very helpful way.

5. *Keep talking.* A final, simple message that reflective listening communicates is that the listener wants the person to keep talking, to keep on sharing herself or himself. This helps the person to feel safe to open up. Roadblocks, on the other hand, tend to make the person feel more distant and to want to stop talking.

Acceptance

If all of these underlying messages were to be summed up in a single concept, it would be *acceptance*. Like faith, the concept of acceptance embraces both broad psychological and deep theological dimensions. Acceptance is the total attitude beneath the process of reflective listening, and it is central to the work of the counselor. But what is meant by this in practice? How can you help a person to feel accepted?

First consider what acceptance is *not*. Acceptance is not the same as approval. Being accepting of someone who is talking to you does not mean that you have to approve of everything that person says or does. You are not asked to approve of or agree with the person, only to accept him or her as a worthwhile human being. You show this acceptance by avoiding the roadblocks and by practicing reflective listening. To accept is *not*

> to approve or disapprove
> to give advice or criticism
> to interpret or reassure
> to question or probe
> to be silent

Rather, to accept is to give all your attention and energy to the process of understanding what the person means and to reflect that meaning back to the person accurately. It is being open, allowing the other person to be as he or she really is, without using masks or filters. It is listening without judging.

The attitude of acceptance is one that pervades one's whole being, of course, and not just the context of counseling. The more accepting you are of yourself, of your own feelings and thoughts, the more able you are to be accepting of other people and to be open to what they have to say. We find that the reverse is also true—that the more you practice the attitude of acceptance toward others, the more you find an inner peace and a tolerance for your own imperfections. This is one reason we said earlier that the practice of reflective listening can leave you a different person. It is not a matter of waiting until you achieve perfect acceptance before you begin to counsel. Were that the case there would be no counselors, for we are all wounded healers. Instead, the very process of reflective listening, through its powerful unspoken assumptions, creates in both listener and speaker a sense of deep acceptance. Rogers called it "unconditional positive regard,"[5] and again it is a very short step to the kind of love that is attributed to God. Perhaps true acceptance, then, is something the counselor never fully achieves but always strives toward. Is it too bold to say that reflective listening, with its underlying attitude of acceptance, gives the person an echo of God's love?[6]

LEARNING TO THINK REFLECTIVELY

If our discussion stopped here, you would have perhaps a glimmer of how the process works but you would probably have little notion of how to go about it. Fortunately, reflective listening is a very learnable skill, and it can be specified. Here again we draw on the original work of Carl Rogers and on the excellent translation of those concepts undertaken by Thomas Gordon.

A first step in learning reflective listening is to realize that any statement can be interpreted in different ways. Because of personal experiences, you tend to interpret words in certain ways. The speaker may have an altogether different intention, and a second listener might come up with still another conclusion.

To think reflectively means to consider different possible meanings, underlying intentions, and feelings in what a person says. Figure 5-1, a diagram adapted from the writings of Thomas Gordon, illustrates this nicely. Whenever a person says something, it begins with an intention. This is within the speaker's mind and is known only to him or her. It is what the speaker *means* to communicate. To do so, the speaker must *encode* this intention into words. This encoding process is subject to many kinds of distortions, for people do not always say exactly what they mean. It is limited by the strictures of our language and the speaker's facility in using it. The message may further be distorted at the encoding stage by anxiety, inattention, and learned habits of (mis)communication. Through the encoding process, words are formed and the speaker speaks.

These words are *heard* with more or less accuracy by the listener. Here again distortion can occur through simple mishearing of the words. This may

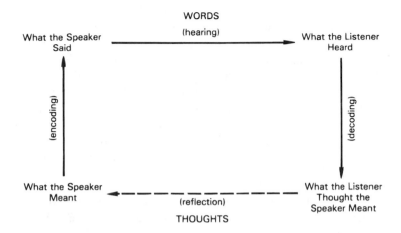

FIGURE 5-1   A Model of Communication. Adapted from Thomas Gordon, *Parent Effectiveness Training* (New York: Wyden, 1970).

occur because the listener is less familiar with the language being used (e.g., the words spoken are in a second language for the listener) but can also occur among the fluent. An example of this is the "whispering down the line" party game where one person whispers a message to the next and so on through a chain of listeners. By the time the message has passed through several dozen people, it may be unrecognizable just by virtue of this second stage: *hearing*. Or suppose a woman asks her husband, "Would you feed the cat?" She means this as a request: "Please feed the cat." Not listening carefully or perhaps being two rooms away, the husband hears: "*Did* you feed the cat?" and answers, "No." If this miscommunication is not cleared up, the woman may be surprised and resentful at his apparent refusal to honor this simple request.

Even if the listener receives the exact words spoken by the speaker, there is still a third very important source of distortion—the process of *decoding* or translating. Here the listener has the challenge of deciding just what the words *mean*. This is an attempt to match the first step in this process, namely the speaker's original intention. What the listener is responding to, however, is a thrice-distorted echo of that intention. Yet most people, reacting to this interpreted meaning, act as if this *were* the speaker's intent, and they respond assuming that they *know* what was meant.

This process is not understood by most people. Their interpretation of the speaker's intent is silently equated with the speaker's actual meaning. It is not surprising that miscommunication occurs.

Reflective *thinking* makes this process conscious, reminding you that your interpretation is only a guess and may not match what was actually meant. It also makes conscious another process that usually proceeds without much awareness—the generating of possible alternative meanings and the decision as to which one is most likely to be correct.

In workshops we have people practice this reflective thinking step in the following manner, which we recommend that you try on your own. Find someone who is willing to work with you on this by being a speaker. This person will say things to you that are somewhat complex in meaning, and your task will be to generate possible aternative interpretations. A good sentence stem that we often give to the speaker is, "One thing that I like about myself is that I . . ." The speaker can complete this sentence in various ways. The listener's response at this stage is to ask a very direct question: "Do you mean that . . . ?" filling in the blank with a possible interpretation, trying to find at least five alternative interpretations. The speaker simply answers "Yes" or "No" to questions. An example:

SPEAKER: One thing that I like about myself is that I am open.
LISTENER: Do you mean that you enjoy being around a lot of people?
SPEAKER: No.
LISTENER: Do you mean that you can talk about your feelings easily?
SPEAKER: Yes.
LISTENER: Do you mean that you are always looking for new things to try?
SPEAKER: (after some thought) Yes.
LISTENER: Do you mean that you are sexually liberal?
SPEAKER: (smiles) No.
LISTENER: Do you mean that you can listen to people without judging them?
SPEAKER: Yes.

Here are five rather different possible meanings of what the speaker said. Notice several things about this process. First of all, there is more than one "Yes," more than one layer of meaning. Sometimes a "Do you mean that" question will raise a possible meaning that the speaker had not considered, and in this case there is the characteristic pause for thought before answering. Often the speaker will feel a strong need to say more than just "Yes" or "No"— to elaborate on meaning. Here you see the beginning of the power of this process to encourage the person to keep talking. Finally, note that even here there is the possibility of misinterpretation. What you meant in asking whether the speaker was "sexually liberal" may not have been the meaning to which the speaker responded. Each person's mental dictionary is unique, and how one person defines or interprets a word may be quite different from another's connotations for the same word.

This is a stage well worth practicing because it teaches you to *think* more reflectively—to stretch your thinking to find alternative meanings. This is the very thought process that underlies reflective listening. Good reflective listening, as we shall see, does not ask questions in this manner, but it *does* attempt to do what these "Do you mean" questions begin to accomplish—to close the cycle of communication shown in Figure 5-1 by checking your own interpretation with the speaker. Here it differs greatly from normal conversation. Instead of reacting to an interpreted meaning with your own material, you form a hypothesis about meaning and check it with the speaker. The result of this is that the speaker delves deeper into his or her meaning and talks more about it. It is the pursuit of this process (rather than the use of roadblocks) that creates the therapeutic relationship.

FORMING A REFLECTION

The ideal reflection is a *statement rather than a question*. It accomplishes the same purpose as the questions described earlier, but it takes the form of a statement rather than an inquiry. The reason for this is subtle. Reflections posed as questions are somewhat more threatening, more likely to throw the person off track. For example: "You're feeling a little jealous?" may lead the person to deny the feeling, whereas the same words without the question feel safer, as if they were the person's own words.

The difference in spoken English is one of inflection. A question turns up at the end, a statement turns down. Try it:

WRONG: You're really angry at your parents? (voice turns up at the end)
RIGHT:　You're really angry at your parents. (voice turns down gently)

It is a subtle difference but an important one. When you ask your reflection as a question, there is a slight communication that you think the person shouldn't feel that way, even if that is not your intent. Making the same reflection as a statement communicates more acceptance and is less distracting to the speaker. You are not asking the person to reconsider but merely helping the person to continue the train of thought without distraction.

A good reflective statement *usually begins with the word "you"*. It says something about what the speaker is thinking or feeling. There are exceptions. For example, "It seems (to you) that nothing is going right (for you) any more." Reflections beginning with the word *I* should be avoided; few good reflections start this way. The essence of a good reflective statement is that it makes a guess about the speaker's meaning. Whether the guess is correct or not is irrelevant because in either event the speaker will provide more information to improve your understanding.

Examples

As with the "Do you mean" questions, there is no single "right" reflection for any given situation. There are numerous possibilities. The following examples are possible reflections to the six statements of the self-assessment given at the beginning of chapter 4. Remember that whether or not the reflection exactly matches the speaker's meanings is irrelevant and that there are numerous possibilities for each situation.

1. Last night Joe really got drunk and he came home late and we had a big fight. He yelled at me and I yelled back and then he hit me hard! He broke a window and the TV set, too! It was like he was crazy. I just don't know what to do.
    POSSIBLE REFLECTIONS:

    > You're really scared.

    > It feels like the end of the rope.

    > Things are getting worse, and you wonder what to do next.

2. My neighbor really makes me mad. He's always bothering us or borrowing things that he never returns. Sometimes he calls us late at night after we've gone to bed, and I really feel like telling him to get lost.
    POSSIBLE REFLECTIONS:

    > It's pretty annoying.

    > You're angry at him, and also you don't want to hurt him.

    > You feel caught between a rock and a hard place.

3. I'm really mixed up. A lot of my friends, they stay out real late and do things their parents don't know about. They always want me to come along and I don't want them to think I'm weird or something, but I don't know what would happen if I went along either.
    POSSIBLE REFLECTIONS:

    > You want to please both your parents and your friends, and there you are stuck in the middle.

    > And in the midst of all this, you're also trying to figure out who *you* are and what you value.

    > It's pretty confusing.

4. My Mary is a good girl. She's never been in trouble, but I worry about her. Lately she wants to stay out later and later and sometimes I don't know where she is. She just had her ears pierced without asking me! And some of the friends she brings home—well, I've told her again and again to stay away from that kind. They're no good for her, but she won't listen.
    POSSIBLE REFLECTIONS:

    > It feels like you're losing you daughter, and that's a sad feeling.

    > You're really afraid for her.

    > You're doing your best, but nothing seems to work any more.

Now it's your turn. For the last two *you* generate at least three possible reflective statements. Compare these statements to the ones that you wrote at the beginning of chapter 4.

5. I really feel awful. Last night I got drunk and I don't even remember what I did. This morning I found out that the screen of the television is busted and I think I probably did it, but my wife isn't even talking to me. I don't think I'm an alcoholic, you know, 'cause I can go for weeks without drinking. But this has got to change.
    POSSIBLE REFLECTIONS:

6. My life just doesn't seem worth living any more. I'm a lousy father. I can't get a job. Nothing good ever happens to me. Everything I try to do turns rotten. Sometimes I wonder whether it's worth it.
   POSSIBLE REFLECTIONS:

GETTING STARTED

This process is more difficult than it looks at first, particularly in "real life" where you don't have as much time to consider your response. In the beginning it may be helpful to have some stem phrases to get the words rolling in reflective form. One such stem, which we do *not* recommend that you use because it has been so overused, is, "What I hear you saying is that you . . ." Here are some other possible stems to use as you practice.

> It sounds like you . . .
> I imagine that you're feeling . . . (one that *does* start with *I*)
> It seems like . . .
> You feel . . .
> So you think that . . .
> You mean that you . . .
> So you . . .
> You . . .

Remember to make it a statement! Your voice tone should go down at the end of the sentence. Turning your voice up makes it a question. Another caution is that you should not get into the habit of relying on these stems. They are for practice, to help you get the words rolling. Stem statements can become very annoying if they are overused, especially if you tend to use the same one time after time.

DEPTH OF REFLECTION

One dimension of reflection that has been studied by followers of Carl Rogers is the depth of reflection.[7] Some reflective statements are fairly superficial. They do little more than repeat a part or all of the content that was spoken. Some people malign this level of reflection by calling it *parroting*, but even such superficial reflections have surprising power in helping people to keep exploring.

As the listener moves away from direct repetition, he or she begins to make a bit of a jump in guessing what was meant. One short jump is to rephrase slightly, to find synonyms from your own mental dictionary and to try them out. A little longer jump is to take the whole content of what was said and paraphrase it, adding meaning that you believe to be there although it has not actually been said. The deepest levels of reflection do just this; they add meaning and capture the underlying feeling instead of simply repeating what was said.

As an example, consider the last of the six self-assessment statements: "My life just doesn't seem worth living any more. I'm a lousy father. I can't get a job. Nothing good ever happens to me. Everything I try to do turns rotten. Sometimes I wonder whether it's worth it." Here are some reflections at each of three different levels.

Simple Repetition

It seems like nothing good ever happens.
Sometimes you wonder if it's worth it.

Partial Rephrasing

Things just aren't going very well.
Nothing you do seems to work.

Whole Paraphrase, Adding Meaning

Things look pretty hopeless, and you can't see them ever getting any better.
Things look very bleak right now, maybe so bleak that you think about ending it all.

Counselors skilled in reflective listening use a mixture of these levels. The deepest reflections are most difficult but also can be most important. In essence they try to capture the underlying meaning of a whole communication, to include in this the person's feeling tone, and to add the next step, almost as if the listener were writing the next sentence of the paragraph.

One potential pitfall in paraphrasing is to leap too far. A guess that is too far afield can be very jarring. It becomes, in fact, a roadblock, namely an interpretation. The person suddenly feels analyzed, and in the process of wrestling with the interpretation may lose the original direction. Here are a few examples of some jumps that would be too far from the statement above.

Interpretations

You're having a midlife crisis and don't know who you are.
Things aren't going well in your marriage.
And you wonder if God accepts you.

Clearly, reflective listening is a continuous dimension, a matter of degree. To stay too close to the original (sometimes the better choice) may be to miss a hidden meaning, but to jump too far may disrupt the whole process.

Sounds complicated? Well, it is. The good news, however, is that as you practice this skill you can learn on your own how to do it better. You develop an intuitive sense of how far to jump. This happens because there is fairly immediate feedback about the usefulness of your reflection.

IMMEDIATE FEEDBACK

When you offer a reflective listening statement, immediate information is provided from the other person as to how it was received. You will know that you reflected well if

The person keeps talking.

The person acknowledges your reflection with some form of "yes" or "no" and goes on clarifying.

The person shows a facial expression change that has been called a "recognition reflex"—a sign that the reflection touched on truth.

The person tells you that you are a good listener, warm, understanding, and so forth; you get an enthusiastic "Yes!" response.

On the other hand you can tell when your reflection has missed the mark.

The person stops talking or changes the subject.

The person becomes defensive and denies a previous statement.

The person shows nonverbal signs of defensiveness.

There is a long pause after your reflection or a "Well . . ."

These are not 100 percent accurate signs. A person may, for example, stop and think quietly for a long time after an excellent reflection. On the whole, however, you can use these types of observation to get feedback about the appropriateness of your reflection.

Practice

At this point we recommend that you get some further practice because the skills of reflective listening cannot be learned in any other way. Here are a few suggestions.

1. Work with a partner. Have that person use the same "One thing I like about myself is . . ." statement or switch it to "One thing about myself that I'd like to change is . . ." This time you respond not with a question but with a reflection. The speaker, in turn, responds "Yes" or "No" but also continues to elaborate and explain further after each reflection. After such elaboration you offer a new reflection based on your new information. Example:

SPEAKER: One thing about myself I'd like to change is that I'm disorganized.
LISTENER: You can't seem to get things done on time.
SPEAKER: No, not so much as I can never find things.
LISTENER: And you think if you kept things in better order, it would be easier.

SPEAKER: Right. And more than that, I just feel like I can't get my life to-
            gether, you know?

LISTENER: There are all the pieces of your life lying around, and you wonder
            how they all fit.

SPEAKER: Yeah, or where it's all going.

LISTENER: Where you are headed, what your purpose is. That must feel con-
            fusing.

SPEAKER: Exactly! I just feel so scattered . . .

This process could continue for quite some time. A relatively simple first statement was elaborated into a deeply personal issue. Notice, also, that the first reflection was "wrong" in that it got a "no" response but that the effect of this reflection was nevertheless quite good. If the reflection is done well, it makes no difference if it's "right" or "wrong." For practice, read through this script aloud, turning each LISTENER reflection *down* at the end and then pursue this process with a partner.

2. This second exercise is more challenging. Again, have a practice partner talk more at length about a current issue that is emotionally important in some way or about a recent experience that included some significant feelings. As listener, respond *only* with reflective statements—no questions, no roadblocks. This is difficult, but it helps to break reliance on other kinds of responses and teaches the counselor that almost always it is possible to reflect instead. Try it!

3. A third type of exercise for learning reflections is to try it in "real life" conversations. As you become more adept with reflective listening, it is easier to make a larger percentage of your responses be reflective statements. Of course, there will be some misses, as in any learning process, but usually people, as they try this new skill, are surprised at how well others respond.

With time the process of reflection becomes natural, so don't be discouraged if it seems difficult or unnatural or "technique-ish" at first. Most valuable skills are difficult and don't feel natural when you begin learning them. Walking, riding a bicycle, driving a car, eating with a fork—remember learning these basics? Or how about eating with chopsticks? All of these things seem strange when one begins. You feel clumsy and wonder if you'll ever do it right, but with practice it becomes completely natural and finally you lose your awareness of the process itself.

Of course, in ordinary conversations you will do more than reflect. Sometimes you will want to ask a question or shift the topic or give your own opinion. We have no magic guidelines to offer for how to mix reflection with other kinds of communication. We can tell you, though, that you will have to practice reflection very consciously if you are to learn it. The easiest thing to do is to fall back into your old habits. If you do take the time to learn reflective listening, you'll be surprised at how *often* it can be used and how much of a difference it can make in relations with others. One rule for the time being is this: Before asking a question or giving advice or using another of the roadblocks, consider whether you could instead use reflective listening.

SOME POINTS OF FINE TUNING

Once you have become comfortable with the basics of reflective listening, you can turn your attention to some more artful fine tuning, to some refinements of skill that you can work on as you practice.

Overshooting vs. Undershooting

People are strange and sensitive creatures and sometimes can be influenced by very small things. Whether a listener turns a reflection up or down at the end can make a difference in how willing the speaker will be to go on. In the same way a person is more likely to accept a feeling reflection and to continue to explore it if it is understated than if it is overstated.

For an example, consider the emotion of anger. There are many words in the English language to describe angry feelings. Some of these are mild words, expressing a small degree of anger. Others portray moderate anger, and still others express a very strong degree of anger. Here are a few:

Mild anger words:	annoyed, irritated, irked, miffed, disappointed
Moderate anger words:	angry, upset, mad, resentful
Strong anger words:	furious, enraged, outraged, irate

Besides the choice of adjectives, there are other ways to make feeling words stronger or milder by modifying them. For example:

To make it milder: a little angry, sort of angry, somewhat angry
To make it stronger: really angry, very angry, quite angry

It makes a difference which word you choose to describe a feeling during reflective listening. In general, overshooting the feeling (overstating it, choosing a stronger expression) has the effect of making the person deny the feeling or at least deny that it is so strong. This seems to interrupt the flow and may cause the person to back off or stop sharing at a feeling level. In general, it seems better to make mistakes on the side of undershooting, by understating the intensity of the feeling. Judge how strong the feeling is, then understate it slightly. The result of this is usually for the person to say something like, "A *little* angry! You bet I'm angry, and more than a little." The person then goes on to talk about the feeling. *When in doubt undershoot.*

Reflecting a Conflict

Another situation that calls for considerable skill from the reflective listener is when a person feels at least two different ways about something.

I want to get married again, but I'm afraid that it will end the same way that it did last time—in a painful divorce.

I'd like to move to Chicago where I could get a better job, but I hate a big city and I don't want to lose my friends here.

I'm curious about the effects of marijuana and how I would feel if I smoked it, but I'm afraid I might lose control of myself.

I know I should stop drinking, but I enjoy getting drunk and besides all my friends drink.

Notice that in the middle of each of these statements is the word *but*. That is the telltale sign of this kind of situation. The person feels one way *but* also feels another. Two feelings or beliefs or values are in conflict. The person is in conflict, one might say.

Conflicts are great occasions of temptation for the counselor, who may be just dying to give advice, to argue one side, to tell the person what should be done. Roadblocks are obvious and direct ways to do this: to give advice, be logical, moralize. But there is also a less obvious way that you may fall into without realizing it, even if you avoid giving direct advice.

This second way of taking sides is to reflect only *one* side of the conflict. If you think of a conflict as an argument within the person, you are then reflecting only one side of the argument. For example, if a person says "I think I'd like to have children, but I'm afraid of the responsibility," you might reflect "You think it would be nice to have kids," or you could choose to say "You wonder whether you'd like having somebody so dependent on you." Both are reasonably good reflections, but there is a problem. Each represents only one side. It's better to get *both* sides into the reflection: "You think it would be nice to have kids, and the idea scares you a little, too." (also understated)

Why so much fuss over this? Because if you take sides by reflecting only one part of the argument, it is very likely that the person will begin to take up the other side. Suddenly, the two of you are slugging it out. You have become involved in the person's internal conflict by making it external. Consider also that the more a person argues one side of a conflict, the more he or she becomes committed to that side. (It's a social psychological principle: I learn what I believe as I hear myself talk.) Thus, you may unwittingly be backing the person into a corner without either of you realizing what is happening.[8]

If, on the other hand, you keep reflecting one side of the conflict, then the other, then back again, and so on, the person is likely to be left more confused. The best way to reflect a conflict is to get both sides at once. After all, the person does feel or believe *both* sides. Trust the individual to work it out, and help by being a clear mirror.

Consider the possible reflections for the drinker's dilemma: "I really feel awful. Last night I got drunk and I don't even remember what I did. This morning I found out that the screen of the television is busted and I think I probably did it, but my wife isn't even talking to me. I don't think I'm an alcoholic, you know, 'cause I can go for weeks without drinking. But this has got to change."

One-Sided Reflections

You think you don't really have a drinking problem.
You can see that your drinking is doing a lot of harm.
You're really upset with what's happening because of your drinking.
It's scary when you can't remember what happened.

Balanced Reflections

On the one hand you don't think you're an alcoholic, and yet you can see that alcohol is doing a lot of damage in your life. That must be confusing for you.
It sounds like you know you have to do something about your drinking, and yet you don't want to think of yourself as an alcoholic.
It doesn't seem that bad, and yet it does.

Using Analogies

What is an analogy? It is pointing out how one thing is like something else. Being frantically busy is like "running around like a chicken with its head cut off" or like "burning the candle at both ends." Ernie Ford used to talk about being "as nervous as a long-tailed tomcat in a room full of rocking chairs." A very shy person may be likened to a turtle or to an unopened flower.

Analogies can be fun. A lot of humor has to do with seeing the similarity between two things that you had not put together before. Analogies can also be very personal, very deep, showing that you really do understand how it is. The trick is to find the right analogy, and some of us are better at that than others.

To select the right analogy, you need to know something about the person, about how he or she thinks. What are the images that he or she would understand? To the person who thinks of chickens as coming in plastic wrap from the supermarket, the analogy "like a chicken with its head cut off" may lack meaning. People who have never used molasses probably won't know how fast it runs in January. To form a good reflective analogy, you must understand two things: first, how the person really feels; second, what image would best capture that feeling for the person. For example:

A teenager from a farming family says, "I just don't know what to believe. When I'm with Joe I feel one way. When I'm home I think my parents are right. When my friends talk to me, I can see their points, too." What is that feeling *like*? Perhaps you as a listener would think of being pushed about in a city crowd, but that image might not work. Maybe it's like being blown around in the wind. What blows around in the wind? A kite? A feather? A tree? A leaf? All of those things might work. Or how about a weathervane? Most barns have weathervanes. So you say, "You feel a little like a weather-vane. If the wind tugs you one way, it feels right to turn that way. But then the wind changes and you feel right turning there, too."

A good analogy often causes the person to "light up" in recognition, to feel very understood. A good analogy is hard to find. Poets work to find just the right analogy to express their subjects. So do good listeners.

Suppose a musician says, "I feel so terribly alone, like I'm in a big void. Inside I'm a very deep person, but when there's nobody to share it with it all seems so meaningless." If you know about music yourself, you will begin thinking about what kind of musical sound would be like that feeling, and perhaps you will say, "It's like the sound of a flute in a big, empty hall."

Of course, you won't always be right. Sometimes your image will not be the one that fits what the listener meant or will fall short of the mark. But that's all right because the person will probably say so and go right on telling you about how she or he really does feel. Good listening is one kind of target practice where there is no penalty for missing.

REFLECTIVE LISTENING WITHIN A COUNSELING SESSION: AN EXAMPLE

The following conversation between Janet and her pastor illustrates how reflective listening can be employed in a counseling session. Janet is fifty-eight years old and has spent most of her life married to George, taking care of their home while doing volunteer work in the community. Four months ago a blood vessel ruptured in George's brain, and one week later he was dead. Now the paster receives a call from Janet, whose voice and tears on the telephone express the need for an immediate visit. The pastor invites her to come to the office later that afternoon.

Verbatim

Commentary

PASTOR: Hello, Janet, come in! I'm glad you came.

JANET: Hello, Pastor. It is nice of you to see me like this.

P: From our short talk on the phone it sounds like you are struggling with some feelings about losing George and being alone

The pastor begins with a summary reflection of what Janet said in their telephone conversation.

J: It's just that it's been such a huge change for me! And it all happened so quickly.

P: You didn't have much time to prepare yourself for it.

Not knowing yet what Janet wants to say, the pastor stays close to her own words but offers a partial rephrasing.

J: No. (She cries a little and the pastor waits silently.) At first people were so wonderful— bringing by food and calling and everything. There was so much love expressed by the people here.

P: And now that seems to be changing.

The pastor reflects the initial, underlying feeling, and takes an interpretive leap, using the reflection technique of "continuing the paragraph."

J: Well, I can understand. People have to get back to their own lives.

Janet confirms the correctness of the pastor's paraphrase.

P: And still you feel alone—a little abandoned.

The pastor again reflects the underlying feeling, using "a little" to understate the feeling.

J: Yes, I guess I do. (She sits silently for half a minute.) Abandoned.

P: By people here and, maybe, by George, too.

Again the pastor makes an intuitive leap in this reflection.

J: I do! (Her facial expression changes markedly.) I get so angry at him! Is that normal? I don't think I ought to be angry. It's not his fault he had a stroke and died

The vehemence of Janet's response and the facial change suggest that the pastor has reflected well.

P: It doesn't seem right to you to be angry, and still that is how you feel. That must be confusing.

Resisting the temptation to advise or reassure this early, the pastor stays with reflective listening.

J: Well, that's just a little part of it. There are so many new things—so many feelings all mixed up.

Janet opens up a new area.

P: You have to do a lot of things that George used to take care of.

The pastor reflects in paraphrase, making a guess about the new area. This is a reasonable reflection but moves away from the emotions that Janet came to explore.

J: Yes—the car, the house, the bills—he did so much. Yesterday I took a bottle of wine out of the cupboard and I realized that I've never learned how to use a corkscrew! Sometimes I don't think I can keep going.

Janet responds to the reflection by focusing on the tasks that face her . . . but then, as clients do, gives the pastor another chance.

P: It can be discouraging to have to face all of that alone.

This time the pastor picks up the feeling in the reflection.

J: It's not that so much. I just don't feel like I have the energy to do everything that has to be done.

Discouraged did not match Janet's own feeling, and she continues to clarify what she means.

P: Kind of tired, like it's hard to get up and face another day.

After a "miss," the pastor stays closer to Janet's own words in rephrasing.

J: Right! Some mornings I don't think I can get out of bed. But I do, and once I get going I feel a little better. And then I get to thinking about something again . . . (she pauses)

This time the reflection was "right on" from her perspective, and she continues to explain her feelings.

P: (after a pause) and the feelings start: sometimes angry, sometimes sad . . .

Again "continuing the paragraph" as a form of reflection.

J: Sometimes *relieved*, even.

Again Janet opens up a new area.

P: Like it's for the better.

Not a bad reflection, but probably over-shooting in intensity.

J: No, not quite. I wish George were here . . . . And yet some days it feels nice just to be on my own. I don't have to answer to anybody. I don't have to cook a meal unless I'm hungry. I don't have to make the bed.

Janet backs off at first, but then resumes her original direction. If a trusting relationship has been established through reflection, it can override small interruptions due to misses or overshooting.

P: It's a new kind of freedom for you. Like a weight has been lifted from your shoulders.

The pastor paraphrased and tries an analogy.

J: That sounds terrible, doesn't it? I don't want you to think that George was a burden. . . . I'm just so mixed up.

Janet reacts as if the analogy, too, were stated too strongly, but then returns to her feelings.

P: So many different feelings: angry, sad, relieved—sometimes all in the same day.

The pastor returns to reflection of emotion and makes a good guess ("all in the same day") based on previous experiences with people in grief

J: I'm up and down, up and down. It wears me out.

P: A little like riding on a roller coaster, an emotional roller coaster.

The pastor tries another analogy.

J: I never did like roller coasters. Too fast.

P: And you wonder where this one is going.

The pastor makes another intuitive leap in this paraphrase.

J: I . . . (cries again)

P: It's something that's painful even to think about.

Uncertain as to the source of her tears, the pastor reflects the crying itself

J: I'm scared! What am I going to do for the rest of my life? George *was* my life!

From this point the counseling session could go on in any of several directions. The pastor could continue with reflective listening, trusting in Janet's inner wisdom to find resolution. The pastor might now offer some statements of hope, regard, and support. They might pray together. In time the pastor might begin to help Janet identify her gifts and find new meaning and direction for her life.

This conversation exemplifies the therapeutic use of reflective listening. Every one of the pastor's responses in this dialogue was a reflective listening statement. This is not to say that a pastor should do *nothing* but reflect. Rather, it is to show how it is possible to stay with a reflective posture even when there is great temptation to depart into other ways of responding and how this can serve to help the client continue exploring his or her own meaning.

WHEN NOT TO USE REFLECTION

Reflective listening is a wonderfully valuable skill. It helps you to understand better than ever before, and it helps other people to grow and to discover new things about themselves. But reflection is not a solution to everything.

There are many times when you will need to do more than reflect. There are times for advice and direction, especially when people specifically ask for it. There are times for asking questions, namely when you need to know something. In helping people change, reflective listening often is just a first step, albeit a very good first one. It is the central skill for the first phase of counseling that we have called *clarification*. For the formulation phase, more direct questions may be needed, and still later it may be time for direction and suggestion. All of these later phases build on the relationship that is established through the reflective process, however, and you can continue to intermix reflective listening as you proceed through later steps of counseling.

There are also times when it is important for you to share things about yourself. One of these is when you have very strong feelings yourself. Chances are that the other person will pick up on your feelings whether or not you express them directly. If you do not acknowledge your reactions directly, the person may misunderstand or misinterpret what is happening, perhaps taking it personally. To deny your own feelings in such a situation is to display the very kind of process that you hope to help your client overcome. Carl Rogers recognized this in pointing to *genuineness* as a third crucial condition for a therapeutic relationship, in addition to accurate empathy and unconditional positive regard.[9]

The sharing of your own internal process is an important part of building a relationship. For therapists this process of self-disclosure must be used judiciously, but it can contribute in important ways to trust. It *is* possible to hide behind reflection. Reflective listening works very well, and the other person may not be aware immediately that you are not revealing anything about yourself. If this complete imbalance continues, however, the relationship can begin to feel more unsafe. Part of the art of relationship building, either inside or outside of the counseling context, is to find that optimal balance between understanding and self-expression, between reflective listening and self-disclosure.

SUPPORTIVE COUNSELING

The term *supportive counseling* is sometimes used to refer to a type of counseling relationship where the goal is maintenance. There is no particular change or choice toward which the counselor and client are working, at least not immediately. Instead, the goal is to help the client to hold on, to persevere, to gain self-esteem or spiritual centeredness. Supportive counseling is sometimes thought of as a second-class intervention, as if it were an antonym for "real" counseling. To the contrary, supportive counseling is a valid and valuable function, one particularly appropriate within a pastoral relationship. Progress made may not be as dramatic as in change- or choice-oriented counseling, but this in no way diminishes the value of this kind of relationship to individuals.

When is supportive counseling appropriate? One good application is when the goals of counseling are unclear but the individual is clearly in distress. This represents a prolonged clarification phase of the counseling process, a longer than usual period of sorting out and relationship building. Supportive counseling is appropriate when an individual has undergone a major transition (such as divorce) and is working through the confusion that often ensues. This particular type of counseling is described in chapter 9. Support is appropriate when an individual is facing an apparently irreversible or unavoidable stress, such as terminal illness. It is appropriate for the lonely and isolated individual, particularly when coupled with other interventions that will eventuate in the development of a better support system for the person (see chapter 20).

Reflective listening is the primary skill to be employed in supportive counseling. A counselor's initial "reflex" responses may be to provide reassurance, consolation, agreement, advice, or other responses from the list of roadblocks in chapter 4. To be sure, there is a time for such responses, and they are often appropriate to include within supportive counseling. Still, we encourage you to consider whether reflective listening might be the better choice when you are about to use a roadblock response and to experiment with what happens when you choose reflections.

SUMMARY

Reflective listening is a valuable and highly useful counseling skill. It is the primary vehicle for exploration during the clarification phase of counseling and forms the core of the relationship in supportive counseling. Based on an underlying attitude of acceptance not dissimilar from the love and grace of God, it helps to create an atmosphere in which transformation can occur. The basic purpose of a reflection is to check and clarify the speaker's intention behind a communication. Reflections are statements rather than questions and attempt to capture the person's meaning. The counselor practicing reflective listening receives immediate feedback from the listener as an automatic part of the communication cycle, thus enabling the counselor to improve his or her listening skills. Analogies, undershooting, and reflection of conflict represent points of fine tuning, special skills to be developed. Reflection is not to be used to the exclusion of other counseling methods, but it can be applied far more often than most counselors realize. A balanced relationship includes self-disclosure as well as reflective listening.

From here, you must go on alone in the process of learning the skill of reflection. Yet you are far from alone, for each time you make the effort to listen reflectively, you learn. Every conversation in which you use reflection teaches you a little more about how to use it accurately and sensitively. It may not always be helpful or enough, but it will seldom be harmful. As the months and years go by, reflection becomes less something that you *do* as a *technique* and more a way of being, a way of relating to other people. For reflective listening changes you as well.

ADDITIONAL READINGS

Books by Gilmore, Gordon, Egan, and Ivey described in chapters 2 and 4 all contain good training material on listening skills. Some other resources on basic counseling and therapeutic skills are the following.

KENNEDY, EUGENE, and SARA CHARLES *On Becoming a Counselor: A Basic Guide for Nonprofessional Counselors* (rev. ed.). New York: Continuum, 1989.

LOUGHARY, HOHN W., and THERESA M. RIPLEY *Helping Others Help Themselves: A Guide to Counseling Skills.* New York: McGraw-Hill, 1979.

MOURSUND, JANET *The Process of Counseling and Therapy* (2d ed.). Englewood Cliffs, NJ: Prentice-Hall, 1990.

SULLIVAN, HARRY STACK *The Psychiatric Interview.* New York: Norton, 1954. This is a classic book on interviewing by the neoanalyst Sullivan.

TRUAX, CHARLES B., and ROBERT R. CARKHUFF *Toward Effective Counseling and Psychotherapy: Training and Practice.* New York: Aldine, 1967. A classic in nondirective, client-centered therapy, including specific training principles and methods based on the research of Carl Rogers and his students.

NOTES

[1]Thomas Gordon, *Parent Effectiveness Training* (New York: Wyden, 1970).

[2]Carl R. Rogers, "The Necessary and Sufficient Conditions of Therapeutic Personality Change," *Journal of Consulting Psychology* 21 (1957): 95–103.

[3]For reviews of treatment process and outcome research on client-centered therapy, consult Sol L. Garfield and Allen E. Bergin, eds., *Handbook of Psychotherapy and Behavior Change*, 3d ed. (New York: John Wiley, 1986), and James O. Prochaska, *Systems of Psychotherapy: A Transtheoretical Analysis*, 2d ed. (Monterey, CA: Brooks/Cole, 1984).

[4]Carl R. Rogers, "A Theory of Therapy, Personality and Interpersonal Relationships, as Developed in the Client-centered Framework," in Sigmund Koch, ed., *Psychology: A Study of a Science* (New York: McGraw-Hill, 1959), vol. 3;

[5]Carl R. Rogers and others, eds., *The Therapeutic Relationship and Its Impact* (Madison: University of Wisconsin Press, 1967).

[6]Paul Tillich, "You are Accepted," in *The Shaking of the Foundations* (New York: Scribner's, 1948).

[7]Charles B. Truax and Robert R. Carkhuff, *Toward Effective Counseling and Psychotherapy* (Chicago: Aldine, 1967).

[8]For a discussion of the therapeutic applications of this principle, see William R. Miller and Stephen Rollnick, *Motivational Interviewing* (New York: Guilford Press, 1991).

[9]Carl R. Rogers, *On Encounter Groups* (New York: Harper & Row, 1970).

6

PERSPECTIVES AND PERSONALITY THEORY

> The well-meaning contention that all ideas have equal merit seems to me little different from the disastrous contention that no ideas have any merit.
>
> —Carl Sagan, *Broca's Brain*

Paul Pruyser once commented that, if he had to choose between diagnosis and treatment as to which were the more important, he would choose diagnosis.[1] We are inclined to agree, particularly when diagnosis is understood not as classification or labeling, but rather as developing a formulation, a perspective, an understanding. To "diagnose" in this sense is to decide how to look at a person and a problem. This is a decision of some consequence because it in turn colors one's view of what, if anything, needs to be done.

Suppose, for example, that an individual who is being counseled shows all the signs of depression. If the counselor believes that this is a biochemical problem and begins thinking in terms of medication, it is natural to seek the consultation of a biological psychiatrist. If the depression is seen as a consequence of lifestyle, the counselor will begin to encourage the person to make some behavioral changes. If the depression is viewed as being stress induced, the sources of stress will be sought and addressed in order to break the vicious cycle. If the problem is seen as having a spiritual base, prayer and the use of scripture may be in order. If the depression stems from a distorted thought process, perhaps the key to peace lies in helping the person to find new cognitive perspectives. If the cause is unresolved grief or negative self-concept or social withdrawal or alcohol abuse or unrealistic guilt or dietary deficiencies or perceived helplessness or marital problems, still other resolutions are indicated. All of these *can* cause depression. To try to do "a little of everything" in counseling a depressed person is as futile as randomly selecting one approach. The key is first to *understand* the problem. Once a comprehensive and accurate understanding is reached, the choice of treatment approach is greatly facilitated.

This is *diagnosis* in its best sense. The word literally means "to know (the difference) between." It is a perfectly good word but does carry with it overtones both of medicine and of labeling. We have chosen instead the term *formulation*, which emphasizes the thinking process that is involved. This is not to dismiss the value of medical thinking or of diagnostic classification systems. Biological factors are crucial in understanding human behavior, and the importance of certain diagnostic categories will become apparent in part V. A good formulation *includes* such considerations but is much broader. It is a comprehensive way of looking at a person and his or her problems—an attempt to bring the big picture into focus without losing the accuracy that is characteristic of more close-up perspectives.

Within psychology, personality theories represent attempts to derive such broad systems of thought for understanding human nature. They suggest the aspects of human experience that are relevant to observe (e.g., overt behavior, dreams, thoughts, family interactions, slips of the tongue, or the individual's own categories of thinking). They provide a language of constructs or concepts to use in talking about people (e.g., ego, reinforcement, anxiety, shadow, games). They suggest how the proposed parts of the personality interact with each other (e.g., stimulus-response, id/ego/superego, parent/adult/child). They create conceptual dimensions on which individuals can be measured (e.g., introversion-extroversion, ego strength, intrinsic versus extrinsic religious orientation, sensing-intuiting, dependency, internal versus external locus of control). Each personality system contains an implicit theory of how change occurs, describing the conditions that are essential to bring about personal change (e.g., working through transference in psychoanalysis; empathy, warmth, and genuineness in client-centered therapy; cognitive restructuring in rational-emotive therapy; changes in social reinforcement patterns in behavior therapy; shifts in communication patterns within family systems therapy).

The alternatives can be bewildering. Yet the course of counseling is inseparable from this process of formulation. How counselors think about problems and people profoundly influences whether and how they will intervene. Furthermore, not all kinds of intervention are helpful; some, in fact, are harmful. For this reason it is important that you be aware of how you think—to know your own underlying assumptions—to put your perspectives in perspective.

AN IMPLICIT PERSONALITY THEORY

Aware of it or not, you already have your own personality theory. Every person, not just a counselor, quietly derives her or his own system for thinking about the causes of human behavior. Many factors contribute to this: books and articles you have read, your professional training, your experiences with the particular people you have known, your successes and setbacks in counseling, the approach of your own therapist if you have been in therapy yourself, the *zeitgeist* of psychology in your locality, input from media, and what your parents told you about why people do the things they do. All of these and more shape your own way of thinking about human nature.

One way of assessing your own implicit personality theory is to consider where you stand in relation to four classic personality theories within psychology. The following Personality Theory Questionnaire consists of twenty-five statements about people in general. After reading each statement, indicate whether you agree more than disagree (A) or whether you disagree more than agree (D). Please: no fence-sitting. For each statement it is possible to quibble with the wording or to defend one side or the other. (In fact, that's the point.) But for each statement, take a stand: Do you more agree or disagree?

Personality Theory Questionnaire

William R. Miller, Ph.D.

For each statement indicate either that you agree more than disagree (A) or that you disagree more than agree with the statement (D).

1. ____D____ In attempting to understand human beings, one should stick to the observable and avoid theory and concepts that cannot be directly experienced or observed.

2. ____A____ Events taking place in the present are systematically linked to events that occurred in one's past.

3. ____A____ A specific piece of human behavior cannot be understood without considering the total person.

4. ____D____ People are basically good (as opposed to neutral or evil). If left to a natural state, uncontrolled by external restraints, they seek health and personal growth while respecting the rights of others to do the same.

5. ____D____ A person's character is largely determined by the time he or she reaches adulthood. The only real changes that one can expect from an adult are small ones, and these occur over long periods of time.

6. ____A____ The so-called "laws of behavior" that are intended to apply to all individuals tell us very little about a person.

7. ____A____ Much of behavior, both normal and abnormal, is directed by unconscious factors of which we have little or no awareness.

8. ____A____ If one is to understand people and their behavior, it is important to have a unifying theory of human personality, even though aspects of that theory may not at present be based on observable facts or empirical research.

9. ____D____ Aggression is an inherent part of human nature, deeply rooted in our basic instincts.

10. _____*A*_____ Given alternatives and support, people are capable of making major and enduring changes in themselves.

11. _____*A*_____ Much of human behavior is motivated by the continuous attempt to increase pleasure and to avoid pain and discomfort.

12. _____*D*_____ People have no inherent values—only those that are discovered or learned through living.

13. _____*A*_____ Learning processes play a major role in the formation of personality and the determination of human behavior.

14. _____*A*_____ It is an important part of counseling to allow the individual to talk and explore his or her experiences without direction or evaluation from the counselor.

15. _____*A*_____ Events that occur early in life are more important in determining one's adult personality and behavior than are those occurring after the person has reached adulthood.

16. _____*O*_____ Looking within the person (instead of to the environment) for the causes of behavior is probably more misleading than enlightening.

17. _____*A*_____ The idea of *self* (inner experiences) or *ego* is crucial to the understanding of behavior and personality.

18. _____*O*_____ Scientific method, in the usual sense of structured observation and experimentation, is not appropriate for the study of psychology in humans.

19. _____*D*_____ People are neither inherently good nor basically selfish. Their "human nature" is determined by some combination of heredity and life experiences.

20. _____*O*_____ It is important for a counselor to be *personally* involved in counseling, revealing his or her authentic feelings to the client.

21. _____*D*_____ Perhaps the most important goal of counseling is to help the individual become aware of and accept his or her own values.

22. _____*D*_____ For the most part, counseling should focus on the client's present experiences rather than events from the past.

23. _____*O*_____ Human behavior is determined by lawful principles; free will has little or nothing to do with it.

24. _____*O*_____ The relationship between a counselor and a client is more than a context in which change happens. It is the relationship *itself* that heals.

25. _____*D*_____ A person is free to be what he or she wants to be.

Having completed the Personality Theory Questionnaire, you can now proceed to score it and to discover where you stand relative to four classic personality theories, which will be discussed in the following sections. First, use the Scoring Scale. Notice that there are four columns with A's and D's arranged in lines next to numbers that correspond to the twenty-five statements of the questionnaire. For each item, circle all of the letters that correspond to your answer to that item. For example, on item 1, if you had answered A (agree more than disagree), you would circle the two A's in that line. Had you answered D, you would instead circle the two D's. For the second item you would circle the middle two letters if you had answered D but the outer

SCORING SCALE

	B	E	H	P
1.	A	A	Ⓓ	Ⓓ
2.	Ⓐ	D	D	Ⓐ
3.	D	Ⓐ	Ⓐ	A
4.	Ⓓ	Ⓓ	A	Ⓓ
5.	Ⓓ	Ⓓ	Ⓓ	A
6.	D	Ⓐ	Ⓐ	D
7.	D	D	D	Ⓐ
8.	D	D	Ⓐ	Ⓐ
9.	Ⓓ	Ⓓ	Ⓓ	A
10.	Ⓐ	Ⓐ	Ⓐ	D
11.	Ⓐ	D	D	Ⓐ
12.	A	A	Ⓓ	Ⓓ
13.	Ⓐ	D	D	Ⓐ
14.	D	Ⓐ	Ⓐ	Ⓐ
15.	Ⓐ	Ⓓ	Ⓓ	Ⓐ
16.	A	Ⓓ	Ⓓ	Ⓓ
17.	D	Ⓐ	Ⓐ	Ⓐ
18.	Ⓓ	A	Ⓓ	Ⓓ
19.	A	A	Ⓓ	Ⓓ
20.	Ⓓ	A	A	Ⓓ
21.	Ⓓ	A	A	Ⓓ
22.	A	A	A	Ⓓ
23.	A	Ⓓ	Ⓓ	A
24.	Ⓓ	A	A	A
25.	Ⓓ	A	A	Ⓓ

two letters if you had answered A. Do this for all twenty-five items, being careful to circle *all* the letters that correspond with your answers.

Next count the number of circles in each of the four columns (disregarding whether it was an A or a D that you circled) Record the four totals below and multiply each by 4.

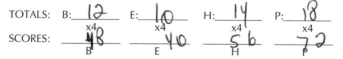

TOTALS: B: __12__   E: __10__   H: __14__   P: __18__

SCORES: __48__   __40__   __56__   __72__
       x4   x4   x4   x4
       B   E   H   P

Each of these scores is intended to indicate the approximate percentage of your agreement with each of four classic viewpoints in psychology:

B = Behavioral

E = Existential

H = Humanistic

P = Psychodynamic or Psychoanalytic

Note that the four psychological viewpoints have a certain amount in common. Here are the score profiles for the four most extreme positions, where the respondent showed 100 percent agreement with one viewpoint:

Radical Behaviorist:	B =	100	E =	44	H =	28	P =	40
Radical Existentialist:	B =	44	E =	100	H =	76	P =	24
Radical Humanist:	B =	28	E =	76	H =	100	P =	40
Radical Psychoanalyst:	B =	40	E =	24	H =	40	P =	100

Your own scores reflect your pattern of convergence with these four major viewpoints. Typically, one or two scores are higher than the others, sometimes substantially so, indicating a stronger agreement with those positions. For others there is more of a flat pattern of scores, representing an eclecticism that may be either open-mindedness or indecision. All orders and combinations of scores are possible. Pastors who have taken this questionnaire have ranged across all four preferences in their highest scores.

FOUR PERSONALITY THEORIES

What are the four secular theories to which these scores correspond? It is difficult to draw a fair and accurate summary sketch of these broad perspectives. They overlap each other, and within each there are some significant variations. Each of these is also a living theory, having changed substantially since its introduction. Still, there are some important differences in emphasis.

Psychodynamic Theories

Among the oldest systems of thinking within psychology and psychiatry are those termed *psychoanalytic* or, more generally, *psychodynamic*. These stem from the influential writings of Sigmund and Anna Freud. Their focus is heavily *intrapsychic*, looking within the individual for unconscious conflicts and other roots of problems that lie below the individual's conscious awareness. Psychodynamic perspectives are also heavily developmental in focus, considering crucial stages of the emerging person and usually emphasizing the importance of early experiences in the formation of personality. The overall concept of the person emphasizes the impulse-bound nature of human nature: the striving for personal pleasure which, if unchecked, could take on demonic proportions. Fictional representations of this perspective are common, as in William Golding's novel, *Lord of the Flies*, and the popular drama, *Equus*. A psychodynamic perspective is consistent with theological and political theories that stress control and the importance of restraining humanity's "natural tendencies." As a consequence, psychodynamic theories also emphasize processes of balance in human adjustment—balancing primitive inner drives with external reality—the process that Freud termed *das Ich* or *the I* and that has been translated as *the ego*. Successful adjustment consists of working out a compromise between the inner and the outer realities. Early psychodynamic theories placed the primary focus on intrapsychic processes, introducing into everyday vocabulary the concept of ego defense mechanisms such as rationalization, projection, and denial. More recently, ego psychology has itself sought a better balance with consideration of the influence of the social environment.

Behavioral Theories

Arising, in part, in reaction to psychodynamic approaches, the early behavioral theories placed heavy emphasis on the observable and tended to eschew hypothesized hidden dynamics such as "the unconscious" and "defense mechanisms." Instead, the focus was on learning, on the ways in which individual behavior is shaped by experience in the social environment. The writings of John Watson, often regarded as the founder of behaviorism, emphasized stimulus-response psychology. Later, the work of B. F. Skinner stressed concepts of reinforcement and punishment, the importance of what *follows* behavior as well as the stimuli that precede it. Enormous quantities of research followed, demonstrating ways in which learning processes shape both animal and human behavior. In a philosophic vein, behavioral approaches have often been associated with Skinner's social pragmatism, which attempts to design environments that will encourage behavior contributing to the overall welfare of the society. Change is a process of *relearning* in this view. Although stereotypes have sometimes confused behaviorism with reliance on punishment for control, as in Orwell's novel *1984* or the Kubrick film *A Clockwork Orange*, emphasis is instead typically given to positive reinforcement and to encouragement for gradual learning. Behavior therapists have often suggested new approaches to difficult personal and social problems, and research has indicated that, for some problem areas, behavior therapies are particularly effective.

Humanistic Theories

Both psychodynamic and behavioral theories view the individual as determined—as being controlled by certain laws of behavior. In reaction to these deterministic views, there arose a powerful third force in psychology. The central and prolific spokesman for this view for four decades was Carl Rogers, although one must also acknowledge the formative influence of Abraham Maslow. Denying that people are controlled by either unconscious or environmental forces, the humanistic psychologists point to purpose, meaning, and values as motivating drives. Rogers in particular maintained a profoundly optimistic view of the essential core of human nature—that if left undistorted an individual would develop naturally toward a positive personal identity that is both uniquely beautiful and respectful of the integrity and rights of other individuals. The person is seen as engaging in a lifelong search toward an inner goal, which is his or her true self. (From a spiritual perspective, this *self* includes transcendent elements, such as the inner voice or the soul.) To the extent that the individual experiences harmony between the perceived actual self and the ideal self, he or she moves in a healthy direction, continuing to grow. Adjustment problems arise out of a discrepancy between the person's actual self and the ideal—that which the person perceives that he or she *should* be. The process of counseling attached to this view has been called *client-centered* or *nondirective* because of the goal that it should be focused on and directed by the client.

Rogers was one of the first psychologists to specify critical conditions for change, which he considered to be understanding, nonpossessive warmth, and genuineness. To the extent that the therapist succeeds in providing these conditions, she or he creates an atmosphere in which clients will grow safely toward their true selves, moving toward self-actualization. The listening skills presented in part II derive primarily from this perspective, although the use of such methods is by no means restricted to a humanistic view of personality.

There are some profound overlaps of humanistic psychology and theology: (a) the emphasis on striving toward an inner goal; (b) the concept of acceptance as a crucial issue in human life; (c) an emphasis on the basic worth and dignity of the individual; (d) a belief in free will, in the choosing of one's own path; and (e) a belief in the individual's ability to repent at will, to change in major ways the course of one's life. To be sure, not all systems of theological thought share these assumptions, but certainly the humanistic theorists have wrestled with these essentially spiritual issues—perhaps because Rogers and others were themselves greatly influenced by religion. It is important to realize that humanistic thought and therapies are not to be equated with the value system that has been called *secular humanism*. The interface between humanistic psychology and religion has been addressed at many points, including the classic dialogue between Paul Tillich and Carl Rogers,[2] the writings of Erich Fromm,[3] and treatises on "Christian humanism."[4]

Existential Theories

Often confused with humanistic views because they overlap, the existential theories represent a fourth distinct perspective on human nature. Like the humanists, existentialists emphasize free will and the search for meaning. The philosophic basis of this view differs from that of Maslow and Rogers, however, and derives instead from the writings of Sartre, Kierkegaard, and

TABLE 6-1 A Comparison of Four Classic Personality Theories

	PSYCHODYNAMIC	BEHAVIORAL	HUMANISTIC	EXISTENTIAL
Model of Motivation	Need gratification	Reinforcement	Self-actualization	Quest for meaning
Origin of the Self	Conflict resolution	Learned	Positive innate plan	Chosen
Model of Adjustment	Balancing	Learning	Growing	Choosing
Model of Healing	Transference	Relearning	Acceptance	Responsibility
Focus of Observation	Unconscious, intrapsychic; memories, dreams, free association	Overt behavior and interactions with the social environment	Current feelings and experiences	Immediate experience
Therapist's Role	Analyst	Teacher	Facilitator	Companion
Key Theorists	Sigmund Freud	John Watson	Abraham Maslow	Viktor Frankl
	Anna Freud	B. F. Skinner	Carl Rogers	Ludwig Binswanger
	Carl Jung	Joseph Wolpe	Erich Fromm	Rollo May
	Alfred Adler	Hans Eysenck		Medard Boss
	Karen Horney			
Philosophical and Theological Roots	Jewish mysticism	Logical positivism	Phenomenology	Existentialism
	Energy physics	Associationism	Humanism	
	Kantian nativism	Social pragmatism		
Contemporary Writers	Salvador Maddi	Albert Bandura	Eugene Gendlin	James Bugental
	M. Scott Peck	G. Terence Wilson	Sidney Simon	Sam Keen
	Margaret Mahler	Arnold Lazarus	Allen Ivey	Irving Yalom
	Heinz Kohut	Michael Mahoney	Ira Progoff	Clark Moustakas
More Recent Developments	Object relations	Social learning	Values clarification	Gestalt therapy
	Ego psychology	Cognitive therapy	Psychosynthesis	Reality therapy
	Self-psychology	Self-control	Intensive journal	

the later existentialists. Popular proponents of existential psychology have included Rollo May, Irving Yalom, Fritz Perls, and Viktor Frankl. The existentialist denies the existence of any absolute purpose or meaning. The only meaning that one has is that which one chooses or makes for oneself. Human beings are neither inherently good nor sinful. They are not slaves and victims of unconscious impulses or of environmental control. One may perceive oneself as being controlled by such forces, but that, too, is a choice. The process of therapy within this perspective involves a shared search for meaning within the larger recognition that there is no meaning except what one chooses. This recognition precipitates an existential crisis, a frightening sense of loneliness and relativity. Such *angst* is seen as healthy, and the symptomatic relief of anxiety is therefore seen as useless or countertherapeutic by the existentialist (as by the psychoanalyst). The only life of integrity is one that is self-directed by an act of will, mindful that within the aloneness of existence all meaning is chosen.

OTHER PSYCHOLOGICAL THEORIES

Cognitive Theory and Therapy

In the 1970s another major approach to counseling emerged. The first popular form, introduced by Albert Ellis, was known as rational-emotive therapy (RET). Ellis's method emphasized "irrational beliefs" as the source of human suffering, seeking to identify and change such beliefs. Unfortunately, the methods of RET became identified and confused with Ellis's own rather antitheistic personal views, which regard virtually any religious beliefs as irrational and pathogenic. Aaron Beck subsequently described systems of cognitive therapy focusing more on the structure or process of thinking which can lead to problems. Again, the emphasis is on thoughts as the origin of negative feelings and maladaptive behaviors. This approach has been further popularized by writers such as David Burns, Arnold Lazarus, and Wayne Dyer and in the self-help organization Rational Recovery. Cognitive therapy will be described in more detail in chapter 12.

General and Family Systems

A general systems perspective is that individual behavior cannot be understood outside its social context. Most often in psychology this context has been the family. In family systems theory, the "problematic" behavior of an individual serves a function within the family, and so the family rather than the individual alone must be seen in order to understand and treat the problem. Although one person may be the identified patient, in fact the key to change lies in the family system. Attempts to change the individual will be resisted by the family, who attempt to maintain status quo. From this perspective, in fact, successful treatment of the individual might be expected to have detrimental effects on the family system, which is destabilized by the change. Family therapists working from a systems or structural perspective usually insist on seeing the whole family, seeking to alter maladaptive rules and communication patterns. Such therapy is typically brief and often dramatic. We would add, however, that research clearly shows that it is possible to be quite successful in working with individuals as well and does not support the view that the family must always be included in treatment for counseling to be effective. *Sometimes* the family needs to be seen along with the individual, and a family systems strategy is one good approach for doing so.

WHAT ABOUT SPIRITUALITY?

How does the spiritual dimension fit into all of this? The pastor is, after all, more than a counselor and is concerned with spiritual as well as mental and physical health. In fact, writers within each of the major perspectives have sought an integration between psychology and spirituality. Scott Peck's popular volumes seek rapproachment between psychodynamic theory and spiritual concerns.[5] Assagioli's system of psychosynthesis explicitly included a higher consciousness as well as an unconscious—the attic as well as the cellar. Erich Fromm, Karl Menninger, Carl Jung, James Fowler, Carl Rogers, and William James all explored this interface of psyche and spirit. Other writers have sought an integration of religious and spiritual issues with behavioral[6] and cognitive psychology.[7]

Whatever the theoretical framework within which one is counseling, it is possible to incorporate the client's spiritual issues and concerns. Although some theorists and other writers within psychology have been explicitly hostile toward religion, spirituality remains an important domain in the lives of many clients, even within secular treatment settings. The research of Rebecca Propst has shown that the positive effect of cognitive therapy can be significantly increased by incorporating clients' spiritual issues into counseling and that religiously oriented counselors may be more effective in doing so.[8] For the pastoral counselor who is comfortable in both worlds, it is easy to move back and forth between psychology and faith issues, emotional and spiritual concerns. It is normal, in healthy individuals, for the psychological and spiritual to be well-integrated aspects of self. The same is true in good counseling.

This is not to say that you should feel *obliged* to raise spiritual issues with every counseling session or individual. Certainly, there are problems that can be resolved without taking a spiritual inventory. Just remember to see the whole person with whom you are working, and do not hesitate to use your other pastoral skills and roles when you are counseling.

SYNTHESIS

At this very moment you, like every other counselor, struggle for a more complete view of human nature. Does it matter which one you choose? In one sense, any theory that helps you to organize your thinking may be helpful. It assists you in knowing what to pay attention to and what to ignore, in coming to a formulation of the individual and his or her situation, in deciding what needs to be done.

Yet in another sense it makes a great deal of difference which view you adopt. Choice of a more restrictive way of looking at reality may exclude from consideration the treatment approach that would be most helpful. In addition, views of human nature are notoriously self-fulfilling. There is more than comic truth to the phrase, "What you see is what you get." How can one find a systematic way of thinking that avoids some of these pitfalls? This is a challenge of integrity for every counselor.

We cannot prescribe for you an ideal perspective. The viewpoints presented here represent only four alternative *psychological* ways of thinking. We do not intend for you to make a choice among these. Rather, we present them to help raise your awareness of overlaps between your own present viewpoint and classic schools of thought within psychology. As a pastor you bring still other perspectives and work from a set of presuppositions that differ from and transcend these systems. The point here is *awareness*, to know what your working assumptions are, to have an organized way of thinking about people and their problems, to recognize how your own assumptions affect your work as a counselor.

There is no single ideal or desirable viewpoint for accomplishing the purposes of counseling. We can, however, say a few things about what should characterize the counselor's thinking process. Whatever system of thought is adopted by a pastoral counselor, the following qualities are desirable and helpful to the counseling process.

1. *Flexible*: a thinking style that is open to new information rather than assumption-bound, seeking the paradigm to fit the individual rather than forcing all individuals to fit into a single mold
2. *Eclectic*: in the best sense, willing to consider perspectives and intervention approaches from a broad range of sources
3. *Practical*: helping you to know what to do next
4. *Pragmatic*: choosing on the basis of helpfulness, interested in information and research on the relative effectiveness of different approaches
5. *Differential*: changing with the individual's needs, rather than having a single perspective or intervention approach for everyone

Each of the perspectives presented in this chapter contains its elements of truth. The challenge is this: to develop a systematic, organized way of thinking about people and their problems that helps you to decide what the problem is, what is causing it, what is missing, and what is needed. This includes using personal beliefs and perspectives while at the same time correcting for the biases that are inherent in them. You already *have* a formulation system, and part of the purpose of this chapter has been to encourage you to become more aware of it. Your present system is a complex confluence of many types of information. From here on you continue to add new perspectives and knowledge, to try out new ways of organizing and synthesizing, to discard biases that interfere.

One important source of corrective information is your clients. The process of reflective listening described in chapter 5 leads toward a more phenomenological perspective, an individualized understanding of the person's reality. Another source of input is new knowledge from the rapidly growing body of research in psychology and other mental health fields, some of which is summarized in part V. In chapter 7, however, we will consider a few central questions and general conceptual frameworks that may be helpful as you ask the questions of formulation: How can I best understand this person and the problems he or she brings, and what can we do together that would be most likely to help?

ADDITIONAL READINGS

The "Dialogues in Contemporary Psychology" series (Richard I. Evans, ed., Greenwood Publishers) consists of volumes containing transcribed discussions with a variety of classic theorists in psychology, including Gordon Allport, Albert Bandura, Erik Erikson, Erich Fromm, Carl Jung, R. D. Laing, Jean Piaget, Carl Rogers, and B. F. Skinner. Consult your library.

Psychoanalytic Theory

BRENNER, CHARLES *An Elementary Textbook of Psychoanalysis* (rev. ed.). New York: Doubleday, 1974.

CAMPBELL, JOSEPH, ed. *The Portable Jung.* New York: Penguin, 1976. Excellent introduction to Jungian psychology.

FABER, HEIJE *Psychology of Religion.* Philadelphia: Westminster Press, 1976. Discusses faith development in relation to psychoanalytic theory.

FREUD, SIGMUND *A General Introduction to Psychoanalysis.* New York: Liveright, 1924. Sigmund Freud's three classic works on religion are *The Future of an Illusion* (New York: Norton, 1961), *Moses and Monotheism* (New York: Vintage, 1939), and *Totem and Taboo* (New York: Norton, 1950).

FROMM, ERICH *Psychoanalysis and Religion.* New Haven: Yale University Press, 1950.

HALL, CALVIN S. *A Primer of Freudian Psychology.* New York: World, 1954.

JUNG, CARL G. *Memories, Dreams and Reflections.* New York: Random House, 1961. Of all the neoanalysts, Jung was the one most interested in and outspoken about religion and spirituality. This is a fascinating autobiographical document containing some of his own religious experiences.

SMITH, JOSEPH H., and SUSAN A. HANDELMAN, eds. *Psychoanalysis and Religion.* Baltimore: Johns Hopkins University Press, 1990.

Behavioral Psychology and Behavior Therapy

EYSENCK, HANS J., and IRENE MARTIN, eds. *Theoretical Foundations of Behavior Therapy*. New York: Plenum Press, 1987.

MILLER, WILLIAM R., and JOHN E. MARTIN *Behavior Therapy and Religion*. Newbury Park, CA: Sage Publications, 1988. An edited volume on the interface of spiritual and behavioral approaches to change.

SKINNER, B. F. *About Behaviorism*. New York: Random House, 1974. This book is Skinner's classic description of radical behaviorism and his own social pragmatism, from a totally secular perspective.

TARLOW, GERALD, and ANNE MAXWELL *Clinical Handbook of Behavior Therapy: Adult Psychological Problems*. Cambridge, MA: Brookline Books, 1989. A practice-oriented handbook that summarizes research literature and clinical approaches for forty-nine specific behavior problems encountered in counseling.

Humanistic Psychology and Psychotherapy

EVANS, RICHARD I. *Carl Rogers: The Man and His Ideas*. New York: Dutton, 1975. An overview of Rogers, with part of the text of a classic debate between Rogers and B. F. Skinner.

FROMM, ERICH *The Art of Loving*. New York: Harper & Row, 1956. Fromm represents an important bridge from analysis to humanistic psychology. Like Jung, he devoted extensive attention to the role of religion and spirituality in human life.

MASLOW, ABRAHAM H. *Religions, Values, and Peak-Experiences*. New York: Viking, 1970. Maslow is often referred to as the founder of the humanistic tradition within psychology.

ROGERS, CARL R. *Client-centered Therapy*. Boston: Houghton-Mifflin, 1951. This is Rogers' first full statement of the client-centered approach to therapy that has been so influential within pastoral counseling.

Existential Psychology and Psychotherapy

ASSAGIOLI, ROBERTO *Psychosynthesis*. New York: Penguin, 1971. Psychosynthesis is a fascinating spinoff of existential therapy, a unique and creative system rich in conceptualization and technique.

BROWN, ROBERT MCAFEE *Elie Wiesel: Messenger to All Humanity*. Notre Dame, IN: University of Notre Dame Press, 1983. Brown struggles as a Christian theologian to integrate the existential and prophetic writings of Elie Wiesel, survivor of the Holocaust.

BUBER, MARTIN *I and Thou*. New York: Scribner's, 1970.

BUGENTAL, JAMES F. *The Search for Authenticity: An Existential-Analytic Approach to Psychotherapy*. New York: Irvington, 1989.

FRANKL, VIKTOR E. *Psychotherapy and Existentialism*. New York: Simon & Schuster, 1968.

———*The Doctor and the Soul* (rev. ed). New York: Vintage, 1986.

KIERKEGAARD, SOREN *The Sickness unto Death: A Christian Psychological Exposition for Upbuilding and Awakening*. Princeton, NJ: Princeton University Press, 1980.

MAY, ROLLO *The Art of Counseling* (rev. ed.). Gardner, 1990.

———*Existential Psychology*. New York: Random House, 1990.

MOUSTAKAS, CLARKE E. *Loneliness*. Englewood Cliffs, NJ: Prentice-Hall, 1990. A small book on a large problem; an existential grappling with the phenomenon of loneliness.

SARTRE, JEAN-PAUL *Existential Psychoanalysis*. Chicago: Regnery-Gateway, 1962.

YALOM, IRVING *Existential Psychotherapy*. New York: Basic Books, 1980.

Cognitive Therapy

BECK, AARON T. *Cognitive Therapy and the Emotional Disorders*. New York: New American Library, 1979.

ELLIS, ALBERT, and ROBERT A. HARPER *A New Guide to Rational Living*. North Hollywood, CA: Wilshire, 1975.

MCMULLIN, RIAN *Cognitive-Behavior Therapy: A Restructuring Approach*. New York: Grune & Stratton, 1981. An interesting approach based on the shifting of perceptions and drawing on gestalt psychology.

Family Systems

FRIEDMAN, ERWIN II. *Generation to Generation: Family Process in Church and Synagogue*. New York: Guilford Press, 1985. A broad presentation of systems theory, integrated with religious perspectives.

HALEY, JAY *Problem-solving Therapy: New Strategies for Effective Family Therapy*. San Francisco: Jossey/Bass, 1976.

Surveys and Integrations

CORSINI, RAYMOND J., and DANNY WEDDING, eds. *Current Psychotherapies* (4th ed.) Itasca, IL: Peacock, 1989. An edited volume surveying systems of psychotherapy.

HALL, CALVIN S., and GARDNER LINDZEY *Theories of Personality* (3d ed.). New York: John Wiley, 1979. This is the standard text on personality theories within psychology.

LARSON, BRUCE *The Meaning and Mystery of Being Human*. Waco, TX: Word, 1978. This fascinating and stimulating book is the outgrowth of a Lilly Endowment project in which Larson participated in a wide range of different therapeutic experiences and then wrote a synthesis to identify common elements of human growth and change. Well worth reading.

PROCHASKA, JAMES O. *Systems of Psychotherapy: A Transtheoretical Analysis* (2d ed.). Monterey, CA: Brooks/Cole, 1984. A superb review and integration of major alternative approaches to therapy.

NOTES

[1]Comment in a workshop in Albuquerque, NM, 8 October 1981. For elaboration of this idea, consult Paul Pruyser, *The Minister as Diagnostician* (Philadelphia: Westminster Press, 1976).

[2]*Paul Tillich and Carl Rogers: A Dialogue* (San Diego: Radio/Television, San Diego State College, 1966); transcript of a conversation a recorded 7 March 1965.

[3]Erich Fromm, *Psychoanalysis and Religion* (New Haven: Yale University Press, 1950).

[4]Harvey Cox, *The Secular City* (New York: Macmillan, 1985); Thomas Molnar, *Christian Humanism: A Critique of the Secular City and Its Ideology* (Chicago: Franciscan Herald, 1978); Daniel Callahan, ed., *The Secular Debate* (New York: Macmillan, 1966); David Eggenschwiler, *The Christian Humanism of Flannery O'Connor* (Detroit: Wayne State University Press, 1972); Miguel de Unamuno, *The Agony of Christianity and Essays on Faith* (Princeton; NJ: Princeton University Press, 1974).

[5]Scott Peck, *The Road Less Traveled* (New York: Simon & Schuster, 1978); *People of the Lie: The Hope for Healing Human Evil* (New York: Simon & Schuster, 1983).

[6]E. P. Bolin and G. M. Goldberg, "Behavioral Psychology and the Bible: General and Specific Considerations," *Journal of Psychology and Theology* 7 (1979): 167–75; Gary Collins; *Christian Counseling* (Waco, TX: Word, 1988); Stephen Hayes, "Making Sense of Spirituality;" *Behaviorism* 12 no. 2 (1984): 99–110; William R. Miller and John E. Martin, eds., *Behavior Therapy and Religion: Integrating Spiritual and Behavioral Approaches to Change* (Newbury Park, CA: Sage Publications, 1988).

[7]Lawrence and C. H. Huber, "Strange Bedfellows? Rational-Emotive Therapy and Pastoral Counseling," *Personnel and Guidance Journal* 61 (1982): 210–12; William R. Miller, *Living as If: How Positive Faith Can Change Your Life* (Philadelphia: Westminster Press, 1985); L. Rebecca Propst, *Psychotherapy in a Religious Framework: Spirituality in the Emotional Healing Process* (New York: Human Sciences Press, 1988).

[8]L. Rebecca Propst, "The Comparative Efficacy of Religious and Nonreligious Imagery for the Treatment of Mild Depression in Religious Individuals," *Cognitive Therapy and Research* 4 (1990): 167–78; L. Rebecca Propst, Richard Ostrom, Philip Watkins, Terri Dean, and David Mashburn, "Comparative Efficacy of Religious and Nonreligious Cognitive-Behavioral Therapy for the Treatment of Clinical Depression in Religious Individuals," *Journal of Consulting and Clinical Psychology* 60 (1992): 94–103.

7

GETTING ORGANIZED: FOUR HELPFUL QUESTIONS

The eternal mystery of the world is its comprehensibility.
—Albert Einstein, *Out of My Later Years*

Formulation is the way in which a counselor reaches an answer to the question, "What do I do now?" Some therapeutic approaches pay relatively little attention to systematic thinking and instead recommend that the counselor follow immediate intuitions or rely upon the power of the healing relationship. Other systems prescribe structured and systematized approaches. Both are appropriate at times. In part II, we recommended that during *clarification* (phase 1) you maintain a client-focused attitude, using reflective listening to explore the client's own thoughts, feelings, and perceptions. During *intervention* (phase 3), on the other hand, research justifies in many cases carefully following a prescribed therapeutic approach for a particular type of problem.

Between the two extremes of openness and structure, and between the phases of clarification and intervention, lies the process of formulation (phase 2). Its purpose is to arrive at an accurate and comprehensive picture of the client and his or her problems. The formulation process is one of systematic yet flexible thinking. It draws together the perspectives and information gained during the clarification phase, combines these with the counselor's own conceptual framework, and points toward appropriate intervention strategies. It requires a unique combination of structure and ongoing openness to new possibilities. In the words of Alvin Toffler, "No single world view can ever capture the whole truth. Only by applying multiple and temporary metaphors can we gain a rounded (if still incomplete) picture of the world. . . . I mistrust those who think they already have the answers when we are still trying to formulate the questions."[1]

As an aid in organizing your thinking, we propose four general questions to be considered during the formulation process.

1. What is troubling this person?
2. What is causing the problem?
3. What is missing?
4. What is needed?

Within each of these questions are many complexities. In this chapter we suggest some simple yet flexible structures that can be used in seeking answers to these four crucial questions.

1. WHAT IS TROUBLING THIS PERSON?

The person who seeks the help of a counselor is often confused. His or her general distress is usually clear, but the exact nature of the problem is not. The trouble touches on many areas—relationships, job, spiritual life, emotions, actions. Just what *is* the problem? What are the relevant areas of the person's experience that should be explored?

We find it helpful, in listening to a client talk during the first few sessions, to think about three general domains of human experience, three interrelated and yet distinguishable pieces of the puzzle. We will call these by their psychological names—*affect, behavior*, and *cognition*—in part because these are good and comprehensive terms and in part because they conveniently begin with the easily remembered letters *A, B,* and *C*.

A. Affect

The term *affect* is used in psychology to refer to the broad domain of human emotions. It is a noun related to the word *affection* and not to be confused with the verb *to affect*.

Human emotions are complicated. In one sense they are phenomenological—they are *experienced*. In this sense no one can tell you what you feel. You are the expert and the final authority on your own feelings. You experience in yourself a rich array of subtle shades of emotion. At the same time, emotions have heavy *physiological* underpinnings. It is possible to observe physiological changes that accompany the experience of emotion: changes in the temperature of the hands and the color of the face, dilation of the pupils of the eyes, perspiration and trembling. Other changes require special instruments to observe: subtle changes in heart rate and blood pressure, in the color of the stomach wall, in the electrical conductance of the skin. All of these are linked to a well-understood portion of the nervous system called *autonomic*, which controls the physiology of emotion. The autonomic nervous system will be discussed in more detail in chapter 14.

These elements of experience, physiology, and expression flow together to form what is called *emotion*. Sometimes the person privately experiences emotions about which no one else knows. At other times those around the individual will perceive that he or she is depressed or angry or stressed through observing changes in the person's appearance or behavior, even though the individual may deny having the feeling. In this latter sense of objective signs of emotion, it is possible to be depressed or stressed or angry without realizing it, without having a conscious awareness of the feeling.

One major area to explore, then, is the area of affect or emotion. What is the person feeling and experiencing now? Are there any indications that the person is unaware of significant emotional changes that are happening within her or him?

B. Behavior

A second domain in which problems can emerge is that of behavior or action. The person may be getting into trouble by virtue of what he or she is *doing*. Social withdrawal frequently exacerbates depression. Heavy alcohol consumption will eventually cause problems for almost everyone. Overcommitting of one's time is a common source of stress and burnout (including among clergy and the most "active" members of a church—see chapters 20 and 21). Relationship problems are frequently related to what each partner does or fails to do. All of these are behaviors, actions that contribute to a problem.

Again, there may be a discrepancy between the person's own experience of his or her behavior and external perceptions of the same actions. A person's perception of his or her own behavior is colored by awareness of the intention behind it, information that is not directly available to others. The perceptions of others are in turn colored by own their interpretations of the behavior, as discussed in chapter 5 on the cycle of communication. There may therefore be conflicting reports about a person's behavior, even when each party is trying to report honestly on the same events.

Beyond feelings, then, another area to consider is behavior. What is the person *doing* (or not doing) that contributes to the overall problem?

C. Cognition

Cognition is a term that is applied to a wide range of mental processes that are difficult or impossible to observe directly. The easiest synonym is *thought*, although even this is too restrictive in its connotations of logical process. Cognition encompasses a person's total perceptual system—the ways in which she or he views the world. It includes but is not limited to the thought processes (such as logic or values) that one uses for combining information received from the outside world. It incorporates a person's belief systems, hopes and aspirations, memories, and biases. It includes the person's vast store of knowledge and information acquired through the course of life experience.

Some problems seem to be driven or maintained by these cognitive processes. Research on depression, for example, suggests that at least some mood problems can derive from particular ways of thinking and that a road out of depression may be found through examination and change of these cognitive processes. Certain memories may be endlessly replayed as if on a tape-recorded loop, creating or exacerbating certain feelings or behaviors. The pastoral counselor is also very interested in the individual's beliefs in the spiritual realm—about ultimate meaning, grace, responsibility, providence.[2]

A third component of an individual's situation to consider, then, is cognition. What and how does the person think, believe, and perceive?

Interaction

These three facets of individual experience are not separate, of course, but are intricately intertwined. Each influences and is influenced by the others. One can think of a circular relationship among these three (Fig. 7-1).

Any problem that an individual has may be centered in one of these three areas, but it is likely to influence all three. The cycle can become a downward spiral as each element contributes to an escalation of problem patterns. The belief, for example, that one is basically unlovable and unacceptable may con-

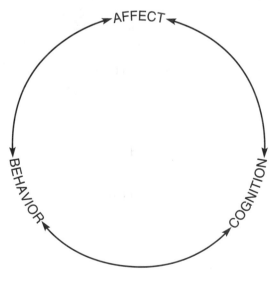

FIGURE 7-1

tribute both to feelings of depression and to the behavior of social withdrawal. The withdrawal in turn creates greater depression and reinforces beliefs that one is isolated and apart from others. The feelings of depression also strengthen thoughts of personal unworthiness and leave the person with little energy to break out of the pattern of withdrawal.

During the clarification and formulation phases, it is helpful to ask how each of these three domains is influenced by and is influencing the problem. What does the person seem to have *too much* or *too little* of in each area? How is the problem showing up on each dimension, and how might each be contributing to a spiral? Frequently, people seek the help of a counselor precisely when they feel caught in such a spiral—when their normal coping skills and styles no longer work and they feel stuck.

Conflict

Another helpful aspect of this model is that it can clarify conflicts or discrepancies. Sometimes a problem emerges because of a lack of consistency or agreement within or among these three aspects of experience. A person may believe things that are inconsistent with his or her own behavior or feelings. For example, a person may

believe that smoking is harmful or wrong but continue to smoke

feel sexually attracted to another person but believe that this is wrong

feel resentful about being taken advantage of but continue to say "yes" to every request

These examples represent, respectively, conflicts between cognition versus behavior, affect versus cognition, and affect versus behavior. Inconsistencies of this kind can be uncomfortable and stressful. Sometimes people find positive ways to resolve such conflicts (e.g., to stop smoking); at other times they resolve them in more destructive ways (such as changing one's belief to "I am too weak to be able to quit, and besides my life isn't worth that much anyhow").

We find it helpful sometimes to use an analogy suggested to us once by Rev. Larry Collins. It is, he said, as if there were within each person a committee. When one gets into a conflict situation, some members of the committee vote one way while others vote in opposition. A certain majority is needed to carry a vote. To complicate matters, some members of the committee are more influential than others. In working on a conflict, it can be helpful to find out who the committee members are and what each one has to say on the issue. The major difference may be between members called *heart* and *head* (affect versus cognition). Or there may be dissenting members within a certain area (e.g., conflicting beliefs). This "committee" idea has been more fully developed within the psychosynthesis concept of subpersonalities.[3]

Understanding different *types* of conflicts can clarify matters further for both counselor and client. There are four. The first of these is the *approach-approach* conflict, in which the individual must choose between two positive or attractive alternatives, such as deciding which of two exciting job offers to accept or which of two seemingly wonderful people to date or to marry. These choices can be stressful, but they are the most benign type of conflict.

A more anxiety-producing conflict is the *avoidance-avoidance* conflict. Here the person must choose between two evils, two negative alternatives. People talk about being caught "between the devil and the deep blue sea" or "between a rock and a hard place." Neither option looks pleasant, but one *must* be chosen. A person may, for example, be increasingly uncomfortable with the nature, purpose, or meaninglessness of his or her work, yet the alternative prospects of unemployment and retraining also look frightening. Such conscience versus "reality" conflicts are the subject of many fictional as well as real-life dramas.

A still more distressing type of conflict is the *approach-avoidance* type. Here a person both wants and doesn't want something. The same person or goal contains both positive and negative aspects. In talking about this kind of conflict situation, a person uses the word *but* a lot. "I want to stay married to my partner, but the drinking is driving me crazy." "I'd like to have children, but I don't have enough time in my life as it is without adding more demands." "I'd like to move to a new city, but I can't face leaving all of my friends." This type of conflict tends to go back and forth in repetitive fashion. The closer one comes to the person or goal about which he or she is conflicted, the more clear the negative aspects become. As he or she draws away, however, the negative aspects fade and the positive reasons to return seem so much clearer. The result is a kind of emotional yo-yo effect.

But worst of all—the grand champion of stressful conflicts—is the *double approach-avoidance* type. Here the individual is caught between two alternatives, both of which contain powerful positive and negative facets. Drawing near to A, one sees the negative aspects of A and feels drawn to the positive in B. On leaving A and approaching B, however, the opposite process occurs and now B looks tainted while A looks attractive. Worse than a yo-yo, this kind of conflict feels like an endless emotional roller coaster ride. A clear counseling example is the married person involved in an affair. The person is powerfully tied to spouse and family by bonds of love and shared years, yet is also drawn to the romantic aura of the new lover. The more he or she recommits to the marriage, the more the drawbacks of the spouse and family become clear and the more idealized the lover becomes. To move away from the family, however, is to clarify the pain of separation and the flaws of the lover, releasing a powerful yearning to return home. The result is an almost unparalleled level of suffering and confusion, depression and craziness.

Solutions to these dilemmas are possible, and methods for helping people to resolve ambivalence are considered in chapter 8. For the time being, however, suffice it to say that, in trying to find an answer to this first question of "What is troubling this person?" it is helpful to consider the three domains of experience, as well as the types of conflict that may exist within and between these domains.

Conflicts exist between individuals as well as within them. This is one reason why the counseling of couples regarding their relationship can be at least twice as challenging as working with one individual at a time. There are not only the intrapersonal patterns of conflict, but also the intricate interactions of each person's affect, behavior, and cognition with the other's. If one begins to work with an entire family, the possibilities can be staggering. Still, it is possible to use the framework provided here to conceptualize each person's situation within the relationship and even to think of types of conflict within the family system as a whole. Nor is this type of element-conflict analysis limited to individuals and families. Similar thinking can be used to understand the interworkings of employer-employee systems, friendships, committees, whole communities, and even the interrelationships between pastors and congregations.

2. WHAT IS CAUSING THE PROBLEM?

A second vital question of formulation is to ask what is *causing* the problem. What is its source, its genesis?

The process often begins with open-ended brainstorming. What *might* be causing the problem? What factors *might* be involved? Here is where a good working knowledge of human psychology can be invaluable. Once a problem has been identified, the counselor still needs knowledge of the kinds of causes that can contribute to this type of problem. Complex patterns such as anxiety or depression are final common pathways for the effects of many different kinds of causes. Many of the chapters in part V are organized around causal factors that contribute to each type of problem and how these can be addressed.

With a list of possible causal influences in mind, the process then becomes one of elimination—weeding out the factors that probably are not important and focusing on the others. Through this process one arrives at the intervention approach(es) most likely to help.

The first task for the counselor is to generate alternative possibilities for what might be causing a problem. Certainly, the tripartite consideration of affect/behavior/cognition can contribute to this creative process, but there is another set of categories to be considered. These represent different types of "causes," and they are four in number. For those fond of mnemonics or alliteration, they all begin with the letter *P*.

Primary Causes

Some problems (though by no means all) can be traced to a primary cause. This is a causal factor that is either *necessary* or *sufficient* (or both) to produce the problem. A "necessary" causal factor would be one that must be present for the problem to occur, whereas "sufficient" causes are those that when encountered by anyone would result in the problem.

The easy examples are biological. A viral organism is the necessary (but not sufficient) cause of influenza. No one has influenza without encountering the virus, but not all who are exposed to the virus contract the disease. A particular chromosomal abnormality is the necessary and sufficient cause of the developmental disorder known as Down's syndrome. Depression often follows certain major surgeries or can be induced by causing certain changes in brain chemistry. Other brain chemistry changes are sufficient to yield consistent syndromes such as Parkinsonism or a psychotic reaction resembling (but not equivalent to) schizophrenia. Some drugs are sufficient causes of change in affect or cognition. As necessary and/or sufficient preconditions for a problem, primary causes are the most direct etiological factors.

With psychological processes it is more difficult to point to clear primary causes that are necessary or sufficient to yield predictable problem patterns. A major loss often sets off a period of depression. Major life changes tend to increase the risk of stress-related illnesses. Fatigue and marital conflict are factors in sexual dysfunctions. After major trauma such as rape or combat, individuals often show a type of psychological shock known as post-traumatic stress disorder. With all of these examples, however, there are the remarkable survivors, those who endure conditions that seem sufficient to cause problems but who emerge apparently unscarred. In psychology, the closest one can usually come to primary causes is to identify conditions that have a very *high probability* of yielding certain types of problems. Exposed to such factors, many or most people would show similar difficulties.

Predisposing Causes

Other causal factors exert their influence over a longer span of time, raising the probability that a person will develop a certain problem *later*. They *predispose* a person, increasing the chances that a problem will emerge.

Again, there are biological examples. For certain types of depression, schizophrenia, and alcohol problems, there is a clear genetic factor involved, although heredity is neither necessary nor sufficient to cause such disorders. A person with a history of these disorders among biological relatives has an elevated risk of developing them herself or himself.[4] Research also points to biological predispositions to certain kinds of stress-related diseases, so that under stress this particular "weak link in the chain" breaks. There is such evidence for predisposition to stomach ulcers, for example.[5]

Certain psychological experiences also predispose a person to problems. Observing significant others handling stress in a certain way—by drinking, taking drugs, or developing vague physical complaints—may predispose a person to use similar maladaptive coping patterns if exposed to similar stress. Certain parenting styles have been linked to later problems among the children.[6] A posttraumatic syndrome induced by exposure to combat or childhood abuse represents a time-bomb type of delayed stress reaction in which a prior period of prolonged trauma surfaces years later in predictable symptoms of depression or rage.[7]

These causes overlap to some extent with those listed as "primary" in that they increase the probability of occurrence of a problem. The distinction is the length of time by which they precede the emergence of the problem. Also, there is less certainty about the problem eventually emerging than is the case with true primary causes. Whenever long periods pass between cause and psychological effect, there is a greater chance that the problem may not emerge or can be averted by intervening life experiences. Predisposing causes, then, are experiences of the past or biological factors that prepare the way for a problem to emerge.

Precipitating Causes

Precipitating causes can be the most misleading because they are the most obvious. These immediately precede the beginning of a problem and so seem to be the definitive cause. A woman has a business setback and enters a period of depression. A man begins drinking heavily after divorce. As should be clear from previous discussion, however, the roots of such a problem may lie much further back (and extend into the present as well, as will be seen shortly).

An event that immediately precedes the onset of a problem may be a total coincidence, unrelated to the problem, or it may represent only "the straw that broke the camel's back"—one small addition to an all but unbearable previous load. Although such factors deserve attention, do not be led to give undue importance to them simply because they correspond in time to the apparent beginning of a problem. It is worth remembering, too, that clients frequently overestimate the importance of precipitating causes for the same reason.

Perpetuating Causes

Finally, there are the perpetuating causes, those that increase the chances that a problem will continue once it has started. These are often overlooked because of an emphasis on the past, but they can be crucial. A problem may start for one reason but continue for another.

Suppose in a congregation there is an individual who is somewhat difficult to get along with and who consequently is avoided most of the time by most of the people. The person lives alone and leads a relatively unrewarding life. Eventually, this relative social isolation, exacerbated perhaps by a precipitating crisis of some kind, results in a depression in which the individual feels genuinely suicidal and makes this known to others. The immediate response of a caring congregation would be to rally around the individual and provide support. People call and stop by regularly to see how the individual is doing. In the middle of the suicidal crisis, the pastor and other people maintain a round-the-clock vigil. Parishioners bring in food and help with the housework. Cards and letters start to arrive, and with time the person starts to feel better. As this happens, the crisis-precipitated support begins to disappear. The calls, cards, and letters stop. Cooking and housekeeping again become lonely tasks.

If this person (consciously or unconsciously) has any sense at all, the depression will return. Life is simply much more interesting and rewarding that way. To get better is to be abandoned. To be depressed is to be supported. The person is in no sense "faking" depression. It is real enough, and it is being powerfully prolonged by the perpetuating influence of this particular social situation.

To understand the causes of a problem, then, it is important to look not only at the past but also at the present and future. Often in this light a person's "problem" makes much more sense. It represents the best way the person knows how to cope, a reasonable adaptation, perhaps, to an unreasonable situation. The question, "What is causing the problem?" extends not only to "Where did it begin?", but also to "What is keeping it going *now*?"

These perpetuating causes can be perplexing for a pastor. Should the congregation "stop caring"? Of course not, and yet the perpetuating influence is clear. The way out in this situation is not for the congregation to abandon the person in sickness *and* in health (though eventually that may happen as people begin to burn out or become "fed up"), but rather for the individual to develop a better-balanced lifestyle with less reliance on aloneness and more investment in the spheres of work and relationships. This issue of balance brings us to another key question in formulation.

3. WHAT IS MISSING?

A third question of importance to the pastoral counselor is, "What is missing here?" People present their problems as they see them but often do not take in the bigger picture. It is the counselor's job to see this larger perspective, to consider the problem within the context of the person's life.

One way to do this is to consider what the person seems to be lacking or avoiding. Fritz Perls, the uncannily intuitive therapist who founded the system known as Gestalt therapy, consistently asked, "What is this person *not* doing, *not* talking about, *not* thinking about, *not* feeling?"[8] Often the absences, the silences, the holes are as informative as the problems the client presents.

One direct approach used by psychologist Sidney Simon is to ask the person, "What do you have *too little of* in your life?" It can be revealing to have the individual name these things, listing everything of which she or he has too little until the possibilities are exhausted. At times, this places in perspective the more conscious problems, which tend to be "too much" in nature. The next intervention question, of course, is, "How can you arrange to have more of these things in your life?"

Another way to consider what's missing is to have a perspective yourself on what it means to have a full and rewarding life. Once when Freud was asked what are the essentials of a happy life, he replied "to love and to work." To these two, psychologist Susan Gilmore added a third area that touches on the spiritual side of personhood—aloneness. She maintained that each person should have a balance of fulfillment in each of three areas—work, relationships, and aloneness.[9]

Work

Bertrand Russell wrote, "Few things are so likely to cure the habit of hatred as the opportunity to do constructive work of an important kind. . . . Consistent purpose is not enough to make life happy, but it is an almost indispensable condition of a happy life. And consistent purpose embodies itself mainly in work."[10] Russell, like Gilmore, was using the term *work* to refer to more than a job. He was referring to the process of doing something constructive, of contributing to the common good. The search for meaning in the area of work is a search for purpose, for a task or a cause, for something to do that is worthwhile. To work is to do. The related theological issue is vocation.

In today's world the nature and meaning of work are changing so rapidly that those of us who inherited the work ethic of the post-Depression era are left in wide-eyed confusion. Alvin Toffler predicted that work in the decades ahead will be totally different from its counterpart in the first three-quarters of this century.[11] It will be decentralized, destandardized, desynchronized. We will work at different places and paces, times and tasks than ever before. Yet the psychological challenge remains the same—to find a purpose, something meaningful to do with one's life. This is not always found in one's job. Churches are filled, at least the more fortunate ones, with people who find meaning in giving of their time and talents in the life of the local, regional, national, or international community. Volunteerism rides on this search for meaningful vocation. When people are given increasing amounts of free time to use as they will, the challenge is still the same. In childhood where, as Gilmore pointed out, one's work is to play, it is the same. In retirement it is the same. What is my purpose? We also ask of ourselves the question that comes second or third when we meet someone new: "What do you *do*?"

The area of work, of purpose, of vocation is important to consider when asking, "What is missing?"

Relationships

A second place where each person must find fulfillment is in relationships. Gilmore describes this as "the art of moving,"[12] because in relationships we are forever moving toward or away from others. Friendship, courtship, love, collegiality, counseling—these are all processes of moving creatively toward another. Life also presents us with many moments when we must gracefully move away from others—the child leaving home, divorce, retirement, transfer, promotion, separation, and the ending of school, of vacation, of counseling.

The process of moving toward and away from others is rich in promise and in problems. The pastoral counselor will frequently meet people wrestling with the difficulties of these transitions. Change is normally difficult. Yet under it all, ideally, is a network of relationships that is sustaining and enduring. To develop this kind of support for oneself, to have sustaining relationships, is another of life's challenges.

Aloneness

To work is to do. To relate is to move. The third life task is existential: to be. Here lies the rich inner world of meaning, searching, choosing, wondering. Like the other two areas, this one can be over- or underemphasized. The person may spend too much time wrestling with internal existential questions or may wrestle with external reality to the exclusion of the inner reality. To find meaning is the third of life's challenges that cries out for fulfillment, and when people find themselves coming up short in this area they may seek the fellowship of a church or the perspective of a pastor.

The questions here are large ones but are familiar to any pastor. Why do we suffer? What is the meaning of life and of death? Why am I here? Why should I choose life instead of death? Is there an ultimate reality and purpose? Who is God, and what is God's intention toward me? The questions and the answers take on many forms, but the search is common to all.

In asking, "What is missing?" the pastoral counselor must also wonder about how the individual experiences and deals with her or his aloneness, with these issues of being.

4. WHAT IS NEEDED?

This fourth and final question of formulation provides the transition to the next phase of counseling, intervention. If the first three questions have been answered carefully, thoughtfully, comprehensively, then the answer to this question may be obvious. But then again it may not.

Here again there is a process of creative thinking. For any problem there is likely to be more than one alternative solution, more than one way in which to proceed. A knowledge of alternative options is helpful, and this includes not only the kind of information to be presented in part V but also a good acquaintance with the resources available in your community and the surrounding area, the skills to be discussed in part VI.

Before proceeding to these alternative interventions, however, we encourage you to entertain yet one more tripartite thinking system. This asks "What is needed?" in a special way, by considering three different possible goals of counseling. These three goals described by Gilmore are important to consider because they represent three different roads to follow. Interventions appropriate in the pursuit of one goal may be irrelevant, premature, or obstructive in the pursuit of a different goal.

Change

The goal that comes to mind most readily when one thinks of counseling is change. Here the goal is for something to be different. The desired change may be in affect, behavior, or cognition or in some combination of all of them. It may include any or all of the areas of work, relationships, and aloneness.

A clarifying question that Gilmore recommended here is, "If our work together were 100 percent successful, what would be different?" Often there are unexpected answers to this question and sometimes just an honest "I don't know."

There are many strategies and interventions for helping people to change.[13] Knowledge of effective psychological change techniques is growing at a dizzying pace so that most professionals find it difficult to keep up with new research even within a specialty area. If you can propose a behavior, cognition, or affect to be changed, the chances are that you can find in the literature several different and even effective ways to begin. It is important not to jump too quickly to the conclusion that change is necessary, however, for there are other possible goals of counseling.

Choice

Sometimes what a person requires is not change so much as choice. In some cases the making of a choice must occur before the person is ready to change. Decisions can be difficult, and the process of helping people in making them involves some special skills. One of these is reflective listening geared especially toward conflict. Another is an ability to recognize and understand different kinds of conflict. Still other ways of helping people in the process of choice are presented in chapter 9. You cannot make a choice for another person, but you can help that person to reach an acceptable decision.

Helping with some kinds of choices requires highly specialized skills and knowledge, as in working with people in the process of choosing a career. Many choices have profound spiritual and moral overtones: abortion, right to die, participation in military service. Some have lifelong implications: whether to get married or to stay married, whether to have a first child and, after the first, whether to have more. Some choices precede change: "Do I really want to quit?" And in complicated ways some choices, such as "How committed am I to this relationship?" intertwine and interact with the process of change. Some involve unusual situations, while others revolve around normal life transitions faced by many, such as how to deal with an aging parent or what to do after retirement.

In life's moments of choice, people often turn to their pastor. In these times it is important to recognize that the only goal of counseling may be choice, that there are special skills for helping people reach decisions, and that it may be quite premature to rush in with the fervor and technology of change.

Confusion Reduction

A third goal of counseling is called by Gilmore *confusion reduction*. This refers to counseling situations where so much of the person's life is up in the air that any attempt to begin specific choice or change processes is doomed to failure because it misses the point: that *everything* seems wrong.

Gilmore described the most common cause of this kind of crisis as "loss of structure." By structure, she meant the person's cognitive structure, the perspectives and unspoken rules by which the person has been living. At various points in the life process, people encounter situations or transitions that cause them to question their entire structure, their whole way of looking at the world. Their ways of organizing reality in the past suddenly no longer work. It is as if all of the pieces of their life were scraps of paper, now thrown into the wind with no way to predict how or when they will come down.

Structure loss can happen at many times and in many ways. It may come when an adolescent goes to college and begins to question the values and religious beliefs on which his or her earlier years were founded. It may come with the now in-vogue midlife crisis, where the meaning of all previous work and relationships is engulfed in a struggle of aloneness. It may come with retirement or with the death of a loved one. Structure is shattered, the foundations shaken, and the individual has a great deal of searching to do.

In this case it is too soon to focus on choice or change, though there probably will be much of both to encounter. Instead, the goal is one of synthesis, of integration, of perspective gaining, of restructuring. Again, the requisite skills for the counselor are special (see chapter 10). The clarification phase of counseling is usually prolonged, and the counselor needs a tolerance for ambiguity and a patience beyond that required in simpler change processes. The client is struggling for an understanding of life, for meaning, and in this struggle may engage the counselor in a questioning of the counselor's own structure. As emphasized by the existential theorists, meaning searches are joint journeys when counselor and client embark on a process as broad as confusion reduction.

SUMMARY

Before proceeding to a case example, it may be useful to sum up what we have discussed thus far. We have proposed four questions that should be in the counselor's mind during the process of formulation. For each of these four questions, we have offered a conceptual scheme for organizing your thinking as you seek an answer. Neither the questions nor the formulation schemes that we have proposed are definitive or complete. There are many other questions that could be asked and other ways to pursue the answer. We do find the system proposed here to be helpful, however, in considering important facets of the counseling situation, in avoiding the overlooking of significant aspects of the problem, in gaining a more complete understanding of the individual with whom we are working, and in reaching a sound plan for intervention.

For your convenience we have summarized the four questions and their respective formulation heuristics in Table 7-1.

TABLE 7-1 Summary of Key Formulation Questions

1. WHAT IS TROUBLING THIS PERSON?
   Consider these three domains of experience:
   Affect: what the person feels, what emotions are involved
   Behavior: what the person does, how the person reacts
   Cognition: what the person believes and thinks
   Also consider whether conflicts exist and of which type:
   Approach-Approach, Avoidance-Avoidance, Approach-Avoidance
2. WHAT IS CAUSING THE PROBLEM?
   Consider four different possible types of causes:
   Primary causes: those necessary or sufficient to cause this problem
   Predisposing causes: factors that render the person more vulnerable
   Precipitating causes: those that immediately precede onset
   Perpetuating causes: those that cause the problem to continue once it has started
3. WHAT IS MISSING?
   Consider the amount of development, investment and balance in these life areas:
   Work: what the person *does*, how the person contributes
   Relationships: how the person moves in relation to others
   Aloneness: who the person *is*, what the person's meaning and sense of
   identity or integrity are
4. WHAT IS NEEDED?
Consider these three possible goals of counseling:
   Change: to cause something to be different
   Choice: to reach a decision
   Confusion Reduction: to sort out, to seek a new life structure

A CASE EXAMPLE*

Fred, a thirty-six-year-old sales manager for a large publishing firm, comes to see his pastor because of a "crisis of confidence." He has been experiencing increasing amounts of "anxiety" at work, to the point that at times it is difficult for him to carry out his regular duties. His family doctor prescribed a tranquilizer, which he has been taking on a regular basis but to no avail. "Sometimes when I am about to go into a business meeting I feel like I just can't go through with it. I feel this terrible sense of panic. I can hardly breathe, I sweat, it feels like my collar is choking me. And then in the meeting I feel like I am going to fall apart—go crazy or break down or something. My self-esteem is completely shot. I don't know what's happening to me." Fred also complains of shifting mood: being up one minute and down the next, unpredictably. These problems began about a year ago and have been getting progressively worse. He had similar problems during his graduate training ten years ago, but they disappeared on the day he earned his M.B.A. "Maybe I'm in a rut at work. Maybe that's it. Maybe I should be doing something else. Is that what this means?"

What Is Troubling This Person?

The most obvious complaints that Fred presents have to do with *affect*. He suffers from feelings of anxiety and moodiness; the emotional distress seems to bother him most.

What about his *behavior*? How does he cope? The fact is that he has continued to perform his duties and has done well. When he experiences panic he nevertheless goes through with his tasks in most cases. Thus far, his emotions have not led him to begin avoiding responsibilities, although at this point he is starting to feel the temptation to do so (and this is one reason why he comes for counseling now). All objective evaluations of his work are superlative. He is well liked by colleagues and superiors, his skills are highly respected and valued, and he has recently received a promotion and a large raise. In fact, no one except Fred (and his wife, with whom he has shared his feelings) seems to notice that he is having problems.

What about his *cognitions*? He talks about suffering from low self-esteem, which points to negative self-evaluation. A little further exploration reveals a deep streak of perfectionism and high expectations, and each promotion that gives him increased responsibilities exacerbates this. It is also clear that he begins thinking about upcoming responsibilities and then begins to become anxious. All of this suggests that there may be important elements in how he *thinks* about his situation.

---

*Throughout this book, wherever actual case materials have been used, the names and identifying details have been altered to protect anonymity.

As for *conflicts*, Fred suggests a possible ambivalence about his present job. Whether this is a cause or an effect of his anxious feelings remains to be determined. Asked further about his work, Fred indicates that he likes what he does and believes that he can do it reasonably well (though not as well as he would like). His main complaint about his work is a sense of emptiness or meaninglessness in what he does.

What Is Causing the Problem?

Making a definite determination of the cause of a problem like Fred's takes some time. Still, the information gained by the pastor during the initial interview provides some basic hypotheses and rules out at least some of the potential causes.

As for *primary* causes, there is nothing apparent in Fred's condition or past that would explain what is happening to him as a simple reaction to a primary cause. He has not abused alcohol or drugs, has had no major traumatic experiences, is in good physical health. To be sure his job is demanding, but no more so than that of many of his peers.

Predisposing causes? Fred cannot recall anyone in his family having had similar problems, although he reports that his mother had bouts of depression at times. Nevertheless, it is conceivable that Fred may be physiologically predisposed to panic attacks—something to keep in mind, even though the probability may be low. Prolonged stress from graduate training and his job might also be considered as a predisposing factor to anxiety problems.

Fred cannot identify any particular "straw that broke the camel's back"—no *precipitating* event that stands out in his mind. The anxiety problem seems to have come on gradually and to have increased in severity with time.

Perpetuating causes, however, seem fruitful for exploration in this case. What keeps the anxiety problems going? What is causing them to increase in severity? The answer may be found not in some event in the dim and distant past, but in Fred's present coping styles. His thinking style would seem to be a particularly good area to explore because anxiety and mood problems can emerge from how an individual perceives and thinks about situations (see chapters 12 and 14). One way to test an idea about a perpetuating cause is to intervene in a way to change the hypothesized cause (in this case, his way of thinking about himself in relation to others) and to see whether this makes a difference in the problem.

What Is Missing?

Fred spends a large amount of his time and energy on his *work*. This seems to have been his main life investment thus far. During graduate training, the goal was to get his M.B.A. Now he pursues advancement and achievement in his company, putting in long hours and often going above and beyond the requirements of his job.

The main *relationship* in Fred's life is with his wife, Susan. They seem to have a close and very strong marriage, and Fred shares most everything with her. Susan, too, is happy with their relationship, though sometimes she would like for them to have more time together. They have no children, by choice. Beyond his marriage, however, Fred seems to have few close relationships, if any. The only friends he can report are acquaintances at work, and he does not talk to them about important or intimate matters. His hobbies are all solitary: stamp collecting, painting, reading. When the pastor asks him whether sometimes he feels lonely, tears come to his eyes.

And *aloneness*? Although Fred spends some time by himself, he seldom uses that time to explore himself and his spirituality in depth. His main complaint about work is that it lacks meaning and that he feels empty. He says that he does not feel in touch with God and that he wishes he were "a more religious person." He wonders, too, where his life is going and just what his life means.

What Is Needed?

For Fred, the most obvious and tempting goal of counseling is *change*. But what is the best approach? Where should the counselor begin? Some plausible possibilities, based on information from the initial interview, might be (a) to teach Fred some methods for relaxation and stress management (chapter 14); (b) to work on altering how Fred perceives and thinks about things, particularly his perfectionism (chapter 12); (c) to listen to Fred emphatically over a period of weeks and see what emerges (chapter 5); or (d) to consider whether there may be a biological basis to Fred's problem and refer him for evaluation by a qualified psychiatrist. It would be premature to choose one of these on the basis of the information from this single interview, but these and other possibilities can be evaluated as avenues toward change as Fred and his pastor continue their work together.

The possibility also exists, however, that the underlying goal of counseling may turn out to be *choice*. Fred's present discomfort may be the surface manifestation of a discontent with his career direction, and he may need most of all some help in sorting out issues of vocation and choosing a life direction.

The confusion in Fred's life may extend still further. There are clear clues in the initial information presented above that it could be quite useful to explore in depth Fred's spirituality, his sense of meaning (or meaninglessness) and direction in life—not only at work but more generally, pursuing a goal of *confusion reduction*. At age thirty-six, Fred has entered what Jung called "the second half of life," often a time of intense searching and reevaluation. The productivity goals of his younger years may be giving way to new yearnings.

His experienced anxiety may be a call to examine in depth the assumptions by which he has been living. And perhaps it is for this reason that Fred, sensing this need, sought out his pastor as a guide for the search ahead, rather than turning to any of the many secular professionals available to him.

All of the possibilities above were raised by what the pastor learned in their very first session. The material is organized around the four questions of formulation from Table 7-1 to illustrate how they can be helpful in guiding the counselor's thinking processes that ultimately lead to third phase of counseling, intervention.

ADDITIONAL READINGS

AMERICAN PSYCHIATRIC ASSOCIATION *Diagnostic and Statistical Manual of Mental Disorders* (4th edition), Washington, DC: American Psychiatric Association, 1994. This is the standard reference volume for psychiatric diagnosis. It contains a wealth of information in addition to specific criteria for each diagnostic category. A brief, paperback version containing only the diagnostic criteria is also published by the APA under the title, *Quick Reference to the Diagnostic Criteria from DSM-IV*.

CARSON, ROBERT C., and JAMES N. BUTCHER *Abnormal Psychology and Modern Life* (9th ed.). New York, Harper Collins, 1992. This is the most enduringly successful textbook on psychopathology, an encyclopedia of current knowledge on abnormal behavior. It is revised every three or four years, so copies of the past (but still useful) edition are often available at low cost.

CIARROCCHI, JOSEPH W. *A Minister's Handbook of Mental Disorders*. New York: Paulist Press, 1993. This is an uncommonly good coverage of the most commonly encountered psychological and psychiatric problems, written from a pastoral counseling perspective. The author, with background in both psychology and theology, presents a balanced and up-to-date perspective on the causes and treatment of mental disorders.

DAVISON, GERALD C., and JOHN M. NEALE *Abnormal Psychology* (5th ed.). New York: John Wiley, 1990. Another highly successful textbook on psychopathology; takes a more behavioral orientation in understanding abnormality. Also revised about every four years.

Moursund, Janet, The Process of Counseling and Therapy (3rd ed.). Englewood Cliffs, NJ: Prentice-Hall, 1993. An enduring textbook on the structure of individual, couples, and family counseling, with a helpful final chapter on "The Care and Feeding of Therapists."

PRUYSER, PAUL *The Minister as Diagnostician*. Philadelphia: Westminster Press, 1976. An intriguing first step toward the application of pastoral concepts to the diagnostic understanding of human problems.

NOTES

[1]Alvin Toffler, *The Third Wave* (New York: William Morrow, 1980).

[2]Paul Pruyser provides a diagnostic structure for considering spiritual dimensions of human problems in *The Minister as Diagnostician* (Philadelphia: Westminster Press, 1976).

[3]Roberto Assagioli, *Psychosynthesis* (New York: Hobbs, Dorman, 1965).

[4]C. Robert Cloninger and Henri Begleiter, eds., *Genetics and Biology of Alcoholism*, Banbury Report 33, (Plainview, NY: Cold Spring Harbor Laboratory Press, 1990); Stephen V. Faraone,

William S. Fremen, and Ming T. Tsuang, "Genetic Transmission of Major Affective Disorders: Quantitative Models and Linkage Analyses," *Psychological Bulletin* 108 (1990): 109–27; A. Marneros, N. C. Andreason, and M. T. Tsuang, eds., *Negative versus Positive Schizophrenia* (New York: Springer Verlag, 1991).

[5]I. A. Mirsky, "Physiologic, Psychologic, and Social Determinants in the Etiology of Duodenal Ulcer," American Journal of Digestive Diseases 3 (1958): 285–314; Shiu-Kum Lam, "An Academic Investigator's Perspective," in Edward A. Swabb and Sandor Szabo, eds., *Ulcer Disease* (New York: Marcel Dekker, 1991), 431–50.

[6]Gerald R. Patterson, "Performance Models for Antisocial Boys," *American Psychologist* 41 (1986): 432–44; Diana Baumrind, "Child Care Practices Anteceding Three Patterns of Preschool Behavior," *Genetic Psychology Monographs* 75 (1967): 43–48; J. Wiggins, "Inconsistent Socialization," *Psychological Reports* 23 (1968): 303–36.

[7]Jeffrey A. Kaylor, Daniel W. King, and Lynda A. King, "Psychological Effects of Military Service in Vietnam: A Meta-analysis," *Psychological Bulletin* 102 (1987): 257–71; Chaim F. Shatan, "The Grief of Soldiers: Vietnam Combat Veterans' Self-help Movement," *American Journal of Orthopsychiatry* 43 (1973): 640–53.

[8]Frederick S. Perls, *Gestalt Therapy Verbatim* (Lafayette, CA: Real People Press, 1969).

[9]Susan K. Gilmore, *The Counselor-in-Training* (Englewood Cliffs, NJ: Prentice-Hall, 1973).

[10]Bertrand Russell, *The Pursuit of Happiness* (London: Liveright, 1930).

[11]Alvin Toffler, *The Third Wave* (New York: Bantam, 1980).

[12]Gilmore, *The Counselor-in Training.*

[13]Frederick H. Kanfer and Arnold P. Goldstein, eds., *Helping People Change*, 4th ed. (Elmsford, NY: Pergamon Press, 1991).

8

BUILDING MOTIVATION

Anyone who willingly enters into the pain of a stranger is truly
a remarkable person.

—Henri J. M. Nouwen, *In Memoriam*

One of the motivations that draws pastors to counseling as a form of ministry
is the desire to make a difference in people's lives. The chapters of part IV are
addressed precisely to this process—how to make a difference. Within the
phases-of-counseling model presented in chapter 2, this represents the third
phase, the process of *intervention*.

To some extent intervention has already begun when you start to listen reflectively and help the individual to clarify the problem. It continues
as you think clearly and formulate the problem because you are developing
a comprehensible view of the problem not only for yourself but also for the
client. Sometimes these two processes—reflective listening and coming to a
comprehensible explanation of the problem—are all that is required. Such
clarification often goes a long way toward helping people get their lives back
on track. It enables them to find and use their own good inner resources for
coping and growing, whereas once they felt confused, lost, and generally
stuck.

At other times, however, the counselor is called upon for further help.
Having clarified and formulated the problem well, the question still remains,
"What should I *do* about it?" Part IV is about doing. Within each chapter practical and usable ideas and methods are presented for helping to make a difference. Chapter 9 deals with the counseling goal of choice and suggests some
strategies that can be helpful in facilitating this process. In chapter 10 the focus
is on the goal of confusion reduction—perhaps least understood of the three
goals—and again alternative strategies are described. In chapter 11 the goal

of change is explored directly, and general strategies are presented for helping people to make changes in their lives. The seven chapters of part V then provide more specific change strategies for particular types of problems often presented to pastors.

This chapter, however, deals with a more general issue in counseling: how to *motivate* people to change. It is a very common frustration for counselors: You know what the person needs to do, but he or she doesn't take that next step. This chapter is designed to give you a conceptual framework for understanding how and why people get stuck in the change process and some tools for helping them get unstuck. Although we are talking mostly about change here, this issue of building motivation can be an equally important precursor to choice counseling (chapter 9) or confusion reduction (chapter 10).

THE STREAM OF CHANGE

Change is not something that one has to begin. It is a continual and inevitable part of existence. Change is occurring in us as we rewrite this book and in you as you read it. With every new day each of us is, for better or for worse, a little different—physically and emotionally, in knowledge and in spirit. Such change is easier to appreciate over longer spans of time. The pastor of a church we once attended would exhort the congregation each year at the season of New Year to consider this question: "In what ways am I different today from how I was one year ago today?" Such self-examination has long been part of religious traditions. Faith calls each of us to examine how we have changed, are changing, and will change.

All of us are changing at this very moment. Thus, when an individual comes to a pastor asking for change, she or he is not asking for something new to be started. The key rather is to channel the ongoing momentum of change that is already occurring. It is helpful to remember this and to look at others through this perspective—that the process of change *is already happening* through a richly complex set of ongoing choices, actions, and emotions.

To be sure, many people come to counselors precisely because they feel stuck, as if change had come to a standstill. They are caught in circular, perhaps self-fulfilling spirals and cannot see the way out. Yet spirals are not static. A person moving in a spiral is still *moving*, progressing in a certain direction, albeit downward or negative at times. What feels like distressing inertia or lack of change is usually, in fact, a distressingly consistent pattern and direction of movement. This very double meaning is captured in the physical principle of *inertia*, which means the tendency of an object to remain either at rest or in a uniform direction of motion until it is acted upon by some external force.

This discussion is belabored a bit because the way that a counselor views the process of change is crucial. The pastoral counselor is an "external force," interacting in this case not with an inert object but with a very alive person capable of self-initiated change of direction. Each of us has the capability for and continual challenge of self-change. It is an unending, unstoppable process from the moment of birth to the moment of death. We are, all of us, changing.

Why, then, do people come asking for *change*, perhaps the most common goal of counseling? It is not because change has stopped, nor is it because change occurs only within counseling sessions. People come for help when it seems to them that their own resources for shifting the direction of change have failed. They have, perhaps, tried everything they know to avert their course from this spiral or headlong plunge toward a destination they dislike or fear. Their self-controls are stuck, seemingly locking them on a course they do not want. Those millions who daily find ways to alter their own course when faced with significant problems are not likely to seek counseling. It is those whose normal skills and resources for adjustment seem to have failed who come asking for change. The desired change may be major and general, as in shifting a total lifestyle or altering a destructive relationship pattern, or may be more specific, as in stopping smoking or getting over an intense fear.

What is the counselor's role when a person comes seeking change? A tempting answer is to show the person how to change. There is something to be said for this direct solution-focused approach, and we will return to such practical change strategies in chapter 11. But for now, let us present you with some pieces of a puzzle.

THE PUZZLE OF CHANGE

Consider one puzzling bit of evidence. Researchers commonly find that, when longer and more intensive treatments (such as psychiatric hospitalization) are compared with briefer and less intensive treatments (such as outpatient counseling), the outcomes are similar.[1] That is, the commonsense notion that more treatment leads to more change is not widely supported. People often do quite well with relatively brief intervention.[2]

Puzzle piece number 2: Most significant changes in people's lives occur without help from mental health professionals. Those of us who work as therapists sometimes forget that most important human change occurs outside the context of any formal therapy. People changed long before there *were* mental health professionals, and most people still change on their own. A growing body of psychological research documents the ability of individuals to engage in self-help processes that are often as potent as those occurring within the confines of formal therapy.[3] Some psychologists have been surprised or dismayed by the publication of such findings, but the data should never have been surprising.

Is counseling, then, all a hoax? Not at all. Research clearly demonstrates the value of certain kinds of treatment for certain kinds of problems. Many specific and effective treatment methods have been developed for helping people change. This kind of research, developing more effective treatment procedures, has been a crucial step forward for psychology as the science of human behavior. It helped to advance psychology from the poorly specified interventions of the past to better-defined therapeutic methods with both known effectiveness and a clearer understanding of *why* they work and for whom. We will discuss some of this research in part V. Further, even relatively brief counseling, at least when it has certain characteristics, can result in significantly more long-term improvement than no counseling.[4]

How can all these things be true? How do the pieces fit together? Part of the answer lies in understanding *how* change occurs.

THE STAGES OF CHANGE

What triggers change? How does it happen? Psychologists are only beginning to find answers to these challenging questions of when and why and how people change. A research team at the University of Rhode Island, headed by Dr. James Prochaska, has been studying change processes for three decades. The team began by trying to understand how people alter addictive behaviors such as smoking, overeating, and alcohol and other drug use by studying self-changers who escaped such problems without professional help. Their initial findings suggested that change occurs in stages rather than in an all-or-none fashion. Further, it seemed that these stages were similar whether the change occurred with or without formal therapy. Said another way, a counselor's job is facilitating a natural change process rather than invoking some sort of magic unique to therapy.

If one is facilitating natural change, then it is important to understand how it occurs. Furthermore, the work of Prochaska and his students suggests that different processes are working at each stage of change, so that the counselor's task may be different depending upon where the client is in readiness for change. What the counselor must do to assist a client depends upon where the client is within this process.

The stages of change have been variously described but are usually conceived as sections of a wheel. The first stage, *precontemplation*, represents a state that precedes change. In the precontemplation state, the individual sees no need for change and is not even thinking about (contemplating) it. The processes that some therapists refer to as "denial" may be operating here— actively dismissing evidence of a problem or any need for change (or for repentence, if viewed theologically). The counselor's task here is to increase the individual's awareness of a possible problem, to create doubt or concern, in a way to *increase* ambivalence. Motivation begins when one perceives a discrepancy between where one is and where one wants to be; with no discrepancy, there is no motivation for change.[5] Some approaches for increasing motivational discrepancy will be outlined later.

The second stage, *contemplation*, is characterized by a greater openness to and even seeking of information and feedback about the problem in question. The individual begins to consider that there may be a problem and to think about the possibility of doing something about it. Yet the person also is reluctant. Contemplators want to and they don't want to—they are *ambivalent*. This is a normal stage in the change process. During this stage the types of conflict described in chapter 7 become particularly apparent as the inconsistency of one's thoughts, feelings, and behaviors is realized. The individual may, for example, gain increased knowledge about the dangerousness of his or her behavior and may come to believe (cognition) that it should be changed. Yet the behavior continues. The person's feelings may now, in the contemplation stage, be a mixture of pleasure or comfort in the old behavior and anxiety or depression about its recognized consequences. Here the counselor's task is to help resolve the ambivalence, to tip the balance in favor of change. This is the task of building motivation for action, and again we will describe some strategies for doing so later in this chapter.

The third stage, *determination*, is a period difficult to specify. It is the period when a certain "critical mass" of motivation is reached and the person comes to the determined decision that something *has* to be done. It may be thought of as the tipping of the balance. During the contemplation stage, increasing weight is placed on the previously lighter side of the scales, the side favoring change. As the weights build up on this side, a moment is reached when the balance tips. More recently, Prochaska's group has downplayed this idea of a critical moment of decision and emphasized instead a gradual process of increasing *preparation* for change.[6] Probably both perspectives are valid. Some people do reach a distinct moment in which they decide, commit, turn around (repent).[7] Others cannot specify such a moment and proceed in small and gradual steps. In any event, the counselor's task at this stage is to recognize that the window of opportunity is open and that the time for action has arrived. If one fails to move at this point, the determination window may close and the momentum be lost, though not irretrievably in most cases. Loss of momentum here merely means that the balance has tipped back in favor of the status quo and that the contemplation process must be resumed.

The second crucial task required of the counselor at the determination stage is the initiation of appropriate change intervention. When the moment arrives (the alcoholic asks, "But what can I do?"; the reluctant husband says, "Well, let's give it a try"), the counselor's next job is to see that the client begins an active change process that is likely to help. Of all the transitions of change, this may be the one that a client is least prepared to negotiate and during which the expertise of a knowledgeable counselor can be invaluable. The "mental health maze" is confusing indeed, with its vast array of alternative professionals, paraprofessionals, treatment approaches, and self-help options. For a given client with a given problem, some interventions are helpful and some are not. Some may even be harmful. The choice that an individual

makes when in the moment of determination is often distressingly random—
who happens to be listed first in the yellow pages (and which yellow pages
title the person chooses), which office happens to be closest geographically,
what self-help book happens to be on the shelf at the bookstore. The counselor can be of assistance here by suggesting optimal alternatives, assuming
that the counselor is informed in these matters. The suggestions may include
self-help strategies, interventions undertaken with the help of the pastor, or
referral to another competent professional.

The choice made at this point can be critical. An effective course of action brings about the desired change and prepares the person to retain the
new direction during the maintenance phase that follows. An ineffective intervention may discourage the individual regarding the possibility of redirection, fostering a pessismism that hinders future attempts.

Action is the fourth stage. During this period the individual takes action to bring about the desired change. It is this stage that has been heavily
emphasized by counselors and other mental health professionals in the past,
assuming that each person they treat is ready for the active change process.
Most of the methods described in the chapters of part V are intended to facilitate movement during this action phase. Even when the active change interventions are facilitated by another professional, the pastor can continue
to provide support during this period, encouraging cooperation with the
therapist and persistence in the sometimes difficult transitions. The process
of change is often slower than clients would like, and additional encouragement may help the person to continue in the slow and gradual steps by
which enduring redirection occurs. If a self-help approach is elected, the pastor can provide valuable support by periodically checking on how things are
going.

A difficult and often ignored stage is *maintenance*. Having made an initial change, the individual faces the challenge of maintaining it. Both therapists and evangelists have been guilty of focusing on action while overlooking
the perhaps more difficult task of maintenance. With many types of human
problems, the more difficult endeavor is not making an initial change but
keeping it. A familiar example is weight loss. It is easy enough to lose weight.
Virtually any diet or exercise program can help to bring this about, at least
for some. The all-too-familiar problem is keeping it off. Often very different
skills are required for the maintenance of change than were required to bring
it about in the first palce. The pastor is in an enviable position for being able
to help during the maintenance phase because of his or her ongoing contact
with many of the people counseled.

The final stage of this model is the reality of *relapse*. Like it or not, backsliding is a high probability with many if not most problems. This need not
be a disaster in most cases, and an increasing array of methods are being developed to prevent relapses or to deal with them when they do occur. Again,
the pastor who is in continuing contact may be able to foresee and prevent

impending relapses or to help place them in perspective and to minimize negative effects when they do happen. The inclusion of a relapse stage in this model should not be seen as a pessimistic element. It is a reality of human nature that people slip back into old and less helpful ways of being from time to time. To suggest to a client that a change will be 100 percent complete is usually to set the person up for failure, disappointment, and self-discouragement. A complete view of change includes the possibility of backsliding and a plan for how to deal with it positively and constructively. In this light, the inclusion of a relapse phase in the model is actually a *hopeful* element because this in turn leads around the wheel again and on through the next stages by which change is made.

Prochaska's model is represented by a "revolving door" diagram, with the stages arrayed as the chambers of a circular door viewed from the top (see Fig. 8-1). Though the normal direction of movement is shown in the diagram by arrows, the door can move either way, so it is possible for a person to double back from the determination stage and resume ambivalent contemplating. The exit from the revolving door is from the maintenance chamber, when the person finds successful means of permanently keeping the change. The corresponding tasks of the counselor, described above, are outlined in Table 8-1.

For a given problem (smoking, drunk driving, exhibitionism), how many times does the person have to go around the wheel before making a permanent exit? The answer for smokers seems to be between three and seven, averaging about four serious attempts before quitting for good. The number of

FIGURE 8-1
A Stage Model of the Process of Change
Adapted from James O. Prochaska and Carlo C. DiClemente, "Transtheoretical Therapy: Toward a More Integrative Model of Change," *Psychotherapy: Theory Research and Practice* 19 (1982): 276–88.

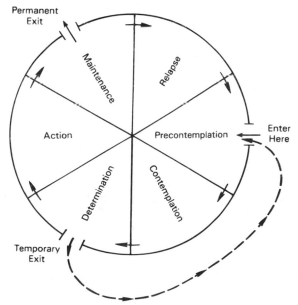

TABLE 8-1   Counselor Tasks and Stages of Change

STAGE OF CHANGE	CORRESPONDING PHASE OF COUNSELING	GENERAL GOALS OF EACH STAGE
Precontemplation	Clarification	Consciousness raising, increase awareness of need for change
Contemplation	Clarification	Increase motivation and commitment to change
Determination	Formulation	Formulate problem, find appropriate intervention (referral?)
Action	Intervention	Take steps toward desired change
Maintenance	Intervention/Termination	Prevent relapse
Relapse	Renew Clarification, Formulation, and/or Intervention	Renew motivation, commitment, and action

attempts needed will vary with the problem and the person, but looking through optimistic eyes, each time around the wheel moves the person one step closer to permanent change.

A useful aspect of this model is in guiding the counselor in knowing how to proceed with a particular client at a given time. Much of what is labeled *resistance* in counseling can arise from an improper choice of strategy. Suppose, for example, that a client is contemplating the possibility of change, and the counselor uses approaches appropriate for the action stage—suggesting steps to be taken in implementing change. What will happen? The client is likely to question whether there is a problem—the central issue in contemplation—and to refuse change recommendations or accept them halfheartedly. Consider, on the other hand, the client who is determined and prepared for change—"I've got to do something; I can't go on like I have been"—and whose counselor uses strategies appropriate for contemplation: "Tell me how you're feeling about this. What was it like when you were younger? When has this happened before? Tell me more." The client will grow restless, wanting to take practical steps but given only questions and requests for more information. In either case, the counselor may lose the client or at least will find it hard going. The problem here is not the client's internal denial, resistance, or defensiveness. The problem is that the counselor has misunderstood the task at hand.

Because the first challenges encountered in the wheel of change are motivational, we will focus in the remainder of this chapter on strategies for increasing motivation and commitment. These strategies are most appropriate in the precontemplation and contemplation stages, although ambivalence often persists or reemerges during action and motivation-enhancing strategies can be useful throughout the change process. Chapters 9 and 10 focus on facilitating choices and reducing confusion (see the discussion of the goals of counseling in chapter 7), strategies for counseling when change is not the current goal, which can also be useful in getting unstuck in the early stages of change. Then, beginning with chapter 11 and through part V, we focus heavily on how to help people who are ready for change in particular problem areas.

STRENGTHENING MOTIVATION AND COMMITMENT FOR CHANGE

Precontemplation

The precontemplation phase provides unique challenges because here one's "client" is usually not the person who is perceived to possess the problem but rather someone else who is concerned about it. Someone calls in distress to ask what they can do about a spouse's or friend's problem: "How can I help him to see?" "How can I persuade her to go get help?" "What can I do about my teenager?" Or perhaps the concern arises in your own mind, as pastor. In other cases it is a conflict with the law that brings a problem to your attention or some other conflict with authorities at school or at work. What is common to all of these situations is that the individual being pointed to may not perceive that he or she in fact *has* a problem.

A caution before we move on: It may be far too simple to try to assign the total problem to an individual. After treating a large number of families with "problem" children, psychologist Steven Johnson decided to ask, "How deviant is the normal child?"[8] In the study that arose out of this important question, Johnson found that the normal, nonproblem child displays a fair number of behaviors that might be labeled "deviant" if closely scrutinized. That is to say, *any* normal person if closely examined for psychological blemishes can be perceived as flawed and labeled as abnormal.[9] Johnson found, in his subsequent experience, that a large percentage of children referred to his clinic for treatment were, in fact, showing behavior patterns that were well within normal range. In evaluating this type of situation, where one individual raises concern about a problem in another, it is wise to try to understand the whole interpersonal picture instead of jumping to conclusions that assign abnormality or blame to a certain person within the situation. Further competent professional evaluation may be called for at this point to determine the extent of a problem. Nevertheless, no matter who "has" the problem (usually much too simple a way of thinking), something typically needs to be done about it, if only because of the dissatisfaction of those who are expressing their concern.

Assuming, however, that there is a significant problem regarding an individual who is effectively in the precontemplation stage, what can be done that may be helpful in encouraging the person on toward the contemplation stage? Here are some general guidelines.

State Your Concern   A most helpful form by which to express a perceived problem to another is to show your concern. This type of concern expresses what one sees happening in the way of specific consequences and does so within the larger context of a positive regard for the individual. The specific negative consequences presented may be happening either to the individual or to those around him or her. Here are a few examples of how different people might express concern:

> SPOUSE: We seem to be fighting more often, and I find myself feeling more and more distant from you, and I don't want that to happen because I love you.
>
> PASTOR: I'm worried about what I see happening to you. You seem to be withdrawing more and more from other people, and you look sad when I see you, even though sometimes you cover it by smiling.
>
> FRIEND: I'm really concerned about how you've been drinking and especially about some of the effects that I see alcohol having on you. Your family seems to be afraid of you. I know sometimes you haven't been able to remember what happened while you were drinking. You've been missing days of work, and honestly you don't *look* good. I want you to know that I'm concerned, that I care about you, and that I want to help however I can.

These statements express specific observed effects, not in an accusatory or confrontational way, but rather within the gentler vehicle of concern. A single expression of this kind may not make a big difference, but the cumulative effect of such expressions—especially if they come from different and significant people—can be substantial.

Avoid Argument   A very unhelpful way to present concern is to get into a "Yes you do"—"No I don't" confrontation. This tends only to back the person further into the corner and to create a greater denial of the problem and more resistance to change. The more an individual is forced to "defend" a position, the more a person becomes committed to it. Thus, it is not a good idea to place the individual in a position where he or she makes statements denying the existence of a problem or the need for change.

Elicit the Person's Own Concern   The exact opposite of argumentation is gently getting the person to talk about his or her own concerns in the problem area. Thus, for example, instead of forcefully presenting a case for the problem the pastor might ask

> "As you know, Leslie has talked to me about some difficulties the two of you are having. I imagine that you have some concerns about your marriage, too, given

how difficult things have been for both of you lately. I wonder what *you* see happening and what concerns you?"

or:

"I know that some of the people who care about you are concerned about your drinking, but I wonder what *your* concerns are. Have you noticed anything about how drinking affects you, perhaps any changes over the years, that concern you?"

or:

"I know that you don't see much of a problem now, but I wonder if you have noticed anything that makes you wonder if you might run into problems in the future? Is there anything that looks like it might get to be a problem unless you do something about it?"

Elicit the Person's Concern for Others

Here the counselor encourages consideration of the situation from the perspective of significant other people—how they see it, how they feel. This is done without implying any label or conclusion about the individual's own "problem." This can be a helpful and face-saving device for encouraging a person in the direction of contemplation. Some examples:

"I wonder how this looks from Gayle's perspective? How does she see this situation? What does she think, and what are her feelings right now?"

or:

"You already know, I think, that your husband and your children are worried about what is happening in your lives right now. They are upset, and because they are such important people in your life, it must be affecting you, too. I think it would be helpful for all of us to get together at least once to talk, so that everybody's feelings are heard. When would be a good time?"

or:

"On the one hand you really don't want to think of yourself as having a 'problem,' and at the same time you're concerned with what you see happening in your family."

One good strategy for eliciting the client's concerns is to ask open-ended questions, rather than those that can be answered with "Yes" or "No" or a brief informational answer. "What brings you here?" "In what ways has this been a problem or concern for you?" "Give me some examples." "When did you first notice this happening to you? Tell me how you got to where you are."

Reflect   After asking such a question, respond for a time with reflective listening, emphasizing the points and feelings that the client offers. The reflective listening skills described in chapter 5 are crucial in making it safer for the individual to begin to contemplate the need for change. Acceptance provides the freedom to consider change. This is precisely the opposite of a head-on confrontational approach that is heavy on advising, suggesting, warning, threatening, admonishing, and using other roadblocks (see chapter 4). Taking an emphatic stance enables the counselor to build a trusting relationship with the client, and within this context it becomes safer and easier to consider advancing through the further stages of change.

Contemplation

When the client has entered the contemplation stage of change and is beginning to consider the need for a shift in direction, the counselor's task becomes roughly that of facilitating a choice—the choice of deciding and committing to change.

An analogy to keep in mind while working with a client in the contemplation stage is that of a balance or scales with two baskets. One side or basket represents the decision to move in a new direction; the other side of the scales represents the decision to stay with or return to previous patterns. The next step in this process—advancing to the determination stage and on to action—literally hangs in the balance.

For the counselor who wishes to help a client to change, the task during contemplation is to place increasing weights on that side of the balance. If the counselor's goal is less directive, the task is simply to allow and enable the client to decide which way the balance will tip.

Very useful information now available from research demonstrates how relatively brief counseling interventions can set change in motion by activating client motivation. In studies conducted in half a dozen countries, several elements have commonly appeared in brief motivational interventions that were found to be effective in initiating behavior change.[10] These can be summarized in the acronym FRAMES and represent six promising components for motivational counseling.

1. Provide Personal **FEEDBACK**   Personally relevant feedback, such as the expressions of concern discussed earlier, can help build motivation for change. Rather than general lectures, this involves specific feedback, expressed in a caring manner.

Particularly in deciding the extent of a problem and the need for change, certain kinds of objective evaluation may be helpful here. This is especially true with problem dimensions that are difficult for the client to observe directly. When an individual comes seeking an evaluation of the seriousness of a drinking problem, we often begin by obtaining some objective data—psychological measures of problem severity and degree of dependency on alcohol, blood tests evaluating how much alcohol has affected the body, perhaps some tests of cognitive capacities known to be affected early by the progression of alcohol-related brain damage. We then review the results of such evaluation with the individual and together decide what needs to be done.

Don't forget, however, to elicit the client's *own* concerns and reasons for change. As suggested earlier, hearing *oneself* express the need for change can be more persuasive than hearing it from others. The client may give voice to his or her thoughts and feelings about the need for change (thereby placing weights on that side of the balance) and may assemble these in one total package of concerns that has never been seen as a whole before. Combined with some additional objective information, this may help to tip the balance.

2. Emphasize the Client's Personal **RESPONSIBILITY** *for Change*   "No one can make you change. It's really up to you. In fact, I couldn't change you (decide for you) even if I wanted to." Such messages have commonly been included in effective brief counseling. They emphasize the client's freedom of choice, underline personal responsibility for change, and help the counselor avoid an unhealthy and unrealistic sense of having to do all the work.

3. Offer **ADVICE**   Now a seeming paradox: advise and encourage. To be sure, it is wise to be a good listener and to make your mistakes on eliciting the client's own wisdom before you offer yours. To be sure, it is the client's ultimate responsibility to change or not to change. Yet there is a place for offering your own wisdom, your pastoral counsel, particularly when it is requested but even, sometimes, when it is not. As we will discuss below, this can be intermixed with the other five elements of FRAMES.

4. Provide a **MENU** *of Options*   Offering one and only one solution runs the risk of it being unacceptable. People seem to respond better to choices—to selecting from a variety of alternatives. We sometimes say, "Let me describe different things that have worked for people, and then I'd like you to consider which of these might be best for you . . ."

5. Continue to Practice an **EMPATHIC** *Counseling Style*   Do not abandon listening and supportiveness as you approach determination and action. Continue to reflect the client's feelings and concerns. Affirm and support your client. Try to keep at least a three to one ratio between your listening and talking. Avoid dogmatic, labeling, or other roadblocking approaches that attempt to persuade a client to change by force of logic, guilt, fear, or other rational or emotive processes. The approach recommended here is one that involves the counselor and client in a joint consideration of the total picture—the client's present situation, evidence of a need for change, factors that discourage change, possible new directions, and the consequences of taking versus not taking a new course. Reflective listening remains a principal skill for the counselor during this process. A good word to describe this stance is *consultative*—consulting together to determine what problems there are and what can be done about them.

6. Provide Encouragement and Optimism for SUCCESS   "You can do it" is a crucial message for people to hear. When they come to counseling, people are often discouraged, disheartened, and demoralized. They need a vision of hope, a lifeline of optimism. Don't forget to provide this sixth element of FRAMES. To be sure, test your optimism against reality, but hope even in the deepest valley of the shadow is one of the great gifts of faith and a vital element in pastoral counseling.

Now for a brief example of how these six elements of FRAMES might be blended together toward the end of an initial counseling session:

> Well, it certainly sounds like you have come to a choice point. A number of things are telling you that it's time for a change: the way you have been feeling anxious and depressed, the feedback you've had from friends, your family's worries, the fact that you've been sick a lot, and the way you're thinking about work all the time. Of course it's your choice what to do—it's up to you whether you go on the way you have been or decide to make a change. I've certainly been concerned about you, and personally I would encourage you to do something about your work load and to take better care of yourself. As we've discussed, there are a number of different ways to start making a change, and I'd be glad to help you sort out which might work best for you. I know this has been hard for you and that you've been under a lot of stress for a long time. I just want to say that I believe you *can* make a real change for yourself and your family here, if you decide to.

Discrepancy as Motivation   One bit of psychological knowledge to keep in mind when you seek to enhance motivation is that it is generally a *discrepancy* that motivates change—a discrepancy between where I am now (feedback) and where I want to be (goal). The clearer it is that there is a gap between one's present and one's desired state, the greater the motivation to get moving, *provided* that the person sees an effective and accessible route toward change.

Here is a rich area for pastoral counseling. What does the person want most in life? What are his or her most central values and goals? What does she or he hold most dear or sacred? It can be helpful to put the "problem" under consideration within this larger focus. Does what the person is presently doing move him or her closer to or further from these values and goals? Motivation for change emerges when one perceives a discrepancy between the present path and an important and desired destination. A method for exploring personal goals and values is presented in chapter 10.

Determination

It is important for a counselor to help clients to strengthen motivation and commitment. It is also important to recognize when a client is *ready* to change. At this point (*determination* in the stages-of-change model), the counseling strategy shifts from motivation building toward action and resolution. How can you tell when someone is approaching determination and readiness to change? Table 8-2 shows seven types of signs that may emerge as this point approaches.

Don't abandon motivational strategies when you see these signs; even as people begin to change, they often remain ambivalent and need continued support for their resolution. It is here, however, that new strategies become important in helping people move toward change. Motivational counseling can raise awareness, pointing to the *need* for change, and offer acceptance and support, which increase the *freedom* to change. But awareness and acceptance will be insufficient if the individual has or sees no alternatives. The person who reaches the stage of determination is at this turning point: "Now that I see the need for change and I want to change, what shall I *do*?" Alternatives provide the *direction* for change.

Alternatives represent new roads to try. The old path is familiar, but redirection requires finding a new one (or several) and setting out on a new course. Here, too, the skilled counselor can be invaluable in providing broader perspectives, new possibilities, unfamiliar resources, new ways of thinking or acting, change programs to begin, one small step in a new direction. Alternatives!

Once a client reaches the determination stage, the perceived presence or absence of effective alternatives is a key to what happens next.[11] The person who is distressed but sees no realistic or effective way to change will seek ways to reduce the distress—denial, avoidance, withdrawal, and other de-

---

TABLE 8-2   Signs of Readiness For Change

1. *Decreased resistance.* The client stops arguing, interrupting, denying, or objecting.
2. *Decreased questions about the problem.* The client seems to have enough information about his or her problem, and stops asking questions. There is a sense of being finished.
3. *Resolve.* The client appears to have reached a resolution, and may seem more peaceful, relaxed, calm, unburdened, or settled. Sometimes this happens after the client has passed through a period of anguish or tearfulness.
4. *Self-motivational statements.* The client makes direct self-motivational statements, reflecting recognition of a problem ("I guess this is serious"), concern ("This worries me"), openness to change ("I need to do something"), or optimism ("I'm going to beat this").
5. *Increased questions about change.* The client asks what he or she could do about the problem, how people change if they decide to, or the like.
6. *Envisioning.* The client begins to talk about how life might be after a change, to anticipate difficulties if a change were made, or to discuss the advantages of change.
7. *Experimenting.* If the client has had time between sessions, he or she may have begun experimenting with possible change approaches (e.g., going to an Alcoholics Anonymous meeting, going without drinking for a few days, reading a self-help book).

From W. R. Miller & S. Rollnick, *Motivational Interviewing.* New York: Guilford Press, 1991.

fensive strategies. By contrast, the person who perceives available avenues for change is likely to try them. Two types of counselor intervention can be helpful at this point: (a) to encourage the person that change *is* possible and can be achieved by taking specific action; (b) to offer the individual not one but several alternative options for beginning the change process, allowing the person to choose the one that seems most appropriate. Research suggests that, when a person is offered multiple choices for intervention, he or she is more likely to accept, stick with, and succeed through the chosen strategy for change.[12]

Action

General strategies for helping people change, once they are ready, are introduced in chapter 11. The information and approaches to be discussed in part V also represent action strategies appropriate for counseling with specific problems.

Maintenance

Supportive contacts continue to be important during the maintenance stage, after active change interventions have ended. The pastor who counsels is often in an ideal position to maintain such supportive contact, not having to wait for the client to initiate further interactions.

The skills that people use to maintain change vary from one problem or life area to another. Still, there are a few general change-maintaining strategies that apply to many areas. These include

> recognizing high-risk situations for backsliding into previous patterns of behavior and either avoiding these or learning how to cope with them
>
> recognizing the early signs of a relapse into previous patterns, and using these as warning bells to renew change strategies
>
> learning to think in ways more consistent with the new direction ("think thin," new self-concept)
>
> obtaining social support for the new direction
>
> altering lifestyle to support the new direction and discourage a return to old ways
>
> preparing an effective "escape" strategy to be used if and when the old pattern returns, thus preventing a slip from turning into a disastrous fall

Strategies such as these are useful in many areas of change, and the problem of relapse prevention is addressed more fully within chapter 16.

Relapse

Finally, no matter how well laid one's plans, the probability is often high that previous behavior patterns will return at some point. The apostle Paul complained, "That which I would I do not, and that which I would not I do." This, too, is part of the human condition. People are necessarily less than perfect in change, as in all things.

A reversion to a previous pattern can (but need not) be quite discouraging. The key here is to prevent the relapse from turning into a self-perpetuating cycle of discouragement, further backsliding, further discouragement, and so on. Self-castigation regarding a slip or relapse is seldom productive and tends instead to feed into a negative spiral. A more productive pattern is to use the relapse for new learning—as a reminder of the importance of change and a signal to renew one's efforts in the new direction. As indicated by Prochaska's model, a relapse can be part of the *positive* spiral that leads to enduring change. When a client returns to the office with hanging head, reporting an incident of backsliding, one potentially helpful response is, "I'm glad that this happened while we are still working together. Let's talk about what happened, try to understand it, and learn how to make it less likely that this will happen in the future." The counselor needs to counteract the client's own discouragement with a vision that sees beyond this moment to the longer process of transformation. Because of his or her symbolic role, the pastor may be uniquely able to give permission for forgiveness, acceptance, and renewed hope.

ADDITIONAL READINGS

For the Counselor

DECI, EDWARD L., and RICHARD M. RYAN *Intrinsic Motivation and Self-motivation in Human Behavior*. New York: Plenum Press, 1985.

KANFER, FREDERICK H., and ARNOLD P. GOLDSTEIN *Helping People Change* (4th ed.). Elmsford, NY: Pergamon Press, 1991. Many specific techniques for facilitating therapeutic change, both in general and with certain types of common problem areas.

MILLER, WILLIAM R., and STEPHEN ROLLNICK *Motivational Interviewing: Preparing People to Change Addictive Behavior*. New York: Guilford Press, 1991. A detailed explanation and practical guidelines for motivating "resistant" clients to change stubborn behavior patterns.

SHELTON, JOHN L., and J. MARK ACKERMAN *Homework in Counseling and Psychotherapy: Examples of Systematic Assignments for Therapeutic Use by Mental Health Professionals*. Springfield, IL: Charles C Thomas, 1974. Helpful guide to the use of homework assignments in counseling, to extend and continue progress between sessions.

SHELTON, JOHN L., and RONA L. LEVY *Behavioral Assignments and Treatment Compliance: A Handbook of Clinical Strategies*. Champaign, IL: Research Press, 1981.

TOUGH, ALLEN *Intentional Changes: A Fresh Approach to Helping People Change*. Chicago: Follet, 1982. Discusses the natural processes involved in change and how one can facilitate them.

For the Client

SIMON, SIDNEY B. *Getting Unstuck: Breaking through the Barriers to Change*. New York: Warner Books, 1988.

NOTES

[1]William R. Miller and Reid K. Hester, "Inpatient Alcoholism Treatment: Who Benefits?" *American Psychologist* 41 (1986): 794–805; Charles A. Kiesler, "Mental Hospitals and Alternative Care: Noninstitutionalization as Potential Public Policy for Mental Patients," *American Psychologist* 37 (1982): 349–60.

[2]Harold Holder, Richard Longabaugh, William R. Miller, and Anthony V. Rubonis, "The Cost Effectiveness of Treatment for Alcoholism: A First Approximation," *Journal of Studies on Alcohol* 52 (1991): 517–40.

[3]Allen Tough, *Intentional Changes: A Fresh Approach to Helping People Change* (Chicago: Follet, 1982); Russell E. Glasgow and Gerald M. Rosen, "Behavioral Bibliotherapy: A Review of Self-help Behavior Therapy Manuals," *Psychological Bulletin* 85 (1978): 1–23.

[4]Thomas H. Bien, William R. Miller, and J. Scott Tonigan, "Brief Interventions for Alcohol Problems: A Review," *Addiction* 88 (1993): 315–336.

[5]E. A. Locke, K. N. Shaw, L. M. Saari, and G. P. Latham, "Goal Setting and Task Performance: 1969–1980," *Psychological Bulletin* 90 (1981): 125–52.

[6]James O. Prochaska and Carlo C. DiClemente, "Stages of Change in the Modification of Problem Behaviors," *Progress in Behavior Modification* 28 (1992): 1183–1218; James O. Prochaska and Carlo C. DiClemente, "The Transtheoretical Approach," in J. C. Norcross and M. R. Goldfried (eds.), *Handbook of Psychotherapy Integration* (New York: Basic Books, 1992).

[7]W. R. Miller, and J. C'deBaca, "Quantum Change: Toward a Psychology of Transformation," in T. Heatherton and J. Weinberger (eds.), *Can Personality Change?* (Washington, DC: American Psychological Association, 1994, pp. 253–280).

[8]Stephen M. Johnson and others, "How Deviant Is the Normal Child: A Behavioral Analysis of the Preschool Child and His Family," in R. D. Rubin, J. P. Brady, and J. D. Henderson, eds., *Advances in Behavior Therapy* (New York: Academic Press, 1973), vol. 4.

[9]David L. Rosenhan, "On Being Sane in Insane Places," *Science* 179 (1973): 250–58.

[10]William R. Miller and Victoria C. Sanchez, "Motivating Young Adults for Treatment and Lifestyle Change," in George Howard (ed.), *Issues in Alcohol Use and Misuse by Young Adults* (Notre Dame, IN: University of Notre Dame Press, 1994, pp. 55–82).

[11]Robert W. Rogers, "A Protection Motivation Theory of Fear Appeals and Attitude Change," *Journal of Psychology* 91 (1975): 93–114; Robert W. Rogers and C. R. Mewborn, "Fear Appeals and Attitude Change: Effects of a Threat's Noxiousness, Probability of Occurrence, and the Efficacy of Coping Responses," *Journal of Personality and Social Psychology* 34 (1976): 54–61.

[12]Edward L. Deci, *Intrinsic Motivation* (New York: Plenum Press, 1975); Edward L. Deci, *The Psychology of Self-determination* (New York: Free Press, 1980); William R. Miller, "Motivation for Treatment: A Review with Special Emphasis on Alcoholism," *Psychological Bulletin* 98 (1985): 84–107.

9

FACILITATING CHOICES

Two roads diverged in a yellow wood
And sorry I could not travel both
And be one traveler, long I stood . . .
—Robert Frost, "The Road Not Taken"

To make a choice is to make a decision, to select among alternatives. Each of us every day makes thousands of tiny choices as well as some more major ones. To write a sentence one must choose from among many thoughts that could be expressed, selecting the one that seems to be clearest and to follow best from what has gone before. So it is with all choices. Facing into the future, people choose from alternative roads the path that seems to follow best from the experiences they have had thus far. To choose is to continue on life's journey.

Sometimes, however, the journey is interrupted. The person comes to a fork or a crossroads so perplexing that it seems impossible to proceed. All or part of the person's life comes to a standstill until the decision is made at last—which way to go?

People work in different ways as they make decisions. Some prefer to make the choice and get it over with, even if the final decision may not be the best possible one. Others prefer to consider all of the options first and to examine each one carefully before that final, sometimes agonizing moment of decisiveness. Each style has its strengths and its weaknesses. The former "decisive" person gets things done more readily but is more susceptible to making hasty, arbitrary, and less than well-considered choices. The latter "deliberative" person usually considers more options and thinks each one through more carefully but may become so caught up in the deliberation that it becomes difficult to make a decision.

No matter what one's style of deciding, it happens from time to time that one encounters a choice too difficult to sort out on one's own. At such times people turn to others for help (though not necessarily for advice) in deciding. (The "deliberative" person may come more readily for such decision-making assistance, whereas the "decisive" individual may be more likely to appear for counseling because of the consequences of decisions already make.) One person to whom people go for help is the pastor.

Some pastors interpret this as an invitation to give advice, to tell the individual what he or she *should* do. Indeed, many people are in part asking for the pastor's own perspective on which course is best. But the challenge to the pastoral counselor is much broader than this, much deeper than merely informing the client of the "right" course. The pastor's own opinion (if indeed it is being asked for) is but one more source of information, one more input to the choice process.

There are several good reasons to resist the temptation to give advice. The first is that this may not be what the person really needs, even if he or she seems to ask, "What do *you* think I should do?" The underlying plea in the choice quandary is, "Help *me* to decide." It is tempting for the client to phrase this as, "Tell me what to do," or "Decide for me," but in a very real sense the counselor cannot. The decision *must* be the individual's. The counselor who works with alcoholics learns quickly the impossibility of making a choice for another. The survivors of a suicide must also come to peace with this reality—that no one can ultimately decide for another.

A second reason to avoid giving advice, especially early in the process, is that this represents a roadblock. It stops the person's own exploration process. Once the counselor has announced a solution, it seems unnecessary and anticlimactic for the person to keep exploring for his or her own answer (though of course it must be so). The first stage of counseling for choice as well as for other goals is *clarification*, and the clarification process is derailed if the counselor gives in to the temptation to advise, warn, persuade, or moralize.

A third simple reason to refrain from advice is that it may not be the *best* advice or solution. Neither counselor nor client can know the answer before the question is clear. What if the individual *takes* the advice? Is the counselor then responsible if it doesn't work out right, or worse, if the result is catastrophic? To offer a quick solution is to suggest that you know better than the individual what he or she should do, what is the right course for him or her to take. It is to assume an illusory amount of responsibility and control, to seem to take charge of that which cannot be yours to command. This is not to say that advice is never called for. It is. Your own perspective can be very important to those who struggle with choice, but it is only one kind of input to the choice process and it must be placed within the proper perspective so that is not misleading or preemptive of the individual's own prerogative process of choice.

The four phases of counseling described in chapter 2 are helpful to remember when counseling toward choice. This perspective recognizes that choice is a process that occurs in steps over time and that different interventions are helpful at different points in this process.

1. CLARIFICATION PHASE

Choice counseling begins with listening. The counselor must come to share the inner world of the decision, the person's own perceived reality about the choice to be made and the alternatives being considered.

The techniques used to facilitate this stage of exploration have already been described in part II. Through reflective listening and the creation of an open and accepting atmosphere for expression, the counselor seeks to understand how the individual perceives the choice, the alternatives of which the client is aware, and how the person *feels* about this choice and the perceived alternatives.

Several processes are occurring during this phase. If the counselor reflects the conflict accurately, capturing not just one side but all sides of the situation, the client is able to attain a more complete picture of the dilemma. This is helpful because typically the individual has been bouncing back and forth between pro and con elements of the conflict without stopping or backing off to get the bigger picture. Reflection, then, *helps the person to see the whole situation*, the whole choice. Second, the reflective process *activates the client's own problem solving capacities*. More alternatives may be discovered, and the relative merits of each may become clearer as the person talks without being interrupted by roadblocks. Third, the person becomes *more aware of the feeling elements of the choice*. Sometimes people try to be totally logical in reaching a decision, ignoring the fact that many decisions are made on rather illogical (or nonlogical) grounds. Reason is one process involved in choosing, but by no means the only one. Reflective listening helps the individual to get in touch with and more fully consider other facets of the choice.

An assumption underlying a reflective approach to choice counseling is that the individual is capable of reaching a good decision if he or she is permitted to explore it within an atmosphere of acceptance. In the clarification phase (as well as later, if the process continues), the counselor seeks to create this atmosphere.

One complexity of the clarification phase is that the client may be trying to decide whether or not to decide! There may be an indication of a threat or the hint of an opportunity, suggesting that perhaps a decision should be made. By listening carefully the pastor helps to clarify whether or not the risk or opportunity is important enough to warrant an active decision. Psychologists Wheeler and Janis suggested that three major components influence a person's motivation to make an active decision: (a) whether the risks or opportunities are serious, (b) whether it is possible to find an effective solution, and (c) whether there is enough time.[1] A person who perceives that one of these three crucial conditions is lacking may "decide not to decide," thus making the decision by default. Thus, one task of clarification may be to help the client decide whether or not to decide.

Counseling on this point can be directed to the three key components listed above: (a) help the individual to assess realistically the seriousness and importance of opportunities or risks being faced, (b) encourage the person (to the extent that it is realistic) that an effective solution can be found, and (c) evaluate whether there is sufficient time to select and enact an alternative. Research suggests that, of these, the second is most powerful. People who believe that no workable solution can be found tend to engage in denial, avoidance, and procrastination, whereas those who believe a solution can be found are more likely to engage in an active and productive search for it.[2]

2. FORMULATION PHASE

The formulation phase in choice counseling involves arriving at a comprehensive picture of the decision that the individual faces. What, in fact, are the alternatives? How is the person "stuck," and how can this inertia be overcome so that the person can resume the journey?

One way to clarify a choice or decision is to specify all of the alternatives that are available. These may be alternative *actions*, or they may be alternative ways of *thinking* or *feeling* about something. (You will recognize the A-B-C system of Affect, Behavior, and Cognition from chapter 7.) If the analogy of the "internal committee" is used, then the question of clarification becomes, "Who are the members of the committee, and how does each one feel or think?"

In some decisions the choices are limited. A few are binary—either/or choices between two and only two mutually exclusive options. Some seemingly binary choices are to have a baby or remain childless, to stay married or get a divorce, to quit drinking or continue drinking, to accept an offered promotion and move or remain in the present position, to have an abortion or continue the pregnancy. Yet even for these there are often more than two options. A woman who decides against abortion can still choose to keep the baby herself or to make an adoption plan. Those who cannot or choose not to have children of their own may still consider adoption, foster parenting, or maintaining special relationships with children they know. The possibilities for a changed relationship offer another alternative when it seems that the only choices are to stay in a marriage the way it is or to divorce. In choices where the alternatives seem few, the counselor's task is both to clarify feelings and values regarding the options that are perceived and to determine whether there may be still other possibilities not yet fully considered. The descriptions of types of conflict in chapter 7 may also be very helpful in understanding (and helping your client to understand) what is happening in a fixed-choice situation: why the roller coaster feelings, why the back-and-forth vacillations between alternatives. Formulating the fixed-choice decision means clarifying the choice to be made, the desired long-range outcome, and the nature of the present conflict. This is accompanied, of course, by continued reflection of feelings and by empathy with the difficulty of the process.

Other decisions are more open ended. The deadlines for decision are less clear, and the choices are many if not infinite. The client may be wondering, "What should be my life work, my career? How should I use my financial resources, and what lifestyle will I choose for myself? What kind of person will I marry, or will I instead explore alternatives to traditional marriage?" These choices are not so much either/or in nature; instead, they involve a long series of or's. Some of the tasks of the counselor are the same as for more fixed choices—to clarify values, explore feelings about the choice, help define the desired outcomes. Yet this kind of choice is also broader and requires additional counselor skills. Clarification of the alternatives here involves more brainstorming and information gathering. What are all of the possible options? To which ones is the individual drawn, and why? Here the clarification and formulation phases blend more quickly into intervention, and as with more fixed choices the process of reflective listening continues to be important throughout the intervention phase.

3. INTERVENTION PHASE

Having clarified the choice to be made, the client's feelings and values, and the available alternatives, the counselor may choose to use any of a variety of choice-facilitating strategies. These are again based mostly on the premise that the client is capable of discovering his or her own decision, rather than having the right answer delivered by an external agent. These strategies will be described in two sets—those more useful in fixed-choice situations and those more applicable in open-ended decisions. Like most binary classifications, this one is too simple, and there is a continuum of kinds of choices between these two extremes. Nevertheless, the grouping of choice interventions in this way can be a helpful organizing tool.

Fixed-Choice Strategies

Fixed-choice strategies are used to help individuals in deciding among a small number of alternatives, usually two or three. They are intended to help the person get a comprehensive view of the whole choice and consider the relative strengths and weaknesses of each option. This process is the same when the person is choosing between attractive alternatives (approach-approach conflict) as well as when all of the options look bad and it's a choice of the lesser evil (avoidance-avoidance).

The "Ben Franklin" Chart   One strategy is to draw up a particular kind of chart attributed to Benjamin Franklin, although it certainly has
been used and recommended by many others. This involves starting with a
clean sheet of paper and drawing a line down the middle (in the case of two-
choice situations). On one side are listed *all* of the reasons favoring one of the
alternatives; on the other side are detailed reasons favoring the other option.
Within each of these two general categories there tend to be two different
kinds of reasons—positive and negative. Suppose that a person is to choose
between alternatives A and B. There are two kinds of reasons for choosing A:
to obtain the positive benefits that are expected to come with choosing A and
to avoid the negative outcomes that might follow if B were chosen. Likewise,
the reasons for selecting B include the positive benefits that are perceived to
come with choosing B and avoidance of the negative outcomes that might follow if A were chosen. (The perceptive reader will note that this represents a
double approach-avoidance conflict, which is what many binary choices are—
especially those that are brought to the attention of a counselor.)

Table 9-1 shows an example. Suppose that you were working with an
individual who is trying to decide whether to remain in a currently distressing marital relationship. If this is reduced to a simple binary choice, the options are "stay" or "leave". The four columns then represent positive reasons
for staying ("What are the benefits of staying?"), the reasons for *not* leaving
("What are the things you fear—the bad things that might happen if you
leave?"), the positive reasons for leaving ("What good things might happen
to you if you leave?"), and finally the reasons for *not* staying ("What are the
things you fear—the bad things that might happen if you choose to stay?").

TABLE 9-1   Example of the "Ben Franklin" Chart Method

REASONS "PRO" (STAY IN THIS RELATIONSHIP)		REASONS "CON" (LEAVE THIS RELATIONSHIP)	
POSITIVE REASONS (REASONS TO STAY)	NEGATIVE REASONS (REASONS NOT TO LEAVE)	POSITIVE REASONS (REASONS TO LEAVE)	NEGATIVE REASONS (REASONS NOT TO STAY)
Shared years	Fear of living alone	Feel happier alone	Stagnation
Stability for the children	Losing the house	Stability for the children	Still young enough to find
Financial security	Growing old alone	Freedom—could	new partner—may
Still feel love		choose my own lifestyle	get older and then finally leave Physical danger when partner is drinking

Getting all of these down on paper can be very instructive (as well exhausting). Usually, the person has been rehearsing all of these reasons mentally, obsessing about them, going back and forth among all of the reasons for and against each course of action like a Ping-Pong ball at a championship match. To see all of them at once sometimes makes the choice clearer. At times all of the reasons pile up on one side. In other cases, as in the example given in Table 9-1, there are roughly equal numbers of reasons in each column.

Not all of the reasons are of equal value, however, which makes for an even more complicated picture. For each of the reasons given (most of which consist of anticipated possible outcomes, positive or negative), it is helpful to ask two questions. First, how *likely* is it that this would really happen if you made this choice? If the client would benefit from seeing this on the chart, it could be expressed as a percentage between 0 percent (certainly would not) and 100 percent (absolutely certain it would happen). This can be important because at times the individual has been grossly overestimating or underestimating the likelihood of a certain outcome. Second, it can be helpful to ask how *significant* it would be for the client if this did actually happen. How good (or bad) would that be? A rating system of numbers or letters can be used if it seems helpful to have this in writing (e.g., 1 = not important at all, to 7 = extremely important). If you or the client is very fond of accounting, you can even calculate cross-products of probability ¥ importance (with appropriate mathematical signs). This goes well beyond the tolerance of most people for quantifying their experience, however, so use your judgment about how far to carry this.

Information Gathering   The process of constructing a choice chart may make it apparent that more information is needed. What in fact happens to people when a certain choice is made, such as reporting a rape? What are the possibilities of a certain outcome occurring, such as being able to adopt? What resources would be needed if one option were chosen? (For example, what does it cost, who would need to help?)

If further information is needed, where can this information be found? Are there books or other written sources that could help, or is there perhaps computer-accessible information? Are there people with whom it would be helpful to talk? The counselor can help in identifying appropriate sources of accurate information and in making any necessary referrals (see chapter 19). It may also be helpful, if another person is to be consulted, to role play that interview with the client in preparation for the real thing, especially if the client is anxious about what to say and how to cope with the needed interview.

Acting Out Alternatives   A further application of role playing in choice counseling is the practice of acting out alternatives. With the counselor taking the role of significant others in the client's life, the client "tries out" alternative expressions and decisions. Alternatively, the trying out can be done in imagination. The client can be asked to relax, close his or her eyes, and imagine that decision A has been made. How are things different? What is happening one year later? Five years later? Then suppose that B has been chosen instead. Now how have things evolved? If nothing else, this exercise can generate clearer items to include in the choice chart as anticipated possible outcomes of the various alternatives.

Role Reversal   A special case of such acting out is role reversal. Here the counselor says something like, "I am going to play the advocate for one alternative. I'm going to argue for choosing A, and I want you to respond to my arguments by supporting B. Then later we will switch roles." In arguing each side, don't use your *own* arguments for each alternative, but rather those that the client sees as salient. The choice chart is a good source for beginning this process. You can argue reasons from one side of the page while the client tries out the alternatives. It is important then to switch roles, so that the client has an opportunity to explore both sides of the issue. It is essential for the client to understand that you are not actually advocating one position or the other but are giving voice to one side of the client's own internal conflict. If this is not made clear, this situation is fertile ground for projection.

Time Out   Neither the counselor nor the client should expect to leave the office with a decision made, nor is the success of this counseling process dependent upon such an immediate choice. Rather, your goal is to help the client see the whole picture.

Having done this difficult work together, it can be useful for the client to allow himself or herself some time to work the decision through. At the end of a session of searching such as this, we often suggest that no decision be made immediately. Rather, the individual should allow the process to continue "unconsciously" for a while. The pastor's way of saying this might be to recommend that the person pray about it. In time, a feeling or intuition emerges for which way to go. The answer comes from within, and we have usually found such answers to be trustworthy. For the heavily logical person who is accustomed to reaching decisions by totally conscious reasoning, this can be both a trying and a worthwhile experience. One of the most rational thinkers of the 20th century, Bertrand Russell, put it this way:

> The best plan is to think about it with very great intensity—the greatest intensity of which I am capable—for a few hours or days, and at the end of that time give orders, so to speak, that the work is to proceed underground. After some months I return consciously to the topic and find that the work has been done.[3]

The process can take days, weeks, months. There is no predicting when the sense of closure will come. It can be understood as the wisdom of the unconscious or the guidance of God. Whatever the time frame and the explanation, it is a real process and one that is usually much preferable to the immediate forcing of a decision.

Open-Ended Choice Strategies

When the alternatives are many, somewhat different strategies may be helpful, although these overlap in part with those already presented.

Brainstorming   Brainstorming is a process used to generate alternatives. The rules are fairly simple. Think of all of the possible alternatives, no matter how unlikely, ridiculous, farfetched, or unrealistic they may be. Do not censor them. Write down every alternative that comes to mind, without worrying about whether it is a good idea or not. The purpose is to divorce the creative idea-generating process from the evaluative idea-eliminating process. To start evaluating before a range of ideas has been presented is to inhibit creativity.

For an individual, this can be a good assignment to complete between sessions. When more than one person is involved in brainstorming, such as a family or a whole committee, research suggests that many more ideas will be generated if every person *individually* writes down all of the ideas and possibilities that he or she can come up with, again without censoring them. This is done before any idea is discussed or evaluated. Then, after each person has had time to use his or her own creativity, a master list of alternatives is produced by compiling all of the lists, again before any idea is discussed. This can generate twice as many options as the alternative of every one voicing ideas as they occur. Somehow the joint generating process decreases each individual's creativity, perhaps because each is inhibited or interrupted by the group or perhaps because each feels less responsibility to be creative when others are actively making suggestions.

Card Sorting Methods   Once possibilities have been generated, the process of evaluation of alternatives can begin. One approach is to use any of a variety of card sorting techniques.

One such technique is a "planning board" method sometimes used in values clarification. Here the individual begins with a set of cards (3 ¥ 5-inch index cards work well, and so do torn-up slips of paper) each of which contains a possible value or alternative. The content of cards may come from lists developed and reused by the counselor, or it may be generated uniquely for each individual. (One list of general values will be provided in chapter 10, but here the needed list is often more specific to the decision at hand.)

The individual then arranges these cards in order of priority—for example, how important each is to him or her personally. It can be helpful to lay all of the cards out on a table, to examine them all, and then to select first, second, third priorities, and so on. This results in a series of forced choices—how important is each element in relation to all of the others? In sorting aspects of vocation, for example, how important is having a high income relative to working around people one likes, having evenings free, and feeling that one's job contributes to human welfare? In considering what an ideal marital partner would be like, how important relatively are intelligence, outgoingness, and sexual attractiveness? (See Table 9-2.)

A variation is first to sort cards into piles. The choice can be binary (important to me versus not important to me) or more complex (five piles ranging from 1: "very important" to 5: "not at all important"). Then within a given pile a rank ordering can be done.

Information Gathering and Special Assessment   As with fixed choices, open-ended choice processes may require the gathering of further information and, in fact, are likely to require it. A client may be asking, "What are the outcomes that I want (values) and what are the different ways to achieve these? What am I best suited for? What are the options?"

This information gathering process may involve the services of a skilled specialist, such as a well-trained career counselor. It may involve the use of

TABLE 9-2   Example Card Lists for a "Planning Board" Strategy

PRIORITIES IN A JOB	PRIORITIES IN A RELATIONSHIP
Good salary	Doesn't make me jealous
Work with people I like	Intelligent
Contribute to human welfare	Physically attractive
Not take work home—evenings free	Likely to grow and change continually
Pleasant work environment	Generally optimistic
My own private work space	Willing to take risks and try new things
Working outdoors	Has a solid career
Working with people	Enjoys touching
Working with facts	Expresses anger easily
Working with ideas	Expresses affection regularly
Working with my hands	Willing to do housework
Good retirement plan	Earns a good salary
Vacation time	Enjoys sports and outdoor activities
Flexible hours	Well liked by my friends
Able to work at home	Likes my friends
Physical labor and exercise	Enjoys sexuality
Work feels meaningful	Initiates sexuality
Opportunity for advancement	Likes to travel
Opportunity for personal growth	Wants to have children
Job security	Shares my religious beliefs
Input to decisions that affect my work	Willing to stay up all night to discuss a problem in our relationship
BLANK CARDS (for additional items not on the list	BLANK CARDS

special assessment procedures that can be helpful in sorting out possibilities, such as a vocational interest test or personality inventory. In some areas there are computerized information systems, which are continuously updated, to help people in the process of considering career options or leisure activities. As more specific options are considered, it can be helpful to talk with someone who has already chosen that path (e.g., to find out more about veterinary medicine by interviewing a veterinarian). A pastor may keep a mental or even literal file of individuals within a congregation or community who have had certain kinds of experience and who would be willing to talk to others about it (see chapter 20).

Fantasy   The creative counselor may also make use of fantasy processes in helping clients in choice. Close your eyes. Imagine yourself five years from now, or ten years from now. How do you look? How are you dressed? Where do you live? What is your life like? How do you spend your time? Who are the people around you? Such fantasy exploration can help to uncover an individual's personal values and goals, dreams and aspirations, fears and expectations.

As discussed earlier, imagining possible scenarios is another way to look at the future. By a *scenario* we mean a fantasy of how the future might be if a particular choice were made. For vital decisions about one's life, such as career, relationships, or lifestyle, it may be informative to have the client create three scenarios of each alternative: (a) the worst possible outcome; (b) the best possible outcome, and (c) the most likely outcome. This technique can help a person become more conscious of hopes and fears attached to various possible alternatives. Things usually turn out better than people's worst scenarios but less stunning than their best ones.

A somewhat more somber fantasy exercise is for clients to write their own obituary. What would they want to be said about them and their lives in retrospect? Or suppose that they knew they had only two years left to live. How would they spend their time? What would their priorities be?

Fantasy exercises such as these can remove the person from the rutted thinking of the present and provide a longer vision or perspective that may be useful in making open-ended choices.

4. IMPLEMENTATION PHASE

With choice counseling, the fourth phase involves actually implementing the choice that has been made. In most cases this need not be a final no-return implementation, but rather can be an experiment, a trying out of the choice to see how it works.

This is not true for all choices. Some are nearly or totally irreversible. Sterilization surgery, announcing the desire for a separation, or resigning from a job may all lead to consequences that are difficult to reverse. In such decisions, the first step can be very difficult and should be taken only after careful consideration.

But the step must come. Choice and decision are private processes, which usually must go public at some level if they are to be implemented. Sometimes the choice is not obvious at first. For example, if a person decides to stop smoking others may not notice for some time because it is difficult to notice the absence of an action. A choice can be made more public and accountable by announcing it, so that others will notice and provide their support.

The first step is to take a first step. William James suggested that this step should be bold, to mark the occasion. Announce that it is happening, and take the first step with flair! Live as if the decision has been made, and you are already implementing it. It is usually best, once a decision has been reached, to begin immediately. "I'll start tomorrow" has been the downfall of many decisions.

Perseverance is important as well. Make a specific plan for implementing the decision and stick to it. Ask others to help (or at least not to make it harder). This is especially important in approach-avoidance conflicts, where resolve weakens for a period of time once the person begins to move away from center. The only escape from such a conflict, especially the double approach-avoidance kind, is to make a decision and then keep moving in that direction.

A third strategy is to prepare for backsliding. Even with the best of intentions, backsliding is likely to occur in many choice situations. It is best to anticipate this possibility and to consider how it will be dealt with. What will the client do if the desire to drink returns one night? What will happen when a lover, who has been told that the affair must end, shows up at the door with flowers at a time when the client is feeling especially lonely? The perceptive counselor will work with the client to anticipate the possible occasions for decision slippage and will lay specific plans for how to deal with such situations should they arise. Direct practice through role playing may help ensure that the individual will be able to follow through with such plans.

Finally, there should be plans for evaluating the decision. At some preplanned point, the counselor and client should get together again and look at how things are going. Did the decision have the anticipated outcomes? Is it time to change plans somewhat or to reconsider the decision? What other options are there? At such points it may be necessary to go back to the beginning and start the choice process over again with clarification, generating of alternatives, and so forth. Not all choices are final, and often clients must retrace their steps back to a crossroads and puzzle again over which way to try next.

Two examples of more complicated decisional processes may help to elucidate these phases of choice counseling. Neither example fits the stages exactly, and each contains it own complexities. Nevertheless, these two common conundrums are worthwhile themes for further explication of the process of pastoral counseling toward choice. The first of these is career decision making.

CAREER/LIFE PLANNING

Career decision making may be one of the most difficult and important choice processes of a person's life and usually is not a one-time decision. In a rapidly changing world with new technologies, shifting values, and emerging lifestyles, it is now ordinary for a person to have three, five, even seven different jobs or occupations in a lifetime.

This means that people will be making decisions about the kind of work they want to do or can do throughout most of their adult lives. Once again the pastor is in an ideal position to encourage and facilitate careful consideration of this issue. For some individuals, spiritual dimensions of career choice are of prime importance. The idea of a "calling" is not limited to the traditional religious occupations, and increasingly people are attempting to listen for inner direction, for a call to life work.

At the same time the vastness of unemployment problems and general economic instability have meant that people looking for jobs feel more desperate than ever. They may feel that they have no time for career planning but simply need a job to put bread on the table or at least to bolster sagging self-esteem. Yet even those in need of immediate income can benefit greatly from a considered process of career/life planning.

With an increasing average lifespan and later retirement, people may spend sixty years or more as workers! Given this span it is well worthwhile to spend some time deciding about career direction. Work in general is beneficial to physical and mental health, but it is even better if the person is working at a job that feels meaningful and productive and is a good fit with his or her own needs and preferences. The general goal of career counseling, beyond assisting with job seeking skills, is to increase the person's chances of achieving this good fit. For the pastoral counselor, the goodness of fit between person and career includes awareness of the spiritual self as well as other considerations, such as physical and psychological factors.

The process of choosing a career direction is often described as including four steps, which correspond roughly to the four phases discussed above. These steps or phases involve answering four questions: Who am I? What are my options? What is the best fit or match for me? How do I get there?

1. Who Am I?

Phase 1 of career decision making is a matter of assessment and clarification. It is important for the counselor to listen to the reasons, feelings, and alternatives that the client brings to the search. It can be helpful for the counselor to go beyond listening by using some standard assessment questions, instruments, or methods to help clarify the individual's values, interests, skills, or abilities. Thus, the usual reflective listening element of the clarification phase may need to be augmented by specialized assessment methods.

Some experts in career counseling believe that *values* represent the cornerstone of career/life planning. This may be especially true for individuals who seek the guidance of a pastor in sorting out vocation, for in choosing a pastor they are asking to be understood in the larger context of values and spirituality. Earlier in this chapter (Table 9-2), an exercise was discussed for clarifying work values, and additional resources for this purpose are provided at the end of this chapter.

Vocational *interests* are another consideration. What does the person like to do, enjoy, find rewarding? Vocational interests are often assessed by using either of two structured inventories—the *Strong Interest Inventory* or the *Self-Directed Search*. Both assess the individual's pattern of interests and then match this to patterns commonly found in major occupations. In essence, such inventories ask, "Which occupations currently contain people who are most similar to this person in interests?" The Strong inventory is the more complicated of the two, and there are certain controls as to who is professionally qualified to administer and use it. Pastors may wish to collaborate with qualified psychologists in using this test. Computerized scoring and interpretation are available. The *Self-Directed Search*, by contrast, is unrestricted, self-scoring, and straightforward in interpretation. A danger in using this or any vocational interest instrument is that the individual may misconstrue interests as abilities. For example, if interests turn out to be similar to those of a physician, the person may conclude that the test points to an *ability* to be a physician. It is crucial to realize that an *interest* inventory is just that—a measure of a person's interests in comparison to those of people already functioning in various occupations. Vocational interest inventories are used in career counseling because people tend to be happier in occupations where they share interests with coworkers. Yet each occupation can benefit from an infusion of "nontraditional" people bringing fresh insights, and interests ought not be confused with abilities.

Skills and abilities are best explored by examining a person's past achievements as well as education, training, and job experience. *Achievements* are broadly defined here as including all activities that a person has done well. Achievements need not be skills for which a person has been paid, nor do they occur only in vocational settings. It can be very useful to ask a client to recall some achievements from childhood. An assignment to help in skill identification involves writing down all of the things that one has done well or of which one is proud. The counselor and client then together look for common threads running through these descriptions of achievements, the underlying skills and abilities. These threads may at first seem unrelated, and they may span several years or even decades. (For more structured formats useful for identifying skills through achievement, consult the additional readings for this chapter.) Through identification of these common threads, the counselor and client begin to clarify the enduring skills that the client uses, the intrinsically interesting abilities that seem to motivate the client regardless of the particular task or achievement at hand. This skill identification process can be enhanced further when conducted in groups where individuals help each other.

2. What Are the Options?

This is the phase of formulation, of generating alternatives. Once the client has become aware of her or his interests, skills, and abilities, the next step is to begin identifying the kinds of jobs in which these skills and interests can be applied. This is a time for broadening the client's perspective, for widening what has often been a kind of tunnel vision. For example, if teaching skills have been evident in many achievements, the individual need not be limited to teaching in public schools. Other options include working in the training division of a company, private tutoring, being a tour guide, teaching skills such as driving or cooking within community settings, or demonstrating products and services.

The formulation phase is a good time to find out what the client would describe as "an ideal job." It can be useful at this stage for the client to talk with others—friends, employers, experts—to find out where they think a person with these particular skills might find satisfying work. Library research can contribute to this as well. A reference librarian can provide assistance through resources such as the *Occupational Outlook Handbook* and the *Dictionary of Occupational Titles*. These two publications suggest occupations that are similar in their requisite skills, interests, and demands.

3. What Is the Best Fit or Match for Me?

Here is the "intervention" phase—evaluating available alternatives, exploring possible directions that fit the client's individual needs and interests. This means still further contact with the real world. One process for gathering relevant input here is the informational or exploratory interview. This involves obtaining the name(s) of one or more people who might be able to provide more information about the kinds of jobs and places that could employ people who have the identified skills. The client then interviews such people to find out more about career possibilities (without asking for a formal job interview). Some counselors keep a list of volunteers who are willing to be the first contact for clients embarking on informational interviewing. These volunteers may come from a range of life experiences—young and choosing a first job, midlife and reentering the job market after years of raising children, midlife and facing a voluntary or mandatory career change, retired and deciding how to spend new free time, and so forth (see chapter 20).

The person in career transition should be very direct in requesting an *informational* interview rather than a job interview. The purpose of the interview is to find out more about a certain vocation. The questions to ask include how the worker spends a typical day or week, what major responsibilities there are, what skills are needed, what the person likes best and least about the job, what other occupations are similar, what other people and places hire individuals with such skills, what are the traditional formal entry level requirements as well as the informal alternatives for entering the field. Finally, the client should always ask for the names of other people with whom to talk for further information and contacts. In the jargon of the career counseling field, this is known as *networking*.

4. How Do I Get There?   After a series of informational interviews, the client begins to narrow the field of choice, both in terms of the kind of job he or she wants and the kind of organization or setting in which to seek a job. When this begins to occur, the client is getting ready for actual job interviews. Before pursuing these interviews or accepting an offer, however, it is helpful for the client to review with the counselor the following questions: *What* is my goal? *Why* is it best? (a very important question) *How* do I get there? *When* will each step occur? *Who* will be affected by this decision, and from whom do I need help? Answers to these questions constitute a career focus.

Having clearer answers to these questions also helps the client to assess the job possibilities being considered. Answering these questions plus reviewing the values, skills, and abilities identified earlier can help the client to undertake career/life planning that is realistic and reflects all parts of life—physical, emotional, psychological, family and interpersonal, and spiritual. A pastor can help a person to consider vocation within this larger context, to balance the important factors and consider the bigger questions like, "What does it mean to be a success?"

Further detailed resources are provided at the end of this chapter for learning more about how to assist clients in career/life planning and job finding.

TIME MANAGEMENT

A second complex type of choice counseling is time management—how to manage and use one's time. This is perhaps the broadest choice issue, encompassing all of one's waking hours and, for the religious person, opening up the larger question of stewardship. Comfortable but effective use of time is often a goal for pastors, too, who find themselves stretched in a dozen directions and answering everyone else's needs but their own.

Time management affects other areas of counseling. When counseling people toward career decision making or toward the development of assertive communication skills (see chapter 15), we have often found that the larger issue is the use of time. Time management may also open up other areas because making decisions about use of time requires thinking about basic lifetime goals and exploring personal values. People in career transition (those who are moving from one kind of work to another, be it from nonpaid home-making to paid employment or from work in the public sector to a position in a profit-making corporation) may need time management skills before they are able to complete the transition. If a person is implementing the career/life planning steps described earlier in this chapter while still working full time, he or she may be overwhelmed by the reality that "looking for a job is a full-time job" and may need assistance in budgeting time to work on career planning in addition to fulfilling regular responsibilities.

Time management is such a general concern in our society, in fact, that it is a fruitful topic to consider in planning adult education programs. Many people today could benefit from increased skills in the stewardship of time.

The most straightforward time management counseling system that we have found comes from the business world and was described clearly and concisely in a little classic by Alan Lakein.[4] Drawing on this system, we will briefly outline four basic steps, paralleling the four general steps of choice counseling described earlier.

1. Clarify Goals

No one can "save" time in the sense of hoarding it or holding it back for later use. One can only decide how to use it, and such a decision requires reflection on goals and purpose. To "manage" time one must first know one's goals for the use of that time.

Lakein's method for clarifying time-use goals is to have the client write answers to three crucial questions. They are best answered rather quickly (perhaps allowing three minutes per question) and without censoring or self-evaluation.

1.   What are your lifetime goals? (These are often quite general.)
2.   What are your goals for the next three to five years? (Here greater specificity may begin to emerge.)
3.   Assume that you will die in six months but will be in perfect health until then and without disablement. How would you spend your time? (The list now becomes even more specific.)

These questions provide three different perspectives on personal goals. Some people find that the answers to questions 2 and 3 flow naturally from the goals stated in response to question 1. Others find very different answers emerging, especially with question 3. According to Lakein, radically different answers to question 3 (relative to 1 and 2) indicate a need for a change in time use priorities. Likewise, a large discrepancy between goals and how the person is *actually* using his or her time is an indication of the need for re-evaluation.

There are many other possible techniques that can be used in this first step of clarifying goals. Educator Sidney Simon has written several useful books on how to explore values and goals (see resources at the end of this chapter). Another helpful method is the pie chart, an empty circle that the client divides into parts by drawing lines from the center to the perimeter (Fig. 9-1). One chart is divided on the basis of how time is actually used each day or week, with each piece of the pie representing a major role or function that the indi-

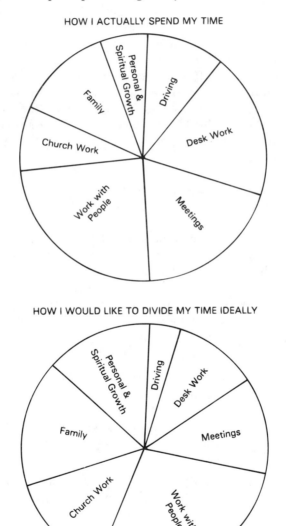

HOW I ACTUALLY SPEND MY TIME

HOW I WOULD LIKE TO DIVIDE MY TIME IDEALLY

FIGURE 9-1   Sample Pie-Charts on the Use of Time

vidual performs and that occupies time. A second pie chart is divided according to how the person would *like* to be distributing his or her time ideally.

A more sensitive goal clarification exercise is to describe what important goals one would leave unaccomplished if life ended tomorrow. What dreams would be unfulfilled? What tasks would be left undone? An exercise mentioned earlier is to write one's own obituary. Assuming that death will occur at a ripe old age, what *ideally* would be said in a eulogy? The purpose in this, as in all step 1 exercises, is to clarify the individual's goals for use of time.

2. Prioritize Goals

All goals are not equally important. The next step is to prioritize them. Lakein's three lists provide a rich range of goals to use in this stage. Even the most general lifetime goals can be prioritized; some *are* more important than others. From the three lists (or from the ideal and real pie charts, or from the obituary exercise, etc.), have the individual arrange the elements in order of importance. (It may be helpful to write each goal on a separate index card so that they can be sorted and arranged more easily.) Narrow the lifetime goals down to a short list, perhaps the top three *major* goals. Often goals from different lists or exercises will overlap and can be combined into a higher-order goal.

3. List Activities

Now the goals become more concrete. For each of the top goals, the person lists all of the activities that might help in achieving it. This is a brainstorming process—no censoring allowed. Do not delete activities because resources seem too limited or others would disapprove, and so forth. Evaluation of these limitations is accomplished later. For this third step the idea is to generate as many actions as possible—the maximal number of alternative ways for approaching the top goals.

4. Schedule the Activities

Finally comes the challenging step of implementation. To begin accomplishing lifetime goals, one must fit the activities that will lead to the goals into the weekly calendar. If the person cannot find at least five minutes in a week to spend on one of the activities, probably that activity should be crossed off the list for the time being. This doesn't mean that it won't be done eventually, only that it won't be done this week. The point is that to reach a goal one has to take action over time, and action—especially new action—usually requires some intentional planning if it is to compete with established habits of time use.

The scheduling of activities should be done on a daily or at least weekly basis. Of course, all of us schedule and carry out many other activities that are not related to lifetime goals, yet having generated a goals-activities list, one is more aware of these activities and is able to schedule them regularly.

Lakein further suggests that everything on the "to do" list be given its own priority: A, B, or C. A is top priority, B is medium priority, and C is lowest priority. The "A" activities should be those that help one to meet the lifetime goals, and they get top priority in planning the daily routine and weekly schedule. The "B" activities, with time, tend to become either "A" or "C" in status. The "C" activities, with lowest priority, may eventually be dropped or may increase in status (possibly because someone else asks about them or puts on some pressure).

Once goals have been set and specific activities have been outlined, it is helpful to have a system of *feedback* about progress toward goals. A very simple one used by many people is a literal "to-do list" from which items are crossed off upon completion. More complex methods of monitoring are described in chapter 11. Some companies publish time-monitoring aids and calendars. The basic principle here is that one needs a source of information, a way of knowing where one is relative to a goal. It is beneficial to have a concrete goal toward which to work, but such goals are meaningless unless one *also* has feedback—a way of knowing one's present status. The absence of feedback and encouragement is a major barrier in implementing change once a goal has been chosen.

Another barrier often encountered at the stage of implementation is *procrastination*. One tip for overcoming procrastination is to break down a big task into smaller ones. Often people keep putting off an "A" activity because it seems too overwhelming. Indeed, "A" activities often are major in scope because they represent important long-range goals. Smaller steps have a better chance of being achieved, and as a consequence a beginning is made toward accomplishing the longer-range goal. Completing a small step also encourages the person to take the next step.

High standards represent yet another potential barrier to implementation of a decision and can contribute to procrastination. When one has very high standards, lifetime goals can seem unattainable, impossibly difficult, scary. It makes sense that one would avoid such goals. In approaching difficult goals it is unrealistic to expect to do it right the first time. Lakein recommends that one adopt a "trial and success" perspective instead. Trial and success means that, even if tackling the "A" task doesn't produce the expected (or right) results the first time, something has been learned and the task can now be accomplished (or attempted) in a different way.

Lakein's writings include many simple and highly practical rules to assist in implementation once the time management decision process has been worked through. Here are just a few examples.

Never handle the same piece of paper twice. Do something with it to make it a different piece of paper. Make a phone call about it, note what to do with it next time it surfaces, discard it, and so forth. Correspondence can be filed into A, B, or C boxes based on priority.

Plan more challenging work for prime time. Each person has a daily period of peak productivity. Some are morning people; others work best in the afternoon or evening. The day can be planned so that more difficult "A" tasks get prime time and more routine activities occur at other times.

Set limits. Most people must turn down opportunities if they are to maintain their direction toward "A" goals. For some it is important to learn how not to say "Yes" when they want to say "No" (see chapter 15). For others the bigger challenge is learning how not to say "Yes" when they want to say "Yes."

The "80/20" rule. Lakein points out that, in many spheres, 80 percent of the desired benefit can be achieved from 20 percent of the time and effort and that exerting the additional 80 percent of the time and effort to reach perfection yields a relatively modest gain of 20 percent. If one can learn to be satisfied with 80 percent rather than perfection, Lakein says, enormous time savings are possible.

It is at this implementation stage that the choice process turns into a change process, as is evident from these practical strategies. A choice is usually not complete without change, without implementation. Change, on the other hand, may lack direction if it is not guided by a clear choice or direction. This chapter has focused on the process of choice, giving two complex examples of how the phases of choice may occur in counseling. Another common goal of pastoral counseling, the process of confusion reduction, will be considered next in chapter 10. A few pragmatics of implementation, of carrying out a decision, are discussed more fully in chapter 11.

SUMMARY

The choice strategies described here proceed from the assumption that the individual will find his or her own best decision. They trust and facilitate the individual's own process of choice, rather than attempting to impose a resolution from without.

The process of choice occurs over time, and the following summary of the developmental phases of choice counseling may be helpful to keep in mind.

1. *Clarification*
   Identify and define the choice, problem, decision, or conflict
   Through reflective listening, clarify feelings about the choice
2. *Formulation*
   Derive a comprehensive picture of the choice situation
   Define the outcomes that are desired
   Define the possible alternatives
   Clarify the type of conflict involved

3. *Intervention*
   Specify possible outcomes with each alternative and values attached to
      each
   Gather additional information needed to make the choice
   Generate additional possible alternatives
   Evaluate the alternatives
   Allow time for the choice process to occur
   Make a choice based upon all information and perspectives available

4. *Implementation*
   Take a first step to implement the choice, and keep moving
   Plan how to cope with the possibility of backsliding
   Evaluate satisfaction with the outcome of the choice
   Reconsider? Return to step 1.

ADDITIONAL READINGS

For the Counselor

AZRIN, NATHAN H., and VICTORIA A. BESALEL *Job Club Counselor's Manual: A Behavioral Approach to Vocational Counseling*. Austin, TX: Pro-Ed, 1980. A specific description of procedures used in the "Job Club," a highly effective service for helping people find employment. Such a service could be provided by a local congregation.

CRYSTAL, JOHN C., and RICHARD N. BOLLES *Where Do I Go from Here with My Life?* Berkeley, CA: Ten Speed Press, 1980. Contains systematic instructions for counselors, instructors, and students in pursuing a process of career planning.

LEWIS, HUNTER *A Question of Values: Six Ways That We Make the Personal Choices That Shape Our Lives*. New York: Harper & Row, 1990. A philosophic examination of the structure of personal and social value systems.

LOUGARY, JOHN W., and THERESA M. RIPLEY *Career and Life Planning Guide* (rev. ed.). Englewood Cliffs, NJ: Cambridge Books, 1988.

For the Client

AZRIN, NATHAN H., and VICTORIA B. BESALEL *Finding a Job*. Berkeley, CA: Ten Speed Press, 1982. A helpful workbook to accompany the job club approach (see Azrin and Besalel counselor's guide above).

BOLLES, RICHARD N. *The Three Boxes of life and How to Get Out of Them: An Introduction to Career/Life Planning*. Berkeley, CA: Ten Speed Press, 1981.

———*The New Quick Job Hunting Map* (rev. ed.). Berkeley, CA: Ten Speed Press, 1983. A short, practical book of exercises designed to help clients identify their skills through achievements. Two versions are available—beginners and advanced. The beginner version is intended for people seeking their first job; the advanced version is intended for people who are changing jobs.

———*What Color Is Your Parachute? A Practical Manual for Job Hunters and Career-Changers* (rev. ed.). Berkeley, CA: Ten Speed Press, 1994. Probably the best-known self-help resource on career change, written by a pastor.

CAMPBELL, DAVID *If You Don't Know Where You're Going, You'll Probably End Up Somewhere Else* (rev. ed.). Allen, TX: Tabor Publishing, 1990. Encourages intentionality and the use of personal strengths in determining one's own future.

LAKEIN, ALAN *How to Get Control of Your Time and Your Life.* New York: NAL/Dutton, 1989. The original self-help book on time management—clear and practical.

WHEELER, DANIEL D., and IRVING L. JANIS *A Practical Guide for Making Decisions.* New York: Free Press, 1980. A general self-help resource on decision-making skills for personal and occupational choices.

WHELAN, ELIZABETH *A Baby? Maybe: A Guide to Making the Most Fateful Decision of Your Life* (rev. ed.). Indianapolis: Bobbs-Merrill, 1980. Excellent, neutral resource for helping people to deal with the decision faced by more and more couples—whether to have a child (or another child).

NOTES

[1] Daniel D. Wheeler and Irving L. Janis, *A Practical Guide for Making Decisions* (New York: Free Press, 1980).

[2] M. E. P. Seligman, *Learned Optimism: How to Change Your Mind and Your Life* (New York: Pocket Books, 1990).

[3] Bertrand Russell, *The Pursuit of Happiness* (London: Liveright, 1930).

[4] Alan Lakein, *How to Get Control of Your Time and Your Life* (New York: NAL/Dutton, 1989).

10

REDUCING CONFUSION

> Are dislocations creative? I believe they can be. Some, of course,
> are destructive. But dislocation, with all its risks, is surely prefer-
> able to stagnation, which is the temptation when we cling too
> powerfully to what we have. When we do that, growth ceases.
> This is living death. . . . We are always being dislocated, mov-
> ing ourselves or being moved (sometimes kicking and scream-
> ing) to somewhere else along the journey. It is precisely
> dislocation that *makes* it a journey.
>
> —Robert McAfee Brown, *Creative Dislocation: The Movement of Grace*

Confusion. It is something that everyone experiences from time to time. More
than an emotion, it is a quandary that involves every level of experience—affect, behavior, and cognition. More than an ordinary crossroads, it seems
rather like being at the hub of a wagon wheel or a spiderweb, with each spoke
or strand representing an equally unknown alternative. When a person has a
high fever, reality is changed and he or she becomes disoriented, less able to
distinguish or choose. Confusion is like a *psychological* fever.

Confusion itself can have several effects on people which can be quite
incapacitating. The person may become preoccupied by the confusion, which
in turn interferes with normal thinking and memory processes and com-
pounds the state of confusion.[1] This can also decrease motivation and generally slow the person down, sometimes to the point of outright depression (see
chapter 12). There is a desperate search for comprehension and understanding. "Most people," Gilligan observed, "will grab onto the first thing that enters into their consciousness that reduces the uncertainty." Confusion may
thus increase the person's vulnerability to highly structured "solutions" such
as religious cults.[2]

Some confusion is brief, even momentary, and is more directed toward
a specific issue. A parent may be confused about how to deal with the crises

and transitions of a troubled teenager. A parishioner may be confused about the meaning of suffering or the doctrine of grace, finding that previous simplistic notions no longer suffice. Sometimes the word *confusion* is used to describe fixed alternative choices (chapter 9) or conflicts (chapter 7), especially if emotional involvement is high.

Another type of confusion, however, is more pervasive. It is a disruption of the total person—of work, relationships, and aloneness. The individual's entire perspective and purpose are questioned. Meaning is shattered. It is like a tapestry coming unwound, a vessel shattered. The feeling is one of being in pieces, and the task for the counselor is to help in putting the pieces together again. It is this kind of shattering of being that Gilmore termed *structure loss* and for which she described the counseling task of *confusion reduction*.[3]

We will address the counseling task of confusion reduction at two levels. First, there is the challenge of *crisis intervention*. Pastors are regularly on the scene within days, hours, sometimes minutes of a crisis: death, injury, fire, violence, medical diagnosis, family disruption. During these early days and weeks, your task is acute—to help manage and alleviate the crisis. As the crisis settles, however, there comes a longer and often more difficult (albeit less intense) process of confusion reduction. Usually, this involves not a reconstruction of the old order, but a seeking of new ways of constructing meaning, often with the addition of some new pieces and the omission or at least relegation of others. We will return to this longer process, but crisis intervention comes first.

CRISIS INTERVENTION

Crises are moments of memorable ministry. We have powerful memories of pastors and their partners who were there for us in times of great emotional need. The crises themselves have faded, but there lingers the remembrance of a hug, shared tears, a simple expression of God's love.

In the midst of crisis, don't expect to have the answers. To be sure, there may be great pain in need of healing and desperate questions of "Why?" and "What now?" By virtue of your calling, you will be a person who wants to help, to heal, to answer, and there may be much you will be able to do. Yet in the midst of immediate crisis, you are first and foremost God's servant. Answers and solutions—real ones—usually take time. Pastoral care starts right away.

There are six things that are usually needed in crisis intervention. These are complex skills that come with experience, but here are the basics.

1. Listen   Encourage people in crisis to talk, and listen to what they have to say. Sometimes it will be hard to hear, full of anger, pain, or fear. To begin with, just listen, and use the skills of reflection and acceptance outlined in chapter 5. Allow and encourage emotional expression. Offer pastoral support, caring, and encouragement. You are probably the best window at this point to God's unconditional love.

2. Assess   While you are listening, begin the process of assessing the crisis. What has happened? What is most needed? The issues are basically the same formulation questions posed in chapter 7. As you listen, think through what specific goals it will be important to address immediately, then in the short run, and then in the long run.

There are some specific assessments to be made in a crisis as well. Is there a risk of suicide? We will address the task of assessing and reducing suicide risk in chapter 13. Is there an immediate need for medical attention? What practical needs must be taken care of—food, clothing, shelter, or other resources? Do the police or other authorities need to be contacted? Are there steps that must be taken now (as following a rape) before an opportunity is lost? What other professional help may be needed? Are there immediate dangers?

In this last regard, it is important to consider whether there is danger of physical violence. Though it is difficult to predict dangerousness in general, there are factors that increase the risk of violence in crisis. In general, times of relationship disruption are more dangerous, such as discovered infidelity or threatened separation or divorce. Is there a history of threats or violence? Are lethal weapons available? Are alcohol or other drugs involved? Is there a specific intention or plan to do harm? In the latter case, all mental health professionals have an obligation to warn those in danger, even if it means violating client confidentiality.

Your overall task here is to assess reality, to get a clearer picture of what has occurred and what is happening now. This leads directly to the remaining tasks of crisis intervention.

3. Help with Understanding   People in crisis often have an anxious feeling of being out of control and are looking for an understanding of what is happening to them. You may need to get additional information to share (e.g., from doctors, police, or family members). You may need to draw on your knowledge of what is normal in crisis and to provide reassurance. Mostly, this involves talking through what is happening and what it means.

4. Focus on Problem Solving   In a crisis situation, you will often need to be more directive than may be your accustomed style in counseling. It is both practically important and therapeutic for you to focus on problem solving (though not, of course, to the exclusion of listening and support). What needs to be done? What problems must be addressed first, and how might that happen? Explore ways of coping.

5. Take Specific Steps   Don't just talk about how to cope. Do it! People in crisis are often immobilized and confused. Work out specific plans, and help take the first steps. Assess what each person in the crisis can and cannot handle at present, and get them involved in active coping. Taking steps to make things better often begins to restore a sense of self-control. Don't forget spiritual coping resources, too.

6. Mobilize Social Support   Whose help can be enlisted for practical and emotional support? Are there people who have survived a similar crisis who might be good companions? Who holds pieces of the puzzle to be solved? Who could provide some of the practical needs? Are there family members to be contacted? Help to increase the immediate social support circle for dealing with the problems to be faced.

It is this combination of loving support and practical problem solving that is the essence of crisis intervention. We have provided a variety of readings at the end of this chapter, which elaborate on the processes and skills of crisis counseling. Issues and methods of grief counseling will be addressed more specifically in chapter 12.

TECHNIQUES OF CONFUSION REDUCTION

The longer-term process of confusion reduction is a complicated task analogous to weaving. The loose ends are slowly drawn together into a fabric that will withstand future tugging and wear. The old weave has unraveled, and the threads and cords must be rewoven, adding new fibers in some places and recognizing others that are now too worn to be used. Yet it is the client and not the counselor who must be the weaver. Again, the inner wisdom of the client is trusted to recognize patterns of meaning as they emerge on the loom of counseling. The counselor stands beside the weaver providing support, lending a hand now and then, occasionally suggesting a color when asked for advice, and most of all believing in the vision and competence of the weaver to create a strong new pattern—a pattern that will emerge naturally from within and that will be unique for every weaver.

It is much easier to *describe* the process of confusion reduction than to *prescribe* techniques for its resolution. The existential psychologists and psychiatrists have been the masters of this description—Rollo May, Viktor Frankl, R. D. Laing. Their writings capture the richness of meaning-weaving. In reading their work, one recognizes the process.

What one does not tend to find in these writings is a description of specific techniques of counseling. Indeed, the existentialists commonly eschew the idea of *techniques*, seeing these as simplistic, mechanistic, misleading. The more practically minded counselor in reading existential psychology asks, "But what do I *do*?" The existential supervisor would probably answer with a knowing and patient smile or perhaps with a rebuff that the task of the counselor is not to "do for" but rather to "be with" the client. The trainee counselor with a tolerance for ambiguity and a fascination for intuition will stay to learn more with wide-eyed wonder, while the more pragmatic counselor walks away shaking his or her head in disgruntled puzzlement at this training that seems to rely upon osmosis.

So here our choice is a difficult one. We can describe the *process* of confusion reduction and hope that you will somehow be able to assimilate it and facilitate it with your own clients. Or we can stick to our promise of providing a "practical psychology" and describe some techniques of confusion reduction at the risk of oversimplifying and mechanizing this fragile process. We have chosen to do the latter, but with some caveats that we hope will put the techniques that follow within a proper perspective.

Caveats

In part II, we described an approach to counseling derived from the insights of Carl Rogers, and we specified some techniques used in this approach. Like Rogers, we believe that the techniques are not themselves the healing process, but only represent it—not unlike the symbols of faith that are "outward and visible signs" of truths that are deeper. Carl Rogers wrote of an *atmosphere* that one should create in counseling, and the word is an interesting one in that an atmosphere is vital to life, yet (ideally) invisible. Similarly, the client-centered writers have described optimal *attitudes* of the counselor—understanding, acceptance, honesty. The techniques of client-centered counseling are not themselves the attitudes needed for counseling. Yet they do represent them, and in a very real sense the use of these methods begins to teach and create the needed perspectives within the counselor. They are a mixture of process and practice.

In the same way the techniques we will suggest here are not themselves the process of confusion reduction. They do, however, help to facilitate the process when properly used, just as reflective listening can facilitate choice and personal exploration. Within the content that emerges when these methods are used, the perceptive counselor will glimpse the deeper process that is occurring. This, then, is our first caveat—do not mistake technique for process.

Second, it is crucial to remember that the client is the weaver and that in the most general sense it is not your task to direct the process. These techniques are not intended to control or shape what happens, only to start the loom working and the shuttle moving.

Finally, we emphasize again that these are not *the* methods for confusion reduction, only some possibilities. They are methods that we have used and found helpful in working with clients in the midst of confusion and structure loss. They have not been proven or tested in scientific research. Neither are they our own creation, for they are variations of techniques that have been widely used within counseling. In your own practice you may well discover other approaches that better fit your personal counseling style. We simply commend these to you as examples, as ways to facilitate the weaving process that underlies them all.

Reflective Listening

Perhaps the most vital technique used throughout the process of confusion reduction is reflective listening. It can be thought of as a device that presses and consolidates each new thread to the total fabric after the shuttle has passed by, leaving this new strand.

The individual in the midst of structure loss has lost touch with self, with a coherent picture of his or her own identity. The person may be quite vulnerable at this point to the imposition of structure from without, and this is one appeal of the religious cults that combine very visible acceptance with a highly structured lifestyle. The counselor, however, seeks not to impose an external structure but rather to bring out the new creation that is already within the individual.

The technique of reflective listening is particularly valuable in this process because it permits clients to hear their *own* material reflected back. It allows people to hear things replayed and to reflect upon and explore them further. This is not redundant. Rather, it helps clients to stay with their own thoughts and feelings long enough to begin to incorporate them into a whole. This is especially useful to the person who has lost the sense of self because it echoes back the content that emerges from that temporarily lost self.

No one is a perfect mirror. The counselor chooses to reflect some elements and not others and thereby influences the process. Rogers himself was forced to acknowledge this when his students demonstrated that he paid selective attention to his client's positive self-statements. Nonetheless, the goal is to reflect back the client's own process.

In confusion reduction, the clarification phase of counseling is often greatly extended. Indeed, clarification and formulation of a coherent structure or meaning *is* the process. When this weaving process has proceeded well along, it may become apparent that there are other choices and changes to work on as well, but considerable clarification is needed before this point is reached. The central counseling skill for clarification is reflective listening.

Storytelling

Remembering that the purpose of confusion reduction is the reconstruction of a coherent sense of self and identity, one approach is to have the person tell his or her story from the very beginning. Biography has long been a popular vehicle in literature, film, and drama. The enormous popularity of books (such as the work of James Michener) and television series (such as *Roots*) which span many generations may be attributable to the fact that they touch the yearning of each of us to be rooted in history. For Jews this history represents the very identity of the people. For each individual, identity is to be found, in part, in developmental history.

The telling of one's life story involves some preparation. The individual is invited to tell, in whatever fashion seems natural, his or her whole life story from the beginning. This can and often does include the showing of childhood and later pictures, mementos, personal creations such as poems or drawings, and any other important symbols of the milestones and transitions along the way.

This takes time. It cannot usually be contained within a typical counseling hour. Although the process can be spread out over several sessions, it is best for the story to proceed uninterrupted, particularly if sessions are separated by more than a few days. For this special session the counselor can agree with the client about a longer meeting time. Two hours are usually adequate, although the time necessary can vary widely for different individuals. If a specific length of time is agreed upon, the client is also more likely to pace the story to reach completion within that time. To increase flexibility, it is usually best to schedule this type of session at the end of the day or at a time when there is a buffer of available time afterward if necessary.

Your role as counselor is that of the interested listener. It is the *telling* of the story by the client that is vital, and the counselor facilitates this by listening with a minimum of interruption. Roadblocks are assiduously avoided, except for occasional questions of clarification. Reflective listening is the primary tool used by the counselor in responding to the story as it unfolds.

As the story progresses, a special type of reflection becomes useful. This is a reflection that ties together elements of the person's history. Here are a few examples of how these reflections might take form:

> "That's a theme that seems to appear again and again—swimming upstream against the current."
>
> "You felt really lost then, perhaps as you had felt before when your family moved to Detroit."
>
> "In the middle of this really bleak period, there was an amazing ray of sunshine—something that had happened to you before, too."
>
> "It's almost like how you felt when . . ."
>
> "And so again you . . ."

It is apparent that these reflections are also interpretations of a kind. They seek to tie together elements of history. The purpose is not so much to invoke a specific insight as to create a sense of connectedness through this process of crossstitching. It is *the same person* who has lived through this life, and the person who lives now is connected to all of these experiences and places and people.

This process of hearing the story from the beginning is also valuable to the counselor. It provides a total perspective within which to understand present experiences (the same process that is valuable for the client). It also provides a large number of details of the person's history that can be valuable in later sessions. These details clarify allusions and associations made by the client and provide a broader range of experiences to which both counselor and client can relate new developments. Further, it is a powerful relationship-building device for the counselor to remember these details and to continue to make cross-stitching reflections like those mentioned above as counseling proceeds. To remember small, seemingly insignificant details about a person is to communicate, "You are very important, and I listen carefully to what you have to say—even to the small details. What you say matters, and I remember it." This does not require you to remember *everything*, but the judicious recall of details previously volunteered by the client can contribute substantially to the building of a therapeutic relationship.

A caution is in order here, however. The use of such details *outside* the context of counseling, particularly in the presence of others, may be disquieting or embarrassing to the individual. It may seem a betrayal of confidence, even though the details seem small and it is not apparent to others that they were given within the context of counseling. Even if the details seem trivial, they may symbolize to the client a vulnerability and the possibility that other, more sensitive details might also be revealed. This is a special concern for the pastor who counsels and who maintains ongoing relationships after counseling has ended.

Finally, this process of storytelling can be valuable within groups as well. Frequently, mutual support groups develop within a spiritual context (see chapter 20), and an increasing number of pastors seek the mutual support of peers through ongoing "sharing" groups. For the past twenty years, we have been involved almost continually in such groups, not as leaders or facilitators but as peer-participants. We find it invaluable to have an ongoing group of friends who know us well and who share our day-to-day, week-to-week experiences—our hopes and fears, joys and sorrows, pains and insights. What has been especially helpful to us been the fact that these few close friends have also shared in our life stories and have understood the context within which new experiences occur. One way to establish such a base of shared experience is for each member of the group to take a full session to trace her or his personal life story, presented and illustrated in whatever manner feels most appropriate. This is perhaps best done after the group has been meeting for some time and has built a modicum of mutual trust. This storytelling can require a long period to complete, since each member fills an entire session. Yet it is an excellent investment in future trust and understanding.

The Card Sort

This exercise has a similar purpose and process. It collects the pieces of the individual's history and begins to place them within a larger context. It may be used instead of or in addition to the life story.

TABLE 10-1   Client Instructions for the Card Sort Technique

1. Obtain a supply of small, blank cards. Unlined 3" x 5" index cards are suitable and easily available.
2. Begin the exercise when you have a span of at least two hours of uninterrupted time. Give your whole attention to this task.
3. Begin by writing or printing on each card one small piece or experience of your life. It may be a name, a place, a feeling, the title of a book or poem, a phrase that is important to you, a date, an idea, an activity, or anything that has had some meaning for you. Put each new piece on a separate card, and write as quickly as you can. Let the process flow. One piece may lead to another, and that to another, and so on. Do not stop yourself or censor—don't try to decide whether or not something is good enough to put on a card. Write down everything you think of.
4. Continue this process until you sense that you have finished, or run out of pieces.
5. Go on to this next step only if you have time to complete it. If not, wait until a later time when you have enough time to do it in one sitting without being interrupted. Go through your pile of cards and sort them into groups that seem to belong together. The groups don't have to be logical or to make sense. Just put together the cards that seem to belong with each other. A group can be just one card or as large as you want. If new pieces occur to you while you are doing this, make new cards and add them. Continue until you have sorted all of the cards into groups.
6. Put a rubber band or paper clip around each group, and bring the stack to the next session.

The assignment is both simple because of its concrete steps and complex because of its open-endedness. This particular technique was taught to us by Susan Gilmore, although it resembles a number of other self-exploration methods. The instructions for clients are specified in Table 10-1.

Reviewing the card sort with the client in many ways resembles the telling of the life story. It also takes a considerably longer time than a normal session in most cases. Your role as counselor is primarily to reflect and to ask occasional clarifying questions. Cross-stitching reflections are valuable, and many details are learned that can be useful in future sessions. It is advisable to complete the review of the card sort in one longer session rather than trying to break it up into several chunks.

A large, open table or floor space is needed. The process begins with any category of cards. Remove the band or clip from a group, and one by one place each card face up, reading what it says and allowing the client some time to explain it. At first it may be helpful to ask a simple question like, "What does it mean? ," but soon a pattern is developed where you read a card and the client clarifies its meaning. The cards are laid out in their groups, usually in vertical columns side by side, similar to the arrangement of cards in solitaire.

You can learn much from this process beyond the many details that are provided. It is instructive to see how many cards there are. There may be card sorts as small as ten cards in two piles or as large as many hundreds of cards.

You are also given a glimpse of how the client *organizes* reality. How many categories are there? How are cards grouped—by feelings, chronologically, by people? This method samples both the pieces of the client's inner reality and the structure by which those pieces are interrelated.

A few practical tips are in order regarding this exercise. First, it is best to avoid giving more detailed instructions. Those given in Table 10-2 are sufficient, and more detail begins to shape what the client brings. For the same reason, the client is asked to obtain the needed cards. If you provide cards, it is a communication as to the ideal size of the final pile. In reviewing the cards, hold each card while the client talks about it, placing it on the table or floor with the other cards only *after* the client has finished explaining it. This helps to maintain a slower and more patient pace, and the laying down of each card represents a step of completion, another piece added to the total picture. Finally, as with the life story, it can be helpful to have a period of "debriefing" after the process has been completed. What did the client experience in completing this exercise? What are his or her reactions now? Are there any cards that should be added now, or any regrouping that seems necessary?

We recommend that before you use this method with clients, you complete the process yourself, perhaps sharing the final result with your spouse, a friend, or a colleague. This provides an insider's view of the experience and what can be learned from it.

What *are* the benefits of this process? They are perhaps greatest precisely for the person in the midst of structure loss because the exercise makes vivid the structure that continues to be present within. Elements of history are reclaimed and regrouped, and a sense of greater wholeness can emerge. The effect may not be immediate, nor should you be disappointed if no rapid change ensues. Beyond this, the exercise also seems to enhance the therapeutic relationship. The client frequently has a sense of having shared a great deal of very personal and important information with the counselor, and if you have maintained a reflective listening stance throughout this sharing, a deepened sense of closeness can result.

It is difficult to detail what you should look for during a card sort. Certainly, themes and consistencies are instructive and are the substance of the reflective cross-stitching described earlier. Patterns of thinking may become apparent, particularly binary black/white patterns that may be related to the individual's distress (see chapter 12). The questions from chapter 7 can be applied here, especially, "What is missing?" A related issue is that of balance. What is given the greatest emphasis, and what is deemphasized? Be aware that one's memories of the past are highly colored by one's present state. To an individual who is profoundly depressed, all of his or her past life also seems to have been gloomy; indeed, it is difficult to recall more positive experiences. For the time being, however, keep such evaluations and interpretations of the card sort to yourself. The experience is complete in itself and should not be marred at this point by your critiques of how the structure might be improved. Remember that the goal here is clarification and understanding, not change.

Value Hierarchies

Conflicts, difficult choices, feeling stuck, and confusion can all arise when personal values clash. An individual going through structure loss or other personal searching can benefit from greater clarity about the goals and values that guide his or her life. More generally, pastors are uniquely concerned with the values that govern the lives of those in their charge and may often be called upon for counseling as people struggle with issues of personal direction and values.

Milton Rokeach, whose work stands as a landmark contribution to the psychology of values, provided a number of helpful perspectives and approaches for counselors.[4] One is that values can be thought of as organized hierarchically within each individual. Some values are quite central and dear to the individual's identity. Others, which might be characterized as beliefs or attitudes, are more peripheral.

Consider the conceptualization of personal organization shown in Figure 10-1. The things that a person says and does (behavior) and the person's passing thoughts reflect underlying attitudes and beliefs. These attitudes and beliefs are themselves more malleable, changing with new knowledge and experience. Beneath these are relatively enduring values, some of which are more central and stable than others. At the very heart of it all is the person's core identity—that sense of self that might be called soul and that contains the person's very essence and ultimate concerns,[5] that which he or she holds dearest.

FIGURE 10-1   Levels of Organization of the Person

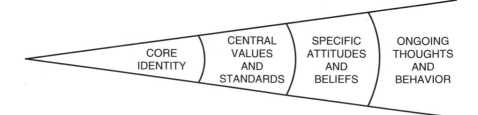

Change is possible at any of these levels. Simple behaviors can be changed in themselves. Attitudes and beliefs can be altered, sometimes with substantial influence on feelings, thoughts, and actions (see chapter 12). In Rokeach's view, the deeper the level of change, the more widespread the ripples and effects. Thus, when deep shifts occur in values or identity, major changes can follow. Similarly, when one value, attitude, or belief is discovered to be in conflict with a deeper, dearer value, sudden and radical change may occur.

There are important reasons, therefore, for helping people to clarify the values that guide their lives. Table 10-2 contains a list of potentially important values that we have used in counseling and research. The approach is modelled after a shorter list used by Rokeach. Each value is described by a key word, which is followed by a brief description meant to clarify its meaning. To use this list in counseling, make one card (a blank three- by five-inch index card works nicely) for each value, with the key word printed in large letters at the top and the clarifying description underneath. There are several ways in which this values card set can then be used.

TABLE 10-2   A Long List of Values[6]

ACCEPTANCE	to fit in with others
ACCURACY	to be correct in my opinions and actions
ACHIEVEMENT	to accomplish and achieve
ADVENTURE	to have new and exciting experiences
ATTRACTIVENESS	to be physically attractive
AUTHORITY	to be in charge of others
BEAUTY	to appreciate beauty around me
CARING	to take care of others
COMFORT	to have a pleasant, enjoyable life
COMPASSION	to feel concern for others
COMPLEXITY	to have a life full of variety and change
CONTRIBUTION	to make a contribution that will endure
COURTESY	to be polite and considerate to others
CREATIVITY	to have new and original ideas
DEPENDABILITY	to be reliable and trustworthy
ECOLOGY	to live in harmony with the environment
FAITHFULNESS	to be loyal and reliable in relationships
FAME	to be known and recognized
FAMILY	to have a happy, loving family
FLEXIBILITY	to adjust to new or unusual situations easily
FORGIVENESS	to be forgiving of others
FRIENDS	to have close, supportive friends
FUN	to play and have fun
GENEROSITY	to give what I have to others

(continued)

TABLE 10-2   *(continued)*

GOD'S WILL	to seek and obey the will of God
GROWTH	to keep changing and growing
HEALTH	to be physically well and healthy
HELPFULNESS	to be helpful to others
HONESTY	to be truthful and genuine
HOPE	to maintain a positive and optimistic outlook
HUMILITY	to be modest and unassuming
HUMOR	to see the humorous side of myself and the world
INDEPENDENCE	to be free from dependence on others
INDUSTRY	to work hard and well at my life tasks
INNER PEACE	to experience personal peace
INTIMACY	to share my innermost feelings with others
JUSTICE	to promote equal and fair treatment for all
KNOWLEDGE	to learn and possess valuable knowledge
LEISURE	to take time to relax and enjoy
LOGIC	to live rationally and sensibly
LOVED	to be loved by those close to me
LOVING	to give love to others
MODERATION	to avoid excesses and find a middle ground
MONOGAMY	to have one close, loving relationship
ORDERLINESS	to have a life that is well-ordered and organized
PLEASURE	to feel good
POPULARITY	to be well liked by many people
POWER	to have control over others
RESPONSIBILITY	to make and carry out important decisions
REALISM	to see and act realistically and practically
RISK	to take risks and chances
ROMANCE	to have an intense, exciting love relationship
SAFETY	to be safe and secure
SELF-CONTROL	to be disciplined and govern my own actions
SELF-ESTEEM	to like myself just as I am
SELF-KNOWLEDGE	to have a deep, honest understanding of myself
SERVICE	to be of service to others
SEXUALITY	to have an active and satisfying sex life
SIMPLICITY	to live life simply, with minimal needs
STABILITY	to have a life that stays fairly consistent
STRENGTH	to be physically strong
SPIRITUALITY	to grow spiritually
TOLERANCE	to accept and respect those different from me
TRADITION	to follow set patterns of the past
VIRTUE	to live a morally pure and excellent life
WEALTH	to have plenty of money
WORLD PEACE	to work to promote peace in the world

One approach is to ask the person to sort through the set of cards and to identify those ten that are most important and the ten that are least important. The top ten can then be placed in order of importance, with the most central and dearest value placed at the top, the second most important next, and so on. (Be flexible here. Some people have trouble identifying just ten and will want to add a few more. Some will give equal rank to two or three. It is the process that is important.) For other people or purposes, it may be useful to prioritize a longer list, perhaps even the entire list.

Such a process can be repeated with different instructions. What are your values *now*? What were your values *ten years ago*? What would you like for your priorities to be *ten years from now*? How would you like your values to be *ideally*? It can also be instructive to ask a client to construct an ideal hierarchy of values from his or her religious perspective.

Starting from the present hierarchy of values, you can ask, "Which of these could you give up and still be *you*?" One by one, the client can examine value priorities starting from the bottom (least important) card, putting them down one by one until he or she reaches the point where the values could no longer be let go without losing a sense of "me."

If a focal problem, such as alcohol, is part of the counseling situation, it can be useful to ask—after the value hierarchy has been constructed— "Where does _____ fit in here?" For example: Where does drinking fit in here? Which values are less important than drinking, and which more important? How many of these values might you give up before you gave up drinking?

Within our present context, however, the primary purpose of this exercise is clarification. It is meant to help the person develop a clearer sense of the guiding, core values of her or his life. As before, we recommend that you try this very personal exercise yourself before using it with clients.

The Case Conference

One more technique that we use frequently in the midst of confusion (either ours or our clients') is the case conference method. A counselor who feels lost and confused as to how to proceed may seek consultation from a colleague or supervisor. In this case, the "professional" who is consulted is the client.

Surprising? Within the framework presented thus far, this is actually quite consistent. We have argued that each person has within herself or himself a wisdom or inner direction and that an important part of the counselor's work is to clarify that wisdom. This is the basic attitude behind reflective listening. In the case conference method, this is made even more explicit. The words used to introduce this approach might be as follows:

"You are looking for direction, and I believe that the direction you seek lies within you, though it may not be at all clear right now. Although this may sound strange, I have a cotherapist who is within you—a part of you that is very wise. I would like to talk to that cotherapist now."

Counselors who have been trained in hypnosis will note some resemblance between this instruction and a variety of therapeutic dissociations that are often used in clinical hypnosis. (This is not itself a hypnotic procedure, however, nor should hypnosis be used by a counselor without extensive training and supervision.)

After the initial instructional set given above, a conversation begins between you and the client. To enhance the switch in roles, the client may be asked to changed chairs. If the client has been sitting in a chair somewhat lower than yours, the chair to which he or she switches could be one that is level with yours. This nonverbally marks the transition. In the new chair, the client becomes a consultant or supervisor. Together you discuss the client in third-person language. The "supervisor" (your client) speaks about the client either by name or in the third person (he/she) rather than in the first person.

What is the purpose of this unusual exercise? First of all, we do believe in the inner consultant within each person, and indeed there is experimental evidence pointing to the existence of a more objective "hidden observer" within each of us.[7] Second, it permits the client to obtain some distance from his or her own present situation and to examine and discuss it from a different perspective. Third, it underlines the collaborative nature of counseling and the responsibility of the client to be directly involved in the process. Finally, full circle to the original point, we find that what emerges from these case conferences is often very helpful. We use this method not only in confusion reduction, but also in choice or change counseling when we seem to have reached an impasse. We consult the "supervisor," ask where to go next, thank the supervisor for the advice, transfer the client back to her or his own chair, and usually proceed to do what the supervisor suggested. All of this must operate within the confines of clinical judgment, of course, but time and again we have found that, when we have run out of insights and ideas, the client has known what was needful. (This technique can be useful even when you do not feel stuck.)

During the exercise, you should mostly ask questions. It may be helpful to open with a general statement such as, "In working with _____ I really seem to have reached a plateau. Our work together so far has been useful, but I'm not sure where to go next, or what would be most helpful. What do you think is happening with _____ now?"

Such questions are asked in absolute seriousness, not in a playful or simulated way. You are genuinely asking for wise advice, and you expect to receive it. Some other questions that we have asked:

"I wonder if we are on the right track, or if somehow we've gotten sidetracked?"

"What do you think _____ needs most right now?"

"Which of these two approaches do you think would be better, or is neither one a good idea?"

"How do you think _____ will be doing two or three years from now?"

"What do you think are the things that matter most to _____?"

A great variety of such questions can be asked, and choice of the appropriate questions relies upon your own judgment and intuition.

A few clients have difficulty in making the transition of roles, and in such cases the exercise may be of little benefit. With encouragement and a little coaching, however, many clients are able to take on the role of a consultant, often with interesting and fruitful results.

SUMMARY

Five different techniques may be helpful in the process of confusion reduction: reflection, storytelling, the life card sort, value hierarchies, and the case conference. Each of these in its own way attempts to help the client in finding a structure with which to move into the future. The counseling process itself is much more complicated than can be captured in techniques, yet these vehicles can be helpful along the way.

Techniques such as these are not comfortable or acceptable for all counselors. A psychoanalytically oriented therapist would reject some of these approaches (and indeed much of what follows) as intrusive, interfering with the natural transference process upon which analytic therapy relies. The true existential therapist would abhor these and all other "techniques." Our more behavioral colleagues might find the methods in this chapter inexcusably "fuzzy," unspecified, and ungrounded in scientific data. Each of these reservations has its merit.

At the same time it is virtually impossible to explicate a practical psychology, useful for pastors, that is agreeable to all theoretical viewpoints. We have chosen in this and other chapters to present practical approaches that we have found most helpful, acknowledging that there is ground for disagreement all along the way. The choices in this chapter are particularly subjective because of a relative lack of scientific research on this more complex process. Nevertheless, the task of confusion reduction is one that you are likely to encounter throughout years of pastoral counseling experience, and a discussion of this process is appropriate here. We hope that from the methods presented, you can find some helpful tools and that through them you can perceive the deeper structural process that is occurring as clients undergo this tumultuous type of transition.

ADDITIONAL READINGS

For the Counselor

AGUILERA, DONNA C. *Crisis Intervention: Theory and Methodology.* St. Louis: C. V. Mosby, 1990. Includes specific counselor guidelines as well as numerous case examples.

CLINEBELL, HOWARD J. *Contemporary Growth Therapies.* Nashville: Abingdon, 1981. Clinebell focuses on therapies with a more general goal of personal discovery and growth, processes relevant in confusion reduction. The writings of existential therapists are also applicable here (see the "Additional Readings" in chapter 6). Especially relevant are Viktor Frankl, *Man's Search for Meaning* (New York: Washington Square Press, 1963), and Rollo May, *Psychology and the Human Dilemma* (New York: Van Nostrand Reinhold, 1967).

EMMONS, MICHAEL L. *The Inner Source: A Guide to Meditative Therapy.* San Luis Obispo, CA: Impact, 1978. A fascinating blend of therapy and spiritual direction. Emmons describes therapeutic uses of imagery and meditation to tap "the inner source" of wisdom and direction.

FIGLEY, CHARLES R. *Helping Traumatized Families.* San Francisco: Jossey-Bass, 1989.

GILMORE, SUSAN K. *The Counselor-in-Training.* Englewood Cliffs, NJ: Prentice-Hall, 1973. Source material on the concept of confusion reduction.

HOFF, LEE ANN *People in Crisis: Understanding and Helping* (3d ed.). Reading, MA: Addison-Wesley, 1989. Contains information and guidelines for specific crisis issues such as rape, physical abuse, divorce, and AIDS.

KENNEDY, EUGENE *Crisis Counseling: The Essential Guide for Nonprofessional Counselors.* New York: Continuum, 1984.

PELLAUER, MARY D., BARBARA CHESTER, and JANE BOYAIJIAN *Sexual Assault and Abuse: A Handbook for Clergy and Religious Professionals.* San Francisco: Harper, 1987.

SWITZER, JUDSON J., and GERALD C. RICHARDSON *Counseling in Times of Crisis.* Dallas: Word, 1987.

SWITZER, DAVID K. *The Minister as Crisis Counselor* (rev. ed.). Nashville: Abingdon, 1986.

———*Pastoral Care Emergencies: Ministering to People in Crisis.* Minneapolis: Paulist Press, 1989.

For the Client

BRIDGES, WILLIAM *Making Sense of Life's Transitions: Strategies for Coping with the Difficult, Painful, and Confusing Times in Your Life.* Reading, MA: Addison-Wesley, 1980. Describes a psychological model of transition, including a "neutral zone" that may seem like a becalmed period of no movement but that is in fact a natural part of the process. Helpful for increasing self-acceptance during a difficult transition or choice.

———*Managing Transitions: Making the Most of Change.* Reading, MA: Addison-Wesley, 1991.

BROWN, ROBERT MCAFEE *Creative Dislocations: The Movement of Grace.* Nashville: Abingdon, 1980. An unusual and very personal book from a modern theologian— an account of his own difficult life transitions and his spiritual understandings and growth through them. Very readable, very helpful.

GLASSER, WILLIAM *Positive Addiction.* New York: Harper Collins, 1985. A book about finding positive, constructive passions in life to replace what has been.

HILLMAN, ROBERT J. *There Is Hope—For Those Who Are Ill and Those Who Care for Them.* Homebush West, NSW, Australia: Anzea Mustard Seed Books, 1992. A short book filled with hope and spirit, authored by a terminally ill pastor. Overseas copies are a bit of a nuisance to obtain but worth it: Anzea Publishers, 3-5 Richmond Road, Homebush West, NSW 2140, Australia.

MOUSTAKAS, CLARK E. *Loneliness and Love.* Englewood Cliffs, NJ: Prentice-Hall, 1972.

SIMON, SIDNEY B., and SUZANNE SIMON *Forgiveness.* New York: Warner Books, 1991. On letting go of the past and moving on.

SKINNER, B. F., and M. E. VAUGHAN *Enjoy Old Age: A Program of Self-management.* New York: Norton, 1983. A large-print book filled with helpful and practical suggestions for easing the transitions into old age.

NOTES

[1]Gina Agostinelli, *Confusion: Its Nature and Imposed Limitations on Capacities* (Doctoral dissertation, Indiana University, 1987).

[2]Steven G. Gilligan, "Ericksonian Approaches to Clinical Hypnosis," in J. K. Zeig, ed., *Ericksonian Approaches to Hypnosis and Psychotherapy* (New York: Brunner/Mazel, 1982).

[3]Susan K. Gilmore, *The Counselor-in-Training* (Englewood Cliffs, NJ: Prentice-Hall, 1973).

[4]Milton Rokeach, *The Nature of Human Values* (New York: Free Press, 1973).

[5]Paul Tillich, *The Dynamics of Faith* (New York: Harper Collins, 1958).

[6]The authors express their thanks to Dr. Dan Matthews, who was helpful in editing and extending this list through his clinical experience in working with an earlier version.

[7]Ernest R. Hilgard, *Divided Consciousness: Multiple Controls in Human Thought and Action* (New York: Wiley Interscience, 1977).

11

PROBLEM-FOCUSED COUNSELING: HELPING PEOPLE CHANGE

> I have not the right to want to change another if I am not open to be changed.
>
> —Martin Buber

Over the years psychologists have come to recognize that change which occurs in counseling is very much like natural change processes that occur in everyday life.[1] Carl Rogers was a strong advocate of this view, departing from previous therapeutic traditions that attributed change mostly to the skill of the therapist (but lack of change to the client's personality or "resistance"). Rogers maintained that true change arises from within the individual, guided by his or her natural process of growth.[2] The counselor's role, he argued, is not to direct change but rather to free up the natural change process within the client. Thus, Rogers' system came to be called *client-centered* or *nondirective counseling*. Similar, perhaps even stronger views regarding the individual's responsibility for choosing and directing his or her own process of change are held by existential theorists.[3]

During the 1970s, the behavioral tradition joined in this trend toward helping people change themselves. This may seem something of a contradiction because early behaviorists emphasized a deterministic model, with the individual's behavior being controlled by stimuli and contingencies from the social environment.[4] Yet there arose within behavior therapy a new emphasis on "self-control" which, in less than a decade, became the dominant behavioral perspective. The basic reasoning is this: If it is possible to specify the conditions by which behavior is controlled and changed, is it not then further possible to teach these as *skills* so that people can learn to control and change their own behavior? This applies some advantages of a behavioral perspective—careful specification of methods and scientific testing of effectiveness—

to the new task of giving individuals greater choice and self-direction through awareness and the application of learning principles in their own lives. Suddenly, behavioral psychology, which had arisen within a deterministic philosophy, had become allied with the powerful social movement toward self-directed change.[5]

The implications for a pastor dealing with day-to-day problems in counseling are quite exciting. One thing that has characterized the work and research of behavior therapists is the attempt to *specify* how people change and how to help them do so. This is not unique to behavioral psychology. It was Carl Rogers, for example, who first subjected his therapeutic theories to scientific test in order to study their effectiveness.[6] But the scientific method has been a part of behavior therapy from its very beginning. Treatment methods are not accepted simply because they sound logical or happen to fit with a certain theory. Rather, the proof of a new technique is its effectiveness relative to other methods (or to no treatment) when examined within properly controlled scientific research.

The result of several decades of such research has been the gradual development of an array of well-specified counseling techniques with known effectiveness. To the degree that a counseling technique can be specified—that the important procedures can be clearly described—it can also be taught to counselors and to clients themselves. Psychologists have studied the effectiveness of paraprofessional therapists (those without professional degrees but who have been taught *specific* intervention skills and who apply them under the supervision of a professional) and have found that when treatment procedures are well specified a paraprofessional counselor can apply them with good results.[7] This is not to say that other aspects of the counseling relationship are unimportant. For example, the effectiveness of paraprofessional counselors in *applying* behavioral counseling methods is influenced by the extent to which the counselors show and apply the skill of reflective listening, described in chapter 5.[8] Likewise, it is clear that characteristics of the client also affect the outcome of counseling.[9] Nonetheless, this does not diminish the importance of the general finding—that it is possible to specify counseling methods—active change strategies—which significantly assist the individual in achieving redirection within a given problem area. The best approach varies considerably from one problem to another and from one individual to another. Yet it is possible to learn strategies that seem to work for most of the people most of the time, at least within a given problem domain, and to learn alternative counseling strategies so that, if one does not work, another can be tried. Further, it is becoming possible in certain areas to select the counseling approach that is most likely to work for a certain type of individual.[10] This kind of knowledge advances counseling beyond dogmatic commitment focused on a single perspective, beyond trial and error, beyond sole reliance upon intuition, to a practice founded on specifiable methods for which we have reasonable hope of effectiveness based upon scientific evidence. For the profession of medicine, this has been the ideal for decades. Within psychology, psychiatry, and counseling, the advent of this perspective is relatively (and disturbingly) recent.

It was an appreciation of the implications of this movement for pastoral counseling that led us to begin giving workshops for pastors and ultimately to the writing of this book. It is difficult even for the research-trained psychologist to keep up with the rapidly growing literature on effective treatment methods. For the pastor, busy with a thousand daily details and frustrated by the jargon and statistics of professional psychology, it is virtually impossible. Sources of information are needed that translate the current findings of clinical research into practical, usable form. In the foregoing chapters we have tried to set this information within a broader context of pastoral counseling. In this chapter and those that follow it, we have attempted to describe specific counseling strategies that can be learned and competently applied by pastors who counsel and that can in turn be taught as self-change skills for clients. Many of these strategies are derived from cognitive and behavior therapies, approaches that have only recently begun to influence the training and practice of pastoral counselors.

PROBLEM-FOCUSED COUNSELING

Seen in a slightly broader light, helping people change represents a kind of problem solving. Confronted with a problem, the individual is faced with the challenge of finding a solution and bringing about the needed change in the environment or in his or her own behavior. (Remember, we're in the *action* stage of counseling here. In earlier stages, such as contemplation, a problem-solving emphasis can be counterproductive—see chapter 8.)

This kind of counseling is, first of all, a particular way of *thinking* about problems. Many people who come for counseling are bogged down in global and depressing conceptions of their troubles: "Everything is wrong!" "My whole life is a mess!" "I just can't cope." "I have a sick personality." These unhelpful ways of looking at problems emphasize two themes:

1. Globalism—*everything* is wrong, the problem pervades every corner of life
2. Personal responsibility for the negative (though often not for the positive)—"It's just how I *am*, my personality, my nature."

Both of these themes, if accepted and followed logically, lead to gloomy predictions about the possibility for things to get better in the future.

In relationships a similar way of looking at things can occur, but this time projected outward. Again the *whole* relationship may be seen to be hopeless, but the problem may now be attributed to the personality of the other (see chapter 18). The two assumptions persist—that the problem is global and can be understood as deriving from how a person "is." Again the prognosis for change sounds poor.

Problem-focused counseling works from different assumptions:

1. That it is worthwhile to be more specific about what the trouble is
2. That change is promoted more by looking at what one *does* than by trying to analyze what one *is*.

To be sure, as discussed in chapter 10, the larger questions of being and global life-meaning are legitimate pursuits in counseling. When the goal is to bring about a *change*, however, it seems to be more helpful to be specific and to think in terms of actions rather than personalities. Thus, an "unfriendly person" is someone *doing* unfriendly things. A "depressed person" may be *thinking* depressing thoughts. A "loner" may be *feeling* lonely and *acting* in isolated ways. Such reframing of a problem from "being" to what the person is "doing" can be important for at least two reasons. First, it inherently contains a greater optimism for change, since it always sounds easier to alter what one *does* than what one *is*. Second, it usually suggests some possible courses of action toward change. If one is doing unfriendly things, the direction for change lies in identifying and altering those actions. If one is thinking depressing thoughts, the direction for change is toward recognizing and replacing the unhealthy thought patterns.

Thus, problem-focused counseling begins with shifting the individual from global and personality-focused ways of thinking toward more specific and action-oriented conceptions of problems. The choice of such a specific focus has several advantages. First of all, it is a place to begin. In facing a global problem, the challenge of change can seem overwhelming, but making a smaller, more specific change seems possible. In the long run, larger change is usually made up of such small steps. Second, it refocuses the person from global distress toward specific coping, a mental shift that in itself is often therapeutic.

Another important part of learning to *think* in this manner is to recognize that your choice of a specific counseling direction represents a *hypothesis* about what *might* be wrong and what *might* help (see chapter 7). You test this hypothesis by trying the change strategy that it suggests and seeing if it works. Whether or not change occurs, information is gained about the nature of the problem and its solution. The point is to see your counseling strategy as one guess, which may or may not be the right one. A general principle here is that if something isn't working within a reasonable time, try something else.

There are many specific change strategies that can be tried. In the following chapters we will describe on a problem-by-problem basis some of the strategies that have been found most helpful. We will particularly emphasize those approaches that are most feasible for use in pastoral counseling. Our present purpose, however, is to give you an overview of general change strategies, organized in an integrated sequence of problem solving that proceeds from problem formulation to strategies of intervention. This organization also uses three broad change-facilitating processes: awareness, acceptance, and alternatives.

AWARENESS

Problem-focused counseling, like problem-solving more generally, begins with an awareness and formulation of the problem. Your own system for conceptualizing problems is an important influence on how your client comes to understand his or her own situation (recall part III). Don't forget, in this process, to attain an understanding of how your *client* conceptualizes the problem as well: What seems to be the core of the problem from the -client's perspective, what might be causing it, what has already been tried, and what does the client imagine might help? Together you and your client develop an awareness and formulation of the problem, which leads directly toward the next step in change.

Three specific tasks are often included as part of awareness building in problem-focused counseling: specifying the problem, setting a goal, and self-observation.

Specifying the Problem

Here the thinking follows the lines of specification suggested above. If the client complains of being anxious, *what* is he or she anxious about? *When* is this feeling worst and when least? *Where* does it happen: Is it tied to particular external events, internal thoughts, and feared events, or does the feeling just seem to occur at random without any warning? *How* does the person feel and recognize the anxiety? If a client complains that a spouse is "inconsiderate," *what* are the overt actions to which this label refers, which "prove" it in the client's mind? This is a process of moving from general complaint to specific description.

One helpful way to get at this is to ask just what the client wants from counseling. One possible question is, "If our work together were 100 percent successful, how would things be different?" In addition, it is helpful to think in terms of what the client would like to have *more* of and *less* of in his or her life. If counseling were successful, what would the client be doing *more* of and *less* of? What would he or she be thinking about more and less? What would the client be feeling more or less of? From global problems (which is what most clients bring), you proceed toward "more and less" thinking in each of the ABC domains of experience described in chapter 7: affect (feeling), behavior, and cognition.

Sometimes things still get bogged down here in labels. "I would be acting more *friendly*." "My spouse would be more *respectful*." This simply is not good enough. What do friendly people *do*? What actions would a respectful spouse do more or less of? How would you *know* if a person had become more friendly or if a spouse had become more respectful?

Sometimes this attempt to specify a problem meets with resistance from the client. Perhaps the client protests that it is senseless to look at such details or wishes to focus on other areas. Remember that resistance (or "denial" or "motivation for change") is an *interpersonal* phenomenon, arising from the interaction between you and the client (chapter 8). When resistance is encountered in problem-focused counseling, we recommend that you consider the following as possibilities.

1. That you have moved too quickly into formulation and intervention and that a longer period of relationship-building (clarification) may be needed.
2. That the goal of counseling, at least at the outset, may not be change but rather choice or confusion reduction
3. That you and the client are working at different stages of change (see chapter 8)
4. That the client is correct in indicating that you are missing an important piece of the picture
5. That what you have suggested is too big a step or that the client does not understand the rationale for your suggestion
6. That you do not fully understand the client's expectations and goals in counseling

Relatedly, we find that the following strategies work well in dealing with client "resistance."

1. Listen empathically to the client's objections, rather than disagreeing or arguing.
2. Discuss specific goals of counseling to be sure that you are in agreement.
3. Share your own thinking with the client, your rationale for choosing the suggested intervention.
4. Ask the client to discuss the pros and cons of taking the next step that you have recommended.
5. Break a complicated task down into smaller, more easily accomplished parts.
6. Ask the client for suggestions of alternative methods by which the same goal might be approached.
7. If an assignment is involved, make a clear and specific agreement about what the client will do and when, and perhaps check in with the client between sessions to monitor progress.

Setting a Goal

The next step, after specifying the problem, is to negotiate a temporary *goal* toward which to work. Here again your process of formulation thinking is key. The goal you negotiate should be one that has a reasonable chance of being accomplished and of making a noticeable difference in the problem. If the goal discussed is a longer-term objective that is likely to require some time to reach, it is wise also to set shorter-term goals for week-by-week or even day-by-day progress. Often it seems more possible to make a specific change today than to approach a larger change over a long span of time. This is one reason for the Alcoholics Anonymous advice, "One day at a time."

The choice of an appropriate short-term goal can be complex, but several general guidelines are helpful. The goal should be

1. not too ambitious, lest discouragement overtake the process of change, yet hard enough to be challenging
2. specific, so that both client and counselor can tell whether it has been reached
3. a concrete step toward longer-term goals
4. acceptable and understood by the client
5. ideally expressed as an *increase* of some kind

This last requirement cannot always be met, but it is helpful to try to increase behavior whenever possible, instead of just suppressing it.

Table 11-1 lists both some inappropriately vague goals and a more specific possible goal in each case. It is obvious that the more specific goals listed in this table do not necessarily address the whole problem. Rather they represent smaller, specific steps toward solution of the problem. This is consistent with the overall purpose of this awareness process. The first strategy of specification is intended to move the person from an inert (and immobiliz-

TABLE 11-1   Broad and Specific Goals in Problem-focused Counseling

BROAD GOALS—TOO GLOBAL, NOT SPECIFIED WELL ENOUGH TO BE ATTAINABLE	SPECIFIC GOALS—CONCRETE, ATTAINABLE, REASONABLE, POSITIVE
Feel less tense	Practice relaxation exercises at least once daily
Be less inconsiderate	Express positive feedback to someone at least five times daily
Be less depressed	Find and do two potentially pleasant activities per day
Be more spiritual	Spend thirty minutes per day in meditation or prayer
Be more productive	Devote a specific thirty-minute block of time each day to _____
Stop nagging the children	Count positive and negative things said to the children and work on increasing the ratio of + to -
Cut down on the use of alcohol and drugs	Keep careful records this week of every drink and other drug use, as well as urges to use them

ing) global conception of the problem toward more active and focused thinking. This second step turns such focus and thinking into specific short-term goals that in turn lead to particular strategies for bringing about change.

Self-Observation

A third common strategy for increased awareness is self-observation. The last two goals in Table 11-1 involve keeping records of one's own behavior. There are several good reasons for careful, structured self-observation.

1. It provides accurate information about one's actual behavior and decreases distortion through either minimalization or exaggeration.
2. It provides a baseline against which change can be evaluated. In particular, it allows the individual to observe small changes in the right direction, giving a kind of encouraging feedback that might not be apparent if self-observation were not undertaken.
3. It raises awareness of the behavior in question, and this in itself is often a powerful motivator of change.
4. It can provide, if done properly, invaluable information about how the behavior in question interacts with situations in the external world. When and where is it best? When and where is the problem worse? These can be crucial cues to help in deciding how to proceed further in the pursuit of change.

The word *behavior* is used above to describe what is being observed, but remember that it is equally possible for a client to observe that which others cannot directly see—his or her own thoughts and feelings. Sometimes the goal of counseling may be to increase or decrease certain specific types of thought (see chapter 12). Observing how one's mood fluctuates with situations can also be very instructive.

Self-observation requires some degree of quantification. It means that something must be counted, measured, or observed. For less tangible targets such as mood, a prearranged rating scale from 1 to 7 or from 0 to 100 can be used. Sometimes it is the *content* that is observed, as in the instruction, "Whenever you feel upset, write down what you were *thinking* just before that." Your job is to help your client choose an appropriate focus and method for observing.

Table 11-2 shows three sample diary forms for self-observation. The first is a self-record card that we have used with heavy drinkers. The individual keeps track of alcohol consumption on a drink-by-drink basis. This is only part of one self-change program for problem drinkers that will be described more fully in chapter 16. Nevertheless, our clients have consistently pointed to this awareness-raising technique as one of the most helpful parts of the program. It provides direct, sometimes surprising awareness of the amount and frequency of drinking. It provides sensitive information about progress as the client keeps such records over the weeks of treatment. A careful examination

TABLE 11-2   Some Sample Diaries

DIARY CARD TO RECORD ALCOHOL CONSUMPTION:
Week Beginning: _____   Card # _____ _____

	DAY	TIME	DRINK TYPE	AMOUNT	WHERE	WITH WHOM
1	11/4	5:50pm	Wine	4 oz	Home	Alone
2	11/4	6:15	Wine	4 oz	Home	With G
3	11/4	9:00	Scotch	1.5 oz	Home	With G
4	11/5	12:30pm	Beer	10 oz	Restaurant	Alice
5						
6						
7						
8						

DIARY FORMAT FOR RECORDING POSITIVE AND NEGATIVE STATEMENTS MADE TO/BY SPOUSE:

DAY	THINGS I SAID		THINGS SAID TO ME	
	+ POSITIVE	− NEGATIVE	+ POSITIVE	− NEGATIVE
Monday	llllll	lll	llll	lllll
Tuesday	lll	ll	llllll	l
Wednesday				
Thursday				
Friday				
Saturday				
Sunday				

DIARY FORMAT FOR RECORDING MOOD:

DAY	TIME	SITUATION	WHAT I WAS THINKING	MY MOOD OR FEELING
Tues	12:30	Jack is late for lunch	"How can he do this to me? He doesn't care."	Angry Depressed

of a few weeks of such records may also reveal very important patterns, such as high-risk situations or predictable antecedents of overdrinking.

The second diary in Table 11-2 is designed to help two people keep notes on positive and negative communications between them. If, for example, a couple is working on increasing positive communications, this diary is an interesting awareness device to use. It may, first of all, raise each person's awareness of just how many negative (or how few positive) things he or she actually says to the other. A day-by-day record of progress toward the goal of more positive communication is made possible, and the very recording of each positive and negative statement raises immediate awareness. A comparison of each partner's diary with the other's can be revealing as well. Perhaps one partner perceives few positives coming from the other, while the other records a considerable number of what were intended to be positive messages. The use of such an approach in working with couples is discussed in chapter 18.

Finally, the third diary in Table 11-2 is an example of a less quantified but still specific diary for raising one's awareness of mood. The individual keeps records of strong feelings as they occur, noting also the situation that seemed to cause this mood and how that situation was interpreted mentally. This three-column approach is discussed further in chapter 12.

Self-observation does not stand alone. Sometimes, in fact, it can be detrimental if it is not followed by other strategies for change. Simply becoming more *aware* of a problem may be of little use if the person then has nothing to *do* about it. Increased awareness without effective alternatives may only lead to lower self-esteem, discouragement, and ultimately to a worsening of the problem. When *combined* with acceptance and alternatives, however, such awareness can be a powerful motivator of change. This is to caution you that self-observation should not be prescribed alone or out of the context of a larger counseling process.

This also raises the more general issue of counseling homework assignments. It is our perspective that *most* important change occurs not during counseling sessions but rather during the application in real life of what is learned. It is somewhat limiting to think of change as occurring for one hour during the counseling session, stopping for the 167 hours that pass until the next session, and then resuming once more as the client enters the counselor's office. Change, as discussed earlier, is a continuous and natural process. The counselor's goal is to facilitate this change process. Some of what occurs during sessions will be facilitative, but problem-focused counselors often make use of homework—of specific assignments for the client to do and practice *between* sessions. Self-observation is just one such assignment, and many more will be suggested in the chapters ahead.

ACCEPTANCE

We have proposed three general processes that help to facilitate change. The first process, raising awareness, is a beginning. Awareness can be a difficult process, however, and one that may require the person to reflect and reevaluate. To see a problem clearly can be to see the world and oneself differently. Sometimes that hurts. Pastors may understand this better than most, dealing regularly with the spiritual phenomena of self-examination, confession, and repentance.

That is why we place second in sequence the process of acceptance. Problem-focused counseling never means forgetting about the *person*. Throughout the problem-solving process, it is important to remember and support the person-focused process of acceptance. Much that is relevant to this topic has already been considered, but three points deserve mention here.

Self-acceptance

Some people act as if prolonged self-reproach were good for them. Having "slipped" or "failed" again, they enter an extended period of self-castigation and self-hatred as if this were a required period of penance and punishment.[12] Such self-degradation can slow the process of change.

Here we must clarify the distinction between self-hatred and awareness of one's shortcomings. Within a theological context, this corresponds to the difference between hating the sinner and rejecting the sin. If we are enjoined not to do the former, presumably this applies to ourselves as well: love your neighbor as yourself. The crucial importance of *awareness* in the change process has already been explained, but many people confuse this with self-devaluation, as if that were vital to repentance. To repent is to turn around, and turning is an action, not a self-defacing feeling or attitude. It is helpful to be aware of a need for change, but not to despise oneself for it. To do the latter is to diminish the crucial change condition of acceptance, which in turn decreases the chance for actual change.

For this reason, acceptance is a key issue in change. It is important to rethink attitudes of self-hatred. Here your pastoral insights can be invaluable. Cognitive restructuring strategies, discussed in chapter 12, can also be helpful in this.[13]

Empathy

A second important source of experienced acceptance is from you, the counselor. The kind of acceptance needed for change is facilitated by the therapeutic condition of empathy, which is manifested (among other ways) in the reflective listening skills discussed in part II. For the counselor, this means that empathic listening is a vital key in helping people change. This is especially important to remember if your first inclination is to rush in with the answer to every problem.

When one wants to change, it is often helpful to talk the situation over with an empathic listener. This is not to be confused with a *sympathetic* listener, who simply agrees. Remember that empathy has nothing to do with agreement and disagreement; it has to do with acceptance and understanding. Here again is the paradox: Being accepted makes it possible to change. A listener who is empathic, who reflects accurately, helps one become clearer about one's own situation and feelings and about what must be done to change.

Social Support

Often it is easier to change "with a little help from friends," with social support from others. The ways in which others can help are numerous. Acceptance is only one of them. Supportive others may enhance awareness by helping to evaluate how the change is coming along, by calling attention back to the issue, or by just being aware of the fact that one is trying to change and asking how it is going. They can help to hold one accountable for change if they agree to a periodic "checking in" about the issue (much as is done with a counselor). They can also help with alternatives, providing additional ideas and support for carrying them out. When undertaking a change it is usually helpful to consider how caring others—friends, family, pastor, coworkers— might be able to facilitate this change, to make it easier. In the same way the friend or pastor who is aware that a person is attempting to make a change might ask, "How can I help?"

ALTERNATIVES

Awareness shows the need, and acceptance provides the support for change, leading directly to the question, "What can I do?" Three general steps are useful here—(a) generating alternatives, (b) selecting and implementing a strategy, and (c) evaluating progress.

Generating Alternatives

A good way of starting when the question is, "What can I do?" is to generate a number of different alternatives. (Remember that this is for a goal of change. To generate many alternatives with a person in the midst of confusion reduction could be countertherapeutic.) Given awareness of the problem and some more specific goals for counseling, how might the person go about pursuing the goals?

This suggestion is a departure from one common model of counseling in general and of pastoral counseling in particular—that once the problem is identified the counselor will provide "the answer." The process suggested here is a much more collaborative one, a search together for possibilities rather than the authoritarian pronouncement of one solution. To be sure, you may provide some valuable ideas and suggestions, but it is at least equally important to help the client mobilize her or his own creative problem-solving resources.

The beginning of this process of generating alternatives is a period of *brainstorming* (chapter 8). This means that, for a period of time, everyone involved generates as many ideas and alternative solutions as possible without stopping to evaluate any of them. "Yes, but . . ." is prohibited here: no quick discounting of alternatives by saying ". . . but that won't work because . . ." The very word *but* is to be avoided during brainstorming. Success in this stage is finding different possibilities without immediate regard to how good they are. You might begin by asking the client to think of how he or she might go about taking the first step toward a goal that has been discussed. Meet ideas with reflection, reinforcing the client's searching for possibilities. If the "but" process begins, encourage the client to move on to more ideas and come back to evaluation later. What else might work? How else could he or she get started? When a client is stuck, you may add a few suggestions but with two precautions. First of all, make *several* suggestions rather than just one. This offers a choice and prevents the client from prematurely attaching to one idea as "the best" just to please you or because it is easier than coming up with alternatives. Second, present ideas as just that: *ideas* to be considered as possibilities. Ideas can be introduced with neutral language such as, "Here are a few things that other people have tried. I don't know if any of these will make sense to you, but they have worked for some people." Some alternatives can then be suggested with an invitation for the client's reaction.

When working with a larger group such as a whole family or (heaven forbid) a committee, the method described in chapter 8 can be used, whereby each person compiles a personal list of alternatives before any of the ideas are openly discussed. This often results in more possibilities than the usual process of an open discussion.

Suppose, as an example, that an individual wants to meet people and make friends. Where can one meet people? There are many more possibilities than most people think. If one tries to think of meeting places per se, the thinking may quickly be limited to our society's traditional spots—namely, bars and churches. But people are *everywhere*! One can meet people in the grocery store, in a park, in a club, at a wedding or funeral, in a shopping center, on a bus or train, at a political rally, at a library, at a dance, at a football game, and so forth. A good general rule for people hoping to meet potential friends is to do the things that they enjoy doing but to do them around other people. This is how they can find other people interested in similar things—in clubs and classes, choirs and jogging tracks, wherever people do what they like to do around others. The exploration of a client's complaint that "There's nowhere to meet people" may in turn reveal other important issues for counseling and change such as shyness, inadequate social skills, or a general lack of outside interests.

To suggest possible strategies for change, you need to *know* some alternatives! The following six methods are general strategies for change, techniques that turn up again and again in writings on behavior change. These focus especially on people's overt *behavior*, what they *do*. There are also various alternatives for altering *moods* and *cognitions*, which will be addressed more fully in chapter 12.

1. Avoidance   One strategy for dealing with negative behaviors (those a person wants to do *less* of) is avoidance. This is the "lead us not into temptation" method. This does not mean avoiding the *problem* itself (trying not to think about it, denying it) but rather avoiding the situations most likely to exacerbate the problem. People often find this helpful during the early stages of change, when their resolution is just beginning to become stronger.

The ex-smoker avoids cigarettes and heavy smokers. The nondrinker does not keep alcohol in the house and stays away from heavy-drinking friends when they are drinking. The idea is not to expose oneself unnecessarily to the places, people, and situations that are most difficult, that pose the highest risk. This is not the *only* possible strategy, but it is one that successful changers have often followed.

2. Active Coping   Avoidance has its problems, however. Sometimes it is difficult to avoid completely as, for example, when an ex-smoker works with or is married to a smoker. In the case of some problems (such as phobias), avoidance is a very *bad* idea because it tends to intensify the problem. An alternative is active coping: "deliver us from evil." Actually, it is not always a matter of "evil" by any means. The general strategy, though, is to confront the fiery furnace, the difficult situation by using active coping strategies. Many of these are suggested in future chapters, and they may include relaxation, self-statements, assertiveness, personal limits, "positive thinking," previously rehearsed coping behaviors, and self-observation.

3. Changing the Environment   A third alternative presents still another possibility. Instead of avoiding a situation or trying to cope with it as it is, this strategy attempts to change the environment or situation itself. Certain simple changes are designed to make life easier by decreasing the need for constant vigilance: placing a child-proof gate across the top of the stairs or keeping the house free of diet-damaging snack foods. Other simple changes reduce the annoyance level of the environment, such as coping with a teenager who likes loud rock music by buying a set of headphones. Still other changes are intended to increase behaviors: placing bright blue sticker-dots at various places in the house or office to remind you to use self-relaxation or buying a good pair of running shoes and a comfortable jogging suit to facilitate exercise. How could the environment be changed to help with this behavior change?

4. Practice   A fourth general behavior change strategy is to practice. All new skills are learned through practice. This can be done first in imagination, thinking through how to do something. How could clients ask a friend for a favor, or what might they say when meeting someone for the first time? Practice can be used in counseling sessions by role-playing situations from real life. You may model a particular skill, such as assertiveness, and then have the client practice it with feedback. Practice can also be assigned as homework, to try out a new strategy and report back at the next session how it went.

5. Extending/Limiting the Range   A fifth possibility is to begin either to extend or to limit the range of situations in which a behavior is practiced, depending upon whether an individual wants to increase or decrease it. A social skill that is learned in one situation can be transferred to another. A client may be encouraged first to try a new skill in a safe situation and then to begin to use it in more difficult and new situations. A person who has difficulty in giving positive feedback to others (making "compliments") may practice this first with the counselor, then with the family, then with friends, working up eventually to the people hardest to praise—perhaps a critical employer or a difficult relative. For new skills that are just being learned, it is best to practice them first in situations where they are easiest, settings most likely to facilitate the behavior to be practiced. Then the person can work on extending the range.

This process also works in reverse. A behavior that the person wishes to decrease may be successively restricted to very limited situations in an attempt to discourage or eliminate it. A person seeking to decrease smoking might decide to smoke only out in the garage, sitting on a certain stool. This restricting strategy has also been helpful with individuals suffering from psychotic thought processes. A person with true psychosis usually is helped substantially by an appropriate antipsychotic medication (see chapter 17), but often there is a lingering pattern of "crazy" thinking. Under these circumstances, the thoughts will get the person into trouble only if they are communicated to other people. One principle for self-control, then, is to restrict "crazy talk" to certain people, preferably a counselor who can help the individual sort it out.

6. Tipping the Balance   Finally, some people find it helpful to set up specific consequences for themselves when they wish to change a behavior. The goal is to tip the balance in favor of the desired change by making it more attractive and the old behavior pattern less attractive. One principle here is positive reinforcement of the new pattern, setting up a rewarding consequence as a kind of celebration of progress. "If I make my short-term goal for the week (day, month), then I will celebrate by . . ." This is done by arranging a sort of contract, an "If . . . then." "If I succeed in reaching my change goal, then I will treat myself to . . ." The treat, of course, should not be something destructive or inconsistent with the goal. A dieter should not celebrate weight loss by an eating binge. (Actually, this *does* happen sometimes. A person engages in a binge after being good and feeling entitled. Such patterns tend to be quite self-defeating in the long run.) Similarly, parents may teach and encourage new behavior by offering a small, special "thank-you" when a child changes in a desired way. Is this bribery? No more than adults' paychecks and bonuses, and it works. The positive reinforcement principle is the same whether it is applied in self-control or to influence the actions of others.

The opposite principle is that of punishment, which also works but must be used with greater caution. An individual may choose to impose a certain penalty if a goal is not reached, as an incentive to make the desired change. Some have given a financial deposit to a friend with the instruction that it is to be donated to charity if the intended goal is not reached. Such penalties should be constructive rather than destructive. Perhaps clients assign themselves something they "should" do or that is "good" for them but that they generally avoid. Some examples (these are very specific to the individual) might be cleaning out the garage, jogging, weeding the garden, or painting the front gate. (Notice, though, that what is a penalty for one may be very enjoyable for other people and therefore would not work.)

The use of these principles of self-change is considerably more complicated than it appears at first. We offer four suggestions in this regard. First of all, people generally have good sense about what will and will not work for them, and the process of joint problem solving between you and your client helps to eliminate unhelpful strategies. (A few tips on selecting appropriate change strategies are contained in the next section.) Second, there is an extended example at the end of this chapter to illustrate how these self-change strategies can fit together. This example applies the strategies to the treatment of insomnia. Third, there are some excellent books describing these processes in greater detail, a few of which are listed with the further readings for this chapter. Finally, the best test of whether a strategy is helpful is whether it works in the individual case (see the section on evaluation later in this chapter).

Selecting and Implementing a Change Strategy

How can a counselor select, from among the many alternatives, the most appropriate strategies for helping people change? There are several general principles.

Rule 1 is to *try first what usually works best*. There is a rapidly growing body of research knowledge on the relative effectiveness of different strategies. Some approaches are, in general, much more effective than others. Those approaches that are more strongly supported by the current scientific literature are emphasized in this book. A few additional resources to help you remain current on developments in the field are suggested in chapter 20.

A second general rule, beyond using those methods that have been found by research to be most effective, is to *try something new*. Typically, the client has already tried a number of things, and if these had worked the person would not be sitting in your office. It is useful to explore in some detail what the person has already tried. For example, a person may have "tried" an antidepressant medication for a week without effect and then discontinued it, not realizing that with many such medications the therapeutic effects are not expected to appear until after two or three weeks of regular dosage. A parent may have "tried" positive reinforcement but may have applied it poorly or in a fashion that would not be expected to work.[14] Before eliminating promising approaches on the basis that the person has already tried them, make sure that the try has been adequate. Beyond this caveat, however, the rule applies—try something new. If "nagging" the children hasn't worked the first 300 times, chances are that the 301st time won't make a difference either. If six months of bed rest has not alleviated chronic pain, it is unlikely that more months of the same will help. If it isn't working, try something new!

The same rule applies to counselors. If you as a counselor treat the person in the same way that everyone else has been dealing with him or her, it is unlikely that you will be able to help. If everyone else has been giving advice, or has been moralizing and criticizing, or for that matter has been loving and supportive, and you do just the same, there is no reason to expect that you will make a difference. Try something new! Similarly, if one of your parishioners has been seeing the same therapist for an extended period without apparent benefit, it may be time to move on. People are extraordinarily reluctant to do this for some reason. In virtually any other service area, a person would quickly change professionals if there were no beneficial outcome. Would a car owner return to the same garage if the car was never fixed? Would a patient return to the family physician if the prescriptions never cured the illness? Still, people imagine that if one year has produced no results, perhaps two years of the same therapy will. This expectation rests on very questionable assumptions about therapy—that the change emanates from the therapist, that long periods of time are required before change begins, or that "true change" cannot be seen over short spans of time. We recognize that some therapists would disagree with us vehemently on this point. Some complain—rightly so in some cases—about "quick-fix" counselors who never take the time to permit a full and complete change in the client. Yet there are far too many cases of the opposite problem—clients who have received years of needless, useless, and expensive psychotherapy for problems that could have been resolved in a matter of weeks or months with proper treatment. Some change processes do indeed take time, and it is unprofessional to recommend termination of a treatment process without due consultation with the present therapist and consideration of the value of what is being done. But the general point remains: If it isn't working, try something else.

Third, we reemphasize that the client's own wisdom is a valuable asset in selecting among alternative approaches. We routinely discuss with our clients some different ways of thinking about their problems and the various change strategies that might be used. A very important kind of information in this process is what the *client* thinks of these possibilities. To be sure, this is not the sole and authoritative basis for choice. Clients can be wrong, too, but frequently they are right. One former client, a creative artist, complained of a peculiar obsession. He reported that every time he settled down to work, he was disrupted by the thought of the face of a person he feared and disliked. He indicated that he thought hypnosis would help him. There was no reason, based on the research literature on obsessions at that time, to believe that hypnosis should work. Rather, a different approach seemed most likely to help. This approach was pursued for several weeks without benefit, and finally the decision was made to try hypnosis as he had requested originally. Within two weeks his obsession was gone.

So there are various things to consider: scientific evidence, what has already been tried, and what the client thinks might work. The fourth and final element is one that simply cannot be specified but that nevertheless remains important. This is your own intuition, a contribution of your life experience. It appears most often as a hunch, an idea that this particular method or special strategy just might be the key. This intuition is not to be given final authority, for like the client's hunches it can be quite wrong. Psychological research has shown time and again that clinical hunches about people can be altogether incorrect.[15] Many counselors make the mistake of giving undue weight to their own hunches at the expense of other kinds of information. Still, in making the final choice of which road to take, given due consideration of scientific evidence and the client's experience, there is a role to be played by your own judgment.

Happily, the initial choice of change strategy need not be the final one. The best source of information about the correctness of a particular approach will be the client's own response to it. It is to this important third issue of alternatives—evaluation—that we now turn.

Evaluating Progress

Think of every counseling intervention as an experiment. You carry out certain steps in the hope of producing a particular kind of change. That is the basic form of all science. An experiment begins with the statement of a hypothesis about the relationship between two events. The simplest form of such a hypothesis is that A causes B: $A \rightarrow B$. Now, if this is true, then changing A should also bring about a change in B. For example, if B, the state of matter (solid, liquid, gas) is related to A, temperature, then changing the temperature (A) should bring about a change in the state of matter (B). This is easily observed by heating ice or freezing steam, an experimental test of the hypothesis that $A \rightarrow B$.

But how does this apply to counseling? The Bs within the counseling setting are the problems that a client brings. The question of *formulation* is "What is causing B?" In the process of formulation, one or more possible A factors are discovered. *Intervention*, then, is actually a test of the hypothesis. If indeed A is causing B, then changing A (intervention) should bring about a change (improvement) in B.

As a simple example, suppose that a client is suffering from disturbing nightmares. Any number of A factors might be hypothesized to be the cause. A good candidate, however, is an elevated level of anxiety or physical tension. Anxiety level can, if fact, function in all four causal roles discussed in chapter 7; it can be predisposing, precipitating, primary, or perpetuating. The hypothesis, then, is that a high anxiety level (A) is causing nightmares (B) and that changing A should bring about a change in B. How could A be changed? A sedative medication would be one possibility, but there are several disadvantages to this strategy. Many of these medications are potentially addicting, and in addition they tend to interfere with normal sleep patterns and to disrupt ordinary dreaming.[16] Another alternative would be to teach the individual how to use self-relaxation skills to decrease tension level (see chapter 14). This suggests a testable hypothesis: that teaching the individual to use relaxation skills should bring about a reduction in the frequency and/or intensity of nightmares. To test the hypothesis, you would teach relaxation to the client (intervention) and together observe whether the use of this skill has any effect on the nightmares. This very hypothesis was tested with thirty-three clients suffering from intense and longstanding nightmares in a study at the University of New Mexico. Of the thirty three, twenty experienced at least an 80 percent reduction in their nightmares and twelve stopped having them altogether.[17]

The key here is evaluating, having some systematic way of observing whether the intervention is actually helping. If B is not observed, then nothing is learned. The counselor who engages in one intervention (A) after another without systematically observing outcome (B) is like the person who tries to learn how to play golf in the fog. The golfer hits the ball, and it may feel good, and he or she may imagine how far it went or how close to the green it fell. Indeed, *some* shots may fall onto the green, but without feedback the golfer never knows *which* ones were successful, and no improvement in the game occurs. Thus, unfortunately, twenty years of experience at counseling may provide very little actual *learning* experience! Feedback is crucial, both to the proper care of the client and to the professional growth of the counselor.

Evaluation is not as difficult or as scary as it may sound. It simply means having a systematic way of observing changes in the problem (B). This is easiest if B can somehow be quantified, translated into a number of some kind. A few of the types of numbers that are commonly used are

Quantity—how many?
Duration—how long?
Frequency—how many in a certain period of time?
Intensity—how much?

An important skill here is to be able to translate a somewhat vague goal into a specific measurable dimension. "I need to spend more time studying" becomes minutes spent in studying per day (duration). "I want to cut down on my eating" becomes number of calories consumed per day (quantity). "I want to feel better" is a bit harder, but might be a daily rating of mood on a scale of 1 to 7 or 0 to 100 (intensity). Each of these can then be observed using a diary form like those described earlier in Table 11-2. Over the weeks of counseling, it is possible to try different approaches and to see which of them seems to make the greatest difference. Without systematic feedback, this information may be lost. It *does* require a little more effort to help your clients devise a system for evaluating and keeping such records, but it is often a good investment of time.

Sometimes a less formal evaluation is sufficient. It may be enough periodically to evaluate together what progress is being made. An example would be the person who wants to lose weight and "weighs in" every six weeks. There are some potential disadvantages of this approach, however, which are worth considering before choosing it. First, sporadic evaluating may deprive the individual of the important regular feedback and encouragement that can occur with continuous records. Second, there can be heavy biasing of self-report if the client's "impressions" are used rather than some more systematic record. Many clients want the counselor to believe that he or she is doing a good job and so tend to overestimate the progress they are making. We observe this from time to time in our clinic for problem drinkers, where we collect both kinds of information. It is not unusual for a client to say, "Doctor, you've done a wonderful job with me. I am so much better, and I can't tell you how grateful I am." Yet the client's own records may reflect very little improvement in the drinking problem. In such cases, relying solely on clients' impressions can be very misleading.

The opposite problem can also occur. Without feedback, important and beneficial change may go unnoticed by the client. This represents a third potential pitfall if there is no evaluation of progress. An example is a family who underwent counseling to help them change the behavior of a "problem" child.[18] We taught the parents some simple techniques for helping their children learn more positive behaviors, some of the same methods described earlier in this chapter. Over a period of months, the records (kept on a daily basis) reflected very clear and major improvement so that the "problem" son had come to resemble the other two boys in the family. Yet the parents complained that "inside he's still a problem kid" and were not sure about the change. Had we been relying only on their impressions we might have abandoned the whole approach as ineffective. Instead we persisted and used the records to persuade the parents that in fact they had succeeded in bringing about a genuine change. Within a few more weeks their attitude, too, had changed (attitudes often change more slowly than behaviors). Long-term follow-ups with the family revealed that this change endured and that they continued to be much happier together.

These general change strategies are not limited to a counseling context. An individual can apply these same general principles to change his or her own behavior, and there are many self-help books based on these principles. It is possible to do the same kind of experimenting with one's own life.

Psychologist Michael Mahoney recommended taking a "personal scientist" approach to one's own problems, trying out different strategies for change and evaluating whether or not they help.[19] This is a healthy view and a more optimistic approach to self-control than the notion that either one "has it" or does not.

AN EXAMPLE OF SELF-CONTROL PRINCIPLES IN ACTION

Some new perspectives on how to think about problems in a specific fashion have been given in this chapter. Many particular strategies for awareness, alternatives, and acceptance have been suggested. It may be helpful, in closing, to consider how these methods can be combined and applied to deal with a common problem: insomnia.

People who suffer from insomnia often make the mistake of drifting into globalism and personal responsibility as they think about the problem. They ask, "What's *wrong* with me?" as if their sleeping trouble meant that there were some great defect in their character. This is encouraged, perhaps, by our language and literary images of being unable to sleep because of a bad conscience. This is sometimes the case, but insomnia is much more common than outstandingly bad consciences. In trying to understand why a person isn't sleeping (not *"can't* sleep"), it can be helpful to take the more specific way of thinking advocated earlier. What is the person *doing* that might be contributing to insomnia, and what is known scientifically about the process of sleep? From this it is possible to derive hypotheses about what might be causing the problem (A) and what might help (change in A) to bring about a change in sleeping pattern (B).

Insomnia is a complex problem, and more thorough and specific discussions are available.[20] The present purpose of this discussion is to use insomnia as an example of how self-change principles can be applied successfully.

At the awareness level, the first step is to specify the problem. This may sound easy: The person isn't sleeping. Yet there are many different kinds of insomnia, and they can have different causes. Is it a problem in *getting* to sleep, lying awake while trying to sleep? Is it a problem in *staying* asleep, waking up in the middle of the night and tossing and turning? Is it waking up in a panic or from a nightmare? Is it waking up too early in the morning and being unable to get back to sleep? Each of these means something different and may require a different type of intervention.

Suppose that the specific problem is mostly in getting to sleep. The person complains of being unable to fall asleep and of lying awake for an hour or more before finally drifting off. An appropriate evaluation measure, then, would be the number of minutes required to fall asleep and perhaps the number of hours slept each night. This is a bit of a problem because the person should not lie awake watching the clock to see how long it takes to get to sleep! Still most people can give a reasonably good estimate in the morning of how long it took to fall asleep the previous night, and the person's own satisfaction with that length of time is, after all, the crucial complaint. A goal might be to fall asleep within thirty minutes (though other people might consider it insomnia if it took them twenty minutes to fall asleep). That is a specific goal, and it is possible to use self-observation to note gradual progress toward the goal. The diary would record simply the approximate time the person first went to bed, fell asleep, and awoke in the morning.

It would be possible to brainstorm many potential solutions to the insomnia problem. The individual may already have tried quite a few: warm milk, counting sheep, reading in bed, or tranquilizers. We will explain a particular approach that has been found to be quite effective in helping people to overcome this kind of insomnia. It combines self-observation, active coping, changing the environment, practice, and limiting the range. For this reason it is a good example of an integrated program of self-change principles and of one that works.[21] It consists of a series of simple rules to follow.

The first rule involves setting a minimum amount of time within which to fall asleep. In the present case, it might be set at thirty minutes. Usually, it is not wise to set this at less than twenty minutes. So rule 1 is: If I do not fall asleep within thirty minutes, I will get out of bed.

The second rule involves limiting the range. The bed is to be used for nothing but sleep and sex. No reading in bed, no eating, thinking, planning, talking, watching TV, or making telephone calls. Bed is for sleeping. This is designed to associate the bed with falling asleep.

The third rule is that, when it is necessary to get out of bed (see rule 1), one must do something. This might be any of the things that one otherwise did in bed when trying to get to sleep, such as reading or watching TV. It might be something unpleasant, which serves as a further incentive to fall asleep: waxing the kitchen floor, cleaning the bathroom, or polishing shoes. Some people find it helpful to get fully dressed when getting out of bed, then to change back into bedclothes when retiring.

The fourth rule is to return to bed when feeling tired. If again thirty minutes pass without falling asleep, rules 1 to 3 are invoked.

The fifth rule is to get out of bed in the morning at the same time no matter what. No sleeping in, regardless of how long one was up.

The sixth rule is no napping. No sleeping during the day. Sleeping occurs only at night and only in bed.

And that's it. Usually a week of strict observation of these rules begins to resolve the problem. The body is literally required to begin sleeping on a more regular schedule (which often was part of the problem in the first place). A majority of people with this kind of insomnia are helped by these rules.

Lest this discussion be dangerously oversimplistic, however, a few caveats are in order. Not *all* sleep-onset insomnia can be cured in this way. Sometimes stress-reduction methods are more helpful (chapter 14). Sometimes depression (chapter 12) is a significant contributor to insomnia. There is a range of physical problems that may be involved, and normal aging also changes sleep patterns. Alcohol and drug abuse can be involved, particularly in restless sleep. This approach is merely the one that is most *commonly* helpful. Like all interventions discussed in this book, it should be undertaken not with the *promise* that it will help but as an experiment, as something to try that might help. Often it does. In this case it will be clear within two or three weeks whether it is going to work, provided the person abides by all the rules. If it is not working, try somethng else! Consultation by a psychologist or physician specializing in the treatment of sleep disorders may be required in more complicated cases. (Readings listed at the end of this chapter may be consulted for a more detailed discussion of insomnia and its treatment.)

Much of what follows in the chapters to come is of this sort. Different types of factors (*A*) will be considered that can cause various kinds of common problems (*B*). Alternative interventions will be suggested, based on change methods that have been found to be commonly helpful. Each is a possibility: Not a miracle cure, a quick fix, or a definitive answer, but a potentially helpful strategy to be tried. This is done within the general framework that we have presented for pastoral counseling—a joint searching, a collaborative exploration of awareness, acceptance, and alternatives.

SUMMARY

General principles of change are common to many therapeutic interventions. Once learned, these principles can be applied in changing a wide range of problems. They focus on what a person *does* (rather than *is*) and on what the person could *do* differently to change. These techniques focus on increasing awareness, acceptance, and alternatives.

Awareness
   Specify the problem
   Set a specific, attainable goal
   Use self-observation to increase awareness and to monitor progress
Acceptance
   Help the client to increase self-acceptance
   Practice empathy during counseling
   Help the client to establish and use a network of social support
Alternatives
   Generate various alternatives through brainstorming
   Consider common change strategies

> Avoid temptation or problematic situations
> Learn active coping skills for difficult situations
> Change the environment to facilitate personal change
> Practice new skills and coping styles
> Extend or limit the range of the behavior in question
> Tip the balance with incentives
> Selection and implementation of a change strategy
> > Choose methods with greater proven effectiveness
> > Try something new
> > Use your own hunches and intuitions as well as the client's
> > Evaluate the effectiveness of the strategy chosen

This last point, evaluation, is important because ongoing feedback is both the best test of the effectiveness of a strategy and your best information source for professional learning. It can be exciting and encouraging, both for your client and for you, to see change actually *happening* as various interventions are tried. Relatively simple self-observation methods can be used to provide systematic feedback of change. Such feedback teaches both you and your clients, clarifying what conditions and strategies are most important in bringing about change. A client thereby is informed of how better to cope with future challenges, while you refine your own counseling skills by discovering what does and does not work for particular types of individuals and problems.

ADDITIONAL READINGS

For the Counselor

HOWARD, GEORGE S., DON W. NANCE, and PENNIE MYERS *Adaptive Counseling and Therapy: A Systematic Approach to Selective Effective Treatments.* San Francisco, Jossey-Bass, 1987. This well-written book describes a systematic, eclectic, and goal-oriented approach to counseling, derived in part from principles of organizational behavior. Guidelines are offered for selecting and individualizing counseling approaches.

KANFER, FREDERICK H., and ARNOLD P. GOLDSTEIN, eds. *Helping People Change: A Textbook of Methods* (4th ed.). Elmsford, NY: Pergamon Press, 1991.

KANFER, FREDERICK H., and BRUCE K. SCHEFFT *Guiding the Process of Therapeutic Change.* Champaign, IL: Research Press, 1988.

SHELTON, JOHN L., and RONA L. LEVY *Behavioral Assignments and Treatment Compliance: A Handbook of Clinical Strategies.* Champaign, IL: Research Press, 1981. A practical guide for counselors in using homework assignments to facilitate progress between consultation sessions, with specific application chapters for anxiety, depression, marital problems, addictive behaviors, chronic pain, shyness, etc.

SWITZER, DAVID K. *Pastoral Care Emergencies: Ministering to People in Crisis.* Mahwah, NJ: Paulist Press, 1989.

WHEELIS, ALLEN *How People Change.* New York: Harper & Row, 1973.

For the Client

CATALANO, ELLEN M., WILSE WEBB, JAMES WALSH, and CHARLES MORIN *Getting to Sleep.* Oakland, CA: New Harbinger Publications, 1990.

WATSON, DAVID L., and ROLAND G. THARP *Self-directed Behavior: Self-modification for Personal Adjustment* (5th ed.). Monterey, CA: Brooks/Cole, 1989. The original book on how to apply behavior change principles to one's own life.

WILLIAMS, ROBERT L., and JAMES D. LONG *Toward a Self-managed Life Style* (3d ed.). Boston: Houghton-Mifflin, 1982. General, readable book on self-change methods.

NOTES

[1]James O. Prochaska and Carlo C. DiClemente, "The Transtheoretical Approach," in J. C. Norcross and Marvin R. Goldfried, eds., *Handbook of Psychotherapy Integration* (New York: Basic Books, in press); Linda C. Sobell, Mark B. Sobell, and T. Toneatto, "Recovery from Alcohol Problems without Treatment," in Nick Heather, William R. Miller, and Janet Greeley, eds., *Self-control and the Addictive Behaviours* (Sydney: Maxwell Macmillan Publishing Australia, 1991), 198–242; Allen Tough, *Intentional Changes: A Fresh Approach to Helping People Change* (Chicago: Follet, 1982).

[2]Carl R. Rogers, "A Theory of Therapy, Personality and Interpersonal Relationships, as Developed in the Client-centered Framework," in Sigmund Koch, ed., *Psychology: A Study of a Science* (New York: McGraw-Hill, 1959), vol. 3.

[3]Viktor E. Frankl, *The Will to Meaning* (New York: World, 1966); Rollo May, *Love and Will* (New York: Dell, 1969); Irving Yalom, *Existential Psychotherapy* (New York: Basic Books, 1980); Ernst Keen, *Three Faces of Being: Toward an Existential Clinical Psychology* (Englewood Cliffs, NJ: Prentice-Hall, 1970); James F. Bugental, *Intimate Journeys: Stories from Life-changing Therapy* (San Francisco: Jossey-Bass, 1990).

[4]Harry I. Kalish, *From Behavioral Science to Behavior Modification* (New York: McGraw-Hill, 1981); Frederick H. Kanfer and Jeanne S. Phillips, *Learning Foundations of Behavior Therapy* (New York: John Wiley, 1970).

[5]Michael J. Mahoney and Carl E. Thoresen, *Self-Control: Power to the Person* (Monterey, CA: Brooks/Cole, 1974); Paul Karoly and Frederick H. Kanfer, *Self Management and Behavior Change* (Elmsford, NY: Pergamon Press, 1982).

[6]Carl R. Rogers and R. Dymond, *Psychotherapy and Personality Change* (Chicago: University of Chicago Press, 1954).

[7]Andrew Christensen, William R. Miller, and Ricardo F. Munoz, "Paraprofessionals, Partners, Peers, Paraphernalia, and Print: Expanding Mental Health Service Delivery," *Professional Psychology* 9 (1978): 249–70; Joseph A. Durlak, "Comparative Effectiveness of Paraprofessional and Professional Helpers," *Psychological Bulletin* 86 (1979): 80–92.

[8]William R. Miller, Cheryl A. Taylor, and JoAnne C. West, "Focused versus Broad-Spectrum Behavior Therapy for Problem Drinkers," *Journal of Consulting and Clinical Psychology* 48 (1980): 590–601; William R. Miller, R. Gayle Benefield, and J. Scott Tonigan; "Enhancing Motivation for Change in Problem Drinking: A Controlled Comparison of Two Therapist Styles," *Journal of Consulting and Clinical Psychology* 61 (1993): 455–61.

[9]For example, see Rudolf H. Moos, John W. Finney, and Ruth C. Cronkite, *Alcoholism Treatment: Context, Process, and Outcome* (New York: Oxford University Press, 1990).

[10]This is increasingly true in the treatment of problem drinkers. For a discussion see William R. Miller, "Matching Problem Drinkers with Optimal Treatments," in Reid K. Hester and William R. Miller, eds., *Handbook of Alcoholism Treatment Approaches: Effective Alternatives* (Elmsford, NY: Pergamon Press, 1989), 175–203. Psychiatric thinking has also moved in this direction: Samuel Perry, Allen Frances, and John Clarkin, *A DSM-III-R Casebook of Treatment Selection* (New York: Brunner/Mazel, 1990).

[11]These same three principles of change have been recognized by Al-Anon, under the names of Awareness, Acceptance, and Action. See Al-Anon Family Groups, *In All Our Affairs: Making Crises Work for You*. (New York: Author, 1990).

[12]Sidney B. Simon, *Vulture: A Modern Allegory on the Art of Putting Oneself Down* (Allen, TX: Argus Communications, 1977).

[13]William R. Miller, "Including Clients' Spiritual Perspectives in Cognitive-Behavior Therapy," in William R. Miller and John E. Martin, eds., *Behavior Therapy and Religion: Integrating Spiritual and Behavioral Approaches to Change* (Newbury Park, CA: Sage Publications, 1988).

[14]William R. Miller and Brian G. Danaher, "Maintenance in Parent Training," in John D. Krumboltz and Carl E. Thoresen, eds., *Counseling Methods* (New York: Holt, Rinehart & Winston, 1976).

[15]An excellent review of research on clinical judgment can be found in Jerry S. Wiggins, *Personality and Prediction: Principles of Personality Assessment* (Reading, MA: Addison-Wesley, 1973).

[16]Institute of Medicine, *Sleeping Pills, Insomnia, and Medical Practice* (Washington, DC: National Academy of Sciences, 1979).

[17]William R. Miller and Marina DiPilato, "Treatment of Nightmares via Relaxation and Desensitization: A Controlled Evaluation," *Journal of Consulting and Clinical Psychology* 51 (1983): 870–77.

[18]Miller and Danaher, "Maintenance in Parent Training."

[19]Michael J. Mahoney, *Self-change: Strategies for Solving Personal Problems* (New York: Norton, 1979).

[20]Robert L. Williams, Ismet Karacan, and Constance A. Moore, *Sleep Disorders: Diagnosis and Treatment* 2d ed. (New York: John Wiley, 1988).

[21]Richard R. Bootzin and Perry M. Nicassio, "Behavioral Treatments for Insomnia," *Progress in Behavior Modification* 6 (1978): 1–45; T. J. Knapp, D. L. Downs, and J. R. Alperson, "Behavior Therapy for Insomnia: A Review," *Behavior Therapy* 7 (1976): 614–25.

12

MOOD, GRIEF, AND DEPRESSION

I do have periods of what to me is incredible depression. As high as I can get, I'm capable of being that low. There are times when I am very sad, times when I'm lonely; there are times when I'm unhappy and when I feel sorry for myself. What have I got to feel sorry for myself about? I have everything. But it has nothing to do with what you've got or where you are. It's the human condition. To run the gamut of these emotions is a great part of the living experience.

—John Denver

This section of our book has been in one way the easiest and in another way the most challenging to write. Having provided a context for pastoral counseling and general strategies for clarification, formulation, and intervention, we turn now to specific methods for dealing with common problems brought to counselors. This is a difficult task because there are no definitive and universal answers, guaranteed counseling formulas, or "quick fix" instructions. People's problems and the process of change itself are complicated and variable. Yet we can and do discuss specific alternative counseling approaches, many of which have been developed and clarified through psychological research over the past three decades. We have tried to emphasize methods that are well specified, where the effective elements of the change process are better understood. Such specification makes it easier for us to explain the method to you and for you in turn to apply it with your clients. We have tried to provide guidelines to help you recognize and understand problems and to know when and how to intervene (or to refer). With each chapter we have again provided a list of further readings and resources for those who wish to pursue a topic in greater depth.

Where research exists on the relative effectiveness of different approaches, we have tended to favor those with better-documented efficacy. We do not mean to imply, however, that the methods presented in the chapters that follow represent *the* way, the only way, or even the best way to intervene with a given individual or problem. Rather, we will describe some perspectives and intervention approaches that we find useful in our own work, that have stood the test of time and research, and that we believe may be helpful and effective when added to the repertoire of the pastoral counselor. We begin in this chapter with some of the most common problems of counseling addressed by pastors: mood, grief, and depression.

WHAT'S NORMAL?

Everyone struggles with sadness, grief, or shifting moods. These are normal, a part of living in a bittersweet world. It is part of pastoral counseling to support people through these changes. For some, however, moods go beyond the limits of normal adjustment and reaction. They become too extreme, prolonged, or debilitating. They become problems and require some kind of intervention.

One kind of extreme is what is known to psychologists as *depression*. More than a feeling of being down or blue, depression is a particular set of symptoms that distinguishes normal and healthy mood states from the extreme and unhealthy. Depression is common. At least 10 percent of all adults will become seriously depressed at some time during their lives, and less severe forms of depression will touch many more of us. Another important though rarer type of extreme mood, manic states, will be discussed later.

MOOD VERSUS DEPRESSION

Many counselors confuse mood with depression, partly because the word *depressed* has a popular meaning as well as a technical one. People say, "I am feeling depressed," or "You look depressed," to refer to mood states of sadness, fatigue, demoralization, even loneliness. For the professional counselor it is important to know the difference between "down" moods and true depression.

Mood is a general term. It refers to how a person feels and generally comes in two varieties—good moods and bad moods. When you ask someone, "How are you?" you may be asking the person to tell you about her or his present mood. The answers given to this general question often reflect this positive-or-negative quality of moods: "Pretty good," "Not so well, really," "Just fine," or "Having a bad day." There are dozens of words that describe particular moods, such as *melancholy, ecstatic, pensive, frivolous, moribund*, or *relaxed.* Our experience of moods, however, is that they are more or less positive or negative. It is quite normal for moods to shift frequently, even rapidly. A particular experience may "pick you up" or "bring you down." Such phrases all refer to mood and have little or nothing to do with true depression.

So what is *depression*? It is a syndrome, a set of symptoms or diagnostic signs that tend to appear together. A head cold is a syndrome, with symptoms including stuffy or runny nose, sneezing, coughing, sore throat, low-grade fever, headache, or other aches and pains. Not all of those signs must be present to diagnose a head cold, but it is the observation of this *set* of symptoms that makes it possible to recognize the head cold and to distinguish it from other kinds of illnesses.

Depression is not an illness in the same sense as a head cold, but it is a recognizable syndrome and one with which every competent counselor must be familiar. Although there is a set of frequent symptoms of depression, it is important to realize that not all of these signs must be present, nor is there any single symptom that *must* be present. As with the head cold analogy used above, any one of the symptoms on the list may be missing, and the syndrome is recognized by the *pattern* of symptoms. This means that the diagnosis of depression is not a simple matter. Many people complain to a pastoral counselor that they are "depressed" but do not, in fact, show the clinical syndrome of depression. Likewise, it is quite possible to be depressed without feeling sad or blue and certainly without appearing dejected to other people. Most people do not understand the difference between mood and depression, but it is vital for the pastoral counselor to do so.

Recognizing Depression

If an individual comes to you complaining of "depression," it is useful first to find out exactly what the person means by this. If you employ the reflective listening skills discussed in chapter 5, an explanation should emerge naturally as part of the clarification phase of counseling. Some people, in saying that they are depressed, mean that they are sad; others mean that they are grieving some loss. Still others mean that they are angry or lonely or fatigued or burned out. Some use this description as an overture to discussing a marital problem or a work crisis or a spiritual search. Listening carefully and reflectively will reveal more about what is meant by "depressed."

As the story unfolds, the process of formulation begins. As part of the first question posed in chapter 7—"What is troubling this person?"—it is vital to be able to recognize a few common syndromes that do occur, that have a kind of life of their own, and that require certain types of intervention. One of these is depression. It bears repeating here that you should be evaluating the possibility of depression *even if the individual is not complaining of sad moods* because depression has many masks. Depressed people sometimes present themselves as angry or cranky. The first indications you see may be multiple physical complaints or a passing mention of problems in sleeping or in concentrating at work. The encountering of any of a set of key indicators should set off a little signal in your mind, prompting you to check more carefully for the possibility of true depression.

The key symptoms of depression are presented in Table 12-1. The number of these that must be observed to diagnose depression is somewhat arbitrary. The current psychiatric convention is to diagnose major depression when five or more are present.[1]

For the pastoral counselor, the important issue here is not one of making a perfect diagnosis but rather of recognizing the syndrome of depression, which calls for particular kinds of action. The pastor is in a uniquely advantageous position to recognize depression for several reasons. First, the pastor has ongoing contact with the people he or she serves and can observe the prolonged periods of unusual behavior typical in depression. Second, the pastor often has been familiar with the person before the onset of the depression and

---

TABLE 12-1 Key Signs of Depression[1]

1. *Depressed mood.* The individual may complain of feeling sad, lost, hopeless, irritable, or empty. These feelings are persistent rather than transitory, occurring almost all day or every day.
2. *Loss of interest or pleasure in usual activities.* Typically pleasurable events and activities are no longer found enjoyable. Sexual drive may decrease. This absence of joy or pleasure may occur even though the individual does not "feel depressed." It is the absence of normal pleasure, a loss of interest in what was previously enjoyed. The individual may withdraw from activities.
3. *Change in appetite.* The person may lose appetite or may begin eating more. This may appear as a noticeable weight loss or gain.
4. *Change in sleep pattern.* Either of two opposites may occur. The individual may begin sleeping more or may suffer insomnia most days.
5. *Change in movement.* The individual may appear physically slowed down, moving and talking more slowly than usual. Conversely, the individual may appear more agitated than usual.
6. *Fatigue.* The person experiences a general lack of energy, tiredness, or difficulty in coping because of feeling "drained."
7. *Feelings of worthlessness, self-reproach, or guilt.* These are particularly likely to be seen by the pastoral counselor. The guilt and self-reproach are out of proportion— excessive and inappropriate in scope or intensity. The person may feel unforgivable, condemned, cursed, or abandoned by God.
8. *Change in thinking and concentration.* A depressed person often has difficulty in concentrating and thinking or in making decisions. Remember that this is a fairly consistent and persistent state and is a change from the person's normal condition.
9. *Suicidal thoughts and acts.* The individual may frequently think about death, wish to be dead, think about committing suicide actively or passively. Actual suicide attempts may be made (see chapter 13).

so is able to compare present with past behavior. This is crucial because all nine of the signs listed in Table 12-1 represent changes from previous behavior. Third, people often turn first to their pastor when feelings and signs of depression emerge. Certain of the signs, particularly guilt, self-reproach, and suicidal thoughts, are especially likely to be brought to the pastor who is perceived as warm, understanding, and open to discussing personal issues.

When in your counseling you encounter one or more of these signs in a client, you should consider whether any of the others might also be present. As the list of symptoms shown by the individual grows longer, the chances increase that the person is suffering not from normal mood fluctuations but rather from clinical depression. In evaluating this, recall that these are *persistent changes* in the person's behavior. They are not there one day and gone the next. The change persists for two weeks or more and often much longer. The average length of a depressive episode is between three and nine months. Also recall that these signs represent changes from the person's previous behavior.

There are important reasons for you to recognize depression and intervene. Depressed people do not always recognize and understand their condition. Yet depression, if not addressed, can contribute to declines in physical health,[2] social relationships, self-esteem, and spiritual life. It is associated with increased risk of suicide (see chapter 13) and alcohol/drug problems. Children and other family members of depressed people also tend to suffer adjustment and relationship problems.[3]

WHAT CAUSES DEPRESSION?

The truth is that there is no single cause of depression; there are many causes. Five major types of factors that can cause depression will be considered here. Any one of these can be sufficient to set off a depressive episode, but more often the cause is more complicated, involving several of these factors. Formulation of the causes of depression in a particular case is a complex process but a vital one because different causes may require different treatment approaches. What works well for depression resulting from one cause may be useless or harmful when the cause is of another type.

These factors can influence *mood* as well as depression. The factors discussed below can result in a low or down mood in the short run. Sustained over time, such factors may then result in longer-term depression so that the individual does not "snap back" from the low mood. This is, in most cases, a matter of degree rather than black-and-white categories. This means that the following causes can fruitfully be considered in working with any client suffering from mood problems, even if such problems are not sufficiently severe to qualify as clinical depression. The five factors can be remembered by the acronym STORC: **S**ituational factors, **T**hought patterns, **O**rganic factors, **R**esponses, and **C**onsequences.

Situational Factors

Some situations are depressing in themselves. Virtually anyone in such situations would experience a change in mood and if the situation is sufficiently prolonged or intense would become depressed. For a variety of reasons, some individuals are more susceptible (predisposing causes) to situationally induced depression, but the importance of the situations themselves must not be overlooked. It is sometimes easy, working with an individual in the confines of a private office, to forget the client's world, his or her external and social realities.

What kinds of situations increase the chances of depression? One factor to consider is *stress*, which will be discussed more thoroughly in chapter 14. Prolonged exposure to stressful situations increases the chances of becoming depressed.[4] Such stressors include time pressure, difficult social relationships, noise and crowding, financial worries, physical pain, threats to health and welfare, and social evaluation.

A second significant situational factor is *loss*. The most obvious kind of loss is the death of a loved one, but grieving may also occur over the loss of a friendship, marriage, job, material possession, pet, or opportunity. A normal grieving process occurs in such situations, and most pastors are familiar with the stages of grieving hypothesized by Kubler-Ross to describe this pattern.[5] In some cases, however, the grief reaction becomes abnormally intense or prolonged. There are no objective criteria to determine how long is "too long." Pastors, who stand beside so many people in the grieving process, are probably better judges of this than most psychologists. There are, however, some helpful guidelines for recognizing abnormal grief reactions; these are described in a section on grief counseling later in this chapter.

There is a third type of situation known to contribute to depression. All of us need a certain amount of positive feedback, caring, and regard from those around us. Sometimes people find themselves in situations or occupations where there is *too little positive reinforcement*. They experience mostly criticism and demands, with relatively little encouragement and support. In relationships this is often called "being taken for granted" or "not appreciated." Living in such situations, relationships, or occupations for prolonged periods can result in an increasing drift in the direction of depression.

Thought Patterns

A second general type of factor believed to contribute to depression is cognitive—how a person thinks. The relationship is complex,[6] but certain patterns or habits of thought do tend to be associated with depression no matter how positive the individual's life situation may be.[7] Thus, sometimes friends are puzzled at the dejection of someone who "has everything" and who seems downcast in spite of "everything going right." Of course, if depressing situations are combined with depressing ways of looking at the world, the effect is still greater.

What kinds of thought patterns foster depression? One common one is *negative self-statements*. Depressed people frequently tell themselves negative things. "I'm no good." "I failed again." "No one ever really loved me." "I'm ugly" (stupid, incompetent, clumsy, weak, or dull—fill in the blank with your own fears). If a friend ever said such derogatory things in so consistent a fashion, that person would not remain a friend for long. Yet quiet, continual self-criticism is the order of the day for some people. Each statement takes a little chunk out of one's self-esteem.

Another kind of thought pattern that may damage one's happiness is what Albert Ellis has called *irrational beliefs*.[8] These are mostly unrealistic expectations of how the world, other people, or oneself should be. Often revolving on concepts of "should," these beliefs may well have important (sometimes distorted) content from prior religious or moral training and thus may emerge readily in pastoral counseling. An example is the belief that "everyone should love me and approve of me for everything that I do, and if anyone disapproves of something I do it is a terrible tragedy which must be remedied right away." Few people, perhaps, would consciously admit to such an extreme belief, but some certainly behave as if it were true. What are the consequences of believing this? First of all, one is likely to be stressed most of the time because the disapproval of others for at least some actions is inevitable for anyone who is not a hermit. Further, a substantial amount of the person's time will be eaten up with trying to make amends for perceived disapproval. This means spending more and more time with those who disapprove and less and less time with those who already are loving and caring. Furthermore, if the individual succeeds in bringing about self-change to please the critics, then there will be another set of people who will almost certainly be displeased (perhaps those who liked the person as she or he was!). Thus, an irrational belief, an unreasonable expectation, leads the person into a cycle of behaviors, thoughts, and emotions that spins in the direction of depression.

A third thought pattern characteristic of depressed people is *selective attention and memory*. Such a person tends to overlook successes and positive feedback and to focus on and remember the negative. One cutting criticism in the company of a hundred loving and positive comments stands out as "the real truth." Looking back over one's life from the vantage point of depression, it looks as though it has mostly been empty, futile, negative. To some extent this is the *result* of depression—people already depressed tend to look at the world through these eyes[9]—but it also becomes part of the self-perpetuating cycle.

A fourth depressing perspective is *pessimism*. Expecting the worst has a way of becoming a self-fulfilling prophecy. People who believe that nothing they do will make any difference soon stop trying. They assume that they are unable to do things and never challenge the assumption. They expect to fail.

One final issue is *guilt*. Earlier we discussed excessive and inappropriate guilt, which implies that there is a normal and appropriate level of guilt. Guilt is not an evil that should be totally eliminated. Guilt is an important element of personal development and social cooperation. The individual who commits antisocial acts without a trace of remorse is at least as pathological as the one who suffers the slings and arrows of outrageously exaggerated guilt. It is the latter of these two, however, who is the more prone to depression. Holding oneself personally responsible and accountable for untoward outcomes can end in depression. By virtue of his or her profession, the pastor is in a uniquely powerful position to help such individuals in dealing with guilt feelings, whether appropriate or inappropriate (a judgment surely difficult to make in some cases). Unlike the psychologist whose tools are often limited to "talking the person out of it," the pastor has at her or his disposal a richer array of concepts, approaches, and rituals appropriate for the resolution of guilt. Significant aspects of the client's own belief system merit exploration here, including forgiveness, grace, and expiation.

Organic Causes

The psychologically oriented pastoral counselor is inclined to look for *psychological* causes when depression is encountered. Indeed, many counselors are trained to eschew biological theories and the use of medical interventions such as medication. Yet it is abundantly clear from current research that certain kinds of depression have important biological roots and can be substantially relieved through the appropriate use of medications.[10] The counselor who is unaware of this biological side of depression is overlooking significant information. Counseling may be quite slow or ineffective with certain types of depression that would respond well to medication. Failure to recognize this, in fact, may substantially endanger the life and welfare of the client, who becomes increasingly depressed by his or her failure to respond to treatment.

What we are saying is this. Sometimes depression responds well to biological treatment. Sometimes it responds well to psychological approaches. If you use only one approach, you will help some but not others. To cling to any single strategy is a dangerous disservice to clients undergoing great suffering and known to have an elevated risk of suicide.

How can you know when a biological approach, such as an antidepressant medication, should be tried? One pragmatic sign is that the depression does not respond to ordinarily effective counseling strategies. The cognitive-behavioral counseling approach to be discussed later in this chapter has been found, in two decades of research, to be at least as effective on the whole as antidepressant medication.[11] Yet neither strategy works for all, and when one approach isn't working, another should be tried.

A second factor to consider is the severity of depression. In addition to the signs of depression listed in Table 12-1, there is a second set of symptoms characteristic of severe depression (sometimes called *melancholia*) that may respond to antidepressant medication. These distinguishing signs are outlined in Table 12-2. Differentiations based on this list are by no means perfect. To the extent that several of these signs are present in a client, however, you are well advised to seek the consultation of a competent biological psychiatrist (see chapter 19).

Some of the signs in Table 12-2 overlap with those in Table 12-1. In three cases (loss of pleasure, guilt feelings, and change in movement), the difference is one of degree—these signs are more likely to appear in severe depression and to appear with greater intensity. Insomnia and appetite change are also characteristic of depression in general, but in the case of melancholia only one type or direction is characteristic: terminal insomnia (rather than onset insomnia or excessive sleeping) and loss of appetite (rather than appetite or weight increase). It is not typical for ordinary depression to be worst in the morning, but this is often characteristic of melancholia. Depression that is more reactive to one's life situation might be expected to be least severe upon awakening and to worsen as the day (and contact with a depressing situation) progresses. Finally, though it is difficult to define, people with melancholic depression sometimes have a sense that their depressed mood has a distinct quality, that it *feels different* from ordinary sadness or grief. Some of our clients have complained of feeling that "something is wrong inside." In any event, it is important to be aware of and recognize this type of depression because it is severe and often responds well to antidepressant medications.

TABLE 12-2   Characteristics of Severe Depression (Melancholia)[1]

1. *Loss of pleasure.* The loss of pleasure from all or almost all activities is particularly characteristic of melancholia. Nothing is enjoyable.
2. *No response to ordinarily pleasant events.* Relatedly, the person does not react to activities or events that normally would be enjoyed. He or she doesn't feel better, even temporarily, when something "good" happens. Nothing seems to help.
3. *Morning depression.* Melancholia depression is frequently, though not always, worst in the morning, and the person begins to feel somewhat better as the day progresses.
4. *Terminal insomnia.* A frequent sleep problem is that of waking up early in the morning (two hours or more before the usual time) and being unable to get back to sleep. This is different from onset insomnia, in which the person has difficulty in getting to sleep in the first place.
5. *Major change in movement.* A major slowing down or agitation may be observed, with a very noticeable change from the person's previous behavior.
6. *Loss of appetite.* If appetite changes, it is in the direction of loss of interest in food. Major weight loss may occur.
7. *Extreme guilt.* Feelings of inappropriate guilt may be particularly strong.
8. *Distinctive quality.* This kind of depression often "feels different" from ordinary experiences of sadness or grief.

In addition to melancholia, there is another type of mood-related (affective) disorder that it is vital to recognize when you see it. Within the general population it is relatively rare (fewer than 1 percent will be so diagnosed in their lifetimes), yet its effects are so potentially devasting and dangerous and it is so readily treatable in most cases that a failure of diagnosis is a serious matter indeed.

This is *bipolar disorder*, also known as *manic-depressive illness*. It is a particular type of disorder or family of disorders, with a partly inheritable cause and a fairly effective treatment. In its classic form, the individual cycles back and forth between episodes of depression (as described above) and *manic* episodes.

The characteristic signs of a manic episode are listed in Table 12-3. Again, remember that these represent *changes* from the individual's previous pattern. A person who has always had poor judgment and high self-esteem and who has always been talkative and restless is not the kind of person being considered here. Furthermore, these are not transient changes, here one day and gone the next. Rather, they are persistent states, lasting at least one week and usually much longer. They tend to begin and end abruptly. The average length of a manic episode is two to three months. It is also noteworthy that manic

---

TABLE 12-3   Key Signs of a Manic Episode[1]

1. *Elevated mood.* The individual may appear excessively cheerful, optimistic, enthusiastic, "on top of the world," though mood may also change in the direction of unusual irritability. This mood is uncharacteristic of the person's normal state, lasts at least a week, and is a definite change from previous mood. The individual may also express quite inflated ideas of his or her own importance and generally shows high self-regard.
2. *Increased activity.* The person becomes more active physically, socially, and/or sexually. Work activity may increase sharply. The person may show or complain of restlessness.
3. *Talkativeness.* The individual becomes uncharacteristically talkative and may appear driven to talk. Speed of speech may increase.
4. *Racing thoughts.* The person complains of racing thoughts, of having a head full of ideas. In listening to the person, he or she may seem to jump rapidly from one idea to another.
5. *Decreased need for sleep.* Not to be confused with insomnia (inability to sleep), this sign involves fewer hours of sleep per night because the person experiences less *need* for sleep.
6. *Distractibility.* The individual may show an unusually short attention span, and he or she is easily distracted.
7. *Poor judgment.* The person shows an uncharacteristic tendency to become involved in high-risk, stimulating, pleasurable activities. Common examples include heavy drinking or drug use, shopping sprees, foolish spending or business ventures, sexual affairs, sudden traveling, or minor law violations.

episodes rarely occur only once. By current conventions, at least three of the seven signs in Table 12-3 are required to diagnose a manic episode.[1]

For better or for worse, people having bipolar disorder do not always show clear manic episodes. It is now generally accepted, however, that people who *do* show manic episodes do have bipolar disorder, and most of them will develop major depressions in time if they have not already done so. The ability to recognize a manic episode for what it is, then, is an important counselor skill. It can save the individual from years of needless suffering, social disapproval, ruined relationships, and sometimes disastrous outcomes. Once again, a pastor who remains in contact with people over extended periods is in a good position to recognize such patterns of change in behavior and to intervene.

Before leaving the biological causes of depression, several other potential factors should be mentioned. A sudden, acute and severe depression is not uncommon after major shocks, especially physical shocks like major surgery or traumas such as rape. Depression can emerge and linger for a time after an illness like influenza or pneumonia. Postpartum depression does not occur after every birth but is common. These kinds of depression tend to pass with time, but their severity should not be underestimated. The days and weeks after a major life event are prime times for pastoral visits.

Attention is also being given to relationships between mood and diet. People who consume large amounts of caffeine, sugar, and carbohydrates may experience mood swings and may fall into a cycle of consuming still more of the quick energy source to fight off a falling mood. This in turn results in still greater mood swings. Such individuals should be evaluated for hypoglycemia. Other people seem to have unique sensitivities to certain food groups, and their mood may be affected. Inquiry about dietary habits can be helpful, particularly in the cases of puzzling mood shifts that occur at predictable times of day and do not seem to obey the rules of other types of causes.

Alcohol or other drug abuse is an important possibility to consider when depression is encountered in a client. Alcohol is a depressant drug. The use of alcohol or other sedative medications can exacerbate depression, as can the abuse of a variety of other substances including tranquilizers, stimulants, and opiates. Routing questions about the person's use of alcohol and drugs will sometimes yield important clues as to the involvement of these substances in depression.

Finally, a seasonal affective disorder is now recognized, in which depression begins predictably during the same two-month period of the year and similarly lifts during a consistent six-day period. As a rule of thumb, this pattern must have occurred at least three times (though not necessarily in consecutive years) before its seasonal nature is recognized. Assuming there is no obvious external explanation (such as family, activity, employment, or social changes with the seasons), a variety of biological factors may underlie such a pattern. Changes in light, allergies, and temperature have been considered as possible causes, and exposure to bright light may offer relief.[12]

Responses: Behavioral and Lifestyle Factors

Certain aspects of an individual's behavior may also contribute to the genesis or exacerbation of depression. A few of the more common ones that you may encounter are discussed here.

One useful area to consider is the person's *social skills*. Often people who are depressed, and particularly those with recurrent depression, are somewhat lacking in important relationship skills. Depressed people tend to create a negative first impression in others. They may not know how to meet people, how to start or carry on a conversation, how to listen effectively to others, or how to give affection or positive feedback. All of these are crucial to the formation of sustaining relationships that form a network of social support. Without these skills, the individual tends to be shut out by others or merely ignored. This in turn leads to social isolation that poses a high risk of depression.

One particular social skill that may be crucial to the avoidance of depression is *assertiveness*, or the ability to express one's feelings and views without alienating others (see chapter 15). Inability to express anger appropriately, for example, can result in a turning inward of the anger, leading to depression. This is related to the general area of social skills because emotional self-expression is crucial to the formation of lasting and sustaining relationships.

A response pattern to which depressed people are prone is *withdrawal*. They may choose simply to avoid people and activities. A pastor may be in a position to notice when someone begins to withdraw and may be able to intervene to reverse this pattern before it can seriously exacerbate depression.

Finally, some severely depressed individuals have exceedingly high *anxiety* levels. Their avoidance of social situations is motivated not by a lack of interest or social skills but by quite disabling levels of interpersonal anxiety. Overcoming depression in such cases includes dealing with these pervasive and often longstanding fears (see chapter 14).

Social Consequences of Behavior

One final class of causes that needs to be considered is the social consequences of the individual's behavior—how others react. There are two general categories here.

The first of these is how others react when the person is *not depressed*. If the individual is mostly ignored, taken for granted, or treated badly by others when showing normal mood, he or she may begin to shift in the direction of depression. An example is a stay-at-home spouse whose daily existence may be fairly unrewarding. No one notices his or her efforts; notice is taken mostly when something goes wrong. Time may be spent mostly in giving, taking care of the needs of children, with little positive input. We noted earlier that a low level of positive reinforcement can generate depression.

The second important class of social consequences is what happens when the individual *becomes depressed*. Other people may react in a way that in essence reinforces depression. In the previous example of the housebound spouse, the working spouse may now begin coming home earlier and paying special attention. The children may start helping more with chores. Friends may call more often, deacons from the church may stop by with home-cooked food and encouraging words, the pastor may pay a few extra visits. If all of this helps and the individual gets through the depression, the social environment may then go back to business as usual and the person is once again abandoned: no more extra visits, home-cooked food, help with the chores, or calls from the pastor.

Under such circumstances any reasonably sane and intelligent person would become depressed again. Life is simply better that way. This is emphatically *not* to imply that such a person is faking depression. Rather, it is possible for such social consequences to push an individual into more frequent and severe but genuine and painful depressions. Research has shown that the extent of suffering from physical pain (for example, back pain or post-surgical pain) can be substantially increased or decreased by the use of such social consequences.[13] Certainly, depression can similarly be influenced, being inadvertently maintained (perpetuating cause) by the responses of others.

At this point you may be dazzled, dozing, or despairing at the complexity of causes of depression. We wish it were simpler, but it is not. Here is an excellent example of why it is crucial to spend quality time on the process of formulation—"diagnosis" in the best sense of that term—to understand what the problem is and what is causing it. To make an incorrect formulation at this point is to waste your time and the client's, spending needless and valuable effort barking up the wrong tree.

FORMULATING THE INDIVIDUAL CASE

Given all of these possible causes of depression and mood problems, how should you go about sorting out the facts in an individual case? There are several practical procedures that can help a great deal in tracking down the probable causes of an individual's depression.

The Client as Resource

One well-informed resource to make use of in searching for the cause of depression is the client. Regard your client as a partner or collaborator in the diagnostic process. To be sure, you may have unique information not likely to be available to the client, but the reverse is also true. A blending of your knowledge of depression and the client's own self-knowledge can be quite fruitful.

To begin, we often explain to the client what depression is and what it is not, clarifying the difference between mood and depression in particular. We further explain that depression can have many different causes and that it is important to find out which of these is most responsible for the client's present state. It is helpful to include a large dose of optimism and encouragement at this point, and indeed it is warranted. There are several points to be noted here: (a) depression is now fairly well understood as a problem that many people encounter; (b) a variety of causes have been identified, and as a result different treatment approaches are available; (c) although no one of these is the right treatment for everyone, it is very likely that within this range it will be possible to find something that helps; (d) overall, the chances of getting through this and feeling better are excellent, and in the process it may also be possible to learn how to prevent future problems. A helpful and reassuring message is, "Although we may not find the right approach immediately, I will work with you until we do."

This said, the search begins. It may be helpful to outline the various kinds of causes of depression outlined above, adapting them, of course, to the language and comprehension level of the client. The general set is, "Here are some of the things that commonly cause depression. As I talk about them I want you to think about which of these you believe might be most involved in your own situation." Very often the client can point to one or two that sound right, and these may represent excellent starting points.

The Rule-out Approach

Another process is to approach the search by process of elimination. There are some types of causes—biological factors, for example—where the client's awareness and knowledge will be insufficient to judge their importance. The detailed lists of key signs presented in the earlier tables of this chapter can be helpful in considering whether further exploration of biological causes may be warranted. Although a client often cannot say directly whether a biological cause is involved, he or she can often report the presence or absence of the key symptoms in Table 12-2 or 12-3.

Likewise, other types of causes may be ruled out as the interview progresses. The client who is constantly involved in social activities and who complains of feeling low in spite of "having everything" probably is not suffering from deprivation of positive feedback. (It *is* possible, however, to have a very busy schedule that is filled with mostly unrewarding or negative activities.) The depressed local president of a social club is less likely to be lacking in key social skills (though it is still a possibility). Through knowledge of the individual and his or her own report, the counselor can begin to eliminate those causes that seem unlikely.

Input from Significant Others

The friends or relatives of the client may also be valuable resources in your search for the causes of depression. Such people would be consulted, of course, only with the explicit permission of the client.

Those who live with and around a person sometimes have very helpful and accurate perspectives on problems that develop. They may notice subtle or longer-term changes in behavior, which can be very important in this sorting process. Two good questions are, "What have you noticed that has changed about _____ over the past few months?" and "What do you make of this?" The specific symptoms in Tables 12-1, 12-2, and 12-3 can be queried. It may also be beneficial to review the list of possible causes with these close companions of the client to obtain their views on likely causal factors.

Another factor to consider here is family history. It may be important to explore whether blood relatives of the client have ever had similar problems. The biologically linked depressions in general and bipolar disorder in particular have strong hereditary components. A pastor who is familiar with the parents, grandparents, or other relatives of the client or who can obtain good information about them may find crucial clues. A family history of what seem to be manic episodes, for example, would indicate a need to explore the possibility that the client is suffering from bipolar disorder, even though the client's present symptoms may be solely those of depression.

Self-observation

A fourth approach is to have the client begin keeping a careful diary of mood similar to that presented in chapter 11 (Table 11-2). This is a useful means for exploring factors associated with the person's mood. What precedes changes in mood? Is there a predictable relationship between mood and time of day? Does the person seem to feel consistently better or worse when doing certain things or being in certain places or with certain people? Reviewing a few weeks of such diary records can be very revealing. A striking lack of correspondence between mood and life events, in turn, may be a clue to consider biological factors.

Trial and Success

A fifth and final approach is to begin trying alternatives to find out what helps. After a reasonable process of elimination, one is often left with several possible causes of the present problem. Trying interventions designed to deal with each of these causes is a viable approach to finding, from the possibilities that remain, the one(s) most likely to lead to solution.

A few cautions are in order here. Change in depression takes time. With most antidepressant medications, for example, no major improvement is expected until after at least two weeks of steady dosage. Cognitive therapy may require two months or so to produce substantial improvement. Initial changes in mood may be small and might well be missed unless careful diary records are being kept. It is important not to discard a viable intervention approach prematurely because of unrealistic expectations as to how quickly it should show results. Depressed individuals are particularly prone to discouragement and may need support to stay with an approach long enough to see results.

On the other hand, persistence with one approach beyond a certain period with no results is potentially harmful. A medication that has shown no beneficial result within one month is not likely to do so. Months of psychotherapy without improvement in depression probably means that the wrong approach is being taken. There is no value in persistence for its own sake, particularly when there are viable alternative approaches.

Third, it is important to know, when an intervention is tried, that it has been done properly. A trial on medication is of no value if the dosage is improper or if the client fails to take it. Likewise, an unsuccessful trial on one medication does not mean that all medications will fail. The same applies to counseling approaches. A method has not been adequately tried if the counselor is poorly trained in its use or if the client does not cooperate in it.

Fourth, the hope here is for trial and *success* rather than trial and error. The counselor and client should accomplish as much ruling-out as possible before beginning trial interventions. It can be exceedingly discouraging for a depressed individual to try one approach after another with no benefit. The ideal is to identify the one intervention most likely to help, based on all information available, and then to give that a complete and fair try. If no improvement is experienced, the second most likely alternative is tried. Preference should be given to treatment strategies with a proven track record in research. There is value in trying *first* the intervention most likely to produce some improvement, if only because this encourages the client to keep on trying this and other approaches.

Finally, avoid prematurely deciding that the whole solution has been found. Depression often arises from several sources, and a successful response to one approach does not necessarily mean that other possibilities should be abandoned. There may be further benefit in additional alternatives.

With all of this said, the trying out of reasonable alternative interventions remains a viable way to proceed, echoing the "personal scientist" approach mentioned in chapter 11. After a careful process of elimination, experimental pursuit of remaining alternatives is quite justifiable. From the client's viewpoint this presents an optimistic picture, too. There are different methods to try, and the likelihood of one of them working is high. Lack of improvement after one approach is not reason for discouragement because you do not put all of your eggs in one basket. Rather, it means that it is time to try something else.

To be sure, this process requires a lot of skill on your part. The skillful counselor is able to support and motivate the client to persist in the pursuit of a solution and is aware of alternative causes and interventions. There are difficult judgment calls: Which approach to try first or how long to persist on one path. Still, there is no good alternative (except, of course, referral). Depression *is* a complicated problem, and there is no one right approach for everyone. Helping depressed people requires competence, patience, confidence, optimism, persistence, and a graceful tolerance for ambiguity.

The hopeful side of this is that there *are* so many sound alternatives. Research of the past twenty years has yielded different approaches with proven value in dealing with depression. It is to these interventions that we now turn.

ALTERNATIVES

To intervene is to conduct an experiment (chapter 11). It is to make one change (A) in hopes of bringing about another (B). The B in this case represents symptoms of depression, and the A factors are the various potential causes and corresponding intervention approaches. Every treatment process is an experiment.

Your first step, then, is to form hypothesis about what the problem is and what is causing it. This leads to an intervention strategy (A) intended to bring about a change in the problem (B). If your formulation is correct and the intervention is sound, then change occurs.

This section outlines the interventions that have been shown to be effective in helping people overcome depression. There are many methods *not* mentioned here, and the omission is intentional. There are quite a few popular but unproven "therapies" on the market. The shelves of bookstores and supermarkets are filled with "self-help" books, most of which have never been exposed to a single scientific evaluation. The originators of these therapies and books often make extravagant claims regarding their effectiveness, but the value of therapeutic approaches must be judged not from authoritarian pronouncements but from carefully conducted research. There is, unfortunately, little quality control in the area of counseling and therapy at the present time.

One of the most important services that you can offer is either to provide or to guide clients to those approaches that have been most strongly supported by current scientific data. This is doubly important with problems such as depression, where counseling can have life-and-death implications because of an elevated suicide risk and where the personal and family suffering involved can be intense.

The interventions recommended below are grouped according to the five classes of causes (STORC) described earlier. It is not possible to describe these in sufficient detail here to prepare you to practice them, in most cases. Rather, what follows is intended to help you in sorting out the *available* alternatives. Resources are provided at the end of this chapter for those who wish to learn more about particular treatment approaches.

1. Situational Factors

Depression, as seen earlier, sometimes arises as a reaction to certain kinds of situations. The general strategy here is to bring about a change in the situation itself. If general *stress* seems to be contributing to the depression, any of a variety of stress-reduction strategies (chapter 14) may lead to an improvement in the long run. If the individual's depression emerges from *relationship* difficulties, it is wise to address these directly (chapter 18) while also working to alleviate the depression.

Another situational factor is loss and bereavement. Special aspects involved in grief counseling are discussed in a separate section at the end of this chapter.

A frequent situational factor in depression about which the pastor can often do something is low levels of positive experience. People need regular positive input and pleasant events, but some neglect these "psychological vitamins" and consequently find themselves running down. In some cases this may be linked to a belief that it is wrong to enjoy oneself or that everyone else's needs must come first. As depression increases, the individual feels still less inclined to do anything social or pleasurable, perpetuating the downward cycle. The means of escape from this spiral is to begin doing those things that are (or at least used to be) pleasant. This often takes some encouragement on the part of the counselor. An instruction we often use is, "The assignment is to *do* it. You are not required to enjoy it." Breaking the inertia is what is important. It also helps to be specific in this counseling process—to help the person plan *particular* activities and times rather than giving a general bit of advice. Some excellent guidelines for this process are provided by Lewinsohn and his colleagues in the self-help and counselor resources listed in this chapter's bibliography. Specific homework assignments involving gradual increases in pleasant activities are a central part of this process, and the pastor is in a good position to keep in regular and even daily contact to encourage and reinforce progress. Don't expect immediate results. The first "pleasant" activities may not be experienced as positive at all. It is helpful to have the client keep a diary of activities and mood so that small changes can be seen. This also permits identification of the more powerful "daymakers"—activities that seem to have a strong positive influence on mood. It can also be helpful to identify activities and events that seem to have the opposite effect—"daybreakers"—and to avoid or change these unpleasant experiences as much as possible, particularly during the period of recovery from depression.

2. Thought Patterns

Jon sat in the office smiling. At twenty-four, he was filled with a missionary zeal and a powerful desire to serve others. Self-sacrifice had been a dominant theme in his home, and his parents were widely regarded as models of unselfish servanthood. He was bright, compassionate, filled with gifts—and he was utterly immobilized by depression. Loss of appetite had left his frame emaciated, and he was unable to concentrate or sleep because of the thoughts turning around in his mind. His thoughts were self-critical, of how he had failed and was failing to reach perfection, of how he was undeserving of God's love. He felt tired all of the time but would not and could not rest.[14]

On the surface his depression might be seen as situational. He had no friends, spent no time in pleasant activities, received ample criticism from his parents and his mentors. An initial suggestion that he back off a bit and take some time for himself, however, revealed an underlying thought process that allowed no such "selfishness" and demanded that others' needs always be put before his own. He saw relaxation as wasteful, sinful, and self-indulgent. Another therapist had told him that his religious beliefs were the cause of his problems, and now he eyed his new counselor suspiciously, perhaps expecting the same.

Our work took some time. Working within his value system, a first step was to help him see that in his absoluteness he was slowly rendering himself incapable of service to others. Service such as he demanded of himself requires health and strength. We discussed how Jesus, his model, had chosen times for rest, for visiting friends, for solitary reflection, and how Jesus had allowed himself to be anointed with oil—an act that his followers rejected as frivolous and wasteful. Such moments, though not the center of Jesus' life or ministry, are remembered in scriptures. They were not relapses or backsliding or evidence of weakness, but rather the essential times of nourishment and recharging that are required for any person and especially for people who would spend their lives in the service of others. Through this reevaluation process Jon began to give himself permission to be well and whole.

Over the past two decades, there has been an explosion of interest in the cognitive therapies, in interventions that seek to change rigid thought patterns and processes that may lead to depression and other problems. Cognitive therapy is a talk therapy, but a very directive one. It departs from pscyhoanalysis, which is a more one-sided talk process focusing heavily on the past. It also departs from Rogers' client-centered therapy in its directiveness. The well-meaning pastor may sit for weeks reflecting the feelings of a depressed individual, but this is unlikely to do anything more than increase the person's awareness of the extent of the depression. That is not to say that there is no value in reflective listening. The relationship-bonding and clarification aspects described in chapter 5 are equally important here. It is only to say that listening is not enough in most cases of depression. A prolonged course of talk therapy might, of course, end in the depression lifting, but then depressive episodes end naturally within a span of months. With depression, the "successful" therapy is always the last one.

Cognitive therapies, on the other hand, have been shown to have specific effectiveness in decreasing the severity and length of depression.[15] There are various systems (see Additional Readings at the end of the chapter), but they have in common the identification and change of problematic thought processes and patterns. Some pastors are concerned when encountering this approach because it examines and challenges individual belief systems. This is not without reason because some therapists, including Albert Ellis, one of the major proponents of cognitive therapy, are adamantly antireligious in orientation and tend to view religious belief systems as pathological.[16] Yet the challenging of people to reexamine their beliefs is not monopolized by therapists. This is, in fact, a rightful part of the pastor's role. Research shows, in fact, that clients' religious imagery can be integrated into cognitive therapy with beneficial results.[17] The issues are complex and controversial, but the new cognitive therapies are challenging and effective tools for the pastoral counselor.

One of the simplest cognitive interventions is to help the individual begin making more positive self-statements; for example, to generate a list of "What's good about me" and then to rehearse these silently. This sometimes has a rapid effect on mood. A resistance that therapists often encounter in this process is the individual's negation of each personal strength or embarrassment at talking or even thinking about these. Recognition of one's own gifts may be confused with boasting or *hubris*, the sin of pride. Many issues of religious training and moral upbringing are involved here, and the pastor is an appropriate counselor with whom to sort these out. Sometimes the simple permission of one's pastor to admit and celebrate these personal strengths can be more powerful than hours of rational discussion from a nonpastoral therapist. Pastoral consideration can also be given to the sin of self-denigration, a sometimes overlooked flipside of the sin of pride, which has been proposed as a particularly important perspective in counseling women.[18]

The *rational-emotive* approach first outlined by Albert Ellis focuses on unhealthy "irrational beliefs" that the individual holds and that predispose to distress.[19] Many of the beliefs that Ellis calls *irrational* do involve themes of a person's faith system—ideals, perfection, good versus evil, or "shoulds." The principles underlying rational-emotive therapy can be disentangled, however, from Ellis's own humanistic atheism. The case example that began this section is one in which it was possible to honor the belief and value system of the client while working within that system to question and change problematic elements. The very basis on which the counselor questioned the absolute ban on "self-indulgence" was, in fact, the client's primary value of service to others.

A cognitive therapy perspective sometimes less offensive and problematic to the pastor is *cognitive behavior therapy*, described by (among others) Aaron Beck, Arnold Lazarus, and David Burns (see Additional Readings at the end of this chapter). The focus is not so much on the specific *content* of beliefs as on the person's *way* of thinking, the *process* of thought. Beck has identified a number of thought processes that may lead to depression, almost regardless of content. Examples are *exaggeration* (blowing something all out of proportion to its importance) and *overgeneralization* (taking one small fact to be representative of the larger picture). A single rebuff may be taken as proof of one's total unlovability or may be misinterpreted as signaling the end of a treasured relationship. *Selective attention to the negative* (overlooking favorable feedback in favor of the unfavorable) is another example that has already been discussed.

A key assumption in any cognitive therapy system is that emotional reactions do not follow directly from events in the external world. In this view, *nothing* necessarily "makes" one angry or upset. The emotion follows only from interpretation of reality.

One useful strategy builds on this premise by increasing the person's awareness of the interpretations or thought processes that occur in the brief instants between events and emotional reactions. Starting with a two-column diary, the person records each strong feeling that occurs during the day (positive or negative) and what events occurred just before that feeling. With the counselor's help, the person then reviews these while asking the question, "What must I have told myself in order to feel this way about that event?" With some experience in this exercise, the individual can then begin keeping a three-column diary (see chapter 11, Table 11-2) that includes not only event and emotional reaction, but also thoughts that led to the feeling. The goal of this procedure is to reveal general themes or thought processes that lead to distress. The overall process from there is to find and practice alternative ways of thinking about or interpreting events, so that the person is not so distressed by them but rather deals with reality in a more healthy manner.

We cannot prescribe for you a set of universally healthy beliefs. There is a great temptation here for counselors to prescribe their own beliefs for others. Yet people are different from one another, and what to one has been a lifelong source of strength and consolation may sound to another like a platitudinous slogan. Cognitive therapy is not the prescription of particular ideologies but rather an individualized search for helpful and healthful ways of restructuring one's thinking away from patterns that lead to depression and debilitation. The three-column diary method can be valuable in identifying the patterns that require change. The next challenge, then, is to find "antidote statements" that will work for *this* individual. The resources of the client's faith can be drawn upon here. Beck also recommends homework assignments to behave in ways that violate the old, maladaptive thought patterns—to live against old beliefs.[20] Techniques of cognitive therapy are complex. To learn more about these helpful counseling methods, consult the resources listed at the end of this chapter.

Many therapists now combine the strategies of cognitive therapy with the more behavioral pleasant-events approach of Lewinsohn, described earlier. Several self-help resources combining these methods are included in the further readings listed at the end of this chapter. The combination of these strategies seems to be quite effective in helping individuals overcome depression.[21] In a study at the University of New Mexico, we found that depressed individuals showed significant improvement after this multidimensional counseling, relative to a waiting list control group. To our surprise, we further found that individuals using a self-help guide and working on their own with minimal counselor assistance were just as successful in overcoming their depression as were those clients chosen at random to receive more intensive counseling in individual or group format.[22] Apparently people, once taught these methods, are able to continue to apply them on their own. Cognitive-behavior therapy is no miracle cure, and it is not effective with every case of depression. Nevertheless, it is a sound approach, well founded in scientific research.

3. Organic Causes

The evaluation and treatment of organic factors in mental disorders is not the province of pastoral counseling or of psychology, but rather of medicine. The psychiatrist's training as a physician qualifies her or him to prescribe the kinds of treatment helpful in addressing biological aspects of depression. Here your role is to recognize the warning signs of severe depression or manic episodes and to refer the client for appropriate evaluation.

Several classes of biologically influenced depression were described earlier. The more rare of these, bipolar disorder, is more strongly influenced by hereditary factors and tends to appear early in adult life, usually during the twenties. Individuals with bipolar disorder usually (but not always) respond well to medication with *lithium*. Unlike most psychiatric drugs, lithium is a simple salt. Taken by a normal individual, it has almost no effect; it is not a mind-altering drug, and there is no temptation to abuse it. For the person with bipolar disorder, however, its effect is often dramatic. To oversimplify a bit, lithium's effect is to decrease the breadth of the mood swings so that the highs are not so high and the lows are not so low. This effect is not immediate but occurs over a period of weeks. A marked therapeutic response to lithium is often used as the final confirmation of the diagnosis of bipolar disorder. Lithium is a dangerous substance in its potential for overdose, but this risk is minor when its use is properly monitored by a qualified psychiatrist, particularly when compared with the substantial risks involved in untreated depressions.

What role can a pastor play in all of this? There are several vital functions in which you can be a major asset. The first of these has already been mentioned—early recognition of the pattern. We have seen a number of people with clear signs of bipolar disorder who have suffered for years, even decades, primarily because no one around them recognized their problem for what it was—a treatable illness. Second, you can help in getting the individual to a properly qualified physician. The specialty being sought here is that of *biological* psychiatry. Many psychiatrists primarily practice talk therapies and are not expert in diagnosis and treatment of biological problems—an expertise that requires constant reading of a rapidly growing technical literature. Third, you can serve as a sounding board for the person's reactions to what is learned. For some, realization that a biological cause has been responsible for their longstanding suffering comes as a great relief; for others it is a bitter pill to swallow. The children of a person with bipolar disorder also need to be informed at some time of the nature of this illness, since they are at high risk. Diagnosis of this condition is not a reason for great concern; to the contrary, it is more likely a cause for thanksgiving because the prognosis, with treatment, is fairly good. Finally, you can help to encourage proper use of the medication. A common problem with lithium is that clients stop taking it. The usual reason is that to some extent they enjoy the ups of manic swings, and lithium reduces these. Unfortunately, lithium is not a medication that can be turned on and off rapidly. The likely result of discontinuation is a major depressive relapse. Often the medication is continued indefinitely because there is no persuasive reason to discontinue it and doing so often results in a recurrence. Should you notice a reappearance of symptoms after successful treatment with lithium, the first question to ask is, "Are you still taking your medication?" Given the dangers associated with excessively high doses of this drug, you should also be aware of some of the symptoms of lithium overdose—hand tremor, nausea, vomiting, diarrhea, abdominal pain, weakness and dizziness. Such symptoms in a person taking lithium merit prompt medical attention.

With bipolar disorders eliminated, there remains a group of depressive disorders that are more likely to emerge during middle age and that often respond well to antidepressant medication. Antidepressants are a large group of medications that affect chemical levels in the nervous system. Different antidepressants affect different chemicals in the brain, and choice of the proper antidepressants is a complex task. Physicians who rely primarily on one or two antidepressants may be insufficiently informed about the available alternatives and their differential qualities. Like lithium, antidepressants have little effect on a person in normal mood. Because they do not alter normal mood states, they are unlikely to be abused and have no real street use except by people attempting to rebound from the depressant effects of other drugs they are using. There is potential for overdose, and many of these drugs are dangerous when combined with alcohol or certain foods. (A pharmacist is a good information source on this issue.) Also, like lithium, the antidepressants do not work immediately. Usually, it takes ten to fourteen days before beneficial effects begin to appear. In fact, immediate relief is more likely the result of placebo effects rather than of specific effects of the medication. Close monitoring by a physician is essential, particularly during early weeks. If there is no beneficial effect within several weeks, it is probable that the dose or the medication needs to be changed. The ineffectiveness of one antidepressant is not evidence that all medications will be unsuccessful. In numerous cases we have seen clients respond well to the second medication prescribed by our psychiatric consultant after having no benefit from the first. An adverse re-action to a medication is particularly important, and the physician should be informed immediately. (Unfortunately, the reaction of the client is often to discontinue the medication and not return to the psychiatrist.) Such adverse reactions usually mean that the dose or medication must be changed, and often this is important diagnostic information.

The referring question, however, is one of evaluation. Does this person's depression, in the opinion of the consultant, have a significant biological com-ponent? The answer, sometimes, should be "no," and one fact that encour-ages us to continue working with a psychiatric consultant is that, in at least a third of the cases referred, the report is "No significant biological problem—continue with counseling." By no means are all depressed people in need of medication. As a conservative guideline, if you are in doubt, refer for evalu-ation to a physician competent in the evaluation and management of affec-tive disorders. Again, it is a *biological* psychiatrist you seek for such an evaluation. Psychiatrists who provide talk therapies are offering a service not substantially different from that of other counselors and therapists.

A *combination* of medication and cognitive-behavior therapy can be more effective than either approach alone.[21] These are not mutually exclusive treat-ment strategies, and each may amplify the effect of the other.

Finally, a word is in order with regard to the use of electroconvulsive (shock) treatment (ECT) for depression. Once widely used in psychiatric hospi-tals, ECT involves passing through the brain and electrical current of suffi-cient intensity to induce a seizure. The danger and trauma associated with earlier forms of ECT have been greatly reduced through sedation, and the use of unilateral ECT (one side of the brain only) has decreased its side effects. ECT has been largely abandoned as ineffective in the treatment for schizphre-nia. It is still in use as a psychiatric treatment for severe depression, however, and not without reason. The primary advantage of ECT is its relatively rapid effect on severe depression. It has been reported to be particularly effective when severe symptoms of melancholia (Table 12-2) are present.[23] Based on present evidence, our own opinion is that ECT may be warranted to bring about rapid alleviation of deep depression, particularly when acute suicide risk jeopardizes the person's life. In most cases, however, satisfactory and comparable results can be achieved with a combination of cognitive-behavior therapy and antidepressant medication.

4. Response (Behavioral) Factors

One type of behavioral factor discussed earlier involves a *skill deficit*. Lacking in a crucial coping skill (often social/relationship skills), the person becomes less and less able to cope and more likely to withdraw and become depressed. In such situations, the way out lies in the direction of learning the needed skill.

Educational resources are often useful. In the area of assertiveness, for example, a wide range of books, tapes, and classes are available (chapter 15). Similar resources for overcoming anxiety problems are discussed in chapter 14. Where could your client learn the needed skills?

One key element in learning a new skill is *modeling*. The person needs to see an effective model, someone who uses the skill well. This need not be a perfect model—in fact, it is often more comfortable and encouraging to learn from someone who makes mistakes and then copes with these well than to observe a flawless performance. Within any congregation there are usually some good models of a wide variety of skills. Chapter 20 discusses how you can develop and use these resources in the counseling process.

A second key element in learning is *practice*. To learn a skill it is essential to have the chance to try it out again and again, preferably in a safe environment. Some people are able to overcome public speaking or performance fears through their involvement in church activities, where it is usually safer to take risks. How could the client find opportunities to practice the needed skill, and how could the pastor help to arrange these?

Finally, it is important to obtain *feedback* in order to learn a new skill. Practice without corrective feedback is of little value. Ideally, this feedback should be strongly positive, encouraging those steps and elements that the person did well. Suggestions for further change also should be included, but these are easiest to hear if they are presented along with (and in favorable balance to) positive feedback.

A second general response factor involved in depression is *avoidance*. As depression grows, there is an increasing tendency for the person to withdraw, to stop trying, to give up. A pastor is often able to observe this happening and to intervene, to call the person out, to give support and encouragement. Avoidance is the opposite of growing. Many problems are prolonged and exacerbated by avoidance, and the first step in overcoming them is to stop avoiding.

5. Social Consequences

Finally, there is the fact that a person's mood and behavior are influenced by the reactions of others. Interventions in this area seek to apply social support systems in such a way as to encourage healthy behavior rather than prolonging unhealthy patterns.

The key principle here is that of *reinforcement*. Behavior that leads to positive consequences is likely to be repeated; behavior that is ignored or punished is less likely to be repeated. The key is to catch people doing something *right* and to notice, acknowledge, and support it. When that shy youngster in the youth group finally speaks up, there should be a warm and encouraging response. When the depressed client comes back and reports to the counselor the successful completion of an agreed-upon assignment, there should be a little celebration.

This is an issue to consider in pastoral visitation. Pastors who restrict their visits to time of crisis and urgent need will see but one side of their flock and also may inadvertently encourage debilitation in some cases if this is the only time that the pastor appears. The same applies to other visitors from the congregation. It is also good to support and visit people at the *strong* moments of their lives, in the process of taking risks and growing.

With most parishioners this may not be a crucial issue. If there are individuals who seem to have been caught in a cycle of depression and rescue, however, it may be a worthwhile expenditure of time to visit and support them during up times as well and to encourage greater social involvement during these times. The message, of course, is not to abandon people in the midst of crisis, but rather to convey that you support them in sickness *and* in health.

THE CASE OF CHARLES

At fifty, Charles was a well-established administrator in a major firm. He was married, had four grown children, owned his home. To an outsider he seemed to have everything. Yet one day he called his pastor and asked for an immediate counseling appointment.

His opening question to the pastor was, "If I kill myself, will I be damned forever?" It was not a question, really, but a cry for help. For years, he said, he had been feeling low. He sensed no love from his family, felt like a total failure at work. For the past two years he had often thought about dying, hoping that it would happen to him in some passive fashion so that he would not be disgraced. Now he was thinking more seriously about killing himself outright. It had gotten that bad.

The pastor recognized immediately two symptoms of a major depression—feelings of worthlessness and suicidal thoughts. Further listening and a few questions revealed several more characteristic signs (see Table 12-1)—fatigue, insomnia, loss of interest in activities. Charles also just seemed to move more slowly, and certainly his mood was depressed. No doubt about it. This was a major depression.

But what was its source? Exploration of the characteristic signs of melancholia (Table 12-2) did not reveal much. Although Charles did report loss of pleasure in almost all of his activities, he experienced no special quality of mood. His depression seemed worst in the evening, rather than in the morning, and his insomnia occurred on trying to get to sleep, not early in the morning. He suffered no loss of appetite or weight, and his slowness did not seem extreme—he was still functioning well at work from all objective signs. Finally, though he felt worthless and bitter, Charles did not evidence exaggerated guilt. Neither was there any indication of a history of manic episodes (Table 12-3), nor a history of this kind of problem in Charles' family background. At least for the time being, biological factors did not seem to be primary candidates as causes of the depression.

The pastor continued to see Charles for several weeks, meeting about twice a week on the average and keeping in touch with some additional telephone calls. During these early weeks the main process was clarification—empathic listening. Although this in itself is not usually enough to help with a major depression, it does help to establish a working therapeutic relationship and often yields important information as well. At the end of this time, the pastor's notes included the following hypotheses:

> *Situational* factors: No major recent stresses apparent; nothing except for last child leaving home, which Charles seems to be pleased about because of conflicts with her. Recently turned fifty. Feels in a rut at work—little positive feedback, no new challenges. Few positive things happening at home; family has little fun together.
>
> *Thought* patterns: Many negative self-statements; extremely critical of others and of self. Perfectionistic. Very pessimistic—does not think things can change for him at work or at home. Helplessness is a theme.
>
> *Organic* causes: Eats well, exercises regularly; no indications of manic episodes. No recent physical traumas, and problem has been chronic for several years.
>
> *Responses*: Social skills seem OK. He just doesn't use them as often as before. Withdrawing, socially isolated. Doesn't express his anger well: alternates between saying nothing and blowing up, mostly at family.
>
> *Consequences*: Can't see any real payoffs for being depressed; in fact he seems to get little reinforcement for anything.

From these notes, the pastor constructed several possible alternatives for intervention and talked them over with Charles to get his reactions.

1. Begin marital or family counseling—work on increasing positive activities and communication together.
2. Work individually on cognitive patterns—find negative thought processes and search for healthier patterns; explore perfectionism.
3. Work on assertiveness as an alternative to the passive/hostile cycle, and explore forgiveness as a theme.
4. Consider evaluation by a biological psychiatrist for possible physical bases of the problem if above strategies do not seem to help.

Charles found idea 2 especially appealing, and thought that idea 1 was much of the problem but that there was no hope for improving his marital situation. He was also willing to talk about #3 and saw this as related to #2. The word *helplessness* particularly seemed to capture his feeling, and he repeated it several times.

Charles and his pastor worked together for almost a year. After about five sessions, the pastor recommended that both Charles and his wife come for counseling, and from there on the three of them worked together. Over the course of the year, there were some angry and difficult sessions. Slowly their relationship moved from icy distance through cautious neutrality and onto the first positive experiences they had shared in years. Charles recognized some of the thought patterns that fueled his anger and depression and identified and practiced some effective "antidote" statements to use in difficult situations. Assertiveness training proved unnecessary after he restructured his anger-fueling thoughts. For Charles, the roots of this depression seemed to lie in his own ways of thinking and in the frozen silence into which his marriage had deteriorated. When these changed, so did his depression. Ten years later he finds both his job and his marriage a source of joy, and he looks forward to retirement as a chance to relax and enjoy life more.

Discussion

There is a wide array of different strategies for intervening to overcome depression. Some of them can be handled directly by a pastoral counselor and some cannot, but in all of them you can play a key role in recognizing the problem, seeking the right intervention, and providing ongoing support. Some of these, such as cognitive therapy, are solid counseling strategies that you can learn to use but are best practiced with specific training and supervision of early cases.

The issues discussed here may be of interest for further exploration as education topics within the local congregation. Many of the techniques that are effective in overcoming depression are also useful in preventing it. Pastors who serve a community may eventually seek to move from crisis intervention toward preventive, positive mental health programs (see chapter 20).

In concluding this chapter, two special issues will be considered as they relate to the practice of pastoral counseling—special aspects of depression in women and unique aspects of bereavement and grief counseling.

DEPRESSION AND WOMEN

For whatever reason, depression is much more commonly diagnosed among women than among men. This is true across cultures. Severe depressions are also more common in women, with the exception of bipolar disorder, which is almost equally common in men.[24] There is reason to believe that predisposition to depression is influenced by the X chromosome and therefore passed from mother to child.[25]

Several issues specific to women and depression should be addressed here. First is the concept of involutional or menopausal depression. For some years it was believed that women during menopause were uniquely predisposed to a severe form of depression that was probably biological in origin. Research data now contradict this idea. There is no particular upsurge in depression during the involutional years in either women or men, and there is no evidence for a unique form of depression tied to these normal hormonal changes. Of course, some people *do* become depressed during menopause, but there is no reason to treat such depressions differently from others.[26]

Second, some women experience regular mood fluctuations with the menstrual cycle. There is wide variation across women, and over 150 different symptoms have been associated with the now popular concept of the "premenstrual syndrome" or PMS.[27] We would offer two cautions here. First, very real biological changes can underlie such mood shifts, and PMS should not be regarded to be a mental disorder. On the other hand, avoid dismissing signs of depression in women as merely due to menstrual changes. This is a too-easy explanation, and there may be other important factors involved.

One type of depression in women that has been well documented, however, is the postpartum reaction.[28] A mild "maternity blues" occurring in the first two weeks (often three to four days) after birth is quite common and involves several symptoms of depression including tearfulness, anxiety, concentration problems, and depressed mood. This rather consistently passes within a few days. In a smaller percentage, however (estimates range from 3 to 30 percent), the signs of depression appear and persist during the months after delivery. More rarely, postpartum women suffer a brief reactive psychosis with hallucinations and/or delusion (see chapter 17), which tends to resolve completely and relatively quickly.

There is no agreement as to the cause of this higher risk of depression after childbirth; no definite biological cause has been identified, and social and psychological factors probably play important roles, given the amount of change that ensues with the arrival of a new baby. It seems that women who have had previous depressive episodes (particularly during pregnancy) are more likely to suffer major postpartum depression.

The pastor's role during the postpartum period includes several potentially important aspects. A pastoral visit during days 3 to 4 after delivery is quite likely to find the mother feeling low (estimated incidence of the blues is 50 percent). No special counseling is needed here beyond normal support and reassurance, as this reaction almost certainly will pass in a few days. Keeping a watchful eye for later depression, however, is important to remember. The best guess currently is that about one mother in ten will become moderately to severely depressed during the months after birth. Two factors seem to be related to the occurrence of depression during this time—a tendency toward depression before pregnancy and an increase in anxiety toward the end of pregnancy. It is also important to recall that in our society mothers are expected to appear happy and that many cover their distress well. A tactful inquiry as to whether the mother has felt depressed since having the baby may bring a grateful rush of tears in such cases. In any event it is important not to confuse significant depression with "the blues." The latter is common and brief and does *not* explain the presence of depression during later weeks or months.

There is no unique treatment for postpartum depression. The chances for recovery are excellent, and the likelihood of a recurrence is relatively small. Pastoral support during this time can be invaluable. If the depression becomes sufficiently severe, other interventions may be required. Should a brief hospitalization be necessary, some hospitals now permit the baby to be admitted with the mother, and this seems to speed adjustment and recovery.

GRIEF

Grief is a specific reaction to a loss. It is a pattern of emotional suffering that begins from the time a loss is anticipated (such as the diagnosis of a terminal illness) and extends through the period of loss and bereavement. The most familiar loss is that of a loved person, but there are other kinds of important losses as well: leaving home, losing a job, theft, disabling injury, or the end of a life phase. "Life is a series of developmental losses," Wolfelt observed. "Therefore, if a person is going to live well, it would naturally make sense that he or she would need to mourn well."[29] Many of the symptoms of depression appear during a normal grief reaction. Because pastors are the most involved of helping professionals in dealing with the bereaved, this special section is devoted to the tasks of grief counseling.

Various writers have described stages through which grieving people pass as they adjust to the loss.[30] In general, these descriptions agree about three basic phases. The first of these is a period of numbness and shock that lasts from several hours to several weeks. People suffering the sudden and unexpected loss of a loved one tend to show a somewhat longer period of numbness. This is followed by a phase of emotional distress, particularly anger and depression. Finally comes the phase of recovery in which the acute distress passes, and the person sets about the task of rebuilding his or her life, which is often quite and forever different.

This is a normal process. It usually follows its own course with or without professional help. It is not clear, in fact, whether one even can or should try to speed it up. People work through the process at different rates and in different ways. Research has found few differences between people receiving formal treatment and those going through ordinary grief adjustment without counseling.[31] The primary task in pastoral counseling here is not to do something to fix a problem, but rather to serve as a supportive companion through the journey of bereavement.

Some Myths about Grieving

A common myth is that it is unhealthy for people to show relatively little emotional response during grief adjustment. We have encountered various individuals who have been told that they were not grieving properly because they were not showing evidence of one or another of the stages described in a popular model of grief adjustment. Some believe that a person who prefers not to talk about feelings is likely to suffer from an impacted grief reaction and to be unhealthy in the long run. These views are not and never have been founded on scientific fact. Present data, in fact, suggest rather the opposite—that it is people who show *extreme* emotional reactions early on who are likely to have more serious adjustment problems in the long run.[31] There is no evidence to suggest that grieving people should be forced to talk about feelings, to "face up to reality," or be otherwise confronted because someone else perceives an insufficient amount of overt expression.

Friends and family members sometimes approach the pastor to express their concern that the bereaved spouse is "not dealing with it" or "should be doing" one thing or another. Unless there is evidence of a truly abnormal grief reaction, it is best to offer reassurance and reflective listening to the family, who may be projecting their own grief process onto the grieving spouse or may be operating from mistaken assumptions as to how grief should or must occur. In the absence of signs of abnormality, it is usually best to trust the individual's own healing process.

The Normal Tasks of Grieving

Various systems of grief counseling have been described. Virtually all of them emphasize certain normal stages, processes, or tasks through which one passes in resolving the state of bereavement. Wolfelt, for example, described five general needs to be addressed:[32]

1. To experience and express outside of oneself the reality of death
2. To tolerate the emotional suffering that is inherent in the work of grief while nurturing oneself both physically and emotionally
3. To convert the relationship with the deceased from one of presence to a relationship of memory
4. To develop a new self-identity based on a life without the deceased,
5. To relate the experience of loss to a context of meaning.

Of course not everyone seeks or needs a counselor to deal with these tasks. When bereaved people *do* choose to talk it over, however, they often seek out their pastor. Here are a few counseling guidelines, based on what is known at present about the normal grieving process.

1. Bereaved people often find it helpful to review the terminal illness or incident that claimed their loved one. Often they want reassurance that everything possible was done, to relieve vague feelings of guilt by omission. It may be very helpful to involve the attending physician in this process if possible. Often the grieving person's contact with the physician was minimal and occurred during the period of numbness and confusion.

2. Encourage the person to talk about feelings. Allow crying if it occurs and use gentle reflective listening. If the person apologizes for crying, it may be a good time to explain that crying is healthy, part of the healing process, and not a reason for embarrassment. Don't neglect the spiritual and religious side, for there are often important feelings and questions here. In general, focus on helping the person feel cared for and understood, rather than trying to make something happen. Support, accept, and reflect the person's emotional expression. Give permission to talk and to feel.

3. During the initial period of shock, it may be helpful to assist the person in making day-to-day decisions, which tend to seem difficult and overwhelming to some at this time. The bereaved individual should be discouraged from making major decisions or choices about the future during this initial period. A caution may be in order regarding telephone callers who occasionally take intentional economic advantage of the bereaved during their period of acute adjustment.

4. If the person chooses to discuss the loved one who has been lost, it is often helpful to encourage him or her to talk about positive memories as well as painful ones. Some pastors include this within the memorial service (for example, having those present say what they remember about the person). When the loss is of a person about whom the bereaved had significant ambivalent feelings, it may be helpful to discuss these directly. If you see a pattern of continued suffering combined with active *avoidance* of memories and associations of the lost, a process of guided mourning may reduce the bereaved's distress,[33] helping the person to confront and talk about the painful memories and cues in an empathic and caring context of counseling.

5. Remember the physical side of grieving as well. Be attuned to changes like weight loss, exhaustion, confusion, and other signs of depression (see above) and anxiety (see chapter 14). Do what you can to help the person maintain good nutrition and fluid intake, exercise, and rest. It is important to take especially good *physical* care of oneself during the stress of bereavement. Keep an eye out for excessive use of alcohol or other drugs.

6. Facilitate social support. The presence of a strong social network of practical and emotional support can be of great comfort during bereavement. This often emerges naturally during the period of acute grief immediately after a loss but may require additional encouragement in the weeks and months that follow. You may be able to help prevent isolation by organizing and encouraging social contact and support through a religious community, self-help groups, or extended family.

7. Help to normalize the person's grieving experience. The bereaved are sometimes distressed or embarrassed to find themselves weeping, fatigued, losing normal appetite, unable to sleep, feeling anxious and tense. The person (or family) may unrealistically expect such experiences to go away within a few days

or weeks. It can be important to reassure the person that these are common and normal experiences in grief which often persist, coming and going in waves, through at least the first year after a major loss. Here, of course, it is also important for you to understand what is and is not normal grieving.

Abnormal Grieving

If grieving is a normal process, what are signs of abnormality? The signs of depression given earlier cannot be used per se, because many of them are common during normal grief. Studies have found that sleeping problems, restlessness, low mood, crying, and fatigue are all quite frequent among bereaved people one year after the loss. During the month after the loss, virtually all of the symptoms of depression (with the exception of suicidal thoughts) are normal.[31]

It is not the case, however, that *anything* is normal during this time. Although transient thoughts of suicide occur, persistent or strong suicidal thoughts, ideas, or actions are not part of the normal grief process and are a warning flag that special attention is needed. After the first month it is unusual for grieving people to show continued weight loss, slowed movement, or pervasive guilt. The compulsion to keep things exactly as they were also bodes ill. Most grieving people begin to make changes in the house and are not inclined to keep things untouched (a process that has been called *mummification*). These are signs of a more serious depression than is normal during grieving, and they indicate the need for special help.

One other caution is that problems that existed before the loss may be exacerbated during the grieving process. This is certainly true of preexisting depression and also of alcohol and other drug abuse. People who have been inclined toward overdrinking or drug misuse frequently increase their substance abuse during the weeks and months after a major loss. For such people this is a period of high suicide risk (see chapter 13), especially for the first six weeks after the loss.

Extreme reactions do occur during grief. Psychotic reactions (chapter 17), though rare, may follow a major loss. Such deterioration is usually rapid and abundantly clear. Unless there was a history of psychotic episodes before the loss, the prognosis for a complete recovery is extremely good. Such major breakdowns should not be confused with certain unusual experiences that are relatively common in the bereaved. It is not uncommon for a bereaved person to have a direct sensory experience of the deceased—to see or hear or smell or feel the presence of the person. Such "hallucinations" were reported by 17 percent of bereaved persons in one formal study, and other data suggest that the actual rate of such occurrences may be much higher.[31] Such experiences by themselves are not cause for alarm, and the individual may wish to discuss with the pastor what these experiences mean. Psychologists are, of course, inclined to regard these as simple hallucinations, projections of the grieving person's mind—as well they may be. Pastors may entertain a broader range of possible interpretations.

SUMMARY

Depression is more than feeling low. It is a syndrome, a set of symptoms that indicates something more serious than ordinary low mood states. Evaluation includes two key considerations—how severe is the problem, and what is the cause? Severity considerations include the following:

1. Is this a major depression? (see Table 12-1)
2. Are there signs of a more severe depression, needing special treatment? (see Table 12-2)
3. Is there a suggestion of manic episodes, indicating the possibility of bipolar disorder requiring medical evaluation? (see Table 12-3)

Many factors can contribute to the development and maintenance of depression.

Situational factors: stress, loss, lack of positive support, trauma

Thought patterns: negative self-statements, irrational beliefs

Organic causes: bipolar disorder (Table 12-2), other chemical imbalances, major physical trauma, dietary factors, alcohol and drug abuse

Response (behavioral) factors: social skills, withdrawal, anxiety

Consequences of behavior: reinforcement of depression, ignoring of healthy and adaptive behavior

A mnemonic for remembering these five categories of causes is STORC.

Formulation is an especially vital phase with depression because the appropriate intervention is guided by the hypothesized causes of the problem. With consultation from the client, a rule-out approach, input from significant others, and self-observation by the client, clues can be obtained as to the most likely candidates for intervention. These can then be tried on an experimental basis to determine whether they produce a beneficial effect ("trial and success" method).

Alternative intervention strategies correspond to the categories of possible causes.

Situational factors:
    Stress reduction
    Increase level of positive support
    Supportive counseling for grief adjustment
Thought patterns:
    Replacing negative self-statements with "antidote" statements
    Identifying unhealthy thought processes
    Cognitive restructuring

Organic causes:
Obtain appropriate consultation from a biological psychiatrist
Biological interventions, as appropriate (medication, diet, etc.)

Response factors:
Teach more adaptive social skills
Discourage avoidance and withdrawal

Consequences:
Support and reinforce healthy, adaptive, risk-taking behavior
Avoid inadvertently reinforcing depressed behavior

ADDITIONAL READINGS

For the Counselor

BECK, AARON T. *Cognitive Therapy of Depression*. New York: Guilford Press, 1987. One of the developers of cognitive therapy describes techniques for counseling with depression.

BLAZER, DAN *Emotional Problems in Later Life: Intervention Strategies for Professional Caregivers*. New York: Springer, 1990. Helpful guidelines for dealing with emotional and practical problems of the elderly.

GITLIN, MICHAEL J. *The Psychotherapist's Guide to Psychopharmacology*. New York: Free Press, 1990. A basic book for therapists on how licit and illicit drugs work.

HOLLIN, CLIVE R., and PETER TROWER, eds. *Handbook of Social Skills Training*. New York: Pergamon Press, 1986. A two-volume paperback set: (1) *Applications across the Lifespan* and (2) *Clinical Applications and New Directions*. Useful chapters on helping clients develop social skills.

HART, ARCHIBALD. *Counseling the Depressed*. Dallas: Word, 1987.

JOHNSON, SHERRY E. *After a Child Dies: Counseling Bereaved Families*. New York: Springer, 1987.

KUBLER-ROSS, ELISABETH *Living with Death and Dying*. New York: Macmillan, 1981.

LEWINSOHN, PETER M., DAVID O. ANTONUCCIO, JULIA STEINMETZ BRECKENRIDGE, and LINDA TERI *The Coping with Depression Course*. Eugene, OR: Castalia Publishing, 1984. This is a clearly structured course, which could be offered within the context of a local congregation. There is an accompanying workbook for participants: RICHARD A. BROWN and PETER M. LEWINSOHN, *Participant Workbook for the Coping with Depression Course*. Eugene, OR: Castalia Publishing, 1984. Also see the Lewinsohn book for clients, below.

NEZU, ARTHUR M., CHRISTINE M. NEZU, and MICHAEL G. PERRI *Problem-solving Therapy for Depression*. New York: John Wiley, 1989. A practical approach integrating behavioral and cognitive strategies.

OATES, WAYNE E. *Pastoral Care and Counseling in Grief and Separation*. Philadelphia: Fortress Press, 1976.

PAYKEL, E. S., ed. *Handbook of Affective Disorders*. New York: Guilford Press, 1992. Encyclopedic reference, particularly strong on biological aspects and treatments of depression and mania.

RANDO, THERESE A., ed. *Parental Loss of a Child*. Champaign, IL: Research Press, 1986. A collection of chapters on the special crisis of losing a child by miscarriage, abortion, stillbirth, sudden infant death, accident, and illness. There are specific readings for clergy and for parents and helpful information about support organizations.

RANDO, THERESE A. *Grief, Dying, and Death: Clinical Interventions for Caregivers.* Champaign, IL: Research Press, 1984.

————*Treatment of Complicated Mourning.* Champaign, IL: Research Press, 1993.

RUSH, A. JOHN, ed. *Short-term Psychotherapies for Depression: Behavioral, Interpersonal, Cognitive, and Psychodynamic Approaches.* New York: Guilford Press, 1982. Includes chapters on a variety of effective approaches, written by leaders in the field.

UNITED STATES PHARMACOPEIA *The Complete Drug Reference.* New York: Consumer Reports Books, 1992. A lay-oriented handbook about prescription drugs. Issued annually, and may be stocked in the reference section of your library.

WILKINSON, JILL, and SANDRA CANTER *Social Skills Training Manual.* New York: John Wiley, 1982. Practical guidelines and procedures for helping clients develop stronger social skills.

WOLFELT, ALAN D. *Death and Grief: A Guide for Clergy.* Muncie, IN: Accelerated Development, 1988. A short, nicely written and very practical guide to grief counseling, specifically for pastors.

WOLFELT, ALAN *Helping Children Cope with Grief.* Muncie, IN: Accelerated Development, 1983.

WORDEN, J. WILLIAM *Grief Counseling and Grief Therapy* (2nd ed.), New York: Springer, 1991.

WRIGHT, H. NORMAN *Self-talk, Imagery, and Prayer in Counseling.* Dallas: Word, 1986. Presents cognitive therapy in a Christian context.

YUDOFSKY, STUART, ROBERT E. HALES, and TOM FERGUSON *What You Need to Know about Psychiatric Drugs.* Washington, DC: American Psychiatric Association, 1992. Another comprehensible resource for nonmedical people.

For the Client

BURNS, DAVID D. *Feeling Good: The New Mood Therapy.* New York: Morrow, 1980. Self-help presentation of well-documented cognitive therapy methods for overcoming depression. Particularly helpful for mood problems based on thinking patterns.

————*The Feeling Good Handbook.* New York: NAL/Dutton, 1990. This is a workbook to help the client proceed through cognitive steps to recovery.

FIEVE, RONALD *Moodswing* (rev. ed.). New York: Bantam, 1989. A useful book for helping people to understand the nature and biology of bipolar (manic-depressive) illness.

GREENBERG, DAN, and MARCIA JACOBS *How to Make Yourself Miserable for the Rest of the Century.* New York: Random House, 1987. A tongue-in-cheek book, pointing out how we make ourselves unhappy through our thinking patterns. Presented in a paradoxical "how to" format. Good for clients with a sense of humor.

KUSHNER, HAROLD S. *When Bad Things Happen to Good People.* New York: Schocken, 1989. A best seller. Rabbi Kushner deals with theological understandings of suffering in this well-written book for parishioners.

LAZARUS, ARNOLD, and ALLEN FAY *I Can If I Want To.* New York: Warner Books, 1988. A short book focusing on cognitive change methods but also suggesting new actions that one can take to counteract unhealthy thought patterns.

LEWINSOHN, PETER M., RICARDO F. MUNOZ, MARY ANN YOUGREN, and ANTOINETTE M. ZEISS *Control Your Depression.* Englewood Cliffs, NJ: Prentice-Hall, 1986. This is an excellent self-help resource, designed to parallel the Coping with Depression course (see counselor materials above) and most closely resembling the self-help manual found to be effective in our study at the University of New Mexico (see note 21).

SELIGMAN, MARTIN E. P. *Learned Optimism: How to Change Your Mind and Your Life.* New York: Pocket Books, 1990. A self-help book focused on how people shape their own reality by the ways in which they perceive and think about themselves and the world around them.

SIMON, SIDNEY *Negative Criticism and What You Can Do about It.* Allen, TX: Argus Communications, 1978. Examines the role of negative criticism in damaging happiness, relationships, and self-esteem.

——*Vulture: A Modern Allegory on the Art of Putting Oneself Down.* Allen, TX: Argus Communications, 1977. An illustrated story on how people put themselves down. Almost a "comic book" format—especially aimed at teenagers but helpful for adults, too.

STAUDACHER, CAROL *Men & Grief: A Guide for Men Surviving the Death of a Loved One.* Oakland, CA: New Harbinger, 1991.

TAGLIAFERRE, LEWIS, and GARY L. HARBAUGH *Recovery from Loss: A Personalized Guide to the Grieving Process.* Deerfield Beach, CA: Health Communications, 1990.

WESTBERG, GRANGER E. *Good Grief.* Philadelphia: Fortress Press, 1962. An enduring little book on grief, written by a pastor.

WOLTERSTORFF, NICHOLAS *Lament for a Son.* Grand Rapids, MI: William B. Eerdmans Publishing, 1987. A Christian philosopher shares his own inner struggles to understand the death of his twenty-five-year-old son. Well written, moving, with deep integrity—it rejects the "easy" answers and moves with sensitivity and warmth toward a spiritual resolution.

NOTES

[1] Based on current diagnostic guidelines contained in the American Psychiatric Association's *Diagnostic and Statistical Manual of Mental Disorders*, 4th ed., rev. (Washington, DC: American Psychiatric Association, 1994).

[2] Carol Slivia Weisse, "Depression and Immunocompetence: A Review of the Literature," *Psychological Bulletin* 111 (1992): 475–89.

[3] Geraldine Downey and James C. Coyne, "Children of Depressed Parents: An Integrative Review," *Psychological Bulletin* 108 (1990): 50–76; Theodore Dix, "The Affective Organization of Parenting: Adaptive and Maladaptive Processes," *Psychological Bulletin* 110 (1991): 3–25.

[4] Ann O'Leary, "Stress, Emotion, and Human Immune Function," *Psychological Bulletin* 108 (1990): 363–82.

[5] Elisabeth Kubler-Ross, *On Death and Dying* (New York: Macmillan, 1969).

[6] Christopher Muran, "A Reformulation of the ABC Model in Cognitive Psychotherapies: Implications for Assessment and Treatment," *Clinical Psychology Review* 11 (1991): 399–418.

[7] David A. Haaga, Murray J. Dyck, and Donald Ernst, "Empirical Status of Cognitive Theory of Depression," *Psychological Bulletin* 110 (1991): 215–36.

[8] Albert Ellis and Robert Harper, *A New Guide to Rational Living* (North Hollywood, CA: Wilshire, 1975).

[9] Jefferson A. Singer and Peter Salvoney, "Mood and Memory: Evaluating the Network Theory of Affect," *Clinical Psychology Review* 8 (1988): 211–51; George E. Matt, Carmelo Vazquez, and W. Keith Campbell, "Mood-congruent Recall of Affective Toned Stimuli: A Meta-analytic Review," *Clinical Psychology Review* 12 (1992): 227–55.

[10]For a review of the literature on biological treatment of depression, consult E. S. Paykel, ed., *Handbook of Affective Disorders* (New York: Guilford Press, 1992).

[11]Leslie A. Robinson, Jeffrey S. Berman, and Robert A. Neimeyer, "Psychotherapy for the Treatment of Depression: A Comprehensive Review of Controlled Outcome Research," *Psychological Bulletin* 108 (1990): 30–49.

[12]Norman E. Rosenthal and Mary C. Blehar, eds., *Seasonal Affective Disorders and Phototherapy* (New York: Guilford Press, 1989).

[13]Francis J. Keefe and David A. Williams, "New Directions in Pain Assessment and Treatment," *Clinical Psychology Review* 9 (1989): 549–68.

[14]The case of Jon is described in more detail in William R. Miller, "Including Clients' Spiritual Perspectives in Cognitive-Behavior Therapy," in William R. Miller and John E. Martin, eds., *Behavior Therapy and Religion: Integrating Spiritual and Behavioral Approaches to Change* (Newbury Park, CA: Sage Publications, 1988, 43–55).

[15]Keith S. Dobson, "A Meta-analysis of the Efficacy of Cognitive Therapy for Depression," *Journal of Consulting and Clinical Psychology* 57 (1989): 414–19; A. J. Rush, "Cognitive Therapy of Depression: Rationale, Techniques, and Efficacy," *Psychiatric Clinics of North America* 6 (1983): 105–27.

[16]Albert Ellis, "The Case against Religion," *Mensa Bulletin* 38 (September 1970): 5–6; Albert Ellis and Eugene Schoenfeld, "Divine Intervention and the Treatment of Chemical Dependency," *Journal of Substance Abuse* 2 (1990): 459–68.

[17]L. Rebecca Propst, "The Comparative Efficacy of Religious and Nonreligious Imagery for the Treatment of Mild Depression in Religious Individuals," *Cognitive Therapy and Research* 4 (1990): 167–78; L. Rebecca Propst, Richard Ostrom, Philip Watkins, Terri Dean, and David Mashburn, "Comparative Efficacy of Religious and Nonreligious Cognitive-Behavioral Therapy for the Treatment of Clinical Depression in Religious Individuals," *Journal of Consulting and Clinical Psychology* 60 (1992): 94–103. See also note 14 above.

[18]Valerie Saiving, "The Human Situation: A Feminine View," in Carol P. Christ and Judith Plaskow, eds. *Womanspirit Rising: A Feminist Reader in Religion* (San Francisco: Harper & Row, 1979, 25–42). Some secular parallels are drawn by Gloria Steinem, *Revolution from Within: A Book of Self-esteem.* (Boston: Little, Brown, 1992). For a thorough discussion see Mary McClintock Fulkerson, "Sexism as Original Sin: Developing a Theacentric Discourse," *Journal of the American Academy of Religion,* 59, (1991), 653–675.

[19]Albert Ellis and Robert A Harper, *A New Guide to Rational Living* (North Hollywood, CA: Wilshire, 1975).

[20]Aaron T. Beck, *Cognitive Theory of Depression* (New York: Guilford Press, 1987).

[21]Michael L. Free and Tian P. S. Oei, "Biological and Psychological Processes in the Treatment and Maintenance of Depression," *Clinical Psychology Review* 9 (1989): 653–88; David O. Antonuccio, Clay H. Ward, and Blake H. Tearnan, "The Behavioral Treatment of Unipolar Depression in Adult Outpatients," *Progress in Behavior Modification* 25 (1989): 152–91.

[22]Michael M. Schmidt and William R. Miller, "Amount of Therapist Contact and Outcome in a Multidimensional Depression Treatment Program," *Acta Psychiatrica Scandinavica* 67 (1983): 319–32. Positive therapeutic effects of a similar self-help manual were reported by Forrest Scogin, Christine Jamison, and Kimberly Gochneaur, "Comparative Efficacy of Cognitive and Behavioral Bibliotherapy for Mildly and Moderately Depressed Older Adults," *Journal of Consulting and Clinical Psychology* 57 (1989): 403–7.

[23]Sidney Malitz and Harold A. Sackeim, eds., "Electroconvulsive Therapy: Clinical and Basic Research Issues," *Annals of the New York Academy of Sciences* 26 (1986).

[24]J. H. Boyd and M. M. Weissman, "Epidemiology," in E. S. Paykel, ed., *Handbook of Affective Disorders* (New York: Guilford Press, 1982). See also note 1 above.

[25]Stephen V. Faraone, William S. Kremen, and Ming T. Tsuang, "Genetic Transmission of Major Affective Disorders: Quantitative Models and Linkage Analyses," *Psychological Bulletin* 108 (1990): 109–27.

[26]M. M. Weissman, "The Myth of Involutional Melancholia," *Journal of the American Medical Association* 242 (1979): 742–44.

[27]Lorna Peterson, *PMS: The Premenstrual Syndrome* (Phoenix, AZ: Oryx Press, 1985); William R. Keye Jr., ed., *The Premenstrual Syndrome* (Philadelphia: W. B. Saunders, 1988).

[28]Valerie E. Whiffen, "Is Postpartum Depression a Distinct Diagnosis?" *Clinical Psychology Review* 12 (1992): 485–508; B. Pitt, "Depression and Childbirth," in E. S. Paykel, ed., *Handbook of Affective Disorders* (New York: Guilford Press, 1982, 361–378).

[29]Alan D. Wolfelt, *Death and Grief: A Guide for Clergy* (Muncie, IN: Accelerated Development, 1988) 13.

[30]The classic description is that of Elisabeth Kubler-Ross, *On Death and Dying* (New York: Macmillan, 1969).

[31]Margaret Stroebe and Wolfgang Stroebe, "Does 'Grief Work' Work?" *Journal of Consulting and Clinical Psychology* 59 (1991): 479–82; Paula J. Clayton, "Bereavement," in E. S. Paykel, ed., *Handbook of Affective Disorders* (New York: Guilford Press, 1982, 403–415).

[32]Wolfelt, *Death and Grief*, 74–80.

[33]Lester Sireling, Daryl Cohen, and Isaac Marks, "Guided Mourning for Morbid Grief: A Controlled Replication," *Behavior Therapy* 19 (1988): 121–32.

13

SUICIDE

Yesterday I suffered so much that I could neither sleep nor eat, which is very unusual for me. I suffer not only from torments which cannot be put into words (there is one place in my new Symphony—the Sixth—where they seem to me adequately expressed), but from a dislike to strangers, and an indefinable terror—though of what the devil only knows. . . . However, it is for the last time in my life.

—Peter Ilich Tchaikovsky
(at the conclusion of work on the *Pathetique* symphony
and shortly before his death, an apparent suicide)[1]

In the course of her or his career, a pastor is called upon to prevent, intervene in, suffer through, reflect on, and interpret countless life crises. Of all of these, perhaps the most emotionally rending is suicide. Threats, attempts, and the potential of suicide leave people with a heavy burden of constant worry and ambiguous responsibility. When suicide occurs, the survivors (including the pastor) are left with a bitter tangle of complicated feelings, thoughts, and memories.

Few pastors will retire without encountering a suicide of someone close to them. Many pastors in the course of their careers are called upon numerous times to intervene with a seriously suicidal individual and to be God's envoy to the survivors in the dark aftermath of a chosen death.

There are no total answers. The most skillful professionals and the most sophisticated psychological tests are woefully inadequate in predicting who will commit suicide and who will not. There are no proven techniques for preventing suicide, nor *can* it be prevented if the individual is genuinely determined to die. No one can completely prepare you to absorb the anger and meet the needs of the survivors.

Still, some practical guidelines and knowledge may be of help. These will be organized in the following four topics: (a) debunking common myths about suicide, (b) evaluating the risk of suicide, (c) intervening with suicidal people, and (d) helping the survivors.

DEBUNKING COMMON MYTHS ABOUT SUICIDE

People who are really serious about suicide don't talk about it. One misconception is that "real" suicides come without warning and that those who talk about doing it are faking or seeking attention. In fact, in a majority of cases of fatal suicide attempts, the individual had told someone of the intention or had made a prior attempt or gesture. People who talk about, mention, joke about, hint at, or allude to suicide should always be taken seriously.

Talking about suicide could make it happen. Some pastors are afraid to bring up the subject of suicide because they are afraid that doing so may increase the chances that it will happen. This is unlikely. Although there are some approaches to avoid (see below), it is unlikely that one could, by inquiring about suicidal thoughts, suggest the idea to someone who has not been considering it. The risk involved in *not* inquiring is ever so much greater.

Once a person has "bottomed out" and started to improve, the risk of suicide is past. This is a potentially dangerous misconception. Suicide can and does occur in individuals who are on the upswing, showing good improvement after a serious depression, for example. One common explanation of this is that the person, while deeply depressed, lacks the energy to commit suicide. As she or he improves, however, the energy may return while the hopelessness remains. It is not uncommon for the survivors to puzzle how suicide could have occurred "just when they were doing so well."

Only [fill in the blank] people commit suicide. The blank in this statement can be filled in with a number of different adjectives, including sick, old, poor, white, or crazy. Although certain categories of individuals are more likely than others to take their own lives, the risk of suicide cannot be dismissed on this basis.

EVALUATING THE RISK OF SUICIDE

It is extremely difficult if not impossible to predict accurately the occurrence of suicide. In part, this is because suicide is a relatively rare cause of death in the United States. A city of 100,000 people is likely to experience between 10 and 15 suicides per year.[2] It is much easier to predict who will have cancer or heart disease, schizophrenia or alcoholism than it is to identify those people who will die by their own hand.

Nonlethal suicide attempts, in contrast, are much more common—perhaps as many as fifty attempts for each actual suicide. Among high school students, 8 to 9 percent report having made one or more attempts.[3] The most common precipitating events for suicide attempts include disturbance in family and other intimate relationships, work problems, and feelings of anger, depression, and hopelessness. In addition, among youth, school problems and boyfriend/girlfriend difficulties are often reported precipitants. A contagion effect has also been observed, whereby one suicide sets off a series of imitation attempts.

Still, there are patterns of risk for actual suicide. These are summarized in Table 13-1. In general, the risk of suicide is elevated for people who are in difficult situations, particularly if there seems to be no escape (such as chronic illness, financial ruin, or divorce), for those who have other problems that result in poor judgment (alcoholism or delusions), and for people who are depressed and severely self-critical. Elderly people are at highest risk of suicide, although there has been an upswing in suicides among those under the age of thirty. One of the highest risk indicators, however, is a previous attempt—particularly if it was a serious one.

What is a "serious" attempt? There are several signs. First of these is the means chosen. Certain methods (firearms, jumping from high places) are much more lethal than others (taking pills, superficial cuts on the wrist). The more lethal the method chosen, the more serious the person's intent to die.

TABLE 13-1   Risk Factors Associated with Suicide[4]

---

1. *Prior Attempt.* One important predictor of suicide is a previous attempt, particularly if the attempt was a serious one. Fatal suicide attempts often follow shortly after an unsuccessful attempt.
2. *Age.* People over the age of fifty are more likely than others to commit suicide, and a suicide attempt in an elderly person is much more likely to be fatal.
3. *Males.* Men are about three times more likely than women to commit suicide, even though women are about three times more likely than men to make an attempt or suicidal gesture. Men are more likely to choose highly lethal methods.
4. *Alone.* Isolated, solitary people have an elevated risk, and divorced people are at highest risk.
5. *Ill Health.* Individuals in ill health, particularly with chronic illnesses that they perceive to be irreversible or terminal, are more likely to take their own lives.
6. *Alcohol and Drugs.* People who abuse alcohol or drugs have a substantially higher risk of suicide.
7. *Depression.* Seriously depressed people have one of the highest risks. It is estimated that approximately 15 percent eventually make a fatal attempt. Particularly at high risk are those who show severe self-criticism or guilt.
8. *Stress.* Risk is elevated in those in the midst of extreme stress such as financial turmoil or stormy marital conflict with threatened separation.
9. *Psychosis.* Confusion, delusions, and hallucinations (see chapter 17) contribute to an increased risk.
10. *Combination.* Combinations of the above factors pose particularly high risk (for example, a male alcoholic, depressed, recently divorced).

Second, serious suicide attempters do not make arrangements to be found in time to be saved and often take precautions to see that they will not be saved. If they are rescued, it is often by accident and through no arrangement of their own. Third, serious attempts are often accompanied by careful preparations. Arrangements may be made for the family to be away, finances may be put in careful order, a note may be left with content obviously intended to be found after death.

Some suicides are impulsive acts, committed in a moment of anger or acute despair. More often, however, the process is one that progresses slowly through several stages. In working with potentially suicidal people, it is useful to keep these stages in mind. These are listed in Table 13-2.

The first step in evaluating suicidal potential, of course, is to ask. You should not be shy or embarrassed about such inquiry. If you are comfortable in asking and treat this as a routine, caring question, the client is likely to answer in an open way. Two practical issues, however, are when and how to ask.

"When" is the easier issue of the two—ask whenever in doubt. Any passing reference or allusion to suicide, any out-of-context reference to death, statements such as "sometimes I wonder if it's worth it"—all of these should alert you to inquire a bit further. The risk factors listed in Table 13-1 should be kept in mind, and particularly when combinations of these occur you should explore the possibility of suicidal thoughts even if no prior mention of them has been made. When in doubt, ask. It is quite unlikely to do harm and may very well be one of the most important questions you can ask.

"How" is a bit more tricky. The inquiry should be made with tact yet without the appearance of hedging or embarrassment. It may be desirable to share with the client your reasons for asking, rather than leaving this reasoning process to the client's own imagination. A form that we have often used is, "Sometimes people who are in the middle of a difficult time like you are going through begin to think about dying or consider the possibility of suicide. I wonder if that is something you have been thinking about." This asks the question in a nonaccusatory fashion, gives permission to answer in

TABLE 13-2   Steps toward Suicide

1. *Decreasing value of life.* First there is a loss of interest or joy in life. No active intent to die is present, but life no longer seems worth living.
2. *Attraction of death.* Next the person begins to think of death as attractive, as a peaceful or desirable alternative. He or she may think increasingly about how nice it would be to die accidentally or of natural causes. One of our own clients at this stage, who had had previous heart problems, began a strenuous program of jogging in hopes of precipitating a heart attack. To his chagrin, he only became more healthy.
3. *Vague thoughts of suicide.* Gradually the person begins to consider vaguely the possibility of suicide. He or she becomes increasingly preoccupied with death.
4. *Planning.* The individual begins to think through how suicide could be accomplished and starts making plans.
5. *Attempt.* Finally, the person makes an actual suicide attempt.

the affirmative if it is true, and gives a reasonable rationale for asking without implying that the counselor sees alarming warning signs in the individual. If the person has already volunteered or alluded to thoughts about suicide, simple reflective listening is probably sufficient to encourage elaboration ("Sometimes things look so black that you think about dying," or just "You think about that sometimes.") The person's first volunteering of thoughts about suicide may be somewhat indirect, and the pastor should be alert for such muffled cries for help (such as, "What happens to a person's soul if he commits suicide?") Coming from a depressed person, questions about afterlife may be just such a plea.

Of course, it is possible that the individual will not answer honestly when asked about suicidal intent. This may be particularly likely if she or he perceives that the pastor will disapprove of or condemn such thoughts. For this reason it is wise, whenever possible, to establish a working relationship, a trusting atmosphere, before charging in with questions. Reflective listening is one excellent way to do this, and the material that is elicited may even render the questions unnecessary. In asking about suicidal thoughts, it is useful to observe the individual closely. A pause in responding or looking away from the counselor may reflect evasiveness. A "No" response presented in a particularly cheerful, smiling way is also suspect.

A few other signs are worth mentioning, though they are neither definite nor frequent. In some cases of suicide with which we are familiar, the person showed a marked sense of peacefulness in the few days before the lethal attempt. This was a noticeable change from the preceding stress and depression and was interpreted by those around the person as a remarkable improvement. In fact, the sense of peace apparently was derived from the decision to die. Also, during the days immediately preceding a planned suicide, the individual sometimes makes final visits or telephone calls to important people. These visits are not labeled as such, of course, but a perceptive person may pick up the finality of it. A special gift may be taken to significant people, perhaps a treasured possession that the individual has had for some time. The message, "I want you to have this"—a seemingly natural albeit unexpected gesture—takes on a terrible new meaning a few days later.

All of this must be tempered, however, by the reminder that *prediction of suicide is extremely difficult*. The vast majority of people showing the signs in Table 13-1 do not commit suicide. There are many more attempts and gestures than actual suicides, perhaps as many as fifty to one. Looking back on the facts of a suicide, it is *always* possible to find some sign or warning that those around the person "should have seen." The problem, of course, is that these same signs are present in many, many other people and there is no known way to identify from this group the few individuals who will actually take their own lives. There is nothing to be gained in looking back and castigating oneself for not seeing it coming, although this is a natural and frequent reaction among the survivors.

INTERVENING

Suicidal thoughts and acts are not in themselves a problem. They are a reaction to a problem. There is no diagnosis of "suicidal," and there is no specific treatment. Rather, what is needed is a resolution of the problems that have led the person to the brink of self-destruction. Suicidal behavior is a cry for help, a sign of just how severe the problem has become.

The most important challenge for a pastor, then, is one of formulation (chapter 7). What *is* the problem, and what needs to be done about it? This is the longer-term picture. Unless the drinking problem, depression, marital stress, or confusion that led to this life-threatening state is resolved, little has changed and the risk of suicide is not decreased. The usual suicide prevention strategies are analogous to detoxification of the alcoholic; this step is an important life-saving measure for the individual, but it does nothing to resolve the problem that led to the crisis.

What are, then, the practical and conventional methods for coping with an acutely suicidal person? The immediate goal, of course, is to bring the person through this crisis period alive. The longer-term goal is to help the individual toward resolution of the underlying problem so that the crisis does not recur.

Listening

It is the middle of the night. Your telephone rings, and you climb out of the deep well of sleep to answer it. The voice at the other end is desperate, crying, confused. Perhaps it is a strange voice; perhaps it is a familiar one. No matter. The person has chosen *you* to call in the midst of a crisis and tells you that suicide may be the only way out.

The best starting point in a situation such as this is reflective listening. First of all, this is probably what the person is looking for at the moment. Listening is unlikely to alienate the person and will probably keep him or her talking. It also gives you time to collect yourself and think about what to do next. Meanwhile, you are establishing or reestablishing some trust by staying with what the person is saying.

Evaluating Severity and Gathering Information

What you will do must depend in part on your evaluation of how serious the situation is. A typical criterion is how far along the person is in the planning process. Is there a specific plan for how the person would commit suicide? Are the means at hand? Is there anyone else with the person? The factors named in Tables 13-1 and 13-2 are also considerations in evaluating severity of risk.

Other information is important. Where is the person now? Has the person been drinking or taken any drug? How close is the nearest friend or relative?

This means that you will probably need to ask some questions. It is unwise to do this too early, however; faced with questions like where he or she is, who is nearby and so on, the seriously suicidal individual may decide to hang up. It is advisable, therefore, to listen reflectively for a period of time and then to intermix questions with reflections.

Support

The next step is to begin providing supportive and stabilizing messages. The content of these cannot be preplanned, but the following are frequently helpful as general themes.

Caring   A person who reaches out is often seeking concern and caring. Statements of positive regard and concern, to the extent that they can be offered honestly, tend to be helpful.

Optimism   The counselor can also provide a sense of optimism to counterbalance the probable pessimism of the client. Suicide is seen as a solution to an inescapable or unbearable situation. Realistic optimism can address the possibility for change, for things being better at a future time.

Perspective   The counselor's perspective acknowledges (rather than denies) how bleak things seem to the client at the moment. That bleakness is seen, however, as a part of a crisis—the entire world looks terrible from the viewpoint of depression. The counselor offers a longer view that includes the likelihood that change will occur, even though at the moment things appear hopeless.

Irreversibility   The counselor further points out that suicide is an irreversible decision, with no room for changing one's mind afterward. The client is encouraged to take a "wait and see" perspective rather than make an irreversible decision now. Some counselors point out that it is always possible to decide later to commit suicide (a statement that is most certainly true).

Responsibility   Finally, many counselors emphasize that the choice is the individual's and make no pretense of being able to take control. This tends to be reassuring to the client and is quite true. No one can make this choice for another.

Contingency Plans

Finally comes the joint decision of what needs to be done. An emergency counseling session may be arranged, either with the pastor or with another professional. The pastor may choose, with the person's permission, to go where the person is in order to talk. (In this case it is wise to take someone along.) The person may be advised to go to a friend's house, or with permission the pastor may call a friend or relative. All of these accomplish what is one common intervention step—to see that the individual is not alone.

Beyond the immediate hour, it is also useful to help the person decide what will happen in the hours ahead. Arrangements for regular contact with other people may be made. Is help needed with regard to work, children, or other responsibilities?

Of prime importance is the initiation of a course of intervention for the problem that precipitated this crisis. What steps can the person take to begin to alleviate the problem? What resources are available in the community? The pastor may, with permission, make an appointment for the person and assist the person in keeping it. Regular follow-up contact from the pastor may also be valuable.

Under certain circumstances hospitalization may be necessary. This is called for when it seems that close supervision is needed for a time to prevent the person from making suicidal attempts. Voluntary admission is one route for the person who feels too shaky and uncertain to manage alone and is willing to be hospitalized. Be well informed of the options available, since many people are quite frightened of psychiatric admission and want to know what it would be like. One caution here is that a blunt statement that "I think you need to be in a hospital" may frighten the person and precipitate a suicidal attempt, particularly if she or he perceives that hospitalization may be forced involuntarily.

Involuntary commitment *is* a possibility, though one to be used only under emergency circumstances. This requires the action of a physician, and in most states there must be clear evidence of danger to self or others. It is wise to have a working relationship with a competent psychiatrist familiar with involuntary commitment procedures, in case the need for this should arise. In the event that the person indicates that he or she has taken or will take potentially lethal actions (taking pills, wounding self), it is best to allow the local police department or rescue squad to handle the situation. The initiation of such actions against the individual's will may well damage the pastor's relationship with him or her and certainly does not resolve the long-term problem, but in life-or-death situations this may be the only viable alternative.

Not all suicide attempts are fatal. In fact, most are not. Many are not serious but are made as pleas for attention and help or as tactics to control others. How does one intervene with a person who makes suicide threats and gestures that are "not serious"? Some advise simple ignoring. Others recommend a paradoxical/confrontational strategy that says, in essence, "All right, go ahead and do it!"

Our own counsel is to treat such cases largely as any other suicide threat or attempt is handled. Precautions should be taken to ensure the person's safety at the present moment. Even "nonserious" people do make attempts, and sometimes such attempts are fatal, albeit by accident. It is best to be conservative and to take every suicidal sign seriously. Beyond the immediate crisis, the intervention is also the same—to determine the problem from which these actions arise and to find an appropriate resolution.

A Case Example

In addition to general principles, sometimes it is helpful to consider a specific example. The following dialogue illustrates how a pastor might handle a telephone call, following the guidelines provided above. We have provided not only the words that might be spoken, but also the thoughts that might be running through the pastor's mind along the way.

SPOKEN WORDS	PASTOR'S THOUGHTS
CALLER: Hello, Pastor, you don't know me. I found your name in the phone book.	Who is this? What does he want?
PASTOR: You're looking for a pastor?	
C: Yeah. I just want to talk.	
P: OK, let's talk.	
C: Well . . . I don't know. Maybe I shouldn't have called.	Sounds depressed. Do I know him?
P: No, it's fine. I have time to talk. Why did you call, . . . and tell me your name.	His voice sounds a little familiar.
C: Uh . . . Todd.	His name's not Todd.
P: What's on your mind, Todd?	
C: I don't know. I just (cries) . . . I just don't know any more.	
P: Sounds like things look pretty bad to you right now; all mixed up.	Ouch! I hope he doesn't think I'm saying *he's* all mixed up.
C: I just don't know if it's worth it . . . living, I mean.	Uh oh.
P: Things look pretty black to you right now. Tell me what's going on.	That's right, emphasize the "right now."
C: My girlfriend—she's got me all messed up. She dumped me.	He's single. Has he been drinking?
P: And you're feeling all alone.	
C: No! Hell, I can get a new girlfriend any time I want.	Sounds sluggish; probably drinking.
P: But still you're feeling bad.	
C: Yeah (silence).	Now what do I say?

P: So your girlfriend left. What else
is going on?

C: I can't find a job. I can't do anything
right.

P: Do you have any family here?   Did I ask that too soon?

C: Nobody who cares about me.
Just my old man.

P: Your Dad?

C: Yeah. He and Mom split,   Keep Dad in mind. You need him.
and he lives here, works at the post office. Should I ask for Dad's name? Not yet.

P: Todd, it sounds like you really
do need to talk. Do you have a
counselor or a therapist?

C: No. What's the use?   He wants me to argue with him. Careful.

P: Well, it just helps to talk to somebody
when you're hurting. I'm glad you called
me.

C: Are you?   That's a real question.

P: Yes, I am. I can hear the pain
in your voice, and I care.

C: Thanks. (cries) I don't know   Here it comes.
what I'm going to do. I'm scared.

P: You're not sure what you might do.

C: I just can't do it any more!

P: Sounds like you've hit bottom.
So now what?

C: I don't know. I'm just sitting here
thinking . . . about killing myself.

P: Things seem that hopeless to   Try to give him some future perspective,
you right now. Listen, Todd I just want   a little hope.
to tell you I understand. I know how
black things can look sometimes.
But it doesn't have to stay that way.
[No answer]   Too quick with the hope.
You know what I mean?

C: I just don't know.   Time to find out how serious he is.

P: You sound pretty scared.
What have you thought about doing?

C: I have these pills here. Or maybe
I'll just go drive over the edge.

P: What kind of pills are they?

C: Sleeping pills. My girlfriend   Maybe that's why he sounds sluggish.
gave them to me.

P: Have you taken any so far?

C: No, I don't think so.

P: You're not sure.

C: I've been drinking.

P: I see. So that's part of why you feel mixed up right now, too. Listen, Todd, . . . is that really your name?

C: No.

P: I didn't think so. Will you tell me?

C: David

P: Listen, David, I'm worried about you. I can't make up your mind for you, but it seems like this is no time to be thinking about killing yourself. You're upset, you've been drinking, and you may have taken some pills already. I know things look bad to you right now—of course they do. But I hope you'll decide to get some help instead. I'd really like to help.

C: (long silence, crying) I don't know what to do.

P: Well, look at it this way. If you're confused, it's better to wait. If you kill yourself, there's no changing your mind later on. Why not wait and see what can happen.

[No answer]

P: Know what I mean?

C: I guess so.

P: But you're right. This is a scary time for you. You're worried. I'm worried. Listen, is there somebody you trust—somebody you care about? A friend, maybe?

C: There's Carol.

P: Your girlfriend?

C: No, she's just a friend. She's married.

P: Somebody who cares about you?

C: Yeah.

P: What would she do if you called her up and asked her to come over?

C: She'd come. Probably bring Mike.

P: Would that be OK?

C: Yeah, I like him.

P: That's what I'd like for you to to, David. Is that OK?

What does *that* mean?

That sounds right.

Now give him some room.

Time for a plan.

The girlfriend?

Good!

Great! Get a commitment.

C: I guess so.   Should I call her?

P: Would you like me to call Carol for you,
or do you want to call her yourself?

C: I'll call her.

P: Right now?

C: Yeah.

P: OK. That's a start. I want to make sure   But what if she's not home when he
you get through tonight OK. Will calling   calls?
Carol do that?

C: Yeah   Now a back-up plan.

P: And if she's not home, how about
if you call me right back.

C: OK.

P: Good. Now, David, I'd like to call you
tomorrow morning to see how you are
and to talk some more. Would that be
all right with you?

C: (pause) OK.

P: Where can I call you?   Please, God.

C: Here. It's 555-8969.

P: OK. I'll call you tomorrow. And right
now you're going to call Carol.
And if she's not there . . .

C: I'll call you back.

P: Good, David. I'll count on it.
Remember—there are people who
care about you. Anything else for now?

C: No . . . Thanks.   Should I say, "God bless you?"
                                               I don't know what God means to him yet.

P: You're welcome. I'll talk to you
in the morning.

HELPING SURVIVORS

In spite of everyone's best attempts to foresee and prevent suicides, they will occur. The one who dies may well be called the suicide victim, but there are other victims whose suffering will continue. These are the survivors.

Although the circumstances surrounding their loss are somewhat unique, the survivors of a suicide seem to face the same process of grieving as those who have lost loved ones to other causes. A sudden suicide may result in a somewhat prolonged period of numbness in the survivors, but other than this their suffering resembles that of others who are bereaved. They have a journey to take—the journey through shock, emotional distress, and recovery. It may be very helpful for them to take parts of this journey in the company of their pastor, but as with grieving in general, the pastor's task is one of availability rather than coercion. There is no single proper way to grieve a suicide. Some talk it through with friends; others pursue the struggle internally. There is no right or preferred method. There are no mandatory stages. The stages of grieving were intended to be descriptive rather than prescriptive, and overt passage through them is not a prerequisite to healthy recovery.

The pastor who wishes to be helpful to the survivors should make his or her availability plain. This might be done with an open-ended invitation or further facilitated via visitation. The general guidelines for grief counseling described in chapter 12 apply here equally well. The survivors may find it helpful to review the suicide and the events leading up to it. Guilt is a frequent issue after suicides, and survivors often seek reassurance that they were not responsible by acts of commission or omission. The "Why didn't I . . . ?" questions are both inevitable and pointless, except in that they lead to an acceptance of the sad reality. A few points may be emphasized by the pastor here.

1. Almost all survivors feel a sense of responsibility, no matter how irrational it is.
2. Looking back, one can always see it coming. The saying that "hindsight is always better than foresight" is doubly true here.
3. Once a person makes the decision to commit suicide, no one can prevent it in the long run.
4. It is impossible to know what was going on in the mind of the person who has died.
5. Suicide is an intensely personal decision, one that cannot be made or even understood by others.

Although it is helpful for the pastor to listen reflectively and to focus on whatever feelings and reactions emerge, there are also no essential feelings that must be elicited. If crying or angry feelings occur, these should be accepted and reflected gently. Likewise, positive memories of the deceased may be explored. More frequent pastoral visits may be needed during the early shock stages of adjustment, and help with day-to-day decisions may be appreciated. The precautions and signs of abnormally severe grief reactions are essentially the same as were described in chapter 12.

In sum, the survivors of a suicide seek an explanation, a meaning, a way of understanding what has happened. They wonder about their relationship to and responsibility for the suicide. There may be special spiritual questions that they wish to discuss with the pastor. In all of this a natural healing process is occurring, a process that—unless it goes seriously astray—leads to healing.

SUMMARY

The risk of suicide should be assessed and explored whenever one encounters indications of possible suicidal thought or behavior. Among the factors associated with elevated risk are prior attempts, isolation, ill health, alcohol and drug abuse, depression, stress, psychosis, being male, and being older. Combinations of these factors increase risk. Yet suicide is not restricted to any particular group, and any mention or other indications of suicidal thought should be taken seriously.

Suicidal intent often develops in phases rather than all at once. At first, life is seen as less valuable and death as attractive. Then thoughts of the possibility of suicide occur, at first vaguely, then more intentionally as plans emerge.

Immediate intervention with a suicidal individual includes empathic listening, evaluating the severity of risk by gathering relevant information, giving supportive and stabilizing messages, and making contingency plans for preventing an attempt. Beyond the immediate crisis, intervention should focus on the problems that contributed to suicidal intent, seeking resolution of these problems to decrease future risk.

Surviving friends and family after a suicide face a difficult adjustment. Although the initial period of numbness may be prolonged, the grieving process resembles that following other kinds of deaths. The pastor who is open and available can be very helpful in resolving some of the residual guilt and in seeking an understanding of the suicide that allows the survivors to go on with their own lives.

ADDITIONAL READINGS

For the Counselor

BECK, AARON T., H. L. P. RESNICK, and DAN LETTIERI *The Prediction of Suicide.* Philadelphia: Charles Press, 1986.

CARSON, ROBERT C., and JAMES N. BUTCHER *Abnormal Psychology and Modern Life*, 9th ed. (New York: Harper Collins Publishers, 1992).

FARBER, MAURICE L. *Theory of Suicide.* New York: Funk & Wagnalls, 1986.

FARBEROW, NORMAN L., and EDWIN S. SCHNEIDMAN, eds. *The Cry for Help.* New York: McGraw-Hill, 1961. Readings on suicide and its prevention.

JEWETT, JOHN *After Suicide.* Philadelphia: Westminster Press, 1980.

PRETZEL, PAUL W. *Understanding and Counseling the Suicidal Person.* Nashville: Abingdon, 1972.

NOTES

[1]Quoted from Modeste Tchaikovsky, *The Life and Letters of Peter Ilich Tchaikovsky* (Plymouth: William Brendon and Son, 1905), 706–7. Letter dated 17 (29) May 1883.

[2]This is the rate of *known* suicides. Some experts believe that many more suicides occur but are registered instead as accidents or death by natural causes.

[3]Anthony Spirito, Larry Brown, James Overholser, and Gregory Fritz, "Attempted Suicide in Adolescence: A Review and Critique of the Literature," *Clinical Psychology Review* 9 (1989): 335–63.

[4]Sources for information on suicide risk include James C. Coleman, James N. Butcher, and Robert C. Carson, *Abnormal Psychology and Modern Life*, 7th ed. (Glenview, IL: Scott, Foresman, 1984); Maurice L. Farber, *Theory of Suicide* (New York: Funk & Wagnalls, 1968); Norman L. Farberow and Edwin S. Schneidman, eds., *The Cry for Help* (New York: McGraw-Hill, 1961).

14

STRESS AND ANXIETY

Therefore do not be anxious about tomorrow, for tomorrow will
be anxious for itself. Let the day's own trouble be sufficient for
the day.

—Matthew 6:34 (RSV)

Pastors in our workshops have sometimes commented, "You don't need to
tell us about stress. We know all about it!" Indeed, pastoral ministry can be
stressful in many ways, and anxiety is no stranger to most who follow this
challenging call. In this second edition, we have added new material to help
pastors deal with stress and take care of themselves (chapter 21).

Yet what *is* stress, really? Is it a situation, an experience, a physical reaction, an emotion? From our perspective, stress, like depression, is all of
these. Rather than being a single event, stress is a sequence of events—some
of them occurring in the outer world and some of them hidden within the individual.

ANXIETY

It may be useful first to consider the popular concept of *anxiety*. This
word has found its way into the vocabulary and the consciousness of almost
everyone these days. Sometimes the word is used to mean "eager" or "excited" ("I'm really anxious to see her again"), but more often it has a negative
tone and refers to an unpleasant internal experience ("I'm feeling anxious
about tomorrow"). Freud's German noun for the latter type, *Angst*, has found
its way into contemporary philosophy and theology.

Everyone has feelings that might be labeled "anxiety." There are many
synonyms to describe such feelings, varying in intensity (unease, distress, agi-

tation) as well as in whether the experience is occurring before (worry, dread), during (panic, terror), or after the feared event (guilt, frustration). None of these are exact synonyms because anxiety is a general concept and describes a wide range of experiences.

With the growth of psychology as a professional discipline, the concept of anxiety has taken on increasing importance and has also come to have different specific meanings and explanations. For Freud it was the sign of a present or impending leak in the psychic dike of defenses, signaling the need for more effective defense mechanisms.[1] For behaviorists it is a learned physical response that can be unlearned.[2] Rogers, in the humanistic psychology tradition, saw it is as the result of a discrepancy between the person's perceived ideal self and the real self,[3] while for existentialists it is a natural and healthy part of existence, of recognizing one's true aloneness and responsibility for meaning.[4] The one thing that was *not* often questioned as these theories and debates arose over the decades was the reality of anxiety itself. Most everyone accepted anxiety as a real "thing," an entity in need of explaining.

As psychologists began developing ways to *measure* anxiety, it was realized that there were several ways to go. It could be observed through *physiological changes* in the autonomic nervous system—the part of the nervous system that is responsible for emotional responses (to be discussed more fully later). It could be observed in the *behavior* of the person, such as nervous movement, speech disturbance, or changes in facial expression. Or it could be observed by asking the person about his or her *internal experiencing*—either directly or via anxiety questionnaires. Many studies used measures from more than one of these dimensions, and that is how the problem was discovered.

Shortly after psychologists began to use these measures, they encountered an unexpected difficulty: none of the measures of anxiety seemed to be related to each other.[5] Each would go up and down without regard for the others, as if they were independent of one another. Slowly the idea of one single entity called "anxiety" had to be called into question. If there really was no one "thing" that is anxiety, then what was being treated? Had all of this been manufactured by language?

Yet in spite of the scientists, people continue to have problems that they label as *anxiety*. It turns out, not surprisingly, that people mean very different things when they use this term, and that an "anxiety" problem may involve any or all of the dimensions mentioned above. For some people an anxiety problem is heavily physical. They have terrifying panic attacks with racing heart, rapid breathing, and the fear of dying; perhaps they have a health-threatening problem such as gastric ulcer or hypertension that is said to be anxiety related. For others, the concern is one of *looking* nervous, and for still others who may look perfectly calm and have no particular physical symptoms, the problem is one of troubling inner thoughts or disturbing confusion.

Remember, then, that when a person says to you that the problem is "anxiety," you don't know much more than you knew the moment before. It is easy to be misled into thinking, "Ah, anxiety! Yes I know what that is, and here is the solution." Yet what you mean by and experience as anxiety may be quite different from the meaning and experiencing of a client. The first step, as always, is careful reflective listening followed by a process of clear-thinking formulation. What *exactly* is the problem, what is causing it, and what if anything needs to be done about it?

STRESS

Just as people were assimilating the concept of anxiety, along came the still more pervasive construct of *stress*. This concept was borrowed from physics, where it refers to the amount of burden placed on an object and the consequent demands made on it. It is a construct measured in force units such as weight and pressure (pounds per square inch) and is used in engineering tasks such as choosing appropriately strong building materials.

In one sense the term *stress* retains this same meaning when applied to people. It can be thought of as an external demand placing a certain burden on the individual and requiring a certain degree of adjustment and coping. Thus, a situation can be "stressful," and an event might be called a "stressor," or just a "stress." But in modern usage this term has also come to include everything that was once subsumed under the name "anxiety"—physical changes, observable reactions, and internal experiences. Thus, it incorporates the totality of the individual's reactions to a situation as well as the situation itself. Stress is not a single event, it is a process.

Remember STORC? (chapter 12) The process begins with *situational* factors, with events occurring in the world. Some things seem to be inherently stressful for almost all people and animals, such as physical pain, loud noise, and crowding. Other situations are uncomfortable for many people, though not all—punishment, evaluation by others, or angry people. Change can be stressful, too, and exposure to prolonged stress has been linked to the development of various physical illnesses.[6] Alvin Toffler's popular book *Future Shock* addressed the effect of rapid change on individuals and societies.[7]

From another perspective, however, nothing is automatically stressful. Stress and anxiety are in the eye of the beholder. A firearm aimed at a person from fifty feet away would evoke no fear if that person had never seen one and did not know its hidden potential. Much of what distresses, frightens, angers, and worries people lies in their own interpretation of the situation. Physical pain that is self-inflicted for religious reasons (as by members of the Penitentes order or in the Native American sundance ceremony) or as part of a program of physical exercise may be experienced in a totally different manner from the same amount of "objective" pain inflicted by another person. Between the physical event that begins the process of pain and the experience of suffering, there are several important steps that account, in part, for why some people cope well with chronic pain or stressors and others do not. (The experience of physical pain is dealt with in a separate section at the end of this chapter.) Stress as a process, therefore, is importantly influenced by how a person *thinks* about or perceives situations.[8] There may even be certain habitual ways of thinking (such as the much-discussed type A personality) that contribute to chronic stress and increased risk of stress-linked diseases.[9]

A third link in the stress chain (S-T-O) consists of *organic* or physical factors. As mentioned earlier, there is a certain part of the nervous system that is directly involved in emotional reactions. Called *autonomic*, this part mediates the general physical responses that accompany the experiences of joy and anger, fear and sadness. The physical responses that are experienced as "anxiety" usually involve arousal of a portion of the autonomic system that is known as the *sympathetic* nervous system. This system is activated by adrenalin, and an injection of adrenalin (either naturally from the adrenal glands or from an external hypodermic needle) results in the kinds of physical changes listed in Table 14-1. Chronic, consistent arousal of this system can result in a physical breakdown of the body and in any of the many diseases that have been linked to stress. Interestingly, the sympathetic system is quite generalized in how it responds in emotional situations, and the physical patterns that occur during fear, anger, and positive excitement are similar. Research long ago showed, in fact, that it is possible to convince people that they are experiencing different emotions even when the physical arousal is identical.[10] It seems that there is one general type of primitive emotional arousal, which by culture we have differentiated into a broad and rich range of differently labeled experiences. Even during depression, this pattern of physical arousal is often present, showing that anxiety and depression can and do coexist.[11]

How a person *reacts* or responds to these situations, thoughts, and physical experiences (S-T-O-R) represents the fourth step in the process of stress. One type of response to stress is aggression (either verbal or physical), which is discussed in chapter 15. Another common response is avoidance—withdrawing from the situation and avoiding future contact. This is a critical res-

TABLE 14-1   Symptoms of Arousal of the Sympathetic Nervous System

Pupils of the eyes dilate (enlarge)
Heart rate increases
Less blood flows to the skin (cold hands)
Breathing rate increases
Digestive processes are inhibited
Mouth becomes dry
Blood pressure increases
Blood sugar concentration rises
Urination is inhibited
Skin changes—"goosebumps," hair standing on end
Sweating increases

ponse in the stress cycle because avoidance tends to increase anxiety rather than decreasing it, particularly if the individual cannot fully avoid the feared situation. Grandma's advice is right—if you fall off the horse, get right back on. To run away and begin to avoid horses is to increase your fear of them. This is a central theme in Jung's psychology—that which we try to avoid invariably comes back to haunt us. Avoidance gives power to that which is feared. This is not to say that it is *never* justifiable to avoid—only that to do so is unlikely to change the stress reaction process. Avoidance is one of the most common reasons for prolonged anxiety problems, and a useful question to ask when dealing with an anxious and stressed individual is, "What is this person avoiding?"

Finally, consider the *consequences* that follow from the person's reactions to stress (S-T-O-R-C). If the aggression or avoidance response results in desirable change (people pay more attention, give in, begin protecting or supporting), the individual may continue to behave in this fashion. Ironically, this tends to reinforce not only the specific reaction pattern but the entire stress process. The person who is rewarded for behaving in a stressed fashion may actually experience greater and more frequent stress. The same, as we shall later see, can also apply to physical pain.

These five links in the chain of stress are the same as those described for depression in chapter 12. These are, in fact, useful steps to consider in understanding *any* emotion as a process, and they will be used again in discussing anger in chapter 15: Situation, Thought, Organism, Response, Consequences.

SOME COMMON ANXIETY PROBLEMS

There are a few common types of anxiety problems with which you should be familiar. The first and simplest of these is a *phobia*, which is an experienced fear and avoidance of a particular kind of object or situation. When asked to confront the feared situation, the individual experiences feelings of dread and worry. When actually faced with it, the person may show physical (sympathetic nervous system) arousal, experience terror, and desperately attempt to escape. One friend of ours, an eminent psychiatrist, suffered from an intense phobia of flying, and his consequent avoidance of airplanes greatly limited his professional opportunities. People may be afraid of elevators, of particular animals, of public speaking, of being evaluated by others, of dating and sex, or of closed-in places. Each of these has a specific Greek-based name, but to name them adds nothing new. The basic point is that a phobia is a specific fear.

One special type of phobia that does deserve attention is *agoraphobia*. This is a particularly disabling phobia because it restricts the person's ability to travel about freely. Agoraphobics fear being away from help or being outside in public (from the Greek *agora* meaning market place). In its most restrictive form, agoraphobia renders the individual unable to leave the home. Many agoraphobics are able to leave home, however, either by traveling with others or by remaining within a certain set of geographic boundaries. Some can trace on a map the region within which they can travel comfortably. Some can drive but not walk outside; others can walk but not drive. In one case, two agoraphobics we knew met each other after some years of individual suffering. One was able to go into a supermarket to shop but was unable to drive there. The other was unafraid of driving but was unable to leave the car. They teamed up to do their shopping.

How does this strange problem arise? Usually it begins as another kind of anxiety problem, namely *panic attacks*. Without warning, the individual experiences massive amounts of autonomic arousal. Any or all of the anxiety symptoms listed in Table 14-1 suddenly flood the person. Just imagine that you are driving down a street or walking through a shopping center, minding your own business, when suddenly—without a warning or an explanation—your heart begins to pound wildly; you start sweating, breathing rapidly, and feeling dizzy; you become nauseous and believe you may vomit or pass out at any moment. This does happen to some people. Out of the blue they are struck by waves of autonomic arousal. These pass shortly and are not especially dangerous, but usually the *person* doesn't know this. Believing that he or she is dying or going insane, the person may consult a sequence of physicians, all of whom will find nothing wrong but who may prescribe tranquilizers. The individual may begin abusing tranquilizers or alcohol or both. Afraid of having another such attack, being out in public, or being away from help, the person becomes more and more restricted, until finally only the home may feel safe. Many of the agoraphobics we have seen have suffered from such problems for many years without ever knowing that this is a recognized syndrome or that it is rather easily treated. As with all phobias, the prognosis for overcoming this problem is excellent, given the proper treatment.

Two other anxiety problems should be mentioned here. An *obsession* is an unwanted thought that intrudes into the person's consciousness. The individual may think about it night and day; it keeps coming back to mind no matter how hard (and partly because) the person tries to avoid it. Thinking the obsessional thought may be associated with anxious feelings. *Compulsions*, on the other hand, are actions that the individual feels compelled to carry out. Common compulsions include repetitive handwashing, excessive cleaning, unnecessary doublechecking (e.g., locks or appliances), following particular routes or backtracking in walking or driving, or other ritualistic acts. Characteristically, the individual feels increasing anxiety until the act is carried out, at which point the anxiety is temporarily relieved. Compulsions are often linked to particular phobias, such as handwashing compulsion combined with a germ or dirt phobia. As in all of these anxiety problems, the person typically recognizes the irrationality of the behavior and may even be ashamed of it, yet feels compelled to continue.

These are not all of the kinds of anxiety problems, nor is it necessary to assign a type or label to every problem. These particular problems are mentioned here because they are common and treatable, and as a pastoral counselor you should recognize them for what they are.

POSTTRAUMATIC STRESS REACTIONS

Another set of problems with which you should be familiar is the psychological shock syndrome that often follows a traumatic experience. The stressor here is not one that is within normal human experience. Rather, it is an exceptional, extreme stress—one likely to produce distress in almost anyone. Some examples are exposure to combat warfare, being assaulted or raped, witnessing the violent death of a loved one, being caught in natural disasters, being tortured, or having a close brush with one's own death.

People react to such traumas in different ways. Some are resilient survivors, coming through the experience with few or no emotional scars. For some the shock is so great that there follows a period of amnesia in which all memory of the event is blocked. This normally passes with time, and memory returns as the person is able to handle it, usually in bits and pieces. A few suffer an acute psychotic episode after a major stress (see chapter 17). This, too, normally passes with time, usually ending as abruptly as it began within a period of two weeks.

For others, however, the damaging effects of a trauma are more long-lasting. Again there are large individual differences. The majority of soldiers exposed to combat do not show major long-range problems, yet this syndrome has been recognized as a serious and enduring problem for a significant number of combat veterans. The severity and duration of the posttraumatic reaction also seem to depend on the kind of trauma. The suffering seems to be greater and more prolonged, for example, when the trauma was intentionally inflicted by another human being than when it occurred as a "natural" accident.

Several characteristic symptoms of the posttraumatic syndrome may not emerge for months or even years after the trauma. These include (a) a high level of nervous arousal (see Table 14-1), reflected in jumpiness, irritability, exaggerated startle reflexes, or difficulty in sleeping or concentrating; (b) re-experiencing of the traumatic events in nightmares, flashbacks (vivid memories or the sensation that one is back in the traumatic situation), or persistent obsessional thoughts; (c) avoidance of situations and stimuli that resemble or remind one of the traumatic situation and distress when exposed to them; (d) an emotional "sealing over" or numbness. The last of these can be the most disabling in the long run. Usually, it is experienced as an inability to feel, particularly to feel positive emotions or to form intimate attachments. The person may feel distant and alienated from former friends and loved ones. A previous emotional sensitivity may be replaced by a flat, numb demeanor. As with depression, the person loses interest and joy in the things that were once rewarding. "I used to write poetry, and I loved to be with people," complained one combat veteran. "Now I feel all cold inside, like I can't feel anything. I can't get close to anybody."

Research on posttraumatic disorders accelerated with recognition not only of the long-term suffering of combat soldiers, but also of the alarmingly high incidence of physical and sexual abuse in society. Studies now indicate that one-fourth to one-third of all women and 11 to 17 percent of all men were victims of sexual abuse before the age of eighteen.[12] In addition to the posttraumatic syndrome described above, victims of childhood abuse commonly suffer from anxiety, depression, guilt, and low self-esteem, as well as sexual difficulties.[13] Advances have been made in understanding the long-term consequences of traumatic stress, though there is still a long way to go. It seems to be helpful to talk through the traumatic event in the presence of understanding others, perhaps others who have been through the same type of trauma. For veterans of the world wars, this was often accomplished on the long boat ride home, but more recent veterans airlifted from a combat zone, the solitary victim of rape, or the assaulted senior citizen may experience an intense isolation that does not allow such therapeutic talking through and may instead continue to avoid talking about the experience. Also helpful are the desensitizing and tension-reducing strategies described in the next section, which presents general intervention strategies for anxiety problems. Treatment by a professional who is particularly knowledgeable about posttraumatic stress—and who keeps up with the expanding research literature—can be quite helpful, and we recommend this kind of assistance. Again, though, be wary—claims are more common than competence.

ALTERNATIVE INTERVENTIONS FOR ANXIETY PROBLEMS

Contrary to what was once believed, it usually is not necessary to root out the historical "causes" of anxiety problems in order to treat them, nor are such problems typically linked to deep-seated personality disturbances. The causes of anxiety disorders are complex, to be sure, but the good news is that a range of effective treatment approaches are now available.

In considering alternatives, it is helpful to think clearly about just *what* the problem is and what its STORC components may be. Such a careful analysis of the problem can be helpful in selecting from among the various alternatives suggested in the following section, most of which have been well supported by clinical research. Once again, it is possible to take an experimental "personal scientist" approach by trying alternatives, starting with the most likely and employing different approaches until one or more are found to help. In certain cases (such as severe or posttraumatic disorders), a professional referral is in order. The main point, however, is that anxiety and stress problems are very treatable. Usually (though not always), the necessary treatment is neither long nor expensive, and in many cases it is possible to use self-help strategies or other methods that can be facilitated by a skillful pastoral counselor.

Changing the Stressful Situation

One optimistic aspect of a STORC conceptualization of emotional problems is that intervention (or prevention) is possible at any of the points contained in the process. The first place where intervention might be considered is with the situation itself, with the stressors.

One consideration here is *lifestyle balancing*. A healthy lifestyle, like a healthy diet, contains a balance of different ingredients. Too much junk food without adequate nutrition leads to long-term health problems. Likewise, mental health problems in general and stress problems in particular may be related to excessive exposure to psychologically noxious situations combined with insufficient nourishing relationships and activities. An interesting awareness exercise for clients is to list all of the activities that take a significant amount of their time in the course of a typical week or all of the people with whom they spend a substantial amount of time. If these are written on small slips of paper or cards, they can then be arranged in order, with the most time-consuming on top and so on down to the least time-involving. The last step in this exercise is to make a subjective rating of each one as mostly nourishing (+), mostly noxious or draining (–) or mostly neutral (0). A list that contains mostly (–) and (0) entries, particularly toward the top, suggests the importance of considering a rebalancing of lifestyle to include more positive and nourishing elements. This is not to say that the goal of living is to avoid the unpleasant and to exist on pure nourishment—only that a healthy balance is desirable and, indeed, vital if one is to function well, without an excessive burden of stress and depression.

Another option is to *neutralize* situational stressors so that they no longer have the power to evoke emotional distress. Almost any individual is unnecessarily distressed by some things. These needless stresses occupy a person's time and energy, rendering the person less able to deal with other challenges or to grow in desired directions. Again, this is not to say that people shouldn't be distressed about anything. A vital faith, in fact, calls people to feel and act on distress about injustice and address the shortcomings of our world and ourselves. Still, there are other needless stresses, and in many cases it is (to the surprise of most clients) possible to *choose* not to be distressed and deterred by these.

How is it possible to neutralize a stress or anxiety response? One well-documented approach is called *systematic desensitization* and makes use of a quite ordinary process of human learning—the process of association. That which is associated with painful and frightening experiences tends to become distressing in itself. An everyday example of this is to be found in the "painful reminders" of past unpleasant experiences—little things that are seen, heard, smelled, tasted, or touched that somehow came to be associated with the pain of that event. This side of the association principle can be used therapeutically to help people avoid unhealthy habits, as will be discussed in chapter 16 on addictions. For the moment, we are interested in the opposite side— that those things associated with pleasant or calming experiences tend to become pleasant or calming in themselves. A favorite chair into which one collapses at the end of the day, a special drink with which to relax, a loving friend with whom one has shared many close times, the suit worn during a particularly rewarding experience—all of these may come to evoke good feelings in their own right. Desensitization takes advantage of this process by systematically associating an anxiety-provoking situation or object with powerful pleasant and calming cues.

The first experimental application of this principle was reported in 1924 by the early psychologist and behavior therapist, Mary Cover Jones.[14] She was asked to help a young child who had developed an intense fear of white and furry objects. Using her knowledge of the association principle, she assembled a set of white furry objects, including a gentle rabbit. The child at first was obviously frightened of these and tried to avoid them. Next she gave the child food to eat and gradually moved the rabbit closer, reasoning that eating is a pleasant and calming activity that might serve to neutralize the child's fear. It worked. After a process of gently closing the gap between child and rabbit while the child was eating, the two shared the same chair happily. The child's fear had been tamed.

No, we're not going to recommend that you have all of your phobic clients over for dinner. This was only the first demonstration of a therapeutic principle that can be applied in many creative ways.

There are two essential elements to this technique. The first is *gradual exposure* to the avoided object or situation. Unlike massive confrontation (such as the height phobic dragging himself up the open fire escape stairs), this strategy aims to be painless. Each step is taken as the person is ready, and the steps are arranged close enough together so that no one step represents a stressful leap. Simple exposure itself (getting back on the horse), particularly if done in a gradual and gentle way, is often sufficient to overcome anxiety. The second element, to be discussed later, is a method for becoming and remaining *relaxed* during practice.

The process of gradual exposure is best accomplished by constructing and then working step by step through a *hierarchy* of situations. Constructing an effective hierarchy is itself a skill that requires some practice and experience. (Resources are provided at the end of this chapter for those who wish to learn this process in greater detail.) An example hierarchy may be helpful. Suppose you are counseling a parishioner who is quite gifted as a singer and in using language, but who is terribly afraid of speaking or singing in public. (Many such people work through their fears in church, which can be seen as a relatively safe place to practice.) A first step would be to construct together a list of many different possible situations that the person finds difficult. Included in this list should be some situations that are only a little challenging, some in the middle range, and some that would be very anxiety-provoking at the outset. (Note that anxiety is defined as *unrealistic* fear, fear of a situation where the actual threat is minimal or nonexistent. There is no point in trying to desensitize a person to a charging bull unless he or she aspires to being a bullfighter.) These situations might be written on blank index cards, one situation to each card. Twenty is a good number of different situations to generate. If a client has difficulty in coming up with different cards, vary parts of the scene like distance (how close to the feared object), time (how long until the feared situation is at hand), size (how large an audience), or confidence (speaking on a known versus unfamiliar subject). With a good set of cards, the next task is to arrange these in order of difficulty. This may be done simply by having the client lay them out on a table and sort them; the more traditional method is to have the client assign each one a rating from 0 (not at all stressful) to 100 (terrifying). The latter method has some advantages in helping the counselor to see big gaps in the list, which may represent steps that are too large. Cards with the same rating should be compared (for example, three 40s become 39, 40, and 41), and any large gaps in the hierarchy should be filled in with new situations. A sample hierarchy for this hypothetical client is shown in Table 14-2.

From this hierarchy several things are apparent. The individual in question seems more frightened by adults than by youth, by larger groups than by smaller groups, by longer talks than by shorter ones, by singing than by speaking, by singing alone than by singing in a group, by giving an unplanned talk than a planned one, and by talking than by reading. All of this is learned by this simple method of generating different situations and then rating them.

The neutralizing strategy of desensitization involves working one's way up through such a hierarchy one step at a time. No step should be too large. Each step is taken only after the previous one has been mastered. This is how almost any skill is learned, and it is an excellent way to overcome fears and anxieties.

There are various ways to progress through a hierarchy. One is *in vivo*—that is, by actually *doing* each step in real life. The steps then become progressive homework assignments. In this desensitization approach no step is

TABLE 14-2   Sample Hierarchy of Situations: Public Speaking Phobia

SITUATION	FEAR RATING
Give a 5-minute practice speech to pastor only	5
Read scripture to youth group (5 people)	6
Speak 5 minutes to youth group (5 people) without advisor there	10
Speak 5 minutes to youth group (5 people) with advisor there	15
Speak 15 minutes to youth group (5 people) with advisor there	20
Give 5-minute practice speech to family (5 people)	25
Sing solo for youth group (5 people)	30
Speak 30 minutes to youth group (5 people) with advisor there	31
Sing solo for family (5 people)	40
Read scripture to adult education group (25 people)	50
Sing as part of an octet at morning worship (100 people)	55
Sing as part of a quartet at morning worship (100 people)	60
Read scripture at morning worship (100 people)	61
Speak 5 minutes to adult education group (25 people)	70
Speak 15 minutes to adult education group (25 people)	75
Sing as part of duet for morning worship (100 people)	79
Speak 30 minutes to adult education group (25 people)	80
Sing solo for adult education group (25 people)	81
Make 1-minute announcement at morning worship (100 people)	84
Give 5-minute talk at morning worship (100 people)	85
Give 15-minute talk at morning worship (100 people)	90
Give unplanned 1-minute speech at morning worship (100 people)	95
Sing solo at morning worship (100 people)	100

forced. Each step is taken only when the person feels ready, encouraged by mastering previous steps. Another approach is to go through the steps in imagination, vividly placing oneself in each progressive situation. This also works well. The point in this second approach is to stay with one step until it can be imagined *without experiencing any anxiety or discomfort*. Various aids can be used to help remain calm while imagining scenes. The one most commonly used is progressive deep muscle relaxation, described in detail later in this chapter. The person becomes completely relaxed and then imagines a scene from the bottom of the hierarchy. If any anxiety or discomfort is experienced, the scene is switched off and the person goes back to relaxing until complete calm is once again achieved. Then the person returns to the scene to try again and repeats this until the scene is mastered, only then moving on to the next most difficult scene. This can be done with the aid of a counselor or as a self-help procedure; materials explaining each of these approaches are listed in the bibliography at the end of this chapter. Other self-calming techniques can be used besides the relaxation method mentioned here. Some people use deep breathing, mediation, yoga, prayer, or exercise to relax. Others use particular images (such as imagining a pleasant and relaxing place or imagining Jesus placing his hand on one's shoulder). The point is to imagine each scene while remaining calm and relaxed. This has been shown to increase the individual's ability to carry out the previously avoided task in real life. Gradual imagining and actual practice, combined with a self-calming technique, are usually quite successful in neutralizing fears.

Another method of neutralizing fears is to rethink them, to look at the feared situations in a different light. It is to this approach that we now turn.

Changing Perceptions

Reality is in the eye of the beholder. We relate not to a "real" world but to the world as we perceive it. Stress and anxiety are caused, in large part, by how we perceive the world. A second major avenue toward relieving stress is through changing these perceptions.

Consider the following experiment. Subjects were informed that they were participating in a study of the effects of noise on problem solving.[15] Each subject was placed in a room, given some complex puzzles to solve, and told that from time to time a loud noise would be played through the speakers in the room. Half of the subjects were given a signal button and told that if the noise ever became unbearable they could press the button and end the experiment, though the experimenter preferred that they not press it. The others were given no such button. No one in the experiment actually pressed the button, but those who had a "panic button" were significantly less stressed by the noise and performed better on problem-solving tasks even though the noise and the problems were identical in both groups. Why do you think this happened?

Consider another experiment on learning.[16] All subjects were told that they would receive a series of painful electric shocks delivered to the skin as part of the experiment. Half were given a "reaction time" switch and told that if they could press the switch fast enough after a signal light came on, they would reduce the intensity of the shock by one-half. The other subjects also participated in the reaction time task but were not told that it would affect the intensity of the shock. In actual fact, neither group had any control over the intensity of shocks, and both groups received exactly the same number and strength of shocks. However, the subjects who *believed* that they had some control rated the shocks as less painful and were less stressed by them.

These and many similar experiments point to the well-established principle that people are less stressed by situations in which they believe they have a certain degree of control, even when the situations are painful or difficult.[17] All else being equal, one is better off believing that one has some influence in what will happen.[18] This phenomenon of perceived control is only one of many aspects of how people perceive the world about them. Things are less stressful when they are understandable, predictable, controllable. The world is much more frightening when it seems incomprehensible, unpredictable, out of control. Note that this is true *whether or not* the person actually has any real degree of control at the moment. The person who believes in his or her ability to change things is less stressed by them, *tries* to change unpleasant situations, and often does so in the long run. On the other hand the belief that "There's nothing I can do" breeds an inaction which, in turn, leaves the person more helpless and out of control over his or her own life.

Not everything is controllable, of course. Sometimes, as Reinhold Niebuhr observed, what is needed is "the serenity to accept the things I cannot change," then moving on with "courage to change the things I can." Sometimes the best way to gain control—and to reduce stress—is by giving up control.[19] The point still is that how one *perceives* a situation has a great influence on how stressed one is by it.

How does all of this translate into practical counseling techniques? Quite nicely, actually. It means that one way to help people be less stressed and anxious about situations is to help them to *think* differently about them, to perceive them in a new light. Most religious faiths include massive doses of this very process—learning to look at the world in a new way, with a new perspective and understanding of what is important and what is not.[20]

We do not prescribe "correct" rethinking patterns for you. The general principle is to seek a new and different way of looking at situations, a way that is less stressful and immobilizing. This is not to say, remember, that one should never be distressed about anything. Being disturbed and moved by injustice, for example, is different from being stressed, frightened, and immobilized. It is not unhealthy to be distressed by the potential of a global catastrophe such as nuclear war. It *is* unhealthy and unhelpful to be numbed and immobilized by this fear, to resign oneself that "there is nothing anyone can do about it." What action one may decide to take toward peacemaking is a matter of individual wisdom and conscience, but if one is numbed and immobilized, then *no* action is taken. The same applies to intensely personal situations. The depressed person who despairs of ever feeling better, the marital partner who sits back and waits "to see how this marriage turns out," the phobic who avoids all contact with the feared situation—all have in common a hidden belief in their own helplessness to change their realities and a consequent passivity. How else might the situation be perceived, what additional perspective (including religious perspective) might help the person feel less stressed, helpless, or immobile?

There is some overlap here with the methods described in chapter 12. It can be helpful to keep a diary of situations that result in feelings of stress, anxiety, worry, or tension. The counselor's question, then, is: "What did you *tell* yourself at that moment which resulted in your feeling this way? What thought passed through your mind? How must you have interpreted this or looked at it in order to come out feeling as you did?" As the stress-producing interpretation and perception patterns become clearer, there are a number of possible counseling interventions that may be useful.

Thought Stopping   One of the simplest methods is to interfere directly with the unwanted thought patterns by stopping them. Even if an anxiety-producing thought comes into awareness, it is not necessary to *continue* thinking about it. Yet people often allow themselves to go over and over a certain thought or worry, dwelling on it as if in thinking it might be resolved. If a particular thought pattern is genuinely unproductive and stressing, a thought-stopping strategy may help. The counselor can demonstrate this method to the client by having the client begin thinking a stressful thought. After about ten seconds, the counselor says, "Stop." (Some prefer to *shout* "Stop!" for emphasis, mildly startling the client, but this is not usually necessary.) "Did you stop thinking about it?" the counselor asks, to which the answer is almost always, "Yes." The point is that the simple instruction, "Stop," is often enough to interrupt a distressing chain of thought. It is possible, of course, for the client to self-administer this instruction. Training can begin by having the client think the distressing thought, then say aloud "Stop," at first loudly, then softly, and finally to just think the word "Stop." In many cases this breaks the train of thought. (Note: With strong obsessions, however, this is not likely to be effective alone and may even have the effect of increasing the person's obsessional thoughts.) For some clients the use of another interrupting phrase such as, "Now wait a minute . . ." may be preferred.

Thought Substitution   A companion strategy is to substitute a new thought for the old one. The diary recording method yields awareness of the thoughts that have been distressing the person. Counselor and client together can work out new ways of thinking, new antidote self-statements to substitute for the previous distressing ones. Some possible examples of substitute thoughts are given in Table 14-3 to help clarify this method, although each individual will come to his or her own best alternatives. When the individual is feeling anxious or stressed, the sequence becomes: (1) Identify the thought that is distressing; (2) Stop it ("Now wait a minute . . ." or "Stop!"); and (3) Say to oneself the new, healthier self-statement to be substituted for the previous distressing one.

Rethinking Arousal   It is possible and helpful to think differently about physical arousal itself. Often a person who is anxious watches and waits for the first signs of autonomic arousal to occur (a change in heart rate, cold hands, or a slight increase in breathing rate) and then becomes anxious about becoming anxious! This results in a spiral of increasing arousal and panic. One approach is to relabel the arousal in a more positive way. One colleague of ours used to show many signs of arousal just before giving a lecture to a large class. Instead of interpreting this as speech anxiety, however, he told himself, "I'm getting psyched up for my class." With this thought in mind, he would proceed to give a stimulating, high-energy lecture. Recall that the physiology of being "excited" and of being "anxious" are similar. Why not, then,

TABLE 14-3   Some Thought Substitution Examples

DISTRESSING THOUGHT	SUBSTITUTE THOUGHT
I can't handle this. I just know I'm going to blow it.	I *can* handle this. I've done it before and I can do it again. It gets a little easier every time.
She sounded so angry! I must have said something wrong. I've done it again—offended somebody. No wonder no one ever likes me.	Now wait a minute! She could have acted that way for many different reasons. And even if she was angry that's no reason for me to panic. God loves us both.
I'm so nervous about this interview! I don't think I can go through with it. What if I get in there and freeze?	What's the worst that could happen? I'd freeze up and not get the job. But I already don't have a job, so what do I have to lose? Besides, it probably won't be so bad. They're people too.
Oh no! I can already feel my hands sweating. This is going to get worse and worse until I completely lose control. Maybe I'll have a heart attack!	Hold on, now. It's just arousal. Maybe I'm just excited about this opportunity. I've felt this way before and nothing terrible has happened. If I just wait it out I'll get through this fine.
If I don't find my wallet I don't know what I'll do! Everything is in there. I'll never be able to remember all of the people I have to call. This is terrible!	Just relax. Getting all excited won't help. I should try to retrace my steps since I saw it last. And even if I don't find it, I know what I need to do.
I'm never going to learn to drive! I've been taking lessons for two months now and still I'm scared to death. If it doesn't get any better this week I'm going to give up.	Now that's just too black-and-white. I'm certainly doing a lot better than when I started, and it's going to take some time to feel completely comfortable. That's no reason to quit now, after coming this far.

be "excited" rather than "nervous"? A certain amount of emotional arousal, in fact, can be helpful. Clients sometimes find it comforting to be educated about exactly what is happening when they become aroused (see Table 14-1). This can take away some of the mystery, making experiences more predictable and understandable. Some clients say, "It's only arousal!" or "It's only excitement." More generally, "It's only . . ." can be a wonderfully reassuring phrase.

Blow-up   Still another rethinking strategy is to ask, "What is the *worst* thing that could possibly happen?"—to blow the fear up to its biggest proportions. The point of this is that often what the person fears is rather vague, unrealistic, or unlikely. The counselor's role in this is to help the person specify exactly what it is that is feared, then consider whether that outcome would really be so bad, and just how likely it is to happen. Here is a brief example drawing on the public speaking phobia described earlier.

PASTOR: All right, so you stand up to make a one-minute announcement in morning worship. What is the worst thing that could happen?

CLIENT: Well, I would get all nervous and I wouldn't be able to think of what to say.

PASTOR: And why would that be so bad?

CLIENT: It would be so embarrassing!

PASTOR: So embarrassing that you would never be able to show your face in church again.

CLIENT: Well, not that bad.

PASTOR: How bad, then?

CLIENT: Well, I would feel funny, like, "What do these people think of me?"

PASTOR: Seems to me that you already wonder that about people!

CLIENT: Well, yes.

PASTOR: But that's the worst that could happen? You would stand up and make a fool out of yourself in front of friends?

CLIENT: Maybe I'd have a whole anxiety attack right there.

PASTOR: Maybe even pass out cold.

CLIENT: Maybe.

PASTOR: How likely do you think that is?

CLIENT: (Smiling) Oh, I don't know.

PASTOR: Pretty unlikely, I'd say. You've handled much more difficult situations in your life without passing out. But even if you did, what would happen?

CLIENT: I guess they'd carry me out and people would be all concerned and I'd have to explain it.

PASTOR: And would that, unlikely as it is, be any worse than the kind of anxiety that you feel so often now?

Like any method, this one does not always work, and sometimes it can backfire. Often, however, the "worst that could happen" turns out to be not so bad or at least extremely unlikely.

Reality Testing   A related approach helps the individual to get a more realistic picture of how likely the feared "disaster" is. Many fears are of the form "if . . . then," with the "then" being a grossly exaggerated or overestimated risk of calamity. Flying in an airplane or riding in an elevator *can* be fatal, but the risk of disaster is much lower than that involved in driving home from work in most cities. There *are* sharks in the ocean, but the number of people actually attacked by sharks each year (only a few in the world) is so small that statistically the sharks in the ocean are about as dangerous as the sharks in your bathtub. Hearing such information, reading about it, and repeating it to oneself as a thought substitution may be helpful for some specific fears. This is not helpful for everyone, but it can be beneficial in dealing with irrational or exaggerated fears.

All of these strategies attempt to decrease the stressful and anxiety-producing aspects of situations by helping the person to *perceive and think* about these situations differently. This is but one link in the chain, but for certain kinds of fears it appears to be a crucial one. Test anxiety, for example, seems to be mostly a problem in concentration and thinking. The person who complains about test anxiety usually is not more *physically* aroused than the rest of the people in the room during an examination. Rather, the difference is in what is going on inside the person's head. The test-anxious student enters the room thinking, "I just know I'm going to blow this one. It always happens to me. I look at the test and I just blank out." Then, on encountering the test itself, the person comes upon an item to which he or she does not know the answer and says, "I knew it! I studied this, and I just can't think of the answer. Probably I won't know the next one either!" The test-calm person sitting in the next chair does something different. Encountering the same difficult item, this student says, "That's a hard one. I'll go on and do the others that I know and then come back, and maybe it will come to me then." Research suggests that such thinking patterns are what distinguish between the "test anxious" and others.[21] Similar patterns apply to any performance-anxiety situation, for such thoughts can occur before and during an athletic competition, a job interview, or a musical recital. Such performance anxiety is often relieved by using a combination of thought stopping and substitution, so that the person spends less time thinking of distressing and unproductive thoughts and more time concentrating on the task itself.

Changing Arousal

Anxiety and stress can be influenced by changing the situation or by altering the person's perception of it. A third general strategy is to influence organismic arousal directly (S-T-*O*).

A wide variety of skills and techniques can can be used to help an individual reduce the kind of autonomic arousal that is often labeled as *anxiety*. The tranquilizers sometimes prescribed by physicians are intended to accomplish this, often through their muscle-relaxant effects. Heavier sedatives may also be used (and abused) for this purpose. These medications have their place and may be useful, particularly in situations of intense and acute stress, but there are some important disadvantages to relying upon medication to decrease arousal. First of all, these drugs do nothing to change the source of the stress. Second, most tranquilizers and sedatives have a high potential for abuse, with the person coming to overuse them in an attempt to cope with various crises or daily mood changes. Many of these drugs are potentially addicting, subject to the development of tolerance requiring increasing dosage for the same effect, and have the potential of fatal overdose, particularly when combined with each other or with alcohol (see chapter 16).

Interestingly, some anxiety disorders can respond well to certain antidepressant medications. The tricyclic antidepressants, for example, have a good track record in the management of panic attacks, with essentially no potential for drug abuse and dependence.[22] As discussed in chapter 12, the consultation of a competent biological psychiatrist is needed here.

What alternatives are there to medication? There are quite effective behavioral treatments for most anxiety disorders, which can be used instead of or in addition to appropriate medication. Different people prefer different methods for relaxing, but various skills are learnable. The one most commonly used by psychologists is the method of *progressive deep muscle relaxation training*, a technique introduced by a physician in 1938.[23] It teaches the individual to accomplish what muscle-relaxant medications are intended to do—to relax the major muscle groups of the body. A brief description will be given here, and the counselor interested in teaching this technique should consult the resources listed at the end of this chapter.

Muscles contain sensors that give the brain information about their state of tension. This makes it possible to feel how tense or relaxed each muscle is. The progressive deep muscle relaxation (PDMR) strategy teaches the person first to recognize tension in muscles by using this information that is available to all of us and then to gain conscious control over the state of tension in the muscles.

This awareness training proceeds in the following fashion. The individual sits or lies down on a comfortable surface—a recliner chair is ideal. With eyes closed, the person tenses one group of muscles at a time, following a set of specific instructions for creating tension. The purpose of this step is to learn how tension feels in each muscle group. The muscle is tensed for a brief period, about seven to ten seconds, and then the tension is released. At this point the muscle relaxes, and the person is asked to attend to how the muscle feels as it changes from tense to relaxed. A typical sequence of tensing exercises is presented in Table 14-4. Each group is usually tensed twice in a row—tense for seven to ten seconds, relax for fifteen to twenty seconds, tense again for seven to ten seconds, then allow the muscle group to relax completely, moving on to the next group after twenty to thirty seconds. There are many variations in the number and length of tension and relaxation phases and in the number and size of muscle groups focused upon. The major value of this approach seems to be the direct training of the individual in the skill of muscular relaxation. It takes some time to acquire this skill, and although tape-recorded instructions are available, the method seems to be substantially more effective when the instructions are given in person, at least during initial learning. With faithful practice between training sessions, a client may learn a helpful amount of self-relaxation skill in six to ten sessions.

Immediate results are not essential, and patience is called for in learning this skill. With adequate training, however, there can be excellent results. Research has shown such training to be helpful in reducing a wide variety of problems, including tension headaches, insomnia, anxiety, nightmares, and even hypertension (high blood pressure).[24]

TABLE 14-4   Typical Progression for Muscle Relaxation

BODY AREA TO BE RELAXED	TENSING PROCEDURE
1. Right hand	Make a fist and squeeze tightly
2. Right wrist, back of hand and forearm	Begin with arm lying flat, palm facing down; bend at the wrist and point fingers upward toward the ceiling
3. Right biceps	Touch hand to shoulder and tense upper arm
4–6. Left hand and arm	Repeat steps 1–3 on the left side.
7. Forehead	Raise eyebrows, wrinkling forehead and tensing scalp
8. Eyes	Press eyelids tightly closed (beware contact lenses!)
9. Nose	Wrinkle up nose tightly
10. Mouth	Press lips tightly together
11. Jaws	Press teeth tightly together (beware excessive pressure)
12. Throat	Press tongue into the roof of mouth
13. Back of neck	Press head back against surface on which it is resting
14. Front of neck	Imagine a force pressing against forehead and resist it
15. Shoulders	Raise shoulders up, trying to touch ears
16. Back	Arch back away from supporting surface
17. Abdomen	Draw in stomach as if trying to touch spine
18. Abdomen	Make stomach wall hard, as if preparing to receive a punch
19. Diaphragm	Take a deep breath and hold it
20. Thighs and abdomen	Lift legs away from supporting surface and hold them up
21. Shins	Point toes back toward head
22. Calves	Point toes away from head (careful not to cramp)
23. Feet	Curl toes downward as if digging them into warm sand (careful not to cramp)

Other relaxation methods are available.[25] Among the candidates are transcendental meditation, yoga, physical exercise, self-hypnosis, prayer, imagery, breathing exercises, and biofeedback. PDMR is most used, however, because it seems to be learnable by most people, requires no special equipment, is fairly easy to teach, and has been shown to be effective in numerous studies. For people whose anxiety appears to be more mental than physical, a method such as imagery or meditation may prove more rewarding than one aimed at physical relaxation (like PDMR or exercise).

There are two general uses of relaxation training methods. The first is to decrease the individual's *overall* level of tension and anxiety. This is accomplished through regular practice and use of the relaxation skill. It may help to practice at a regular time and place each day, building this into the daily routine. The second is for *specific* coping. During early training phases, PDMR is of limited usefulness, since most people cannot, when faced with an immediate crisis, withdraw and practice relaxation for half an hour (though some can). As the person's skill increases, however, shorter and shorter lengths of time are required to induce relaxation, until eventually the person is able to become quite relaxed in a brief period without specific tensing exercises. As this occurs, the person is then able to use the relaxation skill for immediate coping.

The potential applications are many. The individual can relax just before entering a difficult situation, during the challenge, or afterward. A person with sleeping problems can practice relaxation at bedtime. A headache sufferer may be able to avert or relieve head pain by this method. (*Migraine* headaches—which are more severe, often limited to one side of the head, sometimes accompanied by nausea, and often preceded by warning symptoms or "aura" such as lights or sounds—usually require more extensive treatment by a specialist and often respond well to biofeedback training.) Relaxation skill can be used in the process of systematic desensitization, described earlier. Of course, it can also be used just to relax!

Changing Behavior

A fourth possible intervention involves changing behavior—how the person responds (S-T-O-R). Most often this means stopping avoidance patterns and somehow confronting that which has been avoided. It is "getting back on the horse" in a very direct sense.

A desensitization process such as that outlined in Table 14-2 would be such a method if it were carried out in real life. Most of the activities on that list could be arranged with the help of the pastor, so that the person could actually practice and carry out each assignment. Such direct practice can be one of the most rapid means for overcoming fears and avoidance patterns.

There are several things that you can do to help a person experience these small victories. Certainly, helping the person learn a self-relaxation skill is one because this can be useful in reducing the arousal a person feels in attempting each step in the hierarchy. Often a pastor's physical presence and support can be reassuring. The widowed person learning to drive for the first time faces a frightening set of tasks, even after the driver's license has been awarded. A pastor or supportive other might accompany such a person in each new challenge, such as driving through a shopping center or driving on the freeway. The standard "You can do it" encouragement can be valuable at times like these.

It can also be helpful to show the person how—a process that psychologists call *modeling*. Here the usual practice is for you to go first (as in role playing), to show how it might be done. It is *not* important for the model to do the task *perfectly*. In fact, research suggests that a model who makes a few mistakes and then recovers well may actually be more effective than the flawless model because the latter presents a perfection that is easy to dismiss: "I could never do that!"[26] A model who is similar in age, sex, and social standing may be most helpful. The child who is frightened of dogs may be more convinced by another child playing happily with a friendly dog than by a whole line of adults who pet the pup reassuringly. In this regard it can be helpful to obtain the cooperation of a friend or parishioner to serve as a coping model (see chapter 20).

Practice—actually doing the thing that has been feared and avoided—is one of the best antidotes for fear and avoidance. A period of preparation using systematic desensitization in imagination may make the task easier, but often the real and rapid progress begins as the person challenges the fear in real life. One of our colleagues set up a program for people who were shy and anxious about dating.[27] The core of the program that turned out to be most effective was simple practice—just being paired up with a partner (who was also dating-anxious) and going out on "practice dates." For the agoraphobic, the most effective method for overcoming the fear and restriction is to challenge the limits—gradually to exceed the previous restrictions in spite of the fear.[28] This includes learning that panic attacks, if they do occur, are not fatal and can be handled.

Some anxiety disorders are more difficult and require specialized professional help. Agoraphobia, in many cases, is in this category. With proper treatment (which does involve a hierarchy of exposure to the feared situations), this problem *can* be overcome, with substantial improvement usually seen within the course of two to three months. Clusters of compulsive behaviors can also be stubborn problems requiring intensive treatment by a behavioral specialist, though again pastors and others can provide important support in the process.[29] Intense and generalized fears are sometimes best treated by a process known as *flooding*, the reverse of desensitization, in which the therapist induces intense anxiety by exposing the individual to the most-feared items first. (This is a procedure to be used with great caution and not without adequate training and supervision). The best sign that more intensive professional help will be required is the failure of the individual to benefit from the counselor's usual approaches within a reasonable period.

Changing Consequences (S-T-O-R-C)

Sometimes an anxiety problem continues in part because it is reinforced by those around the person. A child's nighttime fears may be maintained partially because they bring special individual attention from the parents. A phobia may permit the individual to protest "I can't" and thus avoid a situation where the underlying reality is "I don't want to" or "I'm afraid I won't be able to." An example from the practice of Dr. Arnold Lazarus was a man who developed a bridge phobia, rendering him incapable of driving across bridges—a rather disabling problem because he lived in San Francisco.[30] The underlying difficulty revolved around a work situation (his job was on the other side of the bridge) with which the client doubted he could cope. After being taught some new social skills for coping with difficult interpersonal situations, the client dealt directly with his new challenges at work and the bridge phobia vanished.

The question to ask here, in considering whether something is reinforcing an anxiety or stress problem, is: "What positive benefits is the person deriving from having this problem, or what unpleasant situations is the person able to avoid by having it?" The intervention here is individualized but involves a change in these consequences. If the maintaining force is a positive payoff (such as special attention in the case of nighttime fear), the solution tends to be to withdraw that payoff in relation to the anxiety, but to provide the desired goal (attention) at other times and in other ways. When the payoff is avoidance, the solution lies in identifying the reasons for avoidance and then coping with these. This might involve reducing an underlying fear or learning a new coping skill. A special application of this type of strategy is discussed later in this chapter, in the section focusing on the problem of coping with chronic pain.

MANAGING PANIC ATTACKS

A few words of practical advice are in order with regard to handling acute panic attacks. These, remember, are sudden large bursts of autonomic arousal (Table 14-1). They are not dangerous and will subside within about five minutes unless the person actively exacerbates the panic. Your basic task in managing an acute panic attack, then, is to help the person remain calm instead of fighting or fearing the panic. The trick is just to ride it out, like surfing a wave.

First, you can help the person understand what is happening. Autonomic arousal results from a natural body chemical, adrenalin, and is a perfectly normal body response. When a person is in real danger, adrenalin prepares the body to deal with the emergency. A panic attack is this same natural reaction, but occurring out of context when there is no real present danger. It's the alarm system going off by mistake. All that is needed is to shut it down. Once adrenalin has been released, it takes the body a few minutes to break it down, and that's what you're waiting for. Often, however, people in the midst of a panic attack fear that they will die, suffocate, pass out, fall down, or go insane. Experiencing these fears, of course, just releases more adrenalin and increases the panic. The point is not to complicate the physical adrenalin rush with mental panic and more adrenalin. There is literally "nothing to fear but fear itself."

Second, help the person avoid hyperventilation—rapid breathing that floods the body with oxygen and itself creates panic-like symptoms of lightheadedness and disorientation which further frighten the person. Hyperventilation can, in fact, set off a panic attack.[31] A simple method to reverse this process is to breathe slowly. If this isn't sufficient, have the person breathe into a paper bag, inhaling his or her own exhaled carbon dioxide, which reverses the spiral. Relaxing and calming, not fighting and avoiding, will cause the arousal to subside.

Some of the strategies covered earlier in this chapter can also be helpful. Physical relaxation or calming self-statements ("It's only adrenalin—all I have to do is wait for a few minutes") can help a person coast through the panic.

In the longer run, it is useful for the person to be aware of the early feelings that precede a panic attack. There are usually some warning signs before the wave of panic passes the point of no return. This is not to say that the person should be *constantly* monitoring heart rate and looking for symptoms—panic sufferers already tend to be hypervigilant in that regard.[32] If the person can be aware of the actual early signs of adrenalin release, however, preventive action can be taken. Instead of exacerbating the panic ("Oh, here it comes! I know this is going to be a bad one!"), sit down, relax, breathe slowly and deeply, make positive self-statements, talk to somebody, get busy with something else, do something fun, withdraw from the stressful situation, and so forth. Like a personal scientist, try different things until something works.

Finally, be aware of the trap of increasing restriction that can develop from panic attacks. In agoraphobia, as mentioned earlier, the person begins to avoid more and more situations and can become housebound. If this begins to happen, it is time to seek the consultation of a psychologist or psychiatrist knowledgeable about panic and agoraphobia.

PAIN AND SUFFERING

Pastors, perhaps more than anyone else except physicians, are called upon daily to confront and deal with the realities of pain and suffering. This section will not tell you why people suffer or help you guide them toward an existential or theological understanding of the puzzle of human suffering. That sort of searching is more the pastor's expertise than the psychologist's. Rather we will discuss suffering here from a different perspective—the physical and psychological events that contribute to it. This has more than an academic purpose. As alluded to in chapter 12, research has suggested several ways in which knowledge of these principles can be used to reduce pain and suffering.[33]

Pain versus Suffering

Pain itself is a sensation; it is pure information conveyed to the brain much as the eye and ear pass along data for the brain to interpret and act upon. When tissue somewhere in the body is being injured and cells destroyed, this information is sent to the brain and self-preserving action is taken (such as pulling one's hand away from the hot surface). The rare people who are born without pain sensors are not fortunate, for they are in constant danger of injury without awareness.

Suffering is an *interpretation* of pain. It involves the addition of an emotional reaction. To some extent this is wired into the human body—we become upset when we are in pain. Yet the distinction is important because it is often possible to alleviate suffering even when nothing can be done about the pain itself. It is altogether possible to dissociate pain from suffering, and there are numerous examples. Nitrous oxide, the "laughing gas" used by some dentists, has the interesting effect (on some people at least) of allowing the individual to experience the pure *sensations* of pain information without suffering, without being upset or distressed about them. Through hypnosis some people can learn to "turn off" their experience of suffering even though the sensations of physical pain are occurring (see below). Other research has explored the workings of a group of natural chemicals in the brain called *endorphins* (literal meaning: the morphine within).[34] Endorphins are produced by the body during times of pain and stress and act much as morphine does. Apparently our bodies have numerous natural resources for decreasing suffering even in the presence of pain information. This is more than what might be called *stoicism*, which presumably is silent suffering. Rather, it is an actual alleviation of suffering, an experiencing of pain with less distress and disability.

To Help the Suffering

Several good strategies are available to help reduce suffering in the presence of pain. None of these requires telling the person, "It's just in your head" (which is both unhelpful and bit insulting). *All* suffering is "in the head" in the sense that the brain is directly involved. There is no point in trying to distinguish between "real pain" and "imaginary pain"—except to ensure that proper medical attention has been received in all cases—because the suffering in both cases is quite real. It is the *suffering* that should be alleviated, and this is not accomplished by trying to convince a person that the pain is not real. The real meaning of this phrase, when used by medical personnel, is usually, "I don't know what else to do for you. I've tried everything I know, and I can't find anything else." Medical approaches focus on pain itself and aim to relieve the sensations of pain. The following approaches aim instead at suffering, regardless of the "actual" pain.

Before embarking on these, however, it is in order to stress again the importance of proper and thorough medical consultation in all pain cases. Pain *is* a warning, a signal—especially when it first arises. It is a message that something is wrong, and no counselor should treat suffering without also ensuring that proper medical diagnosis and any necessary treatment have been undertaken.

Some of the following interventions for suffering can be facilitated by a pastoral counselor. Others, such as biofeedback, require treatment by a professional who has had special training in the technique.

Relaxation   Relaxation itself can be surprisingly helpful. Almost any pain feels worse if the person is tense. An injection in the arm, the aching joint, removal of a Band-Aid from a hairy patch of skin, insertion of a medical examining instrument—all feel more painful when the person's muscles are tensed. Learning to relax in any of the ways outlined earlier may be of considerable help in relieving the suffering that accompanies pain.

Biofeedback   Biofeedback is a technical term referring to the use of an instrument that can provide direct and immediate feedback regarding a person's biological state. There are many such devices. Some measure heart rate; others measure skin temperature or muscle tension. All of these physical states are difficult to experience directly, at least when it comes to detecting small changes. A good example of biofeedback is an instrument that measures the temperature of one's fingertips. This device reads the temperature and feeds it back as a musical tone. As the fingers become warmer, the pitch becomes lower; as they become colder, the pitch rises. By using this device and undergoing a little training, people can learn to adjust the temperature of their fingers at will. How is that useful? It is very useful for people who have a circulatory problem known as Reynaud's disease, which results in painfully cold hands and feet. It also has been found to be helpful for people with migraine headache, as is relaxation training.[35]

Muscle-tension biofeedback can be used to help a person learn to relax a particular muscle group. Therapists sometimes use this along with PDMR if the individual is having difficulty in relaxing certain muscles. The device can detect small changes in muscle tension, and these are fed back to the person—usually in the form of a sound. Again, people can learn to relax muscles at will. Another exciting application of this device uses the process in reverse. Some people who have lost functioning of a certain muscle group through injury or stroke can make use of biofeedback to increase muscular control. Because the device can detect tiny increases in tension, it can be used to retrain muscular functioning. Biofeedback treatment requires some experience and expertise and is usually administered by a licensed psychologist or physician.

Cognitive Control   Sometimes thought substitution, as described earlier, can also decrease suffering by changing the person's perception of the pain information. Athletes on rigorous exercise programs learn to say, "It's only pain," and (for better or for worse) to regard pain as a sign that the workout is doing some good. These examples are not meant to endorse this approach to exercise but to illustrate how pain can be relabeled and given a different meaning. Pain and discomfort are sometimes signs of healing. A thorough explanation from the physician of exactly what is happening may be of some help, making the pain more understandable and interpretable. Sometimes part of the suffering is related to fears and uncertainty about what the pain means.

A dentist we know who is particularly talented in working with children often asks parents to bring a child to the office without giving any expectations about what is going to happen. He takes it from there, talking happily to the child, explaining what he is doing and why (in children's words, of course). As children grow older and sugar starts to work its damage on teeth, there comes the first time it is necessary to use a drill. (Often the parents are so frightened of drills that it is better not to have them in the room, lest they alarm the child even nonverbally.) On this occasion the dentist sometimes says, "This may tickle a little bit or feel funny, but it won't last long." It sounds preposterous to most adults, who long ago confused the pure sensations with their fearful interpretations. Yet sometimes the children in his chair are giggling and laughing at their first drilling. The actual pure *sensation* that accompanies drilling is a kind of tingling, mildly annoying one somewhat like a tickle—especially if it is not accompanied by terror and tension. This skillful dentist learned how to relabel "pain" so that the sensations are not frightening and do not evoke suffering and fear.

These are just examples. Exactly what kind of relabeling or thought substitution might help an individual to become more free of suffering is a matter for your own intuition and creativity. How else could the person think about what she or he is experiencing? Is there a way to perceive it that helps this experience be less frightening, less burdensome, less mysterious, more understandable, more acceptable? We are not advocating platitudes ("It's God's will")—though even these work for some people—but rather new ways of perceiving, of looking at and thinking about pain.

Activity   Immediate, acute pain has meaning. When people break a bone or sprain an ankle, the pain tells them to keep their weight off of it for a while. As the pain continues, however, and becomes chronic (professionals tend to draw the line somewhere between three and six months), its signal value drops. No longer is it healthy to honor the pain and avoid activity (except, of course, where such restriction is necessary). If six months of bed rest have not helped, six more months are unlikely to bring improvement in the pain.

There comes a turning point, then, where (with proper medical supervision) the person must stop regarding pain as an obstacle and start challenging it, start becoming active again in spite of some pain. Proper exercise and activity not only begin to restore physical health but also bring the person back into contact with the outside world in a richer variety of ways, taking the focus off of the pain. This transition sometimes requires the encouragement and even pushing of others. The proper pacing of activity and exercise, combined with relaxation training and cognitive strategies, can yield dramatic reductions in chronic pain.[36]

Distraction   Relatedly, a common strategy that is effective for many people is "to take one's mind off of it." A certain pediatrician we knew had a skillful technique for administering vaccinations to young children in the days when this required multiple injections from a hypodermic needle. He had the child stand directly over a small heat vent in the floor, with elaborate instructions on how to balance on it. In front of the vent, a window looked out into a garden, and the physician next directed the child's attention to the bushes in search of a rabbit who allegedly lived there. The rabbit was described in some detail, as were the places in the garden where the rabbit liked to hide. By the time the child had exhausted the excited search, eyes wide and neck craning to explore every hidden corner, the vaccination was finished.

The general principle is one of attending to something other than the pain sensations. In brief pain situations (such as the dentist's chair), this may be done by listening to music through headphones, taking an imaginary fantasy trip, even planning ahead to the events of the coming days or weeks. In longer-term chronic pain, the distraction principle means involvement in activities, not allowing oneself to be needlessly restricted.

Hypnosis   Hypnosis has had a long and controversial history. To many people this word conjures up magicians, mysterious loss of control, and the humiliating antics of the stage hypnotist's victims. None of these have a thing to do with clinical hypnosis, which largely involves learning the concentration skill of self-hypnosis. Current thinking about hypnosis is that there is no such thing as a deep and mysterious "trance" and that certainly the person is at no point "under the power" of the hypnotist.[37] These are fantasies created by books and films and do not resemble clinical hypnosis. The actual state that is achieved by skillful hypnotic subjects resembles hyperalertness more than sleep. It is, in fact, a mental skill, a practiced focusing of concentration and attention.

Extravagant and unrealistic claims are sometimes made for hypnosis, and there are many charlatans. Hypnosis is not a miracle cure for bad habits, and there is little or no evidence to support its effectiveness in treating most of the problems it has been claimed to cure. Hypnosis *has* been shown, however, to be useful in pain control.[38] In exploring alternatives for the suffering individual, hypnosis can be considered as a viable option. Basically, the skill of hypnosis can help a person to dissociate pain from suffering. Hypnosis has been used successfully to help people go through dental procedures and certain types of surgery without anesthetic. There are various ways to apply hypnotic skill in the alleviation of suffering related to both acute and chronic pain.

Remember that this is a skill, not a miracle cure. The person should not expect to "wake up" without pain. It is also important to choose professionals carefully. There is really no such thing as a hypnotherapist. Hypnosis is but one tool used by professionals. It does not stand alone, and there are various potential dangers in its use. Referral for hypnosis training should be made only to a professional person who has been properly trained and licensed in one of the general helping disciplines (such as psychology, psychiatry, or social work—see chapter 19). Clinics and individuals advertising hypnosis services and making broad claims of effectiveness should be regarded with great skepticism.

Changing Consequences   Finally, it has been demonstrated that a person's suffering can be influenced by how others react to it. Health psychologists now refer to "illness behavior," meaning what the individual does to let others know that he or she is suffering. This may include verbal descriptions, moaning, facial expressions, and other nonverbal cues. Interestingly, illness behavior tends to increase with stress.[39] Most people are inclined to act with compassion in response to such behaviors.

After a certain period of recovery, however, this can become a self-perpetuating pattern. This is particularly likely if the person receives certain positive payoffs *only* after complaining of or showing suffering. Unfortunately, this is exactly how many hospitals function. The person receives pain-relieving medications (which themselves often have pleasant effects) on a "PRN" basis, which translated into practice means only after a sufficient amount of complaining or requesting. Thus, complaints and other pain behaviors are directly rewarded by receiving the desired medication. Hospitals, like pastors, are busy, and it is often the squeaky wheel that gets the attention. If a person wants the company and caring of nursing staff, one way to obtain it is to show pain behavior. This pattern may continue after the person is discharged if the family adopts the same nursing practices. Pain and suffering behavior may also allow the person to avoid certain unpleasant tasks or relationships. As we have pointed out before, this is not at all to imply that people fake pain to get attention and other payoffs. Rather, the fact that such payoffs come *only* after pain behavior—that receiving these positive consequences *depends* on showing pain—actually extends and increases suffering itself.

One of the first people to write about this extensively was a psychologist named Fordyce.[40] He arranged a special pain treatment ward where staff members were carefully trained *not* to reward suffering but instead to reward healthy behavior. At first this sounds inhumane: Break eye contact and look away when the person talks about suffering, and if it continues walk away and come back later. All pain medication was given on a regular time schedule (for example, every four hours), and nothing the patient did had any influence on when and how much medication was given. The results were striking and have been replicated in other settings. Patients reported and experienced less pain and became more active and less disabled. As patients made the effort to begin exercising or talked about things other than suffering, the staff of the ward paid close attention and did all they could to encourage this new pattern. Slowly the pain medication was decreased. In the end most patients were using little medication, experiencing much less suffering (though pain was not gone in most cases), and living more normal, active, productive lives. A more recent alternative approach has been to give patients control over the administration of their own postsurgical drugs by providing a button that releases pain medication. Typically patients given such a button require less medication and experience less pain—a parallel to the research described earlier in this chapter on perceived control.

We add this description because we believe it is important for pastors to consider their own contribution in cases of long-term pain and suffering. Your time and attention can be very important. It is perfectly natural for a pastor to care—to spend long hours listening to accounts of the person's suffering and providing reassurance. Consider the possibility, however, that this well-meaning pastoral function may actually contribute, in the long run, to the perpetuation of suffering. We are in no way advocating pastoral abandonment. In acute crisis and distress, it is a pastor's function to be there. It is also well within the pastoral role to help people search for meaning in their predicaments. But as the predicament continues, it may also be a valuable function to begin reinforcing healthy recovery. This might mean (a) asking less about the suffering and more about what the person is doing to be renewed; (b) showing less interest in reports of suffering but great interest in other topics—particularly ones that involve recovery; (c) being present in the person's struggles to regain normal living—at those moments of victory, breakthrough, and accomplishment; (d) providing direct assistance and encouragement as the individual makes efforts away from disability toward activity and health; and (e) encouraging significant other people in the individual's life to do the same.

A pastor friend of ours some years ago had a heart transplant. Just before he left Stanford Hospital, his physician gave him a piece of advice. "When you get home, ask people to treat you like a normal person. Ask them not to regard you as helpless, not to express sympathy or pity, not to treat you with kid gloves, not to give you special breaks or make allowances. If they see you and treat you as weak and disabled, you will become so. If they see you and treat you as normal and healthy and strong, you will grow in that direction." So it is.

SUMMARY

"Anxiety" is not a single phenomenon but rather a group of elements including physiological, behavioral, and cognitive events. The STORC model, introduced in chapter 12, is also useful in understanding anxiety and stress. Diagnosis of anxiety problems includes identifying which of these elements are involved and what is causing the difficulty. Among common causal factors are situational stressors, thought patterns, exacerbating behavior patterns such as avoidance, and reinforcing consequences.

Some important types of anxiety problems should be recognized: phobias, panic attacks, agoraphobia, obsessions, compulsions, and posttraumatic stress reactions. Although these have a certain amount in common, each requires somewhat different intervention approaches.

Treatment of anxiety problems usually does not require major personality change or excavation of historical roots of the difficulty. Among the alternatives with a track record of success are situational change (such as lifestyle balancing), neutralizing strategies (such as systematic desensitization), cognitive restructuring to alter stress-inducing perceptions, arousal-reducing skills (such as progressive deep muscle relaxation training), practice in confronting and doing that which has been feared and avoided, and alteration of patterns that have encouraged and reinforced fear and avoidance.

Similar strategies have been found to be effective in reducing chronic pain that is unresponsive to the usual medical ministrations. Training in relaxation or biofeedback, cognitive and hypnotic skills, distraction and activity, and differential encouragement of nondisabled actions all hold promise for the relief of physical suffering.

ADDITIONAL READINGS

For the Client

AGRAS, W. STUART *Panic: Facing Fears, Phobias, and Anxiety.* New York: W. C. Freeman, 1985.

BARLOW, DAVID, and MICHELLE CRASKE *Mastery of Your Anxiety and Panic.* Albany, NY: Graywind Publications, 1989.

BENSON, HERBERT, and MIRIAM Z. KLIPPER *The Relaxation Response.* New York: Avon, 1975. A best-seller; teaches a meditative approach to relaxation.

BENSON, HERBERT, and WILLIAM PROCTOR *Beyond the Relaxation Response.* New York: Bantam Books, 1985. An interesting extension of Benson's best-seller, venturing into the spiritual realm.

BOURNE, EDMOND J. *The Anxiety and Phobia Workbook.* Oakland, CA: New Harbinger Publications, 1990. Clear explanations of anxiety problems and specific methods for overcoming them.

CATALANO, ELLEN MOHR *The Chronic Pain Control Workbook: A Step-by-Step Guide for Coping with and Overcoming Your Pain.* Oakland, CA: New Harbinger Publications, 1987.

DAVIS, MARTHA, ELIZABETH R. ESHELMAN, and MATTHEW MACKAY *The Relaxation and Stress Reduction Workbook* (3d ed.). Oakland, CA: New Harbinger Publications, 1988.

DESBERG, PETER, and GEORGE D. MARSH *Controlling Stagefright: Presenting Yourself to Audiences from One to One Thousand.* Oakland, CA: New Harbinger Publications, 1988. Specific help for public speaking and other performance fears.

FREEMAN, ARTHUR, and ROSE DEWOLF *Woulda, Coulda, Shoulda: Overcoming Regrets, Mistakes, and Missed Opportunities.* New York: Harper, 1990.

HART, ARCHIBALD *Adrenalin and Stress.* Dallas, TX: Word Publishing, 1991.

————*Overcoming Anxiety.* Dallas TX: Word Publishing, 1989.

OATES, WAYNE E. *Managing Your Stress.* Philadelphia: Fortress Press, 1985.

RAPAPORT, JUDITH *The Boy Who Couldn't Stop Washing.* New York: Dutton, 1989. Practical information and case examples of obsessive-compulsive disorder.

SELIGMAN, MARTIN *Learned Optimism: The Skill to Conquer Life's Obstacles, Large and Small.* New York: Random House, 1990. A new research-based approach to "positive thinking."

WEEKES, CLAIRE *Peace from Nervous Suffering.* New York: NAL/Dutton, 1990. A classic on how to deal with panic and other anxiety problems.

WOLPE, JOSEPH M., and DAVID WOLPE *Life without Fear: Anxiety and Its Cure.* Oakland, CA: New Harbinger Publications, 1988.

ZIMBARDO, PHILIP G. *Shyness: What It Is, What to Do about It.* Reading, MA: Addison-Wesley, 1990. A self-help book about shyness and how to overcome it.

For the Counselor

BECK, AAARON T., and GARY EMERY, with RUTH L. GREENBERG *Anxiety Disorders and Phobias: A Cognitive Perspective.* New York: Basic Books, 1985.

BERNSTEIN, DOUGLAS A., and THOMAS D. BORKOVEC *Progressive Relaxation Training: A Manual for the Helping Professions.* Champaign, IL: Research Press, 1973. Therapist instructions on teaching relaxation; includes a record with sample script.

CAUTELA, JOSEPH R., and JUNE GRODEN *Relaxation: A Comprehensive Manual for Adults, Children, and Children with Special Needs.* Champaign, IL: Research Press, 1978. Still a solid guide to relaxation training.

FRIEDMAN, MEYER, and DIANE ULMER *Type A Behavior and Your Heart.* New York: Fawcett, 1985. The original book on behavior patterns that have been shown to contribute to risk of heart disease.

MEICHENBAUM, DONALD *Stress Inoculation Training.* New York: Pergamon Press, 1985. A research-based approach for helping people prepare for and cope with stressful situations.

NOTES

[1]Sigmund Freud, *The Problem of Anxiety* (New York: Psychoanalytic Quarterly Press, 1936).

[2]Joseph Wolpe, *The Practice of Behavior Therapy*, 4th ed. (Elmsford, NY: Pergamon Press, 1991).

[3]Carl R. Rogers, "A Theory of Therapy, Personality and Interpersonal Relationships as Developed in the Client-centered Framework," in Sigmund Koch, ed., *Psychology: A Study of a Science* (New York: McGraw-Hill, 1959), vol. 3, 184–256.

[4]Rollo May, *Psychology and the Human Dilemma* (New York: Van Nostrand, 1967).

[5]Peter J. Lang, "The Mechanics of Desensitization and the Laboratory Study of Human Fear," in Cyril M. Franks, ed., *Behavior Therapy: Appraisal and Status* (New York: McGraw-Hill, 1969).

[6]The original life change stressor scale was published by T. H. Holmes and R. H. Rahe, "The Social Readjustment Rating Scale," *Journal of Psychosomatic Research* 11 (1967): 213–18. For more

recent research consult Douglas Carroll, *Health Psychology: Stress, Behaviour and Disease* (London: Falmer Press, 1992); Nicholas P. Plotnikoff, Robert E. Faith, Anthony J. Murgo, and Robert A. Good, *Enkephalins and Endorphins: Stress and the Immune System* (New York: Plenum Press, 1986).

[7]Alvin Toffler, *Future Shock* (New York: Random House, 1970).

[8]Richard S. Lazarus, *Emotion and Adaptation* (New York: Oxford University Press, 1991).

[9]Meyer Friedman and Diane Ulmer, *Type A Behavior and Your Heart* (New York: Fawcett, 1985).

[10]Stanley Schachter and Jerome E. Singer, "Cognitive, Social and Physiological Determinants of Emotional State," *Psychological Review* 69 (1962): 379–99.

[11]Fiona K. Judd and Graham D. Burrows, "Anxiety Disorders and Their Relationship to Depression," in Eugene S. Paykel, ed., *Handbook of Affective Disorders*, 2d ed. (New York: Guilford Press, 1992), 77–87.

[12]Frank G. Bolton Jr., Larry A. Morris, and Ann E. MacEachron, *Men at Risk: The Other Side of Child Sexual Abuse* (Newbury Park, CA: Sage Publications, 1989); Lenore E. A. Walker, ed., *Handbook on Sexual Abuse of Children: Assessment and Treatment Issues* (New York: Springer, 1988).

[13]Bolton, Morris, and MacEachron, *Men at Risk*; Walker, *Handbook on Sexual Abuse*, 66–7.

[14]Mary Cover Jones, "The Elimination of Children's Fears," *Journal of Experimental Psychology* 7 (1924): 382–90.

[15]D. Sherrod, J. Hage, P. Halpern, and B. Moore, "Effects of Personal Causation and Perceived Control on Responses to an Aversive Environment: The More Control, the Better," *Journal of Experimental Social Psychology* 13 (1977): 14–27.

[16]James I I. Geer, Gerald C. Davison, and Robert J. Gatchel, "Reduction of Stress in Humans through Nonveridical Perceived Control of Aversive Stimulation," *Journal of Personality and Social Psychology* 16 (1970): 731–38.

[17]Herbert M. Lefcourt, *Locus of Control: Current Trends in Theory and Research*, 2d ed. (Hillsdale, NJ: Erlbaum, 1982); J. Suls and B. Mullen, "Life Change and Psychological Distress: The Role of Perceived Control and Desirability," *Journal of Applied Social Psychology* 11 (1981): 379–89; S. C. Thompson, "Will It Hurt Less If I Can Control It? A Complex Answer to a Simple Question," *Psychological Bulletin* 90 (1981): 89–101.

[18]Martin E. P. Seligman, *Helplessness* (San Francisco: W. H. Freeman, 1975); *Learned Optimism: The Skill to Conquer Life's Obstacles, Large and Small* (New York: Random House, 1990).

[19]James R. Baugh, "Gaining Control by Giving Up Control: Strategies for Coping with Powerlessness," in William R. Miller and John E. Martin, eds., *Behavior Therapy and Religion: Integrating Spiritual and Behavioral Approaches to Change* (Newbury Park, CA: Sage Publications, 1988), 125–38.

[20]William R. Miller, *Living As If: How Positive Faith Can Change Your Life* (Philadelphia: Westminster Press, 1985).

[21]J. Wine, "Test Anxiety and Direction of Attention," *Psychological Bulletin* 76 (1971): 92–104.

[22]Guy M. Goodwin, "Tricyclic and Newer Antidepressants," in Eugene S. Paykel, ed., *Handbook of Affective Disorders*, 2d ed. (New York: Guilford Press, 1992), 327–43.

[23]Edmund Jacobson, *Progressive Relaxation* (Chicago: University of Chicago Press, 1938).

[24]Edward P. Sarafino, *Health Psychology: Biopsychosocial Interactions* (New York: John Wiley, 1990); D. W. Johnston, "The Behavioral Control of High Blood Pressure," *Current Psychological Research and Reviews* 6 (1987): 99–114; William R. Miller and Marina DiPilato, "Treatment of Nightmares via Relaxation and Desensitization: A Controlled Evaluation," *Journal of Consulting and Clinical Psychology* 51 (1983): 870–77.

[25]Herbert Benson and William Proctor, *Beyond the Relaxation Response* (New York: Bantam Books, 1985); Martha Davis, Elizabeth R. Eshelman, and Matthew MacKay, *The Relaxation and Stress Reduction Workbook*, 3d ed. (Oakland, CA: New Harbinger Publications, 1988); Kenneth L. Lichstein, *Clinical Relaxation Strategies* (New York: John Wiley, 1988).

[26]Allen E. Kazdin, "Covert Modeling and the Reduction of Avoidance Behavior," *Journal of Abnormal Psychology* 81 (1973): 87–95.

[27]Andrew Christensen, Hal Arkowitz, and Judith Anderson, "Practice Dating as Treatment for College Dating Inhibitions," *Behaviour Research and Therapy* 13 (1975): 321–31.

[28]Ronald Rapee and David Barlow, "Psychological Treatment of Unexpected Panic Attacks: Cognitive/Behavioral Components," in Roger Baker, ed., *Panic Disorder: Theory, Research and Treatment* (New York: John Wiley, 1989), 239–59.

[29]Sheri D. Pruitt, William R. Miller, and Jane Ellen Smith, "Outpatient Behavioral Treatment of Severe Obsessive-Compulsive Disorder: Using Paraprofessional Resources," *Journal of Anxiety Disorders* 3 (1989): 179–86.

[30]Arnold A. Lazarus, *Behavior Therapy and Beyond* (New York: McGraw-Hill, 1971).

[31]Ronald Ley, "Hyperventilation and Lactate Infusion in the Production of Panic Attacks," *Clinical Psychology Review* 8 (1988): 1–18; P. Spinhoven, E. J. Onstein, P. J. Sterk, and D. Le Haen-Versteijnen, "The Hyperventilation Provocation Test in Panic Disorder," *Behaviour Research and Therapy* 30 (1992): 453–61.

[32]Anke Ehlers and Peter Breuer, "Increased Cardiac Awareness in Panic Disorder," *Journal of Abnormal Psychology* 101 (1992): 371–82.

[33]Francis J. Keefe and David A. Williams, "New Directions in Pain Assessment and Treatment," *Clinical Psychology Review* 9 (1989): 549–68.

[34]Nicholas P. Plotnikoff, Robert E. Faith, Anthony J. Murgo, and Robert A. Good, *Enkephalins and Endorphins: Stress and the Immune System* (New York: Plenum Press, 1986).

[35]Frank Andrasik, "Relaxation and Biofeedback for Chronic Headaches," in A. D. Holzman and D. C. Turk, eds., *Pain Management: A Handbook of Psychological Treatment Approaches* (New York: Pergamon Press, 1986).

[36]Francis J. Keefe, Julie Dunsmore, and Rachel Burnett, "Behavioral and Cognitive-Behavioral Approaches to Chronic Pain: Recent Advances and Future Directions," *Journal of Consulting and Clinical Psychology* 60 (1992): 528–36.

[37]Theodore X. Barber, Nicholas P. Spanos, and John F. Chaves, *Hypnosis, Imagination, and Human Potentialities* (Elmsford, NY: Pergamon Press, 1984).

[38]Ernest R. Hilgard and J. R. Hilgard, *Hypnosis in the Relief of Pain* (Los Altos, CA: William Kaufmann, 1975).

[39]S. Cohen and G. W. Williamson, "Stress and Infectious Disease in Humans," *Psychological Bulletin* 109 (1991): 5–24.

[40]Wilbert E. Fordyce, *Behavioral Methods for Chronic Pain and Illness* (St. Louis: C. V. Mosby, 1976).

15

ANGER AND AGGRESSION

Violence is the last refuge of the incompetent.

—Isaac Asimov, *Foundation*

Anger probably evokes more ambivalence than any other emotion. It is regarded both as a sign of strength and as a reason for remorse. The wrath of God invokes both fear and awe. People talk about anger as if it were a mysterious force that inhabits them from time to time—"I was overcome by a fit of anger" or "I don't know what came over me." Anger is learned and respected almost as if it were possession by a potent demon. Courts of law make certain allowances for "crimes of passion" and regard murders committed in the sudden heat of anger (second degree) to be less serious than those carried out in the premeditated shade of cool reason (first degree). Some say that it is healthy to "let your anger out." Others seek never to express or even feel anger. It is a most ambivalent and confusing emotion.

Yet like other emotions, anger occurs according to lawful principles. It is predictable, understandable, and subject to self-control. It is a *feeling*, not to be confused with the destructive *behavior* that we will discuss later as "aggression." Angry feelings do not hurt other people. Only certain ways of expressing them do. Anger itself, like anxiety and depression, is a signal—a sign that a change is needed.

In our preceding chapters on depression and stress, we employed a STORC analysis, a psychological method for understanding emotions as occurring in stages. This same type of analysis is helpful in understanding anger, which ordinarily is thought of as occurring suddenly and without control from the person. This will be the last flight of the STORC in this book, although this model can also be used to understand other problem areas. As before, each of the five components of this model will be discussed in examining how anger occurs and—ultimately—how it can be managed.

SITUATIONAL/STIMULUS FACTORS

There are a variety of situational factors that can contribute to feelings of irritability, impatience, resentment, or other forms of anger. *Environmental irritants* fall into this class—noise, inclement weather, perhaps pollution. Being in physical pain can increase irritability and lower the threshold for aggression. Going without sleep has a similar effect.

Frustration is another factor often included here. Frustration can refer to a feeling, but here it is used to refer to the encountering of an obstacle, an obstruction in the path one had intended to follow. Something stands in the way of accomplishing an intended goal, be it a rainy day or a traffic jam, a locked door or a person who moves too slowly. Frustration is an obstacle in the road, and each person chooses how to react to such obstacles. During the World Wars, psychologists were called upon to help in officer selection. One test required the individual to complete a task in cooperation with others, racing against another team working on the same task. Unbeknownst to the candidate, the "teammates" were all part of the evaluation team, and they provided intentional obstacles—incompetent decisions, foolish mistakes, slow pace. The actual test was not how quickly the team finished, but how the officer candidate coped with this kind of frustration. Would the person be incapacitated by such obstacles?

Still another situational factor related to angry feelings and aggressive behavior is *crowding*. Each of us has territorial instincts. As pointed out in chapter 3, each person has a natural distance that is kept in talking to another. Stepping within this distance, getting too close, seems to create discomfort and the person tries to correct it by resuming proper distance. People whose homes are sacked by burglars, who are robbed or assaulted, frequently feel an intense anger that seems to be related to this invasion of territory. Conditions of crowding force a person into a position of restricted territory. The natural range of personal space cannot be maintained. An interesting example is the discomfort that people often feel in elevators, resulting in a fairly predictable sequence of avoidance behaviors: get as far away from others as possible, don't talk, stare ahead blankly and look at the numbers. Prolonged conditions of crowding can contribute to arousal that can be interpreted as anger or stress and is associated with increased risk of aggression.

Some psychologists—Thomas Gordon,[1] for example—have maintained that anger is not a primary emotion but rather is always a secondary emotion. By this is meant that anger follows from another emotion, usually hurt or fear. A person is first hurt in some fashion (embarrassed, injured, humiliated, rejected) or frightened (startled, threatened, worried)—*then* becomes angry in response to the primary emotion. Gordon recommends trying to recover the primary feeling when anger is encountered, to ask what pain or fear was felt first and resulted in the anger. Although this conception of anger as a secondary emotion is debatable, this is a useful question to ask, and often it points to important situational or psychological factors that have triggered the angry feeling.

THOUGHT PATTERNS

Effective approaches to anger management have focused heavily on thought patterns, on cognitive factors that play key roles in anger. As with other emotions, anger does not follow automatically from situations. Nothing "makes" a person angry. It depends on a certain interpretation in most cases. This is especially true of retained anger: holding a grudge, staying mad, or resenting. Just about the only way to keep anger alive is to continue to rehearse injustices mentally. The kind of physical arousal (see below) involved in anger is ephemeral. It passes quickly. To be kept alive, anger must be nourished and fed. This is done by thinking in certain ways. Some people save up their resentments, cherishing and hoarding them until they have enough to justify a tirade or a tantrum (a process that has been referred to as *collecting brown stamps*[2]). George Bach (advocate of "fighting fair") called this *gunny-sacking*.[3] Such metaphors refer to the self-stimulating thought processes that maintain anger over long periods.

A good example of how anger is controlled by interpretation of events can be found in a particular kind of situation. Almost everyone can think of such an occasion. It is a situation in which a person becomes increasingly angry, then suddenly learns one more piece of information and the anger vanishes into pity or remorse or some other gentler emotion. A man was sitting in a movie theater watching a rather moving film. Behind him, a child was conducting a running commentary on every scene. "Oh, now she's going to go to the door. She looks scared! I wonder what's going to happen. Oh, it's George at the door." And so it went. This intruded on the man's enjoyment of the film and angry thoughts built up in his head. "I can see what's happening, for heaven's sake! Will you just keep quiet and enjoy the movie! Why is it necessary to comment on every single thing that happens?" Finally, after whispering inflaming comments to his wife, his rage built to the point where he turned around, ready to scream "Shut up!" There sat a blind man, with a child patiently explaining what was happening on the screen.

These moments remind us how anger depends on one's interpretation of the world. As with depression and anxiety, sometimes things "anger us" (not true, really) because of certain unrealistic or unhealthy assumptions people make about the world, or especially about how the world *should* or *ought* to be. The unspoken, underlying assumption may be, "People should do what I tell them to," or "The world ought to change to suit my needs," or "People should be perfect." Stated outright, these sound a bit foolish, yet sometimes anger revolves around such basic assumptions. People act as if they were true.

The type A personality,[4] which has been implicated as an antecedent of heart attacks and other health problems, revolves on such assumptions. The surface behaviors that mark the type A person include impatience, irritability, fast pace, a "driven" appearance. Beneath such behaviors lie habitual patterns of thought, characteristic assumptions about how the world ought to be organized, efficient, perfect. These exacting standards are applied to self as well as to others, and the type A person goes through the day trying to stay ahead of the ticking clock, critical of "incompetence" or slowness wherever it is encountered—the driver who travels five miles per hour under the speed limit, the cashier who takes too long to check out the customers in line while the next line moves along with seeming speed, the colleague who fails to meet an agreed-upon deadline. Carrying a set of impossible standards and feeling frantic when they are not met, the type A person spends much of each day anxious and angry. This is but one example of how hidden, unspoken assumptions provide an ongoing influence on emotional life and health.[5]

Here is a territory rich in religious material. Shoulds and oughts are the home field of morality. Underlying life assumptions such as "I'm entitled" and "My needs are more important than yours" are directly renounced by most of the major religions of the world. Perfectionism is sometimes (and often wrongly) founded in religious ideals, so that one torments oneself and others for anything short of an ideal. It would be ironic for us to tell you here what you "should" believe or do in this area. There are many variations among religions on issues of ethics and morality and on the attitudes toward self and others that are fostered. We do urge you, however, to examine these beliefs carefully when working with individuals struggling with chronic negative emotions. Some authors, particularly Albert Ellis, have blamed religion for manufacturing mental illness by teaching a morality of should.[6] Others believe that Ellis's condemnation of religion and his assertion that you shouldn't use *should* are every bit as strong and dogmatic as the most fundamental religious systems.[7] Choosing and coming to peace with a personal system of belief is a task for every individual, and it is a task that does not end but changes over the course of human development. Sharing this journey and task is the unique expertise of the pastor, and it is one quite relevant to the full understanding of human emotions.

ORGANIC FACTORS

For decades physiologists have attempted to discern the differences between fear and anger. Both involve arousal of the autonomic nervous system, discussed in chapter 14, and the differences that do exist seem subtle at best. Humans have a nervous system that responds in a very general fashion, left over from our long-ago ancestors. The autonomic system has been described as a "fight or flight" system because arousal seems to prepare us to do one of two things—to fight and defend or to flee to safety. The autonomic system is our built-in emergency kit. It brings about rapid changes in the body that prepare us for emergency action. Without such a system, the human race probably would have vanished like the dinosaurs.

These days people seldom need this system, though it does come in handy in rapid emergency situations. The stressors of life activate this same system, and the body gets ready to flee or fight. The arousal in both cases—fight or flight—is largely the same, and it is quite possible to interpret arousal as either fear or anger, or just as excitement. The interpretation that is made of one's own arousal is yet another cognitive or thought factor. Still the physical arousal itself is real.

Anything that elevates the level of general arousal in the autonomic system, then, may increase the chances of experiencing anger and of acting on these feelings in an aggressive way. Environmental stressors such as noise can increase general arousal if a person is exposed to them regularly.

Another factor worth asking about when counseling angry people is the extent to which they use stimulant drugs. In this context, *stimulants* include all drugs that increase arousal, specifically including caffeine and nicotine. People may take caffeine directly (in stay-awake tablets) or in various beverages (coffee, tea, regular and diet soft drinks) or foods (chocolate). Nicotine, of course, is received mostly by smoking tobacco. People who use large quantities of these drugs are more susceptible to arousal disorders (anxiety, aggression, insomnia, or irritability), and some people are also differentially sensitive to these drugs. Amphetamines and other stimulant drugs—rarely prescribed these days but readily available on the street—have similar and still stronger effects.[8]

There are also some relatively rare but nevertheless real organic problems that can result in sudden outbursts of aggression and violence. Some individuals may be particularly sensitive, becoming violent when even mildly intoxicated.[9] Various forms of brain disorder may also result in sporadic explosions of aggression. Most people with epilepsies are not dangerous in any way (except to themselves, in that they require some protection during seizure for their own safety). Certain people, however, experience violent and explosive episodes that seem to be related to abnormal brain wave activity in the temporal lobes (the section of the brain lying beneath the portion of the head we call the *temples*). In general, aggression resulting from such organic abnormalities tends to be unpredictable and unprovoked. It appears as sudden violence emerging "out of the blue." Such sudden explosiveness requires a thorough examination by a competent neurologist or neuropsychologist familiar with electrophysiology (brain wave measurement). Such disorders, though significant and dangerous, are the exception rather than the rule in aggressive behavior.

A more common biological influence on aggressive behavior is drug intoxication. A variety of drugs impair judgment, alter reasoning, increase arousal, or otherwise increase the likelihood of aggressive outbursts. Prime among these is alcohol, which is associated with a large percentage of crimes of violence. Among other drugs that may increase aggression are stimulants, hallucinogens (such as PCP or "angel dust"), and sedatives. "Cold turkey" withdrawal from addicting substances (alcohol, nicotine, narcotics, sedatives) can also be associated with increased irritability and aggressiveness. In severe withdrawal (delirium tremens), the danger of violence can be great (see chapter 16).

Finally, we should lay to rest an old myth about anger. This is the hydraulic theory—that everyone has a certain level of anger and that it is important for people to "express it" and "get it out," as if draining off the tank or letting steam out of the pressure cooker before it explodes. This is utter nonsense. Nothing in the physiology of anger suggests any kind of cumulative build-up that requires discharge. At a physiological level anger is autonomic arousal, and adrenalin comes and goes quickly. Perhaps more seriously, it has been clear since the early 1970s that nearly all of the evidence on aggression supports just the opposite of a catharsis theory.[10] Aggression begets more aggression. Witnessing violence on television and in movies does not "discharge" anger in the viewer but rather increases the chances that the viewer will be aggressive himself or herself on later occasions. The modeling of aggression makes it easier for others to engage in it. Once someone has thrown the first stone, it is easier for others to follow suit, and for each person to throw a second, and a third. The catharsis model of therapy for anger is not and never has been supported by sound scientific data. There is no demonstrable therapeutic benefit to be gained from the sheer ventilation of angry feelings or from engaging in aggressive acts, even against imaginary targets such as pillows or empty chairs. This hydraulic theory of anger is simply mistaken in its assumptions about how human beings function.

RESPONSES TO ANGER

This is not at all to say that nothing needs to be done with anger, or that it is unnecessary to cope with angry feelings. People respond to their own angry feelings in a wide variety of ways. Some of these are helpful and adaptive; others are harmful and maladaptive.

One response to anger is *aggression*. Aggression is behavior that is intended to do harm. It ranges from an unkind word to the launching of a nuclear weapon. Aggression hurts people and is meant to do so.

Although aggression is much more likely to occur when a person is autonomically aroused (fight or flight, fear or anger), not all violence is done because of anger. Some violence is planned and strategic, intended to accomplish a particular personal or political end. Some individuals, including true psychopaths, commit violence against people and property for personal gain, often without either malice or remorse. Aggression (as modeled by sports) can be either offensive or defensive, although in most conflicts each side regards itself as reacting in defensive or retributive ways to the unprovoked aggression of the other. The likelihood of aggression is further increased by this self-righteous view and by dehumanizing the "enemy" or "opponent" (even though it be your own spouse) and creating new names for them other than their own.

Still, interpersonal aggression is heavily influenced by two things—feelings of anger and acts of aggression (or at least perceived provocation) by others. Research suggests that child abusers were often themselves the victims of severe discipline and violence from their own parents.[11] Aggression begets aggression.

How else do people react to their own feelings of anger? Obviously not everyone becomes overtly aggressive. Some adopt a stance of "passive aggression" consisting of more subtle verbal aggression, withholding of that which is positive, and obstruction. Still others withdraw, escape, turn inside themselves. This is not always unhealthy, by the way. Some people in an inner reflective process are able to rethink the situation, to find a healthier means of looking at it, and emerge with a resolution to then be shared.

Angry feelings that are not resolved, however, can lead to more unpleasant outcomes. People who are angered and unable to express it are likely to drink more alcohol than those not angered or angered but given the opportunity of expression.[12] Indeed, many relapses among alcoholics seem to follow interpersonal conflicts in which angry feelings were not dealt with properly.[13] Certain psychosomatic illnesses such as gastric ulcers have long been linked to unexpressed anger.[14] Psychoanalysts have long attributed depression to anger turned inward against the self, and indeed teaching people how to cope better with angry feelings may help certain individuals in relieving their depression, although there are more generally effective approaches.[15]

Does this seem to contradict what was said earlier about the hydraulic model? It may sound like, "You have to get your anger out; otherwise it will destroy you." Not quite. It's just that people do react to their angry feelings in different ways. Some of these have healthy consequences, and some do not.

CONSEQUENCES OF ANGER-RELATED BEHAVIOR

No one else can react to a person's angry *feelings*, but other people *do* react to their *responses*. When angry feelings become behavior, then the next question is, "What consequences will this have?"

One reason that violence persists is that it can yield immediate rewards. The child who punches another child often gets the toy that was desired (unless there was a hovering enforcer of fairness). The invading army gets the land. The violent spouse "wins" the argument. The abusing parent extracts obedience. Both aggressor and victim are caught in a mutually reinforcing cycle of coercion that has been well described by psychologist Gerald Patterson.[16] From the viewpoint of the aggressor, aggressive behavior is not a problem but a solution. It results in a desired change, achieves a positive end—the toy, the land, the silence, the obedience. From the standpoint of the victim, acquiescence and obedience are rewarded because the pain stops. The bully goes away, hostilities cease, the beating ends, the raised hand is lowered. Both aggressor and victim are rewarded by playing the role. Both are caught in the cycle.

Again, we must be clear what we mean and do not mean. We do not wish to imply that victims "bring it on themselves" or participate willingly. This is a *coercive* cycle. The point is that the aggressor continues because the aggression permits continued control, and the victim continues to obey because, given no escape, this seems the only way to minimize suffering. Counselors are often astounded at how long spouses have endured physical abuse before seeking help. This surprise underestimates the power of the coercive cycle.

Of course, *escape* is also an alternative for the victim, though usually it is not in the immediate interest of the aggressor. This is one of the long-term negative consequences of aggression—people leave. They are alienated, burned out, pushed to the limit. The aggressor ends up alone. Another alternative for the victim, besides flight, is fight. A number of plays, films, and books have asked the question, "Is violence justifiable when the victim gains the upper hand?" The aggressor, in the long run, becomes a victim. People get even, sabotage, fail to cooperate, refuse to come to the rescue, counterattack. The one who lives by the sword dies by the sword, even if the sword is only a sharp tongue.

To understand and intervene on behalf of people who have difficulty coping with anger, one must consider what positive *consequences* are derived from the way in which an individual is currently expressing or coping with angry feelings. Aggression is a powerful temptation; it and other means of dealing with anger, though fraught with suffering at times, are also powerfully reinforced in many cases by their immediate consequences. Typically, these are temporary gains, which in the long run are overtaken by the negative consequences of this chosen way of responding to anger.

ALTERNATIVE INTERVENTIONS

There are many different ways to intervene. The counselor and the client have many choices when it comes to how and where to begin. The following discussion focuses on peacemaking in relationships, with some guidelines given for how to deal with acutely angry people. A few practical considerations will be addressed, and then alternative interventions will be described. Finally, an extended presentation will be devoted to assertiveness, a creative alternative to both aggression and passivity that has come to form the core of many anger management programs.

Counseling and Peacemaking

Although treatment for people who do not deal appropriately with anger is often called *anger management*, the goal should not be understood as the elimination of angry feelings. Anger is a normal emotion. The issue is how the person responds to the emotion—what he or she does with the feeling, how the person behaves when angry.

Helping people to deal in a healthy, constructive, and nonviolent fashion with anger is one form of peacemaking. Approaches to conflict resolution in relationships will be addressed in chapter 18, but for now a few comments about personal and relationship peacemaking are in order. It is increasingly recognized now that peace (both in the sense of personal happiness and in the sense of international harmony) is not the mere absence of hostility. Aggression disrupts peace, but its absence does not create it. To be sure the first step toward peace (in people, relationships, or nations) is the ceasing of active hostilities. This creates a vacuum of sorts into which either peace or resumed hostilities can grow. The suppression of aggression is only a beginning. Peace requires more, something that displaces aggression. That "something" is the active promotion of the welfare of others, an idea which will be explored when alternative responses are discussed later. Remember, then, that the goal of the interventions to be discussed here is not the elimination, denial, or rationalization of anger. Some of the methods described actually do help a person to *feel* less angry and to be less troubled and disabled by angry feelings. Others focus primarily on how the person responds when angry feelings do occur.

Counseling with an Angry Person

Every counselor, sooner or later. must confront people who are very angry. A pastor, who is called to work *among* the people, is even more likely to meet this challenge again and again on hospital wards, in homes, on the job, as well as in the counseling office. It may be useful, then, to consider a few guidelines to remember when these times occur.

A first piece of advice is *listen*—listen like crazy! There is nothing that defuses acute anger more effectively than reflective listening (chapter 5). Some pastors make the mistake of falling into roadblocks—trying to talk the person out of it, distract or humor the person, convince the person that "You don't really feel that way," lecture or reason or moralize. None of these is required, and none of them is very helpful to a person who is feeling angry. A good reflection, on the other hand, acknowledges how the person is feeling without challenging or quarreling. It communicates acceptance (remembering that acceptance is not agreement—for agreement, too, is a roadblock).

Another good reason to avoid roadblocks is that practicing a roadblock makes you a target, a lightning rod. Angry people are looking for targets—for people who look on the defensive or offensive or who behave like victims. Many of the roadblocks look like defensive, offensive, or victim-acquiescent moves. One who practices roadblocks with an angry person is likely to wind up feeling (and being) attacked. Avoid defensive or victimlike stances or behavior that will appear to be a challenge or attack of some kind. To review what these behaviors might be, refer to the list of roadblocks in chapter 4.

Third, make human contact with the person. Using the person's name is one good way. Reflecting feelings and generally relating at a feeling level is another. Angry people are more likely to attack impersonal, faceless victims. (*Attack* is used here in a general sense—not referring just to physical aggression.) Physical contact should be used judiciously—it may establish contact, but it also can be interpreted in a variety of other ways.

Finally, don't assume that you have to *do* something or to fix the problem. Often angry people just want to be listened to, and helpers who rush in with a box of bandages and salves may find themselves unappreciated at best. Anger is a feeling. Reflect it (not only in your manner and nonverbal cues, but in reflective listening statements). Your own demeanor is best kept patient and calm, understanding and personal, though also confident. Unless you are considerably stronger than the angry person, the "Now look here, settle down" approach is risky. Anger subsides with time. Reflection helps the person to calm down and put things in better perspective.

We mentioned earlier that anger is an emotion that evokes powerful and often ambivalent responses. This is as true for pastors as for parishioners. Having a client express anger toward you directly can be difficult to handle. Personal feelings are aroused, and it is tempting to react to these inner reactions rather than responding to the client's needs. Anger may evoke fear, a sense of panic that makes it difficult to stay on a helpful course of counseling. Some respond with feelings of guilt whenever anger is expressed, perhaps out of a deep desire to be liked by all. Other reflexive reactions that anger expression may evoke are defensiveness, contrition, rebuke, appeasement, and attempts to "fix" things. A counselor's own reactions to expressed anger can be so powerful that he or she is tempted to focus inward and slip into a protective pattern. It is usually more helpful to remain focused on the client, to remember that this is an *emotion* experienced by the client, and the best way for maintaining a focus on the client is reflective listening. Here is a brief example.

To set the scene, imagine that a pastor offered an interpretation to a client—that he seems to react to all women as if they were inferiors. His reaction is strong and immediate:

CLIENT: (Loudly) What do you mean? What do you know about anything? You just sit there and give me these ridiculous generalizations. What kind of counseling is that?

PASTOR: You're pretty angry at me. (Resists the temptation to respond defensively and reflects instead)

CLIENT: Damned right I am! I sit here baring my soul and all you can do is give me platitudes. (Often the first few responses after a reflection repeat the anger)

PASTOR: What I say sounds all too simple, too easy. (Churning inside, maybe, but staying with reflection)

CLIENT: Right! Easy answers. Well it's not that easy. (Calming down a bit)

PASTOR: No, it's not. I must have given you the impression that I wasn't listening to you, that I was just passing out standard answers. (Again reflecting)

CLIENT: Well, it just sort of got to me, what you said. (Provides an opening for returning to the touchy topic)

PASTOR: Really irritated you, like it wasn't fair for me to say that. (Reflects again, instead of building a case)

CLIENT: Well, I *don't* think that I react to *all* women in the same way. It's not that simple. (Now willing to talk about it more calmly)

PASTOR: Your feelings about women are more complicated . . .

CLIENT: Yes. Sometimes I do put women down, and . . . (Back on track, now ready to explore a little further)

We hasten to emphasize that reflective listening is not the whole answer in counseling angry people. We recommend this as a helpful way to respond to acutely angry people. It helps them to express themselves, calm down, and develop a working relationship with the pastor. Furthermore, there are times when it is inadvisable for the pastor simply to listen to angry discharges. One of these is in the early sessions of marital counseling (for discussion see chapter 18).

Reflective listening is most useful in individual counseling sessions with a person who is angry *at the time*. Beyond this clarification phase, effective counseling with angry people involves a number of active intervention strategies. These will be elaborated after a few additional practicalities of counseling with angry individuals are explored.

Some Practical Considerations

A few special considerations apply when working with potentially aggressive and dangerous people. One, of course, is self-protection. It is wise to take a companion when visiting a home in the midst of an acute crisis. Having someone nearby during counseling sessions (while still protecting confidentiality) becomes more important. As a professional you also have certain legal and ethical responsibilities when working with potentially dangerous individuals. Most state laws require that a professional who encounters evidence of child abuse report this to the proper authorities, and failure to do so is a punishable offense. Likewise, if a client indicates to the counselor an intent to do bodily harm to another person, it is the counselor's legal responsibility to warn the endangered person. These are two cases in which the usual standards of confidentiality must be broken. The decision to do so is always a difficult one, and it is wise to consult with a supervisor or colleague when possible.

Disclosure of crimes already committed is yet another issue. The law does not require a pastor to violate confidentiality spontaneously in such cases, but the issues are complicated. If the confessed act was a crime of violence that may be repeated against still other victims, for example, your responsibilities to the client are heavily pitted against responsibilities to the social welfare at large. Again consultation with a knowledgeable colleague or supervisor is advisable.

Finally, it should be mentioned that some counselors are simply unsuited to working with angry or aggressive individuals. Acts of violence such as rape or child abuse may be so personally repugnant to some pastors that they are unable to maintain the necessary modicum of acceptance and objectivity required for competent counseling. In such cases, a prompt and sound referral represents the wisest and most helpful form of intervention.

Situational Changes

We turn now to a consideration of intervention options. As has been the case in previous chapters, most of the interventions listed here have received support from scientific research as being effective methods for anger management. The choice of strategies, however, must remain a task for you and your client, who together examine the options and decide which might be most reasonable as a starting place, which might be most likely to help.

Situational changes are usually most appealing to the client. Angry people want to see the problem "out there," and the idea of changing the world to suit them better is usually attractive. This pitfall notwithstanding, there often *are* useful changes that can be made in the situation or lifestyle of the individual to decrease provocation to anger. Sometimes there are fairly simple behavior changes that can be asked of family members, changes which will decrease the degree of provocation while the individual is also learning better coping skills. Decreased exposure to unnecessary irritants—noise, crowds, frustrations—may be helpful. Sometimes a space of alone time eases the tension, especially for the individual who is continually around people both during the day and at home.

A neutralizing strategy such as systematic desensitization (see chapter 14) may also be useful. This seeks to change not the situation, but the person's automatic response to the situation. It breaks the tie between a certain situation and the response of anger and aggression. A hierarchy of scenes could be constructed based on situations in which the person typically becomes angry. These could then be imagined while employing other stress reduction techniques to minimize experienced tension.[17] Is it possible for the person to experience these situations in imagination (and eventually in real life) without becoming aroused?

Thought Pattern Changes

Often a still more effective neutralizing strategy is reevaluation of perceptions and thinking patterns. To remain angry, a person must continue to rehearse inflammatory thoughts. These can be identified by having the person keep a two-column diary (see chapter 12) of situations and angry feelings that resulted from these, then expanding this to a three-column diary so that the intervening column lists the person's interpretations and thoughts that led from the situation to the feeling. An example of such a three-column diary is shown in Table 15-1. The intervening thoughts then are discussed in greater

TABLE 15-1   Sample Three-Column Diary for Anger Management

SITUATION	INTERVENING THOUGHT	RESULTING FEELING
Son left clothing lying on the floor	"I've told him a thousand times about this. He does it just to provoke me."	Frustrated, angry
Automobile I wanted to buy was sold to somebody else before I decided	"I can never make a decision about anything. It's all my fault."	Angry at self, depressed
Garbage was not taken out to be picked up on Tuesday	"Nobody ever does anything to help around here. Why do I have to do everything myself?"	Resentful, angry
Friend did not return my call after promising to do so	"That self-centered creep doesn't have an ounce of consideration for other people."	Hurt, bitter

detail in counseling sessions. How else might the person interpret or think about these situations? Self-defeating and unrealistic aspects in these thought patterns are pointed out, and alternative ways of thinking are considered. The work of Ray Novaco on anger management has provided more detailed methods as well as some encouraging results.[18]

Forgiveness   Again at this point the pastor encounters many issues with moral/ethical and religious content. Perhaps most pertinent of these is the issue of forgiveness. Retained anger represents a failure to forgive and so takes on special significance from a religious perspective. How "to find forgiveness in your heart" is a common challenge with angry people, and this certainly falls within your pastoral role. There are no magic answers, but often people fail to forgive because they confuse forgiveness with any of five other things, all of which it is not. It can be useful to help the person distinguish between forgiveness and these other processes.

First, forgiveness is not the same as *amnesia*. Forgiving and forgetting are different acts. Forgiveness does not require forgetting. In fact, one can hardly forgive that which has already been forgotten! Forgiveness is given in the face of remembering, and if anything it is forgiveness that enables forgetting. Certainly, forgetting is no prerequisite, nor does forgiveness require the promise to forget (which may actually be much more difficult).

Second, forgiveness is not *acquittal*. Forgiveness does not mean that the person is found blameless and without responsibility. To the contrary, forgiveness is only required when responsibility of the individual is recognized. One need not deny responsibility to be forgiven, nor does forgiveness require later denial by either party. Forgiveness is given in the face of responsibility.

Third, forgiveness is not an *award*. It is not earned or given to those most deserving. Forgiveness is given freely, without regard for merit.

Fourth, forgiveness is not *approval*. To forgive an action is not to approve of that action or agree with it. It does not require that the forgiving person say, "I think what you did was OK." In fact, forgiveness is needed only when one does not approve. It is given in the face of disapproval.

Finally, forgiveness is not *acquiescence*. It is not a license to go and do as one pleases in the future. It is not a moratorium on values, a suspension of rules. It is not permission to stay the same, but rather in a mysterious way forgiveness itself inspires and enables change. Forgiveness is given in the face of the knowledge that the future may or may not be different, but also with the enabling hope that it will.

Forgiveness is none of these things. Rather, it is something else—an affirming acceptance of the *person* as distinguished from her or his actions. This is the same acceptance that was discussed in chapter 5 as the basic attitude of the pastoral counselor. It is also, for the pastor, a reflection of that profound kind of love that is attributed to God. Forgiveness is an alternative to anger. Better still, forgiveness is a *response* to anger.

And like its opposite, aggression, forgiveness begets itself. Those who are forgiven are enabled to forgive. There is a relationship between the extent to which a person is accepting of others and the degree of self-acceptance. One who forgives others is enabled to accept forgiveness as well. One who accepts (again not to be confused with approval or acquiescence) personal faults and shortcomings is enabled to extend this same generosity to others.

Organic Factor Interventions

All that was said about autonomic arousal in chapter 14 also applies here. Interventions aimed at reducing physiological arousal level are useful both in stress management and in anger management. After all, the arousal is virtually identical! The regular practice of relaxation, meditation, prayer, or any other calming pursuit can be quite helpful. Angry people often find that a period of physical exertion relieves the tension. This may be why some people have advocated activities like punching a stuffed bag, chopping wood with an ax, or pummeling a pillow. The therapeutic value of these acts has nothing to do with their overtly hostile nature (which may, in fact, be countertherapeutic). The assumption that they help by somehow "working through" the anger is mistaken. Rather it is apparently the large muscle movement that is of value because it reduces tension. A period of swimming, jogging, walking, bicycling, golfing, or rowing would be equally productive without containing the overtones of hostility.

Remember also to check for drug use and abuse. Clients who are consuming large amounts of caffeine, nicotine, or other stimulants can be helped to decrease or cease their use of these substances to diminish chronic arousal (see chapter 16). Alcohol is also frequently involved when people have anger management problems, particularly when there is physical violence. In such cases, attention to the drinking problem is likely to be an essential part of treatment.

Responses to Anger

A key consideration in counseling is how the person responds to his or her own angry feelings. How does this person usually act when angry?

A first step in changing destructive patterns is to decrease aggressive responses to angry feelings. In the case of physical violence, an immediate and complete halt is sought. A psychologist was once seeing a couple for therapy, permitting a number of trainees to observe the sessions (with the couple's knowledge and consent, of course). The husband had been beating his wife almost every time they got into an argument. The trainees sat behind the observation mirror wondering what sophisticated technique the psychologist would use to interrupt this pattern of violence. Her choice was not very complicated: "You've got to stop that nonsense," she advised. "You can't have a loving relationship with someone you're beating up." And from there the psychologist went on to work on their relationship. The violence stopped.

This simple intervention is an example of one possibility in counseling—direct advice. Yes, it's a roadblock, but there are times when direct advice is appropriate. This is one. When your child is about to run out into the street in front of a car, direct intervention is needed first. When physical violence is involved, the cessation of violence takes priority over other necessary changes. In circumstances like this, there is nothing wrong with giving direct advice. Coming from a respected authority, such an injunction may be quite effective, particularly if it is contained within an overall relationship of understanding and acceptance.[19] In fact, *not* to give advice in this situation could be interpreted as tacit approval.

Beyond the ceasing of hostilities, a problem-solving approach seeks alternative responses that the individual can learn. What is being gained (if anything) by the aggression? If it coerces an end to conflicts, a better conflict resolution method is needed (chapter 18). If it drives the family members away and leaves the individual "in peace," perhaps alternative arrangements can be made for some alone time. If it seems to emerge from depression or hopelessness or alcoholism or chronic stress, these problems need to be addressed.

A similar strategy is followed for any other unhealthy pattern, such as extreme withdrawal or overdrinking, that occurs when a person becomes angry. The key is to find and teach a more adaptive alternative that involves neither aggression toward others nor unhealthy passivity. Angry feelings, then, become a cue to begin practicing this new skill (rather than to fall back into old patterns).

Contrary to popular jokes and stereotypes, various psychologists have shown that it can be healthy to talk to oneself![20] In fact, most people do this every day, though usually it is done silently rather than aloud. In counseling, one helps people to *plan* how to talk to themselves when faced with a difficult situation. For example, *before* a situation occurs that is likely to induce anger, the person may learn to say (silently), "Now just take it easy. Remember that things don't have to be perfect. It's not going to help if I get all steamed up, and really there's no reason. I can't expect everything to go as I would like it." *During* a difficult experience, similar self-statements can be made. *After* the experience it is often helpful to review it and remember what one did well, and also those points where things might be done differently in the future. There is no master list of "helpful things to tell yourself" in situations such as this, but you can certainly help a client arrive at a pertinent list of effective self-statements. Self-instruction of this kind is useful in learning any new skill, including a sport like skiing ("Bend your knees, sit back more"). Research has shown had good results in applying such methods with people who are very angry and aggressive[21] and to help hyperactive and impulsive children to increase their attention span and avoid negative behavior.[22] This technique blends previously mentioned cognitive changes with the development of more adaptive alternative responses to anger.

Altering the Consequences of Anger-related Behavior

People sometimes learn maladaptive and harmful ways for dealing with angry feelings and resolving conflicts. One reason that people persist in using such solutions is that they yield some kind of payoff, at least in the short run.

In such cases it is sometimes possible to find ways to remove the reinforcing consequences of the undesirable behavior. Teachers of children often use this method for discouraging aggression. Aggressive behavior is not permitted to pay off—the child who extracts a toy by force is both deprived of the toy and perhaps given some additional penalty. (Unfortunately, at times the personal attention of the teacher can be a reinforcer itself.)

The key here is to understand what payoff has been derived from the response—from aggression, or withdrawal, or from passive-aggressive patterns. In what way does this behavior lead to gratifying results? New arrangements or agreements can be made so that the aggressive (or other undesirable) behavior no longer yields this payoff and instead leads to undesirable consequences. Physical threats or abuse, for example, now lead to being left alone—the family leaves for safer surroundings—rather than to the usual result of terrified acquiescence.

At the same time it is vital to consider how *new* alternative responses, more healthy methods of anger management and conflict resolution, can be made to result in gratifying consequences. Traffic soon becomes snarled in a town with all red lights and no green. Whenever consequences are changed to discourage an undesirable behavior pattern, they should also be altered to encourage a new way of behaving.

THE ASSERTIVE ALTERNATIVE

Some Sample Situations

SITUATION:	A committee chairperson calls a member about attending a special meeting on Wednesday evening. The member has a commitment on Wednesday, which she had mentioned to the chairperson when she agreed to attend.
RESPONSE A:	"Well, I suppose I can come. I guess the other plans I had can be changed."
RESPONSE B:	"I'm sorry, but I do have another commitment on Wednesday. I thought I mentioned that when I said I would come. So I won't be able to make it. Will you fill me in afterwards, and maybe next time our schedules will fit. Thanks! Have a good meeting."

RESPONSE C: "I can't believe you are calling me about a meeting on Wednesday night! I *told* you I was busy Wednesday. How on earth could you forget? How inconsiderate! Maybe I should reconsider my agreeing to be on this committee if this is how you run things."

SITUATION: The congregational newsletter editor has received material late for three months in a row from the chairperson of an important committee. The editor needs the copy on time and doesn't have time to offer to write up material conveyed in bits and pieces.

RESPONSE A: "Oh, uh, hi! Do you think you might be able to give me a minute of your time? I know you're always busy and probably are swamped today so if you can't I'll understand. I was just hoping we could talk about your committee's newsletter material. It seems like it's late sometimes. I wonder if you need some help in writing it up or something, so that it's ready on time."

RESPONSE B: "Hi! I'd been hoping to hear from you today. I need to talk to you. Is this a good time or shall I call back? Good, I'm glad you have time now. You know that I need the newsletter material from each committee on the last day of each month. For three months now your committee's copy has been late. You and your people do such good work and the activities are really important, so I keep holding up the newsletter, but then the mailing is late. What can we do to work out a way for your committee to meet the deadline?"

RESPONSE C: "Well at last I've found you! You've been keeping yourself scarce. I bet you've been avoiding me because you know I have a bone to pick with you. You *never* get your material to me on time. Now how am I supposed to keep our publication on schedule with irresponsible people like you to depend on? If it's not on time next month, I'm going to talk to the pastor about it."

SITUATION: Gary and Joan have offered to house the refugee family that the congregation is sponsoring until an apartment can be arranged. Because of a housing scarcity, the refugee family needs temporary facilities for longer than expected, and this begins to put a strain on Joan and Gary and their family.

RESPONSE A: Joan and Gary mutter to each other and think to themselves about how inconsiderate the congregation is not to offer to help more. They become irritable with the refugee family members, but when someone calls and asks how things are going Gary says, "Oh, I guess all right. It could be better, and we didn't know they would be with us for so long. Our kids feel a little neglected, but I suppose we'll survive."

RESPONSE B: Gary calls the person chairing the refugee committee and asks for help. "Hi! I'm calling to say that Joan and I didn't know what we were in for when we said we'd house the family temporarily. Having them here is disrupting our family life more than we thought it would. Yet we know that to ask them to move would be more disruption for them, and they've experienced so much already. Here's what would help us to house and take care of them . . ."

RESPONSE C: Gary storms into the pastor's office without an appointment, and finding her alone says: "What kind of church is this anyway? How could the refugee committee expect us to do everything for the family—who, by the way, just happen to speak no English, have terrible table manners, and don't eat the food we cook for them. What's wrong with this place? How can you people be so ungrateful? We're not going to put up with this any longer. I want them out and I want them out right away. I don't care what you do with them, just see that we have peace and quiet by tomorrow. This certainly doesn't encourage us to continue being members, you know."

What Is "Assertive Behavior"?

In the above examples, the three responses vary between two extremes, and in each case the middle (B) response is the most balanced or adaptive one. In each case the middle response is also the *assertive* one.

Assertive behavior represents a middle ground between two extremes. At one extreme is an *aggressive* or hostile response which promotes one's own wishes and welfare at the expense of others—without showing regard and respect for the needs and wishes of others (see the C responses above). At the other extreme is a *nonassertive* or submissive response that subjugates one's own feelings and needs in favor of the wishes of others. The former lacks love and respect for others; the latter lacks love and respect for self. The middle ground here is to care for others *and* for oneself—to love one's neighbor as oneself. This is the key defining element in assertive behavior—*respect for others and for oneself.* In addition, a good assertive response is direct, honest, and appropriate, and the nonverbal messages that accompany it match the spoken words.

The first step in helping an individual to be more assertive is a step of awareness, understanding the differences among aggressive, assertive, and nonassertive responses. Table 15-2 clarifies some of these crucial differences.

Nonassertive or submissive behavior emerges from a personal position that Thomas Harris,[23] in his description of transactional analysis, described as "I'm not O.K." Nonassertive individuals consequently ignore their own needs, wants, feelings and ideas, with the result that their communications are often emotionally dishonest, indirect, and inhibited. The motivation is to please others. Writing about assertiveness within a Christian context, David Augsburger described the theological belief underlying nonassertiveness as one of *prizing love and eschewing power.* "Nonassertive love may be said to sacrifice power, and with it justice."[24] The outcome of being nonassertive is failure to achieve desired goals. Nonassertive people may even lose touch with their own desires, needs, wants, and goals. The sacrifice in terms of justice is that the

TABLE 15-2   Differences among Nonassertive, Assertive, and Aggressive Responses

	NONASSERTIVE RESPONSE	ASSERTIVE RESPONSE	AGGRESSIVE RESPONSE
Personal perspective	I'm not O.K.	I'm O.K., You're O.K.	You're not O.K.
General Characteristic of the Response	Ignores and does not express own needs, feelings, ideas	Expresses own needs, feelings, ideas appropriately	Promotes own needs, feelings, and ideas at expense of others
	Permits others to infringe on personal rights and needs	Protects legitimate rights of self and others in a way that does not violate others	Hostile overreaction with intent to humiliate, dominate retaliate, degrade
	Is emotionally dishonest, indirect, inhibited	Is emotionally honest, direct, and expressive	Is emotionally direct and expressive at cost to others
	Submissive, self-denying	Accepting and receptive of self and others	Self-centered, self-serving
Augsburger's perspective	Nonassertive love sacrifices power and with it justice	Assertive love works toward mutual power and dignity	Loveless power exercises control at the expense of caring
Payoff	Avoids confrontation, tension, and conflict	Improves relationships and self-confidence	Vents anger, achieves own way in the short run
Outcome	Personal goals and needs not fulfilled; anger builds	Desired goals may be achieved honestly	Immediate gain usually offset by alienation and hostility from others

nonassertive person is not bold enough to speak out about injustices suffered by self or others.

Aggressive or hostile behavior, by contrast, communicates "You're not O.K." Augsburger's reading of the theological underpinnings of this position (drawing on the writings of Tillich) was that *power is valued more than loving relationships.* Personal needs, wants, feelings, and ideas are promoted to the expense or exclusion of others. The motivation is to dominate or humiliate; the behavior is self-centered and self-serving. The outcome often is the achievement of immediate desired goals, but at the expense of alienation. Aggressiveness breeds aggressiveness in others—retribution, escalation, competition.

Assertive behavior, in Augsburger's words, is a "constructive middle way" that "regards nonassertive flight and aggressive fight as equally extreme, equally futile."[24] Power and love are kept in creative balance and together yield justice. Personal needs, wants, feelings, and ideas are expressed, but not to the exclusion of the ideas, feelings, wants, and needs of others. Remember that the key is respect for others and for self. The intent is neither to please nor to dominate, but to *communicate* with emotional honesty and directness. People who are assertive may achieve their desired goals (though there is no guarantee, and compromise is common), but whatever progress occurs is made without violating or alienating others. Relationships are valued and strengthened, both parties leave the transaction with a positive feeling, and justice is more likely to be served. It is noteworthy that one may be assertive on others' behalf as well as one's own.

Obstacles to Assertiveness

Clients may grasp the differences among nonassertive, assertive and aggressive responses; they may even be able to recite the assertive response for a prescribed situation while sitting within the counselor's office. When it comes to *behaving* assertively in the real world, however, good intentions may be defeated by a variety of obstacles including beliefs, thought patterns, anxiety, or guilt. All of these are *learned* ways of being.

Belief Systems　People who are characteristically nonassertive in their relationships often believe that it is wrong to behave assertively—to ask to be treated with respect, to say no, to ask for time to make a decision, to have alone time, to express anger, to change their minds, to ask for more information, to make mistakes, to express affection openly, to set limits, to disagree. Behaving in such assertive ways may result in severe or at least troubling feelings of guilt. Aggressive people, on the other hand, may have an equally staunch set of beliefs about what is wrong to do—to ask for help, to admit fear or anxiety, to express agreement or support, to compromise, to allow another person to "win," or to decide not to pursue an opportunity. It appears that people who come to pastors for counseling more often need help in developing assertive alternatives to nonassertive or submissive patterns rather than to aggressive ones. Yet pastors certainly encounter aggressive individuals as well, some of whom may perceive themselves as using this forcefulness as "soldiers of the Lord" Nor is it unusual for people to vacillate—to alternate between the two extremes by being passive and acquiescent for a time, then exploding into aggressiveness, then feeling guilty and returning to nonassertiveness.

Part of your task here is to assist the client in identifying the underlying beliefs that serve as obstacles to balanced assertive behavior, some of which may have roots in past religious indoctrination or upbringing that discourages assertive communication patterns. Perhaps the message was that personal needs and feeling are always to be suppressed in favor of others, that obedience to authority is a prime value, that compromise means weakness, or that steadfastness means never being deterred by others. Issues of time use and service are worthwhile to explore here. In our society women are more often given a larger dose of beliefs about what is "acceptable" behavior, usually defined as nonassertive behaviors, whereas men may be more likely to be socialized in the direction of aggressiveness. A same-sex role model of assertive behavior can be very valuable, and it may be particularly difficult here to work with a client of the opposite sex.

Remedies for obstacle beliefs can often be drawn directly from scriptures that are meaningful to the client. "Love your neighbor *as yourself*" can be understood as meaning that it is difficult to serve others when you hate yourself—a balance is needed. Augsberger offers helpful points on presenting assertiveness within a religious belief system.[24] Obstacle beliefs can be reevaluated and restructured with the help of a skilled counselor (see chapter 12).

Anxiety   Sometimes the obstacles to assertiveness are not beliefs and thought patterns but emotional reactions. A person who is quite able to write down an appropriate assertive response for a given situation may be altogether too anxious to carry out the response in real life. This anxiety usually diminishes with practice, and it is helpful to make gradual assignments—perhaps practicing with the pastor first, then with a trusted friend, then in an easier "real life" situation, and so on. The anxiety can also be reduced through the direct methods described in chapter 14, such as deep muscle relaxation and desensitization. Once the initial anxiety barriers are overcome, progress becomes easier both because further action is less anxiety-inducing and because the positive consequences of assertiveness become apparent.

Inertia   Behavior patterns that have been practiced for a long span of time are characterized by a certain inertia—they tend to continue unchanged unless something jolts them from their course or brings about a slow redirection. Often people who behave nonassertively (or aggressively) learned to do so at a very early age. This pattern of behavior was modeled or enforced by parents, reinforced throughout school years, and by now is habitual. It is a comfortable, accustomed way of being. Even though the long-term consequences of this pattern may be quite detrimental, in the short run it seems easiest and most natural.

Whether the obstacles are these or other, often the solution lies in *acting* in a new way, slowly practicing new behavior. As the person tries out new ways of relating, the inertia is broken. The new behavior may prove to be less anxiety-producing than the person had feared, and in any event familiarity and practice tend to reduce anxiety. Likewise, behaving in a new way tends to alter belief systems, bringing beliefs into line with the new actions. Thus, developing skillful assertive behaviors may be the most direct route to overcoming these obstacles in the long run, although special interventions such as anxiety reduction or cognitive restructuring may be helpful in getting the change process started.

Developing Assertive Behaviors

Being assertive involves much more than learning to how to say "no" without feeling guilty, although that is the stereotype. Assertiveness involves a much broader range of communication. Four types in particular will be discussed—positive statements, negative statements, setting limits, and opening horizons.

Positive statements or affirmations do not fit the stereotyped conception of what it means to be assertive. Yet such communications are assertive responses because they represent direct, honest, and appropriate expressions that respect both others and self. Included here are giving positive feedback, making compliments, and expressing affection. Also included are the mirror images of these three—receiving feedback, compliments, and affection. Making requests and asking for help could also be considered positive communications because doing so is taking care of yourself and others.

Negative statements are a focus of popular book titles in the assertiveness area: *When I Say No I Feel Guilty* and *Don't Say Yes When You Want to Say No.*[25] Negative statements and requests *are* one part of assertiveness. These include giving and receiving criticism, refusing requests, and asking for negative feedback.

Setting limits involves preserving one's time and energy, learning to deal with persistent people, and developing social skills that help in self-change endeavors such as losing weight or reducing one's drinking (see chapter 16). Those who fail to set limits find themselves overextended and unable to give complete attention and effort to the tasks at hand.

Opening horizons means taking risks and trying new opportunities—not any and all that come one's way, but selectively. The assertive person is willing to take risks and pursue opportunities that further personal goals or values or the welfare of others. Some specific examples include asking for a raise, choosing a new kind of work, joining an organization that works for social justice, being a foster parent, volunteering at a prison. Such actions open up new possibilities and expand experience.

Teaching Assertion Skills

One of the first important realizations for a client is that assertion skills are not inborn or innate, but are learned and learnable. There is hope for everyone! Likewise obstacles to assertiveness are learned and can be unlearned.

The teaching and practice of assertion skills is a very individualized matter and requires good judgment. Having learned how to make requests does not mean that one should then make them on every possible occasion. Appropriateness is also a defining condition for assertiveness, and it is one of the more difficult judgments at times. Criticism, for example, is probably inappropriate when a seldom seen elderly grandparent does something irritating, or when physical safety is endangered. Assertive communications are heard and responded to differently depending on cultural/ethnic settings, and indeed what *is* assertive varies with culture.

An effective way for helping people learn assertive responses is through role-playing exercises focused on the particular situations in which they need to apply the skill. This can be done in individual counseling, or better still in group counseling or class settings where different perspectives and ideas can be shared. Here are a few steps to follow in directing role-play practice of assertion skills:

1. Identify the problem or situation to which the individual wants to learn assertive responses. Clarify the situation and set realistic goals.
2. Identify what inhibits the person from responding assertively.
3. Generate a list of possible alternative responses the client might use. (The list may well include listening skills as well as direct assertive responses.)
4. Demonstrate the proposed alternative responses for the client—model them, show how it is done.
5. Have the client practice the new responses by role-playing them with the counselor or other group members.
6. Give feedback. Be sure to include a heavy dose of positive encouragement as well as tips on what to change. Also ask for the client's own perspectives.
7. Provide homework assignments that augment these various steps. Possible assignments would included generating alternative ways of responding to a certain situation and writing them down, practicing a new skill in imagination, generating positive self-statements to be used to counteract beliefs that inhibit assertiveness, or practicing a new skill in actual situations.
8. Review assignments. At each session, review how the previously assigned task was carried out, how the client felt about it, or how others responded.

The teaching of assertion skills is a complex matter. These general guidelines provide a structure by which to proceed, and your own style will emerge with further experience. Several excellent books that provide more specific guidelines for counselors are listed in the resource section that follows this discussion. Remember that the general goal is to develop communication skills that provide alternatives to hostility and submissiveness and free the person from these destructive interpersonal patterns. The result is increased effectiveness in accomplishing goals over the long run, not only for oneself but on behalf of others.

SUMMARY

The emotion of anger should not be confused with aggressive behavior. Anger may be harmful to oneself, but it is aggression that harms others. Aggression is one type of response to angry feelings. When dealing with "anger problems" and aggression as a part of the picture in counseling, it can be very helpful to develop a sense of the possible sources of anger and aggression. Among the important diagnostic considerations are the following:

Situational/Stimulus Factors

Are there environmental stressors present (noise, crowding)? Are there frustrations; obstacle to the accomplishment of important goals? Are other emotions (fear, hurt) being transformed into anger?

Thought Patterns

How does the person interpret life events? What habitual underlying assumptions predispose to anger?

Organic Factors

What stimulants does the person use (caffeine, nicotine, amphetamines, diet pills)? Are alcohol and drug abuse a part of the picture? Is there a possibility of brain impairment in cases of explosive violence?

Responses to Anger

How does the person react when feeling angry? What alternative ways of responding does the person have?

Consequences of Anger-Related Behavior

What payoff is received for responding in this way? What needs or wants, met through responding in this way, might otherwise be frustrated? Consider coercive patterns in relationships.

Teaching people how to deal constructively with anger is a peacemaking process. Anger (and aggression) is not an inevitable force or impulse, and the "hydraulic" or "catharsis" model of anger is based on mistaken notions of the nature of human emotions.

In dealing with an angry person in the office, reflective listening is an extremely valuable tool (chapter 5), and "roadblock" responses (chapter 4) may exacerbate anger. A personal empathic stance usually defuses the acute anger and permits counseling to proceed toward resolution of the more enduring roots of the problem. Countertransference is a frequent problem for counselors when clients express anger, and it is important to be aware of your own "reflex" emotions and reactions when anger is directed at you.

A wide variety of alternative interventions exist for helping clients understand and cope constructively with angry feelings. The intervention chosen should be based on a diagnostic understanding of the probable sources of the anger and of anger-related responses. Among the alternatives are the following:

Situational Changes

Alter the environment to reduce exposure to stressors and provocation. Use desensitization or other neutralizing strategy to break situation-induced provocation cycles.

Thought Pattern Changes

Use two- and three-column diaries for analysis of anger patterns. Institute cognitive therapy to find "antidote" self-statements (chapter 12). Consider the theological issue of forgiveness, often involved in anger. Find and change cognitive patterns that are maintaining anger.

Organic Factor Interventions

Decrease arousal level through relaxation, exercise, prayer. Diagnose and treat any related organic factors (such as alcohol abuse). Reduce use of arousing chemicals such as stimulants (for example, caffeine).

Responses to Anger
Intervene directly to prevent future violence. Understand how the client responds when feeling angry. Seek and teach alternative coping skills such as assertiveness.

Consequences of Anger-related Behavior
Identify the payoffs of aggressive or other undesirable responses. Seek ways to remove these payoffs and instead reward alternative ways of resolving conflicts.

Assertiveness represents a middle ground between aggression and passivity. It encompasses both love and justice, manifesting respect for both self and others. Compatible with conflict resolution strategies, it seeks peaceful expression and resolution of problem situations. Assertiveness skills increase one's effectiveness in accomplishing goals while respecting the rights and feelings of other. Assertion can be practiced not only on one's own behalf, but also in promoting the rights and welfare of others.

ADDITIONAL READINGS

For the Counselor

ALBERTI, ROBERT E., and MICHAEL L. EMMONS *Manual for Assertiveness Trainers* (2d ed.). San Luis Obispo, CA: Impact 1990.

AUGSBERGER, DAVID W. *Anger and Assertiveness in Pastoral Care*. Philadelphia: Fortress Press, 1979.

COSGROVE, MARK P. *Counseling for Anger*. Dallas, TX: Word Publishing, 1988. Incorporates scriptural bases for counseling regarding anger.

FEINDLER, EVA L., and RANDOLPH B. ECTON *Adolescent Anger Control: Cognitive-Behavioral Techniques*. New York: Pergamon Press, 1986.

KELLEY, COLLEEN *Assertion Training: A Facilitator's Guide*. La Jolla, CA: University Associates, 1979.

LANGE, ARTHUR J., and PATRICIA JAKUBOWSKI *Responsible Assertive Behavior: Cognitive/Behavioral Procedures for Trainers*. Champaign, IL: Research Press, 1976.

MARTIN, GRANT L. *Counseling for Family Violence and Abuse*. Dallas, TX: Word Publishing, 1987.

MONFALCONE, WESLEY R. *Coping with Abuse in the Family*. Philadelphia: Westminster Press, 1980. Discusses a continuum of family abuse ranging from ignoring and verbal mistreatment to neglect and violence.

NEIDIG, PETER H., and DALE H. FRIEDMAN *Spouse Abuse: A Treatment Program for Couples*. Champaign, IL: Research Press, 1984. Outlines a structured approach for counseling couples who have experienced episodes of spouse violence.

For the Client

ALBERTI, ROBERT E., and MICHAEL L. EMMONS *Your Perfect Right: A Guide to Assertive Living* (6th ed.). San Luis Obispo, CA: Impact Publishers, 1990. This is the original self-help book on assertiveness, first published in 1970. It distinguishes among aggressive, assertive, and nonassertive responses and teaches how to develop responsible assertiveness.

BOWER, SHARON A., and GORDON H. BOWER *Asserting Yourself: A Practical Guide for Positive Change*. Reading, MA: Addison/Wesley, 1991.

LESTER, ANDREW D. *Coping with Your Anger: A Christian Guide*. Philadelphia: Westminster John Knox, 1983.

PHELPS, STANLEE, and NANCY AUSTIN *The Assertive Woman: A New Look*. San Luis Obispo, CA: Impact Publishers, 1987. Teaches assertiveness, with special consideration of women's issues.

SANDERS, RALDOLPH K., and K. NEWTON MALONEY *Speak Up! Christian Assertiveness*. Philadelphia: Westminster John Knox, 1985.

NOTES

[1]Thomas Gordon, *Parent Effectiveness Training* (New York: Wyden, 1970).

[2]Eric Berne, *What Do You Say after You Say Hello?* (New York: Grove Press, 1972).

[3]George R. Bach and Peter Wyden, *The Intimate Enemy: How to Fight Fair in Love and Marriage* (New York: Avon, 1981).

[4]Carl E. Thoresen and Lynda H. Powell, "Type A Behavior Pattern: New Perspectives on Theory, Assessment, and Intervention," *Journal of Consulting and Clinical Psychology* 60 (1992): 595–604; Edward R. Sarafino, *Health Psychology: Biopsychosocial Interactions* (New York: John Wiley, 1990).

[5]Kenneth R. Pelletier, *Mind as Healer, Mind as Slayer* (New York: Delta Books, 1977); Ernest H. Johnson, *The Deadly Emotions: The Role of Anger, Hostility, and Aggression in Health and Emotional Well-being* (New York: Praeger, 1990).

[6]Albert Ellis, "The Case against Religion," *Mensa Bulletin* 38 (September 1970): 5–6.

[7]Allen E. Bergin, "Psychotherapy and Religious Values," *Journal of Consulting and Clinical Psychology* 48 (1980): 95–105.

[8]The relationships between stimulant abuse and anxiety disorders are discussed in the American Psychiatric Association's *Diagnostic and Statistical Manual of Mental Disorders*.

[9]Idiosyncratic Alcohol Intoxication continued to be listed in the 1987 DSM-III-R, the revised *Third Diagnostic and Statistical Manual* of the American Psychiatric Association, but was eliminated from the 1994 DSM-IV because of insufficient evidence for its existence.

[10]Albert Bandura, *Aggression: A Social Learning Analysis* (Englewood Cliffs, NJ: Prentice-Hall, 1973).

[11]Frank G. Bolton Jr., Larry A. Morris, and Ann E. MacEachron, *Men at Risk: The Other Side of Child Sexual Abuse* (Newbury Park, CA: Sage Publications, 1989).

[12]G. Alan Marlatt, C. F. Kosturn, and Alan R. Lang, "Provocation to Anger and Opportunity for Retaliation as Determinants of Alcohol Consumption in Social Drinkers," *Journal of Abnormal Psychology* 84 (1975): 652–59.

[13]G. Alan Marlatt and Judith R. Gordon, *Relapse Prevention* (New York: Guilford Press, 1985).

[14]W. J. Grace and D. T. Graham, "Relationship of Specific Attitudes and Emotions to Certain Bodily Diseases," *Psychosomatic Medicine* 14 (1952): 243–51.

[15]Lynn P. Rehm, Carilyn Z. Fuchs, David M. Roth, Sander J. Kornblith, and Joan M. Romano, "A Comparison of Self-control and Assertion Skills Treatments of Depression," *Behavior Therapy* 10 (1979): 429–42; Leslie A. Robinson, Jeffrey S. Berman, and Robert A. Neimeyer, "Psychotherapy for the Treatment of Depression: A Comprehensive Review of Controlled Outcome Research," *Psychological Bulletin* 108 (1990): 30–49.

[16]Gerald R. Patterson, *Coercive Family Process* (Eugene, OR: Castalia Publishing, 1982).

[17]Joseph Wolpe, *The Practice of Behavior Therapy*, 4th ed. (Elmsford, NY: Pergamon Press, 1991).

[18]Ray W. Novaco, *Anger Control: The Development and Evaluation of an Experimental Treatment* (Lexington, MA: Heath, 1975).

[19]William R. Miller and Stephen Rollnick, *Motivational Interviewing* (New York: Guilford Press, 1991).

[20]Donald Meichenbaum, *Cognitive-Behavior Modification: An Integrative Approach* (New York: Plenum Press, 1977). For a Christian context for self-talk, see H. Norman Wright, *Self-talk, Imagery, and Prayer in Counseling* (Dallas: Word, 1986).

[21]Ray W. Novaco, "Treatment of Chronic Anger through Cognitive and Relaxation Controls," *Journal of Consulting and Clinical Psychology* 44 (1976): 681; "Stress Inoculation: A Cognitive Therapy for Anger and Its Application to a Case of Depression," *Journal of Consulting and Clinical Psychology* 45 (1977): 600–68; Novaco, *Anger Control*.

[22]Donald Meichenbaum and J. Goodman, "Training Impulsive Children to Talk to Themselves: A Means of Developing Self-Control," *Journal of Abnormal Psychology* 77 (1971): 115–26; K. Daniel O'Leary, "Pills or Skills for Hyperactive Children," *Journal of Applied Behavior Analysis* 13 (1980): 191–204.

[23]Thomas A. Harris, *I'm OK—You're OK: A Practical Guide to Transactional Analysis* (New York: Harper & Row, 1967).

[24]David W. Augsburger, *Anger and Assertiveness in Pastoral Care* (Philadelphia: Fortress Press, 1979).

[25]Manuel Smith, *When I Say No I Feel Guilty* (New York: Bantam, 1985); Herbert Fensterheim and Jean Baer, *Don't Say Yes When You Want to Say No* (New York: Dell, 1975).

16

ALCOHOL, DRUGS, AND ADDICTION

That humanity at large will ever be able to dispense with arti-
ficial paradises seems very unlikely. Most men and women lead
lives at worst so painful, at the best so monotonous, poor and
limited that the urge to escape, the longing to transcend themselves if only for a few moments, is and has always been one
of the principal appetites of the soul.

—Aldous Huxley, *The Doors of Perception*

THE ADDICTIVE BEHAVIORS

People tend to think of the addictive behaviors as very different problems. Alcoholism is a disease. Drug abuse is a crime. Smoking is bad habit.
Obesity reflects the sin of gluttony.

Yet from a psychological perspective these seemingly diverse problems
have much in common. Collectively, they have come to be termed the *addictive behaviors*. All of them have, as their central characteristic, a short-term
payoff or pleasure at the expense of a long-term negative effect on health and
welfare: short-term gain, long-term pain. One of the most puzzling aspects of
the addictive behaviors, in fact, is that people often persist in the behavior
long after its negative consequences have become all too apparent. The alcoholic continues to drink in spite of obvious damage to health, family, and
work. The drug addict returns, after a difficult detoxification, to the very substance that induced the addiction in the first place. The smoker continues to
puff two packs a day in spite of the raspy cough, the shortness of breath, and
the scare that prompted a visit to the cardiologist. An overweight person continues to overeat and shun exercise, disregarding dire warnings from the family physician that early signs of heart disease and diabetes are emerging.

Of course, not *everyone* continues such self-destructive patterns. Many do heed the early warning signs, or make a change even before they are in real danger. In fact, research indicates that *most* people who stop smoking, lose weight, or overcome alcohol and other drug problems do so on their own, without professional help. These people never come to the attention of counselors and clinics. Those who come for help have tried to change on their own and failed—thus far, at least. They continue their self-defeating pattern, despite clear danger and consequences.

A second common characteristic of these problems is the immense suffering and expense that they impose on society at large. They are associated with increased risk of serious health problems, the treatment of which costs billions of dollars every year—a cost borne by taxpayers, health plan subscribers, and families. All are associated with premature death. There are up to 200,000 alcohol-related deaths per year in the United States, making alcohol the third leading cause of death after heart disease and cancer and the leading cause among people under the age of thirty. Smoking-related mortalities are twice that number, contributing heavily to premature deaths from cancer and heart disease. Long-term heavy drinkers or smokers die more than a decade earlier than other people, on average. Heavy drinking, drug use, smoking, and overeating are slow (and sometimes not so slow) forms of suicide. Along the way, other people are harmed as well—injured and slain on the highways at the hands of a impaired drivers, killed in drug-related violence, breathing the secondary smoke from others' cigarettes. Enormous amounts of work time and productivity are lost every year because of problems related to these four addictive behaviors. All together, the social costs total hundreds of billions of dollars annually. Hundreds of billions more are spent *buying* the alcohol, drugs, cigarettes, and excess food. There is no way to place a dollar figure on the suffering endured by families in relation to these problems, diseases, and premature deaths.

A third commonality in the addictive behaviors is their propensity to relapse. It is not difficult to stop or reduce these behaviors. What is difficult is *staying* healthy. Mark Twain's quip that "It's not difficult to stop smoking—I've done it dozens of times" is true enough, and true for all the addictive behaviors. Diet books crowd the bookstore shelves, tranquilizers top the best-seller list among prescription drugs, and alcohol/drug treatment centers (and those who fund them) complain of the "revolving door syndrome" with the same people returning again and again. The addictive behaviors are chronic relapsing conditions. (Our colleague, Howard Rankin, once remarked that *life* is a chronic relapsing condition!)

Perhaps you are already reflecting, as many have, on the parallels between addiction and sin.[1] Temptation often has to do with accepting short-term pleasure with long-term risk. The problem of relapse has also been called *backsliding*. We sin *knowing* the risks and consequences. The addictive behaviors have often been described as partially or primarily *spiritual* problems.

Carl Jung, reflecting the writings of Paul, observed an essential opposition of being filled with spirits (alcohol) and being filled with holy spirit. The wages of addiction are indeed death and destruction. Viewing addiction through spiritual eyes can be enlightening, and likewise the study of addictive behaviors is a fascinating field for understanding the broader problems of human transgression.

CATEGORY OR CONTINUUM?

Is addiction a unique condition or a continuum? The idea that people with alcohol problems have a *disease* was promoted originally to reduce moral stigma and to plead for more humane treatment—both worthy goals. The most popular disease model, however, has tended to view alcoholics as categorically distinct from normal people: fundamentally different by virtue of character, genes, physiology, or morals. One implication is that there are two kinds of people in the world—alcoholics who cannot drink and nonalcoholics who can drink as they please with impunity. Such binary thinking also extends to other addictive behaviors.

Yet reality is more complex than this. Alcohol use, problems, and addiction all occur in continuous gradations. There are not two distinct groups: heavy, problematic, addicted drinkers versus normal, problem-free drinkers. About one-third of U.S. adults are nondrinkers, and another third are very light drinkers (one to three drinks per week). [One standard "drink" here is equal to ten ounces of beer, or four ounces of table wine, or one ounce of liquor, all of which contain the same amount of alcohol.] At higher levels of alcohol use, the percentage becomes smaller and smaller. For example, fewer than 10 percent of adults average three drinks a day (twenty per week) or more. Yet there is no distinct demarcation between normal and abnormal drinkers, only a long continuum. Similarly, it is possible to show mild, moderate, or severe problems or dependence. The stereotyped "alcoholics" represent only the tip of the iceberg. Most drunk driving crashes, for example, involve not addicted drinkers, but the much larger number of heavy, problem, and risky drinkers.[2] The idea that one either "has" or "does not have" problems with alcohol (or other drugs, or eating) is an oversimplification.

A better analogy from the medical field is blood pressure. There are people with low, normal, borderline, high, and very high blood pressure—all along the continuum. Where one draws the line between normality and "hypertension" is arbitrary. Currently, a diastolic blood pressure of 90 is regarded as the upper limit of normality, but a person with 89 is not very different from someone with 91, even if measurement were that accurate. It adds nothing to call the person with 91 *hypertensive* and the other *normal*. Depending upon how high the blood pressure, people may need different treatments—cautionary advice, diet, exercise, medication, hospitalization, and so forth. Many other physical problems are like this: blood sugar, cholesterol levels, headaches, and respiratory difficulties.

The line is no clearer with other addictive behaviors. Many commonly abused drugs have legitimate healing uses. When is one's use excessive, problematic, or addictive? The line for "overweight" is a matter of judgment. We are dealing here with continua where the extremes of white and black are obvious, but the middle consists of shades of grey.[3]

One way to understand the continuum is to think of steps along the way, remembering that these steps are not cleanly demarcated but blend into one another. At one end of the continuum is *abstinence*. Those who do not use alcohol or another drug cannot be harmed by using it. As mentioned earlier, about one-third of U.S. adults abstain from alcohol completely. Next comes *use*: the remaining two-thirds are drinkers. Most of these are light or occasional drinkers; the median amount of alcohol consumed by American drinkers is two to three standard drinks per week.

Next along the continuum is *risky use*—drinking in a way that is not yet causing harm but has the potential of doing so. Driving with any amount of alcohol in the bloodstream is risky use. So is intoxication or use of alcohol in association with activities where harm could result from impaired attention, judgment, or reflexes: hunting, water sports, skiing, using power tools, and parenting. Heavy drinking, even if one does not feel intoxicated, is also risky use because of the large number of health hazards associated with steady use. Most experts now recommend as relatively safe limits not more than two standard drinks per day when drinking, with two or more alcohol-free days per

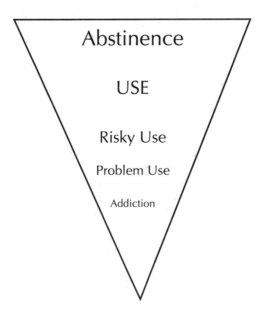

week. The one in eleven who average three or more drinks per day have significantly higher risk of alcohol-related health problems. Incidentally, there is *no* known safe level of drinking for pregnant women. Heavy drinking during pregnancy increases the risk of fetal alcohol syndrome, a pattern of birth defects and permanent disabilities.[4] Even moderate levels of drinking, however, have been associated with later patterns of learning disabilities and behavior problems. The best advice, then, is no drinking at all for women who are pregnant—or who may become pregnant, because there is significant risk from drinking before a woman realizes she is pregnant.

Beyond risky use is *problem use*. Here the person is currently experiencing problems related to his or her own use of the drug. These may be health, family, job, school, financial, social, emotional, or other psychological problems. From the best survey data available, again about one in eleven American adults are currently problem drinkers by this definition—roughly the same as the proportion of heavy drinkers. Finally comes the step of *dependence* or *addiction*, in which the person has increasing difficulty living without the drug. We will discuss these phenomena in greater detail later in this chapter.

Why do we devote an entire chapter to background on addictive behaviors? First, as the above statistics illustrate, these may be among the most common problems you will encounter (whether or not you recognize them) in pastoral ministry and counseling. For over two decades, the current (not lifetime) rate of problem drinking in the U.S. population has been estimated around 9 percent, or one in eleven adults. In one denominational survey, 39 percent of members reported that drinking had been a cause of trouble in their family, and 15 percent said they had been concerned about their own drinking. Among the pastors surveyed, 76 percent said they had been called upon within the past year for counseling related to drinking problems.[5] Add to that smoking, problems with prescription or illicit drugs, and weight problems, and the percentages grow still higher.

A second reason for this chapter is that there is much misinformation and misunderstanding in this area. It is important that you be well informed and up to date on how to understand and address these common problems. Third, there are many options available, and there is much you can do as a pastoral counselor. For several reasons, then, it is important for you to have a competent understanding of the addictive behaviors.

ABUSE AND PROBLEMS

Alcohol and other drug "abuse" has come to be the generic term for problems with these substances. This term implies that there is normal "use" of these substances, but that beyond some point (lying on a continuum), use becomes abuse. This terminology has been criticized on various grounds. Some do not regard any use as normal, and others dislike the pejorative overtones of the term. (A witty colleague has defined alcohol abuse as "mixing fine Scotch with root beer.")

Two general criteria have been used to separate normal use from abuse. One has to do with the level and style of use—when the way or amount one uses exceeds normal limits. This, of course, is a judgment call heavily influenced by what one considers to be normal. The second criterion focuses on continued use despite negative consequences. Table 16-1 lists specific examples within these two categories.

The general category of *abuse*, then, encompasses a broad range of levels and styles of abnormal, risky, and problematic use. Such problems may occur with or without signs of addiction.

THE MANY FACES OF ADDICTION

Of the verb *addict*, Webster says, "to devote or surrender (oneself) to something habitually or obsessively; esp: to accustom (oneself) to the habitual use of a drug."[6] An addiction in the most general sense, then, is a behavior to which one devotes or surrenders oneself habitually or obsessively. (Again, one sees the analogy to being captured or enslaved by sin.) It is in this sense that some writers have expanded the definition of addictive behavior to other problem areas—pathological gambling, workaholism, sexual deviations, destructive relationship patterns, and other compulsions. From a theological perspective, addictive behavior is one working definition of idolatry.

There are several specific phenomena often subsumed under the term *addiction*. Though they can occur together, it is important to distinguish these

TABLE 16-1   Signs of Alcohol/Drug Abuse

ABNORMAL AND COMPULSIVE USE:

Use of abnormally large doses (suggesting high tolerance)
   Example: pint of whiskey or two six-packs of beer or a quart of wine in one sitting; use of prescription drug above recommended dose or for unprescribed purposes
Unsuccessful attempts to stop or reduce use
Secretive use: attempts to conceal amount used
Craving or strong urges or desire to use

CONTINUED USE DESPITE RELATED NEGATIVE CONSEQUENCES SUCH AS:

Interference with ability to fulfill role obligations at work, school or home
Disruption of relationships with friends or family
Legal problems, violence, fights
Periods of memory lapse (blackouts)
Known damage to or neglect of physical health
Taking foolish risks (such as driving while impaired)
Avoidance of or withdrawal from normal social, vocational, and recreational activities
Financial problems

from each other. The presence of one does not necessarily imply the presence of the others, and blending of these different meanings of addiction has been one reason for confusion in this field.

Tolerance

One phenomenon that occurs when a person begins to engage regularly in an addictive behavior is *tolerance*. This means simply that larger and larger doses are required before the desired effect is achieved or—conversely—that a fixed dose has a smaller and smaller perceived effect on the person. Some drugs are more likely to produce tolerance than others. Alcohol, sedatives, tranquilizers, and opiates have a high propensity to produce tolerance. A heavy user of these drugs can tolerate doses that would be fatal for most people. The ability to "hold your liquor" is tolerance. A heavy drinker develops a high tolerance for alcohol. After a period of abstinence, tolerance decreases. Drinkers often mistakenly believe that tolerance is a sign that one can drink safely, without being harmed. Actually, the opposite it true. Tolerance does *not* mean that one can drink large quantities without being physically damaged. It only means that the person can drink large and physically damaging doses *without feeling or showing the effects*. Tolerance is not uniquely tied to drugs. Thrill-seekers sometimes find themselves drawn to ever bigger risks because the old ones are no longer fulfilling.

Physical Dependence

Perhaps the phenomenon most commonly associated with the term *addiction* is *physical dependence*. Here the person experiences physical discomfort, illness, or even life-threatening shock when the drug is withdrawn. In essence, the body has become accustomed to the presence of the drug and has made certain changes to accommodate to its continual presence. This reflects the body's remarkable adaptive capacity. If the drug is then suddenly stopped, however, the body goes into an abnormal state and requires some time to adjust. The unpleasant symptoms that follow are called *withdrawal* or *abstinence syndrome*.

For *alcohol and other sedatives*, the withdrawal syndrome is a complicated and potentially dangerous one. The complete withdrawal cycle is as follows. As inebriation subsides after the last drink, the person begins to become uncomfortable. The discomfort may include headache, agitation, jumpiness, irritability, rapid pulse, feelings of weakness, shakiness (tremor), nausea, sweating, and insomnia. These symptoms, sometimes called *hangover*, typically peak about twelve to twenty-four hours after the last drink. In some cases these are accompanied or followed by hallucinations—seeing, hearing, or feeling things that are not there. A convulsion, similar to an epileptic grand mal seizure, can occur during the first two days of withdrawal.

In more severe cases, another serious phase, known as *delirium tremens* begins around the third day. It begins quickly and usually includes extreme agitation, confusion, and disorientation. All of the symptoms of early withdrawal return, but in more severe form: agitation, fever, rapid and pounding heart, profuse sweating, dilation of the pupils of the eyes, flushing of the skin, gross tremor or shaking, and again possible hallucinations. You may recognize these as related to massive autonomic arousal (chapter 14). Full-blown delirium tremens is a dangerous illness and can be fatal if untreated. Detoxification programs exist for the purpose of bringing people safely through this hazardous period. With proper treatment, the dangerous symptoms and much of the discomfort can be alleviated. A person who is withdrawing and who either has a history of such symptoms or shows early signs of withdrawal syndrome should be taken for supervised detoxification. The vast majority of detoxification today is handled on an outpatient basis, with hospitalization rarely necessary.[7]

Of course, not all heavy or problem drinkers experience such severe withdrawal. In fact, most do not. Physical dependence, as indicated earlier, is a matter of degree. Mildly dependent people may experience only hangovers or notice only some insomnia and agitation for a few days when they quit. A definitive marker of all withdrawal symptoms is that they are relieved or eliminated when the person resumes use of the drug (as in relieving a hangover by having some alcohol—"a bit of the hair of the dog that bit you"). Some people experience no withdrawal symptoms at all. When a full syndrome does occur, however, it is a serious and life-threatening matter.

Probably the most stereotyped withdrawal syndrome is that from *heroin*. Books and films have created the impression that this is an agonizing, horrifying experience involving excruciating pain and suffering, terror, and near death. Physical dependence to heroin is certainly a reality and can occur quite quickly. The withdrawal syndrome, however, is not nearly as difficult or dangerous as that attached to alcohol. In fact, the actual symptoms have been likened to a bad case of flu. Of course, an individual who is *expecting* to go through torturous suffering may have a bad time of it because of the terror at the first signs of withdrawal. Detoxification in a calming atmosphere will usually bring the person through withdrawal with only moderate discomfort.

Nicotine is also an extraordinarily addicting drug. Common withdrawal symptoms include depressed or irritable mood, restlessness and insomnia, difficulty concentrating, anxiety, and a craving for nicotine. Research has shown that heavy smokers adjust their cigarette intake to maintain a constant level of nicotine in the bloodstream.[8] For this reason a mere switch to a lower nicotine brand may not be helpful because the smoker can compensate by smoking more cigarettes, taking more puffs, or inhaling more deeply.

Physical dependence is real. At the same time, addictive behaviors cannot be explained by physical addiction alone. Most problem drinkers, for example, show little or no physical dependence. People abuse drugs, such as hallucinogens, that have little potential for producing a withdrawal syndrome. Relapses occur after people are well past the period of detoxification and withdrawal, so that physical dependence does not explain why people *return* to use after prolonged abstinence. Detoxification alone is quite ineffective in helping people stay free of alcohol and other drugs. Physical dependence is not the whole picture, by any means.

High-Seeking

Another phenomenon sometimes included within the concept of addiction is consistent use of a substance for the purpose of a "high." Here the person is using the drug not (or not only) to avoid the pain of withdrawal, but for its perceived euphoric or other positive effects.

Nicotine is a case in point. It is a stimulant. It goes directly to the brain, arriving about seven seconds after the person takes a puff of a cigarette. Each puff gives a little jolt, a little lift. Some people also report a sense of euphoria from the first few drinks of alcohol (though subsequent drinks tend to have the opposite effect). Cocaine is a substance that directly stimulates pleasure centers in the brain. Laboratory animals quickly learn to press a bar to receive small doses of cocaine and often continue doing so until they drop from exhaustion. Heroin and other opiates simulate the effects of a class of natural brain chemicals known as the *endorphins*—chemicals produced by our bodies that help in pain relief and provide something of a natural high, as is sought by runners.

Psychological Dependence

Yet another face of addiction is *psychological* dependence. Here the person comes to *rely* on the drug to accomplish a certain psychological function, often the altering of mood or alertness. Among the psychological functions for which people rely upon chemical assistance are

> to wake up and become more alert or to stay awake
> to relax or calm down
> to feel good—less depressed or stressed
> to be less shy and become more sociable
> to bolster courage and override fears
> to get to sleep at night
> to feel more sexy or powerful
> to forget or to avoid problems
> to make the world seem more interesting or exciting

to feel more creative or have new sensory experiences

to enhance sexual enjoyment or performance

to suppress hunger

to recover from the effects of other drugs

Any observer of American television and other advertising should not be surprised that people seek chemical solutions for such goals and problems. Television characters are among society's most frequent drinkers, often saying things like, "I need a drink," and using alcohol for any or all of the reasons listed above. Food and drug companies spend huge advertising budgets to educate people that if they ever feel the slightest hunger or distress they should have fast relief. Drinking and cigarette smoking are presented in advertising as routes to sophistication, popularity, excitement, liberation, masculinity, femininity, sexuality, independence, and good taste. Through advertising media, all day every day, people are taught not to tolerate any discomfort but to use substances (including food) to change how they feel.

It is when an addictive behavior has become the *only* or *primary* means by which one is coping with a certain task or problem that psychological dependence has occurred. The food, drug, or compulsion becomes the only (or main) way to get from point A (discomfort) to point B (comfort). Without it, the person has difficulty in coping, at least in this particular area. Like physical dependence, psychological dependence is not a black-or-white phenomenon, but a matter of degree.

Impaired Control

Finally, in any discussion of addiction, the concept of *loss of control* must be considered. Most often used in connection with alcohol and other drug abuse, this is the idea that once a person takes the first dose (cigarette, drink, fix, chocolate chip cookie), the battle is lost. Something mysterious happens to the person, and he or she is no longer capable of self-control. A popular phrase capturing this idea is "One drink, one drunk."

The idea of losing volitional control is part of society's concept of addiction. In alcoholism, it emerged from a nineteenth century European concept of *dipsomania*, used to explain excessive drinking. It implied a brain disorder, triggered in allergic fashion by exposure to alcohol, that rendered the person incapable of self-control. Although some professionals still argue that alcoholism is just such a physical abnormality,[9] most scientists now regard impaired control to be a matter of degree, rather than a black-and-white affair. Juries are also generally unwilling to find defendants not guilty by reason of intoxication. Certain drugs, such as alcohol and cocaine, do impair self-control by altering judgment, memory, and perception, and individuals already prone to impulsivity or other problems with self-regulation are at higher risk in using such drugs.[10]

From a theological perspective, this raises interesting issues regarding the sinfulness of drug abuse. Some have argued, for example, that, although alcohol abuse is a sin, alcoholism is not, by virtue of loss of control.[11] The Presbyterian Church, in a 1986 social policy statement, provided a more complex discussion of this issue, recognizing that as a person becomes more deeply enmeshed in addiction, the *degree* of volitional control diminishes, a condition not unusual in "falling into sin" more generally.[12] In any event, the idea of losing willful self-control has historically been a key part of the concept of addiction.

WHAT DO DRUGS DO?

A full catalog and description of commonly abused psychoactive drugs can itself comprise a sizable book.[13] To oversimplify a bit, drugs of abuse can be thought of as falling into three major categories: ups, downs, and outs.

The *ups* (like cocaine, amphetamine, nicotine, and caffeine) are drugs that increase the level of activity in the nervous system and keep one awake, alert, and aroused. These stimulants also have the general quality of suppressing hunger and fatigue, which is why they have sometimes been used for weight control or given to soldiers in combat. They may also impart a "rush," a powerful and euphoric feeling of well-being.

The *downs*, on the other hand, mostly do just the opposite. They slow down functioning of major parts of the central nervous system and induce drowsiness, incoordination, and often disinhibition (increased talkativeness, risk-taking, and violation of social norms). Drugs that push the body in this direction are sedatives (including alcohol), tranquilizers, opioids (like morphine and heroin), and inhaled volatile substances such as paint, gasoline, and glue. The latter has come to be a particular problem among youth in certain regions and is a special concern because it can rapidly result in brain damage or death. Downers can also impart a feeling of well-being, although this tends to be lost at higher doses or with repeated use.

Finally, the *outs* are those drugs that mostly change perceptions—the experience of reality. These are the cannabis drugs (marijuana and hashish) and hallucinogens such as LSD, psilocybin (mushrooms), and PCP (angel dust). These drugs tend to alter the person's sense of the passing of time and to change sensations and perceptions of the world. They may induce euphoria but sometimes evoke strong negative emotions, particularly in the case of the hallucinogens.

Psychoactive drugs work by acting directly on the brain. Sedatives suppress brain function and in overdose can shut down vital functions of the heart and lungs. Cocaine and other stimulants act on pleasure centers and increase nervous arousal. The opioids resemble endorphins that occur naturally in the brain, overstimulating those particular nerve channels for pain relief

TABLE 16-2   Major Categories of Frequently Abused Drugs

CATEGORY	EXAMPLES	COMMON EFFECTS
Sedatives	Alcohol Barbiturates Tranquilizers	Slowing, incoherence, mood shifts, drowsiness, incoordination, disinhibition
Stimulants	Amphetamine Cocaine Nicotine Caffeine	Elation, agitation, alertness, suppression of hunger, elevated pulse rate and blood pressure, agitation
Cannabis	Marijuana Hashish	Altered sensation, slowed time sense, apathy, increased appetite, rapid heart rate
Hallucinogens	LSD, DMT Psilocybin PCP	Emotionality, strange experiences, altered time sense, hallucinations
Inhalants	Paint Glue Gasoline	Dizziness, sedation, slurred speech, apathy, slowed and uncoordinated movement
Opioids	Heroin Morphine Methadone	Slowing, slurred speech, apathy, poor memory and judgment, drowsiness

and well-being. Hallucinogens alter the activity of other natural brain chemicals, creating unusual experiences.

Table 16-2 provides a short list of frequently abused drugs, organizing them into major categories according to their effects. Each category has the potential for producing psychological and physical dependence. All may induce euphoria and impair judgment.

CHANGING CONCEPTIONS OF ADDICTIVE BEHAVIORS

Why do people become harmfully involved with alcohol, drugs, and other addictive behaviors? Thinking on this subject has changed dramatically over the past century, and it is possible to trace the development of different explanations.[14]

Typically, the earliest explanations are *moral* and attribute the problem to weakness of will or character or willful sin and disregard of societal standards. In this way of thinking, the appropriate response is punishment and other social sanctions. This is currently the dominant model with regard to drunk driving.

Agent explanations, on the other hand, attribute the problem to the drug itself. During the temperance era in the early twentieth century, alcohol was seen as a highly dangerous and addictive drug for all who used it. A logical response in such a view is prohibition, a "war on drugs" to remove the substance from society by making it illicit and illegal.

A dispositional *disease* model of alcoholism was ascendant after the prohibition of alcohol. In this view, only *certain* people (e.g., alcoholics) are incapable of handling the drug, whereas most people can use it safely. The difference is understood as an illness or physical abnormality, which distinguishes the condition from normality. This view of alcoholism is understandably popular with the liquor industry because it de-emphasizes the role of alcohol in creating problems. The appropriate response here is to identify people with the malady and persuade them to avoid the drug.

A *personality* view asserts that addiction problems emerge from an "addictive personality" that is common to all persons with addiction problems. Often this personality is described as dominated by strong and immature defense mechanisms such as denial and projection. From this perspective, psychotherapy might be a sensible strategy for treating such personality disturbance. Currently, popular thinking about alcoholism appears to be a blend of moral, disease, and characterological beliefs.[15]

A true *spiritual* model is found in the origins of Alcoholics Anonymous and the twelve-step fellowships.[16] Here, addiction is described as arising out of defects of character such as self-centeredness and from a spiritual emptiness and hunger. Twelve-step fellowships are not truly *self-help* groups, but rather are *God-help* groups. In this view, the hope for recovery is in turning one's life and problem over to God and asking to be healed. The twelve-step program is a kind of generic spiritual search for God and an attempt to realign one's life to live by God's will.

Biological models point to physical processes that influence addiction. Among these, of course, is the potential of a drug to induce dependence. Research has also focused on genetic predispositions and the effects of drugs on the brain. Prevention and treatment efforts derived from a biological perspective might emphasize counseling those at high risk, or seeking medications to diminish the impact of drugs.

Behavioral models emphasize that addictive behaviors are *habits* subject to learning, modeling, and environmental influence. A process of relearning is called for here, as well as greater attention to the ways in which the environment may be involved in the problem. This view is taken a step further in a *family systems* perspective, which stresses the role of the family in maintaining and treating addiction, and in *sociocultural* models, which emphasize the role of culture, social, and community conditions in the occurrence of these problems.

As is often the case, each of these views contains elements of truth. An historic problem in this field has been an overemphasis on one or another model as *the* Truth, the whole answer to addiction. Most recently, a public health perspective has been emerging as a broader way to conceptualize addictive behaviors.[17] In this way of thinking, three general factors contribute to the problem. First, the *agent* or drug itself (e.g., alcohol, nicotine) is a significant factor and poses risks for any who use it. Were alcohol being introduced as a new drug now, for example, and if we already knew what is known about its effects, it would be unlikely to be legalized. The drugs themselves play a role.

Second, the *host* or individual is also an important part of the picture. Certain people are at greater risk for developing problems when exposed to a particular drug, by virtue of factors such as their gender, genetic make-up, age, and psychological status. Risk and problems vary along a continuum, rather than being limited to a subclass of people (e.g., "addicts" or "alcoholics") who are qualitatively different from other people.

Finally, the *environment* cannot be forgotten and represents the third element of a public health perspective. One cannot fully understand and prevent drunk driving without addressing social conditions that virtually guarantee its occurrence: drive-up liquor windows, the sale of chilled beer at gasoline stations, service of alcohol at large public events, and the building of bars in locations that can be reached only by automobile. Factors such as price, advertising, and availability influence the likelihood of use and related problems. Birth defects and permanent mental and behavioral disabilities occur in children whose mothers drank heavily during pregnancy. Yet these terrible problems cannot be understood and addressed without attending to quality of prenatal care, and to poverty, lack of adequate child care, and other conditions that contribute to maternal drinking.

The point is that no *one* of these factors is sufficient for understanding and addressing the complex problems of addiction. Effective societal countermeasures must include attention to the agent *and* the host *and* the environment.

WHAT CAN A PASTOR DO?

While rightly concerned about the larger picture, pastors also counsel people one at a time, whose lives are harmed or endangered by addictive behaviors. In this regard, it is important to have a working knowledge of treatment options, and we will outline these for you later in this chapter. First, however, we want to describe ways in which you, as a pastor, can be helpful to people with alcohol and other drug problems.

Strengthen Motivation

First, perhaps most importantly, you can help the person build *motivation* for change. Motivation is a significant issue, because many—perhaps most—risky, problem, and addicted users are not quite ready for change. In the language of stages of change presented in chapter 8, they are precontemplators, seeing no need for change, or contemplators who are ambivalent about their situation. These, we find, are the real obstacles to seeking help for 90 percent of smokers, heavy drinkers, and those with other drug problems.

There is a popular idea that pathological defense mechanisms such as denial are part of the "disease" of alcoholism or chemical dependence. In fact, there is no scientific evidence for this assertion, and the data indicate instead that there is no unique alcoholic or addictive personality.[18] People with alcohol and other drug problems are as different from one another as snowflakes. They come from every walk of life, men and women from every racial, age, occupational, and socioeconomic group. Resistance to seeking change is not a personality problem; it is a perception problem. They simply don't see the risk or harm, don't see it as that serious, or don't see the alternatives. That is where you can play a vital role. The motivational counseling (FRAMES) approach outlined in chapter 8 has been shown to be significantly effective in helping people to see and change their risky or harmful use.[19] Even relatively brief (one to three sessions) counseling of this kind has been shown to be effective, sometimes as beneficial as longer treatment.[20]

Provide Support and Understanding

Second and relatedly, there is the way you relate as pastor to those harmfully involved with alcohol or other drugs. The social stereotype is that one has to be confrontational, aggressive, and tough to break through the defenses and be effective. Yet research indicates just the opposite: that the most effective counselors are those who are warm, empathic, supportive, and understanding—good listeners.[21] In other words, the same kinds of approaches that pastors often instinctively use in counseling with other kinds of problems are also helpful here. People with alcohol/drug problems are *people* and respond no better than the rest of us to being coerced, accused, argued with, and confronted.

A word about this word, *confront*. We have been using it here in the sense of an aggressive, directive, pushy, forceful style in which the counselor thrusts the truth upon the client and offers imperative advice. Yet in its etymology, *confront* means to bring face to face. In that sense, confrontation is not a counseling style but a *goal*: to bring the person face to face with a difficult, sometimes painful and scary truth. The question, then, is how best to accomplish this goal: How to help a person see the truth and be changed by it. (Now *there* is a task with which pastors are familiar!) Direct argumentation is just about the *least* effective way of changing a belief, attitude, value, or emotionally charged perception. It is within the safety of a supportive and empathic relationship that people are able to confront truth, to take it in, feel it, and allow it to set them free.

One more point is important here. Therapeutic empathy is not the same as having been there yourself. Some believe that, to help an alcoholic (addict, gambler, etc.), you have to have been one yourself. The same argument is seldom made with regard to depression, schizophrenia, or heart disease, but somehow the notion has gained popularity for the addictive behaviors. Again, research is a helpful resource. Regarding oneself as a recovering alcoholic makes one neither a more nor a less effective counselor for those with alcohol problems.[22] It is not one's recovery status, but other factors such as empathic listening skills that mark the effective counselor.

Don't Diagnose

Diagnostic labels are not the issue but often become a stumbling block. It makes little or no difference whether a client accepts the diagnosis "alcoholic" or "addict," and much countertherapeutic effort is wasted on arguments about labels. Even within Alcoholics Anonymous, where the statement, "I am an alcoholic" is greatly valued, there are strong prohibitions against trying to force this label on another person.[23] It is up to the person to decide. If asked, "Are you saying I'm an alcoholic?" we often say something like, "Labels really aren't important to me. What matters to me is *you*. The important thing is to ask what is happening in your life in regard to [drinking], and what, if anything, you want to do about it."

Know about Change Options

Another real service that you can provide as a pastoral counselor is to help people learn about and explore their various options for change. The really encouraging news, as we shall explain below, is that there are a range of effective alternatives for people who want to make a change in addictive behavior. It is usually a mistake to offer one and only one approach. This sets the person up for failure, since it might not be the right way for that person. Sometimes relapsers move from one treatment program to another, being given basically the same kind of treatment but in different settings. The simple change principle applies here: if what has been tried in the past didn't work, try something else. There are many ways, and the chances are excellent that for any given person there is an effective approach. We try to give this message: "There are many different ways that have worked for people. I will try to help you find the one that is best for you the first time, but if it doesn't work, don't get discouraged. I will stay with you until we find what works for you." Knowing that there is real hope can remove the last obstacles to pursuing change. Your clients need your optimism, as well as your knowledge of different options.

Stay with Your Client

Finally, we advise you to retain an active involvement even when referral is made for formal treatment. Let go of the idea of turning a person over to an "expert" professional or program to be repaired. First of all, formal treatment is by no means the only way that people change. Even after formal treatment is over, the factors that most influence whether a person will relapse have to do with lifestyle and social support: employment, family stability, friends and supportive relationships, stress and anger management, and use of time.[24] Stable spiritual/religious activity is also associated with decreased risk of alcohol and other drug problems.[25] Thus, the ways in which you ordinarily pastor to others are just as vital for those recovering from alcohol/drug problems.

TREATMENT CONSIDERATIONS

Although some claim to have *the* answer, there is no single outstandingly effective approach for people whose lives are enmeshed with alcohol or other drugs. No one approach consistently works for a majority of people, despite common claims of high success rates. In one local survey of treatment alcoholism programs, the lowest success rate quoted was 80 percent, yet none could offer any scientific data to substantiate their claim.[26] This overselling of treatment can have an unfortunate demoralizing effect on clients who fail to respond because it creates the impression that they are in a small minority of failures and that something must be wrong with them. In truth, well over half of those treated in a typical alcohol/drug program—often as many as 80 to 90 percent—relapse at least once during the first two years after treatment. Among smokers, the permanent quit rate on any given try is under 10 percent. That is not reason for alarm; it is simply a perspective that any *one* try may not be enough. Whether people try to change on their own or with the help of a treatment program or professional, it is normal for them to go around the stages of change (chapter 8) several times before achieving long-term stability. In the long run, however, the chances for success are good.

Before we review some of the clinical approaches that have been found to be effective, there are several general issues to consider.

Treatment Settings

The 1970s and 1980s saw a dramatic upsurge in the number of U.S. hospitals and residential programs offering treatment for "chemical dependency," while during the same period most other nations were de-emphasizing this expensive form of care. The reasons for this were more economic than therapeutic, and in the current environment of a health care cost containment crisis the trend is quickly shifting away from hospital-based care. With great consistency, research has shown that inpatient/residential treatment programs are no more effective overall than less expensive outpatient alternatives, for mental health problems in general and alcoholism in particular.[27] They can, however, be immensely profitable businesses, charging $1,000 per day or more for hospital-based counseling delivered at relatively low cost.

Who needs or especially benefits from such more intensive and expensive care? If there is a subgroup more likely to do better in inpatient/residential (versus outpatient) treatment, it seems to be those who (a) have severe problems and dependence and (b) are socially unstable—homeless, poor, without stable jobs or families. More stable and less severely deteriorated people fare at least as well in outpatient treatment, yet this is precisely the group recruited by private hospitals and residential programs. As a crude rule of thumb, if you can afford hospital treatment you probably don't require it; if you can't afford it, it is often unavailable.

Of course, there are special circumstances that warrant hospitalization. These have to do not so much with alcohol/drug problems as with other factors that would justify institutional care even in the absence of substance abuse (e.g., high risk of violence or suicide or concomitant medical illnesses requiring hospital treatment). A homeless, jobless person needs a place to stay long enough to stabilize. As noted above, severe physical dependence does require medical supervision during the detoxification process, but this can be accomplished on an outpatient basis in the vast majority of cases.[28] In any event, continuing counseling or other support in the community is important whether or not hospitalization occurs.

There are also intermediate options between institutional and outpatient care. Halfway houses provide a stable place to live, with minimal treatment, while the person readjusts to the community. Day treatment programs are just the opposite: more intensive treatment during the day, after which the person returns home. More intensive night or weekend programs have also been developed in some areas to accommodate employed people. Two important points to remember about different treatment *settings* are that (a) there are a variety of options and (b) more expensive settings are not necessarily the most effective. Think of a continuum of care (and cost), ranging from self-help and brief counseling at one end to intensive hospital treatment at the other. A reasonable approach is to start with less extensive and expensive options and work one's way up the continuum if previous efforts have not sufficed.

Detoxification

Detoxification is the process of withdrawing from a drug upon which one has become physically dependent. Different drugs produce different withdrawal syndromes, some more severe and dangerous than others. Among the most life-threatening withdrawal symptoms, once addiction has been established, are those induced by alcohol, barbiturates, and other sedative drugs. Withdrawal from narcotics and stimulants can be uncomfortable but rarely life-threatening.

Detoxification can be accomplished in a variety of ways. *Cold turkey* is withdrawal without the use of any drugs. More commonly, treatment programs provide substitute drugs to ease the person down to a sober state with minimal discomfort and danger. Such substitute drugs are used, in practice, for anywhere from a few hours or days (as with tranquilizers for alcohol withdrawal) to a few weeks or months (as with nicotine substitution for smokers) or even years (as with methadone for heroin). Typically, the dose of the substitute drug is tapered off until the person is drug-free.

There is a clear professional consensus, supported by research, that detoxification does not, in itself, constitute effective treatment. The expected outcome of detoxification alone is relapse. Detoxification simply renders the person more ready for change.

Abstinence or Moderation?

A classic debate in the substance abuse field is whether all persons with alcohol or other drug problems must be required to accept a goal of abstinence or whether moderation is an achievable goal for some. With some addictive behaviors (e.g., eating disorders, workaholism), true abstinence is not a realistic choice, but what about those where some clients choose a moderation goal? Here are a few pragmatic points on this complex and controversial subject.[29]

First, whatever their counselors may say about what their objectives must be, clients can and do set their own goals. Several studies have shown that it makes little difference what goal a client is *assigned*; outcomes are determined by other factors.[30]

Second, like it or not, there are moderate and problem-free users of virtually all drugs (unless one considers any use of an illegal drug to be a problem *ipso facto*). Depending upon definitions and populations, between 5 percent and 30 percent of people treated for alcohol problems wind up drinking moderately over long periods.[31] Long-term moderate use of tobacco, cocaine, and heroin ("chipping") seem to be more difficult to maintain but also occur.

Third, with clients who refuse to consider abstinence, your choice as a counselor may be between starting with them where they are or losing them to treatment altogether. Various "warm turkey" strategies exist for working with people who will not agree to abstain.[32] A general goal in these cases is *harm reduction*—to diminish the risk and harm to themselves and others. Any step away from heavy or dependent use is a step in the right direction, and through such successive steps people can often be encouraged ultimately to abstain, whereas an insistence on immediate abstention drives them away from contact with caregivers.

Fourth, it is important to remember that we are dealing with a continuum of severity of problems. For those with severe alcohol problems and dependence, abstinence is clearly the goal of choice. Alcohol studies show, however, that as one moves down the spectrum of severity (refer back to Fig.

16-1), the likelihood of abstinence decreases and the probability of stable moderation increases.[33] Between the prevention (abstinence or safe use) goals at one end of this spectrum and intensive treatments at the other, there are a variety of different approaches.[34] It is the middle range of the continuum—those more numerous people with early, mild, or moderate problem levels—for whom appropriate services have been least available.

Finally, the issue of moderation causes one to grapple with religious and other personal views of drug use.[35] Is any use (of alcohol, tobacco, or a prescription or illicit psychoactive drug) wrong in and of itself? If not, within what limits and for what reasons is it acceptable? Realize, too, that a client's initial views on this issue may well differ from your own. There is merit to being honest about your own beliefs, but it is also wise to consider the likely effect of inflicting disapproval or argument on a client struggling with ambivalence and motivation for change.

EFFECTIVE TREATMENT APPROACHES

The field of addiction treatment is odd in a number of ways. Perhaps more than in any other health field, addiction treatment suffers from an immense chasm between science and clinical practice. The current professional heroes of the addiction field are not researchers like Pasteur, Salk, or Curie, but proponents of treatment strategies unsubstantiated by scientific evidence.[36] Meanwhile, a range of treatment approaches with well-documented efficacy are neglected or even shunned in practice. The same situation would be regarded as ethically unacceptable in the treatment of heart disease, cancer, or other serious illnesses, where failure to provide up-to-date research-proven treatment constitutes malpractice.

As mentioned earlier, a reason for optimism in this field is the array of different approaches with reasonable evidence of efficacy. The description of these alternatives easily fills a textbook of its own.[37] Here we can only describe the major promising treatment strategies for addiction problems.

Medications

Medications used to treat alcohol/drug problems generally fall into four categories. First, there are the *substitute* drugs. In this strategy, the same or a similar drug is given by prescription, with the hope of long-term weaning or at least reduction of risk and harm. Nicotine can be prescribed in patch or chewing gum form, to help smokers quit. In some nations, known and registered addicts are given their drug of choice (e.g., heroin) or a similar drug (e.g., the opiate *methadone,* as in the U.S.) under medical supervision, reducing the risks associated with contaminated needles and a criminal lifestyle and the need to recruit new users to support a drug habit.[38] The substitution of other drugs (e.g., tranquilizers) for alcohol, however, is generally regarded a bad idea because it is ineffective in reducing drinking and can lead to dual addiction.

A second type of medication can *block* drug use. The drug naltrexone, for example, effectively blocks the brain receptors for opiates, so that the injection of heroin yields no high. Disulfiram (trade name, Antabuse) is a prescription drug that when taken daily discourages drinking because any use of alcohol triggers feelings of illness such as nausea, headache, dizziness, and reddening of the face. When taken regularly in adequate doses, such drugs do effectively suppress use. The principal problem is usually in getting the person to take them faithfully.

Active research is ongoing to develop *amethystic* medications that alter the effect of abused drugs without blocking them altogether. Certain antidepressant agents, for example, may decrease drug craving or diminish the euphoric effects of taking alcohol or other drugs.

Finally, psychiatric medications can be helpful in treating other conditions that underlie or accompany alcohol/drug abuse. Antipsychotic medications are perfectly appropriate in treating schizophrenia (see chapter 17). Lithium can be life-saving for people with bipolar disorder, and antidepressants can reduce symptoms of depression (chapter 12). These are not addictive substances and are not abused as street drugs. When such a condition accompanies alcohol/drug abuse or is discovered in abstinence, these medications can be valuable in preventing relapse by addressing the concomitant problem. Unfortunately, some professionals and programs take a "drug-free" philosophy to extremes and deprive clients of these or other nonaddictive and potentially helpful medications.

Teaching Coping Skills

It is unlikely, however, that the mere prescription of any medication will be sufficient to overcome an established drug dependence. Nicotine substitution is relatively ineffective unless accompanied by strategies to help the ex-smoker develop effective drug-free skills for coping with life stresses and challenges. Among the most strongly research-supported treatment components for alcoholism are social skills training, stress management training, and behavioral marital therapy.[39] Note that these approaches do not even focus on alcohol/drug use per se, but on teaching skills for happy and effective living without drugs. In this regard, employment is such an important predictor of sobriety versus relapse that helping a recovering person find a job (or at least meaningful vocation) should be considered a vital part of treatment. It can also be crucial to change friends or social support networks and find new drug-free ways to spend leisure time. Treatment programs teaching lifestyle-focused coping skills have been found to be substantially more effective than traditional treatment focused primarily on alcohol or cocaine use.[40] Again, these findings suggest potentially valuable roles for a pastor in supporting those recovering from alcohol/drug problems.

There are also coping skills directly useful in managing one's own alcohol/drug use. Over thirty studies have documented the effectiveness of teaching less severe problem drinkers how to moderate their use of alcohol.[41] Research is advancing in the area of relapse prevention skills that help people stay sober.[42] Behavior change strategies for cutting down and then quitting tobacco have become a standard part of effective programs for smoking cessation.

Aversion Therapies

People who have a particularly strong attraction to or craving for a drug may benefit from a group of therapeutic procedures that have been studied for over fifty years. The aversion therapies seek to develop a mental/emotional association between the to-be-avoided substance and unpleasant experiences. Perhaps you have had the experience of eating a certain food, then becoming ill, and for some time thereafter losing your taste and desire for that food. There are powerful conditioning processes that can alter one's positive or negative associations. Research evidence is mixed but promising enough to warrant consideration if other strategies have failed to break a pattern of craving and addiction. Certain hospitals (notably the Schick group in the United States) offer an intense form of aversion therapy. A less-expensive alternative sometimes offered in outpatient programs is *covert sensitization*, which pairs a drug with unpleasant events in imagination.

Self-Help Groups

The most widely available source of help in North America is Alcoholics Anonymous (A.A.), a spiritually based fellowship devoted to helping alcoholics recover. Founded in 1935, A.A. continues to grow and numbers its worldwide members in the millions. Research indicates that people who are most likely to affiliate with A.A. are those who look to others for support and help and whose alcoholism matches the pattern emphasized in A.A.: more severe drinking problems with physical dependence and experienced loss of control over alcohol use.[43] The generic twelve-step program has also been extended to address a variety of other problems including drug abuse, overeating, gambling, and compulsive sexuality. Al-Anon and Alateen groups are available for family members and youth.

Pastors are sometimes concerned that twelve-step groups may pose a threat to a client's religious beliefs. In fact, although A.A. emphasizes God as a source of help, it carefully avoids affiliation with any religion and takes no

stand on religious or political issues. In our experience, the spiritual principles (the twelve steps) underlying A.A. are compatible with a broad range of
religious beliefs and ought not pose significant problems for believers, who
may actually find the God-oriented program quite comfortable. Pastoral counseling to integrate personal beliefs with a twelve-step program may be useful. If you undertake such counseling, however, it is essential for you to attend
a number of A.A. meetings to seek an understanding of the program from the
inside.

A variety of other self-help organizations are also currently available in
many areas, including Women for Sobriety and Rational Recovery, which were
explicitly founded for people uncomfortable with twelve-step groups. Very
little research is presently available regarding the efficacy of these groups.

A distinct advantage of self-help groups such as A.A. is the wide network of support they can afford, and at no financial cost. Clients unfamiliar
with A.A. can be encouraged to visit meetings, and you might break the ice
by offering to accompany them. At the same time, research does not suggest
that A.A. is a superior or essential approach to recovery. It is *one* way, and its
founders never claimed it to be more than that. Over 90 percent of those who
try A.A. drop out within six months,[44] but those who stay often swear by it.
Research is just beginning to elucidate how, why, how often, and for whom
A.A. "works."[45]

There are a number of approaches in practice that we specifically do not
recommend because of research evidence on their lack of efficacy.[46] Individual
or group insight-oriented psychotherapies (such as psychoanalysis or other
psychodynamic approaches) have a poor track record with alcohol/drug
problems. General "talk" therapies and counseling in general have not proven
effective, and evidence for hypnosis and acupuncture is also lacking.
Educational lectures and films seem to be of little or no benefit in addiction
treatment. Although popular in the United States, confrontational approaches
("break them down to build them up") are associated with poor outcomes,
especially for people lower in self-esteem. Unfortunately, many current treatment programs (including some very expensive ones) still consist primarily
of a combination of these elements that research has found wanting.

Role of Family Members

Over the years there have been major changes in professional and public opinion regarding the family members of people with alcohol/drug problems. Before and during the temperance era, spouses and other family
members were viewed with sympathy as innocent victims. The rise of psychodynamic thinking brought the notion that alcoholics' spouses were themselves pathological, having chosen their plight to meet unconscious needs,
and thus likely to sabotage any efforts toward recovery. Joan Jackson, in a
classic 1954 article,[47] argued that the suffering and seemingly pathological ac-

tions of family members can be understood as *reactions* to the progression of alcohol/drug problems—as desperate but understandable attempts to adjust to and cope with the family crisis. There followed a welcome reduction in blaming and pathologizing of spouses and family members. Indeed, subsequent research has found no consistent personality patterns among the relatives of alcoholics, although problems such as depression, anxiety, and marital difficulties are common and tend to improve when alcohol/drug problems are treated.

More recently, however, the pathologizing of family members has had a resurgence through two converging movements. Some family therapists have argued that alcoholism is the *result* of dysfunctional family systems or at least that families maintain alcoholism and sabotage recovery to maintain status quo and meet their needs. Writers have described a variety of pathological roles that members allegedly take in dysfunctional families—hero, clown, mascot, lost child, and so forth. A prediction from this viewpoint is that marriages and families should *deteriorate* when a family member in individual treatment recovers from alcohol/drug problems. This is actually the opposite of what is typically observed. Families generally communicate *better* when an alcoholic member is dry, and if you have to guess what will happen to other problems when alcohol/drug abuse is treated bet on improvement.[48] To be sure, *some* personal problems and *some* family problems do grow worse during recovery, signaling a need for specific attention to these areas. Marital stress is particularly likely to increase when only one of two alcohol/drug dependent partners is in recovery. Even in this minority of cases, however, the worsening of family relations is not necessarily evidence that the family "needs" a sick member. The practical need is for sound marital or family therapy (see chapter 18). There is, however, no evidence that a majority of families with an alcohol/drug dependent member are inherently pathological, and many studies have demonstrated effective individual treatment, though family involvement may well be of benefit when feasible.

A second resurgence of family pathologizing has come with the remarkably popular "co-dependency" movement. The core assertion of these writers is that the spouses, children, grandchildren, and other family members of anyone with chemical dependence have an "illness" themselves—the illness of co-dependency. Those who assert their normality are suspected of being "in denial." The list of symptoms of co-dependency is long indeed. Schaef, for example, described the following as symptoms of co-dependency: dishonesty, being out of touch with feelings, distorted feelings, holding onto feelings, control issues, confusion, overreliance on logical thinking, being ego-oriented, perfectionism, being other-oriented, low self-worth, fear, rigidity, judgmentalism, depression, inferiority, grandiosity, self-centeredness, a compromised value system, loss of spiritual base, lack of boundaries, concern with what others think, not trusting your own perceptions, caretaking, making yourself indispensible, physical illness, denial, projection, delusion, fear of abandonment, and gullibility, and she cautioned that "this is not an exhaustive list."[49]

Further, this "illness" has been claimed to afflict not only children of alcoholics, but everyone raised in a dysfunctional family environment. The rate of "dysfunctional" families in the population has been estimated as being as high as 96 percent.

A variety of criticisms have been leveled at the co-dependency or "recovery" movement. Like other diagnostic labels, "(adult) child of an alcoholic" can be stigmatizing and may encourage a "victim" or helpless identity.[50] Feminist critiques have decried the pathologizing of behaviors customarily valued and practiced by women (and by religions) in our society, for example, caretaking, self-sacrifice, and valuing relationships over personal gain. Women (and sacrificial values) may be implicitly devalued as doing one more thing wrong: loving "too much." There is a meaningless circularity to an illness that has dozens of common "symptoms" and afflicts 96 percent of the population. Though often denied, there is at least implicit blaming of alcoholics or dysfunctional families for causing one's own problem, reflected in extreme form in popular books such as *Toxic Parents*. Further, there is simply no scientific evidence for the existence of such unique personality abnormality even among alcoholics themselves, let alone among all their relatives or all members of "dysfunctional" families. The "diagnosis" of co-dependency may, however, lead to damaging misattributions and a failure to recognize and appropriately treat genuine problems such as depression, anxiety disorders, marital distress, and children's behavior problems. Such problems are well understood and treatable, but their attribution to "co-dependency" or "adult child syndrome" may well prolong suffering or contribute to the deterioration of a relationship precisely because the formulation is mistaken (see part III) and effective treatment is therefore overlooked.

We have provided an extended discussion here because the prose of co-dependency books is often moving and persuasive and has specifically found its way into organized religion. It seems to explain pain and problems, much as transactional analysis of the 1970s (which also became popular in religious circles) offered a plausible explanation of alcoholism and other difficulties as "games people play."[51] Neither has led to demonstrably effective treatment. In the absence of scientific evidence to support either the formulation model or a treatment approach, we are concerned for the potentially damaging influence of these views. Their intuitive appeal may lead people to lay (or feel) unwarranted and fruitless blame, to mistakenly attribute their suffering and problems to a nonexistent illness, and thereby to fail to understand and take appropriate action that would be genuinely healing.

In sum, there is no empirical evidence that family members of people with alcohol/drug problems suffer a unique illness or personality disturbance or that any such syndrome is caused by exposure to a dysfunctional family. There are many resilient survivors of exceptionally adverse circumstances,[52] and nothing useful is gained by "explaining" one's current difficulties in this manner. We regard co-dependence to be a fad, a reversion to a long-refuted idea that the families of alcoholics are inherently pathological. We advocate instead Jackson's wise perspective of family members as struggling to survive and cope as best they can. This view leads instead to well-supported approaches that strengthen coping skills, improve family ties and communications, and increase mutual support (see chapter 18). Co-dependence thinking is excess baggage likely to slow the journey or head it off in the wrong direction. Our position in no way minimizes the very real pain often found among family members. To the contrary, we believe that adherence to well-established psychological principles is most likely to lead to effective understanding and alleviation of this suffering.

ADDITIONAL READINGS

For the Counselor

The National Institute on Alcohol Abuse and Alcoholism published three therapist manuals as part of a major research program on the treatment of alcohol problems. Single copies are distributed free of charge through the National Clearinghouse for Alcohol and Drug Information, PO Box 2345, Rockville, Maryland 20852, USA. The three manuals are listed below.

KADDEN, RONALD, KATHLEEN CARROLL, DENNIS DONOVAN, NED COONEY, PETER MONTI, DAVID ABRAMS, MARK LITT, and REID HESTER *Cognitive-Behavioral Coping Skills Therapy Manual: A Clinical Research Guide for Therapists Treating Individuals with Alcohol Abuse and Dependence*. Rockville, MD: National Institute on Alcohol Abuse and Alcoholism (Project MATCH Monograph Series, vol. 3), 1992 (DHHS Publication No. 92-1895).

MILLER, WILLIAM R., ALLEN ZWEBEN, CARLO C. DICLEMENTE, and ROBERT G. RYCHTARIK *Motivational Enhancement Therapy Manual: A Clinical Research Guide for Therapists Treating Individuals with Alcohol Abuse and Dependence*. Rockville, MD: National Institute on Alcohol Abuse and Alcoholism (Project MATCH Monograph Series, vol. 2), 1992 (DHHS Publication No. 92-1894).

NOWINSKI, JOSEPH, STUART BAKER, and KATHLEEN CARROLL *Twelve Step Facilitation Therapy Manual: A Clinical Research Guide for Therapists Treating Individuals with Alcohol Abuse and Dependence*. Rockville, MD: National Institute on Alcohol Abuse and Alcoholism (Project MATCH Monograph Series, vol. 1), 1992 (DHHS Publication No. 92-1893).

Some other helpful resources for counselors are listed below.

AGRAS, W. STUART *Eating Disorders: Management of Obesity, Bulimia and Anorexia Nervosa*. New York: Pergamon Press, 1987.

GITLIN, MICHAEL J. *The Psychotherapist's Guide to Psychopharmacology*. New York: Free Press, 1990. This is a readable desk reference on drugs, including prescription psychiatric drugs, and how they work.

HESTER, REID K., and WILLIAM R. MILLER, eds. *Handbook of Alcoholism Treatment Approaches: Effective Alternatives*, (2nd ed) New York: Allyn & Bacon, 1995. A variety of authors describe different treatment approaches with scientific evidence of effectiveness for alcohol problems and give recommendations about what works for whom.

INSTITUTE OF MEDICINE *Broadening the Base of Treatment for Alcohol Problems*. Washington, DC: National Academy Press, 1990. This is an important public policy statement from the National Academy of Sciences, regarding the need for a broader approach in addressing alcohol problems in society.

INSTITUTE OF MEDICINE *Treating Drug Problems*. Washington, DC: National Academy Press, 1990. A parallel report on the treatment of other drug problems.

McAULIFFE, WILLIAM E., and JEFFREY ALBERT *Clean Start: An Outpatient Program for Initiating Cocaine Recovery*. New York, Guilford Press, 1992. A research-based comprehensive alternative to hospitalization, with specific session outlines, handouts, and so forth.

PRESBYTERIAN CHURCH (U.S.A.) *Alcohol Use & Abuse: The Social and Health Effects*. Louisville, KY: Office of Health Ministries (100 Witherspoon Street, 40202-1396), 1986. One denominations's attempts to forge contemporary health policy on alcohol, with specific recommendations for action.

RAY, OAKLEY S., and CHARLES KSIR *Drugs, Society and Human Behavior* (5th ed.). St. Louis: C. V. Mosby, 1990. This is a best-selling college textbook on drugs and drug abuse.

For the Client

Alcohol Problems

ALCOHOLICS ANONYMOUS *Alcoholics Anonymous: The Story of How Many Thousands of Men and Women Have Recovered from Alcoholism* (3d ed.). New York: A.A. World Services, 1976. The "big book" of A.A., written by its founders and originally published in 1935.

ELLIS, ALBERT, and EMMETT VELTEN *When AA Doesn't Work for You: Rational Steps to Quitting*. Fort Lee, NJ: Barricade Books, 1992.

KIRKPATRICK, JEAN *Turnabout: Help for a New Life*. New York: Doubleday, 1978. The original resource book on the self-help group, Women for Sobriety, written by its founder.

MILLER, WILLIAM R., and RICARDO F. MUÑOZ *How to Control Your Drinking*. Albuquerque: University of New Mexico Press, 1982. A research-tested self-help book for people who want to moderate their drinking.

Eating Disorders   There are thousands of diet and weight control books. The basics of a good plan are gradual weight loss through a healthy, low-fat diet, increased exercise, and a sensible maintenance program. A good pocket-sized food reference can be helpful, such as the American Heart Association's *Fat and Cholesterol Counter* (New York: Random House, 1991). As an example of a sound, comprehensive program, we commend the paperback books of Dr. Peter M. Miller (no relation!), including *The Hilton Head Metabolism Diet* (New York: Warner Books, 1983) and *The Hilton Head Over-35 Diet* (New York: Warner Books, 1989).

A good resource on bulimia is Lindsey Hall and Leigh Cohn's *Bulimia: A Guide to Recovery* (Carlsbad, CA: Gürze Books, 1992).

"Co-dependency"   For reasons discussed above, we do not recommend any of the currently popular self-help books on "co-dependency." Various books have begun to appear for those seeking to escape from the victim identity of the "recovery movement." An example is Stan J. Katz and Aimee E. Liu, *The Codependency Conspiracy: How to Break the Recovery Habit and Take Charge of Your Life* (New York: Warner Books, 1991).

NOTES

¹Gerald G. May, *Addiction and Grace: Love and Spirituality in the Healing of Addictions* (New York: Harper, 1991).

²Institute of Medicine, *Broadening the Base of Treatment for Alcohol Problems* (Washington, DC: National Academy Press, 1990).

³Institute of Medicine, *Treating Drug Problems* (Washington, DC: National Academy Press, 1990).

⁴Current information on fetal alcohol syndrome can be found in the most recent report to Congress on *Alcohol and Health* by the National Institute on Alcohol Abuse and Alcoholism, available in the public documents section of many libraries. The compelling story of the adoptive father of a fetal alcohol child is told by Michael Dorris in *The Broken Cord* (New York: Harper & Row, 1989).

⁵See the appendix to *Alcohol Use & Abuse: The Social and Health Effects: Reports and Recommendations by the Presbyterian Church (U.S.A.)* (Office of Health Ministries, 100 Witherspoon Street, Louisville, KY 40202-1396).

⁶*Webster's Seventh New Collegiate Dictionary* (Springfield, MA: Merriam, 1963).

⁷Outpatient detoxification has long been established to be a safe and cost-effective approach. See C. L. Whitfield, "Non-drug Treatment of Alcohol Withdrawal," *Current Psychiatric Therapies* 19 (1980): 101–19.

⁸Stanley Schachter, "Nicotine Regulation in Heavy and Light Smokers," *Journal of Experimental Psychology: General* 106 (1977): 5–12; Stanley Schachter, "Pharmacological and Psychological Determinants of Smoking," *Annals of Internal Medicine* 88 (1978): 104–14.

⁹James R. Milam and Katherine Ketcham, *Under the Influence: A Guide to the Myths and Realities of Alcoholism* (New York: Bantam Books, 1981). A critique of this view of alcoholism can be found in William R. Miller, "Alcoholism: Toward a Better Disease Model," *Psychology of Addictive Behaviors* 7 (1993): 129–36.

¹⁰William R. Miller and Janice M. Brown, "Self-regulation as a Conceptual Basis for the Prevention and Treatment of Addictive Behaviours," in Nick Heather, William R. Miller, and Janet Greeley, eds., *Self-control and the Addictive Behaviours* (Sydney: Maxwell Macmillan Publishing Australia, 1991), 3–79.

¹¹Anderson Spickard and Barbara R. Thompson, *Dying for a Drink: What You Should Know about Alcoholism* (Waco, TX: Word, 1985).

¹²*Alcohol Use & Abuse: The Social and Health Effects: Reports and Recommendations by the Presbyterian Church (U.S.A.)* (Office of Health Ministries, 100 Witherspoon Street, Louisville, KY 40202-1396).

¹³Oakley S. Ray and Charles Ksir, *Drugs, Society and Human Behavior*, 5th ed. (St. Louis: C. V. Mosby, 1990).

¹⁴William R. Miller and Reid K. Hester, "Treating Alcohol Problems: Toward an Informed Eclecticism," in Reid K. Hester and William R. Miller, eds., *Handbook of Alcoholism Treatment Approaches: Effective Alternatives* (New York: Allyn & Bacon, 1989), 3–13.

[15]Theresa B. Moyers and William R. Miller, "Therapists' Conceptualizations of Alcoholism: Measurement and Implications for Treatment Decisions," *Psychology of Addictive Behaviors* 7 (1993): 238–45.

[16]William R. Miller and Ernest Kurtz, "Models of Alcoholism Used in Treatment: Contrasting A.A. and Other Perspectives with Which It Is Often Confused," *Journal of Studies on Alcohol* 55 (1994): 159–66.

[17]Institute of Medicine, National Academy of Sciences, *Broadening the Base of Treatment for Alcohol Problems* (Washington, DC: National Academy Press, 1990).

[18]Paul Rozin and Caryn Stoess, "Is There a General Tendency to Become Addicted?" *Addictive Behaviors* 18 (1993): 81–7; William R. Miller, "Alcoholism Scales and Objective Assessment Methods: A Review," *Psychological Bulletin* 83 (1976): 649–74.

[19]William R. Miller and Stephen Rollnick, *Motivational Interviewing: Preparing People to Change Addictive Behavior* (New York: Guilford Press, 1991).

[20]Thomas H. Bien, William R. Miller, and J. Scott Tonigan, "Brief Interventions for Alcohol Problems: A Review," *Addiction* 88 (1993): 315–36.

[21]William R. Miller, R. Gayle Benefield, and J. Scott Tonigan, "Enhancing Motivation for Change in Problem Drinking: A Controlled Comparison of Two Therapist Styles," *Journal of Consulting and Clinical Psychology* 61 (1993): 455–61.

[22]For example, see V. Manohar, "Training Volunteers as Alcoholism Treatment Counselors," *Quarterly Journal of Studies on Alcohol* 34 (1973): 869–77.

[23]*Alcoholics Anonymous: The Story of How Many Thousands of Men and Women Have Recovered from Alcoholism*, 3d ed. (New York: A.A. World Services, 1976).

[24]Rudolf Moos, John Finney, and Ruth Cronkite, *Alcoholism Treatment: Context, Process, and Outcome* (New York: Oxford University Press, 1990).

[25]For example, religious involvement is associated with decreased risk of marijuana use: Denise B. Kandel and Mark Davies, "Progression to Regular Marijuana Involvement: Phenomenology and Risk Factors for Near-Daily Use," in Meyer Glantz and Roy Pickens, *Vulnerability to Drug Abuse* (Washington, DC: American Psychological Association, 1992), 211–53. See also Bernard Spilka, Ralph W. Hood Jr., and Richard L. Gorsuch, "Religion and Morality," in *The Psychology of Religion: An Empirical Approach* (Englewood Cliffs, NJ: Prentice-Hall), 1985 257–86.

[26]William R. Miller and Reid K. Hester, "Inpatient Alcoholism Treatment: Who Benefits?" *American Psychologist* 41 (1986): 794–805.

[27]Charles A. Kiesler, "Mental Hospitals and Alternative Care: Noninstitutionalization as Potential Public Policy for Mental Patients," *American Psychologist* 37 (1982): 349–60; U.S. Congress, Office of Technology Assessment, *The Effectiveness and Costs of Alcoholism Treatment* (Washington, DC: U.S. Government Printing Office, 1983).

[28]M. Hayashida, Arthur I. Alterman, A. Thomas McLellan, Charles P. O'Brien, J. J. Purtill, Joseph R. Volpicelli, A. II. Raphaelson, and C. P. Hall, "Comparative Effectiveness and Costs of Inpatient and Outpatient Detoxification of Patients with Mild-to-Moderate Alcohol Withdrawal Syndrome," *New England Journal of Medicine* 320 (1989): 358–65.

[29]For a thorough review of the scientific literature on this subject, consult Nick Heather and Ian Robertson, *Controlled Drinking* (New York: Methuen, 1983).

[30]William R. Miller, "Motivation and Treatment Goals," *Drugs and Society* 1 (1987): 133–51.

[31]William R. Miller, "Controlled Drinking: A History and Critical Review," *Journal of Studies on Alcohol* 44 (1983): 68–83.

[32]William R. Miller and Andrew Page, "Warm Turkey: Other Routes to Abstinence," *Journal of Substance Abuse Treatment* 8 (1991): 227–32.

[33]William R. Miller, A. Lane Leckman, Harold D. Delaney, and Martha Tinkcom, "Long-term Follow-up of Behvioral Self-control Training," *Journal of Studies on Alcohol* 53 (1992): 249–61.

[34]Institute of Medicine, *Broadening the Base of Treatment*.

[35]William R. Miller, "Towards a Biblical View of Drug Use" *Journal of Ministry in Addiction and Recovery*, in press.

[36]Some popular writers who come to mind here are John Bradshaw, Melodie Beattie, Tim Cermak, Terrance Gorski, Anne Wilson Schaef, and Sharon Wegscheider-Cruse.

[37]Reid K. Hester and William R. Miller, eds., *Handbook of Alcoholism Treatment Approaches: Effective Alternatives* (New York: Allyn & Bacon, 1995).

[38]John Marks, "The Practice of Controlled Availability of Illicit Drugs," in Nick Heather, William R. Miller, and Janet Greeley, eds., *Self-control and the Addictive Behaviours* (Sydney: Maxwell Macmillan Publishing Australia, 1991), 304–16.

[39]Harold Holder, Richard Longabaugh, William R. Miller, and Anthony V. Rubonis, "The Cost Effectiveness of Treatment for Alcoholism: A First Approximation," *Journal of Studies on Alcohol* 52 (1991): 517–40.

[40]Nathan H. Azrin, Robert W. Sisson, Robert Meyers, and Mark Godley, "Alcoholism Treatment by Disulfiram and Community Reinforcement Therapy," *Journal of Behavior Therapy and Experimental Psychiatry* 13 (1982): 105–12; Stephen T. Higgins and Alan J. Budney, "Treatment of Cocaine Dependence via the Principles of Behavior Analysis and Behavioral Pharmacology," in Lisa S. Onken, J. D. Blaine, and J. J. Boren, eds., *Behavioral Treatments for Drug Abuse and Dependence* (Rockville, MD: National Institute on Drug Abuse, 1993): 97–121.

[41]Harold Rosenberg, "Prediction of Controlled Drinking by Alcoholics and Problem Drinkers," *Psychological Bulletin* 113 (1993): 129–39. A thorough review can also be found in Nick Heather and Ian Robertson, *Controlled Drinking* (New York: Methuen, 1981).

[42]G. Alan Marlatt and Judith R. Gordon, eds., *Relapse Prevention* (New York: Guilford Press, 1985).

[43]Chad D. Emrick, J. Scott Tonigan, Henry Montgomery, and Laura Little, "Affiliation Processes in and Treatment Outcomes of Alcoholics Anonymous: A Meta-analysis of the Literature," in Barbara S. McCrady and William R. Miller, eds., *Research on Alcoholics Anonymous: Opportunities and Alternatives* (New Brunswick, NJ: Rutgers Center of Alcohol Studies, 1993): 41–76.

[44]"Comments on A.A.'s Triennial Surveys" (New York: Alcoholics Anonymous, 1990).

[45]Barbara S. McCrady and William R. Miller, eds., *Research on Alcoholics Anonymous: Opportunities and Alternatives* (New Brunswick, NJ: Rutgers Center of Alcohol Studies, 1993).

[46]William R. Miller and Reid K. Hester, "The Effectiveness of Alcoholism Treatment: What Research Reveals," in William R. Miller and Nick Heather, eds., *Treating Addictive Behaviors: Processes of Change* (New York: Plenum Press, 1986).

[47]Joan K. Jackson, "The adjustment of the Family to the Crisis of Alcoholism," *Quarterly Journal of Studies on Alcohol* 15 (1954): 562–86.

[48]William R. Miller, Kim E. Hedrick, and Cheryl A. Taylor, "Addictive Behaviors and Life Problems before and after Behavioral Treatment of Problem Drinkers," *Addictive Behaviors* 8 (1983): 403–12.

[49]Anne Wilson Schaef, *Co-dependence: Misunderstood-Mistreated* (Minneapolis: Winston Press, 1986).

[50]J. P. Burk and Kenneth J. Sher, "Labeling the Child of an Alcoholic: Negative Stereotyping by Mental Health Professionals and Peers," *Journal of Studies on Alcohol* 51 (1990): 156–63; Ernest Kurtz, "Commentary," *Annual Review of Addiction Research and Treatment* 1 (1992): 397–400.

[51]Eric Berne, *Games People Play* (New York: Grove Press, 1964); Claude Steiner, *Games Alcoholics Play* (New York: Ballantine Books, 1971).

[52]Norman Garmezy and Michael Rutter, *Stress, Coping and Development in Children.* (New York: McGraw-Hill, 1983).

17

MAJOR MENTAL DISORDERS

I am beginning to realize that "sanity" is no longer a value or an end in itself. The "sanity" of modern man is about as useful to him as the huge bulk and muscles of the dinosaur. If he were a little less sane, a little more doubtful, a little more aware of his absurdities and contradictions, perhaps there might be a possibility of his survival.

—Thomas Merton, *Raids on the Unspeakable*

He sat down in the chair in a misleadingly relaxed slump and said that his name was Mr. Jensen. He wore dark sunglasses behind which his eyes could barely be seen darting about the room, searching. "Where is it?" he asked.

"Where is what?"

"The bug. It's got to be here." The "bug" turned out to mean electronic surveillance equipment. Over the next hour a fascinating tale unfolded of how Mr. Jensen (who the records showed had been discharged from the Navy for medical reasons) had not really been discharged but was now doing undercover work for a top secret research department of the Air Force. Everywhere he went he was followed, and even here—on the locked ward of a mental hospital—he was certain that there were enemy agents. He spoke in a low, almost incomprehensible voice to deter surveillance, which he decided (after finding no microphone in the room) was being conducted from a maintenance truck parked outside at the curb.

"I can't even talk in my car anymore. I took it in to have the radio repaired and they did something to it, so now they can pick up anything I say and they always know where I am." This burly ex-corpsman had been brought to the hospital after threatening several strangers who, he was convinced, had been following him. "Now I see," he said. "They really weren't agents themselves. They were just playing along. It was all a set-up to get me in here." A dawn of realization came over his face, and he shut himself up into an angry and stubborn silence.

WHAT ARE MENTAL DISORDERS?

Madness. Insanity. A nervous breakdown. What are these things, which so frighten people? Can they happen to just anyone at any time? What is it that happens, and is there a way back to sanity?

None of those terms has a precise professional meaning. *Madness* is an old term used to refer to bizarre behavior that others could not understand, that seemed purposeless, senseless, unreasonable. *Insanity* is a legal term, also quite old, and refers to a person's ability to judge right from wrong and to conform his or her behavior to the law voluntarily. It arose because it was thought that certain people commit crimes for reasons beyond their own control and thus should not be treated in the same fashion as those who carry out crimes voluntarily. Finally, *nervous breakdown* is a popular term that refers to almost any form of mental disturbance serious enough to require hospitalization.

PSYCHOSIS

The major problems to which these terms most often refer are those categorized as psychotic. *Psychoses* are conditions that involve a major disruption of the person's sense of reality. The inner reality of psychotic people is usually quite different from that of most people, and so they appear strange, bizarre, or eccentric. Their behavior can be quite alarming to an average person if only because it is so odd. "If she talks so strangely," the average person thinks, "then there's no telling what *else* she might do."

In fact, people with psychoses are not often dangerous. Most are no more likely to harm others than is the average person in the street. Certainly, they are less likely to be harmful than other individuals—such as psychopaths, with whom they are often confused in the public mind. When an "ex-mental patient" commits a major violent crime, it is headline news, but the newspapers are also daily filled with the heinous acts of other people who have never experienced psychosis or been in a mental hospital. The "psychotic killer" is found most often on the pages of fiction or on the silver screen of the movie theater and rarely in real life.

The most common form of psychosis is schizophrenia, a syndrome that has been recognized as a mental disorder since the nineteenth century. The sparse accounts of demon possessions recounted in the Bible suggest that some of these individuals may well have been suffering from schizophrenia or another psychotic pattern. Controversies continue as to how many different psychotic disorders there are, what causes them, and how to treat them, but the reality of the syndrome of schizophrenia is recognized worldwide. It has been estimated that schizophrenia occurs in about 1 percent of the population over the course of a lifetime—a figure that is remarkably consistent across nations and cultures—and it seems to occur about equally among men and women.

We will not belabor the various subtypes here. All require special professional attention. We will focus instead on four issues: (a) How can a pastoral counselor recognize psychoses as they are emerging? (b) What is known about the causes of psychoses, and how is this information useful to you as a pastor? (c) What treatment methods are currently used to treat psychoses? (d) What can you do to help?

Recognizing Psychosis

When psychosis is full-blown as in the case of Mr. Jensen, it is not difficult to recognize that something major is wrong. There are five important categories of symptoms of which to be aware. Not all of these have to be present, and in fact there is no single symptom that is necessary. As in depression, it is the total pattern that confirms the diagnosis. The characteristic symptoms are listed for convenient reference in Table 17-1, and each category will be discussed in a bit more depth.

The first unusual pattern that may be seen in psychosis is *delusion*. A delusion is an unusual belief, an incorrect interpretation of reality that is typically held in spite of contradictory evidence presented by others. The content in some cases is quite bizarre, but in others it is almost believable. The young corpsman, Mr. Jensen, presented his case with such credibility and sincerity that, if one were inclined to believe in elaborate espionage, one could almost accept his story. Imagined plots and schemes are not unusual themes for delusions. Another individual developed an elaborate delusion that the telephone company was planning to destroy her and that every telephone was able to read her thoughts. People with schizophrenia may believe that others are controlling their movements, stealing their thoughts, putting thoughts into their minds, or constantly making reference to them. It is not

TABLE 17-1   Major Signs of Acute Psychosis

DELUSIONS AND UNUSUAL THOUGHT CONTENT
  Odd beliefs that are unchanged by reality input from others
ABNORMAL FORM OF THOUGHT
  Loose associations, neologisms, disorganized or incomprehensible sequence of speech
HALLUCINATIONS
  Voices, sensations, or visions not perceived by others
UNUSUAL EMOTIONAL PATTERNS
  Flat emotions or inappropriate emotions, pervasive lack of pleasure
BIZARRE BEHAVIOR
  Strange actions, postures, repetitive movements, freezing

uncommon for delusions to have strong religious content. Milton Rokeach once encountered three people, all of whom claimed to be Jesus Christ, and he put them in group therapy together, the story of which is told in *The Three Christs of Ypsilanti*.[1] People with pure paranoia (as was the case with the corpsman) often show no other strangeness than this delusion, which may not be revealed to strangers.

Another kind of symptom is disturbance in the *form* of thinking rather than in its content (called for this reason *formal thought disorder*). The most frequent observation here is of loose associations or disorganized speech. The person jumps from one subject to another, apparently following some train of thought that is lost to the listener. There is no recognition that this sequence might not be clear to others, and no attempt is made to provide the usual verbal transitions that ordinary folk, in politeness, insert when they are about to take a leap. The person may also make up new words (*neologisms*) and speak as though others will of course understand what they mean. Essentially, there is a breakdown of reality testing so that the person has difficulty in distinguishing what is internal and private thought from what is available to people in the external world. As the conversation progresses, a feeling of strangeness and incomprehension often emerges in the listener.

Perceptions can also be disturbed in psychosis. The person may have vivid hallucinations, which are sensory experiences unique to the individual. There may be voices no one else can hear, or the feeling of unseen insects crawling on the skin. More rarely, the person will see people or objects where there is nothing. (Visual hallucinations are more common in drug-related states.) But far and away the most common form of schizophrenic hallucination is voices—sometimes a familiar voice and sometimes a strange one. Sometimes the voices talk to each other, sometimes to the person, and sometimes they just talk. They may give orders, harsh criticisms, forecasts of the future, or a running commentary on what is happening (much like normal thoughts, except aloud).

Emotions are also often changed. Most commonly, the person shows little emotional variety—a pattern that is called *flat affect*. There may be very little facial emotional expression. Emotions may be socially inappropriate, as in giggling at a funeral service. The term *anhedonia* describes a common pattern of pervasive lack of pleasure, again a kind of flatness.

Finally, there may be *bizarre behavior*. The person may move in an odd way, rock back and forth repetitively, adopt strange postures, or freeze in a certain position for hours or days at a time. The behavior may be described by others as odd or eccentric.

All of these are major symptoms of schizophrenia and more generally of psychoses. Sometimes these symptoms appear all at once, without warning, but more often there is a period of gradual onset called the *prodromal* phase. A pastor who is able to recognize prodromal changes may be in a position to intervene in a more timely and helpful fashion.

Prodromal changes are sometimes subtle. People may notice a kind of personality change in the individual. Personal hygiene may deteriorate, and the person may begin to withdraw from social contact and normal activities. Emotions start to go flat (rather than depressed or distressed), and little peculiar behaviors or thinking patterns may start to appear in muted form. Speech begins to ramble, to become vague or odd. Work, school, or other social functioning falls off. Most importantly, these represent *changes from the person's previous pattern*. There is a noticeable shift in behavior. Of course, changes similar to these prodromal signs can occur for many different reasons. Prodromal changes are most significant in people who have had psychotic episodes in the past, in that they may foreshadow the occurrence of a new episode.

One particular type of psychosis—brief reactive psychosis—is different. It begins rather suddenly, often in response to some kind of precipitating shock. The symptoms are quite noticeable and usually end as rapidly as they began. In such cases, which probably represent extreme stress reactions, the likelihood is that there will never be another episode. Usually, such episodes last only a week or two and then clear completely. We have seen several such occurrences in our own congregations.

In true schizophrenia, however, the problem is longer lasting, and symptoms rise and dissipate like waves. Episodes are likely to be repeated over a span of years. Schizophrenia—unlike the brief reactive kind of psychosis just described—tends to begin more slowly and gradually. Often the person was not terribly well adjusted before the first episode, and usually this process begins in adolescence or early adulthood. (In the reactive kind of psychosis, in contrast, people often were doing very well before the abrupt beginning of symptoms, and such episodes can occur at any time during life.) In between episodes, the person with schizophrenia may function reasonably well, though not quite at a fully normal and independent level. Some of the prodromal symptoms may linger between episodes.

What Causes Psychosis?

Brief reactive psychosis seems to be a special kind of stress reaction. Though unusual and intense, it does pass fairly quickly and is unlikely to recur. Schizophrenia, however, is a different matter. Although some rare individuals do seem to recover completely after a course of months or years of schizophrenia, this is unlikely. The long-term picture is more often one of gradual deterioration over time, with some individuals managing much better than others.

The causes of schizophrenia are not well understood. There does seem to be a genetic component. Both of a pair of identical twins are likely to develop schizophrenia if one does, although perhaps in 40 percent of cases the second twin does not develop problems, demonstrating that more than heredity is involved. Relationships have been found between schizophrenic symptoms and certain kinds of brain damage, although it is unclear which is cause and which effect. Before the stress-induced brief form of psychosis was differentiated from true schizophrenia, all psychosis was explained as an extreme reaction to anxiety, a view that is no longer warranted. Some widely publicized theorists have attributed schizophrenia to inadequate parenting or to unhealthy family communication patterns, but solid evidence is lacking to support such views.[2] This latter fact is important to the pastor, who may be able to help families in dealing with unwarranted personal guilt felt in relationship to the development of schizophrenia in one member. Clearly abnormal brain chemistry is involved, but the truth is that it simply is not known what causes schizophrenia. There is no sound evidence that it can be *caused* by improper parenting or family style. A similar theory of autism contributed a sad chapter in the history of psychology. A well-known and respected expert postulated that autism (an extremely disabling childhood disorder appearing before the age of three) is caused by "refrigerator mothers" who show insufficient love and warmth toward their babies.[3] The load of guilt subsequently placed on mothers of such children was crushing. In fact, the mothers of autistic children indeed do not hold their babies as often or as closely as other infants are held, but it turns out that this is caused by the fact that autistic children refuse to *be* held and cry and struggle when the mother attempts to do so. Improper parenting seems to have little or nothing to do with causing autism, and the guilt induced in parents was unnecessary and unwarranted. The same mistake should not be made of implying parental or family responsibility for schizophrenia in the absence of substantiating research. It is not surprising, of course, that one finds distress and disturbed communications within a family containing an individual who suffers from schizophrenia—but is this the cause or the result of the syndrome?

Schizophrenia—a psychosis that is severe and persists beyond six months—is probably a biologically based disorder and can properly be thought of as an illness. There are some hereditary links and clear patterns of abnormal brain chemistry. There are medications that often bring about great improvement. Individuals and families can be helped to accept this condition as an illness that needs treatment but for which no one needs to feel guilty or ashamed. It *is* treatable.

Treatment

For the individual with a reactive psychosis, the brief stress-induced type, little treatment is needed beyond supervisory care during the period of intensive symptoms. Hospitalization is often unnecessary, and medications may be used to relieve symptoms. With time, usually a week or two, the crisis is past and the person recovers nicely.

For people with long-term psychotic symptoms, treatment by a competent biological psychiatrist is needed. This is likely to include an antipsychotic medication, far and away the most common means of treatment. There are many different types of medications, and selection of the proper therapeutic drug requires skill and experience. These drugs *do* help in reducing psychotic symptoms and allowing the person to return to independent living. They do not *cure* schizophrenia, but they do help to control the symptoms. Hallucinations, delusions, confused thought process, and bizarre behavior all tend to show improvement with proper medication. Usually, the individual is advised to continue taking this medication after being discharged from formal treatment. The most frequent precipitator of a relapse is the individual's stopping of the medication.

A brief period of hospitalization may be necessary for people in the midst of an intense psychotic episode. Because such people are often confused and in no position to make rational decisions, a procedure of legal commitment may be necessary to have the person hospitalized. The procedures for this vary from state to state, but usually the signature of one or more physicians is required. The physicians usually must certify that the individual is dangerous to self or others or is gravely disabled and unable to function safely on his or her own. The primary purpose of the hospitalization is protection of the person. During hospitalization—typically brief—medication is usually started and the person is stabilized. When symptoms abate and the person seems ready to function independently again (albeit with some assistance in the community), he or she is discharged. The normal period of hospitalization is now a few days or weeks (whereas half a century ago a person admitted to a hospital with a diagnosis of schizophrenia could expect to spend years there, if not the rest of life).

Many communities have now developed *day treatment* centers that provide an intermediate alternative between total inpatient care and minimal outpatient care. In such settings the individual normally comes to the center or hospital in the morning, participates in treatment during the day, and then returns home at night. Treatment often includes training in specific coping and problem-solving skills, group or individual counseling, and monitoring of medications. The goal of treatment is usually to reduce the medication to minimum necessary dosage, to help the person improve social skills and problem-solving abilities, and ultimately to become able to live independently in the community. Not all symptoms disappear. The person may continue to have strange thoughts, for example, but can learn to distinguish these from external reality and to avoid talking about them with other people (which is typically what gets the individual into trouble). The emotional flatness is likely to endure.

In the *long-term* treatment of schizophrenia, there is no advantage in hospitalization. Research indicates that community-based treatment is just as effective as inpatient hospitalization, but the former offers the advantages of being less expensive and of keeping the person in touch with the community and local support networks.[4]

Often it is beneficial to include the family in treatment.[5] Family members will have problems and feelings of their own to deal with, and the family can also be taught skills for living together and caring for the member suffering from schizophrenia. Sometimes family patterns can exacerbate symptoms of schizophrenia, and these can be altered in family therapy. The family can and should be assured, however, that they did not *cause* the schizophrenia, though there are usually important things that they can do to help.

People with schizophrenia often benefit from training in specific coping skills. Community-based programs often include helpful training programs in skills for independent living, relaxation and stress management, and social skills. A group counseling format may be especially beneficial in teaching communication skills such as assertiveness (see chapter 15).

One controversial alternative approach is that advocated by R. D. Laing and John Weir Perry, among others.[6] In this perspective, psychosis is not a biological illness at all but is a normal adjustment process. Advocates of this view reject the use of medication, arguing that this stops the healing process and prevents the person from working through the necessary steps. Laing's Kingsley Hall in Britain and other hospitals in Europe and North America have applied this unconventional approach in treating individuals suffering from psychosis. Claims have been made that this method can produce a permanent cure and that the individual actually recovers and is less likely to relapse than is the case with conventional treatment. These claims are contested by others, who have argued that the "permanent cures" were in fact suffering only from brief reactive psychosis and not from true schizophrenia. Research supporting Laing's claims has been sparse, and it is difficult to judge the merits of this approach.

Finally, regular outpatient visits with a mental health professional can help the individual to avoid rehospitalization and to continue healthy and independent functioning in the community. A pastor can help to identify and provide such support, drawing when necessary on consultation from psychiatric or psychological colleagues. It is wise to maintain a professional relationship with one or more psychiatrists with hospital privileges to facilitate hospitalization if the need should arise among those you counsel. Lacking this, however, an individual can be taken directly to the nearest mental health center or hospital emergency room.

What You Can Do as a Pastor

Even though psychiatric expertise is needed to deal with some aspects of psychosis, a pastor can be of great value as a continuing source of contact and support. This is also true of the larger faith community, which may be able to afford a degree of acceptance and warmth not found elsewhere. Many congregations have welcomed into their midst one or more people struggling with long-term psychosis or other major mental disorders. The support of such a community, or even of a critical small core of people within the community, can be the difference between successful functioning and rehospitalization. During the Middle Ages there grew up in Europe special cities where people with serious mental disorders were taken. Rather than being "hospitals," these were open communities where such individuals were taken in and welcomed. The citizens were tolerant of strange behavior and were not frightened by it. They provided friendly and regular contact with reality. With the rise of hospitals, such communities began to disappear, but the value of this kind of social support is plain. In one study, discharged mental patients chosen at random to receive once-a-week contact with an untrained college student (analogous to the "Big Brother/Sister" approach) were less likely to be rehospitalized than were other patients receiving no such contact.[7] The influence of an entire supportive community can be still greater.

One thing that you can do, then, is to help such individuals become integrated into a supportive faith community. At least a key core of people should be made aware of the individual's special needs and helped to overcome any stereotyped perceptions, fears and hesitations. A few people within a congregation who initiate regular contact, carry on conversations, and interact warmly with these individuals can make an immense difference in the person's quality of life. They can serve as models for others, kindling a larger network of support. A few basics will be helpful to remember.

1. People suffering from psychoses are not especially dangerous. They are more likely to be fearful and confused than aggressive.

2. They often have a somewhat unusual sense of reality and are less inclined to operate by normal social standards as to what is polite and proper. Often such a person says things that are uncannily perceptive but that a "polite" person might choose to overlook or suppress.

3. It is extremely unlikely that one could "say the wrong thing" and precipitate a new psychotic break. These are not especially fragile folks, just somewhat special in how they think and act.

4. It is *not* helpful to "humor" or "go along with" delusional or confused thinking. (The same is true in talking with elderly people who are confused.) It is much more helpful to provide supportive, corrective feedback. A good form for such feedback is a reflective listening statement indicating that you understand how the person sees this situation, followed by a statement of how *you* see it. Try, too, to find the kernel of truth in what the person is saying, and look for the feeling being expressed, rather than dismissing it all as untrue. Suppose, for example, that a man you are visiting insists that this morning he saw his wife, who has been dead for ten years. One response might be: "It's true that you used to see your wife here, but that was a long time ago. She's been gone for ten years now, but I know you still think of her, and still miss her." This gentle, orienting approach helps the person to separate internal from external reality.

5. Social interaction in everyday settings can be extremely helpful and valuable. There is a strong tendency for people with psychosis to become more and more isolated as they are rejected and ostracized by others who do not understand them. This in turn leads to increasingly idiosyncratic and strange patterns of thought and behavior, which further isolate the person.

6. Helpers do not have to be skilled psychotherapists. Ordinary conversing and sharing of recreation and meals can be really beneficial. Sometimes people who have had a long course of illness need help in learning even basic social survival skills—how to shop for food, how to take a bus, how to choose clothing, how to budget money, or how to find a job. (This and many of the other points listed here apply equally to well to retarded citizens, who also need the warmth and support of a community.)

An example of a supportive "orienting" interaction may help here. The woman, Sarah, is about fifty, has had several hospitalizations for paranoid schizophrenia, and lives alone. She comes to the pastor's office complaining that people have been breaking into her house.

SARAH:	They did it again last night. I came home and they had been in there.
PASTOR:	How could you tell? (The pastor here is not seeking to refute the belief but is asking what information the person is basing this perception on. Delusions often have to do with misinterpretation of actual facts.)
SARAH:	The dishes were rearranged on my counter.
PASTOR:	They weren't how you had left them. (reflection)
SARAH:	No. They were moved over to one side and part of the counter was clear, like it had been wiped off.
PASTOR:	What else?
SARAH:	I think my television had been turned on.
PASTOR:	But it wasn't on when you came home.
SARAH:	No, but it felt warm.
PASTOR:	Was anything missing?
SARAH:	No, I don't think so.
PASTOR:	So it seems like somebody broke into your house, moved some dishes around on your counter, and maybe watched your television for awhile.
SARAH:	Yeah. They keep doing that. I don't like it.
PASTOR:	It must be upsetting to you to think that people just come and go in your house as they please.
SARAH:	It is! They have no business in there.
PASTOR:	Have you ever found your door or a window open or broken?
SARAH:	No.
PASTOR:	I wonder how people would be able to get in. I know you had the locks changed last month.

SARAH: And still they get in. Maybe it's the locksmith!

PASTOR: Sarah, let's look at this last time a little more carefully. I know that you think people have broken in, but I'm really not sure myself. It just doesn't make sense to me that somebody would come in there and move your dishes around but not take anything. That's how it has been before, too—nothing has been missing.

SARAH: Once some money was gone from my dresser.

PASTOR: A couple of quarters, I think. But if somebody wanted to steal from you, wouldn't they have taken other things?

SARAH: Maybe they just watch television.

PASTOR: That really doesn't make sense to me either, though, that somebody would go into your house and then just sit there and watch TV. It's not impossible, but it doesn't seem very likely to me. I wonder how else you could explain this.

SARAH: Explain what?

PASTOR: Well, your TV felt warm. But televisions usually do. Is yours the kind that comes on right away when you turn it on, or do you have to wait for it to warm up?

SARAH: Right away. I like that.

PASTOR: Well, that kind has to stay a little warm all of the time. That's why you don't have to wait for it to warm up. That's natural, and it doesn't mean that it has been turned on recently. And I just don't see how somebody could get into your house. Locksmiths are really honest people—they have to be or they lose their businesses—and I don't think it's very likely that your locksmith is breaking in and watching your TV. Do you?

SARAH: I guess not. But I still think people are coming in.

PASTOR: It just feels that way to you. (reflection) I remember you said you come in and just have that feeling that somebody has been there. And then you start looking for evidence.

SARAH: I can tell.

PASTOR: You know, Sarah, I get feelings like that sometimes too. Like when I'm walking into the house alone or walking down a street I get this creepy feeling that somebody is behind me or hiding somewhere. I look around, and nobody is there. Sometimes it's so strong I'm even silly enough to go looking in all of the closets or under the bed. Have you ever done that?

SARAH: Sure. Yesterday.

PASTOR: Well, I do it, too. And you know, there has never been anybody there. Those creepy feelings are just natural things that people get, especially when they are alone. It doesn't mean that there really is anybody there.

SARAH: But the dishes!

PASTOR: Well, I don't know what really happened there. But maybe what happens is that you get this creepy feeling, then you start looking for anything that has been changed. And it's always possible to find something that doesn't seem quite like when you left it. I think probably you moved the dishes away yourself while you were thinking about something else, and just didn't take notice of it. Maybe it was to fix a sandwich or make a cup of tea on the counter. It doesn't matter. I just don't think it's very likely that somebody broke in and cleaned your counter for you. But I *do* understand the kind of feeling that you mean. That's real enough.

This kind of exchange takes some patience. It is not enough to dismiss the person's beliefs as unfounded. It requires some time—reflective listening, helping the person to reason it through and see alternative explanations. Often there are important underlying feelings, expressed almost in symbolic language, that can be talked about. If the person is in the middle of a major psychotic episode, this kind of reasoning probably won't help very much. At other times, though, it can be quite helpful. This sort of patient ongoing reality feedback can help to prevent a piling up misperceptions and confusion that can lead to a new episode or rehospitalization.

You can also keep a watchful eye for important changes. The prodomal signs outlined earlier are vital warnings of a worsening and impending episode. If the person begins to withdraw, show odd behavior or poor hygiene, flatten off emotionally, this is the time to intervene. One question to ask is whether he or she is still taking medication (assuming that a maintenance medication was prescribed—something you should know). If not, resumption of proper dosage may head off more significant problems. Helping the person to resume contact with the proper specialist is also a valuable step at this point. Remember, too, that the confusion and poor judgment accompanying psychosis increase the risk of suicide. Along with depression and alcoholism, psychosis carries an elevated risk for suicidal acts. This is another reason for intervening early at points when symptoms seem to worsen.

PERSONALITY DISORDERS

Another class of major problems is that of *personality disorders*. These are enduring patterns of maladaptive behavior. Unlike many other disorders, they are not reactions to stress, and are not episodic. They do not wax and wane in episodes, like depression or schizophrenia. The two defining characteristics of personality disorders are (a) the consistent pattern of behavior that impairs social functioning and/or causes distress and (b) the longevity of the problem—typically evident since early adulthood, adolescence, or even childhood. Personality disorders are enduring sets of traits that are and always have been characteristic of the individual.

It is fair to say that these diagnoses are among the most debated and revised in psychiatric history. There is a tendency for conditions to be removed from the category of personality disorders once clear causes and effective treatments are discovered. For example, alcoholism and sexual dysfunctions were once widely regarded as deeply rooted personality problems but now are effectively treated and better understood. The number, names, and descriptions of personality disorders typically change each time a new diagnostic manual is published,[8] following debate and votes within the American Psychiatric Association. There was once a move to define an "introverted personality disorder" until Jungian and other clinicians argued persuasively that introversion is not a disorder but a normal personality style.

Another common characteristic of the personality disorders is that they are difficult to treat. Although many volumes have been written to convey people's ideas about causes and proper approaches, research proving their efficacy (with a few exceptions[9]) has been sparse, and no therapeutic method has been shown to be outstandingly effective. Perhaps as effective treatments are found, these patterns, too, will cease to be classified as personality disorders.

The Eccentric Cluster

Current thinking groups the personality disorders into three clusters, differing primarily in the predominant impression that they make on other people. The first of these is a group of personality patterns that tend to strike others as odd or eccentric. *Paranoid* personality, for example, describes an enduring pattern of suspiciousness, short temper, harboring grudges and resentments, and mistrust that permeates all relationships. The *schizoid* character is more a hermit, who actively avoids family and friends, preferring solitude. His or her emotion is generally flat—neither strongly positive or negative—unaffected by and uninterested in others. A *schizotypal* personality is most odd and eccentric in tone. These are typically shy and aloof people, with characteristically peculiar patterns of thought and speech. Their emotion tends to be not flat but inappropriate.

The Erratic Cluster

Unlike the eccentric cluster, personality types in the second cluster are typically involved and engaged with others, often in hurtful, dramatic, and destructive ways. Clearest among these and widely recognized is the *antisocial personality*, sometimes also referred to as *psychopathic* (not to be confused with psychosis). The pattern here is one of consistent conflicts with authorities, remorseless cruelty and damaging behavior, and disregard for the rights and feelings of others. The sensationalist image of fiction and headlines is the "psychopathic killer," but much more typical are repeated acts of vandalism, larceny, fraud, and lying. Almost invariably these acts are evident in the person's history from an early age. The school years are characterized by conflicts with school authorities, parents, or the law. Confronted with unethical or unlawful behavior, the individual often provides elaborate rationalizations and justifications for his or her actions—the victim was "asking for it" or "gullible," or the store "would never miss it, and charges too much anyhow." Most notably absent is a sense of conscience, of social responsibility. This pattern is particularly common in criminal populations and is often associated with alcohol and other drug abuse. There seems to be a genetic risk factor because prevalence increases fivefold in the close relatives of men and tenfold in the close relatives of women with antisocial personality.[10]

Sometimes deception is carried on for the sheer excitement of duping others. Some antisocial individuals carry on false identities or pretenses as *impostors*, claiming elaborate histories of greatness or misfortune, passing themselves off with false credentials as clergy, attorneys, physicians, psychologists, professors, or other professionals—sometimes going to great lengths to steal or otherwise obtain such credentials. Some impostors have practiced their "professions" for years—performing operations, counseling, organizing fund-raising drives—before being discovered and (usually) disappearing to develop a new identity.

People with antisocial personality are difficult to counsel. They are unlikely to remain in counseling, and there is no known effective treatment strategy. The good news is that antisocial patterns tend to abate in middle age. The teens and twenties are the high-risk and most turbulent years. Those who make it through this period without serious consequences (e.g., long-term imprisonment) often level off in their thirties.

A personality disorder receiving increased attention is the *borderline personality*. Although the name suggests a person about to fall over the brink into a psychotic break, the borderline personality is, like other personality disorders, a relatively stable pattern. These individuals tend to function best under conditions of structure, where the rules and limits are clear, and to fall apart in unstructured settings. Sometimes the individual will react to stress or lack of structure with a brief psychotic episode but then characteristically will return to the former state. Individuals with borderline personality often show a pattern of impulsive behavior—engaging in addictive behaviors, sexual indiscretions, suicidal gestures, physical fights, minor crimes such as shoplifting, or indiscriminate spending. Their interpersonal relationships are usually unpredictable and unstable and may (like those of the antisocial personality) be characterized by a manipulative or dramatic quality. Their impulsiveness extends to emotions, and anger control is frequently a problem. Moods may shift rapidly from one extreme to another—dejection, anxiousness, irritability—over a period of a few hours or days. Frequently, these individuals complain of boredom or emptiness in their lives and relationships, and identity confusion is typical. The overall picture is one of long-range instability and unpredictability of mood, behavior, and self-image. Borderline personalities are legendary among mental health professionals for occupying inordinate amounts of time and creating more than their share of chaos, seeking to ensnare the counselor in their emotional intensity, suicidal gestures, and fear of abandonment.

Two other patterns in this cluster are *histrionic* and *narcissistic* personality, both characterized as attention seeking, manipulative, and self-centered. The classic histrionic personality, described since the time of Freud, is melodramatic, needing constant approval, emotionally labile, superficially seductive, and concerned with physical appearance. The archetype is found in the women of Tennessee Williams plays. A narcissistic character is more obsessed with personal importance, intolerant of criticism, feels entitled to adoration and special favors, and doesn't understand the needs and feelings of others.

The erratic personality disorders pose special risks and challenges for pastoral counselors. They are likely, once engaged with a pastor or congregation, to consume disproportionate amounts of time and attention. They are high-maintenance people. They may go from person to person, pastor to pastor, church to church, wreaking interpersonal havoc. Pastors may be drawn into sexual seduction, victimizing scams, intense dependency demands, suicide or violence threats, and rescue fantasies. If you feel yourself being pulled into an uncomfortable relationship, trust your warning bells! Back off, do some checking, talk to a colleague, or seek professional consultation. Some examples of such snares include the person who

> wants constant attention, reassurance, counseling, phone calls but may have little of consequence to say during counseling sessions or, alternatively, always has dramatic emotional tales
>
> comes to pastoral counseling dressed seductively, even if seemingly unaware of the effect of this appearance, or who wants to meet in private places at unusual hours
>
> seems to have little awareness, regard, or concern for how his or her behavior affects you
>
> assures you that only you can understand and help, and draws you into uncomfortable caretaking roles
>
> makes frequent or dramatic suicide threats or gestures, particularly when perceiving abandonment
>
> is vague or evasive about details, or lies to you

Extended faith communities can be important support systems for such people, but it is vital to observe some guidelines in pastoring to them.

1. Set clear limits and boundaries, and stick by them consistently. Do not tolerate unacceptable, personally intrusive behavior.
2. Keep communication flowing among people or groups involved with the individual to avoid manipulation and conning.
3. Use your own feelings of ambivalence and discomfort as a warning signal, and avoid being drawn into destructive interpersonal relationships.
4. Carefully avoid potentially compromising or dangerous situations. Take somebody with you to any crisis or suspicious situation. Avoid counseling without others nearby.

5. Call in professional consultation if you think you may be getting in over your head—preferably *early*.

The Anxious Cluster

The third cluster of personality disorders is characterized by anxiety, fear, and related avoidance. Among the patterns grouped here are the following.

the *dependent* personality characterized by indecisiveness, lack of confidence and self-esteem, strong desire to be taken care of by others, and fear of being on one's own

the compulsive personality—a stubborn and perfectionistic style characterized by a rule-bound conventionality and limited expression of emotional warmth; slavish overconscientiousness and extreme devotion to work, at the cost of family, health, and so forth

the avoidant personality—a pattern of intense fear of rejection and low self-esteem leading to a socially withdrawn lifestyle in spite of a longing for love and acceptance

the negativistic personality—resists routine and expected tasks, exhibits passive-aggressive slowness, reluctantly agrees to do something and fails to follow through, critical of authority, anger about perceived victimization and being taken for granted, resentful

Perspectives on Personality Disorders

Taken together, these three clusters contain vastly different kinds of problems, all regarded as personality disorders primarily because they all represent persistent and maladaptive patterns of behavior that seem quite resistant to change (at least with current treatment approaches). As mentioned earlier, there is no clear "treatment of choice" for such problems, and it is likely that these rather different maladaptive styles require quite different approaches. Real change usually occurs slowly, in small steps over a long period of time, with lots of setbacks. This is due, in part, to our current lack of knowledge and understanding of these disorders. Many other problems, now readily treated, were once considered refractory and embedded in "personality." A pastor and a supportive congregation can be important sources of ongoing care and support. Close cooperation with the individual's primary therapist or support system is highly advisable. And be careful not to burn out your interpersonal resources in the process.

Finally, we add a different caveat. There is a tendency to throw around personality disorder labels in a moralistic, demeaning way, even among mental health professionals. These are easy epithets for people we find difficult: "borderline," "passive-aggressive," "dependent," "paranoid," "narcissistic." The pronouncement of the diagnosis can ring in the ears like a life sentence, conveying chronicity, hopelessness, disapproval, rejection. These labels do not help people. They may momentarily assuage frustration as they cross the lips, but the attitudes they can convey are not healing.

Dealing constructively with people whom the world finds difficult has always been a special challenge of religion. The challenge is to minister in a healing way without being consumed in the process—like a swimmer who carries a struggling, drowning companion for some distance without being pulled under along the way. It's easier if you're not alone. It takes time. You will feel worn out at times. The person may fight against you. You need to keep a clear eye on where you are headed. You must hold the person firmly and lovingly but in a way that does not allow you to be pulled down. You will get tired and need to rest. You will pray. Sometimes the shoreline seems impossibly far away. Sometimes there are waves, sometimes big ones. You may need to call for help. Still the task is to keep the person moving slowly toward the firm ground.

MINISTERING TO THE TRANSIENT

This discussion of personality disorders raises an issue familiar to pastors who work in urban settings—how to deal with transients who drop in at church requesting (or in some cases demanding) assistance. For many pastors, such individuals evoke an intense ambivalence. One the one hand it is the function of a pastor and of a church to minister to those in need. For Judeo-Christian clergy, there is the uncomfortable awareness that Jesus and the prophets would have clearly fit most current definitions of "transient" and "homeless," as would the entire community of the children of Israel during the Exodus. Biblical admonitions to help the stranger at your door are quite strong. Yet it is clear that *some* of those who request aid are doing so deceptively, manufacturing tales of woe and need, and may apply any aid that is provided to untoward ends. For a few, the transient lifestyle poses the excitement of duping the credulous and the challenge of self-support by deception.

The swelling ranks of the homeless and street people clearly include many with major mental disorders. Once warehoused in hospitals, they now roam the streets, marginalized people. Drug problems, especially alcohol problems, are common. To get a job, you need an address. To rent an address, you need a job. The downward spiral can be hard to break, particularly when complicated by major mental problems that are themselves exacerbated by isolation, fear, and deprivation.

How can one sort out legitimate needs from deception—or should one do so? The latter is a value question, of course, and a matter of the balance between resources and demand. For some pastors, it is important to know that the provided assistance will not be used to further a pattern of alcohol and drug abuse, for example. Where resources are limited, it is important to see that they are distributed to the genuinely needy. How can one make such distinctions?

Many urban pastors are considerably skilled in this. Here are a few tips garnered in the course of working with clergy who regularly minister to street people.

1. Coordinate aid. In some cities, the Salvation Army or interdenominational coalitions operate a central service to which many churches refer those in need. When individual pastors provide aid, they register that fact with the coordinating service, along with some identifying information, to help decrease the chances of the same individual soliciting from multiple churches.

2. Check stories. People who drop in at churches to request aid often bring incredible stories. Some of them are true and bespeak a genuine and desperate need for help. Some of them are factitious, designed to deceive and manipulate. Most stories contain elements that can be verified by a telephone call or two, and taking the time to check can help to separate truth from fiction.

3. Provide directly what is needed. A request for food can be answered with groceries. An expressed need for transportation can be answered with the purchase of a nonrefundable ticket or alternative transport. This decreases the chances of aid being misappropriated.

4. Minister to the larger need. When possible, take some additional time to meet more than the immediate need. What are the person's larger physical, psychological, and spiritual needs?

5. Whenever possible, avoid responding impulsively or out of guilt. Some individuals are highly skilled at manipulating emotions with statements like, "I thought this was a church! Aren't you supposed to help the hungry? What kind of pastor are you? I thought I would find help here, but I guess I should just write off the church!" Where there is genuine need, the person will usually be willing to participate in a system of coordinated aid, to have you check on the story, to accept exactly what is requested, perhaps to perform some work in exchange for the assistance provided.

These guidelines are less than complete. There will always be the cases where doubt remains, and often the ultimate decision is one of the heart and of intuition.

OTHER MAJOR DISORDERS

Beyond the psychoses and personality disorders, there are dozens of other major problems that require intensive professional attention. We will mention just a few. In general, the important task is to recognize that there is a significant problem and to help the person find the specialized form of treatment that is needed. Again, a pastor and community also can often provide important support in the long run.

Bipolar Disorder

In chapter 12 we discussed the major mental disorder known as *manic-depressive illness* or *bipolar disorder*. This typically includes both periods of abnormal elation (mania) and periods of abject depression (see Tables 12-2 and 12-3), though only one or the other may appear. In either extreme, the individual's symptoms can take on psychotic proportions. In a manic phase, the person may develop delusions of grandeur (of great personal importance or power), while during a depressive episode, delusions of a more dour tone may emerge (such as the belief that one is condemned and being punished by God or that one is personally responsible for tragedies in the world). Depression and mania can so affect mental state that bipolar disorder is sometimes misdiagnosed as schizophrenia. This is an error of serious consequence because the proper treatments for schizophrenia and for bipolar disorder are different. Here the assistance of a competent psychologist or psychiatrist skilled in diagnosis is essential.

Organic Brain Impairment

Physical damage to the brain can yield long-term problems. This may include various disabilities, a major change in personality, and considerable trauma for family and friends. The human brain has a number of marvelous built-in safeguards but is also exquisitely sensitive to damage. Blows to the head, penetrating head wounds, tumors, circulatory problems and strokes, accidental poisoning, alcohol and other drug abuse or overdose—all can induce permanent brain damage and changes in behavior. There are various disorders involving deterioration of the brain; Parkinson's disease and Alzheimer's disease are examples. Massive nervous degenerations such as multiple sclerosis and infections such as meningitis can also result in profound long-term problems. Competent medical care is an obvious must, and in many communities there are also special services for the victims and families—special nursing and counseling programs, chaplaincies, or support groups. Faith communities can minister effectively by welcoming and providing ongoing support to neurologically impaired people and to their families.

There are common problems among people suffering organic brain impairment. One is impulse control. This can be a psychological threat to others, since we all struggle with issues of self-control, and some theological reflection on the effect and implications of brain impairment is worthwhile.[11] Isolation is also a terrible problem. Stroke victims, for example, often have intact mental capacities but profound difficulty in controlling and generating speech. Those around them misjudge their capacities or simply lose patience with the slow pace of conversation, and a wall of solitude begins to separate the person from normal human companionship. It is sometimes difficult to distinguish and is certainly important to discover what a person can and cannot safely do. Brain injury can impair memory, judgment, perception, thinking, or control of bodily movement but does not necessarily do so. A dramatic incident may lead a family to overgeneralize disability.

There are several helpful functions that you can serve as a pastor of organically impaired individuals. Communication and coordination with the sometimes bewildering maze of health care providers can be an important service. Brain-impaired people (as well as their families) often need desperately to talk, to be listened to with love and patience. You may be able to help in sorting out the right balance between freedom and protection. Through sermons and other contacts with faith communities, you may be able to help people overcome their fear and avoidance and to inspire ministry and support. Sometimes it is as simple as letting people know small, specific ways to be helpful. The basic underlying theme is that, like the terminally ill, brain-impaired individuals tend to be abandoned but are *people* with our common needs for love, companionship, fun, and caring.

Multiple Personality

One relatively rare major disorder worth mentioning is *multiple personality*. This is so rare that the average pastor is unlikely to encounter a single case in the course of a lifetime's work. It is mentioned here both because it has been so popularized via books and films and because it is often confused with schizophrenia. In multiple personality, the individual shows two or more distinct personality forms and switches back and forth among them. Each may have a separate name and may or may not be aware of the existence of the others. Many cases have been traced to extremely traumatic abuse during childhood, but the origins of this disorder are poorly understood and no effective treatment is known (despite tales of spectacular cures in novels). Multiple personality is a favorite choice for people who feign mental illness to attract the attention and interest of therapists.

In any event, this syndrome has absolutely nothing to do with schizophrenia. The confusion arises mostly from popular misconception and from usage of the term *schizophrenic* to mean "divided" or "split." The split that occurs in schizophrenia has no relationship to the splitting of personalities into multiple forms. Rather, it is a splitting from reality. Those rare and unfortunate people who do have genuine multiple personalities do not have schizophrenia, and people with schizophrenia do not show multiple personalities.

Developmental Disorders

Developmental disorders are disturbances in children's normal acquisition of intellectual, social, language, or physical skills. They are usually lifelong deficits, although there are large differences in the extent to which they are disabling. Most developmental disorders are significantly more common in boys than in girls.

Generalized deficits in developmental skills are termed *mental retardation*, typically confirmed by evaluation of adaptive functioning and by intelligence testing that yields an age-appropriate intelligence quotient (IQ) of 70 or below. About 1 percent of the population falls within this range. Some forms of mental retardation, such as Down syndrome, are caused by known chromosomal or hereditary abnormalities. Prenatal health factors are also important contributors to mental retardation, including fetal injury or oxygen deprivation, malnutrition, or exposure to alcohol or other drugs. Drinking during pregnancy is the leading preventable cause of birth defects, including mental retardation, and pregnant women (or those who may be) are therefore best advised to abstain from alcohol altogether. Deprivation of sensory stimulation and physical activity during infancy can itself contribute to developmental delay; conversely, mental retardation can be significantly ameliorated by professionally guided stimulation programs during infant development. Whereas the mentally retarded were once warehoused in institutions, excellent approaches and programs are now available to diminish developmental deficits and increase mental and adaptive abilities. Early recognition and attention from knowledgeable professionals is vital.

A rarer generalized developmental disorder (less than 0.1 percent of the population) is *autism*, which is usually first recognized from the child's lack of normal social behavior. Autistic children appear to be sealed in a world of their own. They do not seek or accept comfort, communication, or interaction with adults or peers. They do not attend to or imitate others and may arch away instead of cuddling when held. Autistic children do not play *with* other children and tend to engage in fixed movements like rocking or making the same body motion over and over again. They are very upset by even small changes in surroundings or routine. The causes of autism have not been fully determined, and there seem to be many contributing physical factors. As mentioned earlier, there is no persuasive scientific evidence that parenting practices play any role in causing this disorder.

A comparatively common developmental problem is *attention deficit hyperactivity disorder*, abbreviated ADHD. Although the signs are typically present in early childhood, this disorder is often not diagnosed until the child enters school, at which point the deficits become apparent. ADHD children have difficulty in focusing their attention for more than a few minutes, in sitting still, in keeping quiet, and in staying out of trouble—in short, all of the things that children are expected to do in ordinary classrooms. They tend to be impulsive and easily distracted, bored, frustrated, or provoked. They are typically active, wiggly, energetic children. One boy we know was nicknamed "Speedy" long before his ADHD was diagnosed. At school, the problem shows up in poor grades and disciplinary infractions. Parents usually complain that the child is disobedient, "doesn't think" before acting, fights, and is generally difficult to manage. ADHD is genetically influenced and particularly common among the biological children (especially sons) of those with alcohol/drug problems or antisocial personality. Because substance abuse and antisocial personality are common in the family histories of children available for adoption, ADHD is also more frequent among adopted children. Medications can be markedly effective, and stimulants (such as Ritalin) often bring about rapid improvement in symptoms, which in turn render behavior management efforts more effective. By the time most ADHD children reach adulthood, there is a substantial reduction in these deficits, though problems often persist.

Family support is crucial for the parents and siblings of children with developmental disorders. Clear information can help the family understand the child and know what to expect. The teaching of special parenting skills can be most helpful. Support groups can provide a much needed place to express feelings and frustrations and to find the strength and companionship to keep providing the extra, demanding care that these children usually require. Good pastoral care and congregational support can be literally a God-send.

Anorexia and Bulimia Nervosa

Anorexia nervosa is a problem most frequent in adolescent girls. The most obvious sign is physical emaciation—the person's body is extremely thin, though this fact may be carefully concealed by style of dress. Despite emaciation, the person usually continues to feel overweight and takes special measures to ensure continued thinness and weight loss. There is a strong and persistent fear of gaining weight. Encouragement to eat more is to no avail. Sometimes even the parents are unaware of the problem, although with time the starvation becomes apparent.

This is a serious problem. Although the chances for recovery without relapse are good, about 15 percent of cases end in death by starvation or complications. This is not a condition to ignore, hoping that it is a phase that will pass. Your most important role here is to have the family get into competent treatment. Family and group therapy have often been used, and it is best to refer to a professional or program with specific experience in the treatment of anorexia. Encourage the entire family to be involved in treatment.

A related condition is *bulimia nervosa*. The bulimic individual appears more normal in weight but shares the anorexic's fear of weight gain and distorted body image. The characteristic pattern in bulimia is binge eating, accompanied by measures to counteract weight gain. These include induced vomiting, stringent exercise, abuse of diuretics or laxatives, or severe dieting. As with addictive behaviors (chapter 16), the bulimic individual often feels out of control, unable to stop the binge-purge cycle.

It is helpful to understand eating disorders yourself. In one case in which we consulted, anorexic relapse was precipitated when one Sabbath morning the pastor greeted a girl with an approving smile, saying, "Well, I see that finally you're putting on a little weight!" This sent the girl into a panic about becoming overweight, and she resumed her former pattern of self-starvation.

Tourette Syndrome

Gilles de la Tourette syndrome is a rare disorder, but one that is important to recognize if you see it, for it is quite treatable. Early symptoms, which usually begin in childhood (between two and sixteen) include muscle spasms (tics), especially of the face. Later, muscle tics may also appear in the shoulders, torso, or extremities. Also common in this disorder are repetitive vocalizations—grunts, barks, throat clearing, coughing—that are difficult for the person to suppress. Many people with Tourette syndrome are also diagnosed with attention deficit hyperactivity disorder (ADHD). About half of Tourette sufferers experience periods of building inner tension that are relieved only by an outburst of some kind, often a string of obscenities. It is the latter in particular that might bring the person to the attention of a pastor. Sometimes the individual or those around the person may entertain the idea of demon possession as an explanation for the apparently uncontrollable outbursts of obscenity. This condition is not to be confused, of course, with the penchant of some to emit a string of obscenities when frustrated. In Tourette syndrome there is an associated sense of compulsion and relief, and this symptom is almost always preceded by a history of tics extending back into childhood.

Without adequate treatment, this is likely to be a lifelong malady. Samuel Johnson, among others, was a lifelong sufferer of Tourette syndrome. The treatment of choice at present is relatively simple: medication, such as haloperidol. Properly medicated, the vast majority of Tourette sufferers show substantial improvement, often after a long series of unsuccessful treatments including various kinds of counseling and psychotherapy. Here is one more example where a prompt and accurate diagnosis of the problem can save the person many years of needless suffering and expensive inappropriate treatment.

SUMMARY

Major mental disorders usually require specialized forms of treatment that are beyond the expertise of the average pastor. Nevertheless, a pastor can provide important assistance and support to such individuals. Types of such help include the following:

1. recognizing the presence of a problem and helping the person to get to the right kind of professional help
2. modeling for others a supportive stance toward persons with major mental disorders as an alternative to fear, rejection, and ostracism
3. providing ongoing support, reality testing, coping skills, and assistance with the day-to-day challenges
4. remaining alert to prodromal signs indicative of a need for renewed treatment
5. supporting the family in caring for the individual

Among the cardinal signs of psychosis are delusions, hallucinations, formal thought disorder (disturbance of the *form* of thought), flat or inappropriate emotions, and bizarre behavior. All of these represent *changes* from the person's prior mode of functioning. Acute reactive psychotic episodes are those that begin suddenly, include extreme symptoms, and typically end abruptly, never to return. These are often stress-induced. Schizophrenia is a psychotic process that develops over a longer span of time and shows a more chronic course. Medications are commonly used to relieve the symptoms of psychosis, although they do not cure the disorder. Hospitalization may be necessary during acute or severe episodes.

Manic-depressive illness is a mood disorder involving extreme periods of mania and/or depression. It, too, can usually be managed but not cured with appropriate medication.

Personality disorders are long-term maladaptive behavior patterns, which change slowly over time. Three currently recognized clusters are characterized by eccentric, erratic, and anxious patterns.

Multiple personality disorder is a rare condition in which the individual shows two or more distinct personalities. Sometimes confused with schizophrenia, it in fact has nothing to do with psychosis and is not particularly responsive to medication. As with personality disorders in general, treatment is usually a long and slow process.

People with organic brain impairment pose special needs and challenges for pastoral ministry. Some brain diseases are permanent and progressive. Recovery from brain injury is usually long, slow, and full of uncertainties.

Other major mental disorders emerge during childhood. Mental retardation and autism represent generalized deficits in the development of normal abilities. Attention deficit hyperactivity disorder and Tourette syndrome pose major difficulties but can often be effectively alleviated by medication and professional care. Anorexia and bulimia are life-threatening eating disorders most common in adolescent and young adult women.

A pastor may be able to save years of needless suffering by recognizing the problem, helping the person and family obtain appropriate and effective help, and providing and arranging much-needed ongoing support within the local faith community. These disorders are not as readily and rapidly treatable as are many other psychological problems, calling for endurance, patience, and consistency of pastoral support.

ADDITIONAL READINGS

For the Counselor

AMERICAN PSYCHIATRIC ASSOCIATION *Diagnostic and Statistical Manual of Mental Disorders*. This standard reference volume—the "DSM"—is available in paperback and contains basic information about psychiatric diagnoses.

ATKINSON, JACQUELINE M. *Schizophrenia at Home: A Guide to Helping the Family*. New York: New York University Press, 1986.

BARNES, MARY, and HOSEPH BERKE *Mary Barnes: Two Accounts of a Journey through Madness*. New York: Ballantine, 1973. A fascinating, disturbing dual account of existentially based treatment of severe psychosis, told from both the patient's perspective and the therapist's.

CLARKIN, JOHN F., ELSA MARZIALI, and HEATHER MUNROE-BLUM, eds. *Borderline Personality Disorder: Clinical and Empirical Perspectives*. New York: Guilford Press, 1992. A range of perspectives and research on borderline personality.

GOODWIN, FREDERICK K., and KAY REDFIELD JAMISON, eds. *Manic-Depressive Illness*. New York: Oxford University Press, 1990. A comprehensive professional volume of information on bipolar disorder.

HOFFMAN, STEPHANIE B., and CONSTANCE A. PLATT *Comforting the Confused: Strategies for Managing Dementia*. New York: Springer, 1991. Advice in nontechnical language—may be particularly useful in nursing home ministry.

JORM, ANTHONY F. *A Guide to the Understanding of Alzheimer's Disease and Related Disorders*. New York: New York University Press, 1987.

MASH, ERIC J., and RUSSELL A. BARKLEY *Treatment of Childhood Disorders*. New York: Guilford Press, 1989. A resource volume handbook for therapists, with solid chapters summarizing research on mental retardation, attention deficit disorder, anorexia, autism, and so forth.

SACKS, OLIVER *The Man Who Mistook His Wife for a Hat*. New York: Harper, 1985. Engaging clinical accounts of people with organic brain impairment, which impart a compassionate understanding of neurological disturbance. A best seller.

SHEAN, GLENN *Schizophrenia: An Introduction to Research and Theory* (2d ed.). Lanham, MD: University Press of America, 1987.

STRAUBE, ECKART R., and ROBERT D. OADES *Schizophrenia: Empirical Research and Findings*. New York: Academic Press, 1992. A technical summary of research knowledge.

VATH, RAYMOND E. *Counseling Those with Eating Disorders*. Dallas: Word, 1986. A book for pastors about bulimia and anorexia nervosa, explaining helpful attitudes and approaches.

Current accurate information about major mental disorders can also be found in textbooks on abnormal psychology, such as those cited in note 2.

For the Client

ATKINSON, JACQUELINE M. *Schizophrenia at Home: A Guide to Helping the Family*. New York: New York University Press, 1986.

DORRIS, MICHAEL *The Broken Cord: A Family's Ongoing Struggle with Fetal Alcohol Syndrome*. New York: Harper & Row, 1989. An excellent first-hand account of a family learning about and coping with fetal alcohol syndrome in an adopted child.

GREENBERG, GREGORY S., and WADE F. HORN *Attention Deficit Hyperactivity Disorder: Questions and Answers for Parents*. Champaign, IL: Research Press.

HOFFER, ABRAHAM, and HUMPHRY OSMOND *How to Live with Schizophrenia* (rev. ed.). New York: Citadel Press, 1992.

SARTON, MAY *After the Stroke: A Journal*. New York: Norton, 1988. A writer's moving first-hand account of recovery from stroke.

TORREY, E. FULLER *Surviving Schizophrenia: A Family Manual* (rev. ed.). New York: Harper & Row, 1988.

U.S. CONGRESS, OFFICE OF TECHNOLOGY ASSESSMENT *Confused Minds, Burdened Families:*

Finding Help for People with Alzheimer's & Other Dementias. Washington, DC: U.S. Government Printing Office, 1990. A government publication, No. OTA-BA-403, which should be available in the public documents section of your library.

NOTES

[1]Milton Rokeach, *The Three Christs of Ypsilanti: A Psychological Study* (New York: Columbia University Press, 1964).

[2]Two enduring standard references on psychopathology are Robert C. Carson and James N. Butcher, *Abnormal Psychology and Modern Life*, 9th ed. (New York: Harper Collins, 1992), and Gerald C. Davison and John M. Neale, *Abnormal Psychology*, 5th ed. (New York: John Wiley, 1990).

[3]L. Kanner and L. Eisenberg, "Notes on the Follow-up Studies of Autistic Children," in P. Hock and J. Zubin, eds., *Psychopathology of Childhood* (New York: Grune & Stratton, 1955).

[4]Charles A. Kiesler, "Mental Hospitals and Alternative Care: Noninstitutionalization as Potential Public Policy for Mental Patients," *American Psychologist* 37 (1982): 349–60.

[5]Ian R. H. Faloon and others, *Family Management of Schizophrenia: A Study of Clinical, Social, Family, and Economic Benefits* (Baltimore: Johns Hopkins University Press, 1985).

[6]R. D. Laing, *The Divided Self: An Existential Study in Sanity and Madness* (New York: Pantheon, 1962); John Weir Perry, *Roots of Renewal in Myth and Madness: The Meaning of Psychotic Episodes* (San Francisco: Jossey-Bass, 1976); Mary Barnes and Joseph Berke, *Mary Barnes: Two Accounts of a Journey through Madness* (New York: Ballantine, 1973).

[7]Gilbert Freitag, Elaine Blechman, and Philip Berck, "College Students as Companion Aides to Newly-Released Psychiatric Patients," in G. Spector and C. Claiborne, eds., *Crisis Intervention: A Topical Series in Community Clinical Psychology* (New York: Behavior Publications, 1973), 2:118—37.

[8]An example of debates over proper definitions of diagnostic categories is found in the American Psychiatric Association's *DSM-IV Options Book: Work in Progress* (Washington, DC: APA, 1991).

[9]Marsha M. Linehan and Heidi L. Heard, "Dialectical Behavior Therapy for Borderline Personality Disorder," in John F. Clarkin, Elsa Marziali, and Heather Munroe-Blum, eds., *Borderline Personality Disorder: Clinical and Empirical Perspectives* (New York: Guilford Press, 1992), 248–67.

[10]American Psychiatric Association, *Diagnostic and Statistical Manual of Mental Disorders*, 4th ed., rev. (Washington, DC: APA, 1994).

[11]Archibald M. Woodruff III, "Ministry to Organic Brain Syndrome Patients," *Journal of Pastoral Care* 38 (1984): 201–8.

18

RELATIONSHIP COUNSELING

You become responsible, forever, for what you have tamed.
—Antoine de Saint-Exupery, *The Little Prince*

People's problems do not occur in a vacuum. People live within a rich network of relationships to others, and so do their problems. For this reason, some therapists have argued that treatment should always involve the family or even the larger social network and that it is impossible to understand or help an individual without including these significant others in the therapeutic process.

We regard this to be a vast overgeneralization, although it does contain a kernel of truth. The social/relationship dimensions of an individual's problems should always be considered. Most "mental health" problems are in fact problems of adjustment, conflicts of some sort between the individual and the social environment. If change is the goal, this may be brought about by changing the individual, the environment, or both. Yet to say that *all* therapy must be family therapy is absurd. Individual counseling can and does provide effective help for many people. An individual approach to treatment does not preclude the making of changes in the person's environment or the requesting of change from significant others.

Sometimes, however, the relationship is the problem. In the treatment of sexual dysfunctions, for example, it is difficult (although not impossible) to work with only one partner because sexuality is necessarily and intimately tied to relationship. Likewise marital conflicts or family crises are best understood not as the pathology of one member but rather as difficulties in the relationship among the members. The counselor's client in such cases is actually not an individual but the relationship itself.

This means that relationship counseling is rather more complex than individual therapy. The counselor relates not only to two individuals, but also to their interrelationships. The complexity is more than additive. The counselor deals not only with two individuals, but also with their past history together, their hidden rules and assumptions in relating, their interlocking and sometimes self-driving patterns of behavior toward one another. The healing process includes not only the essential counseling skills outlined in part II, the formulation process discussed in part III, and elements of problem solving intervention presented in the preceding chapters of parts IV and V, but also a balancing of attention and advocacy for each partner and for their relationship.

There is at present no neat formulation or diagnostic system for relationships, no set of categories or defined problem types to which the counselor can refer. Whereas individual problems have been extensively described and classified, and one can read chapters and books on these different types of difficulties, there is less agreement regarding how to think about and approach the reconciliation of troubled relationships. There has been encouraging progress, however, in the discovery of effective counseling strategies for working with couples and families. In this chapter some helpful frameworks for conceptualizing relationship problems will be provided (with special emphasis on marital discord) and then some alternative intervention approaches will be presented, again with more emphasis on practical application than on abstract theory.

WHAT IS A GOOD RELATIONSHIP?

It would be presumptuous of us to prescribe a single model for the ideal marriage. (The term *marriage* will be used in this chapter recognizing that many people today choose and sustain long-term intimate relationships without entering into a legal contract.) Concepts of ideal marital relationships have been closely tied to both societal standards and religious belief systems. Some have emphasized an asymmetrical relationship in which one partner is the head of the household and the other practices obedience. Others have stressed a more egalitarian model of mutual dependence and independence. Relationships at either of these two extremes can be characterized by happiness or dissatisfaction, by mutual respect or embittered conflict.

Rather than prescribing certain lifestyles or decision-making arrangements, we would point to a few emotional and attitudinal prerequisites for a sound relationship.

1. *A sound relationship is one that occurs between autonomous individuals.* By *autonomous* we do not mean cold, distant, isolated, or unneedful. Rather, we mean that each individual is capable of existing independently and has an identity of his or her own. Psychologist Stephen Johnson cautioned that it is important to establish "autonomous adulthood" before considering marriage, referring to this same ability to exist as an individual in one's own right.[1] This is also the ideal prescribed for marriage by Gibran in *The Prophet.*[2]

2. *A sound relationship is one that is chosen.* Autonomous individuals can choose to depend on others for significant needs, although they do not have to do so. They enter into a relationship out of choice, and they continue in it out of choice. This is the element of will, described by Frankl and others.[3]

3. *A sound relationship is one in which each individual is committed to the growth and happiness of the other.* Erich Fromm and Harry Stack Sullivan, both important theorists on human relationships, emphasized the responsibility of each partner in a loving relationship to support the self-esteem and sustain the positive experiences of the other.[4] This is quite consistent with major precepts of most religions, but it is also ultimately in one's own interest. Love, it is said, cannot be taken but only given. The receiving of love enables the further giving of love. Thus in giving (and only in giving) does one receive, at least in the long run. "You are responsible," says the Little Prince, "for that which you have tamed."[5]

4. *A sound relationship is one in which each partner is open to change and in which each partner has positive skills for requesting and negotiating change from the other.* People who live together need to be able to change. If positive means for eliciting change from the other are not available, it is likely that negative means will be employed.

5. *A sound relationship is one in which each partner shares with the other his or her inner world.* This is intimacy. In a context of mutual trust and respect, the partners communicate to each other their ongoing, present reality—perceptions, reactions, emotions, memories, hopes, plans, experiences, and thoughts. Some people mistake intimacy for the sharing of secrets about one's past. History is a part of intimacy, but a more vital (and more difficult) self-revelation is one's immediate reality. This is riskier than sharing the past because it immediately involves and affects the partner, who in turn reacts.

6. *A sound relationship includes commitment.* Every relationship is marked by its ups and downs. Since the 1960s, however, values have shifted in the direction of independence and personal fulfillment at the expense of commitment to relationship. The core of this ethic might be stated: "I am not responsible for you, nor you for me. If our relationship works out (to my satisfaction), then fine. If not, it's nobody's fault."[6] This perspective, while emphasizing autonomy, fosters the concept of disposable relationships and denies responsibility and commitment. It values independence but not dependability. A sound relationship, we believe, is one that is characterized by endurance and a commitment to working through the hard times that invariably come as part of a shared life.

WHAT HAPPENS TO RELATIONSHIPS?

What goes wrong? Why do so many relationships seem to "go bad"? What happens to bring loving people to the terrible state of embittered, frozen agony with which they sometimes enter the counselor's office?

Our general perspective is that relationships, like all living things, need care and feeding of certain kinds on a relatively constant basis. Without proper care (and even with it to a lesser extent, as part of normal development) there are certain drifts that occur, certain trends away from vitality. If care is ignored for too long, the result is sickness and death of the relationship.

We will outline several of these processes. We emphasize that these are *natural* processes, just as wilting is a natural process for plants that have not been watered, and starvation for organisms that are not fed. Relationships are always changing, either in the direction of growth or away from it. Certain cycles are natural. The point in all of this is not to find fault or establish blame, nor should this instill a pessimism about relationships. To the contrary, the point is a profoundly optimistic one—that if one understands the natural processes in relationships they are no longer mysterious and one is no longer helpless. There are in fact, as we shall see later, a number of things that can be done to promote growth or to encourage recovery when care has been neglected.

Loss of Novelty

One of the first natural processes encountered after initial courtship is loss of novelty. American culture has done much to romanticize romance. Although this has waned somewhat since its peak in the 1950s, many are still believers in the rainbow theory of love. The basic idea is that, when one encounters the right person (finds the "one and only," or encounters "true love," or experiences "the real thing," or any of dozens of other descriptions), there is a special kind of emotional rush that occurs. Hundreds of songs extol the ecstasy of this experience.

And a wonderful experience it is. Perceptions change and the whole world (including the loved one) seems bright and perfect. Physiological arousal goes racing in exciting ways. There is hope, optimism, joy. There's no denying that this is a very pleasant and delightful emotional experience.

But what does it mean? Americans have been taught to interpret this rainbow experience as meaning more than immediate ecstasy. It means that this feeling will last forever, that this is the "right" person, that this person is the ideal mate, and that the marriage will work. Yet in actuality the feeling will fade with time. It always does. This is not to say that it can never be reclaimed or reexperienced in wonderful moments of closeness, for it can. Yet it is normal for such feelings to subside. Nor is this emotional rush a good reason to decide on a permanent relationship (though that is the idea that has been promoted for decades). The rainbow experience is no guarantee of a lasting, rewarding, or even acceptable marriage. Those who experience the rainbow end up with all kinds of marriages, good and not so good, and there are many good and solid marriages in which neither partner ever experienced the rainbow about the other. George Bernard Shaw bemoaned, "When two people are under the influence of the most violent, most insane, most delusive and most transient of passions, they are required to solemnly swear they will remain in that excited, abnormal and exhausting condition continuously until death do them part."[7]

Our clinical experience has even included some individuals who were aroused to rainbow ecstasy by precisely the wrong kind of person. We have known several women who were consistently attracted to men who showed a calm and controlled exterior, with just a hint of a rich emotional interior that might be reached with some effort. In consistent fashion one relationship after another followed the same catastrophic pattern—there was an initial whirlwind romance with excitement and the promise of deep intimacy to come, than a gradual backing away by the man, then an acceleration of efforts by the woman to reach his emotional level, which in turn yielded further closing up and backing away, a final emotional tirade by the hurt and rejected woman, and a bitter and disappointing estrangement. After some months of mourning, a new man was met who, not coincidentally, turned out to show just the same pattern, and it all happened over again—rainbow, courtship, distancing, and estrangement. (It is, perhaps, no coincidence that these women had controlled and emotionally distant fathers who offered just a promise of love and approval but never really came through.)

Lest we imply that only women experience this, we relate the story of another client who came looking for help after the demise of his fifth marriage. He was just on the brink of the sixth when he decided perhaps he should talk to someone. His pattern was to fall madly in love with a modestly but not too attractive woman ten to fifteen years younger than he. These women adored him, found him worldly and experienced, and wanted to be taken care of by him. They were impressed that he never pressed them sexually but was patient and kind, always concerned about their feelings. Sexual intimacy would ensue, followed by a proximal marriage. Then the rainbow would fade, he would find himself no longer feeling the glow, and he began to resent the terrible dependency of this woman. After about half a year (on the average), he would fall in love with someone new, develop an affair, and break off the former marriage to wed his new and true amour.

For all of these people, the painful lesson to be learned was that the rainbow was no magic harbinger of happiness. For these unfortunate people, in fact, the rainbow led them precisely to the wrong kind of mate who fit into an old and rigid program, with quite predictable consequences. This is not the case for all rainbows, of course. Some people are fortunate enough to be drawn to a partner who turns out to be highly compatible, and their relationships grow and become stronger.

The main danger to a marriage here is when one or both of the partners entered the relationship with the expectation either that the rainbow feelings would continue indefinitely or that they at least guaranteed living happily ever after. These expectations may be quite unconscious, but emerge as the rainbow fades and the realities of shared living become apparent. Again there are numerous songs bewailing this transition as if it were a great tragedy, including the B. B. King blues classic, "The Thrill Is Gone." If both people understand that the fading of rainbows is normal and that this does not mean that "love is gone," that they made the wrong choice, or that the marriage is now on a downhill course, then this first transition can be negotiated well and the couple can look for opportunities to experience moments of those same wonderful feelings in the years ahead.

Discrepancies in Expectations

Another normal occurrence early in intimate relationships is the discovery of discrepancies between the partners in what they expected of each other. The previously unseen flaws become more apparent, sometimes leading to the betrayed (and usually untrue) cry, "You're not the person I married!" Issues that had not been clearly discussed prior to marriage also begin to emerge, sometimes revealing surprising differences ("But I thought that you . . ."). Some common areas in which such differences emerge are:

spending time together versus alone
division of labor and roles
socializing ("going out") versus staying in
jealousy
patterns of obtaining and spending money
decision-making style in general
nature and frequency of sex
religious beliefs and practices
children: whether, when, and how to raise them

Decrease in Positives

Positive reinforcement is very high during courtship, perhaps higher than at any other time in one's life. As partners begin living together they may slowly decrease the amount of positive feedback they provide. The small amenities disappear—please, thank you, asking before doing. Each begins to expect the other to keep on giving but slowly stops expressing appreciation or even noticing. From the other's perspective this is often called "being taken for granted." In essence, it means a drop in level of positive feedback and reinforcement. The partners may also share fewer positive events together. Whereas during courtship most of the things they did together were positive, now their shared time may be filled with the instrumental tasks of keeping up a family and household. They simply enjoy fewer things together.

In addition, another natural trend accompanies this shift. Positive feedback from the partner may slowly decrease in its value. Whereas "You really look nice tonight" spoken by an attractive stranger may make your whole day, the same words coming from your spouse may feel just, well, nice. This is in part related to taking for granted, since the words may be demeaned with the unspoken (and incorrect) assumption that a spouse *has* to say such things.

Increase in Negatives

As the power of any given single positive input from the spouse decreases, there seems to be an accompanying increase in the power of negative criticism to motivate change. When a person is consistently warm and positive, ironically enough, each unit of positiveness lessens in its influence.[8] This is the "taking for granted" phenomenon mentioned above. When *negative* input—a "zap"—comes from a consistently positive person, however, it really stings. The recipient is upset, motivated to do something to fix it. This is part of the responsibility of taming. As a person "tames" someone and becomes a consistent source of positive support, his or her negative input becomes all the more potent and painful. That partner is responsible to be aware of this and to temper its use accordingly.

The temptation at this point in human relationships is for people to use negative input when they want something done or changed. With spouse, children, and (to a lesser extent) friends, positive exchange and persuasion may come to seem too slow, too inefficient. A "zap" gets their attention and gets things done. In this way, zapping is reinforced because the zaps "work" and get quick results. Herein is the trap. The temptation is to begin using negative criticism more frequently and, as its effectiveness begins to wane (as it does), to turn up the volume on the negativity. The result is the interpersonal equivalent of an escalating arms race. As negativity of the partner increases, there is further seeming justification for the use of coercive control—threats, sulking, silence, tantrums, criticism, moralizing, faultfinding, blaming, shaming (in short, almost everything on the roadblocks list in chapter 4).

Now, remember that the *reason* coercive control is so effective is precisely because each partner is sensitive, vulnerable to the other. A shared history of positives means increased vulnerability to negatives. Each use of coercive control, however, damages this sensitivity and vulnerability, reverses it in part. If the negative exchanges continue long enough, the result is a pervasive kind of numbness. This is the state, all too often, in which a couple enters the counselor's office. A common statement is, "I just don't feel anything for you anymore." This state *is not irreversible.* The process of overcoming the numbness and recovering loving feelings can, however, be a slow and painful one, and individuals and couples can and do decide that "It's just not worth it."

Of course not all relationships deteriorate to such pervasive numbness, which is the result of prolonged conflict. The point is that there can be a general trend and temptation toward an increasing use of coercive control.

Conflicts, Decisions, Problems, Transitions

In the course of any long-term intimate relationship, the partners encounter important junctures—conflicting needs, difficult decisions, unforeseen problems, and life transitions. Individuals and couples need skills for
coping with such change. When the partners' needs are in conflict, how will
this be resolved? How are important decisions to be made, and who makes
them? When a difficult problem is encountered, how do the partners go about
finding a solution? And when major transitions come for the individuals
(change in job status, illness, new child, death of parents, or symbolic mile-
stone birthdays) what kind of support and change is needed from the partner?

Some couples are better prepared to cope with such frequent and inevitable experiences than others. When crucial skills are lacking for conflict
resolution, decision making, problem solving, and negotiating transitions,
then unresolved crises and resentments can accumulate. In the absence of positive coping skills, too, the temptation is greater to resort to coercive control
attempts or to withdraw from the partner, either emotionally or physically.

Growing Apart

For these or other reasons the partners may begin to grow apart.
Normally, each individual in a relationship continues to grow. If the marriage
was formed early in life before each established an autonomous identity, the
rate and extent of such change can be major indeed. But even a marriage of
mature and autonomous adults is in for significant change as the partners
grow. The question is one of growing together or growing apart. "Growing
together," by the way, does not necessarily mean becoming more similar, as
is mistakenly assumed by some. It means *growing* (changing, improving, expanding, deepening, learning) *together* (in the company of, with the companionship and support of the partner).

The danger is not so much in becoming different. Many partners start
out quite different and, in fact, are attracted to each other for this reason. Rather,
the danger is in losing touch with the other and, consequently, of eventually
living with a stranger. How does this happen? It happens when the partners
have too little contact with each other, communicate too little or too superficially. There may be conspiracies of silence, unspoken agreements not to discuss certain crucial areas. The partners may turn inward for self-protection or
may turn to others—friends, therapist, pastor, a lover—for support. There is
nothing wrong with having a social support system or confiding in a trusted
pastor or therapist, but if this is done *instead* of or to the exclusion of sharing
with the partner, then growing apart is a real danger. This is one reason why
it is risky for one partner in a troubled marriage to enter into therapy alone.

Differences and changes are not fatal for a relationship. They can provide the spice, the renewal, and the richness. Silence, noncommunication, and

withdrawal are the patterns that leave people feeling "estranged" because, literally, they are strangers. They cry out, "I don't know you!" and "You're not the person I married." Coming after years of noncommunication, such statements may be quite true.

Cognitive Changes

The above changes can in turn result in important shifts in how each partner thinks about and perceives the other. The idealized (and perhaps unrealistic) perceptions and images of the partner during courtship fall away. To the extent that the person loved an ideal image rather than the actual partner, this can be quite a shock. But often the initial transition to more realistic perceptions of each other is made without major difficulty.

Yet as the rainbow fades, positives decline, negatives increase, conflicts emerge, and change occurs in the relationship, each partner struggles to develop an understanding of what is happening. Human beings want to understand, to have an explanation, and in the process some rather unhealthy attributions may emerge. Here are a few examples of generalized mind-sets that may result, particularly when coercive control has come to dominate a relationship.

Globalism   There is a tendency to overgeneralize, to take a specific problem and blow it out of proportion. Because one of the trends described above begins to occur, a partner may conclude that the whole marriage has gone bad. Specific experiences and expectations get confused with the entire personality of the other or with the whole relationship.

Projection of Blame   Another natural tendency is to project blame for the situation onto the partner. Most people are reluctant to accept personal blame for what they perceive to be a failure, so to the extent that the marriage is seen as failing, the partner may be held responsible. This is seen in couples who enter the counselor's office with a list of grievances, all of which begin with the word "You . . ." Actually, this is just an example of a more general tendency that people have to see their own actions (especially those that result in negative outcomes) as being committed in reaction to others and the environment, whereas the negative behaviors of others tend to be seen as attributable to their personality characteristics. At an international level the same process can be seen in the escalation of aggression, wherein each side perceives the acts of the "enemy" (itself a key perception) as unjustified provocations and hostilities, whereas its own aggressive acts are perceived as justifiable reactions, retributions, or deterrents.

Basic Pessimism   Here the individual comes to expect that the future of the relationship will be, at best, more of the same if not a downhill process. The person gives up, is resigned to the "reality" of a damaged and damaging marriage. There is no hope or expectation that the partner or the relationship will change or improve. In short, the person feels helpless and hopeless.

Erosion of Trust and Respect   Trust and respect are assumptions made about the partner, ways of perceiving or looking at the partner. To trust a person is to live as if that person's promises will be kept, as if it is safe to be vulnerable around him or her. To respect a person is to live as if he or she is a worthwhile and competent individual, deserving of love.[9] After prolonged coercion and conflict, these basic assumptions may be eroded or even reversed. One may begin to live as if the partner cannot be trusted or respected. If the partner protests this lack of trust or respect, the rather impossible challenge may be issued: "*Prove* to me that you are worthy of being trusted (or respected)." Because trust and respect are chosen ways of looking at another person, however, they are difficult to "earn." The transforming power of trust and respect lies in their ability to transcend trustworthiness and respectability.

Isolation

One final trend that tends to exacerbate all of the above is that toward isolation. David Mace described the devastating isolation of American couples with regard to their marriages.[10] People are taught that marital happiness is natural, that it just occurs, and that one doesn't have to do anything about it. Thus, to have an unhappy marriage is to fail at the most natural and (presumably) easiest of tasks. A similarly erroneous assumption is made about the naturalness of parenting skill.[11] Because many people are taught that marital happiness is natural, people who experience discord in their marriages assume that they are alone, that they are fairly and embarrassingly unique, and that other people have their marriages "together" and resolved. Society teaches that marital problems are private, and not to be shared with anyone else (which, of course, increases the perception that no one else has marital strife). This means that the suffering must be hidden and cannot be shared. Avenues of support that are available for other forms of suffering (illness, death, feelings of sadness or fear) may be closed off by the fierce privatism of the marital bond. The message is that "You shouldn't suffer in a marriage because happiness is natural, but if you do suffer for heaven's sake keep it to yourself." And so the pain goes on in isolated silence.

How Does Love Survive?

After reading this list of potential "drift" tendencies in human relationships, you may wonder how love survives at all—how any relationships endure. It is true that there are many ways in which relationships can drift into unpleasant and unhealthy patterns. These trends are "natural" in the same way that it is natural for a plant to wither without water. If one takes the passive view of marriage—to wait and see how it turns out—then a drift toward storm and stress is likely.

The optimistic side is that there are many things that can be done to prevent negative drift, to reverse it even after it has occurred, and to promote positive growth both for the individual partners and for the marriage relationship itself. This is an active view of marriage—that the partners each have a responsibility to support the growth of the other and of their marriage as well as their own personal growth.

There are also several important roles that can be played by a skillful pastor in promoting stronger relationships. We hope that the preceding material will help you in understanding and thinking about relationships, and how problems emerge in them. This material may be useful in helping the partners to develop a more benign and optimistic view of their situation and relationship. This knowledge can also provide a basis for premarital preparation counseling or more generally in relationship enhancement education. The next section of this chapter is devoted to a presentation of potentially healing actions that can be taken by those who wish to improve the quality of their relationships, actions that you can facilitate as a pastor. Specific counseling interventions will also be considered for helping relationships grow, for dealing with sexual problems, for improving communication within the larger family system, and for counseling those undergoing the difficult transitions of divorce. First, however, we will turn our attention to two important concerns: practical problems unique to relationship counseling and methods for getting off to a good start during the first interview.

SOME PRACTICAL PROBLEMS

In several ways relationship counseling is more complex than counseling individuals. Before discussing intervention approaches, it is worthwhile to consider some of the unique choices and problems that are quickly encountered as one starts counseling couples.

Handling Private Information

One practical problem regards private information—knowledge shared by the counselor with one partner but not with the other. There are no hard and fast rules on how to deal with this. Some counselors assiduously avoid receiving such privileged information in the belief that it causes countertherapeutic alliances and pacts between the counselor and the knowing partner. Indeed, such knowledge can place the counselor in a difficult position. Knowledge, for example, that one partner is having an affair unknown to the other is potentially explosive. Such partners are likely to have different levels of motivation for participation in therapy, with one constantly weighing alternatives unknown to the other. Justifiable anger and resentment may occur in the naive partner who eventually discovers the affair and realizes that the counselor has known all along. It is very difficult to maintain a therapeutic balance when one possesses such loaded information and is sworn to keep it secret from one of the partners being counseled.

There are various ways to deal with this problem. One is avoidance. Some counselors refuse to see partners individually in order to avoid the formation of secret alliances. Some make it clear that any knowledge shared with the counselor is free to be shared with the partner as well. The advantages in this approach are that there are no secrets or subterfuge, and the counselor avoids being drawn into destabilizing and countertherapeutic alliances.

The disadvantage of avoidance is that the counselor, too, may remain naive to crucial information. Further, in spite of the counselor's best efforts, one partner may still provide private information with the request of secrecy, requiring the counselor to make a decision about its use. Such information may come in a letter, a phone call, or a brief remark while the partner is out of the room.

An alternative approach is to live with the possibility of privileged and private information, taking reasonable precautions. You may strongly encourage the knowing partner to share the secret information with the spouse, or you may continue with sessions in hopes of retaining a balanced advocacy. If you wind up in an untenable position, referral may be necessary.

Making the Transition from Individual to Joint Counseling

It is not rare that a pastor begins counseling an individual and then realizes that conjoint counseling involving the spouse is called for. This poses a special challenge because the preceding individual sessions have provided the counselor with a unique alliance with and information about one of the partners. This imbalance is not insurmountable but does need to be redressed. Particularly if the phase of individual counseling has been longer than a few sessions, the joining partner is likely to enter with reservations and anticipations of facing allied opposition. Couples in general enter counseling with the fear that blame will be placed, that the partner will be found to be the innocent victim, and that all of the fault and responsibility for change will fall upon them. This is amplified when one spouse brings the other to see "my counselor."

Methods for overcoming these concerns are described later in tips on conducting the first interview. When conjoint counseling has been preceded by individual work with one partner, special care should be given to the allaying of concerns and the inclusion of the entering partner. This can include an overt assurance that you will be focusing on and advocating for the relationship and not for either individual partner and that blame is neither important nor helpful. "Air time" should also be balanced, perhaps with a slight advantage to the entering partner.

The other side of this process is that the partner who has been enjoying a special and privileged relationship with the counselor now may experience jealousy and a sense of loss. If an alliance against the entering partner was expected, there is also a sense of disappointment and discouragement when this fails to occur. Remember that each of the two partners has special concerns when the transition occurs from individual to conjoint counseling.

Maintaining Balance

This more generally points to the issue of maintaining balance when counseling a couple. Each partner is likely to attempt to entice the pastor into an alliance, particularly where blame concerns are high and counseling is perceived as an adversarial proceeding. Subtle or obvious seductive behavior is one form of bid for alliance. One partner may side with your perceived religious sympathies and beliefs, casting the other as the outsider, the nonbeliever. Rhetorical questions bid for alliance ("Don't you agree, pastor, that . . . ?"). Even the domination of a disproportionate amount of air time within sessions can be a struggle for control of the process and alliance with the counselor.

Balance begins with the first interview. The ground rules of relationship counseling preclude individual advocacy. Within sessions an attempt can be made to provide equal air time for each partner by directing questions to both, differentially reflecting and reinforcing the responses of the more silent partner, sharing material from one and then asking for the other's view or reaction on this same topic. When obvious bids for alliance are made, it may be appropriate to remind the couple that the relationship, the marriage is your client.

Engaging the Uncooperative Partner

Another problem commonly encountered is one partner who is eager for marital counseling with a spouse who is reluctant. Most often this is communicated by the former, who comes individually and complains that he or she would like to improve the marriage but the spouse is unwilling to get help.

The first step is to find out whether the person has, in fact, made a clear and unthreatening request for joint counseling. Often the person has made vague hints about "seeing someone" or merely imagines that the spouse will be unwilling. What were the precise words that were used when the request was made? Sometimes the individual perceives that a clear request has been made when in fact it has not ("I'm not too happy with our relationship and I wonder if we should do something."). What was the spouse's exact response? Again a partner sometimes incorrectly perceives refusal when it was not meant or at least was not absolute ("I don't think so."). Rehearse with the concerned partner how to make a clear, unambiguous, and caring request. The basic elements are (a) an expression of caring; (b) an expression of personal dissatisfaction, as specific as possible; (c) an expression of optimism and desire to have the relationship work; and (d) a specific, time-limited proposal. Example:

> "Jerry, I want to talk to you about something important. I really care about you, and I want both of us to be happy. For the last few months, I just haven't been. I'm not sure what's wrong, but I know that it involves us. I feel lonely, almost— like we're losing touch with each other. And I'm not happy with how we've been making decisions, or avoiding them sometimes. I want to feel happy and close to you again. I know that you've told me you feel satisfied with our marriage as it is, but I'm just not happy with how things are between us. I want to feel closer to you again, and I think it can happen if we both work on it. It's not my fault, it's not yours, but I feel strongly about this—we've got to do something. What I would like to do is to go see Pastor Smith and talk about it. We could just go a few times and see how it goes. But this is important to me. Will you go with me?"

The wording, of course, depends greatly on who the two people are. It can also be helpful to rehearse how the client could respond to anticipated objections and reservations from the partner. A good general strategy is to acknowledge the spouse's feeling or concern and then to repeat the request, rather than trying to launch a counterargument and amass adequate proof.

If the spouse has made a genuine and clear request without success, you may choose to step into the picture by calling and making a direct request. The elements are much the same: (a) an expression of caring and concern; (b) a statement of the partner's specific concerns and feelings and how these involve the spouse; (c) an expression of optimism; and (d) a specific, time-limiting proposal. Example:

> "Jerry, this is Fran Smith. Do you have a few minutes to talk? Good. I think you know that Shelly has come in to see me a couple of times and has been feeling pretty unhappy. I'm concerned and I want to help because I know you both, and I care about what happens to you. I can talk to Shelly alone, but it's just not enough. You're a really important part of Shelly's life, and there's just no way to make real progress on this without your help. I know that you must be concerned about Shelly, and I am, too. I think if we all work together on this, there's a very good chance of things getting better. So I'd like to ask you to come in together a few times just to talk about this situation and where you might go from here. How about this Thursday evening at seven?"

Once again the precise wording is a matter of preference and comfort. This particular request places some pressure on Jerry to come in by implying that to refuse to do so would be to say that Jerry doesn't care or doesn't want to help Shelly. There is also one implication that may take some undoing in the first sessions—that Jerry and Fran are together going to help Shelly. This may increase the chances that Jerry will come in (which is the goal of the call), but it would not be a helpful premise of marital counseling in the long run. Still, the ground rules can be negotiated early, and this problem is minor relative to the difficulty of working without Jerry's presence.

If all requests for joint counseling fail, the dissatisfied spouse has at least three choices—to forget counseling altogether, to enter it alone, or to apply additional pressure. The spouse who feels strongly enough about the necessity of joint counseling may choose to present an ultimatum but should not do so unless he or she is prepared to carry it through. An obvious though extreme one is, "If you aren't willing to come with me for help, then I am leaving." Sometimes pressure of this kind succeeds where gentler tactics fail, but there is always the potential of continued refusal and the person must weigh the alternatives.

It is not impossible to work with one partner to try to improve a marital relationship, though it is something of a handicap. Unilateral disarmament (or other action) always has its risks. Yet it is possible to try to implement some of the interventions described below by working through one partner, and this may be better than no help at all.

The spouse who comes for counseling only under considerable duress also presents special challenges. There is a particular probability of overt or covert hostility from such partners and of sabotage of counseling efforts. The early sessions are crucial in setting the tone of counseling, providing reassurance of balance, and allaying the hostile partner's fears and fantasies about what is going to happen. As in all relationship counseling, perhaps the biggest influence of this kind can be accomplished within a properly handled first interview.

THE FIRST INTERVIEW

The first joint session with marital partners sets the tone, pace, and even content of counseling. It is tempting just to sit back and listen, but this often sets a very bad precedent for several reasons. Often both partners come "loaded" and are expecting to use their ammunition and defend themselves from the other's barrage. Often the partners play out an old tape, an old routine or sequence before the counselor's eyes. There is little therapeutic value in permitting such ventilation and repetition of old patterns. Rather, the first session should make a radical departure from what has been. The first interview should, in fact, already be starting the healing process. In this regard it is vital for you to maintain control of the session, to get off to a good start, and to avoid several important traps. The suggestions that follow are intended to help you do this.

First, the partners should not be permitted to play out their "tapes," their lists of grievances, or even—initially—to talk about how unhappy they are. Here is one place where a passive stance, even if accompanied by sound reflective listening, can be more detrimental than helpful.

Instead, contradicting our usual advice for *individual* counseling, we recommend that you begin by asking certain questions. Keep the answers on track, and don't let the partners stray back to agenda of complaining and blaming. When they do answer these questions, respond with reflective listening. It is also advisable to maintain a good balance of air time in this session—the amount of time that each person gets to talk. If one partner is rambling on or the other is silent, shift the focus intentionally by asking the silent partner for his or her answer to the question or reaction to the other's answer.

What are the questions? First, consider their purpose. It is to refocus the couple on what is good and solid and strong about their marriage and on what they like about each other. There are at least two purposes to this: it provides a counterbalance to the considerable pain that they probably bring, and it has an immediate effect that is positive, which helps both partners feel good about coming back for more. There is a high rate of early drop-out from relationship counseling, and by giving the couple something positive at the very outset you encourage them to stay with the process long enough to help. Now the questions.

> How did you meet?
> What attracted you to him/her?
> What do you remember about your first times together?
> How did you decide to be married?
> What do you like best about him/her now?

It is interesting to ask these questions in a way that does not direct them to one particular partner and to see who answers. One way to do this is to ask while looking dead center between the two people (if feasible). It is informative to see who begins, and the question can then be redirected to the other partner by asking, "Is that how you remember it?" or "What else do you remember?" Use reflective listening as each person answers these questions and be particularly certain to reflect the positive elements in each answer. Remember that a purpose of this is to get each person talking about the positives in their relationship, actually saying the words as well as thinking or hearing them, and reflection encourages this.

Other questions may be used but these are ones we have found helpful. As a rationale or context for these questions, explain that you need the background, the beginnings of their relationship in order to understand the present better. Be alert for diversions from your plan ("*He* decided that we would get married, and you know, that's how it still is. He decides everything! Why

. . .") or hidden zaps ("Well, *back then* she was attractive."). Continually refocus on constructing the positive history of the relationship.

Against this background, it is then less threatening to explore the development of problems. Each person can be asked when he or she first perceived the present problems emerging, and the early history of difficulties can be traced. This also gives the couple more of a time perspective on the problem. Equally important is to ask how they have dealt with these problems so far. What have they tried? What has worked, and what has not? Reflection continues to focus on positive coping attempts, emphasizing efforts that have been made by each with the intention of strengthening their relationship. The positive intent can be emphasized even when the outcome was not optimal ("So you had hoped that having the party would be a lift for Shelly—that was what you wanted, even though it didn't work out that way.") In asking about past coping, be particularly alert for patterns of avoidance—for how the couple has avoided dealing and coping with problems. It can also be enlightening to ask what each would have to do to make the problem(s) *worse*.

Not all of this may be covered in the first session, particularly if you limit the session to the traditional hour. (It is often productive to spend a longer period, up to two hours per session, when working with couples, especially in early sessions.) As the end of the first interview draws near, it is helpful to summarize what has been covered thus far with special emphasis on the positive elements that have emerged. In addition, some general ground rules or expectations for future sessions may be explained here to provide a set or framework for subsequent work together. Here are a few of the points to consider including.

1. The problems you are having are not unusual. There is a general taboo in our society on talking to other people about stresses in marriage, but you are not alone.

2. We are not going to be laying fault or blame, because that accomplishes nothing. This is not a matter of faulty personalities or guilty individuals but of problems in relating to each other.

3. We will be focusing heavily on what can be done, on skills and ideas for breaking out of patterns that make you unhappy and for strengthening your relationship.

4. We will all be working together (if we decide to do so) on your *relationship*, and that will be our focus. No individual headshrinking.

5. Progress in a process like this is not steady. There are periods of quick change as well as long periods or plateaus where change seems too slow. There will also be setbacks along the way. That's all normal.

If the initial contract has been for one or two sessions the contract must be renegotiated at the end of this time rather than assuming that counseling will go on. The question of renegotiation is, "Do you want to continue?" The commitment to continue counseling (sometimes for a fixed number of additional sessions) should not be confused with a commitment to remain in the marriage forever. The latter commitment is much more difficult and often cannot be made before reasonable progress in counseling is seen. Finally, express whatever hope or optimism you can glean. People can and do choose to strengthen their relationships. Low times are part of every marriage, and there are many ways to work toward a stronger relationship.

HELPING RELATIONSHIPS GROW

There are, indeed, many ways to help a relationship grow. Each of the negative trends outlined earlier has a corresponding positive direction and a set of actions that can be taken. We are not going to match these up one-to-one with possible interventions, but each negative drift has its counterpart in the positive actions that follow.

We should also point out that these actions can be applied not only to the healing of damaged marriages, but also in premarital counseling, in enrichment of already strong relationships, and in working with larger family systems. We have included these interventions not only in marital therapy but also in adult education programs and relationship enhancement workshops. As with most human problem areas, early intervention is often much easier than rescue after advanced problems have developed and numbness has set in.

Improving Communication

Difficulties in communication are part of almost any relationship problem. Sometimes it is simply a matter of taking *time* to talk if the couple already has sound communication skills, but more often intervention also includes some training (or at least a refresher course) in basic listening and expressive skills. The following approaches combine these two elements—the structuring of time to talk and training (with practice) in skills for better communicating.

Perhaps the most needed communication skill in most cases is high-quality reflective listening. We have discussed this skill in detail in part II, and the same methods that are so valuable within counseling are also important in other intimate relationships. We frequently teach listening skills as part of the process of relationship enhancement.

A first step is to establish the habit of listening without immediately responding with one's own material. A useful practice exercise here is "silent partner." The assignment is for one partner to talk for a given number of minutes (five minutes is a good place to start) while the other listens without saying a word. The silent partner may use facial expression or other nonverbal methods to communicate listening and understanding but may not respond verbally. A specific topic may be assigned or the content may be left to the choice of the speaker. Then the listener becomes the speaker, and the one who has been speaking becomes the silent partner.

An immediate caveat is in order. It is unwise to give a homework assignment such as this without first trying it out in a session. There are many ways in which an assignment of this kind can go wrong: misunderstanding of the rules, deliberate sabotage, or strong emotional reaction. The usual procedure is to have the partners practice an assignment at least once or twice within sessions in your presence. If these in-session practices go well, the homework assignment for further practice can be made.

A second type of assignment that still provides some safe distance from ordinary face-to-face communication is the "love letter" technique used by the marriage encounter movement. In its usual form, the leader or counselor assigns a specific topic for each partner to write about in personal journal style, expressing thoughts and feelings, perceptions and intuitions, whatever comes to mind (and heart). This writing continues for a specific length of time, varying from five minutes to an hour or more. An equal amount of time is then devoted to sharing these. The partners first exchange journals and read them, then talk about what each has written. Within marriage encounter few guidelines are provided for the content or process of discussion, but once the couple has been taught reflective listening this can be emphasized. There are several potentially beneficial elements of this exercise. It allows each partner to collect and express personal material without being interrupted or distracted. The distance of writing sometimes enables more honest sharing than would occur in face to face communication. The whole process of communicating is slowed down by writing and reading, and in general techniques that slow the flow of communication are beneficial to couples in distress. There is a balance of communication, with each expressing in approximately equal amounts—at least during the writing stage. Finally, the process is time-limiting—ten minutes of writing and ten minutes of discussion (a "ten-and-ten"), or twenty and twenty. The content can be anything assigned by the counselor or mutually chosen by the couple.

Scheduling communication time is often helpful. This may be a regular span of time each day, negotiated blocks of time within each week, or specially arranged appointments. The latter are especially useful when an emotionally charged topic needs to be discussed, but one or both partners are too angry or upset to pursue it immediately. For some couples the problem is not that they are *unable* to communicate but that they just don't do so. Preplanning of time for talking and sharing can in itself be beneficial.

Reflective listening, as any counselor knows, is not an easy skill to learn, but it can be invaluable in intimate relationships. Learning requires not only a cognitive understanding of the concepts and methods but also direct practice with feedback. The practice and feedback methods discussed in chapter 15 apply here. Individuals need information about what they are doing right, coaching on how to improve still further, and lots of encouragement while acquiring this difficult but important skill. Sometimes couples are reluctant to use a "technique" and ask, "But won't my partner know I'm using it?" The answer is that reflective listening is not so much a technique that is used *on* someone, but rather a gift that is given *to* someone. It is a respectful, effortful, and loving way of responding. Both of us apply reflective listening in our own marriage and in our relationships with others (and also fail to do so more often than we would like). This has become such a natural part of relating that we usually are unaware of doing it. With practice, reflective listening becomes part of who you are. In any event, it can be very helpful and healing when working with couples.[12] (Refer back to chapter 5 for details.)

Listening is not enough. A mutual relationship also requires expression of one's own inner world. This involves the concept of assertion, which encompasses the expression of feelings as well as thoughts, positive as well as negative. Teaching even simple expression principles such as the "I message" (starting expressive statements with the word "I") can make a difference in the quality of communication. This and other principles of assertive expression were described in chapter 15.

Many more elaborate communication exercises and games are available; a few are described in resources listed at the end of this chapter. In working with distressed couples, remember to have one or more trial runs with such assignments in supervised sessions before sending the clients home to practice on their own. Likewise, when homework assignments have been given, be sure to ask about them at the outset of the next session. To fail to do this both communicates that the assignment was unimportant and misses potentially valuable counseling information. If it was important enough to assign, it is important enough to discuss and debrief at the following session.

Problem Solving

Another important skill that may require some attention in distressed relationships is problem solving. When faced with a problem, how do the partners go about finding and negotiating a solution? Here are a few points to consider.

1. First, it is wise to make sure that problem solving is what is needed and wanted in a given situation. Some individuals, particularly those who work in problem-solving settings all day, make the mistake of flipping into a solution-seeking mode when in fact the partner only wants to be heard and understood. An example is a working spouse who comes home to encounter a barrage of frustrations expressed by the partner—the phone never stopped ringing all day, the washing machine overflowed, the children were fighting, fourteen projects got started but nothing got finished, dinner burned, and the battery in the car died because the partner left the lights on after an errand.

If the working partner at this moment flips into problem solving and offers to help the partner organize time better so that such things don't happen, the result is likely to be volcanic. Yet the poor problem solver was only trying to be helpful! The error was in misunderstanding what was wanted. Couples can be taught to check channels and make sure they are on the same wavelength. At the simplest level there are two channels—expressing and solving. When one's partner begins to express dissatisfaction of some kind, a good question to ask is, "Do you want me to listen and understand, or are you asking me to help find a solution?" This avoids crossed communications of the kind described in the example above.

2. If problem solving is the task at hand, the next step is to be clear about whose problem it is. Thomas Gordon stressed that the problem belongs to the person who is upset or distressed (or who is *more* dissatisfied).[13] Thus, if Toni leaves the wet bathmat on the floor and Jack is angry about it, it is Jack's problem even though Jack would argue that it is Toni's behavior that "caused" his anger. This is not to say that Toni can cop out by exclaiming, "Well that's *your* problem!" and denying responsibility. Rather, this step clarifies *who* is the upset or offended party. The person whose problem it is then has the responsibility of *expressing*, while the partner's job is to listen reflectively. (Note that expression/listening is the first step no matter which channel you are in—expressing or solving. In the expressing channel, this is the whole process. In the solving channel, the process goes on beyond expression.) Even when the ultimate goal is problem solving, it is best to allow a generous initial period for expressing and listening. A premature launching into problem solving can be as offensive as offering a solution when one is not wanted.

3. There are two good rules to remember about expressing when the goal is problem solving. The first is to say what you would like and what you want in "I message" form. The second is to be as specific as possible. "I want you to be less sloppy" is too vague and general. General feedback changes emotions rather than behavior. If you want a behavior change, be specific: "I would like you to pick up the bathmat in the morning when you are finished with your shower and to put your dirty clothes in the hamper at night." If the expressing partner forgets these rules, the spouse can always ask, "What is it that you would like to have happen?" or "Can you be more specific—what do you want me to do?" Note that the problem may or may not involve the spouse.

4. Once the specific objective has been clarified, brainstorm alternatives. Each partner or family member can suggest alternative solutions, or each may brainstorm individually by writing down ideas that are then shared.

5. Next, the most agreeable alternative is chosen. When the problem does not involve the spouse or the chosen solution is readily acceptable to the spouse, this choice is made by the partner who "has" the problem. The other mostly listens. If, on the other hand, *both* partners are involved, or both "have" the problem, or if the chosen solution is not readily acceptable to the other, then the process of conflict resolution is called for.

6. Finally comes the challenge of implementation. The person whose problem it is and who has chosen an alternative now plans and implements a first step in this direction. The spouse again listens reflectively but may also offer, "Is there anything I can do to help?"

Conflict Resolution

Often *both* partners have feelings about an issue; both are dissatisfied or emotionally involved. In this case it is not as simple as one or the other person having the problem. Both "have" the problem.

The initial steps are largely the same as in problem solving. The partners clarify that they are aiming at finding a solution rather than simply expressing themselves. Then both take a turn at expressing, through "I messages," what they would like to have happen or what they want. Each partner listens reflectively to the other to help in clarifying what is wanted. It can be helpful to require each partner to describe how the other sees the problem, and to continue clarification until each can describe it to the partner's satisfaction. Again, it is important to be as specific as possible. The process of brainstorming follows, with each partner generating as many alternatives as possible.

At the point of choosing an alternative solution, however, conflict resolution requires negotiation. Both partners are involved in the selection of the best alternative. Each possible alternative is considered and evaluated. It may be necessary to return to the brainstorming stage and generate still other possibilities. Finally, an agreement is reached, sometimes in the form of a trade, with each partner agreeing to make a certain change in exchange for a specific kind of help or encouragement from the other. (Usually, it is wise not to arrange direct trades of two emotionally laden changes because of the potential that failure of one partner to comply results in retaliation of the other by likewise violating the agreement.) Sometimes it is helpful to write down the agreement so that each remembers the specific commitments made.

Finally implementation begins. Each starts to carry out the first steps involved in bringing about the desired change. Later the partners may need to evaluate together whether their agreement has worked, and if not, how it should be changed.

Each partner should also recognize a responsibility, when asking for a change from the other, to notice a change when it does occur and to reinforce it. This can be as simple as a "thank you" acknowledgement or as nice as a special backrub, meal, or other treat for the partner in appreciation of the change. Small steps in the right direction should be acknowledged, too, because large changes are usually made up of an accumulation of small changes. The partner who requests a change should also be willing to help and support the making of the change.

We add, again, that this kind of negotiation process assumes a certain degree of mutual good faith. Use assignments and processes such as this at

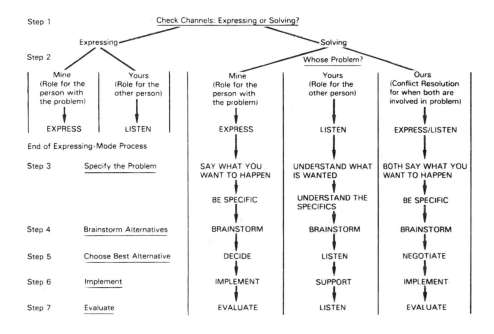

FIGURE 18-1 Expressing, Problem Solving, and Conflict Resolution

your own discretion when the time seems right, and plan ahead, because they can go quite awry without adequate preparation. Sometimes it is necessary to teach one skill before proceeding to another. The learning and exchange of sound reflective listening skills, for example, is often a prerequisite for entering into the more complicated and emotionally charged process of negotiation for change.

Increasing Positives

Another strategy for improving the quality of a relationship is to increase the numbers of positives that are shared and exchanged. The goal is for each partner or family member to increase the positive experiences of the other(s). Here are some possibilities.

1. Each partner writes out a "menu" of positives that he or she enjoys. The list includes smaller and simpler positives as well as larger and more complicated ones. Some of these can be provided by others, and some cannot. Some general types of positives on the list might include the following:

hearing certain words spoken
physical and sexual enjoyments

time and experiences shared with partner
time alone, to be used as one pleases
tangibles that can be purchased
small acts or services
certain activities

These lists are then exchanged, teaching each other what each partner especially likes and enjoys. If desired, separate lists might be prepared (such as
"Positive things I can do for myself" versus "Positive things my partner can
do for me") and shared as appropriate. After exchanging the lists, talk about
them.

2. Each partner can select a particular positive to give to the other, attempting to double it in the week ahead or (if it was not happening at all) to
start helping it to happen. This can be chosen from the list, from a specific verbal request made by the partner, or from one's own creativity. The partners
may tell each other in advance what is going to be increased, or the counselor
may direct each to keep it a surprise.

3. Each partner can secretly choose a particular day in the coming week
to bombard the partner with positives, to greatly increase the overall rate of
positives given. Again, it can be both fun and instructive to keep this "special
day" a secret in advance. With this assignment we have seen some interesting outcomes when the partner is not told in advance which day will be special. Some mistakenly perceive that a preceding ordinary day was the special
day. Others fail to notice the special day when it happens!

4. A general goal can be set of increasing positives to the partner over
the coming weeks. To measure progress on this, each partner can keep track
of positives given and received (without sharing these records with each
other). The counselor again gains information by comparing each partner's
records. Is there a correspondence between the number of positives one partner perceives that he or she gave and the number the other recorded receiving? These records need not be complicated. They can be as simple as hash
marks on a blank index card, or as detailed as a complete diary of positives
given and received. It is important, however, to count every one. (See Table
11-2.)

5. A weekly family conference can be held in which each shares with the
others what positives he or she would like to receive or have happen in the
week ahead. Together the family negotiates which of these would be possible, and all work together to see that they occur. Shared positive experiences
can also be emphasized and planned.

The overall goal in this is to increase the amount of positive exchange
and shared time in the marriage or family. Distressed couples often stop
spending time together or share primarily neutral or negative time. They may
even stop sharing the most fundamental positive times—meals, sitting and
sleeping together, sexual intimacy, simple relaxation. Shared positive recre-

ation may disappear. The restoration of shared and exchanged positive experiences is a basic and crucial step in helping people grow closer again.

Decreasing Negatives

The other side of this coin is to decrease the number and intensity of negatives occurring in the marriage or family. This is a more sensitive issue, and sometimes can be delayed until after positives have been increased to pave the way. In other cases, however, the continuing occurrence of negative events so poisons the springs that no amount of positive exchange can overcome the fear and pain each feels. In any event, the increasing of positives and the decreasing of negatives are complementary goals. Possible steps to be taken are very similar to those just mentioned.

1. Each partner can prepare a list of partner actions that are felt as negative. Here *specificity* is important. What is it that the partner *does* or *says* that feels negative? These lists can be exchanged and discussed. Where distress levels are higher, they can be given first to the counselor, who uses the information as she or he deems appropriate. A simple three-point rating system might be used to indicate which negatives are seen as most hurtful or irritating (3), moderately hurtful or annoying (2), and slightly hurtful or irritating (1). In response to such a list, defensiveness of the spouse may be decreased if he or she focuses on reflective listening and on finding out specifically what it is that is hurtful. Under the best of circumstances, however, this is a difficult list to hear.

2. Each partner can work on one or more specific negatives in an attempt to cut them in half or even eliminate them. Doing so, of course, may itself have unforeseen or negative consequences. To simply "stop complaining," for example, may leave the individual in no better circumstances but also nursing a reservoir of unexpressed anger. Be alert for such possibilities.

3. Decreased negatives can be combined with increased positives if a "special day" strategy is chosen.

4. A general strategy of decreasing negatives can be implemented by having each partner record negatives given and received. Sometimes the very recording process suppresses negative behaviors. Comparison of partner records can provide the counselor with useful information, and the week-by-week records provide feedback on progress toward the goal. It can also be interesting to have each partner make a rough rating of his or her mood at the end of each day, perhaps on a scale of 1 (felt very good all day) to 7 (felt absolutely awful all day). Frequently, the ups and downs of mood can be seen to relate to the rate of positives and negatives coming from the partner or given to oneself (see chapter 12).

5. Family conferences can also, as needed, focus on negative experiences that each member would like to decrease. Depending upon whether or not

these involve other family members, the family can use the problem solving or conflict resolution methods described earlier to help each member toward a more positive balance.

Changes in Thinking

Sometimes positive change in a marriage or family can be aided by a change in thinking, in the assumptions each makes about the other. Earlier it was stated that "trust" and "respect" are chosen attitudes that one person takes toward another. To the extent that one can "live as if" the other is trusted and respected, both often feel increasing levels of trust and respect. Neither trust nor respect requires a certain level of prior proof. They are decisions made by the one who trusts and respects, sometimes in spite of the evidence.

It can be beneficial for you to help clients *reframe* their problems, to think about them in new ways. An example of this is shifting a prior focus on individual fault and blame to a new concentration on patterns in the relationship. Clients can be taught to use their unhealthy thoughts ("It's all his fault," "There she goes again," "Things are never going to get any better") as signals to rethink the situation ("Now wait a minute, I'm in this, too. I recognize this pattern. My partner is feeling angry right now and I need to learn why. What can I do to help resolve this?"). Where unrealistic expectations seem to play a role in marital distress ("People in love never fight," "My marriage should be perfect," "We should feel the same way we did when we first met"), you can help to encourage more realistic expectations (refer to chapter 12).

Perhaps the most helpful system that we have found for understanding and living with differences among people is one which emerges from Jung's personal type theory. The particulars of Jung's system are complex, as is the instrument now most frequently used by counselors working within this system—the Myers-Briggs Type Indicator.[14] Nevertheless, the perspectives of "gifts differing" contain many healing elements, and we regularly use these ideas in our counseling.[15] A few basic assumptions of this system follow:

1. People differ naturally and along understandable dimensions.
2. Differences are valuable, essential, enriching, and to be cherished.
3. Within the normal types described by Jung, it is not "better" to be one type than another. No type is superior, more intelligent or adaptive, healthier or saner. All are preferred ways of perceiving and dealing with the world.
4. Understanding one's own type and how this differs from others is helpful in comprehending, preventing, and resolving human conflicts.

These and other assumptions of this systematic way of thinking encourage people to view themselves and others in healthier ways, to take a nonblaming and constructive view of differences. With couples we have found that this system helps them to understand what their differences are, how these were involved in what attracted them to each other in the first place, and how the continuing differences contribute to both the strengths and weaknesses in their relationships. Resources for further exploration of this system are provided at the end of the chapter.

Finally, we would add a comment about "cognitive lag." It frequently happens in counseling that problem behaviors change before the individuals' perceptions do. In one case a "problem child" shows remarkable change in the behaviors that were causing difficulty, but the parents still complain, "Yes, but deep inside he's still a disturbed kid."[16] In another, both partners in a marriage work hard to increase positives, decrease negatives, and improve communication. After three months of hard work, one or both may say, "But I just don't feel like our marriage is any stronger!" It often happens that if they persist for a few weeks or months longer, the perceptions and thought patterns catch up with the changes that are occurring. In such cases, a bit more patience is often enough. Another possibility, though, is that there are still other problems that have not yet been resolved. In this case a reformulation may be called for and a new intervention may be planned to address the previously unresolved difficulty.

Getting Started

All of the above represent reasonable steps that can be taken to improve the quality of a relationship. Of course, not all of these are called for in all cases. The point is that it is possible to *do* something. Troubled relationships are often characterized by intense passivity and helplessness. Each partner seems frozen into a holding pattern, waiting for the signal that it is safe to land. This passivity, and the interlocking patterns that keep the relationship frozen in its present state, represent some of the most substantial blocks to change.

Even you, as counselor, may get caught up in this passivity. The gloomy basic pessimism can be contagious, and the pastor must take care not to be caught in this gloom. Another common counselor perception is that "there are so many things wrong" or that "the problems have been there for so long" that it seems hopeless to find a place even to start. The remedies we prescribe for these counselor ills are three. First, get off to an optimistic and energetic start by using the methods described earlier (the first interview) to avoid being trapped into the couple's habitual routines. Second, retain a perspective that believes in marriage and the power of individuals to choose and change. Third, get to it! Have the partners begin doing something about the problem. There are many different approaches. As with depression (chapter 12) there may be a substantial resistance to getting started on a particular strategy, but the way out is through starting the change process. The consequences of what the couple has already been doing are known. More of the same is not going to help—otherwise, they would not be in your office. It is time to try something different, to experiment with changes and new ways of relating until at last the relationship begins to grow again in positive directions.

OTHER PERSPECTIVES

We have intentionally presented a particular way of conceptualizing and strengthening relationships. It is a problem-focused approach (chapter 11), which specifies difficulties and seeks solutions. To be sure, this is not the only useful approach for working with couples or families. In chapter 6, for example, we discussed a family systems orientation that focuses on analyzing and destabilizing dysfunctional rules and relationship patterns. We have chosen to emphasize a problem-focused approach because it is well grounded in treatment research, and we find it a more specifiable and teachable approach in working with pastoral counselors. As before, we do not represent ours as the only or always best perspective. We commend it to you as a research-based approach that we have also found effective in our own counseling.

Further Professional Help

Relationship counseling is difficult. There are complexities and pitfalls deeper than the catacombs of typical individual therapy. As with other problems, sometimes it is necessary to call in or refer to a professional with more specialized expertise.

Some guidelines for selecting an appropriate professional for referral will be provided in chapter 19. A few specific comments about marriage and family specialists are included here.

In most communities of at least moderate size, one can find a wide range of practitioners claiming specialty in "marital counseling," "family relations," or "sex therapy." In some areas there are few or no controls on the use of such titles, and virtually anyone can lay claim to them. We recommend that you inquire carefully into the background, training, experience, and credentials of the practitioners available. Licensure or board certification (see chapter 19) in a recognized helping profession (e.g., psychology, psychiatry, social work) is some assurance of adequate qualification, though this also is no guarantee.

There are also myriad approaches to relationship counseling. A large research literature is presently accumulating on the effectiveness of various marital and family therapy methods.[17] Two broad approaches seem to be well supported, although each of these admits to wide individual differences in application among practitioners. The first of these is cognitive-behavioral marital/family therapy, which focuses heavily on patterns of positive and negative exchange within the family and teaches specific skills for negotiating change—the type of approach that we have emphasized in this chapter. Major advocates of this view have included Richard Stuart, Robert Weiss,

Gayla Margolin, and Gerald Patterson.[18] A second approach that has received consistent support has been called a "systems" or "structural" approach to family therapy, mentioned above. This method focuses on communication systems within the family and attempts to alter these power networks in therapeutic ways. Major advocates of this approach have included Jay Haley, Virginia Satir, and Salvador Minuchin.[19] Although the theories behind these two approaches sound rather different and the advocates frequently argue the relative merits of each way of thinking, it is our impression that in actual practice the two are more similar than disparate and that a single common therapeutic process may underlie both. Many other approaches have been popularized, including transactional analysis, gestalt therapy, and psychodynamically-based methods for counseling couples and families, but scientific evidence in support of these has not been forthcoming.

DOMESTIC VIOLENCE

In counseling with individuals, couples, and families, it is important to be attuned to the risks and signs of domestic violence. As relationships drift in a negative direction and control strategies shift toward the coercive, the danger of verbal and physical abuse increases. This danger is greater than many appreciate. It has been estimated that about one in six U.S. couples engage in physical violence over the course of any one year, and over the course of marriages the rate of violence is about one in four.[20] Physical violence against children is even more common.[21] By one estimate, the average pastor (knowingly or unknowingly) sees thirteen to fourteen domestic violence cases each year.[22]

The taboo against discussing marital difficulties with others is doubly strong with regard to family violence. In addition to felt shame and embarrassment, there is the real fear of greater reprisals. Nevertheless, family members will often confide in a trusted counselor who asks the right questions.

Asking about Abuse

When does one ask about potential abuse? Our first advice is similar to what we said with regard to suicidal risk: Always ask if you wonder or see any indication. Verbal and physical aggression are so common in distressed families, in fact, that it is prudent to ask about them routinely. One study found that less than 2 percent of men and 6 percent of women spontaneously listed marital violence among the problems for which they were seeking couples counseling. *When asked directly*, however, in separate individual interviews, "Is there physical abuse or violence in your relationship?" 46 percent of treatment-seeking husbands and 44 percent of wives (56 percent of couples) acknowledged that violence was occurring.[23] Among specific clues and risk factors that should particularly prompt you to inquire carefully are any reference to violence, abuse, weapons, etc.

the presence of alcohol/drug abuse

increasing withdrawal from friends, church, or activities

repeated injuries, bruises, visits to hospital or emergency room, unexplained or vague illnesses, miscarriage

high relationship stress

marital separations or threatened divorce

police visits or arrest

apparent fear or intimidation

What is one asking about? We suggest that you keep in mind three general categories of abuse.

> *Physical violence* involves bodily contact between people that has actual or intended harmful results. This includes pushing, shaking, slapping, hitting, kicking, biting, choking, burning, and so forth.
>
> *Threatened violence* is a communication that expresses to another person an intention or warning of harm. This can include verbal threats, menacing looks or gestures, displaying and handling of weapons, or the inflicting of violence on property or pets.
>
> *Emotional abuse* is a broader category of words and actions intended to inflict psychological harm. Examples are demeaning, name-calling, withholding of affection, intimidating, and expressing disgust or scorn.

How does one ask about potential abuse? There are no specific words right for every situation. In general, be specific, open, unthreatening, and clear. Here are some possible openers:

> "Are you ever frightened of _____? . . . In what way?" "Sometimes when people argue, as you have been describing, somebody loses their cool and pushes or hits. Does that ever happen in your family? . . . Tell me about the last time something like that happened."
>
> "Does _____ ever hurt you? . . . Give me an example."

If you encounter any indication of abuse, persist in exploring the problem. Always take the situation seriously, and it is reasonable to guess that the problem is being understated.

Intervening   Much of what we have discussed in earlier chapters regarding crisis intervention (chapter 10), suicide prevention (chapter 13), and anger management (chapter 15) is directly applicable in dealing with domestic violence. It is important to listen and provide support, but you also have a particular responsibility here to evaluate the degree of potential for danger and harm. Past behavior is generally the best predictor of future behavior, so a starting point is to determine the history and seriousness of violence in the family. Are there any new or escalating circumstances, such as an actual or threatened separation, a discovered extramarital affair, or first police involvement? Are alcohol and other drugs involved? How accessible are lethal weapons? Has anyone (including the victim) seemingly reached a point of desperation? Have there been explicit or implicit threats?

The most urgent purpose of such inquiry is to determine the need for immediate protective measures. Where there is real potential for harm, emergency shelter is needed. It may be vital to remove children from the home for their safety. When the danger of violence is high, it is often wise to notify and involve the local police department. When injury has occurred, prompt medical attention is important, even if the victim insists, "It's not serious." The laws of many states require medical examination and police notification within a relatively short period to document an offense. Most states also have laws requiring professionals to notify child protective services when the abuse or neglect of children is discovered.

Immediate protection is only part of your task, of course, albeit a crucial part. Family violence is rarely an isolated incident, and as with crisis intervention in general, it is important to discover and address the causes of the problem. As a pastoral counselor you may be able to provide an important calming, supportive, and stabilizing influence through your presence, reflective listening, prayer, and concern. Asimov's aphorism, "Violence is the last refuge of the incompetent," reflects a truth: That people resort to violence and coercion when they lack other means for coping. Sorting out the reasons for violence (see chapter 15) is a crucial step toward healing.

SEXUAL PROBLEMS

If discussing family discord or violence is taboo in our society, talking about sexual difficulties is even more so. People are daily bathed in sexual information and programming, sexual humor, and the exploitation of sexual attraction in advertising. Pornography is readily available, and the later decades of the twentieth century were proclaimed to be a "sexually liberated" age. Yet openness about one's own sexual doubts, feelings, and problems remains one of the last areas to be shared even among the closest friends, if ever it is shared at all.

The results of confidential surveys reveal, however, that sexual difficulties are exceedingly common among both men and women. Among men, roughly one in six complains of low sexual desire in spite of normal health; about one in ten has difficulties in attaining or maintaining an erection (pejoratively termed *impotence* in the past), and more than one in three complains of premature ejaculation. Among women, about one-half express difficulties in becoming sexually aroused and do not experience orgasm as consistently as they would like; more than one in six have never experienced orgasm in spite of normal sexual relations (a problem that has been termed, with equal cruelty, *frigidity*).[24]

Taken together, these data assure us that a *majority* of couples are currently experiencing dissatisfaction or difficulties in relating to each other sexually, and that virtually everyone who is not celibate will encounter such problems at some time in his or her life. Sexual problems are not only inevitable but also normal—the majority experience them at any given time.

A variety of factors prevent people from talking with others about sexual feelings and problems. Powerful emotions are attached to sexuality in our society. In addition to sexual arousal itself, people may experience anxiety, guilt, shame, feelings of inadequacy, pride, or embarrassment. Among men in particular, sexuality is the subject of a good deal of competitiveness, humor, and downright deceit, beneath which lie the same emotions mentioned above. This conspiracy of superficiality and silence leaves one with the erroneous impression that it is unusual and shameful to experience sexual dysfunctions, and that people who do are to be regarded with ridicule and scorn rather than compassion and understanding. In this social context it is not hard to understand why people keep their true feelings and experiences to themselves.

Not only are sexual dysfunctions common, they are quite treatable. The success rate depends upon the particular type of problem, but even with the more difficult problems at least half are helped by modern intervention methods, and with some problems the cure rate is virtually 100 percent with proper treatment. We will return to treatment issues later, but there is little reason to continue suffering in silence.

Sexual Dysfunctions

There are no absolute standards of "normal sexual performance" or healthy sexuality, at least not within the realm of psychology and medicine. The conditions that are described in this section are problems only if and when they are distressing and a source of dissatisfaction to the partners involved. All are defined, to some extent, in relation to the partners' happiness and satisfaction. A good example of this relativity is the diagnosis of premature ejaculation. *Premature* obviously is defined in relation to some standard of propriety—a satisfactory latency before ejaculation occurs. There are no standardization tables here. For many centuries rapid ejaculation by men was normative, and neither violated an expectation nor posed a problem—particularly in times and places where little or no importance was placed on female sexual enjoyment. In our present *zeitgeist* of mutual sexual fulfillment, however, ejaculations become "premature" because they fail to meet certain expectations or standards of personal satisfaction. Whether one celebrates or bemoans such changes in societal standards, it is clear that sexual "dysfunction" is closely tied to these expectations and is defined in large part by people's dissatisfaction.

The current understanding of problems in sexual functioning is closely tied to the landmark research of William Masters and Virginia Johnson.[25] To comprehend such problems, they reasoned, it would be essential first to understand *normal* human sexual response. Their controversial and pioneering work provided the first basic information about normal human sexuality.

They greatly helped to advance "sexology" from a field dominated largely by myth and rumor to a professional specialty with scientific knowledge and effective therapeutic interventions.

The Masters and Johnson research led to a description of normal human sexual response as occurring in four stages that are strikingly similar in men and women. The first or *excitement* phase involves a gradual increase in sexual arousal observable in a variety of biological changes. After this initial increase in arousal, there is a *plateau* phase in which arousal levels off and other distinctive physical changes occur. Next is the *orgasmic* phase, an abrupt increase in arousal and the experience of climax or orgasm. Finally comes the *resolution* phase, a sharp drop in arousal accompanied (especially in men) by a decrease in desire and a period of diminished ability for subsequent orgasm. The precise shape and length of this arousal pattern varies widely among individuals. The orgasmic phase may not occur, leaving excitement, plateau, and resolution phases. The plateau may be brief or prolonged. Orgasms may be single or multiple, mild or intense. The basic form and stages of human sexual arousal are fairly consistent, however, which is important in understanding the nature of sexual dysfunctions.

Masters and Johnson regarded this pattern of sexual arousal to be normal and inborn. It is not necessary to learn how to be sexually aroused. The four-stage cycle is natural and, they maintained, occurs unless further factors enter the picture to inhibit or change the pattern. From this perspective, treatment involves the removal of unnecessary obstacles lying in the path of an otherwise natural process.

Types of sexual dysfunction are now classified according to the stage at which they occur.[26] We will offer some detail here to provide you this framework within which to understand sexual problems.

Inhibition of sexual desire, reported by about one in three women and one in six men, involves an inhibition of arousal before it ever gets started. Normal changes in sexual desire do occur with age, health fluctuations, and lifestyle. As with all "dysfunctions," this is a problem only if it distresses one or both of the partners.

Inhibited sexual excitement involves disturbance or absence of physical changes that normally occur during the excitement phase. This is more apparent in men, where it appears as an inability to attain or maintain an erection sufficient to allow sexual intercourse. This problem is reported by about one male in ten at any given point in time; the percentage *ever* experiencing this is considerably larger. In women, the excitement phase changes that parallel male erection are genital swelling and lubrication. Although about half of all women report this as a consistent or frequent problem, this is less disabling and more easily overcome by the couple.

Inhibited orgasm is almost uniquely a female complaint. The woman experiences normal responses during the excitement and plateau phase but does not experience orgasm. Instead, the arousal gradually dissipates after plateau, sometimes (but by no means always) leaving a sense of disappointment or unreleased tension. Most often this difficulty occurs inconsistently. Orgasm may be experienced with certain kinds of stimulation but not others, with one partner but not another, or in seemingly unpredictable fashion. Inhibited orgasm—a long delay or absence of ejaculation—does occur rarely in men (less than 5 percent). Other individuals, about 15 percent of women and a very small percentage of men, have never experienced orgasm in spite of seemingly normal sexual excitement and experience.

The opposite problem of *premature ejaculation* is uniquely a male complaint: too-rapid orgasm. In this case, the man experiences little or no voluntary control over the occurrence of orgasm, and he or his partner (or both) express dissatisfaction with this situation. More than a third of men report this problem, and the actual occurrence is higher when the partner's report is considered as well.

Vaginismus is a rare but distressing condition in which the outer muscles of the vagina spasm and contract, preventing intercourse. Once thought to be caused by deep-seated unconscious conflicts, this disorder can now be treated easily and quickly by a competent sex therapist, and the successful removal of the problem is accomplished in almost all cases.

Finally, *dyspareunia* is the term applied to physical pain experienced by either a man or a woman during coitus. This also is believed to be a relatively rare phenomenon and merits competent medical attention because the cause is often physical.

Causes of Sexual Dysfunctions

Where does normal sexual responding go awry? What factors come to block this natural process, causing the kinds of inhibition and difficulties described above?

There are many possibilities. Certainly, learning factors play a role. Many people learn about sexuality under less than optimal and comfortable conditions. Mistaken beliefs and misinformation abound. People also learn to attach painful emotions to sexual response in some cases—shame, guilt, or fear. Masters and Johnson pointed to two common causes of sexual dysfunctions: (a) *performance anxiety*—the fear of being judged inadequate and (b) the *spectator role*—a kind of dissociation in which the individual, instead of simply experiencing, steps back in consciousness and observes, asking questions like, "How am I doing? Am I getting aroused? I wonder what my partner is feeling," or "I wonder if I'm going to have that problem again." Such thoughts markedly interfere with normal sexual enjoyment and arousal. The most powerful erogenous zone, Masters and Johnson wisely observed, is between the ears.[27]

Contrary to popular belief, physical problems are seldom the cause of sexual difficulties. Certainly, medical problems can be involved, and a physician examination is called for in many if not most cases. Yet the majority of sexual dysfunctions are not due to physical problems. Of the problems listed above, only dyspareunia (painful intercourse) can be traced frequently to a medical problem.

Likewise, only a few decades ago it was believed that sexual dysfunctions were due to profound disturbances in personality. Textbooks on psychotherapy bemoaned the poor prognosis for treating sexual "inadequacies," and indeed the prognosis with traditional psychotherapy was quite poor. The sexual dysfunctions were regarded to be part of the larger class of personality and character disorders.

Much has changed. Sex therapy is now a specialty founded on a scientific understanding of human sexual response, employing well-proven treatment methods that do not rely on personality theory to a significant extent. Treatment is usually brief, includes both partners whenever possible, and is typically successful. This has led to a major revision in thinking about the causes of sexual problems, and the idea that deep-seated character disturbances are at the root of these difficulties has been all but abandoned.

So, in sum, the causes of sexual problems are combinations of the very kinds of factors reviewed in earlier chapters—situational variables, thinking patterns and beliefs, emotional conditioning, rare organic problems, and poor technique.

This prompts us to include a word about language. Few other mental health areas have remained so wedded by language to a moralistic view of causes. The very words that have been used to describe sexual dysfunctions, even by professionals, betray this bias: *inadequacy, impotence* (literally the lack of power), *frigidity,* erectile *failure, technique, achieving* an orgasm, premature or *retarded* ejaculation, *successful* intercourse. The words are loaded with overtones of achievement, competition, shame, and personal blame. It is astounding how recently professional consciousness has been raised as to the overtones of this terminology.

Treatment

The treatment of sexual dysfunctions is a specialized expertise requiring extensive training and supervision.[28] It would be possible to describe a variety of specific techniques that have been developed, but to do so would be to belie the complexity and sensitivity of their application. Standard training in a discipline such as psychology, medicine, social work, or pastoral counseling does not prepare a professional to provide competent treatment for sexual dysfunctions. There are specific treatment approaches to be learned and applied, personal blind spots and inhibitions and biases to overcome. In short, this is no place for an amateur or for a professional who has not had the proper training.

Certification and licensure of sex therapy professionals is still at an early stage. The yellow pages, magazines, news media, and mental health networks are filled with offers from charlatans and ill-prepared "sex therapists."

Recognize that the term *sex therapist* is rarely restricted and can be claimed by *anyone*. This area particularly draws the incompetent, providing voyeuristically stimulating access to the most intimate details of peoples' lives. Referrals should be made with great caution, following some of the suggestions provided in chapter 19.

With regard to your own pastoral counseling, we offer the following recommendations:

1. Maintain an openness to the area of human sexuality, making it safe for people to talk about this intimate area of their lives. A nonjudgmental attitude combined with reflective listening promotes this kind of openness.

2. At the same time avoid exploitation. The details of peoples' sex lives can be interesting and stimulating, but there is no need to elicit and explore these in most cases unless a particular intervention is planned.

3. Where sexual dysfunctions seem to play an important role in relationship problems, refer the couple for treatment of this specific difficulty. This does not require a total turning-over of the case to another professional. Marital counseling, for example, may well continue during or resume after the treatment of sexual dysfunction.

4. Refer to a competent and well-trained professional with specific background in modern methods of sex therapy.

5. Follow up on the referral. Make sure the contact was made, that the couple is satisfied with the process, and that reasonable progress is being made. A collaborative relationship between pastor and sex therapist can be beneficial. Sex therapy often involves issues that have significant moral and religious overtones for individuals. A competent sex therapist may prescribe, for good reason, masturbation, reading of sexually stimulating material, periods of sexual abstinence, or the therapeutic use of a sexual aid such as a vibrator. The question, "Will this help?" is one that can be answered by the sex therapist, but other questions may arise for which you as a pastor can facilitate understanding and progress—"Is it OK to do this?" "Is this wrong?" or "Am I violating my religion?"

A wide variety of self-help books are available in this area. A few of the better ones are listed at the end of this chapter. Most of these are totally unevaluated—little is known about their potential to help or do harm. A few have shown some promise in guiding self-directed treatment of sexual problems.[29] The others listed contain mostly methods that have been well supported when administered by a skilled sex therapist but that are of unknown value in book form. These resources can be used to familiarize you or your clients with modern methods of intervention for sexual problems.

AIDS

Before the 1980s, acquired immune deficiency syndrome (AIDS) was unknown. Its discovery and spread have markedly altered sexual relationships, and first-hand ministry to AIDS victims and their families is an increasingly common pastoral responsibility. The disease begins with infection by the human immunodeficiency virus (HIV), which may yield no symptoms for many years before the disease, AIDS, is diagnosed. During this period, others may be unknowingly infected.

HIV infection requires direct contact with contaminated body fluids and does not occur through touching, hugging, kissing, sharing eating utensils, or breathing the same air. The primary routes of transmission are through sexual intercourse and the sharing (by drug users) of contaminated needles. Five kinds of sexual behavior seem to pose the highest risk for transmission of HIV: extramarital affairs, prostitution, anal intercourse, bisexual relations, and sexual contact with intravenous drug users or other high-risk groups.[30] Risk increases with the number of sexual partners and can be dramatically reduced, but not eliminated, by the use of condoms. Men are more likely to infect their partners than are women, and heterosexual transmission is increasingly common. The use of alcohol or other drugs increases risk of infection, primarily because it is associated with unprotected and high risk sexual behavior.

The worldwide AIDS epidemic will claim millions of lives. The search is ongoing for effective cure and prevention measures, but the fact remains that this cause of death is almost completely preventable—at the individual level, at least—through behavior change. Here is a larger and vital task for pastoral ministry. Your own denomination may have specific programs for addressing AIDS.

Paraphilias

Sexual *dysfunctions*, discussed above, are problems that emerge in normal sexual arousal. A different class of problems is termed *paraphilia* (formerly *sexual deviation*) because the behavior or the source of arousal is considered by society to be inappropriate, abnormal, or criminal.

Paraphilias represent some of the most emotionally loaded disorders, taxing one's ability to maintain a sense of objectivity and understanding. Such behavior can be shocking, repulsive, horrifying to even a seasoned counselor not accustomed to working in this area. Moral and legal issues are directly involved. There is a tendency in our society to see individuals who engage in paraphilias as nonpersons—as deviates, criminals, perverts, sick and disturbed and hopeless people. Law enforcement officials are often highly upset and motivated to "put these people away." Friends and family may be stunned and ashamed.

Such reactions are understandable within the social context, and we do not mean to imply that paraphilias should be approved, permitted, sanctioned, or ignored. We are concerned, however, that in many cases there is no advocate for the offender except, perhaps, a defense attorney. The person is vilified by the public and sometimes the press, abandoned by friends and family, and in some cases sent to prison where brutalization and depersonalization accelerate the problem. If believers are called to minister to the despised and rejected of our land, here are some obvious candidates.

The paraphilias that we will discuss all have in common one fact: The individual is sexually aroused by sources or behaviors that are socially regarded as abnormal. The person may simply prefer and choose this method of sexual excitement or may be incapable of becoming aroused without it.

A more common example is *exhibitionism*, which involves achieving sexual excitement by exposing one's genitals to unwilling and unsuspecting strangers. The shock reaction of the stranger seems itself to be a source of gratification. This is primarily a male phenomenon in our society, although rare female cases have been reported. Exhibitionism should not be confused with exposure to willing audiences for purposes of entertainment.

Voyeurism is a pattern of seeking sexual arousal by watching unsuspecting people undress or engage in sexual activity. The observing itself is arousing, and no attempt is made to contact or assault the victim. Voyeurism or exhibitionism, however, may escalate to more violent crimes.

Transvestism is diagnosed only in heterosexual men and involves dressing in female clothing for purposes of sexual excitement. The cross-dressing is not done for the entertainment of others but is sought for its arousing value.

Some people rely on certain objects (especially articles of clothing) for sexual arousal, a pattern termed *fetishism*, or more rarely engage in sexual acts with animals.

The sexual abuse of children has received increasing attention in recent years. Current estimates indicate that at some time during childhood between one-fourth and one-third of all girls are sexually victimized by an adult; among boys, between one in seven and one in eleven are victims.[31] Some such occurrences are isolated incidents, but others are carried out by adults who prefer and seek arousal through sexual contact with children (*pedophilia*). Again this is predominantly a male problem. Sometimes the child is a stranger but most often is a relative or acquaintance. Interestingly, pedophilia is sometimes associated with otherwise high moral standards and often occurs among men who are married and have intact heterosexual relationships. Sometimes parental abuse of children occurs with the knowledge of the other parent, but often not. Threats or persuasion may be used to keep the child from disclosing what is happening.

Sadism in its true clinical sense means achieving sexual arousal through the inflicting of pain and humiliation on a willing or unwilling partner. Sometimes cooperative partners can be found who are sexually aroused by being physically beaten, bound, or otherwise caused to suffer (*masochism*). In other cases there is a pattern of assaulting unwilling victims. A proportion of rape cases can be accounted for by sexual sadism, although many rapes are primarily violent rather than sexual acts.

Treatment

Although there is a growing body of research on the treatment of paraphilias, society's primary means for dealing with the problem continues to be imprisonment and other forms of punishment. Yet punitive measures have been notoriously ineffective in changing these patterns, neither correcting the problem nor protecting society from these individuals who are ultimately released. In addition, the experience of prison may substantially complicate and expand the problem. Sex offenders are typically the most despised of prisoners and are frequently the targets of physical and sexual violence from inmates as well as scorn and psychological abuse from staff. Imprisonment accomplishes only revenge and a brief removal from society. Upon release, society is left with a free and possibly more dangerous person than it imprisoned.

Promising alternatives have begun to appear. Aversion therapies have been used successfully to suppress arousal attached to the problem pattern, particularly when combined with techniques to increase normal sexual arousal.[32] The teaching of crucial social skills, often lacking in sex offenders, can also be beneficial. The modification of patterns of sexual fantasy is likewise a critical step in changing deviant arousal. Relapse prevention strategies are being tested. Much work still needs to be done, but several things seem clear: (a) It is sometimes possible to alter deviant patterns of arousal and to shift them toward normal patterns. (b) It is often possible to suppress deviant sexual behavior, particularly if it can be replaced by more normal channels for sexual fulfillment. (c) Consequently, it is possible to treat many sex offenders rather than merely imprison them. The prognosis for successful treatment seems to be better for child molesters than for rapists. The importance of confinement of offenders should be decided in part on the seriousness of potential recidivism. Imprisonment may be disproportionately severe for exhibitionists without a history of violence, who are not helped by internment alone. Violent sadism, on the other hand, poses more severe threats to public safety should offenses recur. We reemphasize, however, that confinement alone provides little or no long-term protection for society. Effective treatment, where available, should be undertaken either as an alternative or as a complement to institutionalization.

Homosexuality

Finally, a few words are in order regarding homosexuality. Whereas this was once regarded as a form of sexual deviation, most psychological and psychiatric professionals no longer regard homosexuality to be pathological. Like heterosexuality, homosexuality can be accompanied by either normal or abnormal personal adjustment.

The origins of homosexuality are still unclear. Some experts believe there are substantial inborn determinants, consistent with the report of homosexual people that they recognized or realized their different preference at some time during adolescence. Others emphasize learning factors in the development of sexual preference.[33]

Also unclear is the extent to which sexual preference can be changed once it has been established, whatever its origin. Some people who experience themselves as homosexual are distressed by this fact and seek to change their sexual preference for personal, moral, religious, or psychological reasons. Various approaches have been tried in helping such people to change, and it is fair to say that thus far none has been terribly successful. There are, of course, isolated cases of successful and dramatic change in sexual preference after everything from extensive reconditioning to simple prayer. For better or for worse, there is no guaranteed or even usually effective method that has been identified thus far. Some therapists who have been engaged in research on sexual preference change now dissuade colleagues from pursuing such a treatment goal and regard the pursuit of this goal to be ethically questionable.

At any rate the consensus among mental health professionals since 1980 has been that homosexuality per se does not represent abnormality or psychological disorder.[34] Whether sexual preference should or even can be changed remains unclear. Within faith circles, denominational statements and policies on homosexuality vary widely.

FAMILY THERAPY

The 1970s and 1980s brought a large upswing in the popularity of family therapy, in which all or most members of the immediate or extended family come in for joint counseling. Two major approaches have emerged—behavioral family therapy and family systems intervention—and have been described earlier. A detailed exposition of these methods is well beyond the scope of this book and is available elsewhere in references provided at the end of this chapter. We will, however, try to tie together some loose ends.

By far, the heaviest emphasis in almost all family intervention systems is communication. Thomas Gordon's enduringly popular Parent Effectiveness Training (PET), for example, draws on the basic principles of Carl Rogers' system of personality and interpersonal intervention, focusing heavily on the kind of listening skills outlined in chapter 5 and the negotiation process discussed earlier in this chapter.[35] Transactional analysis also provided a conceptual framework for understanding communication patterns within a family or other social system.[36]

A slightly different emphasis shares Gordon's assumption that parents can learn useful skills for dealing with their children, but draws instead on basic principles of learning. Parents are taught, in essence, to be better behavior changers.[37] Most parents are already trying to shape and change their children's behavior but may be doing so in ineffective or even damaging ways. Behavioral family therapy teaches behavior-change strategies for parents (or teachers) with special emphasis on positive reinforcement. The desired result is not rigidity or a military camp atmosphere, but rather smoother communication, clearer rules, and a higher level of positive exchanges with the family. There is a large scientific literature supporting the effectiveness of this approach for coping with children's behavior problems,[38] and some useful self-help resources have been developed (see Additional Readings at the end of this chapter).

Many of the intervention methods described earlier for marital counseling and enrichment can also be applied to the larger family system. It is often beneficial, for example, to work toward increasing the overall level of positive exchanges within the family. The "family conference" method discussed in this chapter can be used to help all members of the family request and receive help toward reaching positive goals. The negotiation techniques of PET or behavioral family therapy also help to decrease negative exchanges and enduring conflicts.

Like marital and sex therapy, family therapy is a complicated process. The methods described earlier in this chapter may be helpful when applied toward the enrichment of relatively stable families or the resolution of less entrenched or generalized problems. Families with more pervasive and disturbed patterns of difficulty are likely to benefit from the attention of a skilled family therapist experienced in intervening with such entangled networks of individuals. When violence is part of the family, sound treatment is particularly vital, and effective behavioral family therapy approaches have been developed and tested.[39]

Beyond family communication issues, involvement of family members can also be beneficial in treating particular kinds of problems. The successful treatment of anorexia nervosa often involves intervention with the entire family system. The probability of relapse in cases of alcoholism can also be decreased by including the family in treatment. In such cases, when the individual's problems are intimately intertwined with family patterns, it may be shortsighted to seek resolution through individual counseling alone.

WHEN RELATIONSHIPS END

Relationships don't always make it. Sometimes the best (or at least the chosen) route involves dissolution. Divorce and separation are not what anyone intended. Most religions hold that this is not what God intended, but it occurs.

What is your role as a pastor when divorce comes? There are a number of ways in which you can help. The first of these is by not abandoning the individuals involved. If both have been members of the congregation, a difficult period may follow. Both the divorcees and other members of the congregation may perceive a need to "choose." Who will be the friends of each partner? Who will remain in the congregation and who will leave? It's as if friends and social circles must be divided up like property. This is not necessarily so, but is one reason why some individuals become alienated from friends, the congregation, their pastor, and even from their faith, or at least organized religion, during the divorce process.

What's Going On?

When an individual faces the reality of separation, a very difficult adjustment process begins. Stephen Johnson and others have described stages through which many divorcees pass, each requiring a particular adjustment or skill.[40] We will try to distill these into several general processes and indicate how you can help with each one.

The first stage was called by Johnson "separation craziness." This is a period of great emotional flux. The person may experience a kind of roller coaster emotional life—feeling free and on top of the world at one moment, down and in despair and helpless at the next. This is normal. Your counseling task here is to provide support and reassurance, to help the person ride through the emotional swings and begin the process of sorting out her or his life. It is analogous to the clarification stage of counseling, calling for lots of reflective listening.

A process that has been called *denial* may occur, manifested particularly in actions that maintain ties and bonds with the ex-partner. A spouse who has moved out may leave a large number of personal possessions in the house, necessitating continual "stopping by." A partner who "keeps the house" may call the ex-spouse continually to attend to tasks that he or she formerly handled. There may be desperate midnight telephone calls, casual "how are you doing" calls or visits, nonaccidental meetings at places where the spouse is predictably found. All express a reluctance to give up contact, to let go. When children are involved, the picture is still more complicated, since a certain amount of regular contact is inevitable and the children themselves may retain fantasies of reuniting the parents. The crucial step here is *letting go* physically and psychologically, usually in that order. The hanging-on partner is encouraged to stop initiating contact, to give back the key, to move out the final possessions, to find other ways of coping with problems formerly handled by the spouse. There are always rationalizations—it's just more convenient, cheaper, or really not a problem. The fact is that it is difficult to break psychological dependence without a period of physical independence.

Soon there is the task of letting other important people know what has happened. This can be done actively, or the person can wait passively for the news to spread. Invariably, each partner will also encounter acquaintances who do not know and who ask about the spouse. Here the task described by Johnson is that of preparing one's story. An important prerequisite of this is coming to one's own personal explanation of what happened. People have a need to understand what caused a negative experience, to find an explanation that is satisfying. Having done so, the person prepares to tell others. The amount shared will vary with how close one is to the listener. Johnson recommends developing and practicing (with the counselor, perhaps) a longer account for closest friends, a briefer account for acquaintances (maybe two minutes in length), and a very brief statement for general use ("Oh, haven't you heard? It didn't work out."). Rehearsing these various stories with your client can be beneficial in dealing with the question, "How can I tell _____?" Johnson also recommended that the divorced individual take an active role in the telling process, making a systematic pilgrimage to visit every important person and tell the story, at least briefly. This renews the individual's connection with each, resolves some of the discomfort about who knows what, and begins the definition of new relationships independent of the spouse.

Friendships that have involved both partners pose a special challenge. Friends don't know what to do or say. They don't know how to treat each partner, are confused about whether they have to choose, and are reluctant to do so. In this confusion, friends may simply avoid the person out of discomfort. There may also be additional issues, such as an unspoken fear that this single and newly available person may have designs on one's spouse or may threaten one's marriage by showing that it is possible to leave when discontented. For these and other reasons, the divorced person may be thrust out of old friendships with married people. One way to prevent this, in part, is to make the contact and help these friends know how to relate. Johnson suggested taking literally the friendly offer, "If there's anything I can do . . ." and giving friends specific requests for what is needed.

New friendships must also be formed, and the person is thrust suddenly back into the single world. It is tempting at this stage simply to find a suitable new partner and quickly form a new bond, responding to the feeling that one is half a person in search of the other half. Johnson argued persuasively for the establishment of *autonomous adulthood*, which means redefining oneself as a single, individual, worthwhile person. It is logical in this process to seek the company of other single people, but herein lies another shock. Perhaps the last time the person was single and dating was in high school, and the single-person skills one has may be those left over from this turbulent period of adolescence. Badly out of practice, the newly single person quickly encounters the rather assertive world of adult singles and what may seem a callous, casual, and embarrassingly forthright view of sexuality and relationships.

Along the way there is also grieving. The loss of a relationship is in many ways similar to grieving a death, but society provides few overt symbols and rituals to mark the close or transition. There is no funeral, no memorial service, no gathering of supportive family and friends, no formal rite of passage. The stages of shock, anger, or dejection described in chapter 12 also apply here, and you should be alert for them. As with all grieving, the transition and adjustment process is a normal one, but it can become abnormally frozen or prolonged.

There are new skills to learn for many people undergoing divorce. The division of labor that has been typical of many relationships can mean that there are various tasks that have never or seldom been performed by one spouse—cleaning the furnace, servicing the car or putting in gasoline (or even driving itself), cooking a basic meal, washing clothes, putting a fire in the fireplace, operating a cantankerous appliance, or balancing the checkbook. Repairs, maintenance, planning, details, basic survival skills—all may require new learning, and each provides a new frustration and perhaps a painful reminder of how things once were. The way through these problems to autonomous adulthood, of course, is to learn the needed skills. This not only reduces the problems inherent in daily living but also provides a valuable sense of mastery and self-esteem.

There are also major transitions for some—finding a place to live, locating competent child care, finding a job after not working for twenty years. In these major transitions, as in the smaller tasks above, the extended community of a congregation can be invaluable. Some ways in which the faith community can be involved in the helping process are discussed in chapter 20. Some congregations launch a specialized singles ministry to reach out to single adults by providing creative programs, social events, and a helping network for coping with practical problems.

Beyond the crises and transitions of readjustment lie the challenges of developing new intimacy. The scars of a dissolved relationship can leave one reluctant to trust again, anxious about entering into a new commitment. Religious teachings and attitudes on divorce may foster further reservations, as may a subtle sense of duty to the previous spouse (much more intense in the widowed than in the divorced). The intimacy numbness, which in some ways resembles that of posttraumatic shock described in chapter 14, normally passes with time as new relationships grow. A talking-through process with the pastor or other supportive people can be helpful.

This raises the possibility of a specialized support group for people going through the divorce process. One obvious benefit is the mutual support that can be provided by others who are experiencing or have experienced the same adjustment process. A group of this kind is often constituted of people at many different stages in the process—some are still acutely grieving the loss and are riding the emotional roller coaster, others are in the midst of learning needed coping skills, some have told their friends and others are planning to do so, some are beginning new intimate relationships and others cannot imagine even wanting to do so. A developmental model such as that proposed by

Johnson can provide a stimulating structure for a series of meetings, after which the group may choose to continue in a less structured supportive format. A facilitator who has been through the divorce process is often valued, though not essential. In such groups little coaxing is needed to get people to talk. A minimal door-opener unleashes a torrent of personal revelations, questions, searching, emotions. As usual, reflective listening is a crucial skill for the group facilitator in helping the participants grow through awareness, acceptance, and the discovery of alternatives.

Finally, what about the children? Perhaps the biggest contribution that you can make to the future mental health of children experiencing divorce is to help their parents manage conflict. Research indicates that the adverse effects of divorce itself on children are relatively small on average, though there are always exceptions. The negative effect that does occur seems to be most related to continuing parental conflict associated with the divorce. When divorced parents can maintain a reasonably harmonious relationship or at least a low level of conflict, children often manage rather well. Remarriage, by the way, does not seem to significantly influence the overall adjustment of children one way or the other.[41]

SUMMARY

Relationships, like all living things, need regular care and feeding. A sound relationship is one that is chosen by autonomous people who are committed to the growth and happiness of each other, that includes flexibility and methods for change initiated by either partner, and that is characterized by mutual commitment and shared intimacy. Over the natural history of intimate relationships, certain natural changes occur. These can be negotiated well if the individuals are prepared for them, and potential negative aspects of these changes can be avoided. Among these changes are loss of novelty, discrepancies in expectations, decrease in positive and increase in negative shared experiences, conflicts and transitions, growing apart, and certain cognitive shifts. Distressed couples often fail to seek outside help because of common beliefs favoring isolation and discouraging open discussion of relationship problems. Positive change is usually easier when couples seek help sooner, although healing is a real possibility even in very damaged relationships.

Relationship counseling raises special issues and difficulties beyond those encountered in individual counseling. These include privacy of information between partners, transiton from individual to joint counseling, maintaining balanced attention to partners, dealing with uncooperative partners, and responding to the risk and reality of family violence. The first interview often sets the tone for the course of relationship counseling, and it is important to retain control over this session and move it toward positive healing.

There are many strategies for helping relationships to grow or heal. Among the strategies discussed here are improving communication, teaching conflict resolution and problem-solving skills, increasing shared positive experiences and decreasing negative exchanges, altering cognitive patterns, and fostering an active, change-oriented attitude.

More complicated relationship counseling may require skills beyond those of the average pastor. Selection of a competent professional marriage and family therapist is an important process. Both behavioral and family systems approaches to relationship therapy have received support from current research.

Sexual dysfunctions are difficulties commonly encountered in sexual relationships. Survey data indicate that at least half of all couples are currently experiencing such dissatisfactions in their relationships. Sexual dysfunctions are quite treatable and often can be resolved within a relatively short period of competent sex therapy. Pastoral counseling may be helpful in reducing anxiety and fostering more healthy and relaxed attitudes toward sexuality. More direct interventions will usually require the consultation of a properly trained sex therapist, although self-help resources have been found to be helpful in some cases.

Paraphilias involve arousal from sources or behaviors that are considered to be abnormal. Punishment and incarceration may be necessary in certain cases, especially those involving violent sex offenders, but they accomplish little toward the rehabilitation of the individual. Effective treatment is a desirable alternative or addition to imprisonment.

Individuals experiencing the end of an intimate relationship often progress through a series of predictable steps and problems in the transition to single living. Understanding these steps and sharing the journey with others can smooth and speed the transition.

ADDITIONAL READINGS

For the Counselor

Couples Counseling and Relationship Enhancement

CLINEBELL, HOWARD J. *Growth Counseling for Marriage Enrichment: Pre-marriage and the Early Years.* Philadelphia: Fortress Press, 1975.

GUERNEY, BERNARD G., JR. *Relationship Enhancement.* San Francisco: Jossey-Bass, 1977. A classic from a recognized pioneer in the field.

JACOBSON, NEIL S., and GAYLA MARGOLIN *Marital Therapy.* New York: Brunner/Mazel, 1979. Specific, practical strategies for couples counseling.

MACE, DAVID R. *Close Companions: The Marriage Enrichment Handbook.* New York: Continuum, 1983.

MACE, DAVID R., ed. *Modern Marriage and the Clergy*. New York: Human Sciences Press, 1978.

MARTIN, GRANT L. *Counseling for Family Violence and Abuse*. Dallas: Word Publishing, 1987.

MYERS, ISABEL B., and PETER B. MEYERS *Gifts Differing*. Palo Alto, CA: Consulting Psychologists Press, 1980. An introduction to the use of the Myers-Briggs Type Indicator, a valuable and spiritually relevant instrument for assessing and counseling about differences within relationships.

OHLSEN, MERLE M. *Marriage Counseling in Groups*. Champaign, IL: Research Press, 1979.

RASSIEUR, CHARLES L. *Pastor, Our Marriage Is in Trouble: A Guide to Short-Term Counseling*. Binghamton, NY: Haworth Press, 1988.

STUART, RICHARD B. *Helping Couples Change*. Champaign, IL: Research Press, 1980.

VESPER, JOYCE H., and GREGORY W. BROCK *Ethics, Legalities and Professional Practice Issues in Marriage and Family Therapy*. Needham Heights, MA: Allyn & Bacon, 1991.

Families and Family Therapy

FRIEDMAN, EDWIN H. *Generation to Generation: Family Process in Church and Synagogue*. New York: Guilford Press, 1985.

———— *Friedman's Fables*. New York, Guilford Press, 1989. A fascinating set of therapeutic stories. Also available in cassette form. A booklet of discussion questions is available for use with church groups.

LEDERER, WILLIAM J., and DON D. JACKSON *The Mirages of Marriage*. New York: Norton, 1968. A classic family systems view of marriage—clearly written, if somewhat dated.

REKERS, GEORGE A. *Counseling Families*. Dallas: Word, 1988. Reviews family therapy approaches, placing them in biblical context.

WYNN, J. C. *Family Therapy in Pastoral Ministry*. San Francisco: Harper, 1982.

Family Aggression and Violence

NEIDIG, PETER H., and DALE H. FRIEDMAN *Spouse Abuse: A Treatment Program for Couples*. Champaign, IL: Research Press, 1984.

PATTERSON, GERALD R. *Coercive Family Process*. Eugene, OR: Castalia Publishing, 1982. A superb compendium of modern research and family approaches for dealing with aggressive children and adolescents. Patterson's work on the prevention and treatment of aggression is internationally recognized. This is the third volume in an excellent series on families with aggressive children.

Sexuality and Sexual Counseling

DIAMANT, LOUIS, ed. *Male and Female Homosexuality*. Washington, DC: Hemisphere Publishing, 1987.

KAPLAN, HELEN SINGER *The Illustrated Manual of Sex Therapy*, 2d ed. New York: Brunner/Mazel, 1987.

KENNEDY, EUGENE *Sexual Counseling: A Practical Guide for Those Who Help Others*. New York: Continuum, 1989.

MASTERS, WILLIAM H., and VIRGINIA E. JOHNSON *Human Sexual Response*. New York: Bantam, 1981. Their original landmark research on the nature of normal human sexual behavior and its physiology.

For Clients

Relationships

BARBACH, LONNIE, and DAVID L. GEISINGER *Going the Distance: Finding and Keeping Lifelong Love.* New York: Plume, 1993.

BECK, AARON T. *Love Is Never Enough: How Couples Can Overcome Misunderstandings, Resolve Conflicts, and Solve Relationship Problems through Cognitive Therapy.* New York: Harper & Row, 1988.

CALDEN, GEORGE *I Count, You Count: The "Do It Ourselves" Marriage Counseling and Enrichment Book.* Niles, IL: Argus Communications, 1976.

CAMPBELL, SUSAN M. *The Couple's Journey: Intimacy as a Path to Wholeness.* San Luis Obispo, CA: Impact, 1980.

FAY, ALLEN *PQR: Prescription for a Quality Relationship.* New York: Multimodal Press, 1988.

GOTTMAN, JOHN *A Couple's Guide to Communication.* Champaign, IL: Research Press, 1976.

MACE, DAVID, and VERA MACE *How to Have a Happy Marriage.* Nashville, TN: Abingdon, 1977.

STUART, RICHARD B., and BARBARA JACOBSEN *Second Marriage: Make It Happy! Make It Last!* New York: Norton, 1985. Sound advice on relationships in general.

VISCOTT, DAVID *How to Live with Another Person.* New York: Arbor House, 1974.

Family Living and Parenting

DINKMEYER, DON, GARY D. MCKAY, and JOYCE L. MCKAY *New Beginnings: Skills for Single Parents and Stepfamily Parents.* Champaign, IL: Research Press, 1987.

GORDON, THOMAS *Parent Effectiveness Training.* New York: Wyden, 1970. This is the original source book for Gordon's popular PET program to teach communication skills useful in parenting, based on the work of Carl Rogers.

PATTERSON, GERALD, and MARION FORGATCH *Parents and Adolescents: Living Together.* Volume 1: *The Basics.* Volume 2: *Family Problem Solving.* Eugene, OR: Castalia Publishing, 1987, 1989. In our opinion, one of the best skill-building resources for parents of adolescents.

WAGONSELLER, BILL R., and RICHARD L. MCDOWELL *You and Your Child: A Common Sense Approach to Successful Parenting.* Champaign, IL: Research Press, 1979. A good overview of communication and behavior change skills for parents.

Sexuality

BARBACH, LONNIE GARFIELD *For Yourself: The Fulfillment of Female Sexuality.* New York: Doubleday, 1975.

HEIMAN, JULIA, and JOSEPH LOPICCOLO *Becoming Orgasmic: A Personal and Sexual Growth Program for Women* (rev. ed.). Englewood Cliffs, NJ: Prentice-Hall, 1988.

KAPLAN, HELEN SINGER *PE: How to Overcome Premature Ejaculation.* New York: Brunner/Mazel, 1989.

NOWINSKI, JOSEPH *Men, Love and Sex: A Guide to Sexual Fulfillment for Couples.* London: Harper Collins, 1990. A well-written self-help resource to help couples deal with common male sexual dysfunctions, including erectile difficulties and premature ejaculation.

PENNER, C., and J. PENNER *The Gift of Sex: A Christian Guide to Sexual Fulfillment.* Dallas: Word, 1981.

SWITZER, DAVID K., and SHIRLEY A. SWITZER *Parents of the Homosexual.* Philadelphia: Westminster Press, 1980.

WILLIAMS, WARWICK *Rekindling Desire: Bringing Your Sexual Relationship Back to Life.* Oakland, CA: New Harbinger Publications, 1988.

Divorce

FISHER, BRUCE *Rebuilding: When Your Relationship Ends.* San Luis Obispo, CA: Impact, 1981.

KRANZLER, MEL *Learning to Love Again.* New York: Harper & Row, 1977.

LUBETKIN, BARRY, and ELENA OUMANO *Bailing Out: The Healthy Way to Get Out of a Bad Relationship and Survive.* New York: Prentice-Hall Press, 1991.

MEYERS, MICHAEL F. *Men and Divorce.* New York: Guilford Press, 1989.

NOTES

[1]Stephen M. Johnson, *First Person Singular: A Guide to the Good Life Alone* (Philadelphia: Lippincott, 1977).

[2]Kahlil Gibran, *The Prophet* (New York: Knopf, 1923).

[3]Viktor E. Frankl, *The Will to Meaning* (Cleveland: World Publishing, 1969).

[4]Erich Fromm, *The Art of Loving* (New York: Harper & Row, 1956); Harry Stack Sullivan, *The Interpersonal Theory of Psychiatry* (New York: Norton, 1953).

[5]Antoine de Saint Exupery, *The Little Prince* (New York: Harcourt Brace Jovanovich, 1943).

[6]A classic statement of this ethic is found in the "gestalt prayer" of Fritz Perls, which adorned popular posters and is found at the front of his book, *Gestalt Therapy Verbatim* (Lafayette, CA: Real People Press, 1969), 4.

[7]George Bernard Shaw, "Preface," in *Getting Married* (New York: Brentano's, 1911).

[8]Eliot Aronson, "Some Antecedents of Interpersonal Attraction," Nebraska Symposium on Motivation, 1969: 143–73.

[9]William R. Miller, *Living As If* (Philadelphia: Westminster Press, 1985).

[10]David R. Mace, "Marriage Concepts for Research," *Family Coordinator* 24 (1975): 171–73.

[11]Thomas Gordon, *Parent Effectiveness Training* (New York: Wyden, 1970).

[12]A sequence of specific exercises for teaching reflective listening can be found in chapter 10 of William R. Miller and Stephen Rollnick's *Motivational Interviewing* (New York: Guilford Press, 1991).

[13]Gordon, *Parent Effectiveness Training.*

[14]Isabel B. Myers and Mary H. McCaulley, *Manual: A Guide to the Development and Use of the Myers-Briggs Type Indicator* (Palo Alto, CA: Consulting Psychologists Press, 1985).

[15]Isabel B. Myers and Peter B. Myers, *Gifts Differing* (Palo Alto, CA: Consulting Psychologists Press, 1976).

[16]Case description in William R. Miller and Brian G. Danaher, "Maintenance in Parent Training," in John D. Krumboltz and Carl E. Thoresen, eds., *Counseling Methods* (New York: Holt, Rinehart & Winston, 1976), 434–44.

[17]Kurt Hahlweg and Howard J. Markman, "The Effectiveness of Behavioral Marital Therapy: Empirical Status of Behavioral Techniques in Prevention and Alleviating Marital Distress," *Journal of Consulting and Clinical Psychology* 56 (1988): 440–47.

[18]Richard B. Stuart, *Helping Couples Change* (New York: Guilford Press, 1980); Robert L. Weiss, "Contracts, Cognition and Change: A Behavioral Approach to Marriage Therapy,"

Counseling Psychologist 5 (1975): 15–26; Neal E. Jacobson and Gayla Margolin, *Marital Therapy* (New York: Brunner/Mazel, 1979); Gerald R. Patterson and Marion Forgatch, *Parents and Adolescents Living Together* (Eugene, OR: Castalia Publishing, 1987).

[19]Jay Haley, *Problem Solving Therapy*, 2d ed. (San Francisco: Jossey-Bass, 1991). See also *The Power Tactics of Jesus Christ* (New York: Norton, 1989); Virginia Satir, *Conjoint Family Therapy* (Palo Alto, CA: Science and Behavior Books, 1967); Salvador Minuchin, *Families and Family Therapy* (Cambridge, MA: Harvard University Press, 1974).

[20]Gayla Margolin and Bonnie Burman, "Wife Abuse versus Marital Violence: Different Terminologies, Explanations, and Solutions," *Clinical Psychology Review 13* (1993): 59–73.

[21]Gerald R. Patterson, *Coercive Family Process* (Eugene, OR: Castalia Publishing, 1982).

[22]Grant L. Martin, *Counseling for Family Violence and Abuse* (Dallas, TX: Word, 1987).

[23]K. Daniel O'Leary, Dina Vivian, and Jean Malone, "Assessment of Physical Aggression against Women in Marriage: The Need for Multimodal Assessment," *Behavioral Assessment 14* (1992): 5–14.

[24]Ellen Frank, Carol Anderson, and Debra Rubenstein, "Frequency of Sexual Dysfunction in 'Normal' Couples," *New England Journal of Medicine* 299 (1978): 111–15.

[25]William H. Masters and Virginia E. Johnson, *Human Sexual Response* (Boston: Little, Brown, 1966).

[26]The most recent revision of the psychiatric diagnostic system for sexual disorders retains this classification according to the stages of arousal first defined by Masters and Johnson: American Psychiatric Association, Diagnostic and Statistical Manual of Mental Disorders, 4th ed. (Washington, DC: American Psychiatric Association, 1994).

[27]William H. Masters and Virginia E. Johnson, *Human Sexual Inadequacy* (Boston: Little, Brown, 1970).

[28]Joseph LoPiccolo, "Treatment of Sexual Dysfunction," in Alan S. Bellack, Michel Hersen, and Alan E. Kazdin, eds., *International Handbook of Behavior Modification and Therapy*, 2d ed. (New York: Plenum Press, 1990).

[29]For example, see Robert A. Zeiss, "Self-directed Treatment for Premature Ejaculation," *Journal of Consulting and Clinical Psychology* 6 (1978): 1234–41.

[30]J. M. Reinisch, S. A. Sanders, and M. Ziemba-Davis, "The Study of Sexual Behavior in Relation the Transmission of Human Immunodeficiency Virus: Caveats and Recommendations," *American Psychologist* 43 (1988): 921–27.

[31]Frank G. Bolton Jr., Larry A. Morris, and Ann E. MacEachron, *Men at Risk: The Other Side of Child Sexual Abuse* (Newbury Park, CA: Sage Publications, 1989); Lenore E. A. Walker, ed., *Handbook on Sexual Abuse of Children: Assessment and Treatment Issues* (New York: Springer, 1988).

[32]Barry Maletzky, *Treating the Sexual Offender* (Newbury Park, CA: Sage Publications, 1991).

[33]William H. Masters and Virginia E. Johnson, *Homosexuality in Perspective* (Boston: Little, Brown, 1979).

[34]The American Psychiatric Association's *Diagnostic and Statistical Manual of Mental Disorders*, 3d ed. (Washington, DC: APA, 1980), regarded homosexuality as problematic only when the individual indicates that it is unwanted and distressing. The 1994 edition retains only a single line on distress related to sexual orientation.

[35]Gordon, *Parent Effectiveness Training*.

[36]Eric Berne, *Games People Play* (New York: Grove Press, 1964).

[37]Wesley C. Becker, *Parents Are Teachers* (Champaign, IL: Research Press, 1971).

[38]Alan S. Gurman, David P. Kniskern, and William M. Pinsof, "Research on the Process and Outcome of Marital and Family Therapy," in Sol S. Garfield and Allen E. Bergin, eds., *Handbook of Psychotherapy and Behavior Change* (New York: John Wiley, 1986), 565–624.

[39]Gerald R. Patterson, *Coercive Family Process* (Eugene, OR: Castalia Publishing, 1982).

[40]Johnson, *First Person Singular*.

[41]P. R. Amato and B. Keith, "Parental Divorce and the Well-being of Children: A Meta-analysis," *Psychological Bulletin* 110 (1991): 26–46.

19

TERMINATION AND REFERRAL

The end of one thing is the beginning of another. I am a pilgrim again.

—Yuichiro Miura, *The Man Who Skied Down Everest*

The words above are from Miura's journal after the bittersweet conclusion of one of the greatest challenges of his life—to ski down Mount Everest. Having finished this task, he sees that he is a pilgrim once more, one who is on a journey. The end of one thing is the beginning of anothesr.

So it is with pastoral counseling. The end of formal counseling is the beginning of something new for both pastor and client. A new relationship begins. When the client has been a parishioner, one might be tempted to say that an old relationship resumes at the end of counseling. Yet this is not so. A relationship is forever changed, usually though not always for the better, by the intimate sharing that is pastoral counseling.

The process that occurs during counseling is never truly finished, for it is the process of human change and growth. The individual who waited for all change to be accomplished, for all problems to cease before terminating a therapeutic relationship would be in counseling for life. The process goes on after counseling just as it did before and during this period. How then does one know when the time for counseling is over? Furthermore, it often happens that one partner in the counseling relationship senses the need for termination before the other does. Sometimes it is the counselor who reaches this awareness or decision first, and sometimes it is the client. How is this transition made gracefully and properly, and what happens afterward?

WHEN TO END COUNSELING

Sometimes pastoral counseling is brief. Often just a bit of listening, support, advice, or encouragement is needed, and no prolonged counseling relationship evolves. When counseling has extended over a span of time, however, the process of termination poses special issues and challenges, and one must decide when to end this special relationship. (We renew here our advice that there are good reasons to set counseling apart from other pastoral relationships and to have a clear beginning and ending. See chapter 2.)

There are several markers that indicate the time or necessity for ending a process of pastoral counseling. All of them are matters of judgment. The decision to terminate is one to be negotiated between pastor and client. In more difficult cases it can be helpful to consult with a knowledgeable supervisor or colleague. Following are a few common reasons for terminating the process of counseling.

Goal Attained   Sometimes counseling ends because the initial goal has been attained. A choice for which the individual sought counsel has been made; a life change has been accomplished. Of course, the attainment of the originally stated goal does not require termination. Very often the main focus of counseling turns out to be on something other than the first presenting problem.

Reasonable Progress   More often a goal is not fully realized, but reasonable progress has been made. A point is reached where a certain momentum has been started and it is likely that the client will be able to go on alone. The counselor may perceive this first and the client may express some reluctance, particularly if a level of dependence has been established. In such cases the counselor's expression of confidence in the client's ability to carry on can be a healthy message for the client to hear. At other times the client may decide first that it is time to go on alone. In such cases there is little therapeutic value in trying to persuade the individual that it is "too soon" (with the underlying implication that he or she is too weak, is too unsteady, and needs the helping guidance of the counselor). This raises a third reason for termination.

Client Decision   Sometimes a client decides unilaterally to terminate. If the counselor has legitimate concerns, these should be expressed, but it is usually prudent to assist rather than obstruct voluntary termination. The door can always be left open for renewed contact (unless termination is handled in a manner that causes alienation). The message "You're not ready" is usually an unhealthy one, serving the rescue needs of the counselor more than the welfare interests of the client. It is better to make the transition in a way that allows renewed contact without unnecessary obstacles. Some professionals are offended when a client terminates A.M.A.—against my advice—and communicate this in ways that roadblock a return: judgment, criticism, or threat. Others issue dire warnings so that the individual, if deciding to return, must face an embarrassing "I told you so!" The counselor, like the parent, faces the difficult challenge of encouraging and supporting independence even and especially when the outcome is not certain. To see the individual as too weak to go on alone is to risk creating a self-fulfilling prophecy. People are affected by how we see them![1]

Plateau Sometimes a prolonged plateau is reached in counseling, a period where no progress seems to be occurring. Such a period should always call you to reexamine what is happening and to consider alternatives. One alternative is to try something else, to explore a new avenue or begin a new intervention. Another alternative is termination or at least a temporary recess. Any such changes are, of course, negotiated with the client in direct discussion. Simply to announce such a plan is to risk communicating rejection and criticism—"You haven't been changing fast enough, so I'm going to send you away."

Referral Still another possible reason for termination is the realization that other specialized expertise is needed to help the client. Each professional has special skills and limitations. When the client's needs are beyond the expertise and competence of the counselor, referral should be made. Referral does not necessarily require termination of the pastoral counseling relationship. Some referrals are for particular kinds of evaluation or brief intervention, but referral of the individual to another primary care professional is one possible reason for termination.

Leaving Pastoral counselors sometimes leave. Pastors are transferred, accept a new call, retire, and change locations. When this occurs, counseling relationships also end. Usually, there is time to break the news and prepare, and it is best whenever possible for your clients to hear the news from you. With some advance time, you can evaluate progress, decide together what is still needed, and arrange where appropriate for referral.

The situation of a pastor leaving a congregation or parish is a special case that deserves comment. It happens sometimes that former parishioners continue to call a pastor for counseling months or even years after formal dissolution of the pastoral relationship. Some pastors are tempted to continue providing counseling in such cases, in person or by telephone or correspondence, but we strongly advise against it. This is a good example of failure to make an appropriate termination of the special counseling relationship. First, you are probably no longer in the first-hand contact that allows for good judgment and pastoral care. Despite the person's perceptions that only you understand and can help, someone close at hand is a more appropriate counselor. Second, the overall pastoral relationship within which counseling occurred is formally dissolved, yet sustained counseling suggests its continuation—a situation against which many denominations have explicit policies. Third, there is usually a new pastor to whom it would be appropriate for the person to turn. Continuation of a long-distance counseling relationship, like it or not, is an interference with the development of that new pastoral role and leaves you open to many problems. Clients' insistence that "the new pastor doesn't understand" can fit neatly into one's fantasies of irreplaceability or incomparability. Beware. The formal end of a pastoral relationship should be just that. This is not, of course, to dissuade you from *ever* providing short-term pastoral care when former clients call in crisis. Just remember the above, and encourage them to seek local support.

Special Problems   Counseling relationships can become problematic. Any of a variety of processes can compromise the pastor's ability to intervene as an effective and professional counselor. One pitfall to which some pastors succumb is romantic involvement with a client. As discussed earlier, pastors are in many respects ideal targets for transference, and sexually seductive behavior is a not uncommon form of transference. We reiterate that under no circumstances is it therapeutic for a pastor to become romantically or sexually involved with a client. If the pastor experiences the beginnings of problematic countertransference (fantasies, romantic feelings, beginning rationalizations), consultation with a supervisor or senior colleague is urgently in order, and a referral may be necessary.

Likewise, we have mentioned that some counselors are simply unsuited to deal with certain kinds of human problems. Certain problems may shock, disgust, or repulse the counselor. Perhaps an ideal counselor does not have such reactions, but all real counselors do. Other problems may be uncomfortably close to personal difficulties or sensitivities so that the potential for projection and selective blindness is great. Some counseling situations conflict too directly with pastoral roles or basic tenets of faith. The responsible counselor recognizes such situations early and arranges appropriate referral.

Finally, it is altogether possible that a given client may need more intensive counseling than the pastor is willing to provide. Note that here we do not say "able," but "willing." It is the pastor's right and duty to decide how his or her time is best spent. Every counselor must choose which clients to work with and which to refer.

THE ART OF ENDING

Ending counseling is seldom a serious problem. Often counselor and client recognize the nearing of completion at about the same time. There are, however, some points to consider in ending the counseling process gracefully and easing the transition.

No Surprises   It is not wise to spring a decision to terminate on the client—to announce, for example, that this session will be the last. In a way, termination should be discussed from the very beginning of counseling. When will this process be over, and how will client and counselor know when they get there? These issues are addressed more fully later in this chapter when evaluation is discussed. At any rate, counseling should not end (in most cases) with the session in which termination is first discussed. If either client or counselor raises the issue of termination, at least one more session should be planned for wrapping up. This allows both pastor and client to prepare for termination.

Discuss It   Share your perceptions with the client in a nonrejecting way. Indicate what reasons you see for terminating, particularly emphasizing progress that has been made. Ask for your client's views. (Often the client will have been thinking about terminating as well.) A discussion of possible termination does not always lead to the end of counseling, of course. In one case the sharing of our perception that the couple's change process seemed to have come to a standstill led to a relieved revelation by the couple that they, too, had noticed this and were secretly thinking about terminating. This in turn led to a more careful examination of the counseling process and a beneficial change in strategy before the ultimate termination of counseling some months later. Termination is always a matter for discussion and negotiation between pastor and client.

Nonabandonment   It is important to avoid the communication of rejection or abandonment when raising the issue of termination. A negotiating rather than authoritarian stance is one helpful approach—"I have seen you make some very good changes in your life, and I have noticed lately that there seems to be less energy in our sessions and that your mind almost seems to be elsewhere. One reason why this can happen is that the counseling process is nearing the end—you feel a natural completion point approaching. I wonder if you have been feeling any of this?" Such a statement gives permission for the client to express a desire for termination without any "hurting the feelings" of the counselor, while still leaving the door open for the client to say that he or she is not ready to end.

Another nonabandonment strategy is to discuss what further contact, if any, might be helpful. Perhaps sessions less often, with a gradual period of phasing out, would be desirable. What does the client think and want? Here the pastor must be aware of his or her own "need to be needed" and avoid expressing such a question in a way that obliges the client to ask for further help.

In general, the underlying message is, "You will not be alone. I want you to have the help that you need but no more than that. I want you to be able to go on with your life under your own (and God's) power, and I am willing to help you find whatever support is takes for you to get to that point." Also, the door of termination is not a one-way passage. The possibility always exists for resuming counseling if necessary (albeit with another pastor or counselor).

When counseling is terminated, it is important to be sure that you do not abandon the person, particularly if ongoing contact is maintained in the pastoral role. A periodic brief check-back is in order to see how the person is doing. The first few "noncounseling" contacts after formal termination are also important, and the pastor should be alert for signs of avoidance in these—atypical disappearance from or after worship, avoidance of eye contact, or other signs of strained relationship. Some clients retain a moderate feeling of embarrassment and have some difficulty in settling back into a normal pastor-person relationship afterward. It may be helpful to make a few comfortable initiations on more general topics during these early weeks after counseling, if initial signs of avoidance appear. Some of these problems can be prevented if the counselor properly handles the final counseling session.

THE WRAP-UP SESSION

You have approached the end of the counseling process with a client, who has agreed to a final session for wrapping up. What do you do during that last session? Here are some helpful points to include.

Review the Process   Recall what the client's situation was when counseling began and why counseling was begun. Review what you have done together.

Emphasize Change   Summarize the changes that you have observed over the course of counseling, and also ask the client to indicate what changes he or she recognizes. Give encouragement for the change you have seen.

Recognize the Client's Success   Changes that have occurred should be credited to the client. When at the end of counseling a client says, "You have done so much for me," we routinely reply, "I'm glad that you feel good about the process, but it is you who have done the work." This can be reinforced by asking the client to indicate what he or she has done to bring about change. What has worked? Of course, the counselor plays a role in change, but it is important in the wrap-up session to give strong recognition to the client's responsibility for change. Research indicates that clients who attribute change to their own efforts are much more likely to retain those changes than are clients who believe that the transformation was brought about by an external agent such as the therapist, hypnosis, or a drug.[2] Even in cases where a drug has played a role in change, it is the client's courage to recognize the need, decision to use the medication, and persistence in seeking change that make the difference.

Discuss Future Change   What remains to be done? Where does the client want to make still more change or progress, and how will the client go about doing that? What is the next step? What might cause the client to "backslide," and what plans can be made to prevent that?

Inquire about Unfinished Business   It is wise to ask, during a wrap-up session, whether the client has any unfinished business—any questions he or she has been wanting to ask, anything that needs to be said. Here, too, the counselor can raise anticipated issues that might obstruct the transition back to a normal pastoral role. The pastor might ask a parishioner who has been in counseling, "Sometimes at the end of the counseling people feel a little uncomfortable about being a regular layperson in the church again, uncertain about relating to a pastor again instead of a counselor. I wonder if you have any of these feelings, or any unfinished business there?" This question form again gives permission to have or not have such concerns.

Discuss Further Contact   The possibility of further counseling should be discussed, leaving the door open for the client to resume contact if desired. A "check-up" session may be negotiated for several weeks down the road. If a referral is in order, this is discussed (see below).

Exchange Symbols   A variety of nonverbal symbols exist for marking the end of a relationship. Sometimes a client brings a good-bye gift for the counselor. Acceptance of the gift is at the counselor's discretion, but the usual procedure is to accept inextravagant gifts as a symbol of completion. One client brought cheese, crackers, and wine for a final informal symbolic communion. The counselor may choose to use different chairs than have been used for counseling. Some pastors schedule the final session as a lunch (ensuring that the table provides total confidentiality) or agree to a posttermination social visit over coffee, marking the transition to a less formal kind of relationship. Sometimes, weather permitting, a counselor can take a walk with a client during the final session. All of this depends on the counselor's own level of comfort and propriety as well as that of the client. It is wise to be sensitive to the client's own symbols of termination.

Sometimes a final session feels a bit uncomfortable because it seems unnecessary, that there is little to talk about. If this occurs, it is a good sign and further marks the end of the process. Some final sessions are shorter than preceding ones for this reason—there just doesn't seem to be the need for more. What better marking could there be of the end, of the client's readiness to go on alone? If the session is filled with a review of the positive changes that the client has achieved, it will be far from useless. Rather, it represents a consolidation, a closure.

TEMPORARY TRANSITIONS

A few other circumstances require temporary interruptions of the counseling process. In some ways these resemble termination, although counseling is usually resumed afterward.

Vacation

If you are planning to be away on vacation or leave or will otherwise be unavailable for regular counseling sessions, make this fact known to clients well in advance. It is unwise and unprofessional to spring this fact on a client, announcing at the end of a session, "Oh, by the way, I'm going to be out of town for the next three weeks." The more courteous and responsible approach is to give several weeks' notice and to make arrangements for emergency coverage where necessary. We might add here our observation that it is not uncommon for clients to cancel or miss their first session after a counselor's vacation—usually for very sound reasons.

Illness

Other interruptions of counseling cannot be planned. Illness is one of these. When you are ill, sessions need to be postponed. Sometimes this is a marginal decision, and we find that pastors tend to make their mistakes on the side of continuing to "serve" in spite of illness, sometimes exacerbating and prolonging their disablement.

The postponement of sessions due to illness is straightforward, with a few added notes. Rescheduling of sessions, if possible, gives the client a tangible date for the next contact and less of a feeling of being cut off. It can also be helpful, if calls are made personally, to explain that you would be unable to give your very best and that you prefer to reschedule to a time when you can do that.

Some clients are distressed by a therapist's illness and may even feel some personal responsibility for it. Be sensitive to indications of such concerns when counseling is resumed, as these may prove fruitful themes for exploration.

Time Problems

Other unforeseen circumstances can make it difficult to keep appointments. One such circumstance is "running over" with a prior client who is in acute crisis. For instance, if a client is going to be kept waiting more than fifteen minutes, you could leave the session temporarily and explain the situation to the waiting client. A possible communication is, "I'm with a person who is in the middle of a crisis right now, and I need to spend more time than usual. This could take at least _____ minutes more, and I wonder if it would be better for us to reschedule rather than for you to wait and have a shorter time." This communicates your concern for the waiting client and also indicates that you are willing to take special extra time when a person is in need. Seldom do clients resent such a request.

If fees are involved, it is proper to offer that the session postponed under such circumstances be free of charge. A reasonable general standard to use with clients is, "If you miss or have to cancel a session without notice, I will charge you for that time. If I have to miss or cancel a session on short notice, I will not charge you for the next session."

In any event it is usually better to postpone a session than to keep clients waiting for long periods, perhaps forcing a briefer than normal session and a general backing up of your professional schedule. To reschedule one appointment permits you to give your full attention to others. If you find yourself chronically running late or running over, it is time to reevaluate in discussion with a colleague, supervisor, or therapist.

REFERRALS: WHO, WHAT, WHEN, WHERE, AND HOW?

What is a referral? It is an arranged consultation between a client and another professional or community resource. The usual reason for referral is to obtain expertise or resources not available from the counselor. A referral may be made initially if the need is recognized immediately or may be made after a period of counseling when the need is recognized, the limits of the pastor's expertise are encountered, or the counseling process is compromised. It may also be desirable to delay referral until an adequate supportive counseling relationship has been established to avoid giving the person the feeling of being passed from one disinterested professional to another. On the other hand, a prompt referral is called for when a critical need is clear, as in a suicidal depression. Basically, the *when* of referral is when the need arises or is recognized, given adequate preparation. That in turn raises the *how* of referral.

Making the Referral

One important goal in making a referral is to provide a smooth transition. It is helpful to explain to the client the rationale for referral. What is the purpose of seeing this new professional? Why can't you handle it personally? The client should know the specific purpose for the referral. Is it for a brief evaluation, or is a new person going to "take over"? What will your role be?

It is also helpful for you to cut through as much red tape as possible before initiating the referral. It helps to refer the individual to a particular person rather than to a general setting—a hospital, a mental health center, or a clinic. What will happen when the client calls? When feasible, make the call yourself on behalf of the person, facilitating the process of obtaining an appointment. This more than doubles the likelihood that the person will actually get there![3] The more obstacles a person encounters in trying to follow through on a referral, the less likely it is that the new contact will be established.

Real or imagined stigma can also be an obstacle. Some people are willing to talk things over with their pastor but very reluctant to "see someone," particularly if that person is an identified mental health professional. Many individuals retain stereotypes of what it means to see a psychologist or psychiatrist—that it is an admission of weakness or insanity, a shameful breakdown, or a commitment to long-term shrinking on a couch. They imagine that they will be told "the problem is all in your head," that they will have to reveal painful details of their childhood, or that they will be diagnosed as having a faulty personality. You can be very helpful in dispelling these fears, particularly when the referral is being made to a known colleague.

When referrals are made anonymously and without such support, only a small percentage of people actually follow through. Do everything possible to ease the referral and to ensure that it has been accomplished. Don't just give a name and then drop the matter. Follow through. Get back to the person and find out whether the contact has been made and how it went. Call ahead to the professional to whom the person has been referred and arrange to be notified when the appointment has been made and kept. Call while the client is still in your office and schedule an appointment. Offer to accompany the person to the first appointment if that is helpful, serving a supportive pastoral role. If it is important to make a referral, it is equally important to see that the person makes the contact and begins the desired process.

In making a referral it is also desirable to be clear to your colleague about the purpose of the referral. Many counselors have had the experience of referring a client for an evaluation, only to find later that the evaluator has taken the client into long-term psychotherapy. Be specific, both to the client and to the referral professional, as to what the purposes of referral are. If you want an answer to a particular question, be sure to ask it. Provide any relevant information you already have to save time and give the process a headstart. It must be made clear as to whether you are retaining primary counseling responsibility and referring for an evaluation or sending the client with the intent that another professional will take over primary care responsibilities. Many therapists are reluctant to treat a client who is simultaneously in counseling with another professional, and these issues should be clarified carefully.

A longer follow-up, beyond simply assuring that the initial contact was made, is also quite proper. If the client was transferred to another professional for treatment, how is it going? Although one psychologist may be hesitant to monitor the progress of a client once the referral has been made to another psychologist, such ongoing concern is well within the realm of pastoral care. It also provides you with valuable information to be used in deciding where to refer other clients in the future. Remember that, if you want to discuss this with a professional colleague, you will need a formal release of information signed by the client (chapter 3).

Where to Refer

Perhaps the biggest problem in referral for most pastors is knowing whom to trust, where to send a client in need of help. The mental health maze is confusing indeed, and if it is forbidding to the pastor it is even more so to the client. How can you go about identifying and evaluating potential professional resources for referral?

To begin, it may be helpful for us to review the training and qualifications of different types of mental health professionals available to the average pastor as referral resources. Pastors serving in less populated areas, of course, may have to cast a wider geographic net to locate needed resources.

A *psychologist* is an individual whose primary professional training is in understanding human behavior. There are many different subspecialties within psychology—developmental, social, physiological, experimental, industrial, applied, or personality. It is, however, the clinical psychologist who is most often involved in helping people change. The typical clinical psychologist completes a four-year course of undergraduate training with a major in psychology and then a master's degree that requires two or three years and usually includes a major research project called the master's thesis. He or she then must do more intensive work, including a doctoral dissertation, for another two years or so to complete the academic requirements for the Ph.D. degree. An internship is also required, which consists of a full year or two of intensive supervision of clinical work. The normal minimum of training is thus nine years prior to Ph.D. The major focus of training during the latter years is on evaluating and treating psychological problems. One or two years of specialized postdoctoral work may also be completed.

A *psychiatrist* is a physician who completes undergraduate and graduate training in general medicine and then decides to specialize in the treatment of mental disorders. Beyond the normal medical training and a one-year medical internship, the psychiatrist also usually completes a specialized residency in psychiatry consisting of two or three years of intensive supervision. A *biological psychiatrist* is one who specializes in the diagnosis and medical treatment of biologically based disorders, particularly depression and psychoses. Other psychiatrists engage mostly in talking psychotherapies with relatively little medical content. Unlike psychologists, psychiatrists are licensed to dispense medications and to administer certain procedures such as electroshock therapy. Other treatments such as biofeedback may be administered either by a psychologist or a psychiatrist.

When questions of nervous system damage are involved, still another type of professional is consulted. The relevant specialist in medicine is the *neurologist*, who is skilled in evaluating physiological disorders of the nervous system. Testing and evaluation of impairment, on the other hand, is often conducted by a *neuropsychologist*, a psychologist with specialized expertise in brain functions, who also frequently participates in rehabilitation.

A third type of professional who offers direct counseling is the psychiatric *social worker*. The usual training in social work is at a master's level, with the terminal degree being called an M.S.W., though a small percentage continue on to a doctorate or D.S.W. Social work training historically has focused on the adjustment of the individual within the community, and social workers are often quite helpful in identifying relevant community resources and involvements for clients. In recent years social work training has also included an increasing amount of instruction and supervision in treatment procedures, and this is extended in internship training.

Nurses also can obtain specialized training in counseling and sometimes set up independent or group practices. A psychiatric nurse is one whose specialty practical training was in working with individuals diagnosed as having mental disorders.

In some states there are legal standards for the profession of *marriage and family counseling*. The training of such individuals usually includes a master's degree in psychology or related coursework combined with a period of supervised practice. *Alcohol/drug abuse counselors* are now licensed or certified in many states as well, as are mental health counselors more generally.

There are large differences in the extent to which states protect consumers by enforcing minimal criteria on those who would call themselves by these professional titles. Two kinds of laws exist. *Certification* laws are those that restrict a title. Some states, for example, certify psychologists by permitting only certain individuals to use that title. A typical certification law requires passing of one or more examinations, completion of an approved Ph.D. degree and internship, and a minimum period of supervised practice prior to being given the privilege of calling oneself a "psychologist." In states with such laws, no one else may use the title psychologist in the telephone directory or announcements. A stricter type of law is *licensing*, which restricts the practice of certain treatment procedures only to approved individuals. Thus, only licensed physicians may prescribe psychiatric medication (although psychiatric training is not required). In addition, there are national organizations that certify professionals based on minimum criteria. A nationally certified social worker uses the designation *A.C.S.W.* Psychologists who wish to accept insurance payments are usually registered with the National Register of Health Service Providers in Psychology. Board certification procedures exist in psychiatry, psychology, social work, and (in some states) in counseling specialties (marriage and family, alcoholism and drug abuse). Pastoral counselors may seek certification through the AAPC or ACPE (see chapter 20).

You should be acquainted with the laws of your state and what they guarantee about professional qualifications. In many states there are no restrictions on calling oneself a "counselor," "therapist," "consultant," "sex therapist," or "hypnotherapist" (or, for that matter, a "pastoral counselor"). Virtually anyone can lay claim to these titles, be listed in the telephone directory, and advertise in the newspapers. There are also continual changes in state laws, and a few states have at times abolished certification laws so that anyone is allowed to use a professional title.

You should also realize that certification and licensing laws enforce only minimum standards on the use of a title and do not guarantee competence. Some laws likewise included "grandparent" clauses so that those individuals using a title before passage of a law were allowed to continue using it regardless of qualification. Titles are little protection and can be misleading.

Consequently, we recommend that, whenever possible, you become acquainted with the persons to whom you plan to make referrals. One reasonable way to do this is to interview the person regarding her or his interests and qualifications. A responsible professional will be willing to provide this information without defensiveness. Pastors who live in a larger city can try to "take a professional to lunch" once a week for this purpose, but the information can also be obtained in a relatively brief telephone conversation. Alternatively, you could invite professionals to speak as part of adult education events held within your congregation, providing still another sample of how the person thinks and relates to others.

What should you ask? Don't be shy. Ask the hard questions and don't settle for superficial or glib answers. As an introduction, indicate that you are tying to find good referral resources and would like to know more about this person's approach and practice. Again, most professionals will be pleased to respond to such requests. Here are some questions to ask.

1. *Clients.* With what kinds of clients do you like to work? With whom do you work best? Are there particular problems or age groups with whom you have special expertise? (Be cautious of those who answer, "Everyone.")

2. *Training.* What degrees do you hold, and from where? What special training have you had for dealing with the kinds of clients and problems you see?

3. *Approach.* What is your general approach to therapy? What do you do with clients? (A favorite answer here is "eclectic," which is not very informative. It may mean that the person has no particular system for formulating and uses a rag-tag collection of techniques or poorly specified methods. On the other hand it may mean that the person is skilled in a range of alternative interventions and chooses an approach based on reasonable and valid criteria.)

4. *Evidence.* An interesting question to ask, particularly when a specific client or problem area is being discussed, is, "What scientific evidence is there for the effectiveness of what you do? What proof is there that this approach actually helps?" The individual may cite specific research or may dodge by referring vaguely to "many studies" or "my years of professional experience."

5. *Length of Treatment.* How long do you usually see a client? What is the average number of sessions? (The answer ought to be different depending on the pre-

senting problem. Some problems are very easy to treat; others require a somewhat longer course.) This is, of course, also influenced by health care coverage.

6. *Fees*. How are fees determined? Is there a sliding scale? Does the person accept public assistance clients, whose fees are paid (usually on more minimal scale) by the state or federal government? Is payment to be made in advance, on monthly billing, or on time payments? Is the person eligible for health plan payments? Health care coverage is a rapidly changing field but one on which you should remain informed because it affects your referral options.

7. *Credentials*. Is this person certified or licensed in his or her field? By whom? If not, why not? If the person is currently working toward credentials under the supervision of another professional, clarify the extent of supervision and find out more about the supervisor.

8. *Group?* Is the individual part of a professional group, such as a group practice? What other professionals does he or she work with regularly?

9. *Views on Religion*. Here we refer not to a personal statement of faith, but rather to the professional's general views on religion and its relationship to mental health and treatment. How, in the person's opinion, is religion involved in the processes of health and treatment? How comfortable does the person seem in talking about religious issues? How forthright are the answers?

10. *Collaboration*. How willing is the professional to collaborate with you? What about progress reports, consultations, joint sessions as called for?

11. *Recommendations*. Finally, it can be very interesting to ask each professional to recommend other professionals in the same field or related fields with whom he or she has had good experience in making referrals.

Of course you have to find professionals to interview. In a rural area, the possibilities are often quite limited, and it may be necessary to learn about resources in the closest major cities for cases where specialized attention is absolutely necessary. In a large city the problem is just the opposite—too many possibilities. The following are methods that may be helpful in identifying possible referral resources.

1. *Telephone directory*. One comprehensive catalog of resources is your telephone directory. There are perhaps two dozen listings in the yellow pages where mental health resources can be found, and these vary from one area to another. Remember that in many categories, listing provides no guarantee of competence or training.

2. *Universities*. Recommendations may be made by the relevant departments (such as Psychology, Psychiatry, Social Work, or Counseling) of local universities or medical schools. Ask to speak with the chairperson of the department, who may in turn refer you to the most knowledgeable clinical faculty member. This route can be especially useful if you are trying to locate a particular kind of specialty (such as sleep disorders, neuropsychology, or biological treatment of depression). Try to get more than one name if possible.

3. *Colleagues*. Other good resources are the recommendations of colleagues who are familiar with local professionals. Ask everyone who might know—a family physician, other mental health professionals, or parishioners in the field. Often the same few names are mentioned over and over again, and this suggests a worthwhile inquiry.

4. *Organizations*. Certain organizations may also be able to provide the names of qualified professionals. In seeking a stop-smoking program, for example, the local office of the American Cancer Society can often provide suggestions.

5. *Clients*. Finally, an excellent source of information is people who have themselves been in treatment. Whom did they see, and what was their experience? The opinion of consumers must be recognized for what it is—a selective view, albeit an inside perspective.

There are many more resources than traditional professionals. Chapter 20 will explore other community sources of support and how you can identify and help to develop them.

Another possibility is to keep a file of resources for referral, perhaps cross-referenced by problem or expertise area. Index cards work nicely for this purpose, and Figure 19-1 illustrates a possible format. Perhaps the most important part of this card is the "Notes" section, in which you can keep careful records of experiences in making referrals to each individual. How promptly did the client get in to see this person, or was there a waiting list? What was the client's reaction to this professional? Was the client helped? Did the professional send a good report or otherwise collaborate in helpful ways? Notes can also be kept on comments made by other sources, so that a cumulative picture emerges over time. A file containing such information is obviously confidential, containing both client data and hearsay evidence. It can, however, be quite helpful in guiding future referrals.

```
NAME:                                                    Group:

Address:

Telephones       Office:              (24 hour?) _____      Home:

Professional Training:

License/Certification, other credentials:

Specialty areas:


General approach:


Fee arrangements:

              Insurance payments accepted? _____    Public benefits accepted? _____

Recommended by:

Notes:
```

FIGURE 19-1

EVALUATING YOUR OWN COUNSELING

Evaluation. The very word scares people. It conjures up images of report cards, peer reviews, salary determinations, and judgments. Most people seem to avoid evaluations because they think of them as good-or-bad determinations and fear that they will come out in the latter category. But evaluation is also feedback. It means to find out what is valuable. Without feedback, no learning occurs. Feedback helps people to learn what they are doing that is valuable, and what they may need to do differently in the future. For a counselor, this means learning how your clients do in the long run.

Of course, there is some information that is obtained during the counseling process itself and can be useful, but it is also selective. There is a strong tendency for people to tell therapists in general (and perhaps pastors even more so) that they did a good job. "I can't tell you how much you've helped me!" may be a statement with several levels of truth. Those who do research on therapy talk about the "hello/good-bye" effect whereby the client when coming in complains of how terrible things are and when leaving exclaims how wonderful everything is and how much counseling helped. The verbal report of clients during counseling is a source of information but is not always to be taken at face value. In our alcoholism treatment research, for example, we have observed clients who express profuse thanks for treatment and who report that they are much improved but whose drinking seems to be quite unchanged when objective measures or the reports of others are obtained.

Clearly, we are not going to turn you into a psychological researcher. That, too, is a special expertise. But we do recommend that you take some specific measures to gain regular feedback so that you continue to grow and learn. In this sense, "evaluation" consists of professional development. Here are a few suggestions.

1. *Set specific goals.* In discussing formulation and change we suggested that it is helpful to set specific goals for change. Here is yet another reason to do so—without clear goals, it is very difficult to evaluate what happened. If you don't know where you're going, it is difficult to know whether you got there! At the stage of formulation, compile a list of specific goals to be pursued in counseling, and be as specific as you can. This is often helpful to the client, can help keep counseling on track, and gives you a basis for assessing your work.

2. *Baseline.* Whenever possible, also make notes on where the person started. Psychologists call such a starting point a *baseline.* How many drinks or cigarettes per day or how many arguments per week? In considering this it may help to ask, "If you succeed in reaching the goal you have set, how could we tell? How could someone else know that you had achieved it?" This will also help in determining when counseling is over.

3. *Progress checks.* It is helpful to check, on either a regular or periodic basis throughout counseling, what progress has been made toward each of the goals. Self-monitoring (chapter 11) is one way to keep track of progress, though it is not

applicable to every problem. Hospitals and agencies now frequently use this problem-oriented record-keeping format—specifying the goals of treatment at the outset and then charting progress toward each goal as treatment proceeds. Such records of progress also provide a good perspective for clients, who sometimes forget just how far they have come.

4. *Final evaluation.* A part of the wrap-up session can be a review of the initial goals of counseling and a joint evaluation of what progress has been made toward each. This further helps to clarify what challenges the client still faces on each dimension.

5. *Follow-up.* It is also informative to know what happens after the formal counseling process is over. Some therapists make routine follow-up calls or send questionnaires to their clients on the anniversary of termination to check in on how they are doing. A return visit may be offered (often without fee, in fee-charging settings) to review longer-term changes. Such sessions can be very helpful for both counselor and client. The questions may be similar to those asked at wrap-up—What changes have you made, how did you do it, what worked best or helped most, what lies ahead? Follow-up visits are also good continuing care because new or renewed concerns may be identified early and addressed through further counseling.

6. *Collateral information.* Pastors are often in a position to obtain additional information from relatives and friends of the client. This must, of course, be done without jeopardizing the client's privacy and confidentiality. Often it occurs incidentally, as part of regular pastoral duties. Such perspectives from others provide you with further feedback for the counselor. Reports from other professionals when referrals have been made are also useful sources of learning, confirming or disconfirming your initial impressions.

All of these types of information can help you continue sharpening your counseling skills by providing you with feedback. Unless you make an effort to obtain such information, however, you are likely to work in a feedback vacuum that hinders continued learning. This is particularly a problem for pastoral counselors who do not work in a local congregation, where ongoing contact with parishioners offers feedback in itself.

SUMMARY

The process of counseling can come to an end for any of a variety of reasons: attainment of or reasonable progress toward the goal, a unilateral client decision, a progress plateau, need for referral, or special problems interfering with the course of counseling.

Following a few basic principles of transition can smooth the termination of counseling and facilitate resumption of therapeutic contact if needed: (a) avoid surprises—don't announce termination unilaterally; (b) discuss termination plans with the client; and (c) avoid communicating abandonment and maintain continued contact as appropriate. A final wrap-up session can serve to review the progress of work together, to emphasize positive change that has been accomplished and to credit this to the client, to discuss what lies ahead, to reveal unfinished business, to negotiate future contact, and to mark the termination of the counseling relationship. Your vacations, illness, and time limitations may require special provisions within the counseling relationship.

Among the skills helpful in making referrals are (a) clarifying the rationale for referral; (b) cutting through red tape and removing obstacles; (c) relieving fears and concerns about stigma; and (d) providing needed ongoing support through the referral process. It is important to be clear with both client and colleague regarding the purpose of referral.

One key consideration is the type of professional to whom referral should be made. Psychologists, psychiatrists, neurologists and neuropsychologists, social workers and psychiatric nurses, pastoral and marital/family and mental health counselors all offer specialized expertise. Professional certification controls the use of certain titles, whereas licensing laws restrict the practice of certain treatment procedures.

Interviewing potential referral professionals can yield valuable information to use in deciding appropriate referrals. Professionals can be queried regarding preferred clients, training, therapeutic approach and evidence for its effectiveness, anticipated length of treatment, fees, credentials, group support, views on religion, willingness to collaborate, and recommendations for other potential referral resources. Possible referral professionals might be identified through the telephone directory, university departments, colleagues, professional organizations, and the experience of clients themselves.

Continuing professional development depends upon feedback of the results of one's own counseling, which enables ongoing learning. The setting of specific goals and tracking of concrete progress toward those goals can yield such useful information, particularly when combined follow-up contact after counseling has been terminated. Such follow-up visits can also prove valuable as continuing care, assuring the client of the pastor's continued interest and providing early warning signs of the need for resumption of counseling.

ADDITIONAL READINGS

OGELSBY, WILLIAM F. *Referral in Pastoral Counseling.* Nashville: Abingdon, 1978. This volume is out of print but still worth consulting on this topic if you can find a copy.

NOTES

[1]William R. Miller, *Living as If: How Positive Faith Can Change Your Life* (Philadelphia: Westminster Press, 1985).

[2]Stephen Kopel and Hal Arkowitz, "The Role of Attribution and Self-perception in Behavior Change: Implications for Behavior Therapy," *Genetic Psychology Monographs* 92 (1975): 175–212.

[3]L. S. Kogan, "The Short-term Case in a Family Agency: Part II. Results of a Study," *Social Casework* 38 (1957): 296–302.

20

BUILDING A MORE RESOURCEFUL COMMUNITY

> Alike and ever alike we are on all continents in the need of love,
> food, clothing, work, speech, worship, sleep, games, dancing,
> fun. From tropics to arctics humanity lives with these needs so
> alike, so inexorably alike.
>
> —Carl Sandburg, Prologue to *The Family of Man*

YOU ARE NOT ALONE

Every congregation is filled with people in need. The examples given throughout this book are but a few. A pastor who communicates openness and skill
in counseling may soon be overwhelmed by the number and needs of those
who find their way to the private study, and soon they come not only from
the immediate congregation but also from the wider community. In combination with the other demanding roles a pastor must play, this can become a
responsibility that is as taxing as it is rewarding.

Fortunately, you are not alone. We do not mean, though it is true, that
there are many other pastors in the same situation. Neither do we need to remind you that God is with you to provide vision and renewal. Nor are we
making reference to the larger community of professional referral and consultation sources discussed in chapter 19.

Rather, we mean that within every congregation, every community of
people, there are rich and extensive resources to be tapped. Most of the meaningful changes that occur in people's lives happen without any special guidance from a professional helper.[1] People changed, recovered, grew, and
improved long before there *were* professional psychologists, counselors,
physicians, or social workers. Major change is largely self-directed, enabled
by a great sea of informal helpers. When you learn to develop and use this re-

sourcefulness in the local community, you have at your disposal a much larger network of intervention and support. We will discuss five kinds of adjunctive agents that can be employed in the counseling process: paraprofessionals, partners, peers, paraphernalia, and print.[2]

Paraprofessionals

The prefix *para-* means beside, alongside of, or closely related to. In this sense a *para*professional is one who works beside or along with, closely related to a professional helper. Usually, the practice of using paraprofessional helpers includes a careful screening process, training in specific interventions, and ongoing supervision and support. The absence of any one of these elements invites problems. Within these important bounds, however, paraprofessionals can play vital roles in the health of a community. Within the medical sphere, the "paramedic" has become a crucial link in emergency and rescue services. Physician and nursing assistants are also playing an increasing role in general and family practice, performing routine procedures and freeing up physician time for more specialized tasks requiring greater training and expertise.

A similar proliferation of helpers has occurred within the mental health field. Because psychological services are seldom fully *licensed* (restricted to certain trained professionals) and only certain professional titles are controlled by certification, however, it is possible for virtually anyone to set up an independent practice and to claim a title such as "therapist." In this way the public is afforded less protection than in the realm of medicine, where most interventions must be either carried out or supervised by a properly trained and licensed physician.

Paraprofessionals can provide valuable service, but such services should always be offered under the training and supervision of a more highly trained professional. Specific interventions such as relaxation training (chapter 14) are readily learned and taught by paraprofessional helpers, and the outcome for the client is generally as good as when the same procedure is taught by a psychologist. In a research clinic at the University of New Mexico, paraprofessional counselors (students) have been employed as primary intervention agents, following carefully specified treatment procedures under psychological supervision. Over a period of twenty years of studies, successful results have been shown in the treatment of problem drinking, nightmares, anxiety problems, and depression.[3]

What paraprofessionals do *not* have, however, is the broader purview that comes with advanced training. This is especially crucial in the area of formulation—recognizing key syndromes, developing a competent diagnosis and understanding of the problem, understanding the causes and context, and seeing alternative interventions. For this reason we have advocated and emphasized the *para* portion of paraprofessionalism: beside, closely related to a competent professional.

The paraprofessional, then, is a special sort of intervention agent—an extension of the professional helper, a way of providing and extending counseling services without compromising quality.

Who *are* paraprofessionals? They can be trainees en route to an independent level of expertise—medical students, trainee chaplains, psychology or nursing degree candidates. They can be volunteers who are interested in helping. They can be the designated officers of the congregation in positions of service—deacons or elders. The requisite skills vary depending on what the paraprofessional will be expected to do, and this becomes a consideration in the first process—that of screening.

Screening Many people are drawn to being helpers out of their own needs for help. They imagine, at some level, that by working on the problems of others they will be able to work through their own difficulties. This is not a totally misguided motivation, for in learning about people they also learn about themselves. Many who are attracted to helping professions for such reasons do work through some of their problems in the course of training and go on to be competent and responsible professionals. If, however, a person begins intervening in the lives of others while still in the midst of personal turmoil, there is great potential for projection, countertransference, selective blind spots, and harmful outcomes.

One factor to consider in screening potential paraprofessionals, then, is their own state of adjustment. People in the midst of personal distress and disturbance are not prepared to help others and are particularly prone to problems when clients' difficulties and their own are similar. The pastor who works with a congregation over a span of time is in an especially good position to judge the long-term stability and maturity of members who may express interest in being helpers.

Another unhelpful agendum sometimes brought by people who are drawn to helping involves proselytism. The individual's concept of "helping" may center on convincing others to share a particular viewpoint, philosophy or belief system. Two major problems with such an approach are that it is heavily loaded with roadblocks and it tends to propose one solution for diverse problems. Helping, at least in this context, does not involve convincing other people that they are wrong and the counselor is right. Such proselytism is by no means limited to religious perspectives. Numerous forms of "therapy" and "self-help" have attracted advocates who regard their particular approach as the one true light, the only road to health and wisdom.

Screening is more than a one-time process. Further indications of the trainee's appropriateness emerge as training progresses. Some people take naturally to skills like reflective listening, while others seem nearly unable to acquire or sustain such skill even with extensive coaching. Low self-esteem, for example, has been found to be associated with difficulty in learning reflective listening skills.[4] Ongoing supervision is also crucial in ensuring proper ethical and professional practice and is an important continuing form of screening as well as training.

Training   The training of paraprofessionals usually focuses on a specific set of skills to be used in a particular setting, with certain types of individuals, under ongoing supervision. In our own training of paraprofessionals, we have always included instruction in basic communication skills, as discussed in part II. Simple didactic instruction is not sufficient to teach such skills. Extended and repeated role-play and practice with feedback are usually necessary for trainees to break their old communication habits and learn to listen reflectively.

Beyond this, the content of training is specific to the task to be performed. Volunteers to staff a suicide prevention hotline will be taught the kind of material contained in chapter 13. One study at the University of New Mexico used paraprofessionals to train people successfully in skills for coping with chronic nightmares. This required training and supervised practice in conducting deep muscle relaxation training and systematic desensitization. What one teaches to paraprofessionals depends upon the tasks they will perform. In any event, the training procedure usually includes (a) basic counseling skills; (b) a rationale for the particular procedures being used; (c) specific instruction in the intervention methods; (d) role-play practice with feedback; and (e) troubleshooting to prepare trainees to deal with common or unanticipated problems and to recognize the limits of their own abilities. We have found it helpful to use a standardized training manual and to encourage trainees to follow the procedures it specifies. Such a handbook also serves as a reminder of training, a "refresher course" to be reviewed as needed. Some examples are listed at the end of this chapter.

Supervision   Paraprofessionals involved in formal interventions should be closely supervised. Ideally, this includes not only regular supervision meetings but also direct observation and review of the trainee's work. Some clinics provide direct observational facilities (such as one-way mirrors) that can be used with the knowledge and consent of clients. These afford especially rich training and supervision opportunities. Recordings of sessions and co-counseling provide other opportunities for direct review and feedback. Such supervision is not only a safeguard, it is a learning opportunity for the paraprofessionals and provides much needed ongoing support and continuous training.

Some churches and religious groups have initiated paraprofessional programs of this kind, including the Samaritans program, Stephen Ministries, and marriage enrichment encounters. Laypersons who are chosen to complete terms of service within a congregation might be given specialized training and ongoing support, developing skills to be used in home and hospital visitations and selective counseling. Such privileged training may also increase the willingness of laypersons to serve in these capacities, not only by affording an honored and meaningful status to the role but also by providing the kind of preparation and support that helps people feel more adequate and confident in service functions.

Partners

Not every pastoral counselor has the time, resources, or training to manage a paraprofessional program of this kind. A more manageable way of using the resources of a congregation is through the empowerment of "partner" functions. A partner, in this sense, is an ordinary layperson who has certain skills or resources and is willing to share them. A partner differs from a paraprofessional in the extent of training and supervision provided and in the formality and complexity of intervention required. A partner basically is called upon to use her or his ordinary resources and skills to assist others. Here are some examples:

> A man with free time during the day volunteers to help retarded citizens learn how to use the public transportation system.
>
> A woman with many social contacts helps people become aware of the various activities and organizations available in the community and accompanies them to their first meetings to break the ice.
>
> A man who likes to cook teaches basic food preparation skills to those who never learned them, including the newly divorced or widowed.
>
> A widow who has worked through her grief and made a good adjustment spends time with the bereaved, listening to their pain, helping them adjust and learn needed skills, showing that there is life after the death of a loved one.
>
> A English teacher helps refugees improve their language skills after hours.

Every person has skills that are needed by someone else. These can be taught by example, by direct instruction, by modeling and showing how, by encouragement and feedback. Another valuable partner function is the simple sharing of time. Big Brother and Big Sister programs are of this kind. Individuals newly released from an institution badly need this sort of human contact. One study found that psychiatric patients chosen at random (on discharge from the hospital) to be assigned a partner for a minimum of one hour of weekly contact showed significantly better community readjustment than those who had no such partner.[5] Human contact helps.

A pastor who is aware of this can greatly enable such connections. We recommend that you or the church keep a card file containing the names of people who have certain skills and resources and who are willing to be called upon to share them. This is the stewardship of simple gifts—skills in shopping, cooking, decision making, budgeting, map reading, or automobile maintenance. It is a stewardship of time. As clients appear with certain needs, you can approach members of the community who have the needed skills and ask whether they would be willing to be called upon for this particular kind of support. Also, as members of the community live through crucial life experiences and transitions and emerge from them whole and well, ask whether they would be willing to talk about this experience with others in the midst of it. Members of twelve-step fellowships such as Alcoholics Anonymous are often willing to help newcomers find their way into meetings. One study found a rather dramatic difference between alcoholics simply *advised* to go to A.A. versus those (chosen at random) who received a systematic encouragement procedure.[6] In the latter procedure, while the client was still in the office, the counselor telephoned a member of A.A. who had previously agreed to help newcomers. The counselor then put the client on the telephone to talk to this longstanding member of A.A., who in a friendly and encouraging manner offered a ride and companionship to the first meeting. The member/partner later placed a reminder call to the client before the meeting, picked the client up at home, and introduced the client to the meeting. Within this systematic encouragement group, 100 percent of clients got to an A.A. meeting. In the group merely advised to go, none actually got there!

Your card file must, of course, be completely confidential and for your use only. It is a personal resource to use in the course of your own counseling. The cards contain simply the person's name, how to get in touch and the best times to do so, and a description of the skills he or she is willing to share. These cards are then filed according to need areas. Never violate the confidentiality of people in your card file without their specific permission. Anonymity must be strictly protected, for example, for any member of a twelve-step fellowship—only the member has the right to reveal his or her own identity as a member, as an alcoholic, and so forth.

In making a contact between client and partner, it is usually wise to call in advance to ensure that the potential partner is able and willing to help at the present time. Following this clearance, the contact can be initiated by you or by a call from either client or partner. As with the referral resource file, you can keep confidential notes on how each contact proceeded and what the outcome was, to be used in future decisions about partner linkages.

Peers

In both paraprofessional and partner arrangements the relationship is uneven—a person with skills helps another who needs them. With the third kind of adjunct this is not the case. Peers are people in the same boat, on the same level. Perhaps they are ordinary people coming together to form a sharing and support group. Perhaps they are people who all have similar problems, as might be found in Alcoholics Anonymous or Weight Watchers. The benefits of peer linkages are to be found in the mutual support of a common search.

In some congregations, peer support groups already exist and meet on a regular basis. They may be called Bible study, men's breakfast group, prayer circle, women's association, or any of a variety of special interest groups meeting to sew, quilt, feed the hungry, plan worship services, garden, or explore peace issues. Such groups can provide important emotional growth and support for participants, particularly if they meet the following criteria: (a) they meet on a fairly regular basis; (b) they have a consistent membership or at least a core of regular attenders; and (c) they provide an atmosphere in which personal concerns, feelings, and problems can be discussed safely and openly.

Other groups are explicitly designated as sharing and support groups. They are formed and continue to exist to provide a smaller circle of intimacy where each member can talk about life's transitions, large and small. In the ideal, such a group provides a consistent group of loving and caring friends who know one's history, understand something of one's inner world, and share in new experiences and changes. Each member of the group has a safe place to express joys and fears, to struggle with decisions and problems, to share accomplishments and defeats.

Both together and individually we have participated in at least ten such ongoing support and sharing groups, some of which have continued to meet for many years. We have found the communion of these groups to be invaluable. Some began as study groups on scriptures or specific issues; most began with the express purpose of creating a community for personal exploration and support. Some started by the drawing together of an already close group of friends, others by the placing of an announcement in a congregational newsletter inviting anyone to attend who would be interested in participating in a weekly sharing group experience.

There are some important choices to be made in beginning a group of this kind. One is *whether membership will be open or consistent*. The open group permits people to come and go as they wish, with new members entering at any time. Most groups within religious organizations are at least overtly of this type. It has been our experience, however, that meaningful personal growth involves the taking of risks in self-disclosure and that such risks are facilitated by consistent membership. A compromise is to allow an "open period" during which people may come to the group to decide whether or not it will meet their own needs. At the end of this time, participants make a decision either to drop out or commit themselves to continuing. The group then continues with a consistent membership, who gradually grow to feel safer and more willing to risk as they come to know each other better. The constant entry and exit of members greatly disrupts this development of trust. At future points the group may decide to have an open period, allowing new people to consider joining. The addition of new members to a consolidated group offers unique challenges, however, both for old members and for new.

A second important decision is *size*. We have participated in groups as small as three and as large as fifteen where deep personal ties developed over the course of months or years of meeting. We find, however, that an optimal size is between five and ten. This provides enough members so that absences due to traveling or illness are not devastating, yet affords each member a reasonable amount of "air time" during each meeting. If groups grow too large, division into smaller groups can be considered.

A third issue is *duration*. In some groups, members contract with each other to meet a certain number of times and then renegotiate. Others leave duration open, meeting until the group collectively decides to terminate. As mentioned above, a negotiated open trial period of a specified number of weeks may be followed by the continuation of those members who wish to make a longer-term commitment.

A fourth issue is *length of meeting*. Often half an hour is spent at the beginning of meetings with individuals arriving a little late, getting refreshments (if provided), and catching up on superficial chat. Then more personal sharing begins. Consequently, we find that two hours represents a minimum length of time for meetings. Some groups even specify that the first half hour is for socializing and refreshments and that then things "get started."

A fifth issue is *content*. Some groups choose to focus their discussion on specific books, scriptures, issues, readings, topics, consciousness raising, or spiritual disciplines. Others intentionally avoid predetermined topics, focusing instead on whatever each member is experiencing. This is a decision of the degree of structure to be imposed on meetings. Sometimes it is helpful to "get things started" by having a particular content on which to focus. Some groups have structured topics for the first few weeks or months and then change to an unstructured format. Others begin each meeting with content on a particular "exercise" to get discussion rolling and then proceed in a less structured way. Here are some possible structures that have been used by sharing groups.

> Each member tells the group what has happened since the last meeting, both the events and how she or he felt/feels about them.
>
> Each member talks about the best thing that happened this week, the worst thing that happened this week, and (hardest of all) "the thing that is hardest for me to talk about right now."
>
> Each meeting focuses on a chapter, article, or other reading chosen by one or more members to be discussed by the group.
>
> Each meeting focuses on a particular topic chosen by the group during the previous meeting—certain memories, feelings, beliefs, questions, experiences, challenges, or frustrations that are common to members.
>
> A series of meetings is devoted to hearing the life stories of the members (chap-

ter 10). Each member is given one meeting to narrate an autobiographical account. Each member can use whatever media or methods seem best—pictures, poetry, music, or stories. This exercise can be particularly valuable to the ongoing group because it provides a sense of the history of each member, a context within which to understand new experiences that are shared. Some groups choose to do a prolonged retreat or marathon session together when extensive material of this kind is to be covered, rather than spreading it out over several weeks or months of meetings.

Each member specifies something that he or she is working to change, and the group members both challenge and help the person to take specific steps toward the goal before the next meeting.

A sixth issue is *frequency of meetings*. Most often groups meet weekly, and this works well. Some groups meet biweekly, which seems to be an outer limit for sustaining group cohesion (particularly if members periodically miss meetings). One local group practices an interesting balance, meeting for personal sharing on every second and fourth Monday of the month but having a social "fun" meeting (usually dinner out or potluck) whenever a fifth Monday occurs.

This raises another issue, which is the extent to which *socializing* will be mixed with the heavier content of the group. During the early weeks and months of meeting, such time tends to be spent in fairly superficial chatting and intellectualized discussion. This is a fairly normal beginning, a process by which members come to test the waters. Gradually, some members begin to take bigger risks and more personal material is shared. At this point a crucial transition occurs. There may be awkward alternations between light-hearted exchanges and heavy personal sharing and risking, perhaps punctuated by humor and intellectualizing that emerge from discomfort. Here a key decision is made—how much time is going to be spent in socializing and how much devoted to deeper sharing? Some members opt out at this juncture. A related issue is the serving of refreshments, a pleasant addition but perhaps also a distraction for the group and an added responsibility for the host. Each group must negotiate these issues.

Confidentiality is always a key consideration and one to be decided by consensus early in the life of the group. The sharing of difficult and important personal material is usually enabled by and predicated on an agreement of total confidentiality. What is said in the group is to be conveyed to no one else. A specific understanding should be reached as to whether this includes the spouses of members; if material is shared with partners they, too, must understand and respect the agreed-upon confidentiality protections.

Finally, there is the issue of *leader-led versus leaderless* groups. A leader can facilitate a group but is by no means necessary. The dynamics of leaderless groups differ in important ways from those where an identified leader is present.

Should you, as pastor, participate in groups of this kind? Certainly, there is great potential for conflicts of role. If you join as a coparticipant, you will be expected to share personal material in the same way that other members do. If other participants are also members of the congregation, a uniquely strong bond of trust must be established with these particular parishioners. Some pastors find this to be a difficult and conflictual situation. If, on the other hand, you play the role of group leader and facilitator without sharing at the same personal level, different problems tend to emerge in group dynamics. The presence in a group of any nonparticipating "observer" inhibits sharing by members, and this is doubly likely to occur if the leader/observer has projection-rich overlays of authority and morality. Either kind of participation also places you in a uniquely privileged relationship with certain members of the congregation, a differentiation that may prove problematic in later contexts.

Still, pastors can be very lonely people, isolated by their role, having no one except family with whom to share their inner world. For these reasons the community of a personal sharing group can be invaluable. One alternative is to participate in a group constituted of peers or of individuals having no other official relationships with the pastor. We will consider these and other important aspects of maintaining your pastoral health in chapter 21.

Last, in the realm of peers, it should be mentioned that peer support groups can be constituted of individuals struggling with similar problems. The wide variety of "anonymous" twelve-step groups are of this kind, many of which meet in churches and synagogues. A congregation can start support groups for people in certain transitions: new parents, the newly divorced, college students, children of alcoholics, the recently bereaved, family members of those with major diseases, the recently retired. By virtue of their common life changes, such individuals often form lasting bonds and provide mutual support.

Paraphernalia and Print

The shelves of any bookstore are laden with books promising to work miracles in helping people change. There are books to help one lose weight, gain friends, sleep better, improve one's memory, feel less anxious and more zestful, hypnotize oneself, decrease bad habits, have more fun, cope with stress, live longer, find a career, live through divorce or get over lost romances, make a fortune, or become more relaxed, less depressed, more spiritual, less bored, more rational, less procrastinating, more assertive, less indecisive, and more effective on the job, on the tennis court, or in bed. From womb to tomb there are books on how to do it better.

Do self-help books really help? Some of them do and have been shown to be helpful in controlled research.[7] Some are based on methods that work when administered by a skilled counselor but may or may not be effective in self-help form. Yet most, despite their extravagant claims, are based on absolutely no sound evidence at all. In the "Additional Readings" at the end of each chapter, we have tried to be selective in presenting self-help and other materials that we have found helpful in our own work, some of which are well founded in research. We encourage you to consider these and other self-help materials as resources in your counseling work, with several caveats: (a) Always *read* a resource yourself before you recommend it to a client; (b) consider self-help approaches as an alternative, though not a total replacement for personal counseling; and (c) be aware that self-help interventions, like any other intervention, can be ineffective or even harmful and maintain contact with the individual to follow progress or the lack of it. Keep a card catalog of self-help resources, along with notes on how clients responded to each.

When sound self-help resources are identified (and there are many), make them available. This can be done not only through ordinary counseling work but more generally. Many congregations maintain a library of books to be checked out by interested parishioners, and this can be well stocked with carefully selected self-help resources. To facilitate the use of such books, use a check-out procedure that does not provide a public record of who used which book. Some books may be lost through this minimal security system, but it is probably a good investment. A large sticker on the cover bearing the congregation's name may encourage eventual return of books.

Within the counseling process there are at least four ways in which self-help resources can be used. They can be used *instead of formal sessions*, permitting the individual to work on his or her own with minimal counselor assistance. This is our routine procedure for problem drinkers who have not developed serious dependence on alcohol and who want to learn moderation.[8] We provide an initial evaluation session, give the client a self-help resource with the encouragement that research has shown that many people are able to use this method effectively on their own,[9] and arrange a two-week follow-up session to check on progress. If all is going well, this is followed by a six-week checkup, and if progress is continuing at that point an open-ended invitation is issued for further consultation as needed.

A second procedure is to use self-help materials as an *adjunct to counseling*. A client can read such materials while also working with a counselor on the problem. Ideally the procedures advocated in the self-help book and in the counseling sessions are congruent.

A third possibility is for the client to apply self-help methods *to one problem area while counseling is focusing on other topics*. Thus a client who is depressed and who also wants to lose weight may see a counselor for the former while using self-help resources (book or group) to work on weight loss (or vice versa).

Finally, self-help materials may be useful *at the conclusion of counseling*. In one study we found that problem drinkers given a self-help manual at the end of treatment were significantly more likely to continue showing progress than were those not receiving the manual.[10] Thus, self-help resources may be effective in maintaining and extending the gains that have been achieved during the active counseling process.

Paraphernalia? What are those? In addition to books there is a rapidly growing range of other self-help aids. Some of these are so reusable and applicable to common problems that they may be worthwhile resources to have on hand. It is impossible to predict what the burgeoning technology will provide next, but here are some examples of present resources:

> Tape recordings of therapeutic instructions for methods such as progressive deep muscle relaxation
>
> Biofeedback devices for a variety of purposes
>
> The "bell and pad" apparatus for teaching bladder control to children who are bedwetters; this has been well substantiated as a helpful (though by no means perfect) method for overcoming bedwetting and is available commercially.
>
> Videotapes on mental health topics
>
> Videotape equipment to provide feedback as part of programs that teach assertiveness, job-finding and interviewing skills, and other social skills
>
> Board games and other play devices and games with an underlying mental health goal
>
> Portable breath-alcohol analyzers to increase awareness of level of blood alcohol and intoxication
>
> Personal computer software focused on particular counseling tasks
>
> Timers and counters for self-monitoring of various behaviors.

The availability of such resources can be made known through a local congregational newsletter, and they can be shared among several congregations depending upon demand. Again a confidential check-out system is essential.

A newsletter itself can be an important resource. Without jeopardizing confidentiality, an announcement can be made of a special need of which the pastor is aware (with the permission of the individuals involved, of course). Reviews of self-help resources can be published. Upcoming mental health resources and activities can be publicized. Feature articles can focus on common life problems.

A BROADER VIEW OF PASTORAL COUNSELING

Most of this book has focused on pastoral counseling in the traditional sense—formal sessions between pastor and client. People change in many contexts and for many reasons other than formal counseling, however, and a faith community affords many other potentially positive influences on mental health.

Viewed in this way, many if not most of your contacts with people can be thought of as (ideally) promoting mental health. Some possible examples:

> The pastor models good listening skills when others are talking and shows regard for their personal input.
>
> The pastor avoids being a go-between but instead encourages individuals who have feelings or frustrations regarding another parishioner to express them directly.
>
> The pastor respects the value of other people's time and asks, whenever placing a telephone call, "Is this a good time to talk?"
>
> The pastor gives good attention and eye contact even on brief interpersonal exchanges and does not try to "do two things at once."
>
> The pastor sets clear limits on demands for his or her own time, takes consistent leisure and vacation time, and otherwise models a lifestyle that balances work with personal mental health.
>
> The pastor admits mistakes and deals with them in an open rather than defensive manner.

These are not intended to be moral homilies, but rather examples of how the healthy influence of a pastor can extend to even small interactions.

As a pastor you also have an additional avenue open to you. You can not only practice what you preach, but have the opportunity of preaching what you practice! Sermons can be quite influential in communicating basic attitudes and information about mental health and in expressing (intentionally or not) your own approaches and openness to counseling about personal problems. Mental health topics always provide rich material for development, and although not all current psychological maladies were recognized in ancient times, the scriptures invariably speak to these timeless topics of human struggle and suffering.[11] We have expressed cautions earlier regarding the use of case material in sermons, a practice that can provide rich elaboration but which also contains important pitfalls. Another element that affects the willingness of people to seek counseling is self-disclosure. A pastor who is willing to discuss and explore her or his own views and struggles comfortably (carefully distinguishing these from *the* Truth) often enables others to self-disclose as well. This is an issue not only in counseling but in public speaking. Part of the decision to seek or not seek counseling from a pastor is made in response to impressions gained while listening to sermons and other public remarks, even informal ones. A pastor who makes casual public reference to clients' problems, who is defensive in dealing with emotions and other personal material, or who uses roadblocks instead of listening is unlikely to find a queue at the counseling room door. On the other hand, a pastor who honors confidentiality, who self-discloses appropriately and comfortably, who speaks with respect and understanding of human problems, and who listens reflectively rather than firing off advice or other roadblocks is likely to be kept busy in hearing and dealing with the inner struggles of the community.

In chapter 1 we referred to your unique pastoral right of initiation, the ability to intervene when a problem is perceived and at early stages even when a formal request has not been made. Here counseling enters the realm of *prevention*. There are various kinds of prevention, but two will be discussed— secondary and primary prevention.

Secondary prevention refers to the recognition of problems at early stages and intervention before they become more serious. This can include recognizing a high-risk situation even when there is no evident problem at present. You can be present at crucial moments when problems often emerge and when extra support can be valuable—the early days after arrival of a new baby, the approach and aftermath of the "empty nest" when the last child leaves, anniversaries of loss, and other major life changes and transitions including the more obvious ones of bereavement, job loss, and divorce. Many pastors conduct premarital counseling, but few arrange for checkup visits for couples on their first or subsequent anniversaries, when the initial glow has probably abated and some new realities have emerged. Unlike traditional mental health professionals, you do not have to wait for an invitation but rather can initiate when you perceive a need or potential need.

Primary prevention is less focused on a particular subgroup. Primary prevention undertakes to intervene with an entire community (such as a congregation) in a way that will promote mental health and decrease the occurrence of certain problems. Because of the voluntary participation aspects of faith communities, however, interventions necessarily touch only certain parts of the community (whereas in school, for example, there is a captive total population). Much less is known about effective primary prevention than about treatment. More is known about how to help people recover from problems that about how to help them not develop such problems in the first place. In primary prevention, one is treading on uncertain albeit promising ground.

Marriage enrichment has been a favorite primary prevention target in faith communities. There are a wide variety of programs intended to strengthen marriages and decrease the rate of relationship disintegration. We have attended and conducted such experiences, which often occur in retreat settings. The goal is important, and such programs have often been strongly endorsed by pastors who are concerned about the frequent demise of marriages in their midst. Still, we must point out that the actual effects of such retreats are largely unknown. Few adequate scientific evaluations have been conducted on the outcome of such marriage enrichment experiences. It is well to remember, too that although the intent or title of a program may be to *prevent* problems, it is possible to do harm. One painful example was a public school system's program for alcohol and drug abuse prevention. Many schools have such programs, but one particular school commissioned a scientific evaluation.[12] The result? Students who had gone through the program were more familiar and comfortable with these drugs and more likely to be using and selling them. One cannot assume that, because an intervention is called "prevention" or "enrichment," it in fact prevents or enriches anything.

With this important caution, however, we reassert our belief in preventive pastoring—that faith communities *can* provide experiences that promote positive mental health. We have offered adult education classes within church settings on topics such as stress management, time management, assertiveness and anger management, relaxation, communication skills, conflict resolution, coping with mood and depression, sex-role stereotypes, and alcohol and drug problems. Many of these tie in directly to topics of concern to faith communities. Conflict resolution, mediation, and anger management, for example, are of immediate applicability in the search for peacemaking strategies. Time management is an issue of stewardship, both calling people to be more aware of how they use their time and enabling them to manage it better so that they have greater flexibility for discretionary activities such as spiritual growth and service involvement. In designing and offering such educational series, draw on methods that have been best supported by psychological research. Many of the basics of these methods have been covered in previous chapters.

Steps can also be taken toward developing a more supportive community within the congregation. Procedures that increase positive feedback among members are a step in this direction. One example is a "thank you" bulletin board displayed in a public place where all members are invited to place notes expressing appreciation for things that others have done or said. These can be sealed, intended to be found and read only by the addressee, or can be made public by posting for all to see. The invitation for everyone to use the board relieves the pastor or other individuals from the burden of "forgetting" someone. As people begin to exchange appreciations for even small actions and efforts, a rewarding process can ensue resulting in a positive spiral of increased appreciation and lifted mood, which in turn encourages still further actions on behalf of others.

The communication and listening skills discussed in part II can be taught to officers of the congregation, to classes, to couples, or to specially commissioned helpers. As the number of people trained in reflective listening increases, so does the level of helpful communication within the congregation. (Remember that simple instruction is not enough. Learning of these skills requires practice and feedback.)

The Interfaith Counseling Center

As federal aid for mental health services has suffered drastic cuts and local faith communities have perceived the growing need for counseling, some have taken action to set up special centers to offer therapeutic services within a faith context. The interfaith counseling center is a viable model and one that may be an important source of mental health services in the future. An interest in healing has always been a part of faith traditions. From our own experience in setting up and administering such services, we offer the following recommendations and considerations.

1. The counseling services of an interfaith counseling center (ICC) should be clearly distinguished from proselytism for particular beliefs and from membership recruitment. Some "faith counseling centers" strongly advocate particular beliefs and views as part of their interventions. We regard this to be improper counseling and an abuse of vulnerability. One protection against partisan proselytism is to obtain a broad base of sponsorship representing a range of faith communities. One such center with which we consulted was cosponsored by nineteen congregations from nine different faiths.

2. In hiring of clinical staff, primary consideration must be given to professional competence. Quality of training and experience is of prime importance in selecting staff because this ultimately influences the quality of services to be provided. Credibility of staff to other mental health workers and agencies in the area is an important issue. Sensitivity to and positive regard for the religious beliefs and spiritual dimensions of individuals are also essential qualities of staff. Adherence to particular creeds need not be a major consideration in hiring.

3. The skills required to develop and administer such an ICC (including fund-raising and public relations abilities) are not likely to be found in an individual who also has the personal and professional prerequisites for clinical work described above, nor are clinical and administrative responsibilities easily combined. If possible, an executive director who does not carry major clinical responsibilities may be advisable.

4. As with any service system, financing is likely to be the major obstacle. In spite of an excellent record of service and a clear and constant need, the ICC mentioned above was forced to close its doors after three years because of budgetary deficits that exhausted the generous initial grant that permitted the center to open. A feasible and flexible funding plan would include support from a variety of sources including (a) regular contributions by supporting congregations; (b) an initial endowment to cover the probable deficits of early years as well as start-up costs; (c) client fees, which can be expected to cover at most 50 percent of operating costs if a reasonable sliding scale is used; and (d) supplementary support from private foundations, local industries, public charities, and individual donors. The Board of ICC should include individuals who are willing and able to assist in the continuing process of fund raising, as well as professionals expert in mental health services. Health plan reimbursability is a further consideration in staffing patterns.

5. Regular liaisons between the ICC and its sponsoring congregations are vital. Possibilities include an annual meal meeting for pastors of present and potential sponsoring congregations, representation from congregations on an advisory board, presentations of the ICC and its work at the governing board meetings within individual congregations, and talks by ICC staff members within the local congregations.

6. Adequate support staff (secretarial and reception) is essential. Such support is difficult to constitute from part-time volunteers because of the constancy, complexity, and confidentiality of work with an ICC.

All in all, the obstacles are legion. Based on the above considerations, a minimum starting staff would include an executive director/fund raiser, at least one and preferably two clinical staff members, and secretarial/reception staff. There are also initial costs of finding and preparing appropriate office space, obtaining furnishings and supplies. A substantial reserve should be held to cover operating costs for at least two years. Still, the effort is worthwhile, and if these major practical problems can be solved the ICC can be a valuable service to the community at large.

Avoid Negative Influences

In addition to helping provide solutions, the local congregation can take steps to avoid being a part of the problem—to avoid contributing to already problematic situations or creating them.

The first religion-related issue that comes to mind for the average mental health professional might be guilt. Indeed, some pathologically guilty people trace their difficulties to early religious teachings. It is certainly wise to keep a careful eye on the content of education programs for children within the congregation. Even well-intentioned teachings at the wrong time can have a scarring effect. Rabbi Kushner wrote of a young boy whose mother had died and who was told, "Don't be sad. God just needed her more than you did."[13] In this one statement are at least three unhealthy communications: (a) that it is not OK to feel sad; (b) that God was personally responsible for the mother's death; and (c) that this occurred because the boy did not love and need his mother enough.

There are many considerations beyond the content of religious teachings. Chapter 12 discussed how a well-intentioned supportive community can actually prolong depression and pain by reinforcing it selectively. In such cases, support needs to be provided for nondepressed, nondisabled actions. This runs contrary to what most people think of as helpful—to aid and rescue those who are hurting. A pastor who is aware of this possibility of paradoxical effect can consider whether such a contingency is contributing in a particular case and arrange for a more healthy pattern of support.

Yet another risk is that of overloading people who generously give of their time and talents. Burnout is not limited to occupation settings, and talented people sometimes leave a faith community because they feel fatigued and consumed. Talents, like candles, are resources that should neither be hidden under a bushel nor burned at both ends. The time management skills described in chapter 9 are applicable not only for pastors but for others who give their time in service. Likewise the assertiveness skills discussed in chapter 15 are important if one is to maintain a balance between service to others and personal well-being.

TOWARD WHOLENESS

Acknowledging the limitations and shortcomings of organized religion, we still believe that faith communities provide not only powerful potential forces for mental health but also unique contexts within which individuals seek and grow toward *wholeness*. The entire spiritual dimension of humanness has been noticeably bypassed, overlooked, absent in most modern psychological theories and services. The wedding of competent professional care to a context that acknowledges and affirms spirituality is one reason for our continuing commitment to pastoral counseling. People look to their faith communities to foster this sense of wholeness. Like a comprehensive faith, competent pastoral counseling encompasses the whole person—biological, psychological, and spiritual.

Though some stereotype religion as forcing people into a common mold, quite the opposite is true of mature faith communities.[14] The person is valued as an *individual*, a unique creation of God unlike any other, with intended gifts and purpose to be discovered and pursued.[15] People are not just tacitly acknowledged to be unique but are actively called to discover their gifts and purpose and to develop and pursue these to the glory and service of God.

A profound sense of *acceptance* may also be found within the healthy faith community. In part, this acceptance comes of the recognition that each person is an individual and unique creation of the same God. In part, it emanates from the faith's teaching regarding God's love, forgiveness, and acceptance of people in spite of their shortcomings. But perhaps the most tangible manifestation is to be found in the community itself—in this group of seekers taking an active interest in each other's welfare in the course of a long and constant journey. There is an open belongingness to many faith communities that welcomes in the stranger and fosters in its members a sense of strength and support that enables the taking of new risks and actions.

Actions, too, are part of the community. As one is accepted and drawn to awareness both of gifts and of the call to use them, there follows a *challenge to act*. Perhaps the acting involves changing one's own behavior and life pattern toward a chosen ideal. It may mean overcoming performance fears or shyness or lack of confidence. Perhaps it involves "repenting," literally turning again from a diverted course back to one's intended path. Perhaps to act means to serve others in a new or different way, using the gifts one has been given. The faith community calls and enables individuals to act.

Here, too, is the broader context of pastoral counseling. We began this book by saying that people come to pastoral counselors seeking to be *understood* as whole people. They come also to be *allowed* and *enabled* to be whole people. Many of the specific concerns that have been addressed in these chapters represent unnecessary limitations, conditions that block the individual's growth, change, wholeness. The removal and resolution of such obstacles is a crucial part of effective pastoral counseling. It is liberation from a bondage that disrupts not only psychological well-being, but physical and spiritual as well. Yet, as a pastor you have still more to offer than the removal of chains. One who is freed is a pilgrim again, begins a new journey. As a pastor you understand this journey in its wholeness. It is not that you have final answers to be dispensed or definitive road maps to be used by all pilgrims. It is more that you have a vision, a broader way of seeing, a sense of wholeness. On a clear day, you can see the possibilities in people—the hints, perhaps, of what God intended. Through calls to awareness, acts of acceptance, and discovery of alternatives, you urge each individual on toward that still, small inner voice that is forever calling.

ADDITIONAL READINGS ON BUILDING A SUPPORTIVE COMMUNITY

BAROUH, GAIL *Support Groups: The Human Face of the HIV/AIDS Epidemic.* New York: Long Island Association for AIDS Care, 1992.

D'ANDREA, VINCENT, and PETER SALVONEY *Peer Counseling: Skills and Perspectives.* Palo Alto, CA: Science and Behavior Books, 1983. Outlines a program for training laypeople as peer counselors.

EGAN, GERARD *The Skilled Helper: A Systematic Approach to Effective Helping* (4th ed.). Monterey, CA: Brooks/Cole, 1990.

JOHNSON, DAVID W. *Reaching Out: Interpersonal Effectiveness and Self-actualization* (3d ed.). Englewood Cliffs, NJ: Prentice-Hall, 1986.

L'ABATE, LUCIANO *Building Family Competence: Primary and Secondary Prevention Strategies.* Newbury Park, CA: Sage Publications, 1990.

PECK, M. SCOTT *The Different Drum: Community Making and Peace.* New York: Touchstone, 1987.

SELF-HELP RESOURCES

Just about any bookstore now has a section entitled "self-help," which is stocked with volumes of advice on virtually any personal dimension. Remember that *anyone* can author such a book, and there's a lot of nonsense out there. Most books contain homespun advice with no scientific basis. In the sections at the end of each chapter we have tried to help you sort through this maze of offerings by recommending a few of what we regard to be the more reliable resources.

Here are the names and addresses of a few publishers which, in our opinion, carry generally better-quality self-help resources. Each will gladly send you, on request, a free catalog of their current titles.

Castalia Publishing Co.
P.O. Box 1587
Eugene, OR 97440
503-343-4433

New Harbinger
5674 Shattuck Avenue
Oakland, CA 94609
800-748-6273

Impact Publishers
P.O. Box 1094
San Luis Obispo, CA 93406
805-543-5911

Research Press
2612 N. Mattis Avenue
Champaign, IL 61821
217-352-3273

KEEPING UP

Knowledge advances rapidly in psychology, and in order to keep up it is useful to have sources of reliable information and summaries. The following publishers offer generally high-quality practical guidebooks oriented for counselors, and focusing on specific problem areas:

Allyn & Bacon, Longwood Division
(Psychology Handbooks and Guidebooks series)
111 10th Street
Des Moines, IA 50309
800-848-4400

Guilford Press
72 Spring Street
New York, NY 10012
800-365-7006 or 212-431-9800

Word Publishing
(Resources for Christian Counseling series)
Waco, TX 76703
800-933-9673

A variety of journals also provide new material on pastoral counseling and related topics. These include:

Common Boundary
Journal of Pastoral Care
Journal of Psychology and Christianity
Pastoral Psychology

CONTINUING EDUCATION IN PASTORAL CARE AND COUNSELING

As a pastor who counsels, your own resources and skills can be increased by participating in ongoing continuing education opportunities. A number of associations provide or certify opportunities for continuing education in pastoral care and counseling. A listing of clinical pastoral education (CPE) programs is available from:

> Association for Clinical Pastoral Education (ACPE)
> 1549 Clairmont Road, Suite 103
> Decatur, GA 30033-4611

Information about continuing education opportunities for pastoral counselors more generally is available from the American Associate of Pastoral Counselors (AAPC), created in 1964 to promote the ministry of pastoral counseling and the professional competence of pastoral counselors. The AAPC participates in setting professional standards and in certification of pastoral counselors. This organization also accredits training programs, and can provide a list of approved training centers. The address is:

> American Association of Pastoral Counselors (AAPC)
> 9504-A Lee Highway
> Fairfax, VA 22031-2303
> (703-385-6967)

Other organizations of interest for continuing education include:

> American Association for Marriage and Family Therapy
> 1100 17th Street (10th Floor)
> Washington, DC 20036-4601
> (202-452-0109)

> American Protestant Correctional Chaplains Association
> 516 Jordan Drive
> Tucker, GA 30084

> American Protestant Hospital Association
> College of Chaplains
> 1701 E. Woodfield Road, Suite 311
> Schaumberg, IL 60173

> Association of Mental Health Clergy
> 12320 River Oaks Point
> Knoxville, TN 37922

> Canadian Association for Pastoral Education
> P.O. Box 96
> Roxboro, P.Q. H8Y 3E8
> Canada

National Association of Catholic Chaplains
3501 South Lake Drive
P.O. Box 07473
Milwaukee, WI 53207-0473

National Association of Jewish Chaplains
100 East 77th Street
New York, NY 10021

National Institute of Business and Industrial Chaplains
9449 Briar Forest Drive
Houston, TX 77063-1034

National Organization for Continuing Education of Roman Catholic Clergy
5401 South Cornell
Chicago, IL 60615 (312-752-8849)

Special consultation in helping communities set up a local interfaith counseling center is available from:

The Samaritan Institute
2696 South Colorado Blvd, Suite 380
Denver, CO 80222
(303-691-0144)

Stephen Ministries is a program that provides training for increasing pastoral care resources within the local congregation:

Stephen Ministries
8016 Dale
St. Louis, MO 63117-1149 (314-645-5511)

A good source of information on marriage enrichment programs is a national clearinghouse:

Association of Couples for Marriage Enrichment
P.O. Box 10596
Winston-Salem, NC 27108

NOTES

[1]Allan Tough, *Intentional Changes* (Chicago: Follett, 1982). Some accounts of major life transformations, in the style of Ebenezer Scrooge, can be found in William R. Miller and Janet C'deBaca, "Quantum Change: Toward a Psychology of Transformation," in Todd Heatherton and Jon Weinberger, eds., *Can Personality Change?* (Washington, DC: American Psychological Association, 1994), 253–280.

[2]These categories were originally described by Andrew Christensen, William R. Miller, and Ricardo F. Muñoz, "Paraprofessionals, Partners, Peers, Paraphernalia, and Print: Expanding Mental Health Service Delivery," *Professional Psychology* 9 (1978): 249–70.

[3]For example, William R. Miller, Cheryl A. Taylor, and JoAnn C. West, "Focused versus Broad Spectrum Behavior Therapy for Problem Drinkers," *Journal of Consulting and Clinical Psychology* 48 (1980): 590–601; William R. Miller and Marina DiPilato, "Treatment of Nightmares

via Relaxation and Desensitization: A Controlled Evaluation," *Journal of Consulting and Clinical Psychology* 51 (1983): 870–77; Sheri D. Pruitt, William R. Miller, and Jane E. Smith, "Outpatient Behavioral Treatment of Severe Obsessive-Compulsive Disorder: Using Paraprofessional Resources," *Journal of Anxiety Disorders* 3 (1989): 179–86; Michael M. Schmidt and William R. Miller, "Amount of Therapist Contact and Outcome in a Multidimensional Depression Treatment Program," *Acta Psychiatrica Scandinavica* 67 (1983): 319–32.

[4]William R. Miller, Kim E. Hedrick, and Debra Orlofsky, "The Helpful Responses Questionnaire: A Procedure for Measuring Therapeutic Empathy," *Journal of Clinical Psychology* 47 (1991): 444–48.

[5]Gilbert Freitag, Elaine Blechman, and Philip Berck, "College Students as Companion Aides to Newly-Released Psychiatric Patients," in G. Spector and C. Claiborne, eds., *Crisis Intervention: A Topical Series in Community Clinical Psychology* (New York: Behavior Publications, 1973), 2:118–37.

[6]Robert W. Sisson and John H. Mallams, "The Use of Systematic Encouragement and Community Access Procedures to Increase Attendance at Alcoholics Anonymous and Al-Anon Meetings," *American Journal of Drug and Alcohol Abuse* 8 (1981): 371–76.

[7]Robert A. Gould and George A. Clum, "A Meta-analysis of Self-help Treatment Approaches," *Clinical Psychology Review* 13 (1993): 169–86; Russell E. Glasgow and Gerald M. Rosen, "Behavioral Bibliotherapy: A Review of Self-help Behavior Therapy Manuals," *Psychological Bulletin* 85 (1978): 1–23.

[8]William R. Miller, "When Is a Book a Treatment? Bibliotherapy for Problem Drinkers," in William M. Hay and Peter E. Nathan, eds., *Clinical Case Studies in the Behavioral Treatment of Alcoholism* (New York: Plenum Press, 1982), 49–72.

[9]William R. Miller and Ricardo F. Muñoz, *How to Control Your Drinking*, rev. ed. (Albuquerque: University of New Mexico Press, 1982).

[10]William R. Miller, "Behavioral Treatment of Problem Drinkers: A Comparative Outcome Study of Three Controlled Drinking Therapies," *Journal of Consulting and Clinical Psychology* 46 (1978): 74–86.

[11]Gary Collins, *Christian Counseling* (Waco, TX: Word, 1988).

[12]Richard B. Stuart, "Teaching Facts about Drugs: Pushing or Preventing?" *Journal of Educational Psychology* 66 (1974): 189–201.

[13]Harold S. Kushner, *When Bad Things Happen to Good People* (New York: Avon, 1981).

[14]James W. Fowler, *Weaving the New Creation: Stages of Faith and the Public Church* (New York: Harper, 1991).

[15]Elizabeth O'Connor, *The Eight Day of Creation: Gifts and Creativity* (Waco, TX: Word, 1971).

21

PASTORAL SELF-CARE

Hell is truth recognized too late.

—William Sloane Coffin, Jr.

This chapter was not in our first edition. It arose from another decade of experience in working with and training pastors who counsel. This chapter is for you, the *person* who pastors.

Counseling in general is highly personal work. You enter the counseling room armed with nothing but yourself. You, with God's help, are the instrument of healing. Like all sensitive instruments, this one needs to be kept attuned and balanced. If you fail to keep yourself healthy and centered, your counseling and your clients will suffer along with you. The sheep falter when the shepherd is lost.

Pastoral counseling adds even more dimensions to the demands of the healing professions. The high standards and expectations imposed by society on healers are even higher for pastors. The workday is often long. A pastor's life, though rewarding, can also be lonely. In the midst of a life of giving, of constant ministering to others, the question looms: Who ministers to me?

One of the ways in which we have sought to return thanks for our own gifts is by working with pastors who are struggling with personal difficulties. We have found this rewarding work, not only in the quality time spent with pastors, but in the knowledge that by ministering to pastors we are in the long run reaching so many others who will ultimately be upheld through the pastors' own ministries. We urge you to apply this same logic to yourself. Time spent in keeping yourself healthy physically, psychologically, and spiritually is a sound investment on behalf of the many whose lives you could touch in the years ahead. It enables you to keep going, to continue pastoring with renewed energy and vision.

Our hope is that this chapter will support *you*. If we succeed, we will help you to step back for a bit and consider your own needs and how you may need to address them.

Going Down with the Ship

Some years ago we were invited to speak about counseling to a group of pastors on the anniversary commemorating four chaplains who died on the Dorchester. These clergy saw to their own needs last, gave up their life vests for others, and went down with the ship. For this act, they are rightly honored to this day. Yet the image also haunted us as we reflected on what we were going say to these pastors: Going down with the ship. . . . Everyone else first. It somehow captures an essential theme in pastoring that has a profoundly positive as well as a sinister side.

We need not explain or defend to you the merits of sacrificial service. Few enter pastoral ministry without a deep appreciation if not hunger for giving. It is to the other side of this coin that we have found ourselves most often speaking in our therapeutic work with pastors: that unless you are yourself renewed, you are at risk of burning out and of losing, at least in part, your ability to serve. A powerful image here from the Hebrew scripture is the burning bush: To burn without being consumed. That is the critical balance of pastoring.

PASTORAL SELF-EVALUATION

How are you doing in your own life, with regard to a healthy balance? The self-evaluation below is designed to help you think more specifically about where you are personally. There is no hidden dimension to this inventory. It is not a personality x-ray. It cannot be more revealing to you than your own conscious honesty. Rather, it is a *self*-assessment, and that is where change (like repentance) begins. It may be helpful for you to repeat an inventory like this periodically, perhaps annually on the anniversary of your ordination or call to ministry.

A Self-Assessment Inventory

Like the items in the Goldilocks tale, some areas of our lives are too large, some are too small, and some are just right. For each of the areas in this inventory, evaluate honestly whether you have too much of it in your life, too little, or just the right amount. To start with, just circle a rating on the 1 to 7 scale for each area. The items are in no particular order. If an item doesn't apply to you, just skip over it.

TABLE 21-1   Self-Assessment Inventory

	FAR TOO LITTLE			JUST RIGHT		FAR TOO MUCH		IMPORTANCE
The amount of physical exercise that I get	1	2	3	4	5	6	7	_____
Time that I devote to nourishing my own spiritual life	1	2	3	4	5	6	7	_____
Friendship	1	2	3	4	5	6	7	_____
The amount of time that I spend working	1	2	3	4	5	6	7	_____
The amount that I accomplish in my work	1	2	3	4	5	6	7	_____
Playing and relaxing	1	2	3	4	5	6	7	_____
Studying, thinking, and learning	1	2	3	4	5	6	7	_____
Quality time spent with my spouse/partner	1	2	3	4	5	6	7	_____
Quality time with my children and/or extended family	1	2	3	4	5	6	7	_____
Stress and anxiety in my life	1	2	3	4	5	6	7	_____
The amount of food that I eat	1	2	3	4	5	6	7	_____
The amount of rest and sleep that I get	1	2	3	4	5	6	7	_____
My own use of alcohol	1	2	3	4	5	6	7	_____
My own use of other drugs	1	2	3	4	5	6	7	_____
Laughter	1	2	3	4	5	6	7	_____
Prayer and meditation	1	2	3	4	5	6	7	_____
Telling the truth	1	2	3	4	5	6	7	_____
Time in meetings	1	2	3	4	5	6	7	_____
Self-esteem	1	2	3	4	5	6	7	_____
Receiving love from others	1	2	3	4	5	6	7	_____
Loving action toward others	1	2	3	4	5	6	7	_____
Crying	1	2	3	4	5	6	7	_____
A sense of meaning in my life	1	2	3	4	5	6	7	_____
Risk-taking	1	2	3	4	5	6	7	_____
Recreation and enjoyable activities	1	2	3	4	5	6	7	_____
Revealing and expressing myself to others	1	2	3	4	5	6	7	_____
Being organized	1	2	3	4	5	6	7	_____
Social support from friends and family	1	2	3	4	5	6	7	_____
Financial resources	1	2	3	4	5	6	7	_____
Security	1	2	3	4	5	6	7	_____
Changing and growing as a person	1	2	3	4	5	6	7	_____
Intimacy	1	2	3	4	5	6	7	_____
Taking time off	1	2	3	4	5	6	7	_____

TABLE 21-1 *(Continued)*

	FAR TOO LITTLE		JUST RIGHT		FAR TOO MUCH		IMPORTANCE
Professional counseling for myself	1	2	3	4	5	6	7	_____
Expressing anger to others	1	2	3	4	5	6	7	_____
Taking care of my physical health	1	2	3	4	5	6	7	_____
Alone time	1	2	3	4	5	6	7	_____
Pleasant events in my daily life	1	2	3	4	5	6	7	_____
Vacation and leave time	1	2	3	4	5	6	7	_____

After you have rated each area, next go back through the list and ask, "How important is it for me to make a change in this area of my life?" On the IMPORTANCE line write *V* for very important, *S* for somewhat important, and *N* for not important.

If you have a life partner, this next section is to help you consider your relationship from your own perspective. How happy are you with each of these dimensions of your relationship?

TABLE 21-2 **Self-Assessment Inventory: Relationship**

	VERY HAPPY		SATISFIED		VERY UNHAPPY		IMPORTANCE
Amount of time we spend together	1	2	3	4	5	6	7	_____
How we share household chores	1	2	3	4	5	6	7	_____
Communicating with each other	1	2	3	4	5	6	7	_____
Sexual fulfillment	1	2	3	4	5	6	7	_____
How we share responsibility for children	1	2	3	4	5	6	7	_____
My partner's values	1	2	3	4	5	6	7	_____
How we spend our time together	1	2	3	4	5	6	7	_____
How we resolve problems	1	2	3	4	5	6	7	_____
How my partner treats me	1	2	3	4	5	6	7	_____
How we disagree or fight	1	2	3	4	5	6	7	_____
Sharing our spiritual life	1	2	3	4	5	6	7	_____
Physical closeness and touching	1	2	3	4	5	6	7	_____
Doing fun things together	1	2	3	4	5	6	7	_____
How I treat my partner	1	2	3	4	5	6	7	_____
Our social contacts with others	1	2	3	4	5	6	7	_____
My partner's trust and respect for me	1	2	3	4	5	6	7	_____
How we make decisions	1	2	3	4	5	6	7	_____
Having our own separate identities	1	2	3	4	5	6	7	_____
Having common interests	1	2	3	4	5	6	7	_____

Now what?

This exercise may point to some areas of your life that are out of balance. Particularly for those that you have marked as very important, there's no time like the present to move toward a better understanding and a plan for change. The four questions that we suggested in chapter 7 may be helpful in assessing your own situation:

What (if anything) is troubling me?
What is causing the problem(s)?
What is missing in my life?
What do I need to do?

Obviously, we cannot here provide prescriptions for all the areas that might be out of balance, but there may be helpful material elsewhere in this book. Much of what we have provided in prior chapters by way of guidelines for understanding and counseling others may apply equally to you. If, in reviewing this self-assessment, you have unearthed some concerns related to an area discussed in an earlier chapter, it may be useful to reread that chapter with an eye toward your own situation, perhaps also consulting some of the resources suggested at the end of the chapter. If you find you feel stuck in answering the four questions above, it may be helpful to talk it over with a friend, colleague, or other professional.

What follows are some general guidelines derived from our own experience in working with pastors, with some important help and suggestions from a few seasoned pastoral colleagues. We offer these not just (or even primarily) as "solutions" to "problems" but as preventive mainentance ideas—a kind of owner's manual for your self. Again, we present these in no particular order.

PREVENTIVE MAINTENANCE FOR PASTORS

Time

One of the most common sources of distress that we hear from pastors is a sense of too much to do in too little time. Since all of us have the same amount of time each day, this boils down to a matter of trying, feeling, or being expected to accomplish too much.

Some of this just comes with the job. There are many regular demands on a pastor's time, and various parts of ministry could in themselves consume all that you have to give. Trying to meet all or even most of the needs and wants around you is a sure road to emotional and physical exhaustion.

Some of this also varies with the person. Those who are called to servanthood sometimes carry with them on the journey some burdensome baggage. Beware attaching your personal worth to killing yourself on the job. Though there are always those times when you must go above and beyond in ministering, be wary of spending yourself *regularly* past the point of diminishing returns. There comes a point where trying to do more results in accomplishing less, where continuing to give undermines your capacity to give. Here are some common bits of advice for avoiding this pernicious trap.

Keep a Sabbath   There is a very human reason for the biblical insistence on a sabbath. Rest is productive, recharging. Take the sabbath literally and seriously, though for you it may not be the same day of the week as a recognized sabbath. Take off at least a full day each week, away from all pastoral duties and activities. Except for emergencies, observe the twenty-four-hour period absolutely (for example, from sundown to sundown). Do the things that you enjoy, that revitalize you. Don't forget family, friends, fun, nature, silence, and solitude.

Set Your Own Limits   When you are approaching your healthy capacity, cut back on what you are trying to accomplish. Learn to say "No" to new commitments when you are at or approaching your limits. Don't say "Yes" just because something needs doing, and you *could* do it and even do it well. When you are considering taking on something new, ask yourself (or those to whom you report), "What will I *not* do that I am doing now, in order to make space for this?" If you fail to set your own limits, they are likely to be set for you by factors like illness, chaos, and relationship turmoil. Find ways to work less and accomplish more.

Schedule Recreation   Give priority to re-creation time just as you do to busy-ness. Some pastors have used golf in this manner, literally packing a bag and going where there are no telephones. If you fail to schedule some spaces in your life, there may be none.

Set Your Priorities   The requests and demands on your time will far exceed your time and ability to respond. Don't expect or try to meet all needs. Judge new commitments in light of your central values. Where are you spending your time now? How does your time use fit with your core values? Be clear about your values and goals and those of the organization for which you work, and then decide where you can make a difference and devote your time there. Some find it useful to review with others (e.g., a colleague, a church board) how their use of time matches with their own and/or organizational priorities.

Delegate   Sometimes it is tempting to spend time doing things that are more easily accomplished but that could be delegated. Finishing up a mailing may give you a sense of having accomplished something but might not be the best use of your time when someone else could help with it. Develop a larger ministry team (chapter 20) capable of response-ability, and call on them for help.

Physical Health

Pay attention to your body, for it will give you important signs. Slow down when your body tells you. Don't ignore fatigue. Have regular check-ups, even when you are feeling well, and if health risks are found, do what it takes to be well. High blood pressure, for example, typically produces no symptoms or discomfort but is a major cause of illness and premature death. Yet it can be treated effectively in a variety of ways. Even if not an end in itself for you, health increases your ability to minister. If you live to serve, *live* to serve!

This also means practicing health habits, making them part of your regular routine. The major causes of death and disability in developed nations are not acute but chronic diseases, which are closely related to health habits. Eat a sensible and healthy diet. Be sure you get regular physical exercise, perhaps in the company of family or friends. Avoid the drugs that poison so many in today's world. Abstain from alcohol or, if you choose, use it only with great moderation. Abstain from the use of tobacco and illicit drugs.

Mental Health

There are many parallels between physical health and psychological health. There are certain things that we all need some amount of in our lives—psychological vitamins. The Sandberg quote that stands at the opening of chapter 20 reflects this. It is wise to see that each day includes one or more pleasant events, even if small: little things that bring you fun, pleasure, satisfaction, or release. Consider a daily midday nap. Feel your feelings, and have people you can talk to about them. Spend some regular time in touch with family or friends who provide love and support.

The latter can take some doing. There is an occupational hazard of isolation and loneliness. Pastors sometimes feel the need to keep a certain personal distance from their flock, perhaps to avoid being too vulnerable, compromising an understood pastoral role, or appearing to show favoritism. Still, the human need for companionship on the journey is profound. It is important to find those with whom you can regularly share your life, your personal struggles, your inner world. Some pastors come together in small support groups for this purpose. Some find meaningful, supportive relationships outside the group to whom they minister. One's family can serve some of this function, but not all. We are not meant to be alone in our journey.

Commit yourself, too, to keeping your primary relationship and family ties strong and positive. Pastoring in general and counseling in particular require a lot of loving energy. Commit whatever time and energy it takes, then, to keep your own love and family relationships strong, for they are with you through both bright and dark times.

Pastoral ministry can at times bring high doses of demand and criticism, leaving pastors depression prone. Regular habits that support your physical and mental health are important for this reason, too. Recognize the early signs of depression or despair, and know what works best for you. One pastor friend finds that when he feels down he mainly needs physical exercise to break the spiral. Remember, too, that emotional pain is inevitable and that even the worst feelings really do pass. One of the heaviest burdens of grief, depression, and anxiety can be the haunting sense that *it will always be this way*. In truth, grief, when normally expressed, passes with time. So does profound depression. So does deep angst. We know no one of age to whom great pain and sadness have never come. The question is not whether you will escape them, but rather when they visit you how you will respond and to what you will be anchored.

This is not at all to say that you should always be able to pull yourself up by your bootstraps and feel better on your own. If you have read this far in this book, you probably believe in the healing potential of counseling, and counselors are no exception to the rule. In fact, many programs require therapists to experience the benefits of therapy themselves as part of their training. Beware the notion that you should be "above" professional help, not only because this notion deprives you of important support, but also because of what it implies about the nature of your own helping relationships.

We have said much in this book about the special nature of pastoring and counseling and the need for strict professional ethics. A personal level in this is to live your life in such a way that, by habit and discipline, you manifest a moral character. Honesty, trustworthiness, reverence, simplicity, lovingkindness, and compassion—these are not qualities that one inherits or (at least in most cases) that are given in bulk in the suddenness of a moment. They are, all of them, made up of hundreds of thousands of tiny decisions and acts that fill our lives each day. To be honest and trustworthy in the smallest of things is a discipline that literally builds these personal characteristics for the greater things. To begin to make exceptions and limits for truthfulness also imposes new burdens and can open the door to greater indiscretions. There is wisdom in the disciplined practice of character.

In balance to this, we hasten to caution against expecting yourself to be perfect. In *The Spirituality of Imperfection*, Kurtz and Ketcham (p. 5) observed that "Trying to be perfect is the most tragic human mistake," the first temptation offered by the serpent in the garden of Eden. Those who cannot experience forgiveness themselves are diminished in their capacity to extend it to others. Plan to make mistakes. No one is expected to be perfect. [Some Christians are troubled by the injunction, "Be perfect, even as God is perfect" (Matthew 5:48). But the *telos* that is sometimes translated here as *perfect* is the fully developed endstate of a living being, and this command is therefore better understood as, "Be *complete*, be *whole*, be *fulfilled*, be *full-grown*."] One achieves character not by seeking perfection, but simply by observing and practicing it in the smallest details of daily life. This is the balance: to do the best that one can and then to be satisfied that it is truly, in a deep sense, enough.

Spiritual Health

In counseling pastors we find ourselves continually drawn to these questions: How much time do you spend daily in prayer? When and where are your regular times for personal reflection and meditation? What spiritual study are you doing, beyond that which is required for your sermons? The candid answers from pastors in distress are often, "Not much." And so we find ourselves, with some self-consciousness, pointing pastors back to their own spiritual roots and center. There is no better guide. For cut off from this spiritual source, pastors wither and so does their ministry. To work without spiritual connection, no matter how frantically, is to waste your time, to squander your health, to burn and be consumed.

Our experience is that pastors, in time of personal need, are pastors in need of personal time. Spiritual masters withdraw for clarity. It is often precisely when one "has the least time" that time spent in spiritual disciplines is most urgent. The time-honored disciplines of prayer, solitude, meditation, fasting, study, and simplicity—it is for good reason that these have survived for so many centuries. They are spiritual sustenance and survival skills. At the center of pastoring is *theos logos*—the word, the knowledge of God.

Toward Wholeness

If, like sermon-makers, we must put this chapter into three points, they would be these.

1. Keep your life in harmony by balancing work time with rest, priorities, and a perspective of *enough.*
2. Keep yourself physically and psychologically healthy through recreation, exercise, disciplined living, forgiveness, and supportive relationships.
3. Stay centered in spirit. Seek God in the silence. For here is your source, your guidance, the wisdom for how to direct your limited yet ample time and resources.

We respect your faithfulness to your calling. Pastors are among the hardest working of all God's servants. You are God's mobile urgent care center, often first on the scene and usually the last to leave. In the course of your lifetime you will touch countless lives in a highly personal and profound way, some of them over and over again. Don't forget to allow yourself to be cared for as well and to minister to yourself. Each investment in the physical, mental, and spiritual health of your own life will touch many others.

God bless you and keep you.

A FEW FURTHER READINGS FOR WOUNDED HEALERS

CLINEBELL, HOWARD J. *Well Being: A Personal Plan for Exploring and Enriching the Seven Dimensions of Life, Mind, Body, Spirit, Love, Work, Play, and Earth*. San Francisco: Harper, 1992.

DOUGLAS, DAVID *Wilderness Sojourn: Notes in the Desert Silence*. New York: Harper & Row, 1987. A reflective journal from a week's solitude in desert wilderness.

FOSTER, RICHARD J. *Celebration of Discipline: The Path to Spiritual Growth*. New York: Harper & Row, 1978. Practical guidelines for living spiritual disciplines.

KURTZ, ERNEST, and KATHERINE KETCHAM *The Spirituality of Imperfection*. New York: Bantam, 1992. From first-hand accounts of healing through Alcoholics Anonymous, Kurtz and Ketcham extract spiritual themes as remedies for perfectionism: release, gratitude, humility, tolerance, and forgiveness.

MASLACH, CHRISTINA *Burnout: The Cost of Caring*. Englewood Cliffs, NJ: Prentice-Hall, 1982.

PELLETIER, KENNETH R. *Mind as Healer, Mind as Slayer*. New York: Bantam, 1992. A classic on the relationship between stress and health.

PROGOFF, IRA *At a Journal Workshop*. New York: Dialogue House Library, 1975. An introduction to the intensive journal process.

ROHR, RICHARD *Simplicity: The Art of Living*. New York: Crossroad, 1991.

AFTERWORD

We would value your own perspectives on the material offered in this book, and the manner in which we have presented it. What have you appreciated about the book? What have you found true and useful in your own pastoral counseling? To what extent are the special features useful to you—the reference notes, tables, additional readings? Where have we been less than clear, fair, helpful, or complete? What changes would you recommend? Should there be a third edition of this book? What would you have us add or subtract? How could the book be more useful in your pastoral ministry? We will appreciate whatever encouragement and feedback you can provide.

William Miller and Kathleen Jackson
c/o Department of Psychology
The University of New Mexico
Albuquerque, New Mexico 87131-1161

INDEX